AF881200

THE BENCH GUIDE TO

LANDLORD & TENANT DISPUTES IN NEW YORK

FIFTH EDITION

HON. STEPHEN L. UKEILEY
SUFFOLK COUNTY
DISTRICT COURT JUDGE

© 2022 Stephen L. Ukeiley
All rights reserved
ISBN: 978-0-9840432-5-5

For authorization to photocopy, contact Thomas A. O'Rourke, Esq., at Bodner & O'Rourke, 425 Broadhollow Road, Melville, New York 11747, or by telephone at (631) 249-7500. Please outline the specific material requested, the purpose and format of the requested usage, and the number of copies you wish to distribute.

This publication is designed to provide information regarding the subject matter contained herein. The author does not expressly or impliedly warrant the accuracy, reliability, or currentness of the information contained in this publication. This publication is not a solicitation of legal advice nor should it be construed by the user in any manner as providing legal, accounting, or other professional advice or service. This publication is not a substitute for the advice of an attorney or other professional. If you require legal or other expert advice, you should seek the service of a competent attorney and/or other professional.

"Human behavior flows from three main sources: desire, emotion and knowledge."

—Plato

INTRODUCTION

In New York, in excess of 330,000 new Landlord and Tenant summary proceedings are typically commenced each year. However, these are not typical times. Since the onset of the COVID-19 Pandemic ("COVID-19" or "Pandemic") in the early part of 2020, the world has been turned upside down. As of August 15, 2022, of the approximate 92.8 million COVID-19 cases reported within the United States, there were in excess of 1 million deaths. At that time, New York accounted for approximately 5.9 million of the Nation's cases (6.3%) and approximately 70,000 deaths (7%).* My heart goes out to those who have lost loved ones from this virus. To put the enormity of the death toll in perspective, the number of New Yorkers that have passed away exceeds the maximum seating capacities of Yankee Stadium and the JMA Wireless Dome, formerly known as the Carrier Dome.

The Pandemic impacted all walks of life. In addition to the tragic loss of life, millions more have and continue to endure pain and suffering as a direct consequence. The physical, emotional, psychological, and financial tolls have been astounding.

The Courts and Court Staff are included within the collective wake of devastation. Notwithstanding the adversity, the Courts remained open throughout the Pandemic; a remarkable feat given the circumstances. The Courts have adapted, most prevalently with the utilization of virtual proceedings which continue to be available in select cases, including Landlord and Tenant summary proceedings. The value to the public, which relies upon the court system to resolve their disputes, is immeasurable.

If the times were not challenging enough, it is worthwhile to reflect upon the transformation of the Court's day-to-day handling of eviction proceedings that occurred a few months prior to the Pandemic. On June 14, 2019, the

* *See* New York Times Coronavirus Outbreak Online Tracker, Aug. 16, 2022, at https://nytimes.com/interactive.

Statewide Housing Stability and Tenant Protection Act of 2019 was signed into law. The resulting changes pertaining to residential and commercial properties have been significant and widespread. Landlords and Tenants are still adjusting to the new laws, a process stunted by the Pandemic.

We are in the midst of a housing and commercial property crisis. On January 1, 2022, there were approximately 600,000 New York households behind on their rent.** Whether a supply or a demand issue, or both, the daily lives of Landlords and Tenants have been disrupted. In response to this crisis, both the Federal and State governments, in addition to the Courts, enacted a series of measures intended to avoid mass homelessness and the closure of commercial entities, including the allocation of more than $2.6 billion in emergency rental assistance to New Yorkers. The status of eviction proceedings remains a work-in-progress.

The timeless question repeatedly raised in Court—*what are my rights?*—has taken on greater significance for Landlords and Tenants. Regardless of race, age, gender, or socioeconomic status, eviction proceedings are frustrating, and the frustration has been heightened by the Pandemic.

To address these concerns, this is an ideal time for another Edition. *The Bench Guide to Landlord & Tenant Disputes in New York (Fifth Edition)*© ("Bench Guide" or "Fifth Edition") continues to inform and educate those involved in this highly specific and technical area of law. The Fifth Edition is a re-write, which includes recently enacted legislation, nearly 1,000 new references to case law and statutory provisions, and offers a practical perspective to Landlord and Tenant disputes. The reader is taken on a step-by-step journey through each stage of an eviction proceeding, and, similar to the previous editions, the Fifth Edition provides an updated overview of courtroom procedures and protocols. It is my hope that the Bench Guide serves as a practical resource for all involved; Landlords and Tenants, counsel, jurists, professors, students, and the public.

There has been a statewide initiative for Alternative Dispute Resolution ("ADR") in Landlord and Tenant cases which provides an alternative forum for the expeditious resolution of disputes. The importance of legal representation for both Landlords and Tenants is another topical issue.

** *See* Caitlin Dewey, "*'Deluge' of Eviction Cases Expected As Moratorium Nears Its End*," The Buffalo News, Jan. 5, 2022, at https://buffalonews.com (referencing study by National Equity Atlas).

Although significant strides have been made in recent years, and in some locations, the right to counsel has been legislated, unfortunately, there remain many instances where litigants are unrepresented. These individuals are at a distinct disadvantage, and the stakes could not be higher.

The Bench Guide originated eleven (11) years ago from a simple outline I created for quick reference while on the Bench. Five (5) editions later, the Bench Guide remains a comprehensive yet portable, user-friendly resource. A project such as this is never accomplished alone. I am fortunate to have had the privilege of knowing, learning from, and working with so many intelligent, articulate, and passionate individuals who have given endlessly of their time, knowledge, and expertise for which I am extremely grateful. There are too many to name each individual, but you know who you are, and I am honored, appreciative, and grateful for our interactions. Each person has had a positive impact on my life which, in turn, has made me a better person and a better public servant.

More specifically, I express my admiration and respect for my colleagues and friends, the Honorable Andrew Crecca, Suffolk County District Administrative Judge; the Honorable Richard I. Horowitz, Court of Claims Judge and Acting Suffolk County Supreme Court Justice; the Honorable Karen Kerr, Suffolk County Family Court Judge and Supervising Judge of the Suffolk County District Court; the Honorable C. Randall Hinrichs, former Suffolk County District Administrative Judge; the Honorable Madeleine Fitzgibbon, former Supervising Judge of the Suffolk County District Court; the Honorable Arthur D. Spatt, former United States District Court Judge, who unfortunately passed away in June 2020; and the Honorable E. Thomas Boyle, former United States Magistrate Judge for the Eastern District of New York.

Special appreciation to Patrick McCormick, Esq., Nicole Berkman, Esq., Beth Gazes, Esq., and Michele Rosenblatt, Esq. for the exceedingly generous giving of your time and knowledge in addition to the countless hours spent reviewing drafts of the Bench Guide. It was not glamorous, but your input is not only appreciated, but vital to the finished product.

Further appreciation to Phil Gallo, Esq., Associate Court Attorney; Susan Alexander, Esq., Law Clerk to the Supervising Judge of the Suffolk County District Court; Jeff Grabowski, Esq., Court Attorney

Referee Model Guardianship Part; Maeghan H. O'Keefe, Esq., Principal Law Clerk; and Evan Tanenbaum, Esq., Principal Law Clerk for the Suffolk County District Administrative Judge, in addition to my colleagues and peers at the Touro University Jacob D. Fuchsberg Law Center: Elena B. Langan, Dean; Myra Berman, Associate Dean for Experiential Learning & Special Programs & Associate Professor; John Linarelli, Associate Dean for Academic Affairs and Professor of Law; and Rodger Citron, Associate Dean for Research and Scholarship and Professor of Law, each of whom I greatly respect and admire. Further appreciation to Victor Ambrose, Esq.; William Bodkin; James Dantuono, Senior Court Clerk; Lori Distefano; Jeffrey Fried, Esq., former Associate Court Attorney; Lauren Gallo, Esq.; Carol Hernandez; Kelly Hernandez; Mayra Hernandez; Anthony LaPinta, Esq.; Nancy LeJava, Esq., Principal Court Attorney; Carolann McClain; and Michael Rosenthal, Esq. Each of you have been supportive, innovative, encouraging, and insightful, and I have been the beneficiary of your wisdom and experiences. Moreover, to my current and former Landlord and Tenant Law students, whom I collectively refer to as the next generation of attorneys, you are special and impressive in so many ways—"do your job and zealously represent your clients."

Further appreciation to all of the dedicated clerks, Court office personnel, and Court Officers whose commitment and professionalism continue to make the courtroom a functioning forum for the resolution of legal disputes. Finally, I cannot thank enough all of my soccer officiating mentors, assignors, instructors, colleagues, and peers. You are very talented and special both on and off the pitch.

The Bench Guide is dedicated to my beautiful wife and best friend Cynthia and our two wonderful children. I also thank my parents, Richard and Dorothy, my brother Scott, and my entire family who have been an inspiration and supportive of all of my endeavors.

Respectfully,

Hon. Stephen L. Ukeiley
Acting Suffolk County Court and
Suffolk County District Court Judge

FOREWORD

As a result of the onset of the global pandemic in 2020 the entire world as we know it, has been turned upside down. The practice of law, like most other vocations and industries, has been substantially impacted. Cases for a significant period of time have been virtual and appearances remote. Landlord and Tenant Law and the summary proceedings encompassed within such practice have been particularly effected. Rules, regulations, emergency and executive orders, statutes and moratoriums, both state and federal, have been enacted and imposed in response to the ever-changing pandemic, effecting landlords and tenants, commercial and residential, alike.

Delays, frustration and uncertainty regarding housing and tenancies abound make this area of practice particularly challenging.

It is with this in mind that the Hon. Stephen L. Ukeiley, an Acting Suffolk County Court and duly elected Suffolk County District Court Judge, has addressed the current state of Landlord-Tenant Law, particularly with respect to COVID-19, with the publication of the *Bench Guide To Landlord & Tenant Disputes in New York (5th Edition).*© Judge Ukeiley is recognized as an authority on Landlord & Tenant law, having presided over thousands of Landlord and Tenant summary proceedings. The previous four editions of this publication have served as an invaluable resource for judges, legal practitioners, law school educators and students, as well as for landlords and tenants. Judges, attorneys and litigants have relied upon Judge Ukeiley's treatise for guidance since its initial publication in 2011. The Fifth Edition, like the previous four, is comprehensive and thorough, and is an extensive and exhaustive guide to the current state of Landlord & Tenant Law, including the effect of COVID-19 and its ramifications on this area of practice.

Judge Ukeiley is devoted and caring and his passion and his

expertise regarding Landlord & Tenant Law shines through each chapter, citation and verse. We in the legal community are fortunate to benefit from Judge Ukeiley's efforts in the form of the Fifth edition.

Kudos to Judge Ukeiley for keeping us informed about the current state of Landlord & Tenant Law.

Some two years into the global pandemic, with each passing day, we await the return of some normalcy in our vocations and our lives. With perseverance, fortitude and strength we hopefully will soon return to the best of times. The Fifth Edition of Judge Ukeiley's bench guide, a classic in its own right, is a welcome tool to assist us on the way.

Hon. Sandra L. Sgroi (ret.)
Former Assoc. Justice
State of New York
Supreme Court, Appellate Division
Second Judicial Department

ABOUT THE AUTHOR

The HONORABLE STEPHEN L. UKEILEY is a duly elected Suffolk County District Court Judge. He is the Coordinating Judge of the District's Landlord—Tenant Matters and an Acting County Court Judge where he presides in the Guardianship Part of the Suffolk County Supreme Court. Judge Ukeiley also oversees Suffolk County's Landlord—Tenant Alternative Dispute Resolution (ADR) Program, a pilot program he assisted in creating, and is the Chair of the Access to Justice Subcommittee on Eviction Proceedings.

Judge Ukeiley has presided over nearly 85,000 civil and criminal cases to completion, including 16,500 Landlord and Tenant summary proceedings. He has also presided in Suffolk County's Human Trafficking Intervention Court. Prior to taking the Bench, he was the Principal Law Clerk to the Honorable E. Thomas Boyle, former United States Magistrate Judge for the Eastern District of New York, and has also served as the Principal Law Secretary to the Honorable Richard I. Horowitz, Court of Claims Judge and Acting Supreme Court Justice.

Judge Ukeiley is an adjunct professor at the Touro University Jacob D. Fuchsberg Law Center where he has taught Landlord and Tenant Law since 2013. In 2018, he was named the law school's "Adjunct Professor of the Year." He has also taught law classes on Human Trafficking and is a former adjunct professor at both the New York Institute of Technology and Long Island University (C.W. Post Campus).

Judge Ukeiley is a frequent lecturer, and is routinely requested to present on the law to members of the Judiciary at both the New York State Judicial Institute and the New York State Magistrate Association conferences. He is an active member of his hometown Suffolk County Bar Association, where he co-chairs the Landlord and Tenant Law Committee, and previously served as an officer of the Suffolk Academy of Law. In 2017, Judge Ukeiley was named to the New York State Judicial Institute's City/District/Housing Courts Curriculum Advisory Committee. He has also served on the Board of Directors of the Suffolk County Women's Bar Association and is the recipient of numerous Recognition Awards for exemplary service and commitment to continuing legal education.

Judge Ukeiley is the author of all five (5) editions of *The Bench Guide to Landlord & Tenant Disputes in New York*©. He has also written numerous scholarly articles and a Children's Book, *The Silly School*©. In 2014 and 2020, the *Bench Guide* was distributed to over 1,200 Town and Village Justice Courts in New York. Judge Ukeiley also previously authored a regular law column in *The Suffolk Lawyer*, the Suffolk County Bar Association's publication.

Judge Ukeiley earned his Juris Doctor from Hofstra Law School, where he was the Editor-in-Chief of the Hofstra Labor Law Journal, and his Bachelor of Arts from Rutgers University. In his spare time, he has completed eighteen (18) marathons, and is a certified United States Soccer Federation and National Intercollegiate Soccer Officials Association referee of youth, adult, and National Collegiate Athletic Association (NCAA) soccer matches.

CONTENTS

CHAPTER 1

JURISDICTION OF THE COURT

The Housing Parts that hear Landlord and Tenant cases are highly specialized courts.[1] These courts generally include the New York City Civil Courts, the City Courts outside of New York City, the District Courts on Long Island, and the more than 1,200 Town and Village Justice Courts throughout the State.

The authority to preside over residential and commercial Landlord and Tenant disputes is set forth in the New York City Civil Court Act,[2]

1 Jack B. Weinstein, Harold L. Korn & Arthur R. Miller, CPLR Manual § 1.04(q) (David L. Ferstendig ed. 2010). Throughout this Bench Guide, the terms "Housing Part" and "Court" are used interchangeably in reference to the designated parts within the State Courts that have jurisdiction over Landlord and Tenant matters. The term "Housing Court" is actually a misnomer because there are "no separately designated" courts called "Housing Courts" within the State of New York. *See id.* However, in New York City, the judges presiding within the Housing Parts are referred to as Housing Judges. N.Y. City Civ. Ct. Act § 110(e). Although most New York judges presiding over Landlord and Tenant disputes are elected to the Bench, New York City Housing Judges are appointed by the State's Chief Administrative Judge for a renewable term of five (5) years from a list of candidates recommended by the Housing Court Advisory Council.

2 N.Y. City Civ. Ct. Act § 204. In the New York City Civil Courts, residential and commercial Landlord and Tenant disputes are heard in separate courtrooms. *See* Bayview Loan Servicing, LLC v. Lyn-Jay, Inc., 54 N.Y.S.3d 609 (App. Term, 2d, 11th & 13th Jud. Dists. 2017) (holding that "[t]he commercial landlord-tenant part could not entertain the proceeding, inasmuch as it sought, in part, the recovery of a residential premises"); 32-05 Newtown Ave. Assocs., LLC v. Caguana, 22 N.Y.S.3d 139 (App. Term, 2d, 11th & 13th Jud. Dists. 2015) (dismissing residential eviction proceeding commenced in commercial Housing Part); Glebow Realty Assoc. v. Dietrich, 121 N.Y.S.3d 534 (N.Y. Civ. Ct. N.Y. Cnty. 2020) (dismissing without prejudice mixed-use premises case in the commercial Housing Part to allow for the commencement of a new proceeding in the residential Housing Part). Of note, rent stabilization laws may apply to an apartment used both for residential and commercial purposes. *Glebow Realty Assoc.*, 121 N.Y.S.3d at 534 (*citing* Golfinos v. 400 Cooperative Corp., 110 A.D.2d 522, 487 N.Y.S.2d 752 (1st Dep't 1985)).

the Uniform City Court Act,[3] the Uniform District Court Act,[4] and the Uniform Justice Court Act, respectively.[5] The scope of jurisdiction in these proceedings is limited and non-expandable regardless of consent.[6]

A. SUMMARY PROCEEDINGS

The Housing Parts conduct summary proceedings which are "special proceeding[s] governed entirely by statute, and it is well established that there must be strict compliance with the statutory requirements to give the court jurisdiction."[7] As noted by the Appellate Division, Second Department, "[i]n creating the summary proceeding, the Legislature intended to afford a means 'of obtaining a speedy determination and adjudication of disputes over the right of possession of real property.'"[8]

Two (2) types of cases comprise the overwhelming majority of Landlord and Tenant summary proceedings: non-payment and holdover proceedings. It is incumbent upon the Landlord, referred to as the Petitioner in a

---

3 Uniform City Ct. Act § 204.

4 Uniform Dist. Ct. Act § 204.

5 Uniform Just. Ct. Act § 204. *See, e.g.*, Burke v. Aspland, 56 A.D.3d 1001, 867 N.Y.S.2d 759 (3d Dep't 2008); MTC Commons, LLC v. Millbrook Training Ctr. & Spa, Ltd., 31 N.Y.S.3d 922 (App. Term, 9th & 10th Jud. Dists. 2016); Bonham Strand LLC v. Paredes, 2017 N.Y.L.J. LEXIS 3695 (Greenburgh Just. Ct. Dec. 14, 2017).

6 These courts were created by the State Legislature between the years 1962 and 1966. The New York City Civil Court Act was enacted in 1962, and took effect in 1963; the Uniform District Court Act became law in 1963; the Uniform City Court Act became law in 1964, and took effect in 1965; and the Uniform Justice Court Act became law in 1966, and took effect in 1967. The New York City Civil Courts, the City Courts Outside New York City, and the District Courts are further described as Courts of Record of the State. *See* Judiciary Law § 2. Although <u>not</u> included within this category, the Justice Courts are similarly authorized as designated courts.

7 Riverside Syndicate, Inc. v. Saltzman, 49 A.D.3d 402, 852 N.Y.S.2d 840 (1st Dep't 2008) (citations omitted); Jaikarran & Sons, Inc. v. Beecham, 110 N.Y.S.3d 783 (App. Term, 1st Dep't 2018). *But see* Lanz v. Lifrieri, 104 A.D.2d 400, 478 N.Y.S.2d 722 (2d Dep't 1984) (summary proceedings are similar to other civil cases with regard to service and pleading requirements such that absent a showing of prejudice, "[*d*]*e minimis* variations from strict compliance [are] not necessarily jurisdictional defects"); Siedlecki v. Doscher, 931 N.Y.S.2d 203 (App. Term, 2d, 11th & 13th Jud. Dists. 2011) (*de minimis* defect in filing affidavit following personal service).

8 Siegel v. Kentucky Fried Chicken, 108 A.D.2d 218, at 227, 488 N.Y.S.2d 744, 750 (2d Dep't 1985).

summary proceeding, to commence the proper type of proceeding.[9] It should be noted that adherence to Local Court Rules is further required.

A significant distinction between non-payment and holdover proceedings is that a non-payment proceeding presupposes the parties have a valid Landlord and Tenant relationship when the proceeding is commenced.[10] In a holdover proceeding, on the other hand, a valid Landlord and Tenant relationship does not exist.[11] There are various subcategories of holdover proceedings, but the common element is that, notwithstanding whether there once was a Landlord and Tenant relationship, the parties do not have such a relationship when the proceeding is commenced.

Petitioners in both non-payment and holdover proceedings seek to regain "possession" of the subject premises.[12] As a result, the occupant must be in physical possession of the premises when the summary proceeding is commenced.[13] Otherwise, the Court is without subject

---

9 *See, e.g.*, Lakeview Affordable Hous., LLC v. Turner, 121 N.Y.S.3d 510 (App. Term, 9th & 10th Jud. Dists. 2020) (non-payment proceeding was improper type of proceeding); Green v. Palmer, 2021 N.Y.L.J. LEXIS 1067 (N.Y. Civ. Ct. Queens Cnty. Oct. 15, 2021) (same).

10 MHA Realty 1, LLC v. Rostoker, 142 N.Y.S.3d 888 (App. Term, 2d, 11th & 13th Jud. Dists. 2021).

11 *See, e.g.*, Gayle v. Flynn, 143 N.Y.S.3d 497 (App. Term, 2d, 11th & 13th Jud. Dists. 2021).

12 *See, e.g.*, *MHA Realty 1, LLC*, 142 N.Y.S.3d at 888 (purpose of non-payment proceeding is to recover possession due to the non-payment of rent); 36 Main Realty Corp. v. Wang Law Office, PLLC, 19 N.Y.S.3d 654 (App. Term, 2d, 11th & 13th Jud. Dists. 2015) (holding "[t]he primary purpose of a nonpayment summary proceeding is to recover possession of the subject premises") (*quoting* Patchogue Assoc. v. Sears, Roebuck & Co., 951 N.Y.S.2d 314 (App. Term, 9th & 10th Jud. Dists. 2012)); Yau v. Yau, 154 N.Y.S.3d 578 (App. Term, 2d, 11th & 13th Jud. Dists. 2021) (holdover proceeding).

13 2 Hamilton Ave. Co. v. Operation Prom, 2019 N.Y.L.J. LEXIS 2481 (New Rochelle City Ct. July 8, 2019) (holding that "[s]imply put, a summary proceeding cannot lie where respondent did not physically possess the premises when the proceeding was commenced"). The issue of possession is fact-based and case specific. Generally, the surrendering of the keys is an indicator of the relinquishment of possession. However, the Tenant's inability or failure to surrender the keys "is not conclusive that [physical possession of] the premises [has] not been surrendered." *See* Pezzo v. 26 Seventh Ave. South, LLC, 144 A.D.3d 778, 41 N.Y.S.3d 62 (2d Dep't 2016); Johnson v. Marcano, 101 N.Y.S.3d 699 (App. Term, 2d, 11th & 13th Jud. Dists. 2018); First Nat. City Bank v. Wall St. Leasing Corp., 363 N.Y.S.2d 699 (N.Y. Civ. Ct. N.Y. Cnty. 1974).

matter jurisdiction.[14]

After a final judgment of possession has been entered and the Tenant vacates the premises, whether voluntarily or following a lawful eviction, the Housing Part generally no longer retains jurisdiction over the proceeding.[15] For example, following vacatur of the premises, the Court may not amend the money judgment for additional monies (even when contemplated by the parties).[16] Unless waived, the Landlord may seek these items in a separate plenary action for damages.

However, the Housing Part may consider post-eviction applications for contempt[17] and restoring the Tenant to the premises based upon a showing of good cause.[18] In a highly unusual case, the Appellate Term for the Second, Eleventh and Thirteenth Judicial Districts denied the Landlord's post-eviction application to re-execute a warrant of eviction.[19] In *Halsey Homes Corp.*, the Marshal executed the original war-

---

14 *2 Hamilton Ave. Co.*, 2019 N.Y.L.J. LEXIS at 2481; 92 Bergenbrooklyn, LLC v. Cisarano, 21 N.Y.S.3d 810 (App. Term, 2d, 11th & 13th Jud. Dists. 2015) ("[i]n a summary proceeding, the respondent must be in possession of the premises at the time the proceeding is commenced in order for the proceeding to lie"); Clark v. Singletary, 31 N.Y.S.3d 920 (App. Term, 9th & 10th Jud. Dists. 2016) (clarifying that "[j]urisdiction over [the former spouse] had not been obtained because [the former spouse] no longer resided at the premises at the time the nonpayment proceeding had been commenced").

15 *See* Dixon v. County of Albany, 192 A.D.3d 1428, 145 N.Y.S.3d 639 (3d Dep't 2021) ("[t]he execution of the warrant terminates the summary proceeding and the jurisdiction of the court"); Steinmetz v. Oyala, 142 N.Y.S.3d 273 (App. Term, 2d, 11th & 13th Jud. Dists. 2021) (holding "the court no longer retained jurisdiction after the execution of the warrant to entertain landlord's motions").

16 *See Steinmetz*, 142 N.Y.S.3d at 273; Goldburd v. Langer, 112 N.Y.S.3d 859 (App. Term, 2d, 11th & 13th Jud. Dists. 2019); Lee v. Green World Cleaners 1, LLC, 112 N.Y.S.3d 415 (App. Term, 2d, 11th & 13th Jud. Dists. 2018) (notwithstanding stipulation reserving the Landlord's right to seek additional moneys, the Housing Part lacked jurisdiction to entertain the application after the judgment was entered and the Tenant vacated the premises).

17 Civil Practice Law and Rules ("CPLR") § 5104; Judiciary Law § 760. *See* 728 Fulton St., LLC v. Lashley, 156 N.Y.S.3d 643 (App. Term, 2d, 11th & 13th Jud. Dists. 2021) (holding that the Housing Part's authority to decide contempt applications continues following an eviction).

18 Halsey Homes Corp. v. Prince-Bowden, 132 N.Y.S.3d 514 (App. Term, 2d, 11th & 13th Jud. Dists. 2020); Chauncey Equities, LLC v. Murphy, 112 N.Y.S.3d 861 (App. Term, 2d, 11th & 13th Jud. Dists. 2019).

19 *Halsey Homes Corp.*, 132 N.Y.S.3d at 514.

rant unaware that the proceeding had been stayed by the Appellate Division, Second Department. Due to the Court-Ordered stay, the Landlord permitted the Tenant to return to the property following the eviction and, thereafter, sought and obtained a second order from the Housing Part authorizing another eviction.[20] In reversing the order granting the second eviction, the Appellate Term reasoned "[o]nce the [original] warrant of eviction had been [legally] executed, the proceeding was no longer pending and the court was divested of jurisdiction."[21]

B. HOUSING PART DETERMINES "POSSESSION" AS OPPOSED TO "TITLE"

In a Landlord and Tenant summary proceeding, the Court has jurisdiction to determine who is entitled to lawful "possession" of the premises. This is accomplished by the issuance of a judgment of possession. The Court may further issue a money judgment and a warrant of eviction directing either the Sheriff or Marshal to remove individuals and their belongings from the premises after a date certain. For "good cause" shown, the Court may stay the execution of the warrant or, if already executed, restore the Tenant to possession.[22] With few exceptions, this constitutes the extent of the Housing Part's authority to grant relief.

The Housing Parts may <u>not</u> grant declaratory and/or injunctive relief other than staying the issuance and/or enforcement of the judgment

20 The Appellate Term reasoned that the initial eviction was proper because it "[w]as completed before the marshal was served with the Appellate Division's stay order." *Id.* (*citing* Chelsea Marina, Inc. v. Scoralick, 94 A.D.2d 189, 463 N.Y.S.2d 489 (2d Dep't 1983)).

21 *Id.* The Court noted that the order staying execution of the warrant had <u>not</u> been served on the Marshal at the time of the eviction, and, as a result, the "[e]viction here was legally executed," and the Housing Part was divested of jurisdiction. *Id.*

22 Real Property Actions and Proceedings Law ("RPAPL") § 749(3); Lafayette Boynton Hsg. Corp. v. Pickett, 135 A.D.3d 518, 23 N.Y.S.3d 204 (1st Dep't 2016).

and warrant of eviction.[23] The Tenant in a summary proceeding may assert any defense, either legal or equitable, including that the Landlord is no longer the owner of the premises or has a superior possessory interest in the property.[24] The Tenant may further assert that it is the "owner" (if not previously acknowledged and accepted), but only as an affirmative defense (not as an affirmative claim).[25]

The Court's limited authority to determine "possession," as opposed to "title" or "ownership," is significant because the parties may have a dispute over the identity of the rightful owner.[26] As a general matter, the parties retain the right to litigate "ownership" as an affirmative claim in the New York State Supreme Court notwithstanding the outcome of the summary proceeding.[27]

The reader should be mindful that when the Tenant unsuccessfully asserts as an affirmative defense in the summary proceeding that he or she is the owner of the property, the Tenant is barred from re-asserting the

23 *See* Barkagan v. S & L Star Realty, LLC, 185 A.D.3d 643, 124 N.Y.S.3d 868 (2d Dep't 2020) (the "[e]quitable relief sought by the plaintiff in the Supreme Court is unavailable to it in the summary proceeding in Civil Court"); Faith In Action Deliverance Ministries v. 3231 Assoc., LLC, 168 A.D.3d 502, 92 N.Y.S.3d 213 (1st Dep't 2019) (holding the Housing Part "[d]oes not have authority to grant an injunction restraining sale of the property, or to grant the equitable relief sought by plaintiff, namely a declaratory judgment and specific performance"); Robinson v. 47 Thames Realty, LLC, 158 A.D.3d 781, 71 N.Y.S.3d 638 (2d Dep't 2018) (removing holdover proceeding to join Tenants' Supreme Court action where injunctive relief was sought); Barsyl Supermarkets, Inc. v. Avenue P Assoc., LLP, 86 A.D.3d 545, at 548, 928 N.Y.S.2d 45, 48 (2d Dep't 2011) (action seeking declaratory judgment may not be decided by the Housing Part); Jamaica Seven, LLC v. Villa, 128 N.Y.S.3d 410 (App. Term, 2d, 11th & 13th Jud. Dists. 2020) (Housing Part lacks authority to "[d]irect landlord to offer occupant a renewal lease without a vacancy increase"); LA Gem, Inc. v. Fuentes, 110 N.Y.S.3d 198 (App. Term, 9th & 10th Jud. Dists. 2018) (Housing Part lacks authority to direct Landlord "to remove certain charges from tenant's future rent bill").

24 *See* RPAPL § 743; Fizzinoglia v. Capozzoli, 94 N.Y.S.3d 538 (App. Term, 9th & 10th Jud. Dists. 2018) (the Housing Part may "[a]ddress any interposed legal or equitable defense" in a summary proceeding); *Yau*, 154 N.Y.S.3d at 578 (the equitable affirmative defense of constructive trust may be asserted in a summary proceeding).

25 *Fizzinoglia*, 94 N.Y.S.3d at 538; Jacob Marion, LLC v. El Bey, 36 N.Y.S.3d 47 (App. Term, 2d, 11th & 13th Jud. Dists. 2016).

26 *See, e.g.*, Thane v. Thane, 149 N.Y.S.3d 883 n.2 (N.Y. Civ. Ct. Queens Cnty. 2021).

27 *See* Nissequogue Boat Club v. State, 14 A.D.3d 542, 780 N.Y.S.2d 71 (2d Dep't 2005).

claim in a subsequent action.[28] However, where the defense is not raised in the Housing Part, a claim for ownership (e.g., by adverse possession), may be litigated in the Supreme Court provided the action is commenced within sixty (60) days from the entry of the Housing Part's judgment.[29]

C. PROCEEDING MUST BE COMMENCED WHERE THE PROPERTY IS LOCATED

The Petitioner must commence the summary proceeding in the appropriate court. A proceeding to regain possession of real property in New York City must be commenced in the New York City Civil Court within the same county (or borough) where the property is located.[30] A proceeding involving property in a city outside New York City must similarly be brought in the City Court located within that city's geographical limits,[31] and the Justice Courts may only hear cases regarding properties located within their particular municipalities.[32]

The District Courts pose a venue challenge similar to that experienced in the New York City Civil Courts. The District Courts are exclusively situated on Long Island, in both Nassau County and the five (5) western Towns of Suffolk County: Babylon, Brookhaven, Huntington, Islip, and Smithtown.[33] As a result of having multiple District Court courthouses within the western portion of Suffolk County, proceedings to regain possession of real property must be commenced in the District Court located within the same Town where the property is located.[34]

28 *Id.*

29 *Id.*; *see* RPAPL § 749(2).

30 N.Y. City Civ. Ct. Act § 303.

31 Uniform City Ct. Act § 204.

32 Uniform Just. Ct. Act § 204.

33 The Unified District Court Act applies to five (5) of the ten (10) Towns that comprise Suffolk County. The eastern portion of the County—the Towns of East Hampton, Riverhead, Shelter Island, Southampton, and Southold—are not within the jurisdiction of the District Court.

34 Uniform Dist. Ct. Act § 303. The reader should be mindful that there is only one (1) District Court located within Nassau County. This Court, which is located in Hempstead, services all three (3) of the County's townships—Hempstead, North Hempstead, and Oyster Bay.

D. STATUTE OF FRAUDS

A rental agreement twelve (12) months or less in duration need not be in writing.[35] Accordingly, a month-to-month tenancy may be based upon an oral agreement because the term of the tenancy is for less than one (1) year (i.e., one month) regardless of the number of times the monthly tenancy is renewed.[36]

However, a rental agreement longer than one (1) year must be memorialized to be enforced.[37] This is because the Statute of Frauds, codified at General Obligations Law § 5-703, provides that "[a] contract for the leasing for a longer period than one year,...of any real property, or an interest therein, is void unless the contract or some note or memorandum thereof, expressing the consideration, is in writing, subscribed by the party to be charged, or by his lawful agent thereunto authorized by writing."[38]

The failure to execute a written agreement when required renders the lease void. At minimum, "[t]he [writing] must designate the parties, identify and describe the subject matter, and state all of the essential terms of a complete agreement."[39] In *Fisher v. Burke*, the Housing Part held that a series of text messages that adequately detailed the terms of a tenancy constituted a valid rental agreement.[40] Although not raised in the Court's decision, it would appear that a rental agreement longer than one (1) year in

---

35 *See, e.g.*, Sawicka v. Schwimmer, 187 A.D.3d 957, 130 N.Y.S.3d 711 (2d Dep't 2020) (the Statute of Frauds does not apply where the parties' oral rental agreement "[d]id not contemplate any specific lease term, let alone a term exceeding one year [resulting in an at-will tenancy]").

36 Mulford v. Borg-Warner Acceptance Corp., 115 A.D.2d 163, 495 N.Y.S.2d 493 (3d Dep't 1985) (Statute of Frauds does not apply to a month-to-month tenancy).

37 *See* LaCarrubba v. Outdoors Clothing Corp., 65 N.Y.S.3d 622 (App. Term, 9th & 10th Jud. Dists. 2017) (oral five-year (5-year) lease agreement unenforceable).

38 General Obligations Law ("GOL") § 5-703(2).

39 Rouzani v. Rapp, 203 A.D.2d 446, 610 N.Y.S.2d 600 (2d Dep't 1994).

40 151 N.Y.S.3d 620 (N.Y. Civ. Ct. Kings Cnty. 2021) (comparing text messages to an exchange of letters) (*citing* Bernstein v. 1995 Assoc., 185 A.D.2d 160, 586 N.Y.S.2d 115 (1st Dep't 1992)). In *Bernstein*, the Appellate Division, First Department held that the rental agreement was enforceable where counsel accepted, without objection, a letter containing the parameters that "[s]ufficiently set forth the area to be leased, the duration of the lease and the price to be paid, [and] fair market value." 185 A.D.2d at 162, 586 N.Y.S.2d at 117.

duration based upon an exchange of text messages would not be enforceable because text messages are generally not subscribed (i.e., unsigned).[41]

E. CONCURRENT JURISDICTION

The New York State Supreme Court and County Court have concurrent jurisdiction over eviction proceedings.[42] Notwithstanding this authority, the vast majority of summary proceedings are commenced in the Housing Parts specifically created to resolve Landlord and Tenant disputes in an expeditious and efficient manner.[43] Where an existing summary proceeding affords "complete" relief, "[t]here is no further basis for invoking the equitable jurisdiction of [the] Supreme Court."[44] Parenthetically, the Federal courts do not have subject matter jurisdiction over State summary proceedings.[45]

When related litigations are pending in multiple courts, there is a presumption against staying the Housing Part proceeding because the Landlord is "entitled by statute to an expeditious determination of its claim that it is wrongfully being denied possession."[46] This

41 *Fisher*, 151 N.Y.S.3d at 620.

42 Cabrera v. Humphrey, 192 A.D.3d 227, 140 N.Y.S.3d 609 (3d Dep't 2021) (holding that "[t]hrough the constitutional grant of broad authority, [the] Supreme Court may entertain such special [eviction] proceedings to remove tenants"); Extell Belnord LLC v. Uppman, 113 A.D.3d 1, 976 N.Y.S.2d 22 (1st Dep't 2013); Chelsea 18 Partners, LP v. Mak, 90 A.D.3d 38, 933 N.Y.S.2d 204 (1st Dep't 2011); Carter v. Levian, 2010 N.Y. Misc. LEXIS 5660, at *4 (Nassau Cnty. Sup. Ct. Nov. 12, 2010).

43 L.B. v. Stahl York Ave. Co., 188 A.D.3d 421, 131 N.Y.S.3d 865 (1st Dep't 2020) (noting the "strong preference" to resolve eviction proceedings in the Housing Parts).

44 *See* Brecker v. 295 Cent. Park W., Inc., 71 A.D.3d 564, 898 N.Y.S.2d 23 (1st Dep't 2010).

45 *See* Kahaleel v. Vanreil, 2019 U.S. Dist. LEXIS 14753 (E.D.N.Y. Jan. 30, 2019).

46 Hillside Park 168, LLC v. Zaman, 117 N.Y.S.3d 426 (App. Term, 2d, 11th & 13th Jud. Dists. 2019); Hillside Park 168, LLC v. Hossain, 110 N.Y.S.3d 863 (App. Term, 2d, 11th & 13th Jud. Dists. 2018) (error to stay summary proceeding where Tenant could assert the same defenses in the holdover proceeding); 2094-2096 Boston Post Rd., LLC v. Mackies Am. Grill, Inc., 41 N.Y.S.3d 452 (App. Term, 9th & 10th Jud. Dists. 2016); DiStasio v. Macaluso, 16 N.Y.S.3d 791 (App. Term, 9th & 10th Jud. Dists. 2015) (error to stay summary proceeding pending the conclusion of Respondent's matrimonial action); Zabala v. Mealie, 2021 N.Y. Misc. LEXIS 4799 (N.Y. Civ. Ct. Kings Cnty. Aug. 27, 2021) (denied Tenant's request for a stay pending appeal of motion decided after hearing date scheduled).

is particularly the case where the claims in the Supreme Court action could be heard in the Housing Part.[47] Moreover, the Appellate Term for the First Department has held that it is improper to stay a holdover proceeding while awaiting a final decision on the Tenant's housing discrimination claims (which were based upon race and ethnicity) pending before the New York Commission on Human Rights.[48]

1. REMOVAL AND CONSOLIDATION

The New York State Supreme Court may remove a summary proceeding to join an existing action where common issues of law and/or fact are raised and there is no resulting prejudice.[49] CPLR § 602 provides, "[w]here an action is pending in the supreme court it may, upon motion, remove to itself an action pending in another court and consolidate it or have it tried together with that in the supreme court."[50] In *Wei v. Lee*, the summary proceeding was removed and consolidated with a Supreme Court declaratory judgment action because both actions involved the same parties and property and "[r]esolution of [the] action [would] necessarily decide the issues…in the Summary Proceeding, and the two should be consolidated in the interest of

47 *2094-2096 Boston Post Rd., LLC*, 41 N.Y.S.3d at 452; *DiStasio*, 16 N.Y.S.3d at 791.

48 Cooper Sq. Mut. Hous. Assn. II Hous. Dev. Fund Co., Inc. v. Mumford, 125 N.Y.S.3d 831 (App. Term, 1st Dep't 2020) (holding that where discrimination claims were filed after service of a second termination notice, "[t]he 'summary' remedy made available by RPAPL article 7 should not be delayed indefinitely while [respondents'] agency complaint [winds] its way through the administrative process").

49 *See* CPLR § 602; *Barkagan*, 58 A.D.3d at 780, 68 N.Y.S.3d at 758 (granting removal of summary proceeding to join Supreme Court action where "[t]he lease provisions preclude the [Tenant] from asserting counterclaims in the summary proceeding and the equitable relief sought by the [Tenant] in the Supreme Court is unavailable to it in the [the Housing Part]"); Robinson v. 47 Thames Realty, LLC, 158 A.D.3d 780, 68 N.Y.S.3d 758 (2d Dep't 2018) (granting removal and consolidation due to similar facts and common issues based upon the same transactions and there being no prejudice); Rogin v. Rogin, 90 A.D.3d 507, 936 N.Y.S.2d 109 (1st Dep't 2011) (granting removal to join Supreme Court action, in part, because the Plaintiff-Tenant "[s] eeks an equitable remedy, an injunction, which the [Housing Part] cannot grant"); Pass v. Garden Court Hous. Dev. Fund Corp., 2019 N.Y. Misc. LEXIS 2152 (N.Y. Cnty. Sup. Ct. May 2, 2019) (same).

50 CPLR § 602(b).

judicial economy."[51]

Notwithstanding any common issues of law or fact, consolidation may be denied where the actions are at "[m]arkedly different procedural stages and consolidation would result in undue delay in the resolution of either matter."[52] Applications for removal have also been denied where the requests were made "on the eve of trial" and for dilatory purposes.[53]

2. ALTERNATIVE ACTIONS TO RECOVER POSSESSION

Actions for ejectment and partition are alternative approaches to regaining possession of real property in the Supreme Court. Both actions are beyond the jurisdictional authority of the Housing Part and require the movant to demonstrate an ownership interest and immediate right to possession.

a. EJECTMENT (RPAPL ARTICLE 6)

An ejectment action to recover possession pursuant to Article 6 of the RPAPL is commonly associated with a declaratory judgment action for the termination of the parties' rental agreement. Ejectment is also available where a summary proceeding is prohibited, such as when a lease provision fails to necessarily terminate the lease upon a breach[54]

51 2021 N.Y. Misc. LEXIS 558 (Kings Cnty. Sup. Ct. Jan. 15, 2021).

52 *Stahl York Ave. Co.*, 188 A.D.3d at 421, 131 N.Y.S.3d at 865 (denying motion to consolidate non-payment proceeding with lead-paint personal injury action).

53 Winters v. Rokoszak, 94 A.D.3d 1009, 943 N.Y.S.2d 122 (2d Dep't 2012) ("[r]emoval would not have been in the interest of the proper administration of justice" due to the lateness of the request); Eastside Exh. Corp. v. 210 E. 86th St. Corp., 2018 N.Y. Misc. LEXIS 6167 (N.Y. Cnty. Sup. Ct. Dec. 11, 2018) (denying motion for removal when used as a delay tactic).

54 *See* Peekskill Hous. Auth. v. Dunlap, 134 N.Y.S.3d 614 (App. Term, 9th & 10th Jud. Dists. 2020) (summary proceeding improper where lease termination provision did not include an automatic expiration date); Graves v. Hasan, 996 N.Y.S.2d 504 (N.Y. Civ. Ct. Kings Cnty. 2014) ("[i]t is well-settled that because such termination [i.e., where the lease provides for a condition upon which a breach allows the Landlord to exercise his or her reserved right to declare the lease terminated] is not an automatic expiration of the lease by lapse of time, it is not an expiration within the meaning of RPAPL § 711[,]" and, as a result, an ejectment action, as opposed to a summary proceeding, is required). For a discussion about conditional limitations and conditions subsequent within rental agreements, *see* Chapter 4, subdiv. D, *infra*.

or where either a co-tenant or joint tenant seeks ejectment against a co-tenant who "[o]usted [the movant] or did some other act amounting to a total denial of his right."[55]

To prevail on a cause of action for ejectment, the movant must demonstrate that he or she: (1) is the owner of an estate in tangible real property; (2) possesses a present or immediate right to possession of the real property; and (3) the defendant is in possession of the estate.[56] Common law principles, other than those statutorily amended, are applicable in an action for ejectment.[57]

It is well-established that where the parties have an existing tenancy of a definite term, the Tenant must be afforded notice prior to the commencement of an action for ejectment.[58] However, no notice, other than perhaps a mandatory non-renewal notice, is required when the Tenant holds over following the expiration of the lease and the parties do not create a new tenancy.[59]

The notification requirement is more complicated for a tenancy of an indefinite term, such as a month-to-month tenancy. There appears to be a split between the First and Second Judicial Departments on this issue. In the First Department, a month-to-month Tenant must be provided at least thirty (30) days notice, the equivalent to the statutorily required predicate notice period to terminate a month-to-month tenancy in

---

55 RPAPL § 633.

56 Noamex, Inc. v. Domsey Worldwide, Ltd., 192 A.D.3d 817, 144 N.Y.S.3d 77 (2d Dep't 2021). *Cf.* Blake Rising, LLC v. Atlantic Collision, Inc., 186 A.D.3d 551, 128 N.Y.S.3d 658 (2d Dep't 2020) (denying summary judgment where Plaintiff failed to demonstrate a right to immediate possession).

57 *See* Kosa v. Legg, 816 N.Y.S.2d 840 (Kings Cnty. Sup. Ct. 2006) (detailing the history of RPAPL Article 6 ejectment actions compared to RPAPL Article 7 summary proceedings).

58 *See, e.g.*, 406 W. 48th LLC v. Vaituzis, 74 A.D.3d 549, 902 N.Y.S.2d 351 (1st Dep't 2010) (Tenant in rent-stabilized apartment entitled to notice pursuant to the Rent Stabilization Code prior to commencement of ejectment action).

59 Alleyne v. Townsley, 110 A.D.2d 674, 487 N.Y.S.2d 600 (2d Dep't 1985) (holding that "[n]o statute abrogates the common-law rule that notice is unnecessary to maintain an ejectment action against a tenant who wrongfully holds over after expiration of a fixed and definite term"); Sheila Props., Inc. v. A Real Good Plumber, Inc., 74 A.D.3d 779, 904 N.Y.S.2d 709 (2d Dep't 2010) (same); *Kosa*, 816 N.Y.S.2d at 840 (same).

New York City, before an ejectment action may be commenced.[60] In the Second Department, several courts have adopted the common law's six (6) month notice period because the common law remains "unchanged, unless explicitly modified by statute," and RPAPL Article 6 did not "[s]pecifically abolish[] the common-law six-month notice requirement for ejectment actions in cases involving month-to-month tenants."[61]

The prevailing party in an ejectment action is entitled to recover up to six (6) years of damages.[62] There is an exception to the rule that an ejectment action must be brought in the Supreme Court. The New York City Civil Courts may also adjudicate an action for ejectment but only when the "assessed valuation" of the property does <u>not</u> exceed $50,000.[63]

60 *See, e.g.*, Lai v. Watson, 2021 N.Y. Misc. LEXIS 6203 (N.Y. Cnty. Sup. Ct. Nov. 30, 2021) (although 90 days notice was given, only thirty (30) days was required to terminate month-to-month tenancy prior to commencing ejectment action); Aurora Assoc., LLC v. Hennen, 2017 N.Y. Misc. LEXIS 72 (N.Y. Cnty. Sup. Ct. Jan. 6, 2017) (denying motion for summary judgment due to insufficient proof that at least thirty (30) days notice was given to month-to-month Tenant prior to commencement of ejectment action).

61 *See, e.g.*, Paz Rentals LLC v. Bryer, 2021 N.Y. Misc. LEXIS 1276 (Kings Cnty. Sup. Ct. March 22, 2021) ("[w]here the landlord accepts rent after the lease has expired this thereby creates a month to month tenancy, and six months' notice is required"); North Flats LLC v. Bradshaw, 2021 N.Y. Misc. LEXIS 49 (Kings Cnty. Sup. Ct. Jan. 4, 2021) ("[s]ince the defendants are tenants for an indefinite term, before the plaintiff can seek to eject the defendants from the premises, or any portion thereof, the plaintiff was required to serve the defendants with a six-month notice to quit"); *Kosa*, 816 N.Y.S.2d at 840 (holding "[t]he common-law requirement of a six-month notice to quit before a tenant may be removed through an ejectment action applies to month-to-month tenancies").

62 RPAPL § 601; *see* 542 Holding Corp. v. Prince Fashions, Inc., 46 A.D.3d 309, 848 N.Y.S.2d 37 (1st Dep't 2007).

63 N.Y. City Civil Ct. Act § 203(j), as amended by Constitutional Amendment approved in November 2021, increasing the New York City Civil Court's jurisdictional limit from $25,000 to $50,000. *See generally* 111-39 76th Rd. LLC v. Greenberg, 2021 N.Y.L.J. LEXIS 528 (Queens Cnty. Sup. Ct. June 3, 2021).

b. PARTITION (RPAPL ARTICLE 9)

When a party no longer wishes to share equal interest in real property with another party, the movant may seek to sever and divest their interests in an action for partition.[64] Partition is an equitable remedy, and generally may "[o]nly be sought by a person holding or possessing the real property as a joint tenant or tenant in common."[65]

A joint tenancy is defined as an "[e]state held by two or more persons jointly who have equal rights to share in its enjoyment during their lives, and where each joint tenant has a right of survivorship."[66] Survivorship in real property constitutes a "right of automatic inheritance" and, as a result, upon the passing of one (1) joint tenant, the deceased's property rights are inherited by the other joint tenant without consideration for the rules of intestate succession.[67]

In a tenancy-in-common, the co-tenants share equal rights to possession of all or a portion of the property as if each co-tenant is the sole owner of the premises. An example of tenants-in-common include, but is not limited to, siblings bequeathed equal ownership in the family residence.

An out-of-possession tenant-in-common maintains an equal right to possession even where the co-tenant has exclusive physical possession of the property.[68] The out-of-possession co-tenant is further insulated from a claim for adverse possession for a period of ten (10) years.[69]

To establish a claim for partition, the movant must establish ownership rights and the right to possession.[70] Partition is "[n]ot absolute and

---

64 RPAPL § 901(1).

65 Trotta v. Ollivier, 91 A.D.3d 8, 933 N.Y.S.2d 66 (2d Dep't 2011).

66 *See* PHH Mtge. Corp. v. Burt, 176 A.D.3d 1242, 112 N.Y.S.3d 231 (2d Dep't 2019); Goetz v. Slobey, 76 A.D.3d 954, 908 N.Y.S.2d 237 (2d Dep't 2010) (noting that a joint tenancy "[d]epends on the maintenance of the unities of title, interest and possession; and the destruction of any of these unities leads to a severance of the tenancy, and to the creation either of a tenancy in common or of several tenancies"); Bushell v. Bushell, 133 N.Y.S.3d 783 (Kings Cnty. Sup. Ct. 2020).

67 *PHH Mtge. Corp.*, 176 A.D.3d at 1242, 112 N.Y.S.3d at 231 (*citing Trotta*, 91 A.D.3d at 8, 933 N.Y.S.2d at 66).

68 Myers v. Batholomew, 91 N.Y.2d 630, 674 N.Y.S.2d 259 (1998); 169 MLS Realty Corp. v. One 69 Skill Corp., 197 A.D.3d 1079, 153 N.Y.S.3d 505 (2d Dep't 2021).

69 RPAPL § 541.

70 Korn v. Korn, 190 A.D.3d 1043, 139 N.Y.S.3d 701 (3d Dep't 2021).

may be precluded where the equities so demand...or where partition would result in prejudice."[71] As a practical matter, the parties' respective interests should be determined prior to the granting of partition.[72]

A claim for rent or use and occupancy may accompany a partition action, but absent an agreement or physical ouster, a tenant-in-common will generally not be liable to a co-tenant for the occupation of the premises.[73] The physical partition of property is "[t]he preferred method [of divestiture] and is presumed appropriate" unless it is shown that such action would result in "great prejudice."[74] Where "great prejudice" would result, the property may instead be sold at a public auction.[75] If the sale of the property is directed, an accounting may be required to determine the parties' proportionate share of the proceeds.[76]

F. INJUNCTIONS

Parties to a lease may seek relief other than possession and rent arrears that are beyond the jurisdictional authority of the Housing Part. These claims may include an injunction, which is interim temporary relief intended to maintain the parties' respective positions (the *status quo*) pending a final resolution of the underlying dispute. Whether seeking a *Yellowstone* injunction to toll "the clock" for curing an alleged breach of the lease or a preliminary injunction to enjoin certain

---

71 Manganiello v. Lipman, 74 A.D.3d 667, 905 N.Y.S.2d 153 (1st Dep't 2010); *see* Kosovsky v. Kosovsky, 187 A.D.3d 504, 130 N.Y.S.3d 314 (1st Dep't 2020) (granting partition and directing sale of cooperative apartment owned by Plaintiff and her stepson absent "great prejudice").

72 Wardally v. Wardally, 186 A.D.3d 531, 126 N.Y.S.3d 378 (2d Dep't 2020).

73 Perretta v. Perretta, 143 A.D.3d 878, 39 N.Y.S.3d 495 (2d Dep't 2016) (*citing* Jemzura v. Jemzura, 36 N.Y.2d 496, 369 N.Y.S.2d 400 (1975)).

74 *Id.*

75 Khotylev v. Spektor, 165 A.D.3d 1088, 87 N.Y.S.3d 58 (2d Dep't 2018); *Trotta*, 91 A.D.3d at 8, 933 N.Y.S.2d at 66.

76 *Khotylev*, 165 A.D.3d at 1088, 87 N.Y.S.3d at 58 ("[i]n light of the parties' dispute as to their respective entitlements to the proceeds from the sale of the property, an accounting is necessary to determine the parties' respective interests in the property"); Rozenberg v. Perlstein, 200 A.D.3d 915, 158 N.Y.S.3d 233 (2d Dep't 2021) (granting an accounting pending allegations of wrongdoing).

conduct, the application may not be heard in the Housing Part. As indicated previously, when a summary proceeding is pending in the Housing Part, removal and consolidation of related actions in the Supreme Court is a possibility.[77]

1. YELLOWSTONE INJUNCTION

For commercial properties, if a Notice to Cure for a specific breach of the rental agreement is served, the Tenant may seek to toll the "cure period" by obtaining a *Yellowstone* injunction.[78] The application for a *Yellowstone* injunction is typically made in conjunction with a declaratory judgment action in the Supreme Court. The Supreme Court's decision on the injunction is not an "adjudication on the merits of the validity of [the] landlord's termination of the lease and [does] not constitute law of the case."[79]

A *Yellowstone* injunction is intended to maintain the *status quo* during the pendency of the dispute.[80] The Tenant must provide the Landlord with notice of the application for injunctive relief in accordance with the terms of the parties' lease.

To obtain a *Yellowstone* injunction, a commercial Tenant must demonstrate that it: (1) holds a commercial lease; (2) received a Notice of Default, Notice to Cure, or other indicator that the rental agreement may be terminated; (3) made application for the injunction prior to the termination of the rental agreement; and (4) is capable of curing

77 For a discussion about removal and consolidation, *see* Chapter 1, subdiv. E(1), *supra*.

78 *See* First Nat'l Stores, Inc. v. Yellowstone Shopping Ctr., Inc., 21 N.Y.2d 630, at 637-38, 290 N.Y.S.2d 721 (1968); 146 Broadway Assocs., LLC v. Bridgeview at Broadway, LLC, 164 A.D.3d 1193, 84 N.Y.S.3d 241 (2d Dep't 2018); Hopp v. Raimondi, 51 A.D.3d 726, at 728, 858 N.Y.S.2d 300 (2d Dep't 2008).

79 60G 542 Broadway Owner, LLC v. Prince Fashions, Inc., 111 N.Y.S.3d 166 (App. Term, 1st Dep't 2018) (citations omitted); River Park Residences, LP v. Richman Plaza Garage Corp., 17 N.Y.S.3d 385 (App. Term, 1st Dep't 2015).

80 Graubard, Mollen, Horowitz, Pomeranz & Shapiro v. 600 Third Ave. Assocs., 93 N.Y.2d 508, at 514, 693 N.Y.S.2d 91 (1999); *146 Broadway Assocs., LLC*, 164 A.D.3d at 1193, 84 N.Y.S.3d at 241.

the breach by means other than vacating the premises.[81] Courts typically grant the application with "[f]ar less than the showing normally required for the grant of preliminary injunctive relief."[82]

The District Court, similar to other local Housing Parts, may not issue injunctive relief, thus the need to make the application in the Supreme Court. The request for a *Yellowstone* injunction must be made before the rental agreement terminates, whether upon its own expiration or the date specified within the Landlord's notice.[83] An untimely request for a *Yellowstone* injunction may be fatal to the Tenant's claims because Courts are generally "[p]owerless to revive [a terminated or] expired lease."[84] In other words, the Court is without authority to "re-

---

81 *See* Gap, Inc. v. 44-45 Broadway Leasing Co., LLC, 191 A.D.3d 549, 143 N.Y.S.3d 6 (1st Dep't 2021) (injunctive relief granted); 80 Broad Retail Assoc., LLC v. BSD 80 Broad LLC, 187 A.D.3d 534, 130 N.Y.S.2d 666 (1st Dep't 2020) (same); Artcorp. Inc. v. Citirich Realty Corp., 168 A.D.3d 515, 92 N.Y.S.3d 225 (1st Dep't 2019) (to obtain a *Yellowstone* injunction, there is no requirement to demonstrate a likelihood of success on the merits). *Cf.* Gap, Inc. v. 170 Broadway Retail Owner, 195 A.D.3d 575, 151 N.Y.S.3d 37 (1st Dep't 2021) (*Yellowstone* injunction denied when the request was made after the cure period expired); Bliss World LLC v. 10 W. 57th St. Realty LLC, 170 A.D.3d 401, 95 N.Y.S.3d 183 (1st Dep't 2019) (denying *Yellowstone* injunction where Tenant failed to procure adequate insurance, thereby resulting in a retroactive period for which there can be no coverage).

82 *Bliss World LLC*, 170 A.D.3d at 402, 95 N.Y.S.3d at 185; Trump on the Ocean, LLC, v. Ash, 81 A.D.3d 713, at 716, 916 N.Y.S.2d 177, 181 (2d Dep't 2011) (*citing* Post v. 120 E. End Ave. Corp., 62 N.Y.2d 19, at 24-25, 475 N.Y.S.2d 821, 823 (1984)). *Cf.* Faith In Action Deliverance Ministries v. 3231 Assoc., LLC, 168 A.D.3d 502, 92 N.Y.S.3d 213 (1st Dep't 2019) (enjoining commencement of summary proceeding and sale of the premises where movant demonstrated irreparable harm, a likelihood of success on the merits, and a balancing of the equities favoring injunctive relief).

83 *See Gap, Inc.*, 195 A.D.3d at 575, 151 N.Y.S.3d at 37; 255 Butler Assocs., LLC v. 255 Butler, LLC, 173 A.D.3d 649, 103 N.Y.S.3d 589 (2d Dep't 2019).

84 *Post*, 62 N.Y.2d at 24-25, 475 N.Y.S.2d at 823; 276-43 Gourmet Grocery, Inc. v. 250 W. 43 Owner LLC, 143 A.D.3d 432, 38 N.Y.S.3d 187 (1st Dep't 2016); Barsyl Supermarkets, Inc. v. Avenue P Assocs., LLC, 86 A.D.3d 545, at 546-47, 928 N.Y.S.2d 45, 47 (2d Dep't 2011). *But see* Audthan LLC v. Nick & Duke, LLC, 181 A.D.3d 503, 121 N.Y.S.3d 245 (1st Dep't 2020) (granting *Yellowstone* injunction because Courts have "[p]ermitted tenants such as plaintiff to rely on a longer cure period under the lease where, as here, there is evidence that the cure could not be effected in the shorter period, and that the tenant has made a diligent effort to cure"); Village Ctr. for Care v. Sligo Realty and Serv. Corp., 95 A.D.3d 219, 943 N.Y.S.2d 11 (1st Dep't 2012) (application for *Yellowstone* injunction timely, even when made after the initial cure date and service of the notice of termination, where lease contemplated Tenant's inability to cure the default within the cure period).

write" a lease by extending the deadline for curing the default.[85] Delays attributable to administrative error by the Clerk of the Court will not be held against the party seeking relief.[86] However, the application will be denied where the Tenant fails to "[d]emonstrate that it was [both] willing and able to cure its default."[87]

A *Yellowstone* injunction may be granted due to the non-payment of rent where the lease provides that the tenancy will be terminated if the rent is not paid in a timely manner following service of a Notice to Cure.[88] Although the overwhelming majority of *Yellowstone* injunctions involve commercial properties, the relief has been granted on limited occasions in proceedings involving residential properties.[89]

It is unclear whether *Yellowstone* injunctions continue to be available in residential cases. In 2008, the Appellate Division, Second

85 *Trump on the Ocean, LLC*, 81 A.D.3d at 716, 916 N.Y.S.2d at 181.

86 S & Y Grace Corp. v. Boston Post Food Corp., 189 A.D.3d 720, 140 N.Y.S.3d 5 (1st Dep't 2020) (granting *Yellowstone* injunction where the Clerk improperly rejected Tenant's Amended Complaint filed and served as a matter of right pursuant to CPLR § 3025(a)).

87 Good Fortune Rest., Inc. v. Kissena Group, LLC, 185 A.D.3d 1013, 126 N.Y.S.3d 371 (2d Dep't 2020).

88 3636 Greystone Owners, Inc. v. Greystone Bldg., 4 A.D.3d 122, 771 N.Y.S.2d 341 (1st Dep't 2004) (*citing* Lexington Ave. & 42nd St. Corp. v. 380 Lexchamp Operating, 205 A.D.2d 421, 613 N.Y.S.2d 402 (1st Dep't 1994) (holding that a *Yellowstone* injunction may be obtained due to the non-payment of rent where the lease provides that such non-payment is a conditional limitation which results in the automatic termination of the lease, thereby negating the Landlord's obligation to serve a rent demand, and further permitting commencement of a holdover proceeding as opposed to a non-payment proceeding)). The distinction is significant in that where the tenancy is terminated prior to the commencement of a summary proceeding, a holdover proceeding is proper which, dissimilar from a non-payment proceeding, would bar any opportunity for the Tenant to cure (i.e., pay) to avoid an eviction unless consented to by the Landlord. *See Lexington Ave. & 42nd St. Corp.*, 205 A.D.2d at 421, 613 N.Y.S.2d at 402. For a discussion about the differences between non-payment and holdover proceedings, and when the payment of rent arrears avoids the eviction, *see* Chapter 4, subdiv. C(1), *infra*.

89 *See Hopp*, 51 A.D.3d at 728, 858 N.Y.S.2d at 300; Caldwell v. American Package Co., Inc., 57 A.D.3d 15, 866 N.Y.S.2d 275 (2d Dep't 2008) (residential Tenants with a lease commercial in form); Gabai v. 130 Diamond St. LLC, 932 N.Y.S.2d 760 (Kings Cnty. Sup. Ct. 2011) (although *Yellowstone* injunction may be extended to residential Tenants where the Landlord served a rent demand for the non-payment of rent, the Tenant must demonstrate "[s]ome equity or defense that could not be raised in the summary proceeding").

Department noted that RPAPL § 753(4), which requires the Court to stay issuance of the warrant of eviction for ten (10) days to allow the Tenant an opportunity to cure the breach, only applied to residential dwellings within New York City.[90] The residential property at issue in *Hopp v. Raimondi* was located outside New York City, and, therefore, beyond the scope of protections afforded pursuant to RPAPL § 753(4). In granting the injunction, the Appellate Division went to great lengths to reconcile the geographic discrepancy.[91] Thereafter, in 2019, RPAPL § 753 was amended to expand the stay protections to all residential properties regardless of location. Due to the fact the ten (10) day stay pursuant to RPAPL § 753 is available in residential cases, the need for a *Yellowstone* injunction is diminished.

A commercial Tenant may not waive within a rental agreement its ability to seek a *Yellowstone* injunction in a declaratory judgment action.[92] In December 2019, the Legislature enacted RPL § 235-h in response to the Court of Appeals' decision in *159 MP Corp. v. Redbridge Bedford, LLC*. In that case, the Court upheld a commercial lease provision waiving the Tenant's ability to seek declaratory relief, including a *Yellowstone* injunction.[93] Real Property Law § 235-h now prohibits any such waiver, and a lease provision waiving the right to seek declaratory relief is null and void and against the public policy of the State.[94]

---

90 RPAPL § 753; *Hopp*, 51 A.D.3d at 728, 858 N.Y.S.2d at 300.

91 *Hopp*, 51 A.D.3d at 728, 858 N.Y.S.2d at 300.

92 Real Property Law ("RPL") § 235-h (effective Dec. 20, 2019).

93 33 N.Y.3d 353, 104 N.Y.S.3d 1 (2019). The Court reasoned that sophisticated parties were free to waive this right, in part, because "[t]he right to commence a declaratory judgment action, although a useful litigation tool, does not reflect such a fundamental public policy interest that it may not be waived by counseled, commercial entities in exchange for other benefits or concessions." *Id.* This is no longer the case. *See* 159 MP Corp. v. Redbridge Bedford, LLC, 2021 N.Y. Misc. LEXIS 2718 (Kings Cnty. Sup. Ct. April 9, 2021) (noting that RPL § 235-h may not be applied retroactively).

94 RPL § 235-h. *See* Redbridge Bedford v. 240 Bedford Ave. Realty Holding Corp., 145 N.Y.S.3d 275 (App. Term, 2d, 11th & 13th Jud Dists. 2021).

2. PRELIMINARY INJUNCTION

A party to a residential or commercial lease may also seek a preliminary injunction in the Supreme Court by demonstrating with clear and convincing evidence: (1) a likelihood of success on the merits; (2) irreparable harm; and (3) a balance of the equities favoring injunctive relief.[95] "The decision to grant or deny a motion for a preliminary injunction rests in the sound discretion of the motion court, and generally [the Appellate] Court will not disturb such determination absent unusual or compelling circumstances."[96]

A motion for a preliminary injunction similarly requires prior notice to the non-moving party.[97] Where a Tenant seeks a preliminary injunction, rather than a *Yellowstone* injunction, the Landlord's failure to serve a Notice to Cure is "irrelevant" because the Tenant was not afforded a "cure" period.[98]

a. IRREPARABLE INJURY

It is well-established that a preliminary injunction should not be granted where the movant may be compensated with money damages (i.e., there is no irreparable injury when monetary relief provides an "adequate remedy").[99] However, a business' "[l]oss of good will and damage to customer relationships, unlike the loss of specific sales, is not easily quantified or remedied by money damages," and may constitute

---

95 CPLR § 6301. *See, e.g.*, *Faith In Action Deliverance Ministries*, 168 A.D.3d at 502, 92 N.Y.S.3d at 213; Jones v. Park Front Apts., LLC, 73 A.D.3d 612, 901 N.Y.S.2d 46 (1st Dep't 2010).

96 Karr Graphics Corp. v. Spar Knitwear Corp., 192 A.D.3d 673, 144 N.Y.S.3d 64 (2d Dep't 2021) (*citing* Chana v. Machon Chana Women's Inst., Inc., 162 A.D.3d 637, 80 N.Y.S.3d 61 (2d Dep't 2018)).

97 CPLR § 6311.

98 City of New York v. Red River Partners, LLC, 2011 N.Y. Misc. LEXIS 5865 (N.Y. Cnty. Sup. Ct. Dec. 8, 2011).

99 Eastview Mall, LLC v. Grace Holmes, Inc., 182 A.D.3d 1057, 122 N.Y.S.3d 848 (4th Dep't 2020) (denying Landlord's motion to enjoin Tenant from early vacating and termination of lease where the lease contained a liquidated damages provision). *Cf.* Soundview Cinemas, Inc. v. AC I Soundview, LLC, 149 A.D.3d 1121, 53 N.Y.S.3d 157 (2d Dep't 2017) (vague and conclusory assertions about the inability to pay rent do not establish irreparable injury).

irreparable harm.[100] In a residential case, it has been held that the eviction of an individual receiving governmental financial rental assistance from a "long-time home" constituted irreparable injury.[101]

b. LIKELIHOOD OF SUCCESS ON THE MERITS

In *Karr Graphics Corp. v. Spar Knitwear Corp.*, the Appellate Division, Second Department held that a preliminary injunction was proper, in part, because the Tenant "[d]emonstrated that it has a likelihood of success on the merits of its claim for a judgment declaring that it validly exercised its option to renew the lease...."[102] The Court further held that the other prongs of the standard were satisfied because the Landlord failed to provide a notice of intent to enforce the "option window," which was required within the rental agreement, and the clear benefit of maintaining the *status quo* pending a resolution of the underlying claims.[103]

c. UNDERTAKING

CPLR § 6312 requires the posting of an undertaking for the "[p]urpose of compensat[ing] the enjoined party for damages incurred by reason of the injunction in the event it is determined that the beneficiary was not entitled to the injunction."[104] Although left to the discretion of the motion court, the amount the moving party posts must be "rationally related" to the potential damages demonstrated by the enjoined party.[105]

---

100 Marcone APW, LLC v. Servall Co., 85 A.D.3d 1693, 925 N.Y.S.2d 752 (4th Dep't 2011).

101 *Jones*, 73 A.D.3d at 612, 901 N.Y.S.2d at 46.

102 *Karr Graphics Corp.*, 192 A.D.3d at 673, 144 N.Y.S.3d at 64 (finding unpersuasive Landlord's interpretation that any breach, regardless of whether the breach had been cured, constituted a forfeiture of the Tenant's right to renew the lease).

103 *Id.*

104 CPLR § 6312(b); *Karr Graphics Corp.*, 192 A.D.3d at 673, 144 N.Y.S.3d at 64 (*citing* Hofstra Univ. v. Nassau County, N.Y., 166 A.D.3d 863, 87 N.Y.S.3d 248 (2d Dep't 2018)).

105 *Karr Graphics Corp.*, 192 A.D.3d at 673, 144 N.Y.S.3d at 64 (undertaking fixed in the amount of $30,000 was reasonable, and request for a higher amount was "unsubstantiated and speculative"); *Hofstra Univ.*, 166 A.D.3d at 863, 87 N.Y.S.3d at 248 (*citing* Olympic Ice Cream Co., Inc. v. Sussman, 151 A.D.3d 872, 54 N.Y.S.3d 690 (2d Dep't 2017) (reversing Order of Supreme Court directing $2.5 million undertaking when said amount was speculative)).

Public entities and officers, including the "[s]tate, a domestic municipal corporation or a public officer [on] behalf of the state or of such a corporation," are exempt from the undertaking posting requirements.[106] Although a public entity or agency, similar to a private party, may be liable for the amount fixed by the Court, it is <u>not</u> required to post an undertaking as a condition for the issuance of the injunction. Instead, the amount fixed by the Court constitutes the maximum amount the enjoined party may recover in the event the injunction is later determined to have been improperly issued.[107]

G. MECHANIC'S LIEN

A contractor who performed labor and/or supplied materials to improve the premises with the consent of or at the request of the property's owner may maintain a lien for the value of the labor and/or materials.[108] A contractor may foreclose upon the lien against the Landlord's property where the Tenant contracted with, but failed to pay in full, the contractor for the work performed at the premises.[109] A special proceeding to foreclose upon the lien is beyond the jurisdiction of the Housing Part and, instead, may be brought in the Supreme Court.

The Court of Appeals reasoned that a direct relationship between the contractor and Landlord was <u>not</u> required when the Landlord consented to the repairs.[110] However, an affirmative act by the Landlord is typically required to demonstrate consent, and the Court will review the "[o]wner's overall course of conduct and the nature of the relationship between the owner and the lienor" to assess whether consent, as

106 CPLR § 2512.

107 *Id.*; *Hofstra Univ.*, 166 A.D.3d at 863, 87 N.Y.S.3d at 248; Town of Putnam Val. v. Cabot, 50 A.D.3d 775, 856 N.Y.S.2d 166 (2d Dep't 2008); State of New York v. 735 Bedford LLC, 2020 N.Y. Misc. LEXIS 10776 (Kings Cnty. Sup. Ct. Aug. 13, 2020).

108 Lien Law ("Lien Law") § 3 (Mechanic's Lien on Real Property); *see* Seibel v. Ramsay, 2022 N.Y. Misc. LEXIS 2448 (N.Y. Cnty. Sup. Ct. May 11, 2022).

109 Ferrara v. Peaches Café LLC, 32 N.Y.3d 348, 91 N.Y.S.3d 349 (2018).

110 *Id.*; *see* Lien Law § 3.

defined within Lien Law § 3, was demonstrated.[111]

Agreeing to a lease term detailing specific improvements to the property has been deemed sufficient to satisfy the consent requirement.[112] Absent such a lease provision, the Court will look to the property owner's overall conduct and the nature of the relationship to determine whether the Landlord consented to the contracted work.

111 Shapiro v. Luxury One Corp., 2019 N.Y. Misc. LEXIS 13820 (Bronx Cnty. Sup. Ct. Aug. 26, 2019) (denying motion to dismiss proceeding due to factual dispute regarding consent).

112 *Ferrara*, 32 N.Y.3d at 348, 91 N.Y.S.3d at 349.

CHAPTER 2

RECENT LEGISLATION IMPACTING RESIDENTIAL TENANCIES

Legislation has recently been enacted that marks a significant shift in policy regarding several longstanding Landlord and Tenant law principles. Some of the changes pertaining to residential properties are discussed in this Chapter.

A. THE HOUSING STABILITY AND TENANT PROTECTION ACT (2019)

On June 14, 2019, the Statewide Housing Stability and Tenant Protection Act of 2019 ("HSTPA") was signed into law.[113] The HSTPA, which was enacted in response to a severe housing shortage,[114] contains fifteen (15) sections and implements widespread changes to both rent-regulated and non-regulated

113 Housing Stability and Tenant Protection Act of 2019, A.8281/S.6458 (Ch. 36 of the Laws of 2019). A subsequent chapter amendment was passed on June 20, 2019 and signed by the governor on June 25, 2019 (the "Chapter Amendment").

114 *See* 335-7 LLC v. City of New York, 2020 U.S. Dist. LEXIS 102425 (S.D.N.Y. June 11, 2020). In 2018, reportedly more than 188,000 New York residents were unable to afford their rent, and, the following year in New York City, the number of homeless persons surpassed 78,000, with approximately 43,000 of those families including children. *Id.*

premises.[115] These provisions may not be applied retroactively.[116]

For rent-controlled and rent-stabilized premises, the HSTPA, *inter alia*: (1) makes permanent the rent regulations that were previously due to expire;[117] (2) repeals de-regulation statutes for both "high income" (household income over $200,000) and vacant apartments when statutory thresholds are exceeded;[118] (3) authorizes the continuation of preferential rent (rates below the regulated rent) in lease renewals;[119] (4) extends the look-back period for rent overcharge claims to six (6) years (previously four (4) years) and eliminates a loophole that negates liability (treble damages) when refunds are offered prior to a judicial or administrative adjudication;[120] (5) provides counties discretionary authority to implement rent stabilization ordinances and create local rent guidelines boards when the local rental vacancy rate falls to five percent

---

115 The changes were significant, and the reader should remain current on the present state of the law.

116 *See* Regina Metro. Co., LLC v. New York State Div. of Hous. & Cmty. Renewal, 35 N.Y.3d 332, 130 N.Y.S.3d 759 (2020) (holding that the "[n]ewly enacted overcharge calculation provisions [of the HSTPA] may not be applied retroactively") (emphasis added); Kuzmich v. 50 Murray St. Acquisition LLC, 187 A.D.3d 670, 135 N.Y.S.3d 368 (1st Dep't 2020) (same regarding rent overcharge); Harris v. Israel, 191 A.D.3d 468, 119 N.Y.S.3d 800 (1st Dep't 2021) (holding that the provisions of Part I of the HSTPA, specifically the non-renewal of leases for rent-stabilized apartments, may not be applied retroactively); Rochdale Vil. v. Baker, 2021 N.Y. Misc. LEXIS 4474 (N.Y. Civ. Ct. Queens Cnty. May 4, 2021) (same regarding restrictions on monetary relief set forth in Part M, at RPAPL § 702).

117 HSTPA, Part A; ADMINISTRATIVE CODE OF THE CITY OF NEW YORK ("NYC ADMIN. CODE") § 26-504. *See* B.G.R. Realty LLC v. Stein, 120 N.Y.S.3d 552 (App. Term, 1st Dep't 2020) (as clarified by subsequent legislation, the HSTPA repealed high rent vacancy deregulation, and in no way "[r]e-regulated units that had been legally deregulated under previous rent laws").

118 HSTPA, Part D.

119 HSTPA, Part E; NYC ADMIN. CODE § 26-511.

120 HSTPA, Part F; NYC ADMIN. CODE § 26-516(a)(2). *Cf.* CPLR § 213-a(8) (action based upon fraud). *See Regina Metro. Co., LLC*, 35 N.Y.3d at 332, 130 N.Y.S.3d at 759 (noting that the statute of limitations on rent overcharge claims is six (6) years); Gridley v. Turnbury Vil., 196 A.D.3d 95, 149 N.Y.S.3d 243 (2d Dep't 2021) (same). The Appellate Division, First Department concluded that the statute of limitations for rent overcharge claims may be extended where "there is evidence of fraudulent conduct on the part of the landlord." Fuentes v. Kwik Realty LLC, 186 A.D.3d 435, 130 N.Y.S.3d 16 (1st Dep't 2020); Stafford v. A & E Real Estate Holdings, LLC, 188 A.D.3d 583, 132 N.Y.S.3d 636 (1st Dep't 2020); 40-40-40-38 78th St. v. Murillo, 147 N.Y.S.3d 687 (App. Term, 2d, 11th & 13th Jud. Dists. 2021).

(5%) or below;[121] (6) repeals the "vacancy" and "longevity" bonuses that permitted rent increases up to twenty percent (20%) and an additional six-tenths percent (.6%), respectively, and further prohibits local rent guidelines boards from implementing their own bonus rates;[122] (7) limits the "owner use" exception, which avoids automatic renewal of the Tenant's lease, to one (1) apartment (previously the Landlord was permitted to assert the exception on an unlimited number of apartments);[123] and (8) restricts rent increases for major building capital improvements ("MCI") and individual apartment increases ("IAI").[124]

Due to the potential impact upon many Tenants within a rent-regulated apartment complex, class actions have resulted when similarly situated Tenants asserted (or could potentially assert) the same or similar claims based upon a policy decision or the Landlord's conduct.[125] For example, in *Borden v. 400 E. 55th St. Assocs., L.P.*, the Court of Appeals certified the class of Tenants within a rent-regulated apartment complex notwithstanding the Tenants' waiver of their rights to recover non-mandatory statutory penalties (i.e., treble damages).[126]

Part M of the HSTPA is titled The Statewide Housing Security and Tenant Protection Act ("Housing Security Act") and is applicable on a statewide basis to all residential properties (both regulated and

---

121 HSTPA, Part G; EMERGENCY TENANT PROTECTION ACT OF 1974, ("ETPA") § 14(b).

122 HSTPA, Part C; NYC ADMIN. CODE § 26-510(j).

123 HSTPA, Part I; NYC ADMIN. CODE §§ 26-408(b)(1) (rent control), 26-511(c)(9)(b) (rent stabilization).

124 HSTPA, Part K; NYC ADMIN. CODE §§ 26-405.1 (rent control), 26-511(c)(6),(13), 26-511.1 (rent stabilization).

125 *See, e.g.*, Borden v. 400 E. 55th St. Assocs., L.P., 24 N.Y.3d 382, 998 N.Y.S.2d 729 (2014) (rent overcharge claim); Chernett v. Spruce 1209, LLC, 200 A.D.3d 596, 161 N.Y.S.3d 48 (1st Dep't 2021) (same); Casey v. Whitehouse Estates, 197 A.D.3d 401, 153 N.Y.S.3d 6 (1st Dep't 2021) (same).

126 *Borden*, 24 N.Y.3d at 382, 998 N.Y.S.2d at 729. The factors for class certification are: (1) the class size and practicality of joining all of the members; (2) commonality of questions of law or fact; (3) whether the claims and defenses are typical of the class; (4) adequacy of the representation and ability to protect the interests of the class; and (5) the justification of the result. *Id.*; CPLR § 901(a). *See also* Maddicks v. Big City Props., LLC, 163 A.D.3d 501, 84 N.Y.S.3d 4 (1st Dep't 2018) (reasoning that "[c]lass actions may be appropriate where the members of the class include former tenants, who may be unaware of their rights").

non-regulated premises).[127] In addition to eliminating attorney's fees in the event of a default by the Tenant,[128] the Housing Security Act, *inter alia*: (1) defines the term "rent" and limits money judgments;[129] (2) modifies rent demand requirements;[130] (3) renders non-payment proceedings moot when rent arrears are paid prior to the hearing;[131] (4) amends month-to-month tenancy notice requirements;[132] (5) imposes mandatory written notice requirements prior to rent increases of at least five percent (5%) and where the Landlord refuses to re-new an expiring lease;[133] (6) limits late fees (to the lesser of $50 or five percent (5%)) and other expenses, including background and credit checks, to the actual cost or $20, whichever is less;[134] (7) expands the time to respond to the Petition, including permitting in-person denials on the return date;[135] (8) requires the granting of an initial request for an adjournment, regardless of reason, for at least fourteen (14) days unless both parties agree to a shorter adjournment;[136] (9) expands the Court's stay authority;[137] (10) increases the notice period the Sheriff or Marshal must provide prior to an eviction to fourteen (14) days (previously seventy-two (72) hours);[138] (11) requires additional language to be included within the warrant of eviction, including the earliest date

127 HSTPA, Part M.

128 *Id.* at § 8; RPL § 234.

129 HSTPA, Part M § 11; RPAPL § 702.

130 HSTPA, Part M § 12; RPAPL § 711.

131 HSTPA, Part M § 13; RPAPL § 731.

132 HSTPA, Part M §§ 6-7; RPL §§ 232-a, 232-b.

133 HSTPA, Part M § 3; § RPL § 226-c.

134 HSTPA, Part M § 10; RPL § 238-a(1). Payment may be demanded prior to the tenancy, but only after the background and credit checks (and proof of payment) have been provided to the prospective Tenant. *See* RPL §§ 238-a(1)(a),(b). The fee is automatically waived when a prospective Tenant submits a background check and/or credit report prepared within the previous thirty (30) days. A lease provision that waives or minimizes these restrictions is void as against public policy. *Id.*

135 HSTPA, Part M §§ 14-16; RPAPL §§ 732, 733, 743.

136 HSTPA, Part M § 17; RPAPL § 745.

137 HSTPA, Part M §§ 21-22; RPAPL §§ 753, 756.

138 HSTPA, Part M § 19; RPAPL § 749(2).

an eviction may take place;[139] (12) imposes criminal and civil liability for unlawful evictions;[140] (13) establishes mitigation responsibilities for residential Landlords;[141] (14) places limits on the retention of security deposits;[142] (15) expands protections against retaliatory evictions;[143] and (16) prohibits the Unified Court System from disseminating information regarding residential tenancies to third-party vendors.[144]

In addition, the Housing Security Act makes it unlawful pursuant to RPL § 227-f to decline to offer a prospective Tenant a lease on the basis that the individual was "involved in a past or pending" eviction proceeding. There is a rebuttable presumption of a violation of RPL § 227-f when a lease is not offered to a prospective Tenant following the Landlord's inspection of Court records or the retention of "information from a tenant screening bureau."[145] The Attorney General has standing to pursue injunctive relief and civil penalties between $500 and $1,000 for each violation on behalf of the aggrieved party.[146]

Part N of the HSTPA implements additional restrictions on evictions involving cooperative apartments and condominiums.[147] Part O expands protections to mobile home owners and manufactured home park Tenants.[148]

139 HSTPA, Part M § 19; RPAPL § 749(1).

140 HSTPA, Part M § 24; RPAPL § 768.

141 HSTPA, Part M § 4; RPL § 227-e.

142 HSTPA, Part M § 25; GOL § 7-108.

143 HSTPA, Part M § 2; RPL § 233-b.

144 HSTPA, Part M § 26; Judiciary Law § 212.

145 HSTPA, Part M § 5; RPL § 227-f(1). *See generally* LNV v. Amin, 127 N.Y.S.3d 740 (N.Y. Civ. Ct. Bronx Cnty. 2020) (analogizing RPL § 227-f (refusal to rent provision) and RPAPL § 757, which requires the sealing of summary proceedings involving foreclosed premises).

146 RPL § 227-f(2).

147 *See, e.g.*, Building and Realty Inst. of Westchester & Putnam Counties, Inc. v. New York, 2021 U.S. Dist. LEXIS 174535 (S.D.N.Y. Sept. 14, 2021) (noting Part N increased the Tenant approval threshold to convert a building into a cooperative apartment or condominium from fifteen percent (15%) to fifty-one percent (51%)).

148 For a discussion on manufactured home parks and mobile homes, *see* Chapter 10, *infra*.

B. RENT REGULATION

In New York, rent regulation was the government's response to the "[h]ousing shortage following World War II."[149] Rent regulation refers to rent control and rent stabilization laws, which were designed "to prevent speculative, unwarranted and abnormal increases in rents"[150] and, at present, impact more than one (1) million households in New York City alone.[151]

The New York State Division of Housing and Community Renewal ("DHCR") regulates the rents of rent-controlled and rent-stabilized apartments and resolves disputes in administrative proceedings independent of the courts. The DHCR is required to prepare annual public reports and maintain a centralized electronic data retention system.[152]

1. RENT CONTROL

In 1946, after the lifting of Federal restrictions following World War II, New York enacted the State's initial version of rent regulation with the passage of the Emergency Housing Rent Control Law. In 1962, the State ceded authority over rent control to New York City with the passage of the Local Emergency Housing Rent Control Act and, thereafter, the New York City Rent and Rehabilitation Law, which effectively limits the amount of rent that may be charged to Tenants or their successors who since 1971 have continuously resided within a residential building

149 Rent Stabilization Ass'n of N.Y.C., Inc. v. New York State Div. of Hous. & Cmty. Renewal, 83 N.Y.2d 156, at 164, 608 N.Y.S.2d 930, 932 (1993). The New York City Rent Stabilization Law was held constitutional under the Takings, Contracts, Due Process and Equal Protection Clauses of the United States Constitution. *See* Harmon v. Markus, 2011 U.S. App. LEXIS 4629 (2d Cir. March 8, 2011), *cert. denied*, Harmon v. Kimmel, 132 S.Ct. 1991 (2012).

150 Georgetown Unsold Shares, LLC v. Ledet, 130 A.D.3d 99, 12 N.Y.S.3d 160 (2d Dep't 2015).

151 *See* 335-7 LLC v. City of New York, 524 F. Supp.3d 316 (S.D.N.Y. 2021); Emily Nonko, "*Everything You Need to Know About Rent Regulation in New York City*," New York Curbed, Jan. 3, 2020, at https://ny.curbed.com.

152 HSTPA, Part L.

constructed prior to February 1, 1947.[153]

Several years later, in 1983, the State re-claimed authority over rent control and designated DHCR as the governing agency.[154] Notwithstanding the transfers of control since inception, rent-control regulations have remained relatively intact.[155] Rent increases are based upon a Maximum Base Rent ("MBR") determined by DHRC, as adjusted by a Maximum Collectible Rent ("MCR"), and a five-year average of rent increases.[156]

The grounds (or justification) for a Landlord to re-gain possession of a rent-controlled apartment within New York City are codified at § 26-408 of the New York City Administrative Code and promulgated at § 2204.2 of Title 9 of the New York Codes, Rules and Regulations ["N.Y.C.C.R."]. The grounds for eviction include, but are not limited to, the Tenant's: (1) failure to pay rent;[157] (2) failure to cure a violation of a substantial obligation of the tenancy following service of a ten (10) day Notice to Cure;[158] (3) willful violation of a substantial lease obligation resulting in "serious and substantial injury to the landlord" within the three (3) month period prior to the eviction proceeding;[159] (4) committing or permitting nuisance and/or objectionable conduct at the premises;[160] (5) causing substantial damage to the premises either with

153 *See* City Rent and Rehabilitation Law, NYC Admin. Code §§ 26-401 to 26-415 (rent control within New York City). *See generally* 335-7 LLC v. City of New York, 524 F. Supp.3d 316 (S.D.N.Y. 2021) (description of the history of rent regulation in New York); Equity Properties Corp. v. Joy, 48 A.D.2d 630, 368 N.Y.S.2d 514 (1st Dep't 1975) ("[t]he purpose of the rent control laws is to protect the tenants in possession [of premises constructed before 1947] and to return apartments becoming vacant after June 30, 1971 to the free market").

154 *See* City of New York v. State Div. of Hous. & Cmty. Renewal, 97 N.Y.2d 216, 739 N.Y.S.2d 333 (2001).

155 *See* Brookford, LLC v. State Div. of Hous. & Cmty. Renewal, 142 A.D.3d 433, 36 N.Y.S.3d 39 (1st Dep't 2016).

156 *See* New York State Attorney General website, "*Residential Tenants' Rights Guide,*" at 7, at https://ag.ny.gov; *see* Nonko, "*Everything You Need to Know About Rent Regulation in New York City,*" at New York Curbed, at https://ny.curbed.com.

157 NYC Admin. Code § 26-408(a).

158 *Id.* at. § 26-408(a)(1); 9 New York Codes, Rules and Regulations [N.Y.C.R.R.] § 2204.2(a)(1).

159 NYC Admin. Code § 26-408(a)(1); 9 N.Y.C.R.R. § 2204.2(a)(1).

160 NYC Admin. Code § 26-408(a)(2); 9 N.Y.C.R.R. § 2204.2(a)(2).

intent or by means of gross negligence;[161] (6) substantial interference with the Landlord's or other Tenants' "comfort and safety" within the same or adjacent building;[162] (7) unlawful occupancy of the premises;[163] (8) use of the premises for "immoral or illegal" purposes;[164] (9) refusal to execute a renewal lease on the same terms not in excess of one (1) year;[165] (10) unreasonable denial of access to the premises that prevents the Landlord from making required repairs;[166] and (11) with exceptions, after obtaining a certificate of eviction from DHCR, the Landlord demonstrates an "immediate and compelling" need to occupy the premises as his or her primary residence or the primary residence of an immediate family member.[167] Except for an eviction proceeding due to the non-payment of rent, the Landlord must provide the Tenant written notice prior to the commencement of a summary proceeding in accordance with 9 N.Y.C.R.R. § 2204.3.

The primary Tenant of a rent-controlled apartment may transfer the tenancy to a family member provided the successor family member resided within the apartment as his or her primary residence for the two (2) immediate consecutive years, or, if the successor is either a senior citizen or a disabled person, then the immediate consecutive period of not less than one (1) year, prior to the primary Tenant's permanent vacating.[168] There are exceptions to the continuous residency requirements which include "temporary relocation" for military duty,

---

161 NYC Admin. Code § 26-408(a)(2); 9 N.Y.C.R.R. § 2204.2(a)(2).

162 NYC Admin. Code § 26-408(a)(2); 9 N.Y.C.R.R. § 2204.2(a)(2).

163 NYC Admin. Code § 26-408(a)(3); 9 N.Y.C.R.R. § 2204.2(a)(3).

164 NYC Admin. Code § 26-408(a)(4); 9 N.Y.C.R.R. § 2204.2(a)(4).

165 NYC Admin. Code § 26-408(a)(5); 9 N.Y.C.R.R. § 2204.2(a)(5).

166 NYC Admin. Code § 26-408(a)(6); 9 N.Y.C.R.R. § 2204.2(a)(6).

167 NYC Admin. Code § 26-408(b)(1).

168 9 N.Y.C.R.R. § 2204.6(d)(1). The statute defines an eligible "family member" for succession rights as a "[s]pouse, son, daughter, stepson, stepdaughter, father, mother, stepfather, stepmother, brother, sister, grandfather, grandmother, grandson, granddaughter, father-in-law, mother-in-law, son-in-law, or daughter-in-law of the tenant; or any other person residing with the tenant in the housing accommodation as a primary residence who can prove emotional and financial commitment, and interdependence between such person and the tenant"). 9 N.Y.C.R.R. § 2204.6(d)(3).

matriculation as a full-time student, and hospitalization.[169]

Although rent-controlled succession rules for family members are similarly applicable to rent-stabilized premises, the obligations and requirements are not identical.[170] Absent an appropriate succession transfer, a regulated apartment may no longer qualify for such relief, and, once a rent-controlled apartment is permanently vacated, it typically becomes subject to the rent stabilization laws.[171]

Not surprisingly, the number of rent-controlled apartments have dramatically declined over the past several decades. During the 1950s, there were approximately two (2) million rent-controlled apartments in New York City, but today that number has dropped to below 20,000.[172] In addition to New York City, rent control regulations have been instituted in portions of Albany, Erie, Nassau, and Westchester counties; i.e., municipalities that have not legislatively "declared an end" to the post-World War II housing emergency.[173]

2. RENT STABILIZATION

In 1969, New York City established rent stabilization laws with the passage of the Rent Stabilization Act as "a means to control a perceived penchant toward unreasonably high rent increases" amidst the housing

---

169 9 N.Y.C.R.R. § 2204.6(d)(1).

170 *See* 90 Elizabeth Apt. LLC v. Eng, 64 N.Y.S.3d 486 (N.Y. Civ. Ct. N.Y. Cnty. 2017) (noting that "[s]uccession propositions applying to tenancies subject to the Rent Stabilization Law are not congruent with those applying to tenancies subject to the Rent Control Law").

171 *See* New York State Attorney General website, "*Residential Tenants' Rights Guide,*" at 7, at https://ag.ny.gov.

172 *See* Nonko, "*Everything You Need to Know About Rent Regulation in New York City,*" New York Curbed, at https://ny.curbed.com (citing a 2019 survey, the median gross rent for a rent-controlled apartment in New York City was approximately $1,039 per month).

173 *See* New York State DHCR website, Office of Rent Administration, "*Rent Programs Overview,*" at https://hcr.ny.gov. *See also* EMERGENCY HOUSING RENT CONTROL LAW, N.Y. UNCONSOL. LAW §§ 8581 to 8597 (McKinney 2002) (rent control outside New York City). Sections 26-403.1 (High Income Rent Deregulation) and 26-403.2 (Increase in Maximum Collectable Rent) of the NYC ADMIN. CODE (rent control in New York City) and section 8582-a of the EMERGENCY HOUSING RENT CONTROL LAW were repealed by the HSTPA.

crisis during the Vietnam War.[174] Rent stabilization limits the amount of rent charged and the frequency of rent increases, and further provides protections against unwarranted evictions in the form of mandatory lease renewals.

Rent stabilization laws apply to each of the following privately-owned residential buildings: (1) buildings constructed between February 1, 1947 and December 31, 1973, having six (6) or more apartments; (2) buildings constructed prior to February 1, 1947, provided the Tenant took possession after June 30, 1971; (3) buildings constructed or renovated on or after January 1, 1947, having specified tax benefits and three (3) or more apartments; and (4) on many occasions, rent-controlled apartments that have become vacant.[175]

The Court of Appeals reasoned that rent stabilization imposes "a less onerous burden on the property owner" than rent control.[176] The legislative history further provides that "[i]n promulgating a rent stabilization regime, as opposed to rent control, legislators sought to balance the interests of landlords and of those tenants who occupy their apartments as primary residences."[177]

The justification for the removal of a Tenant from a rent-stabilized apartment within New York City mirrors the eleven (11) grounds

174 *See 335-7 LLC*, 524 F. Supp.3d at 316 (noting the City Council's position that "unless residential rents and evictions continue to be regulated and controlled, disruptive practices and abnormal conditions will produce serious threats to the public health, safety and general welfare"); Building & Realty Inst. of Westchester & Putnam Cntys., Inc. v. New York, 2021 U.S. Dist. LEXIS 174535, at *5-8 (S.D.N.Y. Sept. 23, 2020).

175 New York State DHCR website, "*Rent Stabilization and Emergency Tenant Protection Act*," at https://hcr.ny.gov. *See* RENT STABILIZATION LAW, NYC ADMIN. CODE §§ 26-501 to 26-520 (McKinney 2000) (rent stabilization within New York City). Sections 26-504.1 (Exclusion of Accommodations of High Income Renters), 26-504.2 (Exclusion of High Rent Accommodations), and 26-504.3 (High Income Rent Decontrol) of the NYC ADMIN. CODE (rent control in New York City) were repealed by the HSTPA. *See generally* Boyd v. Assanah, 2019 N.Y. Misc. LEXIS 1060 (Kings Cnty. Sup. Ct. March 8, 2019) (noting that the units need not be in compliance with building and town codes for rent stabilization to apply); Robrish v. Watson, 26 N.Y.S.3d 216 (App. Term, 2d, 11th & 13th Jud. Dists. 2015) (housing accommodation for ten (10) rooms in a residence built prior to 1974 is subject to rent stabilization). A "housing accommodation" is defined as the "part of any building or structure, occupied or intended to be occupied by one or more individuals as a residence, home, dwelling unit or apartment." *See* 9 N.Y.C.R.R. § 2520.6(a).

176 Braschi v. Stahl Assocs. Co., 74 N.Y.2d 201, 544 N.Y.S.2d 784 (1989).

177 *Georgetown Unsold Shares, LLC*, 130 A.D.3d at 99, 12 N.Y.S.3d at 160.

previously discussed when seeking to re-gain possession of a rent-controlled apartment.[178] The Tenant's failure to occupy the rent-stabilized apartment as his or her primary residence may constitute an additional basis for refusing to re-new the lease and, if necessary, commencing a summary proceeding after providing the Tenant the requisite written notices: (1) thirty (30) days prior to commencing the summary proceeding and (2) between 90 and 150 days prior to the expiration of the lease.[179] Other than the failure to pay rent, a written notice pursuant to 9 N.Y.C.R.R. § 2524.2 must be served on the Tenant prior to the commencement of a summary proceeding. If the Tenant pays the rent and is otherwise in compliance with the other material terms of the tenancy, then the Landlord is generally precluded from seeking possession and is obligated to offer either a one-year or two-year renewal lease.[180] Owners of rent-stabilized buildings must further file annual building registrations with the Office of Rent Administration.[181]

Outside New York City, rent stabilization is authorized by the Emergency Tenant Protection Act ("ETPA"), which was passed in 1974. Rent stabilization was initially only available outside New York City within portions of Nassau, Rockland, and Westchester counties where the vacancy rate was five percent (5%) or less.[182] However, Part G of the HSTPA expanded opt-in discretion to all counties declaring housing

---

178 The grounds to recover possession of a rent-stabilized premises are set forth at 9 N.Y.C.R.R. §§ 2524.3 and 2524.4. For a sampling of eviction grounds, *see* footnotes 157—167 and accompanying text, *supra*.

179 9 N.Y.C.R.R. §§ 2524.2[c](2), 2524.4[c]. *See generally* 700 Bklyn Realty, LLC v. Bklyn Realty, LLC, 154 N.Y.S.3d 732 (App. Term, 2d, 11th & 13th Jud. Dists. 2021). For additional information on recovering possession of rent-stabilized premises and the Landlord's refusal to renew the tenancy for cause, including the Tenant's failure to occupy the premises as his or her primary residence, *see* Chapter 6, subdiv. C(16)-(18), *infra*. The affirmative defense of succession rights is discussed in Chapter 11, subdiv. A(10), *infra*.

180 9 N.Y.C.R.R. § 2524.1.

181 New York State DHCR website, "*Rent Stabilization and Emergency Tenant Protection Act*," at https://hcr.ny.gov.

182 ETPA §§ 8621 to 8634 (McKinney 2007) (rent stabilization outside New York City). Rent stabilization in these jurisdictions is typically applicable to buildings constructed prior to 1974 containing not less than six (6) apartments. *See* New York State Attorney General website, "*Residential Tenants' Rights Guide*," at 8, at https://ag.ny.gov.

emergencies that have rental vacancy rates at five percent (5%) or below.

The ETPA further authorized the creation of Rent Guidelines Boards ("RGB") that regulate rent increases for rent-stabilized apartments, lofts, hotels, and single room occupancies. For rent-stabilized apartments and lofts in New York City, the 2022 and 2023 rent increases were narrowly approved by the RGB. The RGB voted by a 5 to 4 margin to raise rents three and one-quarter percent (3.25%) for one-year and five percent (5%) for two-year lease renewals between October 1, 2022 and September 30, 2023.[183]

C. GOOD CAUSE EVICTIONS

Excluding New York City, at the time of publication three (3) New York municipalities required residential Landlords to provide justification or "good cause" for commencing an eviction proceeding. Generally, good cause eviction laws apply to evictions for a breach of a material lease provision and the refusal to offer renewal leases. In other words, good cause eviction ordinances require the Landlord to offer a new lease and refrain from terminating a market-rate tenancy unless the Tenant breaches one (1) or more of the municipality's good cause ordinances, such as the failure to pay rent or other infractions.

On November 15, 2021, the City of Poughkeepsie became the State's third jurisdiction, following Albany[184] and Newburgh,[185] to adopt a good

183 *See* Greg David and Rachel Holliday Smith, "*Rent Guidelines Board 3.25% Hike is Biggest in Nearly A Decade*," The City, June 21, 2022, at https://thecity.nyc/housing/2022/6/21/23177932/rent-guidelines-board-increase.com. The previous increase was one and one-half percent (1.5%) for one-year lease renewals (last six (6) months only) and two and one-half percent (2.5%) for two-year renewals between October 1, 2021 and September 30, 2022. *See* RGB Order No. 53, June 23, 2021.

184 Albany City Code, Loc. L. F, Art. XIII, Prohibition of Eviction Without Cause (July 19, 2021). The ordinance was found to be unlawful by the Albany County Supreme Court on June 30, 2022.

185 Newburgh City Code, Loc. L. 6-2021, Ch. 240, Art. III, Prohibition of Eviction Without Good Cause (Oct. 25, 2021).

cause eviction ordinance.[186] Approximately four (4) months later, on March 7, 2022, the City of Beacon became the fourth municipality to enact good cause eviction legislation.[187] Parenthetically, in December 2021, the Hudson Common Council voted against a good cause eviction ordinance after preliminarily approving a version two (2) months earlier.[188]

On June 30, 2022, the City of Albany's good cause eviction ordinance was declared null and void, thereby decreasing the number of municipalities with good cause eviction ordinances (excluding New York City) to three (3). In *Pusatere v. City of Albany*, the Court held that the City of Albany's eviction ordinance (Local Law F) was pre-empted by State law because the State does not impose a good cause eviction requirement on non-regulated residential premises.[189]

---

186 The good cause grounds to evict a residential Tenant pursuant to the Poughkeepsie ordinance, Local Law 21-04, include the following: failing to pay rent at a reasonable rate; violating a legal obligation under the lease other than the failure to surrender possession; failing to cure a breach following receipt of a ten (10) day written notice; nuisance conduct or causing property damage; interfering with the quiet use and enjoyment of others; permitting or participating in illegal activity at the premises; refusing to permit the Landlord reasonable access to make repairs or to show the premises to a prospective purchaser; Landlord's good faith intent to use the premises as a personal residence; Landlord's good faith entering into a contract for the sale of the premises; and the Tenant's bad faith rejection of a reasonable written lease renewal offer. *See* POUGHKEEPSIE CITY CODE, Ch. 12, Housing, Loc. L. 21-04, Prohibit Evictions Without Good Cause, (Nov. 2021).

187 *See* Mike Benischeck, "'*Good Cause Eviction' Law Passes in Beacon: What It Does, Why It Was Argued*'," Poughkeepsie Journal, March 8, 2022, at https://amp.poughkeepsiejournal.com/amp/9428908002. The Beacon ordinance further requires, *inter alia*, that a Landlord obtain approval from the Court before increasing a Tenant's rent by more than five percent (5%). *Id.*

188 *See* Noah Eckstein, "*Good Cause Law Fails in 5—5 Tie*," Columbia-Greene Media, Dec. 22, 2021, at https://hudsonvalley360.com. The council vote was deadlocked at five (5), with one (1) abstention. *Id.*

189 *See* Lucas Willard, "New York Judge Strikes Down Albany's 'Good Cause' Eviction Law," WAMC Northeast Public Radio, June 30, 2022, at https://www.wamc.org/news/2022-06-30/new-york-judge-strikes-down albany-good-cause-eviction-law. The decision is *Pusatere v. City of Albany*, Index No. 909653-22 (Albany Cnty. Sup. Ct. June 30, 2022).

CHAPTER 3

THE GOVERNMENT'S RESPONSE TO THE COVID-19 PANDEMIC

On January 15, 2022, the New York eviction moratorium ended. The following week, the total number of COVID-19 cases within the United States had risen above 70 million, and approximately 864,000 of those cases tragically resulted in death. New York accounted for more than 4.6 million cases (or 6.6%) and approximately 63,000 deaths (or 7.3%).[190]

In response to the Pandemic, which New York defined as the period between March 7, 2020 and January 15, 2022 ("the COVID-19 Period"), the Federal and State governments enacted several laws and regulations. The Courts similarly implemented procedures and protocols to apply the newly enacted legislation and a framework for remaining operational during this very challenging period. The reader should be mindful that much of the COVID-19 specific legislation has expired, and subsequent legislation may further impact existing laws.

The government's handling of the Pandemic will be studied for generations. The author does <u>not</u> express an opinion, express or implicit, on the effectiveness of any of the measures.

190 *See* N.Y. Times Coronavirus Outbreak Online Tracker, dated Jan. 22, 2022, at https://www.nytimes.com/interactive.

A. NEW YORK COVID-19 PANDEMIC LAWS

1. TENANT SAFE HARBOR ACT

On June 30, 2020, the Tenant Safe Harbor Act ("TSHA") was enacted.[191] The TSHA, which applies to residential properties only,[192] bars an eviction for the non-payment of rent where the Tenant or lawful occupant suffered a "financial hardship" during the COVID-19 Period.[193] In other words, a residential Tenant who suffered a financial hardship during the COVID-19 Period may not be evicted for the failure to pay rent that became due during that same period.[194]

The burden of establishing a financial hardship rests with the Tenant.[195] When the affirmative defense is established, the Court may award a prevailing Landlord a money judgment for the full amount of rent owed, but without a judgment of possession or a warrant of eviction.[196]

The unpaid rent must have accrued during the COVID-19 Period. In determining whether a financial hardship was suffered, the Court

---

191 TENANT SAFE HARBOR ACT (A.10290B/S.8192) (Ch. 127 of the Laws of 2020).

192 *Id.*; *see* Cabrera v. Humphrey, 192 A.D.3d 227, 140 N.Y.S.3d 609 (3d Dep't 2021) (noting the TSHA "[i]s limited to summary eviction proceedings based on non-payment and does not apply to holdover proceedings").

193 TSHA § 2(1).

194 It has been held that where a settlement was reached prior to the COVID-19 Period, but the Tenant failed to remain current on rent obligations during the COVID-19 Period and in breach of the parties' agreement, the TSHA remained a viable defense. *See, e.g.*, 516 Realty NY LLC v. Hamner, 2021 N.Y.L.J. LEXIS 1151 (N.Y. Civ. Ct. N.Y. Cnty. Dec. 8, 2021) (holding that a "current rent first" provision within a stipulation prior to the COVID-19 Period "[c]annot be deemed to waive the tenant's rights under a statute that had not even been adopted when the stipulation was signed, [and, as a result,] enforcement of the 'current rent first' provision [and permitting execution of the warrant of eviction] would violate the Tenant Safe Harbor Act"); *see also* 110-50 Realty v. Melgar, 139 N.Y.S.3d 778 (N.Y. Civ. Ct. Queens Cnty. 2020) (reasoning that to deny the applicability of the TSHA "[w]ould result in an illogical situation where a tenant at imminent risk of eviction would lack recourse to TSHA protections, while a tenant less at risk (i.e., those without judgments and warrants issued against them) would enjoy ample protections under the statute").

195 *110-50 Realty*, 139 N.Y.S.3d at 778.

196 TSHA § 2(3). As discussed in Chapter 5, subdiv. B(2)(a), *infra*, the TSHA created an exception to the well-established principle that the Housing Part may only issue a money judgment "concomitant" with a judgment of possession and warrant of eviction.

considers the Tenant's or lawful occupant's: (1) income prior to the COVID-19 Period; (2) income during the COVID-19 Period; (3) liquid assets; (4) eligibility and receipt of government financial assistance, including cash assistance, supplemental nutrition assistance, disability assistance, home energy assistance, unemployment insurance, and emergency rental assistance; and (5) any additional relevant factors.[197] Demonstrable proof of one (1) of the above factors is sufficient to invoke the defense.[198]

As discussed later in this chapter, the Tenant's submission of a COVID-19 Financial Hardship Declaration Form constitutes *prima facie* evidence, in the form of a rebuttable presumption, that a "financial hardship" was suffered. This means that to defeat the affirmative defense, credible evidence to the contrary is required.

The statute does not specify whether an award of possession is permissible in a non-payment proceeding where the Tenant suffered a financial hardship and the Landlord seeks a money judgment for rent arrears that accrued both during the COVID-19 Period and beyond. There have been mixed outcomes in the various Housing Parts, and the reader should become familiar with the policies of the particular jurisdiction in which the case is heard.

The TSHA does not have a sunset date, and, as a result, continues to be in effect. As a practical matter, the impact of the statute will cease when residential claims for unpaid rent through the COVID-19 Period

---

197 TSHA § 2(2).

198 *See 110-50 Realty*, 139 N.Y.S.3d at 778.

have been adjudicated.[199]

2. EMERGENCY EVICTION AND FORECLOSURE PREVENTION ACT OF 2020

On December 28, 2020, the COVID-19 Emergency Eviction and Foreclosure Prevention Act of 2020 ("CEEFPA") was signed into law.[200] CEEFPA, similar to TSHA, applied to residential premises only. CEEFPA initially implemented a sixty (60) day stay on eviction proceedings and a 120 day stay on the commencement of new actions.[201]

The statute required that a Hardship Declaration Form written in the Tenant's primary language accompany each notice served upon the Tenant.[202] The submission of a completed Hardship Declaration Form stayed the proceedings and prohibited the commencement of new actions.[203] The Hardship Declaration Form included the following checklist items, any of which was sufficient to create a rebuttable presumption of financial hardship during the COVID-19 Period: (1) a significant loss of household income; (2) an increase in necessary out-of-pocket work or health expenses; (3) childcare responsibilities or attending to an elderly, disabled, or sick family member that impacted efforts to obtain meaningful employment or increased necessary out-of-pocket expenses; (4)

---

199 TSHA § 2(1). Parenthetically, for the period September 29, 2020 through June 25, 2021, TSHA protections were extended to cases involving holdover Tenants where the Petitioner's underlying claim was for a breach other than the non-payment of rent. *See* Executive Order ("EO") 202.66, dated Sept. 29, 2020, and as further extended by subsequent orders. In January 2021, the Appellate Division, Third Department, upheld enforcement of EO 202.66. *See Cabrera*, 192 A.D.3d at 232-33, 140 N.Y.S.3d at 614 (holding that "[b]ecause these executive orders [including EO 202.66, 202.71 and 202.78] prohibit enforcement of residential evictions, without any exceptions for holdover proceedings or warrants issued based on stipulations, [the] Supreme Court was precluded from ordering enforcement of the warrant to evict respondents"). Thereafter, during a downturn in positive COVID-19 cases and approximately one (1) year following the passage of the TSHA, EO 202.66 was rescinded, effective June 25, 2021. As a result, the TSHA defense remains limited to residential cases in both non-payment proceedings and a limited category of holdover proceedings where the basis for the eviction proceeding is the failure to pay rent.

200 COVID-19 Emergency Eviction and Foreclosure Prevention Act of 2020 (A.8241/S.9114) (Ch. 381 of the Laws of 2020).

201 *Id.* at Part A §§ 2, 4.

202 *Id.* at Part A §§ 1(4), 3.

203 *Id.* at Part A § 6.

moving expenses and difficulties securing a new residence; and (5) any other factor that significantly reduced income or increased expenses.[204]

The Hardship Declaration Form was not subject to challenge. The exception to this rule was where the Landlord claimed the Tenant was "[p]ersistently and unreasonably engaging in behavior that substantially infringe[d] on the use and enjoyment of other tenants or occupants or cause[d] a substantial safety hazard to others," i.e., nuisance or objectionable conduct.[205]

On May 4, 2021, CEEFPA was extended to August 31, 2021.[206] However, on August 12, 2021, the United States Supreme Court held in *Chrysafis v. Marks* that Part A of CEEFPA resulted in an unconstitutional deprivation of Landlords' rights due to there being no mechanism to challenge the Tenant's financial hardship claim.[207] The Court reasoned that precluding an opportunity to challenge a Tenant's unilateral declaration of "financial hardship" was a denial of Due Process and fundamental fairness principles.[208] The remaining sections of CEEFPA expired on August 31, 2021.

---

204 *Id.* at Part A §§ 1(4), 11. A stay would also result where the Tenant indicated on the Hardship Declaration Form that relocating "pose[d] a significant health risk due to a household member's increased risk for severe illness or death due to age (over 65), disability or pre-existing condition," commonly referred to as the Medical Hardship. *Id.* at Part A § 1(4).

205 *Id.* at Part A § 9. A hearing was required to initially determine whether the objectionable conduct was continuing. The Landlord was not permitted to amend the Petition to assert a nuisance or objectionable conduct claim, if not previously alleged, but instead was required to commence a new proceeding. *Id.*

206 Legislation extending CEEFPA (S.6362/A.7175) (amending Ch. 381 of the Laws of 2020).

207 141 S.Ct. 2482 (2021) (reasoning that CEEFPA "[v]iolates the Court's longstanding teaching that ordinarily 'no man can be a judge in his own case'"). On September 4, 2020 and August 3, 2020, the Centers for Disease Control and Prevention ("CDC") issued temporary eviction moratoria halting residential evictions for qualifying Tenants due to the COVID-19 Pandemic. The CDC orders, similar to the TSHA, prohibited evictions without negating the Tenant's obligations to pay rent. On June 29, 2021 and August 26, 2021, the United States Supreme Court held that the CDC eviction moratoria exceeded the agency's statutory authority because the policies set forth therein required congressional approval. *See* Alabama Ass'n of Realtors v. Department of Health and Hum. Servs. (I), 141 S.Ct. 2320 (June 29, 2021); Alabama Ass'n of Realtors v. Department of Health and Hum. Servs. (II), 141 S.Ct. 2485 (Aug. 26, 2021). Of note, in *Alabama Ass'n of Realtors (I)*, the Supreme Court permitted the first CDC moratorium to remain in effect a few additional weeks until July 31, 2021, the order's sunset date, "[t]o allow for [a] more orderly distribution of the congressionally appropriated rental assistance funds." 141 S.Ct. at 2320.

208 *Alabama Ass'n of Realtors (I)*, 141 S.Ct. at 2320.

3. EMERGENCY PROTECT OUR SMALL BUSINESSES ACT OF 2021

Approximately two (2) months following the passage of CEEFPA, on March 9, 2021, the COVID-19 Emergency Protect Our Small Businesses Act of 2021 ("CEPSBA") was enacted.[209] CEPSBA was the commercial counterpart to CEEFPA.[210]

This statute, similar to CEEFPA, neither provided a defense for unpaid rent nor prohibited the issuance of a judgment of possession or a warrant of eviction.[211] Instead, both laws were intended to stay eviction proceedings during the Pandemic until such time as deemed appropriate.

To be eligible for the statute's stay protections, a commercial Tenant was required to be an independently owned and operated entity from New York with fifty (50) or fewer employees, and not dominant in its field.[212] The representations asserted within the CEPSBA Hardship Declaration Form were similar to those for residential properties under CEEFPA.[213] However, a commercial Tenant had to further attest that any governmental financial assistance previously received did <u>not</u> make the commercial Tenant whole for losses sustained during the COVID-19 Period.[214]

The law also prohibited the use of self-help by commercial Landlords.[215] CEPSBA was extended through August 31, 2021, at which time the law sunset.[216]

4. EMERGENCY RENTAL ASSISTANCE PROGRAM OF 2021

On April 16, 2021, the COVID-19 Emergency Rental Assistance Program of 2021 ("ERAP") was enacted for the purpose of distributing

---

209 COVID-19 Emergency Protect Our Small Businesses Act of 2021 (A.3207/S.471A) (Ch. 73 of the Laws of 2021).

210 *Id.* at Part A §§ 1, 3-11.

211 *Cf.* TSHA § 2(1) (affirmative defense prohibiting issuance of either a judgment of possession or a warrant of eviction due to the non-payment of rent where a residential Tenant suffered a financial hardship during the COVID-19 Period).

212 CEPSBA, Part A § 1(3).

213 *Id.* at Part A § 1(4).

214 *Id.*

215 *Id.* at Part A § 2.

216 Legislation extending CEPSBA (S.6362/A.7175) (amending Ch. 104 of the Laws of 2021).

billions of Federal dollars in rental assistance, in addition to $100 million in State funding.[217] By the end of 2021, the State had received more than 290,000 ERAP applications and either disbursed or committed to pay over $2 billion.[218]

The Office of Temporary and Disability Assistance ("OTDA") is the agency charged with overseeing ERAP. Several municipalities, including Onondaga County, the cities of Rochester and Yonkers, and the towns of Hempstead, Islip, and Oyster Bay on Long Island, opted to administer ERAP independently from the State.[219]

ERAP funding may be obtained for the Tenant's primary residence within the State.[220] The applicant must demonstrate that rent is owed during the COVID-19 Period and either the household income is below eighty percent (80%) of the area's median income,[221] or the household: (1) qualifies for unemployment benefits; (2) experienced a reduction in household income; or (3) experienced a financial hardship, either directly or indirectly, due to COVID-19, and the failure to obtain ERAP assistance may result in homelessness.[222]

---

217 COVID-19 EMERGENCY RENTAL ASSISTANCE PROGRAM OF 2021 (A.3006/S.2506), Part BB (Ch. 56 of the Laws of 2021). The federal portion of the financial assistance was provided in two (2) installments. On December 27, 2020, Congress passed the Consolidated Appropriations Act of 2021 which allocated $25 billion in emergency rental assistance. *See* Pub L. 116-260, 134 Stat. 1182, § 501 (2020). On March 11, 2021, Congress allocated an additional $21.55 billion. *See* AMERICAN RESCUE PLAN ACT OF 2021, Pub. L. 117-2, 135 Stat. 4, § 3201 (2021). In early 2022, New York was expected to receive an additional $27 million in rental assistance funds from Congress. *See* Sarina Trangle, "*New York is Slated to Get Only 3% of New Rent Relief Sought*," Newsday, Jan. 5, 2022, at https://www.newsday.com/business/new-york-rent-relief-money-left-1.50468633. Parenthetically, ERAP expires on September 30, 2025. ERAP, Part BB § 3.

218 *See* Office of Temporary and Disability Assistance website, at https://otda.ny.gov.

219 Residents of these municipalities may apply for ERAP funding through the State portal if the household income is between 80% and 120% of the area's median income. *See* Office of Temporary and Disability Assistance website, "*Emergency Rental Assistance Program (ERAP)—Apply For ERAP*," at https://otda.ny.gov.

220 ERAP, Part BB, Subpart A § 5.

221 Effective September 15, 2021, ERAP assistance was made available for households with incomes between 80% and 120% of the area median income. *See* Office of Temporary and Disability Assistance website, "*Emergency Rental Assistance Program (ERAP)—Eligibility*," at https://otda.ny.gov.

222 ERAP, Part BB, Subpart A § 5.

ERAP assistance can cover up to twelve (12) months of rent arrears and/or utilities accrued during the COVID-19 Period, with the potential for an additional three (3) months where the Tenant is a member of a "rent burdened household" (i.e., thirty percent (30%) or more of household gross monthly income is utilized for rent).[223] When ERAP funding is accepted (and there is no option for the Landlord to decline), the Landlord agrees that: (1) the arrears are deemed paid in full; (2) late fees are waived; (3) the rent may not be increased for, at minimum, one (1) year following the initial ERAP payment; (4) the Tenant may not be evicted due to an expired lease or a holdover for at least twelve (12) months following the initial ERAP payment (unless there is a new breach or the rental unit is within a building containing four (4) or fewer units and the Landlord or an immediate family member of the Landlord intends to immediately occupy the unit as a primary residence); and (5) notification of the ERAP protections have and will continue to be provided to the Tenant as required.[224]

The submission of an ERAP application stays a pending residential eviction proceeding (both non-payment and holdover proceedings) and prohibits the filing of a new action until there is a final determination of ERAP "ineligibility."[225] A final determination occurs when the ERAP appeals' process has been exhausted.[226]

Both the Landlord and the Tenant may apply for ERAP funding, and where applied for by the Tenant, the Landlord must assist by providing

223 *Id.* at Part BB, Subpart A § 9(1).

224 *Id.* at Part BB, Subpart A § 9(2)(d). The Court must also notify the Tenant of available ERAP assistance programs. *Id.* at Part BB, Subpart A §§ 6, 11. The New York Courts' website listed the Hardship Declaration Form in twenty (20) different languages. *See* New York Unified Court System website, "*Coronavirus and the New York State Courts—Hardship Declarations*," at https://nycourts.gov. *See generally* PR IVC Rosemont Prop. LLC v. Jeanty, 2022 N.Y. Misc. LEXIS 2938 (Suffolk Cnty. Dist. Ct. June 29, 2022) (holding that the Landlord "does not possess the right to dissolve the stay by refusing to accept ERAP funding and/or refusing to provide required input for the application to be completed....").

225 ERAP, Part BB, Subpart A § 8.

226 *See* Administrative Order ("AO") No. 34/22 of the Chief Admin. Judge of the State of New York, dated January 16, 2022.

the requested documentation and/or relevant information.[227] The Landlord's failure to participate in the application process may constitute a waiver of the right to receive financial assistance and an affirmative defense in an eviction proceeding. An uncooperative Landlord may further be barred from commencing future court proceedings to recover rent for the same period.[228]

---

227 ERAP, Part BB, Subpart A §§ 6(3), 9(2)(b); *see PR IVC Rosemont Prop. LLC*, 2022 N.Y. Misc. LEXIS at 2938.

228 ERAP, Part BB, Subpart A § 9(2)[c].

5. AMENDMENTS TO THE EMERGENCY RENTAL ASSISTANCE PROGRAM

On September 2, 2021, Governor Kathy Hochul signed into law several amendments to ERAP ("ERAP Amendments").[229] The ERAP Amendments extended the eviction moratorium for most properties (residential and commercial) through January 15, 2022, including those within municipalities that opted out of the State's ERAP program,[230] and re-established many of the prior policies set forth within CEEFPA and CEPSBA.[231] Excluding the rebuttable presumption created by the Hardship Declaration Form, the ERAP Amendments expired on January 15, 2022.[232] However, as discussed below, the ERAP Amendments modified some of the original ERAP provisions and, as a result, those provisions remain in effect since ERAP is <u>not</u> scheduled to sunset until 2025.

---

229 Amendments to the Emergency Rental Assistance Program of 2021, amending Subpart A of Part BB (Ch. 417 of the Laws of 2021).

230 As stated previously, the cities of Rochester and Yonkers and the Towns of Hempstead, Islip, and Oyster Bay on Long Island elected to operate ERAP programs independent of the State's program.

231 The ERAP Amendments further: (1) authorized the resumption of cases in their ordinary course where a Hardship Declaration Form had <u>not</u> been submitted; (2) required the Landlord to attach a Hardship Declaration Form to all notices served on the Tenant; (3) prohibited default judgments absent written notice; (4) vacated residential default judgments issued both prior to December 28, 2020, and between August 13, 2021 and September 1, 2021; (5) prohibited self-help in commercial cases; and (6) stayed execution of previously issued warrants where a Hardship Declaration Form had <u>not</u> been submitted until after the Court conducted a conference. ERAP Amendments, Part B, Subpart A §§ 2, 6 (commercial cases); Part C, Subpart A §§ 4, 5 (residential cases).

232 In November 2021, Governor Hochul announced that the State would cease accepting ERAP applications because the $2.4 billion emergency rental assistance funds allocated to the State had been exhausted. *See* Mihir Zaveri and Matthew Haag, "*New York to Stop Accepting Applications for Pandemic Rental Aid*", N.Y. Times, Nov. 12, 2021, updated Nov. 15, 2021, at <u>https://www.nytimes.com/2021/11/12/nyregion/new-york-pandemic-rental-aid.html</u>. At that time, the State was receiving approximately 10,000 additional applications per week. *Id.* By decision dated January 6, 2022, a New York State Supreme Court Justice directed the State to continue to accept ERAP applications notwithstanding the anticipated insufficiency of funds, thereby affording each additional applicant a stay pending a final determination on eligibility. *See* Hildalgo v. New York State Office of Temporary and Disability Assistance, 2022 N.Y. Misc. LEXIS 1984 (N.Y. Cnty. Sup. Ct. Jan. 6, 2022) (granting injunctive relief directing the State to continue to accept ERAP applications, in part, because the State may prospectively be eligible for unspent ERAP funds from across the country in March 2022).

A separate Hardship Declaration Form was created for residential[233] and commercial[234] tenancies, and the Forms continue to constitute *prima facie* evidence of financial hardship and create a rebuttable presumption in favor of the Tenant.[235] The legislation further included section 9-a, which created an exception to the automatic stay where the Landlord demonstrated in a holdover proceeding that the Tenant "*intentionally*" caused significant damage to the premises or "*persistently and unreasonably*" engaged in conduct that substantially infringed upon the use and enjoyment of others or resulted in a safety hazard.[236]

This remains the current standard for lifting the stay when "objectionable conduct" is alleged within a holdover proceeding notwithstanding the Tenant's pending ERAP application. The resulting hearing typically will require a twofold determination: (1) whether the objectionable conduct occurred and (2) if so, whether the objectionable conduct is continuing.

233 The Hardship Declaration Form for residential properties required the Tenant to attest that during the COVID-19 Period he or she was (a) "[e]xperiencing financial hardship, and unable to pay [the] rent in full or obtain alternative suitable permanent housing" due to the following: (1) significant loss of household income; (2) increase in necessary out-of-pocket expenses related to performing essential work or health impacts; (3) attending to a family member (child, elderly, disabled and/or sick) negatively impacted the household member's ability to earn income or increased out-of-pocket expenses; (4) moving expenses and difficulty in securing a new residence; or (5) other factors that significantly reduced income or significantly increased expenses or (b) moving would "pose a significant health risk due to a household member's increased risk for severe illness or death due to age (over 65) or disability or pre-existing condition." ERAP AMENDMENTS, Part C, Subpart A § 1(4).

234 A commercial Tenant was required to submit a Hardship Declaration Form attesting that due to the COVID-19 Pandemic, the business: (1) suffered a significant loss of revenue; (2) experienced a significant increase in necessary expenses related to purchasing and providing protective equipment to employees or installing same within the leased premises; or (3) would suffer a hardship if the business was required to move. The designee was further required to attest that the public financial assistance previously received by the commercial Tenant did not "fully make up for the business's loss of revenue or increased expenses." *Id.* at Part B, Subpart A § 1.

235 *Id.* at Part B, Subpart A §§ 9, 11 (commercial cases), Part C, Subpart A §§ 9, 11 (residential cases). The rebuttable presumption was of little consequence for commercial properties because the TSHA affirmative defense only applies to residential tenancies.

236 ERAP AMENDMENTS, Part A § 6; *see* ERAP, Part BB, Subpart A §§ 8, 9(d), 9-a (emphasis added).

Similar to its predecessor, the ERAP Amendments do not permit the Landlord to amend the Petition to assert an objectionable conduct claim, but rather requires the commencement of a new proceeding.[237] Where a judgment was previously awarded based upon objectionable conduct, a hearing is also required to determine whether the conduct is continuing.[238]

The reader should be mindful that the Due Process concerns raised by the United States Supreme Court in the *Chrysafis* decision were addressed by statute and Administrative Order 261/21, dated September 8, 2021.[239] As discussed further below, Administrative Order 261/21 implemented a procedure for Landlords to challenge both the merits of a Tenant's financial hardship claim and the automatic stay resulting from the submission of a Financial Hardship Declaration Form.[240]

The Landlord's challenge in Administrative Order 261/21 is specific and limited to the automatic stay resulting from the submission of a Financial Hardship Declaration Form. Since the Hardship Declaration Form no longer results in a stay, that portion of the Administrative Order is of little consequence. The opportunity to challenge the Tenant's financial hardship claim was not extended to ERAP applications. In fact, there is no mechanism for a Landlord to challenge the automatic stay resulting from the submission of an ERAP application (except for objectionable conduct as described above).

6. LANDLORD RENTAL ASSISTANCE PROGRAM

In October 2021, the State established a $125 million Landlord Rental Assistance Program ("LRAP") to assist residential Landlords where the Tenant either previously vacated the premises or was unable or unwilling to apply for ERAP assistance.[241] LRAP applications were accepted between October 7, 2021 and November 21, 2021.

237 ERAP AMENDMENTS, Part A § 6; *see* ERAP, Part BB, Subpart A § 9-a(1),(2); *see PR IVC Rosemont Prop. LLC*, 2022 N.Y. Misc. LEXIS at 2938.

238 ERAP AMENDMENTS, Part A § 6; ERAP, Part BB, Subpart A §§ 8, 9(d), 9-a.

239 *See* Chrysafis v. Marks, 141 S.Ct. 2482 (2021).

240 *See* Chapter 3, subdiv. B(3), *infra*.

241 *See* David Brand, "*More Than 1,600 NY Landlords Apply For COVID Relief Rent on New Fund's First Day*," City Limits, Oct. 8, 2021, at https://citylimits.org.

LRAP provided up to twelve (12) months of rent arrears for residential households whose rental amount was at or below 150% of the fair market rent for the county. To be eligible, a Landlord was required to submit documentary proof of rent arrears that accrued during the COVID-19 Period and attest that no fewer than three (3) attempts were made, at least two (2) of which were in writing, encouraging the Tenant to apply for ERAP assistance.[242]

Landlords receiving LRAP funding further agreed that: (1) the payment was in full satisfaction of rent obligations for the time period; (2) late fees were waived; (3) the rent would not be increased for one (1) year; and (4) an eviction would not be sought due to an expired lease or holdover tenancy for one (1) year. An eviction could be sought earlier for a new breach or in dwellings with four (4) of fewer units where the Landlord or the Landlord's immediate family member sought to immediately occupy the property as a primary residence.[243]

B. EXECUTIVE AND ADMINISTRATIVE ORDERS

Several Executive Orders ("EO") and Administrative Orders ("AO") were also issued regarding evictions and court operations. In June 2021, during a downward trend in COVID-19 positive diagnoses, the governor rescinded virtually all prior EO pertaining to evictions (and foreclosures).[244] Some of the AO issued by the Honorable Lawrence K. Marks, Chief Administrative Judge of the State of New York, are discussed below.

1. ADMINISTRATIVE ORDER 244/21 (Aug. 13, 2021)

Administrative Order 244/31 implemented a monitoring system that required the Landlord to submit a "Notice of Pending or Completed Rental Assistance Form" in each case where ERAP funds had been received or the

242 *See* Office of Temporary and Disability Assistance website, "*Landlord Emergency Rental Assistance Program (LRAP)—Eligibility*," at https://otda.ny.gov.

243 *Id.* at "*Landlord Emergency Rental Assistance Program (LRAP)—Frequently Asked Questions*," at https://otda.ny.gov.

244 *See* Executive Order No. 210, dated June 24, 2021, rescinding Executive Orders Nos. 202 through 202.11.

Landlord had knowledge (or reasonable knowledge) that an ERAP application was pending.[245] The court system has since been granted partial access to OTDA's computer database to monitor the status of ERAP applications which is useful in determining whether a mandatory stay is applicable.

2. ADMINISTRATIVE ORDER 245/21 (Aug. 13, 2021)

On August 13, 2021, the Chief Administrative Judge further authorized the *immediate* resumption of residential eviction proceedings with limited exceptions.[246] As a result, residential eviction proceedings were permitted to proceed unless the matter was stayed by statute, administrative directive, or, for a brief period, then-existing CDC Orders.[247]

All residential eviction proceedings commenced before March 17, 2020 required a status or settlement conference with the Court before resuming. In addition, the AO authorized eviction proceedings to be conducted either remotely or in-person.

3. ADMINISTRATIVE ORDER 261/21 (Sept. 8, 2021)

In AO 261/21, the Chief Administrative Judge extended the mandatory stay for both residential and commercial cases through January 15, 2022 where a Hardship Declaration Form was submitted.[248] In order to comply with the *Chrysafis* decision, a protocol for applying challenges to a Tenant's financial hardship claim was implemented.[249]

To challenge the validity of the Hardship Declaration, the Landlord was required to provide notice and a sworn written statement setting forth a good-faith basis to dispute the hardship. If a good-faith basis to challenge the hardship was presented, the Court was required to conduct a hearing on further notice to the Tenant. If the challenge was

245 *See* Administrative Order No. 244/21 of the Chief Admin. Judge of the State of New York, dated Aug. 13, 2021.

246 *See* Administrative Order No. 245/21 of the Chief Admin. Judge of the State of New York, dated Aug. 13, 2021.

247 For a discussion about the CDC eviction moratoria, *see* footnote 207, *supra*.

248 *See* Administrative Order No. 261/21 of the Chief Admin. Judge of the State of New York, dated Sept. 8, 2021.

249 *Id.*

sustained, the stay was lifted and the case resumed. Otherwise, the case remained stayed. The reader should be mindful that the Landlord's ability to challenge the validity of a hardship declaration does not extend to ERAP applications other than the limited exception where objectionable or nuisance conduct is alleged in a holdover proceeding.[250]

The Chief Administrative Judge also authorized the resumption of default judgment applications in residential cases, but only after a hearing on notice to the Tenant.[251] Default judgments awarded both prior to December 28, 2020 and between August 13, 2021 and September 2, 2021 were vacated, and those matters were restored to the Court's Calendar upon the Tenant's written or oral request. There were no similar requirements regarding commercial properties.

Warrants issued prior to September 2, 2021 were required to include language that a Hardship Declaration Form was served on the Tenant (with dates) and either the Hardship Declaration Form had not been returned or the Tenant was not entitled to a stay because: (1) the Court determined the hardship claim was invalid or (2) the Tenant caused significant property damage, was persistently and unreasonably engaging in nuisance behavior, or posed a safety hazard to others (with a description of the behavior).[252] Regardless of the status of the case, if an ERAP application was not pending, the Court was required to inform the Tenant of ERAP and the application process. Finally, the ban on commercial Landlords utilizing self-help was extended through January 15, 2022.

4. ADMINISTRATIVE ORDER 34/22 (Jan. 16, 2022)

AO 34/22 was the first Administrative Order following the expiration of the eviction moratorium. The AO once again directed that all residential and commercial cases could resume in the ordinary course,

250 *See generally* footnotes 207–208 and 239–240 and accompanying text, *supra*.

251 Administrative Order No. 261/21 of the Chief Admin. Judge of the State of New York, dated Sept. 8, 2021.

252 *Id.* Where the Tenant caused property damage or engaged in objectionable conduct, a hearing was required to determine whether the conduct was continuing.

subject to ERAP and applicable stays.[253]

For the purpose of an ERAP stay, the AO and accompanying memorandum reiterated that a final eligibility determination does not occur until the ERAP appeal process has been exhausted. The Administrative Order further permits default judgments in residential cases, but the application must be made "*on motion*." In addition, warrants that were issued between March 17, 2020 and September 2, 2022, in both residential and commercial cases, may not be executed until after the Landlord makes a "*motion on notice to the tenant*" to vacate the stay.[254]

The AO noted that the Hardship Declaration Form no longer constituted grounds for a stay of the proceedings (although it remains *prima facie* evidence of financial hardship), and the Form need not continue to be served upon Tenants. Due to ongoing health and safety concerns after the COVID-19 Period, eviction proceedings continued to be heard remotely for a significant period of time. At present, the decision whether to proceed remotely or in-person, or in a hybrid fashion, remains left to the discretion of the Court.[255]

---

253 *See* Administrative Order No. 34/22 of the Chief Admin. Judge of the State of New York, dated Jan. 16, 2022.

254 *Id.* The Landlord's motion would be granted where the Court determined that: (1) the warrant was initially issued in accordance with the laws in effect at the time of issuance and (2) no further stays were applicable. *Id.* Residential cases commenced prior to March 17, 2020 continued to require a Court conference before proceeding.

255 *Id.* In New York City, summary proceedings are further governed by the provisions set forth in Directives and Procedures Nos. 217, 221 and 222, dated August 16, 2021 and January 16, 2022, of the Administrative Judge of the New York City Civil Court.

CHAPTER 4

TYPES OF SUMMARY PROCEEDINGS

The Housing Parts throughout the State handle an exceedingly large number of eviction proceedings. In 2019, approximately 262,000 eviction proceedings were commenced, of which nearly eighty percent (80%) were non-payment proceedings.[256] Although the number of cases precipitously declined in both 2020 and 2021 due to the COVID-19 Pandemic, a staggering number of New Yorkers remain affected and the volume will undoubtedly rise following the expiration of the eviction moratorium.

A. RIGHT TO COUNSEL

It is well-established that an individual does not have a constitutional right to either: (1) housing or (2) counsel in an eviction proceeding.[257] Rather, all rights pertaining to housing are created by statute.[258] In *Lindsey v. Normet*, the United States Supreme Court confirmed that "[a]bsent [a] constitutional mandate, the assurance of adequate housing and the definition of landlord-tenant relationships are legislative…functions."[259]

Unfortunately, far too many litigants (both Landlords and Tenants) appear in the Housing Parts without counsel. As a result, there have been

256 *See* New York State Unified Court System Activity Reporting System, Jan. 1, 2019—Dec. 31, 2019.

257 *See* Lindsey v. Normet, 405 U.S. 56, 92 S.Ct. 862 (1972) (holding that the Constitution does not provide a "[g]uarantee of access to dwellings of a particular quality, or any recognition of the right of a tenant to occupy the real property beyond the term of [the] lease"); Tri-State Gen. Remodeling Contractors, Inc. v. Baijnauth, 753 N.Y.S.2d 327, 331 (N.Y. Civ. Ct. Bronx Cnty. 2002) (no right to counsel in a civil case).

258 *Lindsey*, 405 U.S. at 56, 92 S.Ct. at 862.

259 *Id.*

plenty of cases "lost" on both sides due to no reason other than the *pro se* litigant's lack of familiarity with the laws, standards, and court procedures.

Many litigants are under the mistaken impression they do not need legal representation, while others are in the more perilous position of being unable to afford counsel. Regardless of the reason, a litigant appearing in the highly specialized Landlord and Tenant Housing Parts without legal representation is at a distinct disadvantage.

In 2017, New York City became the first city in the United States to enact a Right to Counsel Law (also referred to as Universal Access to Counsel Law) for unrepresented Tenants and other occupants facing eviction.[260] The Universal Access to Counsel Law guarantees, at no expense to the litigant, the assignment of counsel and "full legal representation" of each Tenant and occupant having a household income at or below 200% of the Federal Poverty Guidelines.[261] Tenants and other occupants who do not qualify for "full" representation are guaranteed "brief legal assistance" prior to the first court appearance.[262]

In 2021, approximately 100,000 individuals from 42,000 households across New York City received legal assistance pursuant to the Right to Counsel Law.[263] Approximately seventy-one percent (71%) of those occupants were provided "full legal representation."[264]

In some areas of the State, including Albany, Binghamton, New York City, and Rochester, to name a few, the Legal Aid Society may represent Tenants facing eviction.[265] This is not the case on Long Island, where

---

260 *See* NYC ADMIN. CODE § 26-1301 (Local Law No. 136 of City of New York).

261 *Id.* at §§ 26-1301, 26-1302.

262 *Id.* "Brief legal assistance" entails a "singular consultation" with counsel prior to appearing before a judge. *Id.* at § 26-1301.

263 *See* Office of Civil Justice, New York City Human Resources Administration, "*Universal Access to Legal Services: A Report on Year Four of Implementation in New York City*," Fall 2021, at 3.

264 *See* City of New York website, "*New York City's First-in-Nation Right-to-Counsel Program Expanded Citywide Ahead of Schedule*," Nov. 17, 2021, at https://www1.nyc.gov/office-of-the-mayor/news/769-21/new-york-city-s-first-in-nation-right-to-counsel-program-expanded-citywide-ahead-schedule.

265 *See, e.g.*, Langdoc v. Warden, 141 N.Y.S.3d 678 (Albany City Ct. 2021); Lawler v. Canfield, 114 N.Y.S.3d 621 (Watertown City Ct. 2019); 2115 Washington Realty, LLC v. Hall, 2017 N.Y.L.J. LEXIS 1198 (N.Y. Civ. Ct. Bronx Cnty. May 11, 2017).

the Nassau Suffolk Law Services Committee, Inc. ("Committee") staffs many of the Long Island Housing Parts with attorneys who primarily represent Tenants of limited financial means. The Committee, which is not affiliated with the Court, may also represent a Petitioner in limited circumstances, such as when the owner has a mental health illness. The Court has no authority to assign the Committee in any particular case.

The reader should be mindful that there are additional housing agencies and clinics available to provide legal advice and services. Moreover, the Court will appoint a *guardian ad litem* where the Tenant is incapable of protecting his or her rights.[266]

B. NON-PAYMENT AND HOLDOVER PROCEEDINGS

A common mistake by Landlords is commencing the wrong type of summary proceeding. If a Landlord brings a non-payment proceeding when a holdover proceeding was proper, or vice versa, the proceeding may be dismissed and the Landlord will have to restart the process.[267]

The primary relief in a summary proceeding is a judgment of possession and a warrant of eviction, with or without a money judgment. The rules pertaining to non-payment and holdover proceedings apply

---

266 *See* CPLR § 1201; 229 W. 109 St. Realty Corp. v. Ichida, 127 N.Y.S.3d 691 (App. Term, 1st Dep't 2020) (holding "[t]o the extent the court believed that the surviving tenant was incapable of defending her rights, the remedy is to appoint a *guardian ad litem*"); 952 St. Marks Ave. HDFC v. White, 115 N.Y.S.3d 604 (App. Term, 2d, 11th and 13th Jud. Dists. 2019) (in dismissing the proceeding, noting that the Housing Part's refusal to allow the non-attorney court-appointed *guardian ad litem* to pursue plausible avenues challenging petitioner's claims did not result in a waiver of defenses); WHGA Renaissance Apts., L.P. v. Jackson, 37 N.Y.S.3d 809 (App. Term, 1st Dep't 2016) (*guardian ad litem* appointed where Tenant suffered from paranoid schizophrenia and was "incapable of adequately defending her rights"); 120-128 Sherman LLC v. Collins, 2020 N.Y.L.J. LEXIS 1455 (N.Y. Civ. Ct. N.Y. Cnty. Sept. 23, 2020) (explaining that "[t]o ensure both sides may have a fair and equitable resolution a *guardian ad litem* was appointed on tenant's behalf to better assist if [Adult Protective Services] was required"); Vanbur Estates LLC v. Quick, 2018 N.Y.L.J. LEXIS 1173 (N.Y. Civ. Ct. Kings Cnty. April 11, 2018) (reasoning that "[a]n individual who requires a [*guardian ad litem*] cannot be found to have waived defenses by failing to interpose them at the inception of the proceeding").

267 Greenport Preserv., L.P. v. Heyward, 160 N.Y.S.3d 734 (App. Term, 2d, 11th & 13th Jud. Dists. 2021) (dismissing non-payment proceeding because the tenancy was terminated prior to commencement of the action, and, as a result, a holdover proceeding was required).

to both residential and commercial properties with limited exceptions as discussed throughout this Bench Guide. In both types of proceedings, the purpose is to allow a petitioner with legal standing an opportunity to recover the possession of real property.[268] Accordingly, in both non-payment and holdover proceedings, the Tenant or occupant must be in possession of the premises when the summary proceeding is commenced.[269]

Perhaps the most obvious difference between non-payment and holdover proceedings is that the parties in a non-payment proceeding have a valid Landlord and Tenant relationship when the proceeding was commenced, typically demonstrated by the existence of a rental agreement, and the Landlord claims that the Tenant failed to pay some or all of the rent due pursuant to that agreement.[270] By contrast, in a holdover proceeding, the Landlord and Tenant relationship was either terminated or it expired when the summary proceeding was commenced, or such a relationship never existed.[271]

In accordance with RPAPL §§ 711 and 713, holdover proceedings may be maintained where: (1) the parties had a rental agreement that expired on its own terms and the Tenant remains in possession without

---

268 *See, e.g.*, MHA Realty 1, LLC v. Rostoker, 142 N.Y.S.3d 888 (App. Term, 2d, 11th & 13th Jud. Dists. 2021) (non-payment proceeding); Fountains-Clove Rd. Apts., Inc. v. Gunther, 47 N.Y.S.3d 212 (App. Term, 2d, 11th & 13th Jud. Dists. 2017) (same); 36170 Realty v. Boyd, 2021 N.Y.L.J. LEXIS 264 (N.Y. Civ. Ct. Kings Cnty. April 2, 2021) (holdover proceeding).

269 92 Bergenbrooklyn, LLC v. Cisarano, 21 N.Y.S.3d 810 (App. Term, 2d, 11th & 13th Jud. Dists. 2015) (noting "[t]he rule is that, in a summary proceeding, the respondent must be in possession of the premises at the time the proceeding is commenced in order for the proceeding to lie").

270 *See MHA Realty 1, LLC*, 142 N.Y.S.3d at 888; West 152nd Assoc.. L.P. v. Gassama, 119 N.Y.S.3d 801 (App. Term, 1st Dep't 2019); Underhill Ave. Realty, LLC v. Ramos, 29 N.Y.S.3d 850 (App. Term, 2d, 11th & 13th Jud. Dists. 2015) (action dismissed where Section 8 tenancy expired prior to commencement of non-payment proceeding); Green v. Palmer, 2021 N.Y.L.J. LEXIS 1067 (N.Y. Civ. Ct. Queens Cnty. Nov. 3, 2021); Aa Kodosh Holdings v. John, 2018 N.Y.L.J. LEXIS 3681 (N.Y. Civ. Ct. Kings Cnty. Nov. 7, 2018).

271 *See* Barton v. Truesdell, 183 A.D.3d 979, 123 N.Y.S.3d 271 (3d Dep't 2020); Xheng v. Fu Jian Hong Guan Am. Unity Assoc., Inc., 168 A.D.3d 511, 92 N.Y.S.3d 227 (1st Dep't 2019); Gayle v. Flynn, 143 N.Y.S.3d 497 (App. Term 2d, 11th & 13th Jud. Dists. 2021); 400 W. 59th St. Partners LLC v. Oyolesi, 2021 N.Y. Misc. LEXIS 6309 (N.Y. Cnty. Sup. Ct. Dec. 8, 2021).

paying any additional rent or use and occupancy;[272] (2) the new occupant entitled to possession seeks removal of the former lessee who remains in possession beyond the expiration of the lease;[273] (3) the property has been sold by an execution against the occupant and the title under the sale was perfected;[274] (4) the parties' rental agreement was terminated due to a breach of a material condition;[275] (5) the parties' month-to-month tenancy was terminated by the Landlord;[276] (6) the occupant is a squatter having unlawfully taken possession of the premises;[277] (7) the property was purchased by a new owner following the former owner's failure to pay property taxes and the redemption period expired;[278] (8) the new owner seeks to regain possession of a post-foreclosed property;[279] (9) the occupant is a Tenant of a life tenant

272 RPAPL § 711(1); *see generally* Jamaica Ave., LLC v. H. Carpets Inc., 153 N.Y.S.3d 834 (N.Y. Civ. Ct. Queens Cnty. 2021).

273 RPAPL § 711(1); Spira v. Douglas, 121 N.Y.S.3d 783 (N.Y. Civ. Ct. Bronx Cnty. 2020).

274 RPAPL § 713(1); Federal Home Loan Mtge. Assn. v. Perez, 968 N.Y.S.2d 317 (App. Term, 9th & 10th Jud. Dists. 2013).

275 *See, e.g.*, Eighteen Assoc., LLC v. Court St. Pizza, Inc., 122 N.Y.S.3d 482 (App. Term, 2d, 11th & 13th Jud. Dists. 2020).

276 *See, e.g.*, Double Down Realty Corp. v. Avalone, 2021 N.Y.L.J. LEXIS 305 (N.Y. Civ. Ct. N.Y. Cnty. April 14, 2021).

277 RPAPL § 713(3); 1st Mtge. Corp. v. Hall, 187 A.D.3d 742, 130 N.Y.S.3d 385 (2d Dep't 2020).

278 RPAPL § 713(4); AJM RE Holdings VIII, LLC v. Cortese, 965 N.Y.S.2d 691 (Nassau Cnty. Dist. Ct. 2013).

279 RPAPL § 713(5); Halsey Homes Corp. v. Prince-Bowden, 132 N.Y.S.3d 514 (App. Term, 2d, 11th & 13th Jud. Dists. 2020); JVJC Corp. v. Hampton, 121 N.Y.S.3d 507 (App. Term, 9th & 10th Jud. Dists. 2020) (occupant may not challenge validity of foreclosure proceeding in a summary proceeding).

following the termination of a life estate;[280] (10) the occupant entered into a license agreement or tenancy-at-will that the Landlord revoked or terminated;[281] (11) the licensee of a licensor remains in possession after the licensor no longer has a right to possession of the premises;[282] (12) the occupant is the former owner who conveyed title to a third party but refuses to vacate the premises;[283] (13) the proposed purchaser remains in possession after failing to finalize a contract for sale, the performance of which was to be completed within ninety (90) days;[284] and (14) the tenancy was incidental to employment from which the occupant has been terminated.[285]

C. THE DIFFERENCE BETWEEN THE "AWARD" AND "ISSUANCE" OF JUDGMENT

The distinction between the "award" and "issuance" of the judgment is significant. The "award" occurs when the Court, either following a trial (which is called a hearing in a summary proceeding), a motion for summary judgment, on default, or pursuant to a Stipulation of Settlement

280 RPAPL § 713(6); Fallarino v. Fallarino, 56 N.Y.S.3d 414 (App. Term, 9th & 10th Jud. Dists. 2017); Novakovic v. Novakovic, 890 N.Y.S.2d 758 (App. Term, 2d, 11th & 13th Jud. Dists. 2009). A life estate is an agreement that provides the occupant exclusive "[p]ossession, control and enjoyment of the property for the duration of his or her life." *Novakovic*, 890 N.Y.S.2d at 759; Bradly v. Lumer, 2019 N.Y. Misc. LEXIS 1717 (Suffolk Cnty. Dist. Ct. 2019) (noting that a "[l]ife tenant has the right to exclude all other[s] from the possession of the subject premises during his or her life and the remainderman or reversioner has no right to possession of the premises for the duration of the life tenancy"). The Housing Part may not establish a life estate, but it must entertain the claim as a defense when asserted. *See* Great Jones St. Realty Corp. v. Chimsanthia, 157 N.Y.S.3d 851 (App. Term, 1st Dep't 2022); Paladino v. Sotille, 835 N.Y.S.2d 799, 802 (App. Term, 9th & 10th Jud. Dists. 2007). For a discussion on life estates, *see* Chapter 11, subdiv. A(4), *infra*.

281 RPAPL § 713(7); Aloni v. Oliver, 138 N.Y.S.3d 788 (App. Term, 1st Dep't 2021).

282 RPAPL § 713(7)[c]; Marine Terrace Assocs. v. Kesoglides, 884 N.Y.S.2d 552 (App. Term, 2d, 11th & 13th 2009).

283 RPAPL § 713(8); *see generally* 1692 Rockaway LLC v. Prashad, 142 N.Y.S.3d 925 (N.Y. Civ. Ct. Kings Cnty. 2021).

284 RPAPL § 713(9); LaManna v. DiDonato, 842 N.Y.S.2d 674 (App. Term, 9th & 10th Jud. Dists. 2007); *see generally* Militello v. Chilvas, 824 N.Y.S.2d 764 (Buffalo City Ct. 2006).

285 RPAPL § 713(11); 329 Union Bldg. Corp. v. LoGuidice, 4 N.Y.S.3d 807 (App. Term, 2d, 11th & 13th Jud. Dists. 2015).

negotiated by the parties, determines that the Landlord is entitled to lawful possession of the premises. The award, while necessary, is just one (1) step in a progression of steps required to terminate the tenancy.

The "issuance" of the judgment follows the "award," and occurs when the Court signs the judgment of possession and warrant of eviction. In a non-payment proceeding, when the Landlord is the prevailing party, it is well-established that the rental agreement is retroactively deemed to have been terminated as of the date the proceeding was commenced.[286] However, as discussed *infra*, the HSTPA has slightly altered this calculation because the tenancy is no longer terminated upon issuance of the judgment and warrant. Instead, the tenancy is terminated when the warrant of eviction is executed (i.e., the eviction is carried out by the Sheriff or Marshal) or, alternatively, the Tenant voluntarily vacates the premises.[287]

To obtain the judgment of possession and warrant of eviction following the "award," the Landlord <u>must</u> submit the appropriate paperwork with the Clerk of the Court. Although many parties file the paperwork immediately or within days of the award, the Landlord may do so within a reasonable period of time.[288]

If the prevailing party is <u>not</u> represented by an attorney, the Clerk may

---

286 Fisk Bldg. Assocs., LLC v. Shimazaki II, Inc., 76 A.D.3d 468, at 469, 907 N.Y.S.2d 2 (1st Dep't 2010); NRP LLC I v. Elo Mgmt. LLC, 59 N.Y.S.3d 244 (App. Term, 1st Dep't 2017); Fifth Ave. Ctr., LLC v. Dryland Props., LLC, 2020 N.Y. Misc. LEXIS 30 (N.Y. Cnty. Sup. Ct. Jan. 2, 2020) (holding "[i]t is settled that the issuance of a warrant of eviction annuls the relationship between a landlord and tenant").

287 *See* 636 Apt. Assoc., JV v. Mayo, 130 N.Y.S.3d 649 (Mt. Vernon City Ct. 2020) (holding that the "[n]ew RPAPL § 749(3), enacted under the [HSTPA], which applies to the instant matter, no longer terminates the landlord tenant relationship upon issuance of a warrant of eviction," but instead affords greater protections until the execution of the warrant).

288 Typically, an unreasonable delay in submitting for the judgment may preclude issuance unless an adequate explanation for the delay is provided. At minimum, the delay may raise questions as to whether the parties entered into a new tenancy, such as by the acceptance of money for a subsequent period, that would bar the eviction. It is within the discretion of the Court to restore the matter to the Calendar for the purpose of confirming or denying the relief. In cases pending in the Supreme Court, when directed to do so, the prevailing party is required to submit a proposed judgment within sixty (60) days of the filing of the decision. *See* 22 N.Y.C.R.R. § 202.48. The failure to submit the judgment in a timely manner constitutes an "abandonment" of the action unless good cause is shown. *Id.*; Clarke v. Parkway Vill. Equities Corp., 984 N.Y.S.2d 631 (Queens Cnty. Sup. Ct. 2014).

provide the requisite forms to obtain the judgment and warrant.[289] Where the Landlord is represented by counsel, the attorney may be required to submit a proposed judgment and warrant for the Court's consideration.

1. PAYMENT OF ARREARS PRIOR TO EXECUTION OF WARRANT (NON-PAYMENT PROCEEDINGS)

In 2019, the HSTPA amended RPAPL § 731 by codifying at subdivision 4 that the Tenant's payment of the rent arrears prior to the hearing renders a non-payment proceeding moot.[290] The statute further provides that if the Court "awards" a judgment in favor of the Landlord following a hearing on the merits, then the Tenant's payment of the amount "awarded," or the depositing of the moneys with the Court, prior to the execution of the warrant of eviction results in the vacating of both the judgment of possession and warrant of eviction.[291] Accordingly, the Tenant would be permitted to remain in possession of the premises, and the summary proceeding would effectively be dismissed.

There is an exception to this rule when the Landlord demonstrates that the Tenant's failure to pay the arrears was due to "bad faith" (then

---

289 The fee for a transcript of judgment in the Housing Parts is $6.00, except in the Town and Village Justice Courts where the fee is $2.00. *See* N.Y. City Civ. Ct. Act § 1911; Uniform City Ct. Act § 1911; Uniform Dist. Ct. Act § 1911; Uniform Justice Ct. Act § 1911.

290 *See* Regency Vill. Mgmt. v. Rodriguez, 121 N.Y.S.3d 510 n.2 (App. Term, 9th & 10th Jud. Dists. 2020). Prior to the legislative amendment, the same outcome was achieved in a litany of decisions. *See, e.g.*, New York City Hous. Auth. v. Torres, 61 A.D.2d 681, at 682 n.1, 403 N.Y.S.2d 527, 529 (1st Dep't 1978) (regarding premises within New York City, "[a] timely tender bars entry of final judgment and therefore logically it must bar issuance of a warrant which is based on that final judgment"); Melick v. Ken's Serv. Stat., Inc., 2014 N.Y. Misc. LEXIS 3874 (App. Term, 9th & 10th Jud. Dists. Aug. 21, 2014) (same for premises situated outside New York City); *see also* Keita v. Ottman, 946 N.Y.S.2d 67 (App. Term, 2d, 11th & 13th Jud. Dists. 2011) (where the "[f]inal judgment in [the] nonpayment proceeding [was] satisfied prior to the issuance of the warrant" and the deadline set forth in the parties' settlement, Landlord's motion to restore the case to the calendar for the purpose of scheduling an inquest against the John Doe and Jane Doe was properly denied); Chester Mamaroneck Gardens, L.L.C. v. Riggsbee, 733 N.Y.S.2d 324 (App. Term, 9th & 10th Jud. Dists. 2001) (arrears offered after entering Stipulation of Settlement, but prior to issuance of judgment).

291 RPAPL § 749(3); Jamaica Seven LLC v. Douglas, 155 N.Y.S.3d 528 (N.Y. Civ. Ct. Queens Cnty. 2021).

the warrant and judgment would stand).[292] In other words, with the lone exception of bad faith, in both residential and commercial non-payment proceedings, the Tenant may avoid an eviction and remain in possession of the premises when the amounts owed are paid prior to the execution of the warrant of eviction. When the parties have a honest dispute regarding the amount of rent owed or the Court awards an abatement of rent in favor of the Tenant, presumably there will be no finding of bad faith.[293]

If the Landlord refuses to accept the Tenant's tender of the full amount awarded, the Tenant may deposit the monies with the Clerk of the Court which similarly stays issuance or enforcement of the judgment and warrant.[294] Thus, the Landlord has no choice but to accept the Tenant's payment.[295] Although funds deposited with the Court are maintained in an interest bearing account, applicable Court and statutory fees will be deducted from the amount tendered to the Landlord.

In a holdover proceeding, the Tenant is not afforded the same opportunity to avoid an eviction because the tenancy was terminated prior to the commencement of the summary proceeding. Since holdover proceedings are typically commenced for reasons other than unpaid rent, a prevailing Landlord, other than for good cause shown, generally need not be concerned that the proceeding will be dismissed or the occupant will be permitted to remain in possession by paying the amount owed. For residential properties, the reader should review the statutory stays pursuant to RPAPL § 753 as discussed in Chapter 15, *infra*.

---

292 RPAPL § 749(3).

293 *See generally 636 Apt. Assoc., JV*, 130 N.Y.S.3d at 649.

294 RPAPL § 751(1) (outside New York City); *see* Sfaelos v. Farrugia, 2002 N.Y. Misc. LEXIS 1361 (App. Term, 9th & 10th Jud. Dists. July 5, 2002).

295 *See 636 Apt. Assoc., JV*, 130 N.Y.S.3d at 649. *Cf.* Chelsea Ridge NY, LLC v. Clarke, 983 N.Y.S.2d 201 (App. Term, 9th & 10th Jud. Dists. 2013) (offering to pay less than the full rent is not a valid tender); *see also* Kew Gardens Realty Co. v. Bank, 958 N.Y.S.2d 61 (App. Term, 2d, 11th & 13th Jud. Dists. 2010) (Tenant failed to provide sworn proof that the offer to pay rent arrears was made prior to the issuance of the final judgment).

2. ATTORNEY'S FEES NOT RECOVERABLE WHEN ARREARS PAID PRIOR TO THE AWARD OF JUDGMENT

As discussed in Chapter 5, *infra*, other than statutory costs and interest, RPAPL § 702 limits the monetary award in a residential summary proceeding to rent arrears and use and occupancy. Unless waived, additional lease obligations, such as attorney's fees, may be enforced in a separate plenary action for damages.

Regardless of the forum, it is well-established that in a non-payment proceeding the Landlord may not be awarded attorney's fees when the Tenant pays the rent arrears prior to the award.[296] The payment of the arrears prior to the "award" means that the Landlord did not prevail with respect to the central relief sought; i.e., a possessory judgment, and, as a result, attorney's fees may not be recovered.[297]

The reader should note the unusual outcome in *40-50 Brighton First Rd. Apts. Corp. v. Shneyerson* where attorney's fees were improperly awarded to the Landlord notwithstanding the Tenants' payment of the arrears prior to the award. In that case, the Appellate Court reasoned that it was powerless to rectify the error because the Tenants did not appeal that portion of the decision.[298]

Real Property Law § 234 prohibits an award of attorney's fees when

---

296 Sherwood Suffolk Co. v. Panorama Catering, Ltd., 128 N.Y.S.3d 780 (App. Term, 9th & 10th Jud. Dists. 2020); 40-50 Brighton First Rd. Apts. Corp. v. Shneyerson, 130 N.Y.S.3d 194 (App. Term, 2d, 11th & 13th Jud. Dists. 2020) (since the arrears were paid at the hearing, "[l]andlord did not prevail in the proceeding with respect to the central relief sought, because there was no possessory judgment which included arrears, and, thus, landlord was not entitled to an award of attorney's fees in the first instance, much less prejudgment interest on those fees"); *Regency Vill. Mgmt.*, 121 N.Y.S.3d at 510 (holding that "[w]here, as here, full payment is made prior to the hearing date and the landlord does not obtain a final judgment of possession in a nonpayment proceeding, the landlord does not prevail with respect to the central relief sought and is not entitled to attorney's fees").

297 *See Sherwood Suffolk Co.*, 128 N.Y.S.3d at 780; *40-50 Brighton First Rd. Apts. Corp.*, 130 N.Y.S.3d at 194; Babylon Vill. Equities v. Mitchell, 816 N.Y.S.2d 279 (App. Term, 9th & 10th Jud. Dists. 2006). *Cf.* 1974-76 Lafontaine Ave. Terr. Corp. v. Rogers, 920 N.Y.S.2d 243 (App. Term, 1st Dep't 2010) (holding that Petitioner "substantially prevailed on the central issues" when "all rent arrears [were recovered] pursuant to the 'so ordered' stipulation of settlement" following issuance of a possessory judgment and, as a result, Petitioner was entitled to recover attorney's fees).

298 *40-50 Brighton First Rd. Apts. Corp.*, 130 N.Y.S.3d at 194 (holding that "[w]hile there is no basis for the award of attorney's fees to landlord, in light of the fact that tenants did not appeal from [the] final judgment awarding landlord legal fees, that award cannot be disturbed").

the Tenant defaults in a summary proceeding involving residential property.[299] Attorney's fees are similarly unrecoverable in a summary proceeding against a Section 8 Tenant.[300]

3. EARMARKED FUNDS

Rent payments are applied towards the oldest arrears.[301] However, when the Tenant writes in the memo portion of the check that the rent payment is to be applied to a particular month, the Landlord must apply the earmarked funds to the designated month(s).[302]

For example, if in the middle of June the Tenant tenders a check equal to one (1) month's rent and designates that the funds are for the June rent, then those funds, if accepted, must be applied to the June rent even if the rent for the months of April and May had not been paid. The failure to apply the earmarked payment to the appropriate month (i.e., June) would presumably result in a defective rent demand and, in turn, dismissal of the proceeding.[303] The reader should be mindful that the Landlord's acceptance of rent for a month following the months in which arrears are owed does not preclude the commencement of a non-payment proceeding.[304]

---

299 Magnano v. Stewart, 145 N.Y.S.3d 329 (Ossining Just. Ct. 2021).

300 *See Regency Vill. Mgmt.*, 121 N.Y.S.3d at 510 (noting that an attorney's fees provision, even when denoted as "additional rent" in the lease, is not enforceable against a Section 8 Tenant).

301 *See generally* Greater Centennial Homes Hous. Dev. Corp. v. Nicholas, 2019 N.Y.L.J. LEXIS 1729, at *6 (Mt. Vernon City Ct. May 22, 2019).

302 Neptune Dev. Corp. v. Kalogiannis, 116 N.Y.S.3d 474 (App. Term, 9th & 10th Jud. Dists. 2019); Greenbrier Garden Apts. v. Eustache, 31 N.Y.S.3d 921 (App. Term, 9th & 10th Jud. Dists. 2016); Rosewall Gardens Assoc. v. White, 2021 N.Y. Misc. LEXIS 3324 (N.Y. Civ. Ct. Bronx Cnty. May 17, 2021).

303 *See, e.g.*, EOM 106-15 217th Corp. v. Severine, 112 N.Y.S.3d 861 (App. Term, 2d, 11th & 13th Jud. Dists. 2019); 1 Beach 105 Realty LLC v. Murphy, 2020 N.Y.L.J. LEXIS 1865 (N.Y. Civ. Ct. Queens Cnty. Dec. 18, 2020).

304 *See Greenbrier Garden Apts.*, 31 N.Y.S.3d at 921.

D. CONDITIONAL LIMITATION VS. CONDITION SUBSEQUENT (HOLDOVER PROCEEDINGS)

The difference between a "conditional limitation" and a "condition subsequent" is another nuance of Landlord and Tenant summary proceedings. A holdover proceeding based upon a conditional limitation is permitted. A conditional limitation is a provision that provides for the early termination of the lease when a certain event occurs.[305] There is no discretion for the Landlord to terminate the lease when considering a conditional limitation. Rather, the termination is automatic upon the occurrence of a specific event.[306]

The failure to include a termination provision within the lease will likely result in the dismissal of a holdover proceeding.[307] The most common example of a conditional limitation is where the lease expires by its own terms on a date certain.[308] Another example is a lease provision that provides, in the event of a breach by the Tenant (such as the failure to maintain adequate insurance for the premises), the lease automatically terminates following expiration of a notice to cure (without a remedy). In this situation, "[t]he direct cause of the expiration of the lease is the lapse of time fixed in a notice, not the breach itself."[309]

The Appellate Term has held that a holdover proceeding may be based upon the non-payment of rent when the lease includes a

---

305 *See generally* Nordica Soho LLC v. Emilia, Inc., 992 N.Y.S.2d 600 (App. Term, 1st Dep't 2014); SRI Eleven 1407 Broadway Operator LLC v. Mega Wear Inc., 144 N.Y.S.3d 289, n.6 (N.Y. Civ. Ct. N.Y. Cnty. 2021).

306 *See* Robert F. Dolan, Rasch's Landlord and Tenant Including Summary Proceedings ("Dolan") §§ 23:25 to 23:27, at 184-87 (4th ed. 2010). *Cf.* St. Catherine of Sienna Roman Catholic Church v. 118 Convent Assocs., LLC, 988 N.Y.S.2d 405 (App. Term, 2d, 11th & 13th Jud. Dists. 2014) (lease triggering event that gives the Landlord an "option" of terminating the tenancy "[c]reates a condition, and not a conditional limitation . . ., and a holdover summary proceeding cannot be based thereon").

307 *See* 1900 Albemarle, LLC v. Solon, 72 N.Y.S.3d 517 (App. Term, 2d, 11th & 13th Jud. Dists. 2017).

308 *See generally* Perrotta v. Western Reg'l Off-Track Betting Corp., 98 A.D.2d 1, at 5, 469 N.Y.S.2d 504 (4th Dep't 1983). *See* Dolan § 23:29, at 190-91.

309 Peekskill Hous. Auth. v. Dunlap, 134 N.Y.S.3d 614 (App. Term, 9th & 10th Jud. Dists. 2020).

conditional limitation that the tenancy will terminate if rent is not timely paid following service of a default notice.[310] The Court reasoned that because the Landlord and Tenant relationship was terminated prior to the commencement of the summary proceeding, the holdover proceeding was proper and "not void as against public policy."[311] The Appellate Term for the First Department reached a similar conclusion with regard to a commercial property.[312]

On the other hand, a holdover proceeding based upon a "condition subsequent" is not permitted. A condition subsequent is a lease provision that gives the Landlord the option of terminating the tenancy if a certain event occurs (e.g., if the Tenant breaches the lease, then the lease is terminated at the discretion of the Landlord). Under these circumstances, a summary proceeding is improper because the fulfillment of the condition does not result in the early termination of the lease, and the Landlord would instead have to commence an action for ejectment to regain possession in the Supreme Court.[313]

---

310 *St. Catherine of Sienna Roman Catholic Church*, 988 N.Y.S.2d at 405; Stadt v. Durkin, 2012 N.Y. Misc. LEXIS 1525 (App. Term, 9th & 10th Jud. Dists. April 2, 2012).

311 *Stadt*, 2012 N.Y. Misc. LEXIS at 1525. The following year the Appellate Term held that where the warranty of habitability defense is established in a holdover proceeding, the summary proceeding must be dismissed. *See* Windy Acres Farm, Inc. v. Penepent, 971 N.Y.S.2d 652 (App. Term, 9th & 10th Jud. Dists. 2013); *see also* 156 E. 37th St. LLC v. Eichner, 113 N.Y.S.3d 484 (N.Y. Civ. Ct. N.Y. Cnty. 2019) (holding that a "conditional limitation providing for the forfeiture of a tenancy upon nonpayment of rent is void as against public policy as it deprives tenants of their right to interpose a breach of warranty of habitability claim").

312 C & A 483 Broadway, LLC v. KLMNI, Inc., 26 N.Y.S.3d 723 (App. Term, 1st Dep't 2015); Great Location N.Y., Inc. v. Seventh Ave. Fine Foods. Inc., 13 N.Y.S.3d 850 (App. Term, 1st Dep't 2015).

313 *See Perrotta*, 98 A.D.2d at 1, 469 N.Y.S.2d at 504; Watervliet Hous. Auth. v. Bell, 262 A.D.2d 810, 694 N.Y.S.2d 484 (3d Dep't 1999); JCF Assoc., LLC v. Sign Up USA, Inc., 101 N.Y.S.3d 700 (App. Term, 2d, 11th & 13th Jud. Dists. 2018) (holdover proceeding dismissed when the lease was not terminated); Fourth Hous. Co., Inc. v. Bowers, 39 N.Y.S.3d 350 (App. Term, 2d, 11th & 13th Jud. Dists. 2016) (dismissing holdover proceeding because the lease did not "[p]rovide that the term of the lease shall automatically expire upon the lapse of time fixed in [the] notice"); Chen v. Salvador, 145 N.Y.S.3d 780 (N.Y. Civ. Ct. Queens Cnty. 2021) (dismissing summary proceeding when "[t]he predicate notices do not [purport a] cognizable cause of action under a provision of the lease that would permit early termination").

CHAPTER 5

JUDGMENTS

For approximately one-third of residential Landlords, up to twenty percent (20%) of their family's household income is derived from rental properties.[314] With so much at stake for both Landlords and Tenants, an understanding of the relief available in a summary proceeding is critical. The Housing Part may award a prevailing Petitioner: (1) a judgment of possession; (2) a money judgment; and (3) a warrant of eviction. A money judgment may also be awarded in favor of the Tenant for a successfully asserted counterclaim.[315]

A. JUDGMENT OF POSSESSION AND WARRANT OF EVICTION

The judgment of possession and warrant of eviction are the ultimate relief in a summary proceeding.[316] The judgment and warrant direct legal possession of the property back to the Petitioner and authorize an eviction should the Tenant refuse to voluntarily surrender possession by a date certain. In both residential and commercial non-payment proceedings, the warrant must be vacated when the rent arrears are paid prior to the eviction unless the Tenant withheld payment in "bad faith."[317]

314 *See* Kristen Broady, Wendy Edelberg, and Emily Moss, "*An Eviction Moratorium Without Rental Assistance Hurts Smaller Landlords, Too*," Brookings Institute, Sept. 20, 2020, at https://www.brookings.edu/blog/up-front/2020/09/21/an-eviction-moratorium-without-rental-assistance-hurts-smaller-landlords-too/.

315 RPAPL § 743.

316 *See* Grand Concourse Estates LLC v. Ture, 2018 N.Y.L.J. LEXIS 3759 (N.Y. Civ. Ct. Bronx Cnty. Nov. 18, 2018).

317 RPAPL § 749(3). Conversely, in a holdover proceeding, since the Landlord and Tenant relationship was terminated prior to the commencement of the summary proceeding, the judgment of possession and warrant of eviction stand even where the Tenant offers to pay the amount owed prior to the eviction.

B. MONEY JUDGMENTS

A prevailing Landlord may be awarded a money judgment without regard to amount because the court's maximum dollar jurisdictional limit does not apply to summary proceedings.[318] To enforce the money judgment, the Landlord may file the judgment with the County Clerk's Office and invoke the enforcement mechanisms pursuant to CPLR Article 52.[319]

The Tenant's financial obligations accrue when the rent becomes due,[320] which under common law is at "the end of the rental period."[321] However, as a practical matter, the parties typically negotiate an earlier accrual date, routinely the 1st day of each month.[322] Where the lease is terminated early, unless otherwise agreed, the Tenant may not recover rent paid "in advance,"[323] and the Tenant remains obligated for previously accrued rent arrears.[324]

---

318 N.Y. City Civ. Ct. Act § 204; Uniform City Ct. Act § 204; Uniform Dist. Ct. Act § 204; Uniform Just. Ct. Act § 204. *See generally* Burke v. Aspland, 56 A.D.3d 1001, 867 N.Y.S.2d 759 (3d Dep't 2008); Edgemont Assoc., LLC v. Goldman, 97 N.Y.S.3d 55 (App. Term, 9th & 10th Jud. Dists. 2018); MTC Commons, LLC v. Millbrook Training Ctr. & Spa, Ltd., 31 N.Y.S.3d 922 (App. Term, 9th & 10th Jud. Dists. 2016); BLDG ABI Enter., LLC v. 711 Second Ave. Corp., 2019 N.Y. Misc. LEXIS 6456 (N.Y. Cnty. Sup. Ct. Nov. 20, 2019).

319 Cantalupo Constr. Corp. v. 2319 Richmond Terr. Corp., 141 A.D.3d 626, 34 N.Y.S.3d 616 (2d Dep't 2016) (civil contempt generally not available to enforce a money judgment obtained in a summary proceeding).

320 Eujoy Realty Corp. v. Van Wagner Comms., LLC, 22 N.Y.3d 413, 981 N.Y.S.2d 326 (2013); Bri Jen Realty Corp. v. Altman, 146 A.D.3d 744, 48 N.Y.S.3d 670 (2d Dep't 2017); Trinity Centre LLC v. Prosurance Brokerage Assoc., Inc., 2020 N.Y. Misc. LEXIS 2534 (N.Y. Cnty. Sup. Ct. May 11, 2020) (holding "[t]he claim is pled sufficiently for all rents that had come due at the time of the filing of the action").

321 *Eujoy Realty Corp.*, 22 N.Y.3d at 413, 981 N.Y.S.2d at 326 (citations omitted).

322 *Id.* (holding that "[w]hen a lease sets a due date for rent, that date is the date on which the tenant's debt accrues").

323 1251 Ams. Assoc. II, L.P. v. Rock 49th Rest. Corp., 831 N.Y.S.2d 360 (App. Term, 1st Dep't 2006). Pursuant to the HSTPA, an advance for a non-rent stabilized residential property may not exceed one (1) month's rent. *See* GOL § 7-108(1-a).

324 *Eujoy Realty Corp.*, 22 N.Y.3d at 413, 981 N.Y.S.2d at 326 (where the rental agreement required payment of the annual rent on January 1st, the Tenant's termination of the lease on January 8th did not negate its obligation to pay the full year's rent).

1. "RENT" DEFINED

The term "rent" refers to the negotiated dollar amount to occupy property pursuant to a rental agreement. The HSTPA defines rent as "[t]he monthly or weekly amount charged in consideration for use and occupation of a dwelling pursuant to a written or oral rental agreement."[325] RPAPL § 702 further provides that "[*n*]*o fees, charges, or penalties other than rent may be sought in a proceeding pursuant to [Article VII]*."[326] A lease provision to the contrary is unenforceable.[327]

Although unpaid rent and use and occupancy may be included within the money judgment, it is not entirely clear whether RPAPL § 702 allows for lease items identified as "added" or "additional" rent. Prior to the HSTPA, "added rent" items, such as attorney's fees, utilities, and potentially late fees, were routinely awarded to a prevailing Landlord provided the amounts were reasonable.

However, it would appear that RPAPL § 702 precludes the award of "added rent" items in a residential summary proceeding.[328] In *Beco v. Ritter*, the Appellate Division, Third Department held that the Landlord's two-tiered rent payment schedule, which amounted to "discounts" for early rent payments, constituted an impermissible late fee in contravention of RPL § 238-a.[329] The Court also cited RPAPL § 702 for the proposition that the late fee "[i]mposed a penalty that may not be

---

325 RPAPL § 702.

326 *Id.* (emphasis added). The reference to the larger "Article VII," as opposed to section 702, which pertains to residential dwellings only, raises the issue whether the restriction on monetary relief was extended to commercial properties.

327 *Id.*; *see generally* 25-31 Ontario St. v. Anthony, 115 N.Y.S.3d 645 (Cohoes City Ct. 2019).

328 *See, e.g.*, Magnano v. Stewart, 145 N.Y.S.3d 329 (Ossining Just. Ct. 2021); 950 Rutland Rd. Co. LLC v. Lord, 2021 N.Y.L.J. LEXIS 588 (N.Y. Civ. Ct. Kings Cnty. June 22, 2021); *see also* 56-11 94th St. Co. L.L.C. v. Jara, 116 N.Y.S.3d 866 (Queens Cnty. Civ. Ct. 2019); Regency Vill. Mgmt. v. Rodriguez, 121 N.Y.S.3d 510 (App. Term, 9th & 10th Jud. Dists. 2020) (in dicta, implicitly stating same). *See also* William J. Niebel, "*The Process Due When Rent Is Due: Residential Non-payment Evictions in New York After COVID-19*," 49 N.Y.R.P.L.J. 5 (2021) (asserting that "RPAPL 702 was enacted to end the practice of labeling items as 'additional rent' in a lease....").

329 190 A.D.3d 1150, 140 N.Y.S.3d 294 (3d Dep't 2021). The Court further concluded the fees were grossly disproportionate to any actual damages sustained by the Landlord. *Id.*

sought in a summary proceeding."[330]

The decision was non-specific as to whether the fees were denied because they were either excessive or impermissibly "sought" in a residential summary proceeding, or both.[331] The distinction is significant because the *Beco* decision is binding in all of the Judicial Departments until the United States Supreme Court, the Court of Appeals, or any of the other Appellate Divisions address the issue.[332]

The Ossining Justice Court similarly interpreted the *Beco* decision and RPAPL § 702 as precluding all monetary relief in a summary proceeding other than rent, use and occupancy, and statutory costs and interest.[333] In *Magnano v. Stewart*, the Court, citing both *Beco* and RPAPL § 702, denied the prevailing Petitioner's request for attorney's fees, an unpaid electric bill, and the costs of a locksmith because the Landlord "[m]ay not recover any other fees, charges, or penalties within this summary proceeding."[334]

A question to be reconciled is whether RPAPL § 702 is applicable to commercial premises.[335] Until there is binding precedent, conflicting decisions may result. However, as a general matter, the restriction on the monetary relief is limited to the summary proceeding because, unless waived, either party may pursue a lease obligation that could not be addressed in the Housing Part in a separate plenary action for damages.[336]

---

330 *Id.*

331 *See id.*

332 *See generally* Evolution Mkts., Inc. v. Penny, 889 N.Y.S.2d 882, n.12 (Westchester Cnty. Sup. Ct. 2009); Zheng v. Lin, 2021 N.Y.L.J. LEXIS 280 (N.Y. Civ. Ct. Queens Cnty. April 7, 2021).

333 *Magnano*, 145 N.Y.S.3d at 329.

334 *Id.*

335 Although RPAPL § 702 is titled "Rent in a *Residential* Dwelling," the statutory definition of rent set forth therein references Article VII of RPAPL which includes both residential and commercial properties. Counterclaims are authorized pursuant to RPAPL § 743.

336 *See* 172 Van Duzer Realty Corp. v. Globe Alumni Student Assistance Assn., Inc., 24 N.Y.3d 528, 2 N.Y.S.3d 39 (2014) (holding "[b]ecause the [Housing Part] was without authority to address a claim for the balance of rent due under the acceleration clause in [landlord's] holdover proceeding[, landlord] was not barred from pursuing damages for [tenants'] breach"); Fifth Line, LLC v. Fitch, 167 A.D.3d 847, 91 N.Y.S.3d 135 (2d Dep't 2018).

2. USE AND OCCUPANCY

The term "use and occupancy" refers to the fair and reasonable value to occupy real property in the absence of a rental agreement.[337] Even though the value of "rent" and "use and occupancy" may be identical, it is not necessarily the case and the terms are not interchangeable.[338] Both Appellate Terms for the Second Department have held that a Landlord may not be awarded use and occupancy in a summary proceeding when the Landlord does not prevail on the issue of possession (i.e., a judgment of possession must be awarded to recover a money judgment in a summary proceeding).[339]

Use and occupancy is generally calculated by multiplying the daily pro-rated value of the reasonable monthly value of the property by the number of days the Tenant was in possession without a rental agreement.[340] For residential properties, the Landlord generally need not retain an expert to demonstrate the reasonable value of the property. Rather, the Landlord may rely upon the rent set forth within the expired or terminated lease.[341] In commercial cases, the testimony of a

337 Nisim v. Ramirez, 152 N.Y.S.3d 208 (App. Term, 2d, 11th & 13th Jud. Dists. 2021); London Paint & Wallpaper Co., Inc. v. Kesselman, 138 A.D.3d 632, 30 N.Y.S.3d 90 (1st Dep't 2016); Ministers, Elders & Deacons of Reformed Protestant Dutch Church v. 198 Broadway, Inc., 579 N.Y.S.2d 543 (N.Y. Civ. Ct. N.Y. Cnty. 1991).

338 2114 Realty LLC v. Estate of Sanabria, 2021 N.Y.L.J. LEXIS 874, at *21 (N.Y. Civ. Ct. Kings Cnty. Sept. 1, 2021) (noting that "[r]ent derives from a contract or an agreement, while use and occupancy derives, literally from use and occupancy of a place and from a sense of equity, fairness and ultimately from a desire to 'balance equities'"); *Magnano*, 145 N.Y.S.3d at 329.

339 *See* Lakeland W. Capital XI, LLC v. Uvino, 134 N.Y.S.3d 125 (App. Term, 9th & 10th Jud. Dists. 2020) (petition dismissed); Esposito v. Larig, 36 N.Y.S.3d 899 (App. Term, 2d, 11th & 13th Jud. Dists. 2016) (same).

340 *See generally* Madden v. Juliet, 13 N.Y.S.3d 850 (App. Term, 9th & 10th Jud. Dists. 2015) (in small claims action, use and occupancy awarded for the sixteen (16) days the Tenant remained in possession following lease termination, or 16/30 of the monthly rent); Sap V/Atlas 845 WEA Assocs. NF LLC v. Jannelli, 918 N.Y.S.2d 691 (App. Term, 1st Dep't 2010) (occupants permitted to remain in possession provided pro-rated use and occupancy tendered "identical to the rent they had been paying").

341 *See Nisim*, 152 N.Y.S.3d at 208 (holding that use and occupancy "[c]an be based upon, among other things, proof of the rent paid under an expired lease"); Warner v. Lyon, 115 N.Y.S.3d 806 (App. Term, 2d, 11th & 13th Jud. Dists. 2019) (same); Vanchev v. Mulligan, 41 N.Y.S.3d 722 (App. Term, 2d, 11th & 13th Jud. Dists. 2016).

licensed appraiser or realtor is more commonly required.[342]

Both rent and use and occupancy may be included within the money judgment,[343] and any amounts not obtainable may be sought in a separate plenary or small claims action following the Tenant's surrender of the premises.[344] The distinction between "rent" and "use and occupancy" is further useful in denoting the parties' relationship. Unpaid "rent" refers to a period when the parties had a valid rental agreement, and "use and occupancy" references a period when the parties did not have such an agreement (e.g., after the lease expired).

a. ISSUED CONCOMITANT WITH A JUDGMENT OF POSSESSION

It is well-established that a money judgment must be issued concomitant with a judgment of possession.[345] In other words, the Housing Part may not issue a money judgment in favor of the Landlord unless it also issues a judgment of possession. The reasoning is that where a judgment of possession is unwarranted, the Housing Part is not the appropriate forum to adjudicate monetary claims stemming from the tenancy. Instead, the Landlord may seek the monetary relief in a separate plenary or small claims action.

---

342 *See generally* Rubenstein v. Mayor, 161 A.D.3d 1202, 78 N.Y.S.3d 716 (2d Dep't 2018) (the Court rejected the opinions of both expert witnesses because their "methods of contrasting the comparable leases was 'unverifiable'"). *Cf.* 98-48 Queens Blvd. LLC v. Parkside Mem. Chapels, 2020 N.Y.L.J. LEXIS 1381 (N.Y. Civ. Ct. Queens Cnty. Sept. 9, 2020) (attempting to avoid delay, the Court "set interim use and occupancy at the last rent rate" and the parties could revisit the rate via expert testimony or other available evidence at the upcoming hearing on the merits).

343 *See, e.g.*, 39-50 24th St. Realty Corp. v. Ol' Bridge Café Inc., 138 N.Y.S.3d 853 (N.Y. Civ. Ct. Queens Cnty. 2021).

344 *See, e.g.*, Messam v. Neisca, 129 N.Y.S.3d 612 (App. Term, 2d, 11th & 13th Jud. Dists. 2020).

345 *See* FBD Realty, LLC v. Rego Park N.H., Ltd., 152 N.Y.S.3d 767 (App. Term, 2d, 11th & 13th Jud. Dists. 2021) (the money judgment may only be awarded "[c]oncomitant with an award of possession"); TAM Med. Supply Corp. v. American Ind. Ins. Co., 2021 N.Y. Misc. LEXIS 6346 (App. Term, 9th & 10th Jud. Dists. Dec. 10, 2021) (same result in a commercial non-payment proceeding) (*citing* Fieldbridge Assoc., LLC v. Sanders, 139 N.Y.S.3d 474 (App. Term, 2d, 11th & 13th Jud. Dists. 2021)); Carney Realty Corp. v. Elite Tent & Party Rental, 156 N.Y.S.3d 808 (App. Term, 9th & 10th Jud. Dists. 2021).

Accordingly, when the Tenant vacates the property during the pendency of a summary proceeding, a prevailing Landlord must be awarded a judgment of possession to also be awarded a money judgment. There has been a litany of cases supporting this outcome where the issue of possession is resolved while the case is pending.[346]

Due to the COVID-19 Pandemic, the Legislature created an exception to the rule. Section 1 of the TSHA prohibits the issuance of either a judgment of possession or a warrant of eviction "[a]gainst a residential tenant or other lawful occupant that has suffered a financial hardship during the COVID-19 covered period for the non-payment of rent that accrues or becomes due during the COVID-19 covered period."[347] However, in that same situation, the statute expressly permits the issuance of a money judgment (without a judgment of possession or warrant of eviction) for the full amount of rent owed in a summary proceeding.[348]

346 *See* Sowalsky v. E. F. MacDonald Stamp Co., 294 N.Y.S.2d 1016 (3d Dep't 1968) ("[a] landlord is entitled to a final order awarding possession, provided such an order is warranted by the evidence, notwithstanding the fact that tenant has removed from the premises subsequent to the commencement of the summary proceedings"); Four Forty-One Holding Corp. v. Bloom, 266 N.Y.S. 233 (App. Term, 1st Dep't 1933) ("Where the proceeding is properly instituted for non-payment of rent,...it is not a 'sufficient cause' to defeat the proceeding that the tenant has given up possession after the service of the precept. The landlord, if justified in instituting such proceedings, under the existing statute is entitled to a final adjudication of the rights of the parties and, in a proceeding of a legal character such as this, those rights are to be determined as they existed at the time the proceedings were commenced"); Eastrich No. 80 Corp. v. Patrolmen's Benev. Ass'n of New York City Tr. Police Dep't, 688 N.Y.S.2d 409 (App. Term, 1st Dep't 1999); Erick James LLC v. Bruna, 141 N.Y.S.3d 294 (N.Y. Civ. Ct. Bronx Cnty. March 1, 2021) ("The Courts of this state have found that 'jurisdiction is not divested merely because of the removal of the respondent subsequent to the commencement of the proceeding'").

347 TSHA § 1.

348 *Id.* at § 3.

b. RULE AGAINST APPORTIONMENT

The "rule against apportionment" is another consideration in determining the amount of the money judgment. This rule applies to rent, but not use and occupancy.[349]

The Tenant is liable for an entire month's rent (i.e., rent is not to be apportioned) as soon as the month's rent becomes due even if the tenancy is terminated prior to the end of that month. Therefore, when the tenancy is terminated after a month's rent has become due (i.e., typically when the tenancy is terminated between the 2nd and final day of the month), there is no need to consider the apportionment of the monetary relief because the entire month's rent may be awarded in the summary proceeding.

Otherwise, where the occupant has been in possession of the premises without a rental agreement for any portion of a particular month, the Petitioner may be awarded use and occupancy, which must be "apportioned." This is accomplished by pro-rating the fair and reasonable value of occupying the premises by the precise number of days the Tenant remained in possession without a rental agreement.[350] For example, if the monthly rent was $600 (and was paid in full), but the Tenant remained in possession for ten (10) additional days following the termination of the lease, then the Landlord would be entitled to use and occupancy in the amount of $200 ($600/30 x 10 days).

Unless waived, when possession is no longer an issue, the Landlord may commence a plenary action to recover use and occupancy.[351] If the Landlord is seeking possession following the termination or expiration of the lease, then a holdover proceeding is permitted after the appropriate predicate notice or notices have been served.

---

349 *Warner*, 115 N.Y.S.3d at 806 (holding that "[l]iability for use and occupancy terminates when the tenant's actual use of the subject premises ends, as the rule against apportionment, which applies to rents, does not apply to use and occupancy); Seabury v. Galloway, 130 N.Y.S.3d 188 (App. Term, 9th & 10th Jud. Dists. 2020) (rent may not be apportioned); Rossi v. Scott, 52 N.Y.S.3d 248 (App. Term, 9th & 10th Jud. Dists. 2017) (use and occupancy must be apportioned, that is, absent a tenancy, the occupant is liable only for the actual days in possession); Priegue v. Paulus, 988 N.Y.S.2d 525 (App. Term, 9th & 10th Jud. Dists. 2014) (same).

350 *See, e.g.*, *Vanchev*, 41 N.Y.S.3d at 722.

351 *See Messam*, 129 N.Y.S.3d at 612; Rustagi v. Sanchez, 999 N.Y.S.2d 798 (App. Term, 2d, 11th & 13th Jud. Dists. 2014).

3. TRADITIONAL "ADDITIONAL RENT" ITEMS

Whether "additional rent" items continue to be available in commercial summary proceedings (they are not permitted in residential cases) remains to be determined. As a general matter, failing to seek an item that may be awarded in the summary proceeding bars seeking same in a subsequent plenary action because that would "constitute an improper splitting of a cause of action."[352] In addition, the doctrine of *res judicata* precludes the re-litigation of a claim that was fully adjudicated in a prior proceeding.[353]

If "added rent" items are still permitted in a commercial summary proceeding, to be awarded in the Housing Part, the item must be identified within the rental agreement as either "added" or "additional" rent.[354] For example, if the rental agreement states that a prevailing Landlord is entitled to attorney's fees, but the lease fails to identify the fees as "additional" or "added" rent, then the attorney's fees would not be recoverable in the summary proceeding.[355] Instead, the fees

352 Acierno v. Faldich, 782 N.Y.S.2d 509 (App. Term, 9th & 10th Jud. Dists. 2004); *see* Caracaus v. Conifer Cent. Sq. Assoc., 158 A.D.3d 63, 68 N.Y.S.3d 225 (4th Dep't 2017); See Why Gerard, LLC v. Gramro Entm't Corp., 94 A.D.3d 1205, 941 N.Y.S.2d 350 (3d Dep't 2012); Landmark Props. v. Olivo, 62 A.D.3d 959, at 961, 881 N.Y.S.2d 110 (2d Dep't 2009).

353 *See* 32nd Jabez Corp. v. Meekang, Inc., 194 A.D.3d 414, 143 N.Y.S.3d 203 (1st Dep't 2021).

354 *See* Thomas Jefferson Owners Corp. v. Lokshin, 134 N.Y.S.3d 129 (App. Term, 2d, 11th & 13th Jud. Dists. 2020) (inspection fees and attorney's fees); Regency Vill. Mgmt. v. Rodriguez, 121 N.Y.S.3d 510 (App. Term, 9th & 10th Jud. Dists. 2020) (attorney's fees); Sokolow v. Neumann-Werth, 86 N.Y.S.3d 370 (App. Term, 2d, 11th & 13th Jud. Dists. 2018) (attorney's fees); Jacoby v. Cabrera, 110 N.Y.S.3d 202 (App. Term, 9th & 10th Jud. Dists. 2018) (utilities and late fees); Martin Operating Corp. v. Andrew Bernstein, Inc., 61 N.Y.S.3d 191 (App. Term, 1st Dep't 2017) (commercial lease provision for 20% real estate tax increase as "additional rent"); *98-48 Queens Blvd. LLC*, 2020 N.Y.L.J. LEXIS at 1381 (real estate taxes in commercial lease).

355 *See* Attia v. Imoukhuede, 57 N.Y.S.3d 674 (App. Term, 9th & 10th Jud. Dists. 2017) (following breach of stipulation of settlement, application for attorney's fees denied, in part, because the lease was not introduced to establish that attorney's fees were negotiated as "additional rent"); *see generally* 125 Ct. St., LLC v. Nicholson, 115 N.Y.S.3d 817 (App. Term, 2d, 11th & 13th Jud. Dists. 2019) (same); Oakwood Terrace Hous. Corp. v. Monk, 36 N.Y.S.3d 48 (App. Term, 9th & 10th Jud. Dists. 2016) ("[s]ince landlord did not submit a copy of the proprietary lease, it failed to demonstrate that late fees and legal fees are collectible in this summary proceeding as 'additional rent'").

would have to be sought in a subsequent plenary action for damages in the Civil Part of the Court or other court of competent jurisdiction. "Additional rent" expenses not yet incurred are not available in a summary proceeding under any circumstance.[356]

A general lease provision stating that all "costs" incurred by the Landlord are deemed "additional rent" has been enforced notwithstanding the omission of the phrase "added rent" in the specific lease section at issue (i.e., a one-time general "additional rent" provision incorporates all of the sections within the lease).[357] The Landlord is generally required to submit a copy of the rental agreement to substantiate a financial award.[358]

a. ATTORNEY'S FEES

In New York, prevailing parties are generally required to pay their own attorney's fees because the fees are "treated as incidents of litigation, rather than damages."[359] An exception exists where attorney's fees are "[a]uthorized by agreement between the parties or by statute or court rule."[360] In Landlord and Tenant proceedings, a lease provision

356 40 Rector Owner LLC v. City of New York, 137 A.D.3d 700, 29 N.Y.S.2d 282 (1st Dep't 2016) ("[n]o indication that plaintiff incurred any attorney's fees" regarding re-letting the premises); Inland Diversified Real Estate Serv., LLC v. Keiko New York, Inc., 36 N.Y.S.3d 407 (App. Term, 9th & 10th Jud. Dists. 2016) (Petitioner must demonstrate the utilities were "actually paid"); Madden v. Juliet, 13 N.Y.S.3d 850 (App. Term, 9th & 10th Jud. Dists. 2015) (inadequate proof attorney's fees were paid); Walden Ctr. Assocs., L.P. v. Cardenas, 930 N.Y.S.2d 177 (App. Term, 9th & 10th Jud. Dists. 2011) (painting, cleaning, and re-letting charges).

357 *See Inland Diversified Real Estate Serv., LLC*, 36 N.Y.S.3d at 407 (a single paragraph within the lease provided that "all of the costs that tenant is obligated to incur pursuant to the lease are deemed 'additional rent'"). The summary proceeding was dismissed for other reasons; namely, the Landlord's failure to introduce the bills, or other proof, demonstrating payment was made. *Id.*

358 *125 Ct. St., LLC*, 115 N.Y.S.3d at 817; LA Gem, LLC v. Fuentes, 110 N.Y.S.3d 198 (App. Term, 9th & 10th Jud. Dists. 2018); Nachajski v. Siwiec, 55 N.Y.S.3d 693 (App. Term, 2d, 11th & 13th Jud. Dists. 2017); *see also* Evans v. Tracy, 951 N.Y.S.2d 85 (App. Term, 9th & 10th Jud. Dists. 2012) (denying award of attorney's fees where Landlord failed to produce the rental agreement); 6 W. 20th St. Tenants Corp. v. Dezertzov, 146 N.Y.S.3d 464 (N.Y. Civ. Ct. N.Y. Cnty. 2021).

359 Ambac Assur. Corp. v. Countrywide Home Loans, Inc., 31 N.Y.3d 569, 81 N.Y.S.3d 816 (2018).

360 *Id.* (*quoting* Congel v. Malfitano, 31 N.Y.3d 272, 76 N.Y.S.3d 873 (2018)).

is typically the genesis for the consideration of attorney's fees and, in such instances, fees may be awarded in the appropriate forum where the Landlord is the prevailing party.[361]

To be considered the prevailing party in a summary proceeding, the Landlord must be awarded the central relief sought, i.e., possession of the property.[362] Although the Court may consider other factors, such as abatement of rent and mixed outcomes, in a non-payment proceeding, the Appellate Term for the Ninth and Tenth Judicial Districts has succinctly stated that where the Landlord does not "[o]btain a judgment of possession for the rental arrears, it was not the prevailing party."[363]

When a Tenant defaults in a residential proceeding (i.e., fails to appear in court when required), although possession, unpaid rent, use and occupancy, and a warrant of eviction may be awarded, the law prohibits an award of attorney's fees.[364] Any agreement to the contrary is unenforceable as a matter of law.[365] Parenthetically, under no circumstance may a Landlord recover attorney's fees against a Section 8 Tenant

---

361 *See* 43rd St. Deli, Inc. v. Paramount Leasehold, L.P., 178 A.D.3d 411, 113 N.Y.S.3d 695 (1st Dep't 2019).

362 *Id.*

363 Sherwood Suffolk Co. v. Panorama Catering, Ltd., 128 N.Y.S.3d 780 (App. Term, 9th & 10th Jud. Dists. 2020) (emphasis added). *See also* Blinds to Go (U.S.), Inc. v. Times Plaza Dev., L.P., 191 A.D.3d 939, 143 N.Y.S.3d 91 (2d Dep't 2021) (denying attorney's fees where "[i]n this highly litigated and contentious action, notwithstanding numerous motions, trials, hearings, and appeals spanning more than 17 years, neither party has obtained the central relief each seeks so as to constitute a prevailing party"); FAC Preserv. HDFC v. Moreno, 150 N.Y.S.3d 496 (App. Term, 2d, 11th & 13th Jud. Dists. 2021) (residential holdover proceeding dismissed); Hillside Park 168, LLC v. Benjamin, 120 N.Y.S.3d 565 (App. Term, 2d, 11th & 13th Jud. Dists. 2019) (although the Tenant had been evicted, denying non-specific attorney's fees request encompassing multiple summary proceedings with mixed outcomes); *see generally Madden*, 13 N.Y.S.3d at 850 (holding where the money judgment was approximately one-third less than the amount claimed, "it cannot be said that [Petitioner] was the prevailing party"); 4702 Chiel Kurtz Realty, LLC v. Molano, 947 N.Y.S.2d 757 (App. Term, 2d, 11th & 13th Jud. Dists. 2012) (holding neither party prevailed where the money judgment was reduced by approximately one-third due to the Landlord's breach of the warranty of habitability).

364 RPL § 234.

365 *Id.* (the statute provides that "[a]ny waiver of this section shall be void as against public policy"). The statute does not differentiate between summary proceedings and plenary or small claims actions.

in a summary proceeding.[366]

The award of attorney's fees must be reasonable and just.[367] In determining the reasonableness of the attorney's fees requested, the Court may consider "counsel's testimony and records as to the nature, extent and necessity of the legal services rendered on landlord's behalf in the [summary] proceeding."[368] The fees must have been incurred in the proceeding for possession, and not connected to another action or unrelated proceeding.[369] A party awarded attorney's fees is further entitled to interest on the award from the date of the Court's determination.[370]

Where the rental agreement provides for attorney's fees in the event of a breach, the breach specified within the lease must constitute the basis for terminating the tenancy to recover the fees.[371] For example,

366 *Regency Vill. Mgmt.*, 121 N.Y.S.3d at 510 (holding that "even if the lease contains a provision deeming attorney's fees additional rent, that provision would not be enforceable, since tenant is a Section 8 tenant and such fees cannot be considered rent as to a Section 8 tenant and cannot be recovered in a summary proceeding against such a tenant"); Greenburgh Hous. Auth. v. Hall, 58 N.Y.S.3d 874 (App. Term, 9th & 10th Jud. Dists. 2017) (same).

367 *See* W6 Facility X, LLC v. West 6 Care Ctr., Inc., 169 A.D.3d 968, 95 N.Y.S.3d 95 (2d Dep't 2019).

368 600 Realty Heights, LLC v. Paula-Molina, 26 N.Y.S.3d 216 (App. Term, 1st Dep't 2015); 125-127 Allen St. Assocs. v. Lin, 26 N.Y.S.3d 214 (App. Term, 1st Dep't 2015); APF 286 Mad LLC v. RIS Real Props., Inc., 13 N.Y.S.3d 849 (App. Term, 1st Dep't 2015); Zi Chang Realty Corp. v. Chen, 2020 N.Y.L.J. LEXIS 787 (N.Y. Civ. Ct. N.Y. Cnty. April 14, 2020).

369 East Aurora Coop. Mkt., Inc. v. Red Brick Plaza LLC, 197 A.D.3d 874, 153 N.Y.S.3d 252 (4th Dep't 2021) (declining attorney's fees for services rendered in a different case on appeal); 40-50 Brighton First Rd. Apts. Corp. v. Henderson, 27 N.Y.S.3d 310 (App. Term, 2d, 11th & 13th Jud. Dists. 2015); Hawthorne Gardens Owners Corp. v. Jacobs, 17 N.Y.S.3d 382 (App. Term, 9th & 10th Jud. Dists. 2015); *see generally* Sardis v. Sardis, 53 N.Y.S.3d 904 (Suffolk Cnty. Sup. Ct. 2017) (shareholder's derivative suit).

370 *See* Quadracci v. Freeman, 195 A.D.3d 560, 146 N.Y.S.3d 472 (1st Dep't 2021) (*citing* Solow Mgmt. Corp. v. Tanger, 19 A.D.3d 225, 797 N.Y.S.2d 456 (1st Dep't 2005) (holding that attorney's fees "[r]epresent a conditional award or prerogative which does not mature until the underlying action or proceeding has been determined[, and in] the court's opinion that establishes the appropriate date from which interest should flow")).

371 *Sokolow*, 86 N.Y.S.3d at 370. *See generally* LG Funding, LLC v. Johnson & Son Locksmith, Inc., 170 A.D.3d 1153, at 1154, 96 N.Y.S.3d 640 (2d Dep't 2019) (since "New York public policy disfavors any award of attorneys' fees to the prevailing party in a litigation, a contract assuming that obligation must be strictly construed to avoid reading into it a duty which the parties did not intend to be assumed") (citations omitted).

in *Sokolow v. Neumann-Werth*, the prevailing Landlord was denied attorney's fees because the month-to-month tenancy was not terminated due to a breach specified within the lease.[372]

The Court has limited discretion to deny attorney's fees based upon "equitable considerations and fairness."[373] For example, denial of an attorney's fees application is appropriate where "[b]ad faith is established on the part of the successful party or where unfairness is manifest."[374] A lease provision authorizing attorney's fees merely for maintaining a summary proceeding, regardless of the outcome or fault, is similarly unenforceable.[375] In addition, a stay on the execution of the warrant of eviction does not alter the Petitioner's status as the prevailing party.[376]

As a general matter, the Court is not bound by the amount of attorney's fees set forth in the rental agreement[377] or the fee agreement between counsel and the client.[378] Absent a lease provision to the contrary,

372 *Sokolow*, 86 N.Y.S.3d at 370.

373 *See* Greenbrier Garden Apts. v. Eustache, 31 N.Y.S.3d 921 (App. Term, 9th & 10th Jud. Dists. 2016).

374 *Id.* (attorney's fees denied where Landlord misapplied earmarked rent payments and failed to respond to Tenant's request for information). *Cf.* Round Dune, Inc. v. Filkowski, 197 A.D.3d 748, 153 N.Y.S.3d 166 (2d Dep't 2021) (attorney's fees permitted where the award was not "manifestly unfair" and there was no evidence of "bad faith"); Win Feng LLC v. Lawrence, 110 N.Y.S.3d 774 (App. Term, 1st Dep't 2018) (awarding attorney's fees absent "unfairness or bad faith by landlord").

375 *See* Krodel v. Amalagated Dwellings Inc., 166 A.D.3d 412, 88 N.Y.S.3d 31 (1st Dep't 2018) (lease provision requiring Tenant to pay attorney's fees for commencing action against Landlord is "unconscionable and unenforceable"); Weidman v. Tomaselli, 365 N.Y.S.2d 681, 691 (Rockland Cnty. Ct.), *aff'd*, 386 N.Y.S.2d 276 (App. Term, 9th & 10th Jud. Dists. 1975).

376 *600 Realty Heights, LLC*, 26 N.Y.S.3d at 216. The stay "[h]as the effect of temporarily depriving the prevailing party of the ability to use the methods specified by law," but it does not change the prevailing party's status. *See generally* Pokoik v. Department of Health Servs., 220 A.D.2d 13, 641 N.Y.S.2d 881 (2d Dep't 1996) (describing stays pursuant to CPLR § 5519).

377 *See* Queens Fresh Meadows, LLC v. Newberry, 2 N.Y.S.3d 310 (App. Term, 2d, 11th & 13th Jud. Dists. 2014).

378 338 W. 46th St. Realty, LLC v. Leonardi, 930 N.Y.S.2d 177 (App. Term, 1st Dep't 2011) ("[a]lthough a fee arrangement between the attorney and his or her client may be indicative of what is a reasonable fee, it is not determinative") (*quoting* Manufacturers & Traders Trust Co. v. Dougherty, 11 A.D.3d 1019, 782 N.Y.S.2d 477 (4th Dep't 2004)).

attorney's fees may not be recovered against a Subtenant.[379]

b. LATE FEES

For residential properties, RPL § 238-a(2) provides that, where the rent is more than five (5) days late, the Landlord may recover a late rent fee equal to five percent (5%) of the monthly rent or $50, whichever is less.[380] A late fee provision is unenforceable against a Tenant in a rent-stabilized apartment.[381]

As indicated previously, the Appellate Division, Third Department held that late fees are not available in residential summary proceedings.[382] To recover a late rent fee, regardless of the forum, the Landlord must provide the Tenant written notice (by certified mail) that the rent was not received within five (5) days of the due date.[383] The failure to provide this late notice "may be used as an affirmative defense" in a non-payment proceeding.[384] A lease provision limiting or altogether waiving the late fee notice is void.[385]

Prior to the HSTPA, several residential late fee cases had held that a five percent (5%) or greater late fee provision was excessive,

379 *See* Oakdale Manor Owners, Inc. v. Raimondi, 29 N.Y.S.3d 848 (App. Term, 9th & 10th Jud. Dists. 2015).

380 *See* Beco v. Ritter, 190 A.D.3d 1150, 140 N.Y.S.3d 294 (3d Dep't 2021) (holding that a "discount" in excess of forty percent (40%) for paying rent early amounted to an unlawful late fee). The Appellate Division, Third Department reasoned that the early payment "discount" was "[n]o different than if [Landlord] charged [Tenants] a flat $375 late fee each time they failed to pay their rent in a timely manner." *Id.*

381 *See* Bandil Farms Inc. v. New York State Div. of Hous. & Cmty. Renewal, 190 A.D.3d 403, 140 N.Y.S.3d 13 (1st Dep't 2021).

382 *Beco*, 190 A.D.3d at 1150, 140 N.Y.S.3d at 294.

383 RPL § 235-e(d) (HSTPA, Part M, § 9).

384 *Id.*

385 *Id.* at § 238-a(3) (HSTPA, Part M, § 10).

unconscionable, and unrecoverable.[386] Courts had similarly held that a $5.00 per day late fee (i.e., $150 per month), which accounted for seventeen percent (17%) of the monthly rent,[387] and a rent "discount," which essentially amounted to a late fee with penalty, were also unenforceable.[388] Moreover, a four percent (4%) late fee was denied against a Guarantor in a plenary action.[389]

Late fees are more commonly associated with commercial premises.[390] In commercial cases, the Landlord is not required to provide the Tenant a five (5) day late rent reminder notice.[391] However, where the Landlord fails to demand late fees in several delinquent rent notices, the fees may be deemed to have been waived if sought after the arrears have been paid.[392] Usurious and disproportionate late fees are unen-

---

386 *See, e.g.*, Wilsdorf v. Fairfield Northport Harbor, LLC, 950 N.Y.S.2d 494 (App. Term, 9th & 10th Jud. Dists. 2012) (10% late fee); Diversified Equities, LLC v. Russell, 31 N.Y.S.3d 920 (App. Term, 2d, 11th & 13th Jud. Dists. 2016) (holding that a 13% late fee was "excessive and grossly disproportionate to any damages" sustained due to the late payment of rent); 67-26 Dartmouth St. Corp. v. Silberman, N.Y.L.J., Apr. 2, 1996, at 30, col. 1 (App. Term, 2d & 11th Jud. Dists. 1996) (5% late fee); Bonham Strand, LLC v. Paredes, 72 N.Y.S.3d 516 (Greenburgh Just. Ct. 2017) (5% late fee).

387 Rock v. Klepper, 885 N.Y.S.2d 713 (Plattsburgh City Ct. 2009).

388 Park Haven, LLC v. Robinson, 3 N.Y.S.3d 286 (App. Term, 2d, 11th & 13th Jud. Dists. 2014). *Cf.* de Socio v. 136 E. 56th St. Owners, Inc., 111 N.Y.S.3d 515 (N.Y. Civ. Ct. N.Y. Cnty. 2018) (awarding $50 late fee per month for eight (8) months which was below the usury rate).

389 Cleo Realty Assoc., L.P. v. Papagiannakis, 151 A.D.3d 418, 56 N.Y.S.3d 294 (1st Dep't 2017).

390 *See, e.g.*, VRA Family L.P. v. Salon Mgt. USA, LLC, 183 A.D.3d 614, 123 N.Y.S.3d 195 (2d Dep't 2020); Brixmor SPE 6 LLC v. H & N Holding Group, LLC, 2022 N.Y. Misc. LEXIS 381 (N.Y. Cnty. Sup. Ct. Jan. 6, 2022); Empire LLC v. Sharapov, 2020 N.Y. Misc. LEXIS 358 (N.Y. Cnty. Sup. Ct. Jan. 31, 2020) (awarding late fees and referring matter to a Special Referee for computation); 39-50 24th St. Realty v. Ol' Bridge Café, 2020 N.Y.L.J. LEXIS 1961 (N.Y. Civ. Ct. Queens Cnty. Feb. 17, 2021) (10% late fee).

391 181st Wash. Hgts. Assoc. LLC v. Children's Place, Inc., 150 N.Y.S.3d 232 (N.Y. Civ. Ct. N.Y. Cnty. 2021); 41 E. 11th St., LLC v. WSIP Realty Corp., 118 N.Y.S.3d 405 (N.Y. Civ. Ct. N.Y. Cnty. 2020).

392 *See* Monica King Contemporary LLC v. Kedzkidz Realty II, LLC, 2022 N.Y. Misc. LEXIS 418 (N.Y. Cnty. Sup. Ct. Jan. 26, 2022) (waiver of late fee during COVID-19 Period where the Tenant "[m]ade the payments before [Landlord] sought to impose the late fees and interest payments"). The Court noted that due to the Pandemic, the Landlord "[s]ent bills but did not seek immediate collection. It was only after [Tenant] paid it anyway, and gave the six months' termination notice, that the [Landlord] tried to charge interest and late fees." *Id.*

forceable in all proceedings.[393]

c. RECIPROCAL ATTORNEY'S FEES

Real Property Law § 234 is applicable to residential leases that contain an attorney's fees provision in favor of the Landlord, but does not include similar relief in favor of a prevailing Tenant. According to RPL § 234, all such leases are automatically deemed to include a reciprocal attorney's fees (and expenses) provision in favor of the Tenant if the Tenant prevails in the summary proceeding or the Landlord fails to perform its obligations under the lease.[394]

A Tenant may seek attorney's fees either as a counterclaim in the summary proceeding or in a separate plenary action. If asserted in the summary proceeding, the Tenant may orally assert the counterclaim on the Record (i.e., the counterclaim need not be in writing) on the return date of the Petition pursuant to RPAPL § 743.[395] The purpose of the statute is to dissuade unscrupulous Landlords from engaging in improper conduct while offering an incentive to expeditiously resolve Landlord and Tenant disputes.[396] A lease provision waiving the Tenant's RPL § 234 rights to attorney's fees is void as against public policy.[397]

Real Property Law § 234 applies to residential eviction proceedings,

---

393 *See, e.g.*, TY Bldrs. II, Inc. v. 55 Day Spa, Inc., 167 A.D.3d 679, 90 N.Y.S.3d 47 (2d Dep't 2018); *see also* Nomad 28th St., LLC v. W.J. Enter. Inc., 120 N.Y.S.3d 585 (N.Y. Civ. Ct. N.Y. Cnty. 2020) (claim in excess of $400,000 in late fees on an award of $526,294); Regatta Prop. LLC v. 21 S. End Hudson Inc., 113 N.Y.S.3d 486 (N.Y. Civ. Ct. N.Y. Cnty. 2019) (denying claim for ten percent (10%) late fee, or 120% per year).

394 RPL § 234; *see, e.g.*, W54-7 LLC v. Perrin, 183 A.D.3d 448, 121 N.Y.S.3d 863 (1st Dep't 2020).

395 655 Country Rd., Inc. v. Caltagirone, 101 N.Y.S.3d 701 (App. Term, 9th & 10th Jud. Dists. 2018).

396 *See* 251 CPW Hous. LLC v. Pastreich, 124 A.D.3d 401, at 404, 1 N.Y.S.3d 32, 36 (1st Dep't 2015) (reasoning that since "[i]t is a remedial statute, Real Property Law § 234 'should be accorded its broadest protective meaning consistent with legislative intent'") (citation omitted); Marsh v. 300 W. 106th St. Corp., 95 A.D.3d 560, 943 N.Y.S.2d 525 (1st Dep't 2012) (holding "[t]he overriding purpose of the legislation is to provide a level playing field between landlords and tenants, 'creating a mutual obligation that provides an incentive to resolve disputes quickly and without undue expense'").

397 RPL § 234; *see* Gorman v. 69-73 Greene St. Owners, LLC, 2016 N.Y. Misc. LEXIS 124 (N.Y. Cnty. Sup. Ct. Jan. 12, 2016).

including actions by shareholders against a cooperative corporation to correct defective property conditions.[398] However, RPL § 234 does not extend to administrative proceedings such as those before the Division of Housing and Community Renewal.[399]

A common dispute for the Courts to resolve is the applicability of the statute where the case is resolved with a mixed outcome or the Landlord voluntarily discontinues the proceeding prior to a hearing. The Appellate Division, Second Department held that reciprocal attorney's fees may only be awarded where the Tenant prevails "in a [Landlord-Tenant] controversy that has reached an 'ultimate outcome.'"[400] As such, the Court's dismissal of a summary proceeding "without prejudice" may result in the denial of the Tenant's attorney's fees because there was not a final determination.[401]

It has been held that a general lease provision providing for the recovery of attorney's fees incurred "in any action or summary proceeding" resulting from a breach by the Tenant is sufficient under RPL § 234, and a prevailing Tenant may be awarded fees as a result.[402] In addition, attorney's fees have been granted where the lease authorized fees

398 *See* Trump Vill. Section 4, Inc. v. Vilensky, 2019 N.Y. Misc. LEXIS 901 (Kings Cnty. Sup. Ct. Feb. 19, 2019) (*citing* Cohan v. Board of Dir. of 700 Shore Rd. Waters Edge, Inc., 108 A.D.3d 697, 969 N.Y.S.2d 547 (2d Dep't 2013)); Hartman v. WVH HDFC, 142 N.Y.S.3d 790 (N.Y. Civ. Ct. N.Y. Cnty. March 31, 2021).

399 Schuette v. Brookford LLC, 200 A.D.3d 479, 155 N.Y.S.3d 76 (1st Dep't 2021); *251 CPW Hous. LLC*, 124 A.D.3d at 401, 1 N.Y.S.3d at 32.

400 J.P. & Assocs. Props. Corp. v. Krautter, 128 A.D.3d 963, 9 N.Y.S.3d 626 (2d Dep't 2015); 125 Ct. St., LLC v. Sher, 94 N.Y.S.3d 539 (App. Term, 2d, 11th & 13th Jud. Dists. 2018) (denying Tenant's claim for attorney's fees notwithstanding dismissal of proceeding due to a defective rent demand because the award "should await the ultimate outcome of the nonpayment dispute").

401 *J.P. & Assocs. Props. Corp.*, 128 A.D.3d at 963, 9 N.Y.S.3d at 626; *see also* Horatio Arms, Inc. v. Celbert, 972 N.Y.S.2d 813 (App. Term, 1st Dep't 2013) (Tenant's claim for attorney's fees premature where summary proceeding dismissed due to improper service).

402 Bunny Realty v. Miller, 180 A.D.2d 460, at 461, 579 N.Y.S.2d 952 (1st Dep't 1992); Stephen, LLC v. Zucchiatti, 890 N.Y.S.2d 371 (N.Y. Civ. Ct. N.Y. Cnty. 2009).

to offset the costs to recover possession and re-rent the premises.[403]

Determining whether the Tenant was the prevailing party "requires an initial consideration of the true scope of the dispute litigated, followed by a comparison of what was achieved within that scope . . .[,] that is, whether the tenant has obtained the 'central relief sought.'"[404] In other words, if a mixed outcome is not "substantially favorable" to either party, then neither will be deemed the prevailing party.[405]

In *de Socio v. 136 E. 56th St. Owners, Inc.*, the Housing Part denied both parties' requests for attorney's fees after granting a fifty percent (50%) rent abatement.[406] The Court concluded that since the gravamen of the case concentrated on the warranty of habitability, where the Landlord and Tenant each "received approximately half of the net recovery sought," neither could be deemed the prevailing party for the purposes of an application for attorney's fees.[407]

A prevailing Tenant must demonstrate the reasonableness of the fees sought,[408] and a hearing is required where the amount of the fees is disputed.[409] For example, fees incurred for unsuccessful motion practice in

403 Casamento v. Juaregui, 88 A.D.3d 345, at 354-55, 929 N.Y.S.2d 286, 292-93 (2d Dep't 2011), *rev'g*, 907 N.Y.S.2d 99 (App. Term, 2d, 11th & 13th Jud. Dists. 2010); *see* Graham Ct. Owners Corp. v. Taylor, 24 N.Y.3d 742, 5 N.Y.S.3d 348 (2015); *Marsh*, 95 A.D.3d at 560, 943 N.Y.S.2d at 525; *but see* Hamilton v. Menalon Realty, LLC, 829 N.Y.S.2d 400, 402-03 (App. Term, 2d & 11th Jud. Dists. 2006) (lease provision unenforceable); Fragiacomo v. Pugliese, 816 N.Y.S.2d 826, 827-28 (App. Term, 9th & 10th Jud. Dists. 2006). *See also* 303 E. 37th Sponsors Corp. v. Goldstein, 918 N.Y.S.2d 400 (App. Term, 1st Dep't 2010) (denying reciprocal right to attorney's fees where the lease was in contravention of the New York City Rent Stabilization Code).

404 *J.P. & Assocs. Props. Corp.*, 128 A.D.3d at 963, 9 N.Y.S.3d at 626 (citations omitted).

405 *See* 339-347 E. 12th St. LLC v. Ling, 921 N.Y.S.2d 781 (App. Term, 1st Dep't 2011) (eleven percent (11%) rent reduction awarded but Tenant did not prevail since claims for punitive and treble damages were denied); 157 E. 57th St. LLC v. Birrenbach, 801 N.Y.S.2d 779 (App. Term, 1st Dep't 2005) ("Considering the tenant's failure to establish that the mold condition remained unremedied — an allegation which, in the words of the Trial Judge, framed the 'central factual dispute' litigated below — we agree that the outcome of the case was not substantially favorable to the tenant and that tenant did not achieve prevailing party status").

406 111 N.Y.S.3d 515 (N.Y. Civ. Ct. N.Y. Cnty. 2018).

407 *Id.*

408 *655 Country Rd., Inc.*, 101 N.Y.S.3d at 701.

409 *Id.* (holding it was error "to award tenant attorney's fees without first conducting a hearing to determine the reasonableness of tenant's counsel's fees").

the Appellate Courts have been deducted from the award.[410] Similar to a Landlord's request, the Court may deny a prevailing Tenant's counterclaim for attorney's fees when the award is "[m]anifestly unfair or where the successful party engaged in bad faith."[411] In addition, *res judicata* necessitates denial of attorney's fees where the claim was previously adjudicated.[412]

When the Landlord voluntarily discontinues a summary proceeding, the Tenant's RPL § 234 claim may be denied where the proceeding was brought in good faith and the Tenant was the cause of significant delay.[413] In *Anello v. Fiedler*, following fifteen (15) months of litigation, including motion practice, an appeal that was abandoned, and discovery exchanges initiated at the Tenant's behest, the Landlord immediately sought to discontinue the summary proceeding after a new affirmative defense arose (ironically, the defense resulted from the excessive delays); namely, the Tenant was turning age 62 which would defeat the underlying claim.[414] The Appellate Term for the Second, Eleventh and Thirteenth Judicial Districts reasoned that it would be unjust to further penalize the Landlord by imposing attorney's fees where the Landlord prosecuted the proceeding in good faith and the Tenant was the cause of "substantial delay and expense."[415]

---

410 Megan Holding LLC v. Conason, 18 N.Y.S.3d 579 (App. Term, 1st Dep't 2015).

411 *251 CPW Hous. LLC*, 124 A.D.3d at 401, 1 N.Y.S.3d at 32. *See also* Parkview Apts. Corp. v. Pryce, 95 N.Y.S.3d 125 (App. Term, 9th & 10th Jud. Dists. 2018) (although holdover proceeding was dismissed after the default judgment was vacated, counterclaim for attorney's fees denied due to "overwhelming proof" the Tenants had breached the lease).

412 Hodge v. 26 Ct. Assocs., LLC, 28 N.Y.S.3d 648 (App. Term, 2d, 11th & 13th Jud. Dists. 2015).

413 *See* Anello v. Fiedler, 159 N.Y.S.3d 315 (App. Term, 2d, 11th & 13th Jud. Dists. 2021); 526 W. 158th St., HDFC v. Ramon, 137 N.Y.S.3d 617 (App. Term, 1st Dep't 2021).

414 *Anello*, 159 N.Y.S.3d at 315 (second owner use proceeding discontinued because the "[l]andlord was unable at that time to meet the heightened requirements [pursuant to the Rent Stabilization Code 2520.6(p)] triggered by [the] tenant turning 62 years old over a year after the commencement of that proceeding"); *526 W. 158th St., HDFC*, 137 N.Y.S.3d at 617 (denying Tenant's RPL § 234 claim where the underlying proceeding "did not appear frivolous and landlord asserted good faith reasons for its [prompt] decision to withdraw the claim after discovery raised questions about the nature of tenant's occupancy").

415 *Anello*, 159 N.Y.S.3d at 315 (*citing* the Housing Part, "[l]andlord should not be penalized for choosing to discontinue the proceeding immediately upon becoming aware, one week before tenant turned 62, that the affirmative defense based upon tenant's age had ripened and would be interposed").

On the other hand, where the alleged defects to the premises are remedied prior to the commencement (and therefore, the subsequent discontinuance as well) of the summary proceeding, the Tenant's RPL § 234 claims for attorney's fees may be granted.[416] In *Isaly-Liceaga v. Pickarski*, the Appellate Division, First Department awarded the Tenant's attorney's fees because the record demonstrated that the remedial measures to abate the noise complaints (i.e., the installation of rugs and suitable floor padding) were completed before the summary proceeding was commenced and, as a result, the "ultimate outcome [was] in [Tenant's] favor, whether or not such outcome [was] on the merits."[417]

To be awarded attorney's fees, the Tenant need not be required to pay counsel. For example, in *Maplewood Mgmt., Inc. v. Best*, the prevailing Tenant, who was represented by a governmentally funded agency and was under no obligation to pay for the legal services rendered, was awarded attorney's fees.[418] The Appellate Division, Second Department reasoned that "[i]t would significantly thwart the accomplishment of the Legislature's intent…if the courts were to hold that the statute requires those landlords who have brought meritless eviction proceedings to pay for their tenant's attorneys' fees only when the tenant himself is of sufficient financial ability to afford his own attorney."[419]

4. ACCELERATED RENT AND SURVIVAL CLAUSES

The Housing Part has subject matter jurisdiction over rent arrears, but not future rent or future use and occupancy. Therefore, in a summary proceeding, the Landlord may not be awarded rent not yet due even where the lease includes an acceleration clause.[420]

The Court considers an "accelerated" rent provision (i.e., a lease provision that states all remaining months' rent becomes immediately due

416 *See* Isaly-Liceaga v. Pickarski, 199 A.D.3d 413, 153 N.Y.S.3d 847 (1st Dep't 2021).

417 *Id.*

418 Maplewood Mgmt., Inc. v. Best, 143 A.D.2d 978, 533 N.Y.S.2d 612 (2d Dep't 1988); *Trump Vill. Section 4, Inc.*, 2019 N.Y. Misc. at LEXIS 901.

419 *Maplewood Mgmt., Inc.*, 143 A.D.2d at 979, 533 N.Y.S.2d at 613. *See also* Blum v. Stenson, 465 U.S. 886, 104 S.Ct. 1541 (1984) (attorney's fees awarded for representation by the Legal Aid Society pursuant to the Civil Rights Attorney's Fees Awards Act of 1976).

420 *See, e.g.*, LC Apts. LLC v. Trovato, 151 N.Y.S.3d 343 (Monroe Cnty. Sup. Ct. 2021).

upon termination) to be damages which are not recoverable in a summary proceeding. Unless waived, the Landlord may commence a plenary action in the Supreme Court to enforce the accelerated rent provision.[421]

If an acceleration clause is omitted from the lease, then the Landlord may still recover the ongoing rent obligations in a subsequent plenary action (but at a much slower pace) provided the lease contains a survival clause. The slower pace is attributable to the prohibition against the Landlord asserting a claim for unpaid rent until after the rent has become due. This means that during the pendency of the subsequent plenary action, the Landlord may amend the pleadings each month to include a new month's rent as it becomes due.[422]

The omission of a "survival" clause from a rental agreement has significant ramifications on the post-lease termination rights of the parties because the termination of the lease generally ends all future rights and obligations under the agreement. An exception exists where the lease provides that post-lease termination the parties remain liable for "damages" and financial obligations under the rental agreement.[423] Otherwise, claims not yet accrued at the time of the lease termination, including accelerated

421 *See* University Sq. San Antonio, Tx. LLC v. Mega Furniture Dezavala, LLC, 198 A.D.3d 1284, 155 N.Y.S.3d 252 (4th Dep't 2021); 172 Van Duzer Realty Corp. v. Globe Alumni Stud. Assist. Assoc., Inc., 102 A.D.3d 543, 959 N.Y.S.2d 39 (1st Dep't 2013) (doctrine of *res judicata* does not preclude subsequent plenary action because enforcement of acceleration clause is not available in a summary proceeding), *mod. on other grounds*, 24 N.Y.3d 528, 2 N.Y.S.3d 39 (2014); 30 Broadway, LLC v. Grand Centr. Dental, LLP, 96 A.D.3d 934, 947 N.Y.S.2d 545 (2d Dep't 2012); Ross Realty v. V & A Fabricators, Inc., 42 A.D.3d 246, at 250-51, 836 N.Y.S.2d 242 (2d Dep't 2007); Trumbull Equities, LLC v. City.com Media, LLC, 2015 N.Y. Misc. LEXIS 1240 (Queens Cnty. Sup. Ct. April 8, 2015).

422 Pikoulas v. Hardina, 36 N.Y.S.3d 340 (App. Term, 9th & 10th Jud. Dists. 2016); 299 Broadway, LLC v. James A. O'Malley, P.C., 2021 N.Y. Misc. LEXIS 5959 (N.Y. Cnty. Sup. Ct. Nov. 18, 2021).

423 L'Aquila Realty, LLC v. Jalyng Food Corp., 148 A.D.3d 1004, 50 N.Y.S.3d 128 (2d Dep't 2017) (the lease "specifically provided that [Tenant] would remain liable for rent after eviction"); H.L. Realty, LLC v. Edwards, 131 A.D.3d 573, 15 N.Y.S.3d 413 (2d Dep't 2015) (Guarantor liable in plenary action where the lease contained a survival clause and the guaranty was not rescinded in the stipulation of settlement between Landlord and Tenant); *see* Chelsea 8th Ave., LLC v. OA 21st LLC, 2019 N.Y. Misc. LEXIS 4610 (N.Y. Cnty. Sup. Ct. Aug. 13, 2019). *Cf.* Fifth Line, LLC v. Fitch, 167 A.D.3d 847, 91 N.Y.S.3d 135 (2d Dep't 2018).

rent, are forfeited and unrecoverable in a subsequent plenary action.[424]

C. DAMAGES ARE NOT RECOVERABLE

The Housing Part may not award a money judgment for "property damages" caused by the Tenant or the Tenant's guests.[425] Similarly, the Landlord may not recover the security deposit or other unspecified items beyond the jurisdiction of the Housing Part.[426]

From a practical perspective, it is in the Landlord's interest to wait until the occupants vacate the premises before seeking property damages because the extent of the damage cannot be assessed until possession reverts back to the Petitioner. Accordingly, the Landlord ordinarily reserves the right to commence a plenary action (civil lawsuit) for such relief and other damages.[427] However, the Housing Part may award damages on the Tenant's counterclaim.[428]

---

424 Kings Park 8809, LLC v. Stanton-Spain, 48 N.Y.S.3d 266 (App. Term, 2d, 11th & 13th Jud. Dists. 2016); Patchogue Assocs. v. Sears, Roebuck and Co., 951 N.Y.S.2d 314 (App. Term, 9th & 10th Jud. Dists. 2012) (noting that "had the subject lease included a survival clause, tenant would have remained liable for monetary obligations arising under the lease, even if this summary proceeding had resulted in an award of possession in landlord's favor").

425 *Ross Realty*, 42 A.D.3d at 246, 836 N.Y.S.2d at 242; Bedford Gardens Co. v. Silberstein, 269 A.D.2d 445, 702 N.Y.S.2d 884 (2d Dep't 2000); *see also* Rostant v. Swersky, 79 A.D.3d 456, 912 N.Y.S.2d 200 (1st Dep't 2010) (Housing Part may not award damages to Petitioner-Tenant seeking to be restored to possession); BLDG ABI Enter., LLC v. 711 Second Ave. Corp., 2019 N.Y. Misc. LEXIS 6456 (N.Y. Cnty. Sup. Ct. Nov. 20, 2019).

426 *See, e.g.*, Hines v. Ambrose, 907 N.Y.S.2d 437 (App. Term, 9th & 10th Jud. Dists. 2010) (security deposit).

427 *See* Burke v. Aspland, 56 A.D.3d 1001, 867 N.Y.S.2d 759 (3d Dep't 2008); Chelsea 18 Partners, LP v. Mak, 90 A.D.3d 38, 933 N.Y.S.2d 204 (1st Dep't 2011); Messerschmidt v. Romney, 112 N.Y.S.3d 410 (App. Term, 9th & 10th Jud. Dists. 2018).

428 *See generally* RH 528 W. 159 St. L.P. v. Timofeeva, 147 N.Y.S.3d 866 (App. Term, 1st Dep't 2021). For a discussion regarding counterclaims in summary proceedings, *see* Chapter 8, subdiv. C(2), *infra*.

D. INTEREST, COSTS, AND DISBURSEMENTS

A summary proceeding based upon a breach of a lease agreement (typically, but not exclusively non-payment proceedings) "sounds in contract" and, as a result, a prevailing Landlord (or Tenant on a counterclaim) may be entitled to prejudgment interest.[429] However, in a non-payment proceeding or plenary action based upon the failure to pay rent, where the Landlord fails to deposit the Tenant's rent checks, the right to prejudgment interest (and attorney's fees) is waived.[430]

A prevailing Landlord may further be entitled to recover statutory costs and disbursements.[431] The reader should refer to the rules of the Court in which the case is pending for available costs and disbursements. Statutory costs include, but are not limited to, a fee for each "necessary" Respondent served and, if the award is based upon a default, an additional fee may be awarded to secure an affidavit (or additional sufficiently detailed sworn statement within the original affidavit of service) from the process server stating that the Tenant is <u>not</u> presently in the military.[432] The affidavit stating the Tenant is not a member of the military is required only when the Tenant does <u>not</u> appear in Court.[433] Unlike the affidavit of service for the Notice of Petition and Petition, a non-military affidavit may be filed any time prior to

---

429 CPLR § 5001. *See, e.g.*, Solow v. Wellner, 86 N.Y.2d 582, at 589-90, 635 N.Y.S.2d 132, 135 (1995); Moore v. Beautiful Spaces, 192 A.D.3d 591, 146 N.Y.S.3d 45 (1st Dep't 2021); Chip Fifth Ave. LLC v. Quality King Distribs., Inc., 2021 N.Y. Misc. LEXIS 745 (N.Y. Cnty. Sup. Ct. Feb. 26, 2021).

430 B.N. Realty Assocs. v. Lichtenstein, 96 A.D.3d 434, 949 N.Y.S.2d 1 (1st Dep't 2012) (attorney's fees denied).

431 *See, e.g.*, N.Y. City Civ. Ct. Act §§ 1906-a, 1908; Uniform City Ct. Act §§ 1906-a, 1908; Uniform Dist. Ct. Act §§ 1906-a, 1908; Uniform Just. Ct. Act §§ 1903(d),(m), 1908. *But see* CPLR § 1102(d); Boyle v. Bishop, N.Y.L.J., Apr. 25, 1978, at 11, col. 1 (App. Term, 9th & 10th Jud. Dists. 1978) (holding a "poor person" pursuant to CPLR § 1102(d) is <u>not</u> liable for costs).

432 At the time of publication, the amount awarded for the affidavit is $5.00 except in the Justice Courts where the amount is $1.50. *See* N.Y. City Civ. Ct. Act § 1906-a; Uniform City Ct. Act § 1906-a; Uniform Dist. Ct. Act § 1906-a; Uniform Just. Ct. Act § 1903(d),(m).

433 Unitrin Advantage Ins. Co. v. 21st Century Pharmacy, 158 A.D.3d 450, 67 N.Y.S.3d 826 (1st Dep't 2018) (denying default judgment where non-military affidavit of service not provided).

submitting an application for the issuance of the final judgment and warrant of eviction.[434]

A prevailing Landlord appearing *pro se* is entitled to recover the filing fee ($45.00 in the Housing Parts except the Town and Village Justice Courts where the fee is $20.00) for commencing the proceeding.[435] The filing fee may <u>not</u> be recovered when the Landlord was represented by counsel.

434 *See* Avgush v. De La Cruz, 924 N.Y.S.2d 307 (App. Term, 9th & 10th Jud. Dists. 2011).

435 *See* Letter to Hon. Matthew T. Crosson, Formal Op. No. 90-F6, 1990 N.Y. Op. Atty. Gen. 25 (August 8, 1990).

CHAPTER 6

PREDICATE NOTICE

In 2020, approximately 44.8 million of the nation's 128 million households (or 35%) rented the homes in which they lived.[436] In New York, the percentage of households renting was even higher, at nearly forty-five percent (45%).[437]

The occupants of both residential and commercial properties must be served with notice of the alleged breach of the lease, the reason for terminating the tenancy, or any other grounds for seeking the return of the premises before a summary proceeding may be commenced.[438] This notice is referred to as a predicate notice.

A. STANDARDS

The predicate notice must "state the facts necessary to establish the existence of grounds for [an] eviction."[439] The notice must further "provide the necessary information to enable the tenant to frame a defense and to meet the tests of reasonableness and due process."[440]

436 *See* "*Renting Statistics*," iProperty Management, updated Nov. 30, 2021, at https://ipropertymanagement.com/research/renting-statistics; "*Number of US Households in 2022/2023: Demographics, Statistics, & Trends*," Finances Online, https://financesonline.com/number-of-us-households.

437 "*Renting Statistics*," iProperty Management, updated Nov. 30, 2021, at https://ipropertymanagement.com/research/renting-statistics.

438 *See generally* U.S. Bank Trust, N.A. v. Augustine, 159 N.Y.S.3d 661 (N.Y. Civ. Ct. Queens Cnty. 2022).

439 Great Jones St. Realty Corp. v. Chimsanthia, 127 N.Y.S.3d 689 (App. Term, 1st Dep't 2020); 888 E. 96th St., LLC v. Hargrove, 111 N.Y.S.3d 494 (App. Term, 2d, 11th & 13th Jud. Dists. 2018).

440 Broadhurst Willows Apts. v. Wooten, 143 N.Y.S.3d 518 (N.Y. Civ. Ct. N.Y. Cnty. 2021); 155 W. 81st St. Assocs. v. Waldman, 2019 N.Y.L.J. LEXIS 624 (N.Y. Civ. Ct. N.Y. Cnty. March 6, 2019).

The predicate notice is evaluated for sufficiency "[i]n view of the attendant circumstances, and courts look to whether the notice could 'have materially misled or confused the tenant or hindered the preparation of [the] defense.'"[441] Non-specific, overly broad allegations lacking sufficient detail to allow for the preparation of a meaningful defense may render the predicate notice defective.[442] Parenthetically, a lease provision specifying the manner and upon whom the predicate notice must be served will generally be enforced.[443]

1. THE NOTICE IS AN ELEMENT OF A PRIMA FACIE CASE

A defect in the service or content of the predicate notice may result in the dismissal of the proceeding. The reader should be mindful that a dismissal based upon a defective predicate notice does not raise jurisdictional issues—neither personal jurisdiction nor subject matter jurisdiction.[444] Instead, the reason for the dismissal would be the failure to make a *prima facie* case. This is because the predicate notice is an element of the Petitioner's case and a condition precedent for maintaining the proceeding.[445]

---

441 1506 Wallco LLC v. Guzman, 135 N.Y.S.3d 795 (N.Y. Civ. Ct. Bronx Cnty. 2020) (*quoting* Oxford Towers Co., LLC v. Leites, 41 A.D.3d 144, 837 N.Y.S.3d 131 (1st Dep't 2007)). The "salutary purpose" of the predicate notice requirements is "to discourage baseless eviction claims founded upon speculation and surmise, rather than concrete facts." *See* Site 15 Affordable Assoc. LLC v. Merkinson, 2021 N.Y. Misc. LEXIS 4965 (N.Y. Civ. Ct. N.Y. Cnty. April 5, 2021) (*quoting* London Terrace Gardens, LP v. Heller, 975 N.Y.S.2d 710 (App. Term, 1st Dep't 2009)).

442 *See* 157 Broadway Assoc., LLC v. Berroa, 112 N.Y.S.3d 854 (App. Term, 1st Dep't 2018).

443 146 Flushing Ave. v. 66S Fusion, Inc., 147 N.Y.S.3d 868 (App. Term, 2d, 11th & 13th Jud. Dists. 2021); Omansky v. 160 Chambers St. Owners, Inc., 155 A.D.3d 460, 64 N.Y.S.3d 212 (1st Dep't 2017) (strict enforcement of lease provision requiring Tenant to provide renewal notice within sixty (60) days of lease expiration); 575 Warren St. HDFC v. Barreto, 983 N.Y.S.2d 203 (App. Term, 2d, 11th & 13th Jud. Dists. 2013); 1626 Second Ave., LLC v. Notte Rest. Corp., 880 N.Y.S.2d 225 (N.Y. Civ. Ct. N.Y. Cnty. 2008) ("Service of notices must be done in accordance with the lease provisions in order for service to be proper").

444 Marmon Realty Group, LLC v. Khalil, 148 N.Y.S.3d 822 (App. Term, 2d, 11th & 13th Jud. Dists. 2021) (predicate notice does not involve personal jurisdiction); Nguyen v. Perparim, 116 N.Y.S.3d 467 (App. Term, 1st Dep't 2019) (same); *see also* 541 Ct. St. v. Zheng, 147 N.Y.S.3d 868 (App. Term, 2d, 11th & 13th Jud. Dists. 2021) (holding that "subject matter jurisdiction is conferred by statute and is not impacted by defects in a predicate notice itself or in the service thereof").

445 *See* Mautner-Glick Corp. v. Glazer, 148 A.D.3d 515, 48 N.Y.S.3d 587 (1st Dep't 2017); *146 Flushing Ave.*, 147 N.Y.S.3d at 868.

The "burden remains with the landlord to prove [this] element of its case at [a hearing on the merits]."[446] In other words, the Petitioner cannot prevail at the hearing absent adequate proof the predicate notice was sufficient and properly served.[447] This rule applies even where the Tenant fails to raise the defense during the hearing.[448]

The Tenant may move to dismiss the proceeding <u>prior</u> to a hearing by motion to dismiss or for summary judgment based upon a defective predicate notice. For example, in *1646 Union, LLC v. Simpson*, the Appellate Term for the Second, Eleventh and Thirteenth Judicial Districts granted summary judgment and dismissed the holdover proceeding due to the Landlord's failure to serve a predicate notice.[449] The Court reasoned that "[p]roof of compliance with such a statutory notice requirement is a necessary element of a holdover proceeding…and a landlord cannot be awarded possession where a valid notice of termination has not been served."[450]

As a general matter, defects in the predicate notice may <u>not</u> be

---

446 W54-7 LLC v. Schick, 829 N.Y.S.2d 399 (App. Term, 1st Dep't 2006).

447 *See, e.g., Mautner-Glick Corp.*, 148 A.D.3d at 515, 48 N.Y.S.3d at 587 (affirming dismissal of holdover proceeding where "proper service of the [predicate] notice was not established at the hearing"); Gristmill Realty, LLC v. Roa, 133 N.Y.S.3d 383 (App. Term, 9th & 10th Jud. Dists. 2020) (denying default judgment application where the Petition failed to allege a proper rent demand was served).

448 Metro Plaza Apts., Inc. v. Buchanan, 204 A.D.3d 45, 162 N.Y.S.3d 543 (3d Dep't 2022); Chinatown Apts., Inc. v. Lam, 51 N.Y.2d 786, 433 N.Y.S.2d 86 (1980). *See* Green v. Palmer, 2021 N.Y.L.J. LEXIS 1067 (N.Y. Civ. Ct. Queens Cnty. Nov. 3, 2021) (where Tenant defaulted, non-payment proceeding dismissed, in part, due to the predicate notice and the lease identifying different people as the Landlord); *see generally Mautner-Glick Corp.*, 148 A.D.3d at 515, 48 N.Y.S.3d at 587; Concourse Green Assoc., LP v. Patterson, 46 N.Y.S.3d 474 (N.Y. Civ. Ct. Bronx Cnty. 2016) (holding "[a]n adequate notice is a required condition precedent, and if the notice of termination is insufficient, the proceeding must be dismissed").

449 113 N.Y.S.3d 459 (App. Term, 2d, 11th & 13th Jud. Dists. 2019).

450 *Id.* (citations omitted); *see* Ocean Bay Rad LLC v. Battle, 2021 N.Y. Misc. LEXIS 7057 (N.Y. Civ. Ct. Queens Cnty. Nov. 12, 2021) (dismissing non-payment proceeding where the predicate notice was "outside of the scope of the agreement of the parties"); Building Mgmt. Co. Inc. v. Etienne, 134 N.Y.S.3d 177 (N.Y. Civ. Ct. Queens Cnty. 2020) (granting Tenant's motion to dismiss proceeding where the notice of termination was defective); A & J Estates v. Grindley, 2019 N.Y.L.J. LEXIS 2863 (N.Y. Civ. Ct. Queens Cnty. Aug. 14, 2019) (dismissing holdover proceeding where an officer of the Landlord signed the termination notice in his individual capacity without any reference to the corporate party to the rental agreement).

waived. Exceptions to this rule exist where the error was *de minimis*, such as an inconsequential faulty description of the premises (e.g., stating the property was at 32 Wilson Road when the formal address was 32 Wilson Street);[451] where the rent demand listed an "approximate good faith amount of rent owed";[452] or where the parties voluntarily entered into a Stipulation of Settlement resolving the summary proceeding.[453]

2. THE NOTICE MAY NOT BE AMENDED

The Landlord is constrained by the predicate notice served, and the notice may not be amended to cure defects, change names, or provide additional information.[454] Since the predicate notice is prepared days, weeks, or, in some circumstances, months prior to the commencement of the proceeding, a significant number of days may pass before any deficiencies are discovered.

For the Landlord, an improper predicate notice may result in significant delay and additional expense because another notice must be served prior to the commencement of a new proceeding.[455] A defective

451 *See*, Kit Ming Corp. v. Tsang, 2001 N.Y. Misc. LEXIS 564 (App. Term, 1st Dep't June 1, 2001) (describing the premises as a "basement store" instead of a "ground floor store").

452 Moniaci v. Kelly, 152 N.Y.S.3d 216 (App. Term, 9th & 10th Jud. Dists. 2021).

453 448 LLC v. Butcher's Choice Meat Mkt., 113 N.Y.S.3d 792 (App. Term, 2d, 11th & 13th Jud. Dists 2019); Fieldbridge Assoc., LLC v. Holmes, 52 N.Y.S.3d 246 (App. Term, 2d, 11th & 13th Jud. Dists. 2017).

454 *See* DLB of NY, LLC v. Billan, 139 N.Y.S.3d 744 (App. Term, 1st Dep't 2021) (vacating judgment because the predicate notice "cannot support any request for possession or relief sought with respect to [a] second [separate] property"); Hollis Partners, LLC v. Artis, 152 N.Y.S.3d 546 (App. Term, 2d, 11th & 13th Jud. Dists. 2021); Chen v. Salvador, 145 N.Y.S.3d 780 (N.Y. Civ. Ct. Queens Cnty. 2021); *Green*, 2021 N.Y.L.J. LEXIS at 1067.

455 *See* NRP, LLC II v. El Gallo Meat Mkt., Inc., 2003 N.Y. Misc. LEXIS 1325 (App. Term, 1st Dep't Oct. 17, 2003); 1834 Caton v. Edwards, 2019 N.Y.L.J. LEXIS 1727 (N.Y. Civ. Ct. Kings Cnty. May 22, 2019). *But see* Marie France Realty Corp. v. 325 E. 14th St. Corp., 126 N.Y.S.3d 840 (App. Term, 1st Dep't 2020) (holding that the "30-day notice of cancellation used by landlord in connection with the prior...holdover proceeding against tenant was sufficient to serve as a predicate for the instant holdover proceeding brought on the same grounds [the following month], where the new proceeding was commenced the next business day after the initial proceeding was dismissed, and where tenant was caused no discernible prejudice"); 890 Park LLC v. Rosenfeld, 946 N.Y.S.2d 66 (App. Term, 1st Dep't 2011) (non-renewal notice from prior proceeding sufficient because the earlier proceeding "had not been terminated at the time of commencement," and there was no discernible prejudice).

notice further places the Tenant in a much stronger negotiating position because if a settlement is not reached, then the summary proceeding will likely be dismissed.

3. AUTHORITY TO SIGN THE NOTICE

In the absence of a statutory obligation or lease requirement, the Landlord's attorney or agent may sign the predicate notice on behalf of the Landlord.[456] This authority extends to situations where the rental agreement states that the Landlord must personally terminate the tenancy provided the Tenant has knowledge, or reason to know, the attorney or agent is authorized to act on behalf of the Landlord.[457]

4. ASSERTING ALTERNATIVE GROUNDS FOR TERMINATION

A predicate notice (and Petition) asserting alternative theories for an eviction may be adequate.[458] In *1506 Wallco LLC v. Guzman*, the Appellate Division, First Department concluded that "[a]lthough the notice to cure was based on an illegal sublet and the notice of termination identified an additional ground of non-primary residence, the

456 *See* Kwong v. Eng, 183 A.D.2d 558, at 560, 583 N.Y.S.2d 457 (1st Dep't 1992); *see* 808 Columbus Commercial Owner LLC v. Quik Park 808 Garage LLC, 154 N.Y.S.3d 411 (N.Y. Civ. Ct. N.Y. Cnty. Oct. 22, 2021) (noting omission of lease provision requiring the predicate notice to be signed by the Landlord); Davidson v. Myers, 112 N.Y.S.3d 878 (Nassau Cnty. Dist. Ct. 2019).

457 Ashley Realty Corp. v. Knight, 73 A.D.3d 500, at 501, 901 N.Y.S.2d 204, 205 (1st Dep't 2010); Port Royal Owners Corp. v. Navy Beach Rest. Group, LLC, 60 N.Y.S.3d 628 (App. Term, 9th & 10th Jud. Dists. 2017); Courtney House LLC v. Goetz, 41 N.Y.S.3d 448 (App. Term, 1st Dep't 2016). *Cf.* Siegel v. Kentucky Fried Chicken of Long Island, Inc., 108 A.D.2d 218, at 220, 448 N.Y.S.2d 744, 746 (2d Dep't 1985) ("[a] notice of termination signed by an agent or attorney who is not named in the lease as authorized to act for the landlord in such matters, *and which is not authenticated or accompanied by proof of the latter's authority to bind the landlord in giving such notice*, is legally insufficient to terminate the tenancy"), *aff'd*, 67 N.Y.2d 792, 501 N.Y.S.2d 317 (1986) (emphasis added); Kesselman v. London Paint & Wallpaper Co., Inc., 42 N.Y.S.3d 573 (N.Y. Civ. Ct. N.Y. Cnty. 2016) (dismissing proceeding where Respondent had "reasonable basis to be confused" regarding the authority of the predicate notice's signatory).

458 *See, e.g.*, 3657 Realty Co. LLC v. Jones, 52 A.D.3d 272, 859 N.Y.S.2d 434 (1st Dep't 2008); *1506 Wallco LLC*, 135 N.Y.S.3d at 795. *See also* Kern v. Guller, 40 A.D.3d 1231, 835 N.Y.S.3d 764 (3d Dep't 2007) (holding it permissible to assert both a non-payment and a holdover proceeding in the same action because "[i]nconsistent causes of action may be pleaded in the alternative") (*citing* CPLR § 3014).

allegations in both were identical, and sufficiently apprised respondent of the grounds on which she would have to defend the proceeding."[459]

A similar result was achieved in *Kew Gardens Portfolio Holdings, LLC v. Bucheli* where the Appellate Term for the Second, Eleventh and Thirteenth Judicial Districts concluded that the predicate notice that described the occupants as licensees or, in the alternative, squatters, was "sufficient to permit occupants to prepare a defense."[460] The Court reasoned that the "[o]ccupants are in the best position to know the circumstances under which they entered into occupancy, and they pointed to no prejudice or confusion resulting from the alternative pleading."[461] Notably, the predicate notice required for licensees and squatters is identical (i.e., ten (10) days).[462]

The content and service requirements for predicate notices vary based upon the parties' relationship. Some of the common predicate notices associated with summary proceedings are discussed below.

B. NON-PAYMENT PROCEEDINGS

The Landlord <u>must</u> make a written "demand" for the payment of rent arrears <u>prior</u> to the commencement of a residential or commercial non-payment proceeding.[463] A written rent demand "permits the tenant to choose between timely paying the rent demanded therein—thus preserv-

---

459 *3657 Realty Co. LLC*, 52 A.D.3d at 272, 859 N.Y.S.2d at 434. *Cf.* Willie Lilley, Care of My Ideal Property v. Molina, 115 N.Y.S.3d 801 (App. Term, 2d, 11th & 13th Jud. Dists. 2019) (dismissing holdover proceeding where predicate notice and Petition "[c]learly were not prepared on the personal knowledge of Willie Lilley, and which allege, in the alternative, that occupant is a licensee, sublessee or assignee of a prior tenant and do not allege that occupant is a squatter").

460 130 N.Y.S.3d 878 (App. Term, 2d, 11th & 13th Jud. Dists. 2020).

461 *Id.* The Appellate Term held that its earlier decision in *City of New York v. Bullock*, which concluded that the assertion of alternative claims in either the predicate notice or the Petition was impermissible, no longer represented the law and, as such, should <u>not</u> be followed. *Id.* (*citing* City of New York v. Bullock, 606 N.Y.S.2d 552, 554 (N.Y. Civ. Ct. Kings Cnty. 1993), *aff'd*, 630 N.Y.S.2d 652 (App. Term, 2d, 11th & 13th Jud. Dists. 1995)).

462 *See generally id.*; *1506 Wallco LLC*, 135 N.Y.S.3d at 795.

463 *See* Greenport Preserv., L.P. v. Heyward, 160 N.Y.S.3d 734 (App. Term, 2d, 11th & 13th Jud. Dists. 2021); Oakwood Terr. Hous. Corp. v. Monk, 36 N.Y.S.3d 48 (App. Term, 9th & 10th Jud. Dists. 2016).

ing the landlord-tenant relationship—or surrendering possession."[464] If after the rent demand period the Tenant neither pays the arrears nor vacates the premises, the Landlord may commence a non-payment proceeding.[465] Parenthetically, effective June 14, 2019, the HSTPA eliminated oral rent demands as an acceptable predicate notice (i.e., rent demands now must be in writing).[466]

The statute of limitations for unpaid rent is six (6) years which "[r]uns on each payment of rent from the date it becomes due."[467] The reader should be mindful that the doctrine of laches may preclude a Landlord from recovering a money judgment for any portion of the rent that is considered stale; i.e., unpaid rent that inexplicably was not sought in a timely manner and, if now permitted to be recovered, would result in prejudice to the Tenant.[468]

1. FOURTEEN (14) DAY RENT DEMAND

A rent demand must be served on all of the Tenants.[469] Subtenants and other occupants that are not parties to the lease (i.e., they have not agreed to pay rent to the Landlord) are not entitled to a copy of the rent

464 *Greenport Preserv., L.P.*, 160 N.Y.S.3d at 734.

465 *Id.*

466 *See* RPAPL § 711(2) (HSTPA, L. 2019, c. 36, Part M, § 12).

467 *See* CPLR § 213(2); Arnav Indus., Inc. v. Pitari, 82 A.D.3d 557, 918 N.Y.S.2d 479 (1st Dep't 2011); *see* Dee Cee Assoc. LLC v. 44 Beehan Corp., 148 A.D.3d 636, 51 N.Y.S.3d 41 (1st Dep't 2017); Flatbush Builders, Inc. v. Dubresil, 2017 N.Y.L.J. LEXIS 2298 (N.Y. Civ. Ct. Kings Cnty. Aug. 16, 2017). With respect to rent overcharge claims against a Landlord, the HSTPA amended CPLR § 213-a by extending the statute of limitations to "six years [previously it was four (4) years] before the action is commenced or complaint is filed." HSTPA, L. 2019, c. 36, Part F, § 6.

468 *See* 817 W. End Co. LLC v. DeLong, 2021 N.Y.L.J. LEXIS 381 (N.Y Civ. Ct. N.Y. Cnty. May 5, 2021) (laches defense sustained where Landlord seeks "rent some twenty-one months after it allegedly started to accrue and the absence of any impediment to [] bring a lawsuit earlier"). *Cf.* S & H Clinton Assocs., LLC v. Cherry, 148 N.Y.S.3d 823 (App. Term, 9th & 10th Jud. Dists. 2021) (denying laches defense absent a showing of both an unreasonable delay in commencing the proceeding and prejudice to the Tenant); Ollie Assoc. LLC v. Santos, 116 N.Y.S.3d 865 (N.Y. Civ. Ct. Bronx Cnty. 2019) (denying summary judgment due to issues of fact regarding the laches defense). For a discussion on the equitable defense of laches, *see* Affirmative Defenses, Chapter 11, subdiv. A(3), *infra*.

469 RPAPL § 711(2).

demand.[470] The rent demand must state that the Tenant is required to pay the unpaid rent or, alternatively, return possession of the premises.[471] The demand must further specify the period for which rent is owed and a good faith approximate sum of the arrears.[472]

The rent demand period for residential and commercial properties is at least fourteen (14) days (had previously been three (3) days).[473] This requirement is strictly enforced.[474] In other words, the Landlord must wait at least fourteen (14) days after the rent demand is served before commencing a non-payment proceeding.[475] The date the rent demand is served is not included within the fourteen (14) day calculation.[476]

Accordingly, the earliest day that a non-payment proceeding may be commenced is the fifteenth (15th) day following service of the rent demand. For example, if the rent demand is served on the 2nd day of the month, then the Landlord must wait until the 17th day of the month to

---

470 *See* 2626 Equities LLC v. Morilloz, 120 N.Y.S.3d 719 (N.Y. Civ. Ct. Bronx Cnty. 2020) (holding that the occupant was "[n]ot in default of an obligation to pay rent pursuant to an agreement with Petitioner [and failed to] provide the Court with any case that stands for the proposition that a mere occupant of an apartment is entitled to a written rent demand pursuant to RPAPL § 711(2)").

471 RPAPL § 711(2).

472 Rochdale Vill., Inc. v. Chadwick, 153 N.Y.S.3d 749 (App. Term, 2d, 11th & 13th Jud. Dists. 2021) (sum sought in rent demand not a good faith estimate because "at a minimum, 63% constituted use and occupancy and not rent"); Thomas Jefferson Owners Corp. v. Lokshin, 134 N.Y.S.3d 129 (App. Term, 2d, 11th & 13th Jud. Dists. 2020) (dismissing proceeding where a substantial amount demanded included improper fees); 125 Ct. St., LLC v. Sher, 94 N.Y.S.3d 539 (App. Term, 2d, 11th & 13th Jud. Dists. 2018) (rent demand not a good faith approximate of amount owed). *Cf. Moniaci*, 152 N.Y.S.3d at 216 (rent demand proper where it "fairly apprise[d] the tenant of the periods for which rent is allegedly due and [approximately] what amounts").

473 RPAPL §§ 711(2), 735; WFHA Creston Ave. LP v. Votaw, 2020 N.Y.L.J. LEXIS 436 (N.Y. Civ. Ct. Bronx Cnty. 2020).

474 *See, e.g.*, Schleimer v. Clarksville Inn Rest., 121 N.Y.S.3d 517 (App. Term, 9th & 10th Jud. Dists. 2020) (non-payment proceeding dismissed where rent demand required payment or surrender of the premises within ten (10) days); *WFHA Creston Ave. LP*, 2020 N.Y.L.J. LEXIS at 436. *Cf.* 60 W. 190th St. LLC v. Rodriguez, 123 N.Y.S.3d 413 (N.Y. Civ. Ct. Bronx Cnty. 2020) (fourteen (14) day rent demand proper).

475 RPAPL § 711(2).

476 General Construction Law § 20; *see* Gottesman Family Props., LLC v. Medi-System Renal Care Mgmt. Servs., LLC, 53 N.Y.S.3d 799 (App. Term, 2d, 11th & 13th Jud. Dists. 2017) (case prior to the enactment of the HSTPA).

commence a non-payment proceeding.[477]

a. RENT DEMAND MUST BE TIMELY

An issue that confuses many Landlords is the timing of service. If rent is due on the 1st day of the month, then the rent demand for that month may not be served until the 2nd day of the month, at the earliest. This is because unless the lease specifies otherwise, the rent is not considered late until 12:00 a.m. on the 2nd day of the month. In this scenario, a rent demand made on the 1st is defective, and may result in the proceeding being dismissed.

Only a non-party over the age of eighteen (18) may effectuate service of a timely rent demand.[478] To be proper, service of the rent demand must be completed in the same manner as service of the Notice of Petition and Petition.[479] This means that the written demand may not simply be mailed to the Tenant, whether by regular, overnight delivery, or certified mail.[480] Rather, the demand must be: (1) personally delivered; (2) left with a person of suitable age and discretion; or (3) left in a conspicuous place following reasonable efforts to ascertain personal delivery. Follow-up mailings by certified and regular mail are required where the latter two (2) methods of service are utilized.[481]

An exception to the fourteen (14) day rent demand involves manufactured home parks and mobile homes. Where a manufactured home park owner seeks to evict a Tenant for the non-payment of rent, the owner must first provide the Tenant, who may be the owner of the

477 *See Gottesman Family Props., LLC*, 53 N.Y.S.3d at 799 (non-payment proceeding dismissed, and money judgment in amount of $354,436.17 vacated, where proceeding commenced one (1) day early).

478 CPLR § 2103(a).

479 *See* RPAPL §§ 711(2), 735. *See, e.g.*, Joseph v. Lyu, 97 N.Y.S.3d 55 (App. Term, 2d, 11th & 13th Jud. Dists. 2018) (attempts at service at the premises when Landlord was aware the commercial Tenant had not opened for business failed to satisfy the "reasonable application" standard).

480 Merrbill Holdings, LLC v. Toscano, 100 N.Y.S.3d 610 (App. Term, 9th & 10th Jud. Dists. 2018).

481 For additional requirements regarding proper service, *see* Chapter 9, subdiv. B, *infra*.

mobile home, a thirty (30) day written notice.[482] The notice must similarly be formally served in accordance with RPAPL §735.

b. CONSUMER DEBT COLLECTION LAWS (RESIDENTIAL PROPERTIES)

The rent demand for residential property must comport with the Federal Fair Debt Collection Practices Act ("FDCPA") because the non-payment of rent is considered a "consumer debt."[483] The FDCPA prohibits communications with a consumer debtor: (1) at inconvenient times (generally between 9:00 p.m. and 8:00 a.m); (2) where the consumer debtor is represented by counsel; and (3) where the consumer "[n]otifies the debt collector in writing that the consumer refuses to pay a debt or that the consumer wishes the debt collector to cease further communication...."[484]

The FDCPA further prohibits the threat of violence or other criminal acts against the consumer, the use of obscene or abusive language, and the making of false or misleading statements in an attempt to persuade the consumer to pay the debt.[485] The statute is not applicable to commercial or corporate entities because the FDCPA defines a "consumer" as "any *natural person* obligated or allegedly obligated to pay a debt."[486]

To prevail pursuant to the FDCPA related to a Landlord and Tenant dispute, the Tenant must demonstrate that: (1) the Tenant is a "consumer" within the meaning of the FDCPA; (2) the defendant is a "debt collector"; and (3) the defendant engaged in conduct in violation of the

---

482 RPL § 233(b)(2). For a discussion on manufactured home parks and mobile homes, *see* Chapter 10, *infra*.

483 *See* 15 U.S.C. § 1692 *et seq.* (2006); Romea v. Heiberger & Assocs., 163 F.3d 111, 115 (2d Cir. 1998). In *Romea*, the United States Second Circuit Court of Appeals reasoned that since residential rent arrears are a "debt" under the FDCPA, communications regarding the arrears, including the rent demand, are subject to the statute. *Romea*, 163 F.3d at 115.

484 15 U.S.C. at § 1692c.

485 *Id.* at §§ 1692c, 1692d, 1692e.

486 *Id.* at § 1692a(3) (emphasis added). *See generally* Castillo v. Balsamo Rosenblatt & Cohen. P.C., 930 N.Y.S.2d 789 (N.Y. Civ. Ct. Kings Cnty. 2011).

statute.[487] A "debt collector" is defined as a person "[w]ho uses any instrumentality of interstate commerce or the mails in any business the principal purpose of which is the collection of any debts, or who regularly collects or attempts to collect, directly or indirectly, debts owed or due or asserted to be owed or due another."[488]

Counsel may be considered a debt collector pursuant to the statute and, as a result, the attorney is responsible for complying with the FDCPA when seeking to recoup rent arrears on behalf of a Landlord.[489] An action to enforce the FDCPA may be brought in Federal Court within one (1) year from the date the violation occurred.[490] The statute of limitations is intended to "protect defendants by ensuring that the action is filed within one year of the most recent date on which the defendant is alleged to have violated the FDCPA."[491]

A prevailing Plaintiff is entitled to recover actual damages, plus costs and reasonable attorneys' fees.[492] Although violations of the FDCPA may result in a claim against the offending issuer, non-compliance with the FDCPA does <u>not</u> necessitate dismissal of a summary proceeding.[493]

The FDCPA, which was enacted to curtail unsavory debt collection practices, is a strict liability statute that imposes liability for the "false representation of the character, amount, or legal status of any debt" regardless of intent.[494] Misstatements within a rent demand fall within the purview of the statute.[495] For example, in *Brake v. Slochowsky & Slochowsky, LLP*, the United States District Court for the Eastern District of New York denied Defendant's motion to dismiss the FDCPA

---

487 *See* Green v. Forster & Garbus, LLP, 2021 U.S. Dist. LEXIS 203571 (E.D.N.Y. Oct. 21, 2021) (credit card debt dispute).

488 15 U.S.C. § 1692a(6).

489 *See, e.g.*, Lee v. Kucker & Bruh, LLP, 958 F. Supp.2d 524 (S.D.N.Y. 2013).

490 15 U.S.C. § 1692k(e).

491 *Green*, 2021 U.S. Dist. LEXIS at 203571 (*citing* Padilla v. Payco Gen. Am. Credits, Inc., 161 F. Supp. 2d 264, 273 (S.D.N.Y. 2001)).

492 15 U.S.C. §§ 1692(a)(1),(3).

493 *See* Dearie v. Hunter, 705 N.Y.S.2d 519, 520 (App. Term, 1st Dep't 2000); Arrey v. Beaux Arts II, LLC, 101 F. Supp. 2d 225 (S.D.N.Y. 2000).

494 15 U.S.C. § 1692e(2)(A).

495 *See, e.g.*, Sanchez v. Ehrlich, 2018 U.S. Dist. LEXIS 69849 (S.D.N.Y. March 29, 2018).

claim where the Defendant law firm, relying upon an outdated rent ledger, erroneously demanded thousands of dollars in unpaid rent.[496] The Court succinctly concluded that the Tenant could prevail at trial on the FDCPA claim because "[t]he disputed debt involve[d] a garden-variety nonpayment with no legal uncertainties as to the falsity of the debt collector's representation."[497]

Several years earlier, in *Lee v. Krucker & Bruh, LLP*, the United States District Court for the Southern District of New York granted partial summary judgment against the Landlord's attorneys due to a single inflated rent demand. The Court noted that counsel was strictly liable for damages, plus attorney's fees, notwithstanding their reliance on an inadvertent error by the Landlord's billing office which failed to credit a partial rent payment.[498]

The implementation of suitable procedures to avoid errors in the rent demand may constitute a viable defense to the otherwise strict liability statute.[499] However, in *Lee*, there was no indication that a credible maintenance procedure had been implemented by the attorneys, and, the matter was reportedly settled for approximately $130,000 ($22,000 in damages and $108,000 in attorney's fees).[500]

2. FIVE (5) DAY LATE RENT REMINDER (RESIDENTIAL PROPERTIES)

For residential properties, RPL § 235-e(d) requires the service of a second written reminder (or notice) <u>prior</u> to the commencement of a non-payment proceeding. The statute provides that a written five (5) day late rent reminder <u>must</u> be served when the rent has <u>not</u> been

496 504 F. Supp.3d 103 (E.D.N.Y. 2020). The law firm prepared two (2) rent demands seeking $2,130.81 and $1,711.75 in rent arrears, respectively, plus legal fees and a "carrying" charge. However, the Tenant was current on rent payments, and multiple summary proceedings were dismissed by stipulation. *Id.*

497 *Id.*

498 *Lee*, 958 F. Supp.2d at 524; *see Sanchez*, 2018 U.S. Dist. LEXIS at 69849 (denying Landlord's motion to dismiss Section 8 Tenant's FDCPA claim).

499 *Lee*, 958 F. Supp.2d at 524.

500 *See* Josh Barbanel, "Eviction-Case Settlement Worries Landlord Lawyers," THE WALL ST. JOURNAL, at http://www.wsj.com/articles/SB10001424127887323608504579022850361952282, Aug. 20, 2013.

received within five (5) days of the due date.[501] This reminder, unlike the fourteen (14) day rent demand, is to be served by certified mail (i.e., not formal service).[502] The failure to provide the five (5) day late rent reminder may constitute an affirmative defense in a non-payment proceeding.[503] In *PPT Mgmt., LLC v. Accu-Serve Process Service, Ltd.*, the Nassau County District Court dismissed the non-payment proceeding where the Landlord mistakenly served a five (5) day rent demand as opposed to a fourteen (14) day rent demand plus a five (5) day late rent reminder.[504]

C. HOLDOVER PROCEEDINGS

In a majority of holdover proceedings, the Landlord must demonstrate that the Tenant was in possession of the premises beyond the expiration or termination of the tenancy and continues to remain in possession at the time the proceeding was commenced.[505] According to common law, when a Tenant remains in possession following the expiration of the lease without entering into a new agreement or paying any additional money, the parties continue to be bound by the terms of the expired lease.[506]

Remaining in possession beyond the expiration or termination of the tenancy represents one (1) of several, fact-specific relationships set forth within the RPL and RPAPL that allow for the commencement of a holdover proceeding to regain possession of the premises absent a Landlord and Tenant relationship.[507] The predicate notices commonly

---

501 RPL § 235-e(d).

502 *Id.*

503 *Id.*

504 Index No. 000352-22 (Nassau Cnty. Dist. Ct. June 13, 2022) (unpublished decision).

505 *See* RPAPL § 711(1).

506 Zheng v. Fu Jian Hong Guan Am. Unity Assn., Inc., 168 A.D.3d 511, 92 N.Y.S.3d 227 (1st Dep't 2019).

507 RPAPL § 713. *Cf.* JCF Assoc., LLC v. Sign Up USA, Inc., 101 N.Y.S.3d 700 (App. Term, 2d, 11th & 13th Jud. Dists. 2018) (holdover proceeding not permitted where parties entered into an agreement for billboard advertising that did not include the granting of a possessory interest to real property).

associated with holdover proceedings are discussed below.

1. REFUSAL TO RE-NEW LEASE (RESIDENTIAL PROPERTIES) (30, 60, OR 90 DAYS)

For residential premises, where the Landlord chooses not to re-new an expiring lease, the Tenant must be served with a written predicate notice prior to the expiration of the tenancy.[508] Before October 12, 2019, the Landlord could allow the lease to expire and commence a holdover proceeding without any prior notice. This is no longer the case.

The requisite notice period that must be provided when the Landlord does not intend to re-new the tenancy is thirty (30), sixty (60), or ninety (90) days. The precise determination is based upon the "cumulative amount of time the Tenant occupied the residence or the length of the tenancy in each lease, whichever is longer."[509] These notice requirements also apply where the Landlord seeks to terminate a residential month-to-month tenancy.[510]

If the Tenant occupied the premises for less than one (1) year and the rental agreement is also for a period of less than one (1) year, then the Landlord must provide at least thirty (30) days notice prior to the expiration of the tenancy.[511] Where the Tenant either occupied the premises for more than one (1) year but fewer than two (2) years or the rental agreement is for at least one (1) year but less than two (2) years, then no fewer than sixty (60) days notice is required.[512] Finally, if the Tenant occupied the premises for more than two (2) years or the rental agreement is for at least two (2) years, then at least ninety (90)

508 *See generally* Langdoc v. Warden, 141 N.Y.S.3d 678 (Cohoes City Ct. 2021); 64 Van St. LLC v. Cuevas, 2020 N.Y.L.J. LEXIS 705 (N.Y. Civ. Ct. Queens Cnty. March 25, 2020).

509 RPL § 226-c(2)(a).

510 *See, e.g., 64 Van St., LLC,* 121 N.Y.S.3d at 584; Sukaj Group LLC v. Mallia, 121 N.Y.S.3d 847 (N.Y. Civ. Ct. Bronx Cnty. 2020).

511 RPL § 226-c(2)(b); *see generally* Wisdom v. Byfield, 146 N.Y.S.3d 469 (N.Y. Civ. Ct. Kings Cnty. 2021) (subtenancy).

512 RPL § 226-c(2)[c]; 1629-1631 St. John's Place LLC v. Castillo, 2021 N.Y. Misc. LEXIS 6510 (N.Y. Civ. Ct. Kings Cnty. Dec. 17, 2021); *64 Van St., LLC,* 121 N.Y.S.3d at 584.

days notice is required.[513]

The failure to provide the appropriate notice prior to the expiration of the tenancy renders any proposed changes to the rental agreement a nullity and, further, the tenancy continues under the terms of the existing lease until an appropriate notice is sent and the notice period has expired.[514] The right to notice may not be waived in a rental agreement.[515] Parenthetically, the statute does not specify the manner in which the predicate notice must be served.[516]

2. RE-NEW LEASE WITH FIVE PERCENT (5%) OR GREATER RENT INCREASE (RESIDENTIAL PROPERTIES) (30, 60, OR 90 DAYS)

The notice provisions set forth within RPL § 226-c also apply when the Landlord seeks to re-new a residential rental agreement with a rent increase of at least five percent (5%).[517] This means that the Landlord must provide the Tenant at least thirty (30), sixty (60), or ninety (90) days notice prior to the expiration of the tenancy when the Landlord's offer to re-new the tenancy is conditioned upon the Tenant agreeing to a rent increase of at least five percent (5%).[518] The failure to provide timely notice results in the continuation of the lease (with the same terms) until an appropriate notice is served and the notice period has expired.[519]

The length of the requisite notice again depends upon the Tenant's occupancy and the length of the lease, whichever is greater. If the Tenant was in possession and/or had a lease for less than one (1) year, then at least thirty (30) days notice is required. Where the Tenant was in possession between one (1) and two (2) years or the rental agreement

513 RPL § 226-c(2)(d); Livian v. Soblesohn, 2021 N.Y. Misc. LEXIS 6209 (N.Y. Civ. Ct. Queens Cnty. Oct. 22, 2021); *Sukaj Group LLC*, 121 N.Y.S.3d at 847; Doyle v. Riquelme, 147 N.Y.S.3d 889 (N.Y. Civ. Ct. Kings Cnty. 2020); Denis v. Fisher, 115 N.Y.S.3d 650 (N.Y. Civ. Ct. Queens Cnty. 2019).

514 RPL § 226-c(1).

515 *Id.*

516 *Id.* at § 226-c.

517 *Id.*

518 *Id.*

519 *Id.*

was for at least one (1) year but less than two (2) years, at least sixty (60) days notice must be provided. Finally, if the lease was for at least two (2) years or the occupancy exceeded two (2) years, then at least ninety (90) days notice is required.[520] The statute is again silent on the manner in which service is to be effectuated.[521]

3. MONTH-TO-MONTH TENANCY

A month-to-month tenancy may result by express agreement or by operation of law such as when a rental agreement of longer than one (1) month expires and the Tenant remains in possession and continues to pay for the additional time without entering into a new rental agreement.[522] A month-to-month tenancy need not be in writing because the term (regardless of the number of consecutive months the tenancy continues) is completed within less than one (1) year, and, therefore, the tenancy is not subject to the Statute of Frauds.[523]

A party wishing to terminate a month-to-month tenancy must provide a predicate notice. If the Landlord fails to provide the appropriate notice, then the tenancy continues until an appropriate written notice is served and the termination date set forth therein passes.[524] If the Tenant fails to provide a proper notice before vacating the premises, liability for the current month's rent, plus an additional month's rent for properties outside New York City, may attach.[525]

Similar to non-payment proceedings, the notice terminating a

520 *Id.* at § 226-c(2).

521 *Id.* at § 226-c.

522 *Id.* at § 232-c; Zielinski v. Kiwak, 110 N.Y.S.3d 210 (App. Term, 2d, 11th & 13th Jud. Dists. 2018); Priegue v. Paulus, 988 N.Y.S.2d 525 (App. Term, 9th & 10th Jud. Dists. 2014).

523 GOL § 5-703(2); 28 Mott St. Co., Inc. v. Summit Import Corp., 34 A.D.2d 144, 310 N.Y.S.2d 93 (1st Dep't 1970); 72nd St. Assocs., LLC v. Persson, 13 N.Y.S.3d 853 (App. Term, 1st Dep't 2015) (oral agreement extending lease two (2) years barred by the statute of frauds).

524 RPL § 226-c(1).

525 *See* Skurka v. Elkoulily, 936 N.Y.S.2d 61 (Nassau Cnty. Dist. Ct. 2011); *see also* Hickey v. Trahan, 31 N.Y.S.3d 921 (App. Term, 9th & 10th Jud. Dists. 2016) (rent for month-to-month tenancy may not be apportioned); Deban v. Hoevener, 950 N.Y.S.2d 491 (App. Term, 9th & 10th Jud. Dists. 2012) (same).

month-to-month tenancy must be in writing and "timely, definite [and] unequivocal."[526] The notice is not capable of amendment,[527] and a termination notice signed by counsel that fails to specify counsel's authority to issue the notice may be defective where the authority to act on behalf of the Petitioner was not previously known to the Tenant.[528] However, a defect in the predicate notice that "could not have materially misled or confused the tenant or hindered the preparation of [the] defense" may be overlooked.[529]

526 *See* United Veterans Beacon House, Inc. v. St. James, 781 N.Y.S.2d 628 (App. Term, 9th & 10th Jud. Dists. 2003). *Cf.* Barrett Japaning Inc. v. Bialobroda, 998 N.Y.S.2d 305 (App. Term, 1st Dep't 2014) (improper to re-serve a four and one-half (4½) year-old termination notice from a prior proceeding).

527 *See* Chinatown Apts., Inc. v. Lam, 51 N.Y.2d 786, at 787, 433 N.Y.S.2d 86 (1980). Prior to October 12, 2019, outside New York City a Landlord was permitted to provide either an oral or written notice, and, if in writing, the notice need not have been formally served. *See* Spangenberg v. Chaloupka, 229 A.D.2d 482, at 483, 645 N.Y.S.2d 514 (2d Dep't 1996) ("service by mail is complete upon mailing regardless of delivery"). Where the Petitioner identifies a procedure for mailing in the regular course of its business, there is a "presumption of mailing" and receipt of the document. *See* We're Assocs. Co. v. Rodin Sportswear Ltd., 288 A.D.2d 465, 734 N.Y.S.2d 104 (2d Dep't 2001); *see also* Expressway Vill., Inc. v. Denman, 893 N.Y.S.2d 736, 737 (Niagra Cnty. Ct. 2009) (Court notice sent via regular mail is presumed to have been received by the recipient when the notice was not returned as "undeliverable").

528 *See* Smith v. Country Serv., Inc., 831 N.Y.S.2d 350 (App. Term, 9th & 10th Jud. Dists. 2006); HSBC Bank, USA, N.A. v. Jeffers, 958 N.Y.S.2d 646 (Nassau Cnty. Dist. Ct. 2011). *Cf.* GRP/AG REO 2004-1, LLC v. Friedman, 792 N.Y.S.2d 819, 821 (Ramapo Just. Ct. 2005) ("[P]etitioner's attorney was clothed with authority to issue the [termination] notice by virtue of his prior activity known by the respondents and/or their attorneys").

529 *See* Oxford Towers Co., LLC v. Leites, 41 A.D.3d 144, at 145, 837 N.Y.S.2d 131 (1st Dep't 2007) (emphasis added).

a. WITHIN NEW YORK CITY

i. RESIDENTIAL PROPERTIES (30, 60, OR 90 DAYS)

RPL § 232-a governs the termination of month-to-month tenancies within New York City.[530] For residential properties, the Landlord must provide the Tenant at least thirty (30), sixty (60), or ninety (90) days notice prior to commencing a holdover proceeding.[531] A notice terminating a month-to-month tenancy must be in writing and formally served in the same manner as the Notice of Petition and Petition.[532]

The appropriate number of days notice for terminating a month-to-month tenancy is governed by the same factors set forth within RPL § 226-c. RPL § 232-a specifically refers to RPL § 226-c regarding the notice period.[533]

Since, by definition, a month-to-month tenancy is for less than one (1) year, the requisite notice given to the Tenant must be at least thirty (30) days unless the Tenant's occupancy has been for more than one (1) year. In other words, if a month-to-month Tenant occupied the premises for less than one (1) year, then at least thirty (30) days written notice must be given; more than one (1) year but fewer than two (2) years, then at least sixty (60) days written notice is required; or if the Tenant occupied the premises for more than two (2) years, then at least ninety (90) days written notice is required.[534]

Neither RPL § 232-a nor RPL § 226-c specify a requisite notice period when a residential Tenant seeks to terminate a month-to-month tenancy in New York City. In *25-86 41st St. LLC v. Chong*, the Queens County Supreme Court noted that "[i]t is undisputed that a month-to-month tenant has a right to terminate the tenancy at any time."[535]

---

530 *See, e.g.*, Lai v. Watson, 2021 N.Y. Misc. LEXIS 6203 (N.Y. Cnty. Sup. Ct. Nov. 30, 2021).

531 RPL § 232-a.

532 *Id.*

533 *Id.*; *see e.g.*, *64 Van St., LLC*, 121 N.Y.S.3d at 584.

534 RPL § 226-c(2)(c),(d).

535 2021 N.Y. Misc. LEXIS 4078 (Queens Cnty. Sup. Ct. July 9, 2021).

ii. COMMERCIAL PROPERTIES (30 DAYS)

To terminate a commercial month-to-month tenancy within New York City, the Landlord must provide at least thirty (30) days written notice.[536] The Landlord need not consider either sixty (60) or ninety (90) days notices unless the rental agreement provides otherwise.[537] Similar to residential properties within New York City, RPL § 232-a omits any reference to the notice that must be served by a commercial Tenant seeking to terminate a commercial month-to-month tenancy.

b. OUTSIDE NEW YORK CITY

i. RESIDENTIAL PROPERTIES (30, 60, OR 90 DAYS)

For month-to-month residential properties outside New York City, as of October 2019, a Landlord seeking to terminate a month-to-month tenancy (similar to New York City month-to-month residential tenancies) must follow the notice period requirements of RPL § 226-c; i.e., thirty (30), sixty (60), or ninety (90) days notice.[538] In 2019, the Legislature deleted the term "Landlord" from RPL § 232-b which had previously required the Landlord to provide at least one (1) month notice. This is no longer the case as the current notice period is set at either thirty (30), sixty (60), or ninety (90) days.

If the Tenant seeks to terminate a residential month-to-month tenancy outside New York City, then at least one (1) month notice is required (without need for consideration of a longer notice period unless agreed to within the rental agreement).[539] The failure to provide the appropriate notice may result in an additional month of rent obligations.[540] The manner of service for the notice is not specified within the statutes.

---

536 RPL § 232-a.

537 *Id.*; Aviv Dev. Corp. v. Weathers, 2020 N.Y.L.J. LEXIS 1203 (N.Y. Civ. Ct. Queens Cnty. July 29, 2020).

538 RPL § 226-c.

539 *Id.* at § 232-b. *See Hickey*, 31 N.Y.S.3d at 921 (holding that "a month-to-month tenant who vacates during the month is liable for the entire month's rent").

540 *Deban*, 950 N.Y.S.2d at 491 (holding that month-to-month Tenants who vacated on the 8th day of the term were obligated to pay an additional month of rent); Smith v. Woodson, 929 N.Y.S.2d 203 (App. Term, 2d, 11th & 13th Jud. Dists. 2011); Downes v. Obadiah, N.Y.L.J., Feb. 8, 2000, at 29 (App. Term, 9th & 10th Jud. Dists. 2000).

The relevant statutes similarly do not specify whether the termination date must coincide with a particular date (i.e., the anniversary date of the tenancy or the last day of the term).[541] Prior to October 12, 2019, when at least one (1) month notice was required, it was well-established that a month-to-month tenancy outside New York City could only be terminated (absent consent) on the final day of the rental term (typically, but not always, the last day of the month).[542]

Thus, if a month-to-month tenancy was commenced on the 1st day of the month, then the termination date, at the earliest, is the final day of the following month, which for the majority of months is the 31st. For example, presume that the month-to-month tenancy commenced on March 1st, and the Landlord seeks to terminate the tenancy by serving a predicate notice on April 6th. The earliest lease termination date is May 31st (i.e., the final day of the term at least one (1) month following service (April 6th) of the notice).[543] In this scenario, the Landlord could also select a termination date of June 30th, July 31st, August 31st, or the final day of any subsequent month, provided at least the minimum number of requisite days notice is given to the Tenant.

Whether the termination date continues to be the final day of the term remains to be determined. The reason for the uncertainty is that the relevant statutes are silent on this point and the well-established practice in New York City that the Landlord merely needs to wait the requisite number of days (regardless of the day of the term the date

541 RPL § 232-b.

542 *See* Anthi New Neocronon Corp. v. Coalition of Landlords, Homeowners & Merchs., Inc., 155 N.Y.S.3d 30 (App. Term, 9th & 10th Jud. Dists. 2021) (*citing* Sills v. Dellavalle, 9 A.D.3d 561, 780 N.Y.S.2d 193 (3d Dep't 2004)); Oz v. Stolpen, 1992 N.Y.L.J. LEXIS 8822 (N.Y. Civ. Ct. N.Y. Cnty. Dec. 9, 1992 (noting prior summary proceeding was dismissed because the predicate notice "[d]id not require removal on the day on which the term expired").

543 *See Anthi New Neocronon Corp.*, 155 N.Y.S.3d at 30.

falls) before commencing the proceeding.[544] Now that a "month notice" has been deleted and replaced with a specific number of days, similar to the requirements for terminating New York City month-to-month residential tenancies, the question to be resolved is whether the New York City method for selecting the termination date (i.e., count the number of days as opposed to selecting a final day of the term) will be adopted outside New York City.

ii. COMMERCIAL PROPERTIES (1 MONTH)

When either party seeks to terminate a commercial month-to-month tenancy outside New York City, then at least one (1) month notice must be provided to the other party.[545] RPL § 232-b does not specify a particular manner of service for the notice.[546]

c. TYPE OF PROCEEDING TO TERMINATE A MONTH-TO-MONTH TENANCY

When a Tenant remains in possession following the expiration of the lease (after proper notice has been provided) and pays moneys for an additional period without entering into a new rental agreement with the Landlord, a month-to-month tenancy is established.[547] If the Tenant thereafter stops making payment without properly terminating the tenancy, there is a split in the Appellate Terms as to whether a non-payment or a holdover proceeding is appropriate.

In the First Department, the Appellate Term has held that the Landlord's recourse is to commence a holdover proceeding, as opposed to a non-payment proceeding, after giving thirty (30), sixty (60), or

544 *See generally* Lila Group LLC v. Cordero, 2007 N.Y.L.J. LEXIS 2303 (N.Y. Civ. Ct. Kings Cnty. Aug. 29, 2007) (New York City residential dwelling). The lease in *Anthi New Neocronon* involved residential property outside New York City that was terminated approximately four (4) months prior to the enactment of the thirty (30), sixty (60), and ninety (90) day notice requirements. *Anthi New Neocronon Corp.*, 155 N.Y.S.3d at 30. In other words, although a ninety (90) day notice was served, the applicable law at the time required one (1) month notice. *Id.*

545 RPL § 232-b.

546 *Id.*

547 RPL § 232-c; Bahamonde v. Grabel, 939 N.Y.S.2d 226 (App. Term, 9th & 10th Jud. Dists. 2011).

ninety (90) days notice.[548] In a month-to-month tenancy, the Landlord and Tenant have an agreement for the payment of the current month's rent. The Court reasoned it would therefore be inconsistent to permit a non-payment proceeding for a future month in which there is no such agreement.[549]

On the other hand, the Appellate Term for the Ninth and Tenth Judicial Districts within the Second Department has held that the Landlord may commence either a non-payment or a holdover proceeding because RPL § 232-c is inapplicable to month-to-month tenancies. The rent demand and commencement of the non-payment proceeding is considered a permissible election to "[t]reat the holdover tenants as tenants for a new term" on "[t]he same terms as were in the expired lease."[550]

4. LEASE EXPIRED BY ITS OWN TERMS (COMMERCIAL PROPERTIES) (NO NOTICE)

For commercial properties, it appears that absent a lease provision to the contrary, a predicate notice is not required to terminate a rental agreement that expired on a date certain (e.g., a lease that expired by its own terms on December 31, 20__).[551] As a result, where a commercial Tenant holds over without paying for the additional time (and thereby does not create a month-to-month tenancy), the Landlord need not provide a predicate notice before commencing a holdover

548 RPL § 226-c(2).

549 *See* Krantz & Phillips, LLP v. Sedaghati, 2003 N.Y. Misc. LEXIS 58 (App. Term, 1st Dep't Jan. 23, 2003); 320 W. 111th St. HDFC v. Lang, 2020 N.Y.L.J. LEXIS 1520 (N.Y. Civ. Ct. N.Y. Cnty. Oct. 7, 2020); 554-558 W. 181st St. LLC v. Cochrane, 110 N.Y.S.3d 793 (N.Y. Civ. Ct. N.Y. Cnty. 2018); Eshaghian v. Adames, 957 N.Y.S.2d 635 (N.Y. Civ. Ct. N.Y. Cnty. 2010); 1400 Broadway Assocs. v. Lee & Co. of NY, Inc., 614 N.Y.S.2d 704 (N.Y. Civ. Ct. N.Y. Cnty. 1994).

550 Tricarichi v. Moran, 959 N.Y.S.2d 372 (App. Term, 9th & 10th Jud. Dists. 2012). *See Priegue*, 988 N.Y.S.2d at 525; Zheng v. Lin, 2021 N.Y.L.J. LEXIS 280 (N.Y. Civ. Ct. Queens Cnty. April 7, 2021).

551 *See* Arverne Ltd. Profit House Corp. v. Taft's Dental, P.C., 99 N.Y.S.3d 851 (N.Y. Civ. Ct. Queens Cnty. 2019) (noting that "[a] holdover relationship after a [commercial] lease expires by its own terms does not require statutory notice prior to a holdover proceeding") (emphasis added); BGB Realty, LLC v. Annunziata, 820 N.Y.S.2d 841 (App. Term, 9th & 10th Jud. Dists. 2006).

proceeding.[552]

It is well-established that the Landlord may not hold the Tenant to a new rental term or re-new the expired lease without consent. In other words, although the Landlord may be entitled to a money judgment for use and occupancy, the Landlord may not unilaterally elect to re-new the expired lease based on the holdover. An exception may apply where the expired lease contained an automatic lease renewal provision and an appropriate reminder notice was provided.[553]

5. TENANCY-AT-WILL (30 DAYS)

A tenant-at-will was initially granted lawful possession of the premises without restriction or limitation for an indefinite period of time pursuant to an agreement with the Petitioner, with or without an agreed amount of consideration (compensation) for the occupancy.[554] A tenant-at-will has complete and unfettered access (exclusive possession) to all or a portion of the property notwithstanding the absence of an agreement for the payment of rent *per se* or a fixed termination date.[555]

A tenancy-at-will may result when a homeowner agrees to have someone maintain their primary residence while the owner spends an undetermined amount of time at a second home or alternative residence. If the owner grants the occupant complete and "exclusive" possession to the primary residence (or to a portion of the primary residence) for an unspecified period while "away," then the parties have

---

552 RPL § 232-c.

553 *See* Affirmative Defenses Chapter 11, subdiv. C(2), *infra*.

554 *See generally* Waldman v. Abt, 156 N.Y.S.3d 831 (N.Y. Civ. Ct. Kings Cnty. 2021) (noting the occupant's sharing of the premises (i.e., the absence of "exclusive" possession) renders the occupancy to be a license, rather than a tenancy-at-will).

555 Rodriguez v. Greco, 927 N.Y.S.2d 819 (App. Term, 9th & 10th Jud. Dists. 2011); *see* Nextel of New York, Inc. v. Time Mgmt. Corp., 297 A.D.2d 282, at 283, 746 N.Y.S.2d 169 (2d Dep't 2002); DiStasio v. Macaluso, 16 N.Y.S.3d 791 (App. Term, 9th & 10th Jud. Dists. 2015); Sherhan v. Numyal Food, Inc., 862 N.Y.S.2d 709, 712 (App. Term, 2d & 11th Jud. Dists 2008) ("[w]hether...exclusive possession or control of any specific area is granted is of great importance in determining whether a license or a lease is constituted") (citation omitted); City of New York v. Utsey, 714 N.Y.S.2d 410, 412 (App. Term, 2d & 11th Jud. Dists. 2000).

entered into a tenancy-at-will even "without the reservation of rent."[556]

The critical elements of a tenancy-at-will is that exclusive possession is given to the occupant for an indefinite period of time.[557] When the owner plans to return to the primary residence, a tenant-at-will is entitled to at least thirty (30) days written notice, not necessarily one (1) month, prior to the commencement of a summary proceeding.[558] The thirty (30) days need not end on any particular date. Since the termination notice ends the tenancy-at-will prior to the commencement of the eviction proceeding, a holdover proceeding is appropriate when the tenant-at-will fails to voluntarily vacate the premises.

RPL § 228 permits the Landlord to provide more than thirty (30) days notice; i.e., no fewer than thirty (30) days notice is required. The termination notice must be formally served unless the parties agree otherwise.[559]

6. LICENSEE (10 DAYS)

Similar to a tenancy-at-will, a license is for an indefinite duration. However, unlike a tenant-at-will, a licensee does not have exclusive, unfettered access to the premises.[560] Rather, a licensee is prohibited from accessing or using portions of the property and/or is required to share the premises with other occupants.[561]

A Landlord and Tenant relationship does not exist where the

556 *See* Carbonella v. Carbonella, 43 N.Y.S.3d 766 (App. Term, 2d, 11th & 13th Jud. Dists. 2016); 109-111 1st Ave., LLC v. Fromholz, 799 N.Y.S.2d 165 (App. Term, 9th & 10th Jud. Dists. 2004).

557 Fizzinoglia v. Capozzoli, 94 N.Y.S.3d 538 (App. Term, 9th & 10th Jud. Dists. 2018); Chu v. Lee, 972 N.Y.S.2d 143 (App. Term, 2d, 11th & 13th Jud. Dists. 2013).

558 RPL § 228.

559 *Id.*

560 Zhu v. Li, 138 N.Y.S.3d 792 (App. Term, 2d, 11th & 13th Jud. Dists. 2021).

561 *Id.*; *Wisdom*, 146 N.Y.S.3d at 469.

occupant is a licensee.[562] The RPAPL authorizes commencement of a holdover proceeding in the Housing Parts to evict a licensee following formal service of a written ten (10) day Notice to Quit in the manner set forth in RPAPL § 735.[563]

A licensee was initially given legal permission to enter the premises.[564] Case law has elaborated that a licensee is a person who lawfully gained entry to the subject premises with the express or implicit permission of the owner, or pursuant to a "[p]ersonal, revocable, non[-] assignable privilege from the owner, without possessing any interest in the property, and who becomes a trespasser thereon upon revocation of the permission of the privilege."[565]

Due to the restrictive nature of the relationship, the rights of a licensee are limited.[566] By definition, a licensee does <u>not</u> have a possessory interest in the premises and, therefore, a licensee "[c]annot maintain an unlawful entry and detainer proceeding" for an illegal eviction pursuant to RPAPL § 713(10).[567] An example of a licensor and licensee relationship is when an adult child, who previously left the family home, "returns" to the home with parental consent, but instead of entering into a tenancy for a fixed duration, it is mutually understood that the stay is temporary (e.g., may only stay "for a little

---

562 *See generally* 645 Brooklyn Realty, LLC v. Beecher-Sakil, 138 N.Y.S.3d 789 (App. Term, 2d, 11th & 13th Jud. Dists. 2021) (denying summary judgment where there was "[a]n issue of fact with respect to occupant's affirmative defense asserting that she was not a licensee, but rather a tenant"); Federal Nat'l Mtg. Assoc. v. Simmons, 12 N.Y.S.3d 487 (App. Term, 1st Dep't 2015) (licensee holdover proceeding dismissed where Respondent entered into possession as a Tenant pursuant to a proprietary lease).

563 RPAPL § 713(7); Russian Orthodox Convent Novo-Diveevo, Inc. v. Sukharevskaya, 166 A.D.3d 1036, 91 N.Y.S.3d 101 (2d Dep't 2018). RPAPL § 713 lists the grounds for commencing a summary proceeding following service of a ten (10) day Notice to Quit where a Landlord and Tenant relationship does <u>not</u> exist. *Id.* at § 713.

564 RPAPL § 713(7).

565 Rosenstiel v. Rosenstiel, 20 A.D.2d 71, at 76, 245 N.Y.S.2d 395 (1st Dep't 1963) (citations omitted).

566 *Zhu*, 138 N.Y.S.3d at 792.

567 Andrews v. Acacia Network, 70 N.Y.S.3d 744 (App. Term, 2d, 11th & 13th Jud. Dists. 2018); Felli v. Catholic Charities of Steuben County, 175 A.D.3d 1065, 108 N.Y.S.3d 624 (4th Dep't 2019).

while").[568] Consideration in the form of payment and/or the adult child performing "work around the house" does not convert the relationship into a tenancy due to the open-ended duration of the occupancy. Another example of a licensee is when a paramour enters the residence of a partner with consent (the couple are not married), but for an unspecified period of time.

If the licensee does not vacate the premises following service of a ten (10) day notice, a holdover proceeding may be commenced in the Housing Part. Real Property Actions and Proceedings Law further permits a holdover proceeding to regain possession from a guest of a Tenant (i.e., licensee of the Tenant) when the Tenant is no longer in possession. This is the case notwithstanding the lack of privity between the Landlord and the former Tenant's licensee.[569]

Although a Notice to Quit must clearly denominate the parties' relationship and the relief sought, the RPAPL omits any specific requirements regarding the content of the notice revoking a license. Accordingly, a determination on the sufficiency of the notice is left to the discretion of the Court. For example, an otherwise clearly labeled ten (10) day written notice that failed to include the date when the occupant was required to vacate the premises was deemed adequate notice.[570] However, in another case, a Notice to Quit that incorrectly identified the parties' relationships was held to be defective.[571] The inclusion of incomplete and/or incorrect information, such as omitting

568 *Zhu*, 138 N.Y.S.3d at 792; Great Jones St. Realty Corp. v. Chimsanthia, 157 N.Y.S.3d 851 (App. Term, 1st Dep't 2022) (holding that "[t]he RPAPL contains no language exempting individuals with some familial relationship to a petitioner from eviction as licensees"); Aloni v. Oliver, 138 N.Y.S.3d 788 (App. Term, 1st Dep't 2021) (license holdover proceeding proper where the licensee and "[p]etitioner resided together in the apartment in a family-like 'romantic relationship'").

569 RPAPL § 713.

570 *See* Washington Mutual Bank, F.A. v. Hanspal, 856 N.Y.S.2d 27 (App. Term, 9th & 10th Jud. Dists. 2007); *see also* Westhab, Inc. v. Alston, 97 N.Y.S.3d 57 (Mt. Vernon City Ct. 2018) (although there are no statutory specific requirements pertaining to the content of a Notice to Quit, inaccurate information may result in dismissal).

571 *See* Willie Lilley, Care of My Ideal Property v. Molina, 115 N.Y.S.3d 801 (App. Term, 2d, 11th & 13th Jud. Dists. 2019) (dismissing proceeding where predicate notice asserted Respondent was "licensee, sublessee or assignee of a prior tenant," but the occupant was in fact a squatter).

the facts upon which the proceeding is based or failing to properly define the type of occupancy, may similarly render the notice defective.[572]

7. SQUATTER (10 DAYS)

A squatter is an individual who initially gained possession to the premises without the permission or consent of the lawful occupant and remains in possession without permission, or, if at some point after unlawful entry permission to occupy was granted, it has since been revoked.[573] A squatter is entitled to a written ten (10) day predicate notice formally served pursuant to RPAPL § 735 prior to the commencement of a holdover proceeding.[574]

From a practical perspective, the owner of the premises will typically seek the removal of a squatter by contacting law enforcement. If, however, law enforcement does not require the individual to vacate the property, the owner's remedy is to commence a holdover proceeding after providing proper notice.[575] For residential properties, the use of self-help to remove an occupant, such as changing the locks, is impermissible and constitutes a class A misdemeanor subject to up to one (1) year in jail and a fine between $1,000 and $10,000.[576]

The reader should be mindful that if the Court determines that the occupant "lawfully occupied the dwelling unit for [at least] thirty (30) consecutive days" or had an existing rental agreement, then the rights associated with a tenancy may attach.[577] An essential element in

572 Hecsomar Realty Corp. v. Camerena, 113 N.Y.S.3d 463 (App. Term, 1st Dep't 2019) (dismissing licensee holdover proceeding where occupant was a squatter who entered the premises without permission); *Cf.* Retained Realty Inc. v. Zwicker, 7 N.Y.S.3d 245 (App. Term, 1st Dep't 2014) (licensee holdover proceeding dismissed where occupant entered possession pursuant to a rental agreement); *but see* United Veterans Beacon House, Inc. v. St. James, 781 N.Y.S.2d 628 (App. Term, 9th & 10th Jud. Dists. 2003) (improper identification of Tenant as a licensee did not warrant dismissal absent a showing of prejudice).

573 DOLAN §§ 35:14 to 35:16, at 537-40 (4th ed. 2010). *See Hecsomar Realty Corp.*, 113 N.Y.S.3d at 463.

574 RPAPL § 713(3).

575 *See* 21st Mortgage Corp. v. Hall, 187 A.D.3d 742, 130 N.Y.S.3d 385 (2d Dep't 2020).

576 *Id.* at § 768(2).

577 RPAPL § 768(1).

establishing a squatter is that the individual initially entered possession without lawful permission. In other words, it is the status of the initial entry of the current occupancy that is significant in determining whether the occupant is a squatter; particularly when there was a "break" from a prior possession. For example, in *Mervco Holding LLC v. Gindi*, the Housing Part noted that the unlawful re-entry after having previously surrendered possession made the former Tenant a squatter, which required notice pursuant to RPAPL § 713(3), because the re-entry was not part of the continuous original tenancy, but instead a new possession which was without permission.[578]

8. POST-FORECLOSURE (10 OR 90 DAYS OR LONGER)

There have been occasions where Tenants have been evicted following foreclosures due to no fault of their own. These cases may involve "short sales," mortgage defaults, and other attempts at reconciliation between the lender and the former owner. Until mid-2009, when the owner lost title in a foreclosure action, the occupants were entitled to the same predicate notice as a squatter; i.e., a ten (10) day Notice to Quit.[579] Both the Federal and State governments have since enacted legislation enlarging many of the notice requirements for occupants of foreclosed dwellings.

The Federal Title VII Protecting Tenants at Foreclosure Act ("PTFA"), which originally took effect on May 20, 2009, substantially expanded the notice provisions for "bona fide Tenants" of foreclosed residential premises and properties involving federally-related mortgage loans.[580] A "bona fide Tenant" is defined as an individual rightfully in possession of the premises having entered into an agreement with the then owner, or other person with a superior interest in the property,

578 120 N.Y.S.3d 717 (N.Y. Civ. Ct. N.Y. Cnty. 2020).

579 RPAPL § 713(5).

580 PROTECTING TENANTS AT FORECLOSURE ACT OF 2009, Pub. Law No. 111-22, §§ 701-04, 123 Stat. 1660 (2009). The statute expired on December 31, 2014. However, in June 2018, section 304 of the Economic Growth, Regulatory Relief, and Consumer Protection Act restored the PTFA. *See* ECONOMIC GROWTH, REGULATORY RELIEF, AND CONSUMER PROTECTION ACT, Pub. Law No. 115-174, 132 Stat. 1296 (2018).

prior to the Notice of Foreclosure.

Absent a new agreement, the purchaser of the dwelling at a foreclosure "cannot look to a lease agreement in an effort to hold occupants liable for [the] payment of rent."[581] In addition, pursuant to RPAPL § 713, the "continued occupancy" by the former tenant following the foreclosure generally does not establish a Landlord and Tenant relationship between the new owner and the former Tenant.[582] However, the new owner may seek use and occupancy (not rent) for the time the former Tenant was in possession of the premises after gaining title, although in many instances, the new owner foregoes such moneys to gain possession at the earliest date.

The new owner must provide a bona fide Tenant with at least ninety (90) days written notice (see page 414 for service rules) prior to the commencement of a holdover proceeding. A bona fide Tenant with a written lease is entitled to remain in possession of the foreclosed property for either the ninety (90) day notice period or the remainder of the lease, whichever is greater, except where the new owner intends to occupy the property as a primary residence, in which case, a ninety (90) day notice will suffice regardless of the number of months remaining on the lease.[583] As a practical matter, a bona fide Tenant will present a copy of the lease to justify the extended notice period.

If the lease was executed after the filing of the notice of pendency in the foreclosure action, then the lease is voidable subject to the new owner's exercising of the option to void the agreement.[584] The new owner must void the lease (as opposed to terminating the lease) due to the foreclosure, which confirms the absence of a "landlord-tenant relationship" between the Tenant and the new owner, prior to commencement of a proceeding for possession pursuant to RPAPL § 713(5).[585]

581 U.S. Bank Trust, NA v. Alston, 162 N.Y.S.3d 909 (Pleasant Valley Just. Ct. 2022).

582 *Id.* (*citing* United Security Corp. v. Suchman, 307 N.Y. 48 (1954)).

583 Protecting Tenants at Foreclosure Act of 2009 § 702(a)(2).

584 Lakeland W. Capital XI, LLC v. Uvino, 134 N.Y.S.3d 125 (App. Term, 9th & 10th Jud. Dists. 2020).

585 BH 2628, LLC v. Zully's Bubbles Laundromat, Inc., 61 N.Y.S.3d 809 (App. Term, 2d, 11th & 13th Jud. Dists. 2017).

The reader should further be mindful that the Supreme Court's findings in the foreclosure proceeding may not be challenged in the Housing Part.[586]

A bona fide Tenant does not include the mortgagor (former owner) or the child, spouse, or parent of the mortgagor under the contract. In addition, a bona fide tenancy must be the result of an "arm's length transaction," and the rent may not be substantially less than the fair market value. If the rent is for a significantly reduced amount, then the rent must have been reduced or subsidized by a Federal, State, or local subsidy.[587]

An occupant who is not a bona fide Tenant is entitled to a written ten (10) day notice that must be formally served in accordance with RPAPL § 735.[588] The Notice to Quit may not be amended or re-served following commencement of the summary proceeding because, similar to other predicate notices, the notice is a prerequisite, and the Petition must accurately allege that the occupant "remained in possession after the expiration" of the date set forth within the notice.[589]

Under the HSTPA, if an occupant is removed from the premises following either a property or tax foreclosure, then the Court records of the summary proceeding relating to the lessee are sealed and "deemed confidential."[590] According to the express language of the statute, it appears that the eviction (i.e., removal), and not the summary proceeding, results in the sealing of the records in a post-foreclosure eviction summary proceeding.[591]

---

586 *See* JVJC Corp. v. Hampton, 121 N.Y.S.3d 507 (App. Term, 9th & 10th Jud. Dists. 2020); Kushnir v. Hartman, 110 N.Y.S.3d 862 (App. Term, 9th & 10th Jud. Dists. 2018); Nassau Homes Corp. v. Shuster, 941 N.Y.S.2d 539 (App. Term, 9th & 10th Jud. Dists. 2011); M & T Mortgage Corp. v. Larkins, 910 N.Y.S.2d 763 (App. Term, 2d, 11th & 13th Jud. Dists. 2010).

587 Protecting Tenants at Foreclosure Act of 2009 § 702(a)(2); Wilmington Trust, N.A. v. Holmes, 130 N.Y.S.3d 630 (N.Y. Civ. Ct. Queens Cnty. 2020).

588 RPAPL § 713(5); U.S. Bank Trust, N.A. v. Augustine, 159 N.Y.S.3d 661 (N.Y. Civ. Ct. Queens Cnty. 2022); *Wilmington Trust, N.A.*, 130 N.Y.S.3d at 630.

589 TD Bank, N.A. v. Yeshiva Chofetz Chaim, Inc., 17 N.Y.S.3d 386 (App. Term, 9th & 10th Jud. Dists. 2015).

590 RPAPL § 757 (HSTPA, L. 2019, c. 36, Part M, § 23).

591 *Id.*

A lessee in possession who was not joined in the mortgage foreclosure action may remain in possession of the foreclosed dwelling for the remainder of the lease.[592] This is because a Tenant is a necessary party to the foreclosure action, and the failure to name the Tenant "[l]eaves that party's rights unaffected by the judgment and sale, and the foreclosure sale may be considered void as to the omitted party."[593] However, a month-to-month Tenant is not a necessary party to the foreclosure[594] and, as a result, a month-to-month Tenant need not be named in the mortgage foreclosure action.[595]

If the foreclosed premises contains multiple families living independently in separate units or consists of both a residential apartment and a commercial store, then the owner must commence a separate summary proceeding for each independent area.[596] The PTFA does not create a private right of action for relief, but rather is intended to protect the rights of those impacted by the foreclosure.[597] New York has enacted a

---

592 1426 46th St., LLC v. Klein, 60 A.D.3d 740, at 742, 876 N.Y.S.2d 425 (2d Dep't 2009). A lease longer than three (3) years not recorded with the County Clerk is void as against a bona fide purchaser for value whose interest is first recorded. *See* RPL § 291; Hi-Rise Laundry Equip. Corp. v. Matrix Props., Inc., 96 A.D.2d 930, 466 N.Y.S.2d 375 (2d Dep't 1983).

593 Development Strategies Co., LLC v. Astoria Equities, Inc., 924 N.Y.S.2d 308 (App. Term, 9th & 10th Jud. Dists. 2011) (internal citations omitted); NYCTL 2012-A Trust v. Phillip, 145 A.D.3d 684, 43 N.Y.S.3d 96 (2d Dep't 2016). A party acquiring an interest in real property by conveyance recorded following the filing of the notice of pendency of the mortgage foreclosure action is not a necessary party to that action and "[i]s bound by all proceedings taken in the action...to the same extent as a party." Green Point Savings Bank v. St. Hilaire, 267 A.D.2d 203, 699 N.Y.S.2d 458 (2d Dep't 1999) (*citing* CPLR § 6501).

594 Eastern Savings Bank, FSB v. Whyte, 2016 U.S. Dist. LEXIS 45880 (E.D.N.Y. April 4, 2016).

595 *Id.* (*citing* In re Roberto Oligbo, 328 B.R. 619, 638 (Bankr. Ct. E.D.N.Y. 2005)); *see* 585 A.P. Lenox Assocs. v. 585 Lenox Ave. Assocs., 194 A.D.2d 380, 598 N.Y.S.2d 264, 265 (1st Dep't 1993).

596 *See* Bayview Loan Servicing, LLC v. Lyn-Jay, Inc., 54 N.Y.S.3d 609 (App. Term, 2d, 11th & 13th Jud. Dists. 2017) (noting that in New York City, residential and commercial eviction proceedings are commenced in separately-designated courtrooms); Loan First Cent. Savings Bank v. Yglesia, 2012 N.Y. Misc. LEXIS 4911 (App. Term, 9th & 10th Jud. Dists. Oct. 11, 2012).

597 Nativi v. Deutsche Bank Nat'l Trust Co., 2010 U.S. Dist. LEXIS 51697, at *9-10 (N.D. Cal. May 24, 2010).

statute comparable to the PTFA regarding judgments of foreclosure issued after January 13, 2010.[598]

To prevail in a holdover proceeding, the successor owner has the burden of proving: (1) ownership or other superior possessory interest over the occupant; (2) compliance with the relevant statutory notice provisions; and (3) that the occupant is not a bona fide Tenant with an existing lease.[599] In *Bank of Am. v. Owens*, the post-foreclosure proceeding was dismissed because the lender required a response to its questionnaire within five (5) days in lieu of service of a proper ten (10) day notice.[600]

RPAPL § 713(5) provides that a certified copy of the deed must be "exhibited" (i.e., presented for inspection) to the occupants prior to the commencement of a summary proceeding.[601] Attaching a certified copy of the referee's deed to the Notice to Quit that is formally served either personally upon a person of suitable age and discretion at the premises[602] or by conspicuous place service (i.e. "nail and mail")[603] satisfies the exhibition requirement. In *Plotch v. Dellis*, the Appellate Term for the Second, Eleventh and Thirteenth Judicial Districts adopted

598 RPAPL § 1305. Under New York law, the notice period for a bona fide Tenant is generally the greater of ninety (90) days or the duration of the rental agreement provided the Tenant is not the owner of the premises and the rent is not substantially less than the fair market rental value. The protections afforded Tenants pursuant to Federal "statutory schemes" and State rent regulations are applicable, and, therefore, must also be considered. *See id.*

599 Bank of Am., N.A. v. Owens, 903 N.Y.S.2d 667, 671 (Rochester City Ct. 2010). *See also* First Nat'l Bank of Chicago v. Silver, 73 A.D.3d 162, at 169-70, 899 N.Y.S.2d 256, 262 (2d Dep't 2010) (holding the foreclosing party has the burden of demonstrating compliance with the Home Equity Theft Prevention Act).

600 *Bank of Am.*, 903 N.Y.S.2d at 667.

601 *See* 769 E. LLC v. Ofori, 121 N.Y.S.3d 760 (N.Y. Civ. Ct. Bronx Cnty. 2020) (dismissing holdover proceeding where neither the referee's deed nor a certified copy of the deed was exhibited to the occupant).

602 *See* Midfirst Bank v. Ajala, 130 N.Y.S.3d 593 (App. Term, 9th & 10th Jud. Dists. 2020) (*citing* Plotch v. Dellis, 75 N.Y.S.3d 779 (App. Term, 2d, 11th & 13th Jud. Dists. 2018)); *Kushnir*, 110 N.Y.S.3d at 862; U.S. Bank Trust, N.A. v. Hayes, 94 N.Y.S.3d 809 (Mt. Vernon City Ct. 2019).

603 Federal Home Loan Mtg. Corp. v. McGibney, 114 N.Y.S.3d 554 (App. Term, 9th & 10th Jud. Dists. 2018); Citibank, N.A. v. Colucci, 110 N.Y.S.3d 202 (App. Term, 2d, 11th & 13th Jud. Dists. 2018).

substituted service as a viable form of service and, in doing so, further held that its prior ruling in *Home Loan Servs., Inc. v. Moskowitz,*[604] which held that personal delivery was the only acceptable form of service of the deed, was no longer the established law.[605]

Counsel may "subscribe" the accuracy of a certified copy of the deed by preparing an attorney certification pursuant to CPLR § 2105. In *Plotch*, although the original deed filed with the Court bore an original seal, the copy served lacked the same official marking. The Court nonetheless held that service was proper because counsel certified the original to be a "true and complete copy" of the original, which was also served on the occupants.[606]

Due to the high volume of foreclosures, there have been questions regarding the standing of foreign banks (out of state) to commence summary proceedings. Pursuant to Banking Law § 200, foreign banks that loan money within New York may "commence actions to enforce obligations under those mortgages" and, as a result, they have standing to commence a summary proceeding.[607]

9. TENANCY BY SUFFERANCE (30 DAYS)

A tenancy by sufferance is a hybrid situation where the occupant previously had lawful possession of the premises but refuses to vacate following termination of the primary Tenant's possessory interest. A tenancy by sufferance may result when a Subtenant, who was not named in the underlying summary proceeding, fails to leave after the Tenant vacated the premises due to the termination or expiration of the Tenant's rental agreement.[608]

Describing the relationship as a "tenancy" is a misnomer because the relationship is not that of Landlord and Tenant, but rather a claim

604 920 N.Y.S.2d 569 (App. Term, 2d, 11th & 13th Jud. Dists. 2011).

605 *Plotch*, 75 N.Y.S.3d at 779.

606 *Id.*

607 *See* First Wisconsin Trust Co. v. Hakimian, 237 A.D.2d 249, at 250, 654 N.Y.S.2d 808 (2d Dep't 1997); Deutsche Bank Nat'l Trust Co. v. Fleurimond, 2016 N.Y. Misc. LEXIS 1259 (Kings Cnty. Sup. Ct. Feb. 29, 2016).

608 *See, e.g.*, Mastas v. Extra Closet, Inc., 553 N.Y.S.2d 582 (N.Y. Civ. Ct. Kings Cnty. 1990).

by the occupant for adverse possession. The owner must provide a tenant by sufferance a thirty (30) day written notice, not necessarily one (1) month, prior to commencing a holdover proceeding, and the notice must be formally served in accordance with the CPLR and RPAPL.[609] Similar to a tenancy-at-will, the thirty (30) days need not end on any particular date, only that no fewer than thirty (30) days must be provided following service of the notice.

10. UNLAWFUL ACTIVITY (NO NOTICE TENANT/5 DAYS TO LANDLORD)

A rental agreement is void when the premises are used for "any illegal trade, manufacture or other business."[610] If the Tenants participate in a federally assisted income housing program governed by the United States Department of Housing and Urban Development ("HUD"), a local public agency may seek to evict the Tenants pursuant to either (1) the strict liability standards set forth in 42 U.S.C. §1437d or (2) the intent-based standards pursuant to RPAPL §§ 711(5) and 715.[611]

Under the federal statute, the decision to commence an eviction proceeding is within the discretion of the public housing agency.[612] When the public agency elects to proceed in this manner, the local housing agency's administrative procedures and protocols must be

609 *See* RPL § 228; Dolan § 30:39, at 446-47 (4th ed. 2010). *See also* Pondview Corp. v. Russand, Inc., 809 N.Y.S.2d 483 (Rockland Cnty. Sup. Ct. 2005); Lippe v. Professional Surgical Supply Co., Inc., 503 N.Y.S.2d 254 (N.Y. Civ. Ct. Queens Cnty. 1986).

610 RPL § 231; Shuhab HDFC v. Delacruz, 2020 N.Y.L.J. LEXIS 869 (N.Y. Civ. Ct. N.Y. Cnty. May 6, 2020). The owner or any Tenant within 200 feet of the premises has standing to seek an injunction to enjoin the continuation of the unlawful business. RPL § 231(6).

611 New York City Hous. Auth. v. Williams, 957 N.Y.S.2d 637 (N.Y. Civ. Ct. Bronx Cnty. 2010). Section 1437d(l)(6) of Title 42 of the United States Code provides that "any criminal activity that threatens the health, safety, or right to peaceful enjoyment of the premises by other tenants or any drug-related criminal activity on or off such premises, engaged in by a public housing tenant, any member of the tenant's household, or any guest or other person under the tenant's control, shall be cause for termination of [the tenancy]."

612 Department of Hous. and Urban Dev. v. Rucker, 535 U.S. 125, 122 S.Ct. 1230 (2002).

followed.[613] An advantage for the Petitioner is that it need not establish that the Tenant had actual "knowledge" or a "reason to know" of the unlawful activity.[614] Congress authorized no-fault evictions under these circumstances because "[r]egardless of knowledge, a tenant who 'cannot control drug crime, or other criminal activities by a household member which threaten the health or safety of other residents, is a threat to other residents.'"[615]

However, an eviction proceeding pursuant to the State provisions of RPAPL §§ 711(5)[616] and 715 requires a showing that the Tenant "knew or should have known" of the unlawful activity.[617] In *551 W. 172nd St. LLC v. Taveras*, the Appellate Term for the First Department dismissed the holdover proceeding because the evidence failed to establish that the Tenant knew or reasonably should have known that her adult son was selling drugs from the residence.[618] The evidence must further

613 *See, e.g.*, Matthews v. Hernandez, 2009 N.Y. Misc. LEXIS 4726 (N.Y. Cnty. Sup. Ct. April 28, 2009), *reargument granted*, 2009 N.Y. Misc. LEXIS 6015 (N.Y. Cnty. Sup. Ct. July 10, 2009).

614 *Rucker*, 535 U.S. at 125, 122 S.Ct. at 1230.

615 *Id.*

616 A special proceeding may be maintained where "[t]he premises, or any part thereof, are used or occupied as a bawdy-house, or house or place of assignation for lewd persons, or for the purposes of prostitution, or for any illegal trade or manufacture, or other illegal business." *See* RPAPL § 711(5).

617 *See* 551 W. 172nd St. LLC v. Taveras, 95 N.Y.S.3d 124 (App. Term, 1st Dep't 2018); Beautiful Vill. Assocs. Redevelop. Co. v. Gomez, 966 N.Y.S.2d 788 (App. Term, 1st Dep't 2012); *see also* Douglas v. New York City Hous. Auth., 126 A.D.3d 647, 4 N.Y.S.3d 495 (1st Dep't 2015) (eviction upheld following arrest and conviction of Tenant's son for drug activity at premises); Waterside Plaza Ground Lessee, LLC v. Hirsch, 18 N.Y.S.3d 582 (N.Y. Civ. Ct. N.Y. Cnty. 2015) (holding the Tenant knew or should have known the premises was utilized for the sale of heroin); *but see* WHGA Renaissance Apts., L.P. v. Jackson, 37 N.Y.S.3d 809 (App. Term, 1st Dep't 2016) (whether the Tenant had the capacity to know or should have known that her son was engaged in unlawful drug activities in the apartment is a question of fact). *Cf.* 518 W. 184th St. LLC v. Guzman, 7 N.Y.S.3d 818 (App. Term, 1st Dep't 2015) (elderly Tenant, who suffered from epilepsy, depression, and memory loss, did not have the requisite knowledge or reason to know that her adult son was using the premises to sell drugs); Second Farms Neighborhood HDFC v. Lessington, 932 N.Y.S.2d 763 (App. Term, 1st Dep't 2011) (Petitioner failed to prove that "the subject premises were used to facilitate trade in drugs and that the tenant knew or should have known of the activities and acquiesced in the illegal drug activity in the apartment").

618 *551 W. 172nd St. LLC*, 95 N.Y.S.3d at 124.

credibly establish that the premises were used "customarily or habitually" for illegal purposes, rather than a sporadic or isolated incident.[619]

A predicate notice is not required to be served upon the occupants, and the Landlord need not terminate the tenancy prior to commencing a summary proceeding pursuant to RPAPL § 711(5).[620] Recognizing the possibility that a Landlord may not be inclined to actively pursue an eviction, whether due to participation in the unlawful activity, acquiescence, or fear of retribution, RPAPL § 715(1) authorizes additional parties to commence a summary proceeding.

Both law enforcement agencies, such as a District Attorney's Office, and other Tenants residing within 200 feet of the premises have standing to commence an eviction proceeding to remove the occupants engaged in unlawful activity.[621] Where an authorized party other than the Landlord seeks to commence a summary proceeding, the interested party must first provide the Landlord a five (5) day written notice stating that a summary proceeding to remove the occupants will be commenced unless, within the notice period, the Landlord makes application for the removal of the occupants or, if having already done so, "good faith" measures are implemented to obtain a judgment and warrant of eviction.[622] Service of the five (5) day notice is to be made "personally upon the owner or landlord of the premises so used or

619 Riverside Park Comm., LLC v. Ventura, 2012 N.Y. Misc. LEXIS 4857 (N.Y. Civ. Ct. N.Y. Cnty. Oct. 12, 2012); New York City Hous. Auth. v. Grillasca, 852 N.Y.S.2d 610 (N.Y. Civ. Ct. N.Y. Cnty. 2007). *Cf.* 436-438 Assocs. v. Alvardo, 981 N.Y.S.2d 635 (N.Y. Civ. Ct. N.Y. Cnty. 2013) ("the mere fact that an arrest occurred at the subject apartment does not establish any guilt or that the subject apartment was used for illegal trade, manufacture, or other illegal business").

620 Spira v. Spiratone, Inc., 561 N.Y.S.2d 881 (N.Y. Civ. Ct. Queens Cnty. 1990); 410 Lenox Ave. Apts., Inc. v. Community II Supermarket, Inc., 516 N.Y.S.2d 432 (N.Y. Civ. Ct. N.Y. Cnty. 1987).

621 RPAPL § 715(1). The Court held that the District Attorney's letter requesting commencement of a holdover proceeding due to drug activity at the property, a copy of the search warrant, and the criminal lab reports constituted a sufficient termination notice. *See* Paul Robeson Houses Assoc., L.P. v. Harris, 58 N.Y.S.3d 875 (App, Term, 1st Dep't 2017).

622 RPAPL § 715(1).

occupied, or upon his agent."[623]

To prevail, the party bringing the proceeding must demonstrate the unlawful activity and the occupant's requisite knowledge. For example, in *New York City Hous. Auth. v. Fashaw*, the Housing Authority commenced a summary proceeding at the direction of the New York County District Attorney based upon alleged illicit drug activity at the residential property. The Housing Part dismissed the proceeding due to an inadequate showing of "customary and habitual" illegal drug activity at the premises and/or sufficient proof that the Respondent had constructive knowledge of the unlawful activity.[624]

In *People v. F.B.*, the Appellate Division, First Department denied the District Attorney's motion to unseal the criminal records of the Tenant that it sought to introduce as evidence in the summary proceeding.[625] The Court held that unsealing was inappropriate because the District Attorney was <u>not</u> acting as a law enforcement agency pursuant to Criminal Procedure Law § 160.55(1)(d)(ii).[626]

When RPAPL § 715 is invoked, the Petitioner's case takes "precedence over any similar proceeding thereafter brought" by the Landlord.[627] However, where the Landlord prosecutes a summary proceeding in good-faith, and reaches a settlement with the Tenant, the Landlord's decision prevails and a non-Landlord interested party may neither compel the Landlord to pursue an appeal nor pursue an appeal on its own.[628]

---

623 *Id.* The occupants in possession of the premises and the owner (or Landlord) <u>must</u> be named Respondents in a summary proceeding commenced pursuant to RPAPL § 715(1). *Id.*

624 *See* New York Hous. Auth. v. Fashaw, 46 N.Y.S.3d 475 (N.Y. Civ. Ct. N.Y. Cnty. 2016).

625 155 A.D.3d 1, 63 N.Y.S.3d 314 (1st Dep't 2017).

626 *Id.*

627 RPAPL § 715(1).

628 *See* 37-01 31st Ave. Realty Corp. v. Mohammed, 906 N.Y.S.2d 679 (App. Term, 2d, 11th & 13th Jud. Dists. 2010) (law enforcement agency's five (5) day notice does <u>not</u> take priority over Landlord's good-faith efforts to resolve the controversy).

11. VICTIM OF DOMESTIC VIOLENCE (10 DAYS)

The Real Property Law acknowledges the plight of victims of domestic violence and offers assistance with regard to residential leaseholds. Specifically, RPL § 227-c allows for the early termination of the tenancy (at the discretion of the Tenant) where an order of protection has been issued in favor of the Tenant due to domestic violence.

An application to terminate the tenancy must be made in the Criminal Court that issued the order of protection.[629] The statute provides that when an order of protection is in effect, the Tenant may terminate the tenancy after providing the Landlord and all co-Tenants ten (10) days written notice.[630] The Criminal Court must entertain the application, even where the underlying domestic violence dispute has been resolved, provided the order of protection remains in effect.[631]

The Tenant has the burden of demonstrating both: (1) a substantial risk of physical and/or emotional harm to the Tenant and/or his or her children if they remain in the premises (notwithstanding the order of protection) and (2) the Tenant made, but the Landlord refused, a request for early lease termination.[632] If the Criminal Court grants the Tenant's application for early lease termination, the termination date must be between thirty (30) and one hundred fifty (150) days following the due date of the next rent payment.[633] The Court's granting of the request is conditioned upon the Tenant being current on all rent payments through the termination date.[634] Finally, a lease provision waiving the rights afforded under RPL § 227-c is void as against public policy.[635]

A Tenant must generally affirmatively assert RPL § 227-c as a claim for the statute's early lease termination provisions to apply. However,

629 RPL § 227-c(2)(a).

630 *Id.*

631 *Id.*

632 *Id.* at § 227-c(2)(b).

633 *Id.* at § 227-c(2)(d).

634 *Id.* at § 227-c(2)[c].

635 *Id.* at § 227-c(4).

in *Riverwalk on the Hudson, Inc. v. Culliton*, the Albany City Court implemented the statute's protections *sua sponte* in a non-payment proceeding brought against the victim and her abusive husband.[636] The Housing Part noted that the victim had vacated the premises due to her husband's (co-Tenant) abusive behavior, and neither the victim nor the husband appeared in Court. Instead, testimony was taken from the victim's mother who described the abusive conduct. At the conclusion of the hearing, the Court severed the victim's financial obligations under the lease based upon RPL § 227-c, dismissed the Petition against her, and issued a default judgment against the defaulting husband only.[637] The Court reasoned that it would be "shockingly unjust and unfair" to enforce the joint and severability clause of the lease in a manner that a victim of domestic violence would have "[t]o pay the rent of her abuser."[638]

12. NOTICE TO CURE

A Notice to Cure provides the Tenant with notice of an alleged breach(es) of the lease that must be corrected during a "cure period" or the tenancy will be terminated.[639] The Notice to Cure must be served in the manner set forth within the rental agreement.[640] If service requirements are not specified, then the service provisions of the RPAPL and CPLR would presumably suffice but, at a minimum, proof of service should be memorialized.

The Notice to Cure must instruct the Tenant of the condition(s) that must be cured or the lease provision(s) claimed to have been breached

636 87 N.Y.S.3d 852 (Albany City Ct. 2018).

637 *Id.*

638 *Id.*

639 Lucky Dollar, Inc. v. Mount Cavalry Pentecostal Church, 2016 N.Y. Misc. LEXIS 474 (N.Y. Cnty. Sup. Ct. Feb. 8, 2016) (Notice to Cure for failing to maintain liability insurance defective due to lack of specificity).

640 *See* 146 Flushing Ave. v. 66S Fusion, Inc., 147 N.Y.S.3d 868 (App. Term, 2d, 11th & 13th Jud. Dists. 2021) (service of Notice to Cure untimely due to conflicting lease provisions); Benben v. DiMartini, 791 N.Y.S.2d 868 (App. Term, 9th & 10th Jud. Dists. 2004) (service of notice of default governed by the terms of the lease; not CPLR § 2103(a), which is applicable "only from the summons through post-judgment notices").

and the consequences for failing to cure the deficiencies.[641] Otherwise, the Notice to Cure is defective.[642] Since the Notice to Cure may not be amended, if the lone breach described within the notice is the Tenant's objectionable conduct, then the proceeding will be dismissed where the conduct ceases following service of the Notice to Cure.[643]

For commercial properties, the time to cure any defects may be extended by the Tenant obtaining a *Yellowstone* Injunction prior to the expiration of the cure period.[644] The cure period may also be extended based upon the parties' conduct. For example, in an illegal-sublet holdover proceeding, the cure period was extended to the commencement date of the summary proceeding where the parties had engaged in "extensive settlement negotiations" and, in the interim, the Landlord accepted a sublet application and payment.[645] If the Tenant fails to cure the deficiencies prior to the expiration of the cure period, then the subsequent termination notice must state a factual basis for the breach in order to demonstrate non-compliance with the Notice to Cure (i.e.,

---

641 *See, e.g.*, NY Kids Club 125 5th Ave. LLC v. Three Kings, LLC, 133 A.D.3d 850, 19 N.Y.S.3d 74 (2d Dep't 2015); Westhampton Cabins & Cabanas Owners Corp. v. Westhampton Bath & Tennis Club Owners Corp., 62 A.D.3d 987, 882 N.Y.S.2d 124 (2d Dep't 2009); 1346 Park Pl. HDFC v. Wright, 34 N.Y.S.3d 561 (App. Term, 2d, 11th & 13th Jud. Dists. 2016); Avalonbay Communities Inc. v. Visicaro, 2021 N.Y.L.J. LEXIS 1277 (Yonkers City Ct. Jan. 12, 2022).

642 Alir Inc. v. Jimenez, 2020 N.Y.L.J. LEXIS 1922 (N.Y. Civ. Ct. Bronx Cnty. Jan. 13, 2021); Kings Thorn LLC v. Walters, 116 N.Y.S.3d 862 (N.Y. Civ. Ct. Bronx Cnty. 2019); First Hous. Co. v. Orozco, 2019 N.Y.L.J. LEXIS 3063 (N.Y. Civ. Ct. Queens Cnty. Aug. 29, 2019). When the Landlord accepts rent with knowledge of a breach of a lease provision, the breach may be waived. If the lease contains a 'no waiver' provision, then the parties' intent is significant in determining enforcement of the Notice to Cure. *See* Jefpaul Garage Corp. v. Presbyterian Hosp. in the City of New York, 61 N.Y.2d 442, 474 N.Y.S.2d 458 (1984); Atkins Waste Materials, Inc. v. May, 34 N.Y.2d 422, 358 N.Y.S.2d 129 (1974).

643 *See generally* Tomfol Owners Corp. v. Hernandez, 201 A.D.3d 453, 156 N.Y.S.3d 732 (1st Dep't 2022) (Tenant alleged to have engaged in objectionable conduct vacated the premises following service of Notice to Cure due to a fire in the apartment).

644 *See, e.g.*, JDM Washington St. LLC v. 90 Washington St., LLC, 200 A.D.3d 612, 160 N.Y.S.3d 27 (1st Dep't 2021); Hargraves v. Tyler Towers Owners Corp., 189 A.D.3d 795, 136 N.Y.S.3d 119 (2d Dep't 2020). For a discussion on *Yellowstone* Injunctions, *see* Chapter 1, subdiv. F(1), *supra*.

645 Mansfield Owners, Inc. v. Bridgeman, 31 N.Y.S.3d 922 (App. Term, 2d, 11th & 13th Jud. Dists. 2016).

justification for commencing the summary proceeding).[646]

13. NOTICE TO TERMINATE DUE TO A BREACH OTHER THAN FOR THE NON-PAYMENT OF RENT

A Notice to Terminate a lease based upon a breach other than the non-payment of rent must state the consequences for failing to vacate the premises by the termination date. The Notice to Terminate is a "[c]ondition precedent to validly terminating the lease."[647] The parties should review the lease provisions regarding predicate notice and the manner in which the notice must be served. Regardless of any heightened obligations, the Landlord may not file a summary proceeding until after the termination date set forth in the notice.

The Notice to Terminate must: (1) unequivocally and unambiguously state the Landlord's basis for recovering possession; (2) advise the Tenant of the termination date; (3) be signed by the Landlord (or attorney or agent known by the Tenant); and (4) notify the Tenant that a summary proceeding will be commenced if the Tenant does not vacate the premises by the termination date.[648] The Notice to Terminate the tenancy must further identify the breached lease provisions so that the Tenant may adequately prepare a defense.[649]

646 BEC Continuum Owners v. Taylor, 2018 N.Y.L.J. LEXIS 1821 (N.Y. Civ. Ct. Kings Cnty. May 30, 2018).

647 *See* Metro Plaza Apts., Inc. v. Buchanan, 204 A.D.3d 45, 162 N.Y.S.3d 543 (3d Dep't 2022).

648 *See generally id.*; MKBH Mgmt. LLC v. Strachin, 149 N.Y.S.3d 883 (Mt. Vernon City Ct. 2021).

649 *Metro Plaza Apts., Inc.*, 204 A.D.3d at 45, 162 N.Y.S.3d at 543 (holding Notice of Termination was defective where "[i]t did not set forth the factual predicates, instead merely paraphras[ed] the lease and underlying regulation"); 69 E.M. LLC v. Mejia, 29 N.Y.S.3d 849 (App. Term, 1st Dep't 2015); *see also* 157 Broadway Assoc., LLC v. Berroa, 112 N.Y.S.3d 854 (App. Term, 1st Dep't 2018) (holding that "[b]road, unparticularized allegations were too generic and conclusory to describe a nuisance in violation of [the Rent Stabilization Code]").

14. SECTION 8 HOUSING (SIMULTANEOUS SERVICE ON PUBLIC HOUSING AUTHORITY)

A federal Section 8 subsidized rental program, such as the Housing Choice Voucher Program pursuant to 42 U.S.C. § 1437(f) and 24 C.F.R. § 982 *et seq.*, offers rental assistance to qualifying households. Under the Housing Choice Voucher Program, the Landlord and Section 8 Tenant enter into a lease agreement for at least one (1) year.[650] In addition, the Landlord enters into a Housing Assistance Payment ("HAP") contract with the local Public Housing Agency ("PHA") which authorizes the PHA to send the rent-subsidized payments to the Landlord.[651]

For rent-stabilized premises, the Landlord's acceptance of a Section 8 rent subsidy is a "term and condition" of the tenancy that continues upon lease renewal.[652] Section 8 Tenants are required to re-certify their income annually, and the failure to do so constitutes a basis for termination from the program.[653]

a. GROUNDS FOR TERMINATION

Once obtained, there is "[n]o law, order, rule, request or direction that imposes upon a Section 8 recipient the obligation to preserve his subsidy."[654] In other words, participation in the Section 8 program is voluntary, and the Tenant's failure to maintain these benefits, absent a

650 *See* 24 C.F.R. § 982.309(a). An initial lease for a duration of less than one (1) year may be approved by the Public Housing Agency where the shorter term improves the Tenant's housing opportunities and the term represents the "prevailing local market practice." *Id.* at § 982.309(a)(2).

651 *Id.* at § 982.1(b).

652 Rosario v. Diagonal Realty, LLC, 8 N.Y.3d 755, 840 N.Y.S.2d 748 (2007) (holding that once accepted, the Landlord may not change the terms and conditions by "opting out" of the Section 8 rent subsidy payments in a renewal lease); Valentine Towers v. Torres, 145 N.Y.S.3d 755 (App. Term, 1st Dep't 2021) (holdover proceeding dismissed upon reinstatement of Section 8 subsidy).

653 Riverview II Preserv., L.P. v. Brice-Frazier, 13 N.Y.S.3d 852 (App. Term, 9th & 10th Jud. Dists. 2015); *Alir Inc.*, 2020 N.Y.L.J. LEXIS at 1922. If the Department of Housing Preservation and Development terminates a Section 8 program, the Tenant has four (4) months to challenge the determination in an Article 78 proceeding. *See* CPLR § 217(1); Banos v. Rhea, 25 N.Y.3d 266, 11 N.Y.S.3d 515 (2015); Torres v. Hernandez, 2005 N.Y. Misc. LEXIS 8563 (N.Y. Cnty. Sup. Ct. March 23, 2005).

654 Grand Concourse E. HDFC v. DeJesus, 84 N.Y.S.3d 318 (N.Y. Civ. Ct. Bronx Cnty. 2018).

lease violation, is <u>not</u> a basis to terminate the lease.[655]

The grounds for terminating a Section 8 tenancy include: (1) a "serious or repeated violation" of the lease; (2) violation of Federal, State, or local law; (3) criminal activity that threatens the quiet use and enjoyment of others; (4) drug-related criminal activity; and (5) for other good cause shown.[656] The failure to pay the rent falls under the category of a "serious violation" of the lease.[657]

b. TENANT RESPONSIBLE ONLY FOR THE TENANT'S SHARE OF THE RENT

A Section 8 Tenant is only responsible for his or her portion of the rent,[658] which according to the Brooke Amendment of the United States Housing Act, is limited to the greater of thirty percent (30%) percent of the family's monthly adjusted income, ten percent (10%) of the family's income, or other amount determined by the public agency.[659] In *Harborview Props. I, LLC v. Valentin*, the Justice Court held that a Landord "[m]ay not pursue the tenant for non-payment of rent owed by DSS, since it would exceed the lawful amount that tenant is

---

655 Jarvis Realty v. Smith, 2019 N.Y.L.J. LEXIS 2213 (N.Y. Civ. Ct. N.Y. Cnty. June 26, 2019).

656 *See* 42 U.S.C. § 1437-f(d); *Rosario*, 8 N.Y.3d at 755, 840 N.Y.S.2d at 748. The term "other good cause" includes: (1) a failure to accept a new lease by the family; (2) family history of disturbances or destruction of the premises; (3) owner's intended use of the premises for personal reasons or another purpose non-residential in nature; and (4) business or economic reasons such as the sale of the premises. 24 C.F.R § 982.310(d).

657 24 C.F.R. § 982.310(a)(1). The termination of a Section 8 Tenant's rent subsidy may be challenged in an Article 78 proceeding in Supreme Court; not a summary proceeding. *See* 60 St. Nicholas Ave. HDFC v. Edwards, 13 N.Y.S.3d 853 (App. Term, 1st Dep't 2015).

658 *See* Seabury v. Galloway, 130 N.Y.S.3d 188 (App. Term, 9th & 10th Jud. Dists. 2020); McDonnell v. Mitchell, 100 N.Y.S.3d 610 (App. Term, 9th & 10th Jud. Dists. 2018) (reducing the money judgment to reflect the Section 8 Tenant's share of the rent).

659 *See* 42 U.S.C. § 1437a; 24 C.F.R. § 982.54. *See also Riverview II Preserv., L.P.*, 13 N.Y.S.3d at 852 (dismissing summary proceeding where rent and electricity charges exceeded thirty percent (30%) of the Tenant's monthly adjusted income).

responsible for as a Section 8 voucher recipient."[660]

In a non-payment proceeding, "added rent" items, such as attorney's fees and late fees, may not be awarded against a Section 8 Tenant under any circumstance.[661] However, the Tenant may be responsible for use and occupancy (the full amount) if the Tenant holds over following termination of the Section 8 Agreement.[662] The failure of the PHA to pay the Landlord its proportionate share of the rent is not grounds to terminate the tenancy.[663]

A Federal rent subsidy payment must be applied to the month the payment was received and may not be utilized for prior arrears.[664] When the lease expires, a Section 8 tenancy (for leases entered into after 1995) may be terminated in the same manner as other tenancies absent an agreement to re-new.[665]

However, where a Section 8 tenancy is terminated or expires by its own terms, a non-payment proceeding may not be commenced to "recover the Section 8 portion of the rent even after the subsidy has terminated."[666] For example, in *Underhill Ave. Realty v. Ramos*, the Appellate Term for the Second, Eleventh and Thirteenth Judicial

---

660 94 N.Y.S.3d 538 (Greenburgh Just. Ct. 2018); *see* Regency Vill. Mgmt. v. Rodriguez, 121 N.Y.S.3d 510 (App. Term, 9th & 10th Jud. Dists. 2020); Port Chester Hous. Auth. v. Turner, 734 N.Y.S.2d 805 (App. Term, 9th & 10th Jud. Dists. 2001); Douglas v. Nole, 867 N.Y.S.2d 16 (Nassau Cnty. Dist. Ct. 2008).

661 *Regency Vill. Mgmt.*, 121 N.Y.S.3d at 510; Greenburgh Hous. Auth. v. Hall, 58 N.Y.S.3d 874 (App. Term, 9th & 10th Jud. Dists. 2017).

662 Zappala v. Caputo, 851 N.Y.S.2d 62 (App. Term, 9th & 10th Jud. Dists. 2007); McCurdy v. Williams, 953 N.Y.S.2d 550 (App. Term, 2d, 11th & 13th Jud. Dists. 2012); Community Props. v. McCloud, 2003 N.Y. Misc. LEXIS 905 (App. Term, 9th & 10th Jud. Dists. June 3, 2003).

663 24 C.F.R. at § 982.310(b); *Harborview Props. I, LLC*, 94 N.Y.S.3d at 538.

664 Ioppolo v. Haerle, N.Y.L.J., Oct. 30, 2001, at 20, col. 6 (App. Term, 9th & 10th Jud. Dists. 2001).

665 *See* Numme v. Lemon, 741 N.Y.S.2d 384 (App. Term, 9th & 10th Jud. Dists. 2002). The lease of a Section 8 Tenant entered into prior to 1996 was automatically renewed absent "good cause" for an eviction. *Id.* The automatic renewal provision was subsequently eliminated by 42 U.S.C. § 1437f(d)(1)(B)(ii), which inserted the phrase "*during the term of the lease*" when referencing reasons to terminate the tenancy. *Id.* (emphasis added).

666 Ocean Bay RAD LLC v. Battle, 2021 N.Y.L.J. LEXIS 1267 (N.Y. Civ. Ct. Queens Cnty. Jan. 10, 2022).

Districts dismissed the non-payment proceeding following the Section 8 Tenant's holding over after the tenancy was terminated due to the Landlord's predecessor's "refus[al] to issue a renewal lease."[667] In other words, mere approval of a Section 8 subsidy is insufficient to re-establish a Landlord and Tenant relationship and, due to the absence of an agreement for the payment of rent, a non-payment proceeding is improper.[668] Instead the Landlord may commence a holdover proceeding and seek to recover use and occupancy.[669]

The HUD Handbook, Federal regulations, and Section 8 rental agreements set forth the prerequisites for terminating a Section 8 tenancy. Strict compliance with these provisions, in addition to the RPAPL and RPL, is required regarding the content and service of notices, recertification documents, and lease termination.[670] The Landlord must further comply with the RPAPL and RPL in the preparation and service of predicate notices, such as a proper rent demand.[671]

The predicate notice must be simultaneously provided in writing

667 29 N.Y.S.3d 850 (App. Term, 2d, 11th & 13th Jud. Dists. 2015).

668 Parkville Realty Assn. v. Woodward, 140 N.Y.S.3d 349 (App. Term, 2d, 11th & 13th Jud. Dists. 2021); Rutland Rd. Assoc., L.P. v. Grier, 55 N.Y.S.3d 694 (App. Term, 2d, 11th & 13th Jud. Dists. 2017).

669 *See* Casco Bay Realty, LP v. Concepcion, 121 N.Y.S.3d 505 (App. Term, 9th & 10th Jud. Dists. 2020); *Underhill Ave. Realty, LLC*, 29 N.Y.S.3d at 850 (noting that the Landlord may commence a plenary action for use and occupancy).

670 *See, e.g.*, 2013 Amsterdam Ave. Hous. Assn., L.P. v. King, 98 N.Y.S.3d 775 (App. Term, 1st Dep't 2019); Crotona Park Redevlop. LLC v. Williams, 2020 N.Y.L.J. LEXIS 418 (N.Y. Civ. Ct. Bronx Cnty. Feb. 24, 2020); SEBCO IV Assocs. LP v. Colon, 115 N.Y.S.3d 614 (N.Y. Civ. Ct. Bronx Cnty. 2019).

671 *See, e.g.*, Rippy v. Kyer, 885 N.Y.S.2d 713 (App. Term, 9th & 10th Jud. Dists. 2009); Clinton Arms Assocs. v. Robinson, 2020 N.Y.L.J. LEXIS 771 (N.Y. Civ. Ct. Bronx Cnty. April 8, 2020).

to both the Tenant and PHA.[672] The rationale for simultaneous service upon the agency is to afford the PHA ample opportunity to withhold payments and to monitor the Landlord's conduct and the conditions of the premises, and to make a determination whether intervention on behalf of the Section 8 Tenant is required.[673]

In addition, a notice terminating the tenancy must, *inter alia*, "advise [the] tenant that 'he/she has 10 days within which to discuss termination of the tenancy with the owner,'"[674] and further give notice that a Tenant with a disability may request a reasonable accommodation to partake in the hearing.[675] With regard to the Petition, it must allege the relevant regulatory status of the tenancy (e.g., Section 8) and the Landlord's compliance with Section 8 regulations and requirements.[676] The omission of a germane allegation, while a defense to the proceeding, does not necessarily render the Petition jurisdictionally defective (i.e., depending on the defect, the proceeding may be able to

672 24 C.F.R. § 982.310(e); 700 Brooklyn Realty, LLC v. Bklyn Realty, LLC, 154 N.Y.S.3d 732 (App. Term, 2d, 11th & 13th Jud. Dists. 2021); Vanbur Estates LLC v. Quick, 2018 N.Y.L.J. LEXIS 1173 (N.Y. Civ. Ct. Kings Cnty. April 11, 2018); Douglas v. Latimer, 901 N.Y.S.2d 905 (Nassau Cnty. Dist. Ct. 2009); Lamlon Dev. Corp. v. Owens, 533 N.Y.S.2d 186, 191 (Nassau Cnty. Dist. Ct. 1988) (holding the failure to simultaneously serve notice on the public housing authority is a jurisdictional defect). In addition to personal delivery, 24 C.F.R. § 247.4(b) permits service of the termination notice on an individual of suitable discretion at least eighteen (18) years of age or on a minor under the age of eighteen (18) "[e]mancipated to act on his or her own behalf, including the ability to execute a contract or lease." *But see* Cromwell Towers Redev. Co., L.P. v. Blackwell, 966 N.Y.S.2d 345 (App. Term, 9th & 10th Jud. Dists. 2012) (dismissing summary proceeding where termination notice was served on the Section 8 Tenant's 16-year-old son).

673 *Douglas*, 901 N.Y.S.2d at 905.

674 *2013 Amsterdam Ave. Hous. Assn., L.P.*, 98 N.Y.S.3d at 775 (dismissing summary proceeding where notice stated in violation of HUD requirements that the Landlord "may" meet with the Tenant to discuss lease termination, when the Landlord was "required" to meet with the Tenant before terminating the tenancy, if requested).

675 *Id.*

676 Brookwood Coram I, LLC v. Oliva, 15 N.Y.S.3d 710 (App. Term, 9th & 10th Jud. Dists. 2015); East 168th St. Assocs. v. Castillo, 79 N.Y.S.3d 485 (N.Y. Civ. Ct. Bronx Cnty. 2018).

continue).[677]

c. SOURCE OF INCOME

Several local governing authorities have enacted ordinances that make it unlawful to refuse to offer a lease to a prospective Tenant based upon source of income considerations (i.e., recipient of financial assistance). These ordinances generally provide that a prospective Tenant's income is a non-factor in determining whether a lease should be offered, provided the prospective Tenant's income is obtained from a lawful source. For example, New York City, Nassau County, and Suffolk County, to name a few, have implemented such provisions.[678] Where source of income legislation has been enacted, the law is routinely enforced by the municipality's Office of Human Rights.[679]

15. CHRONIC RENT DELINQUENCY (NO NOTICE)

Absent a lease provision requiring notice, a Landlord need <u>not</u> serve a predicate notice prior to commencing a holdover proceeding due to

677 433 West Assocs. v. Murdock, 276 A.D.2d 360, 715 N.Y.S.2d 6 (1st Dep't 2000); Harway Terrace, Inc. v. Petropiento, 155 N.Y.S.3d 29 (App. Term, 2d, 11th & 13th Jud. Dists. 2021); *Rippy*, 885 N.Y.S.2d at 713; Bennett v. Brooks, 153 N.Y.S.3d 833 (Mt. Vernon City Ct. 2021).

678 NYC ADMIN. CODE 8-107(5)(a); NASSAU COUNTY LOCAL LAW No. 9-2006 (Nassau County's Human Rights Law); SUFFOLK COUNTY LOCAL LAW No. 25-2014, § 528-9 (Suffolk County's Human Rights Law). Exceptions to the Suffolk County law include, but are not limited to, where the individuals at issue are under the age of eighteen (18), age 55-and-over communities, and owner occupied single- and two-family dwellings. SUFFOLK COUNTY LOCAL LAW No. 25-2014, at § 528-9[C]. *See, e.g.*, Yorkville Plaza Assoc., LLC v. Reynolds, 146 N.Y.S.3d 382 (N.Y. Civ. Ct. N.Y. Cnty. 2021).

679 *See, e.g.*, NYC ADMIN. CODE 8-107(5)(a); NASSAU COUNTY LOCAL LAW No. 9-2006; SUFFOLK COUNTY LOCAL LAW No. 25-2014, § 528-9. In *Olivierre v. Parkchester Preservation Co., L.P.*, the New York State Supreme Court, in showing deference to the regulations of the State and New York City Divisions of Human Rights, held that a Landlord may <u>not</u> impose income guidelines on a Tenant who is the recipient of a subsidy that guarantees the rent and any damages that may be caused by the Tenant. *Olivierre*, Index No. 452058/22 (N.Y. Cnty. Sup. Ct. July 28, 2022) (unpublished decision).

the Tenant's "chronic non-payment" of rent.[680] Chronic non-payment of rent is different from the occasional non-payment of rent and, as a result, the Landlord has the option of commencing a non-payment proceeding (predicate notice required) or a holdover proceeding (no predicate notice).

This is the case even where the rental agreement states that a non-payment proceeding is required.[681] The reasoning is that where the Tenant chronically fails to pay rent on time, a holdover proceeding is appropriate because there has been a violation of a substantial obligation of the leasehold.[682]

A Landlord will typically demonstrate that "[i]t was compelled to bring numerous nonpayment proceedings within a relatively short period of time and that the tenant's non-payment was willful, unjustified, without explanation, or accompanied by an intent to harass the landlord…."[683] Although the number and frequency of the non-payment proceedings are considered, they are "[r]elevant only in the context of the entire circumstances surrounding the alleged withholding of rent."[684] A chronic non-payment proceeding may <u>not</u> be substantiated from just one (1) missed payment of rent.[685]

The case law has resulted in varied outcomes. For example, summary judgment was awarded in favor of a Landlord who commenced five (5) non-payment proceedings over three and one-half (3½) years

680 Definitions Personal Fitness, Inc. v. 133 E. 58th St. LLC, 107 A.D.3d 617, 967 N.Y.S.2d 647 (1st Dep't 2013); 3363 Sedgewick, L.L.C. v. Medina, 723 N.Y.S.2d 592 (App. Term, 1st Dep't 2000).

681 *Definitions Personal Fitness, Inc.*, 107 A.D.3d at 617, 967 N.Y.S.2d at 647.

682 *See* Adam's Tower Lim. P'ship v. Richter, 717 N.Y.S.2d 825 (App. Term, 1st Dep't 2000); Time Equities Assoc. LLC v. McKenith, 113 N.Y.S.3d 479 (N.Y. Civ. Ct. N.Y. Cnty. 2019).

683 25th Realty Assocs. v. Griggs, 150 A.D.2d 155, 540 N.Y.S.2d 434 (1st Dep't 1989); *Time Equities Assoc. LLC*, 113 N.Y.S.3d at 479 (seven (7) non-payment proceedings in seven (7) years).

684 Prince Holding 2012 LLC v. Simmons, 2021 N.Y.L.J. LEXIS 803 (N.Y. Civ. Ct. N.Y. Cnty. Aug. 6, 2021).

685 Spencer Scott Group LLC v. Nahas, 2022 N.Y.L.J. LEXIS 130 (N.Y. Civ. Ct. Richmond Cnty. Feb. 23, 2022) (holding "[a]lthough there is no magic number of proceedings required to maintain a chronic rent delinquency, there must be a history of more than one").

and, in each of those proceedings, the Tenant failed to assert a viable defense.[686] Similarly, chronic non-payment of rent claims have been successful after: (1) six (6) non-payment proceedings were commenced in four and one-half (4½) years[687] and (2) four (4) non-payment proceedings were commenced in three (3) years.[688]

On the other hand, it has been held that two (2) non-payment proceedings over the span of five (5) years failed to give rise to a chronic non-payment holdover proceeding.[689] The Housing Part similarly held in *279 E. 92nd St. Corp v. Grose* that three (3) non-payment proceedings in six (6) years was insufficient to state a chronic rent delinquency claim when the non-payment of rent on all three (3) occasions was due to the Tenant's medical condition which resulted in her "[g]oing on disability for months at a time."[690]

In *FM United LLC v. Dulle-Wollin*, the Appellate Term for the First Department held that the Landlord's execution of a renewal lease, which was required pursuant to the Rent Stabilization Code, did <u>not</u> warrant dismissal of the chronic non-payment of rent holdover proceeding.[691] The Court reasoned that since the Landlord was required to continue with the tenancy, and did not overtly act in a manner inconsistent with lease termination, the "act of renewing the lease was not one of free will but [rather] of adhering to the requirements of law."[692]

---

686 Tenth St. Holdings, LLC v. McKowen, 31 N.Y.S.3d 924 (App. Term, 1st Dep't 2016); *see generally* Rosa v. New York City Hous. Auth., Straus Houses, 160 A.D.3d 499, 76 N.Y.S.3d 5 (1st Dep't 2018).

687 Zevrone Realty Corp. v. Gumaneh, 37 N.Y.S.3d 209 (App. Term, 1st Dep't 2016); *Definitions Personal Fitness, Inc.*, 107 A.D.3d at 617, 967 N.Y.S.2d at 647 (Tenant's motion for an injunction denied where Landlord commenced ten (10) non-payment proceedings in seven (7) years).

688 GIT LEB, LLC v. Golphin, 38 N.Y.S.3d 830 (App. Term, 2d, 11th & 13th Jud. Dists. 2016). *Cf.* Fleetwood Holdings I, LLC v. Smith, 109 N.Y.S.3d 567 (Mt. Vernon City Ct. 2018) (holding that three (3) meritorious non-payment proceedings within twenty (20) months does <u>not</u> constitute chronic delinquent rent).

689 3424 Dekalb Assocs. v. Pabon, 2019 N.Y.L.J. LEXIS 383 (N.Y. Civ. Ct. Bronx Cnty. Feb. 6, 2019).

690 2017 N.Y.L.J. LEXIS 1187 (N.Y. Civ. Ct. Kings Cnty. May 10, 2017).

691 5 N.Y.S.3d 327 (App. Term, 1st Dep't 2014).

692 *Id.*; Grandview Park Assoc., LLC v. Lundy, 105 N.Y.S.3d 815 (Mt. Vernon City Ct. 2019).

However, where the Landlord voluntarily re-news the lease, a holdover proceeding for the chronic non-payment of rent is improper because a holdover proceeding presumes the parties do not have a Landlord and Tenant relationship when the proceeding is commenced (i.e., a non-payment proceeding would be required).[693]

16. NUISANCE (RENT-STABILIZED PREMISES) (7 DAYS)

The Landlord of a rent-stabilized property in New York City may terminate the tenancy of a Tenant whose conduct arises to a nuisance or who allows others to partake in such conduct within the premises. The Tenant is entitled to at least seven (7) days written notice prior to the commencement of a holdover proceeding.[694] The notice, which is not an opportunity to cure,[695] must be sufficiently detailed to provide the Tenant a reasonable opportunity to prepare a defense.[696]

The New York Codes, Rules and Regulations at 9 N.Y.C.R.R. § 2524.3(b) provides that a "nuisance" occurs where the Tenant: (1) with malicious intent or by gross negligence, "substantially" damages the premises or (2) "engages in a persistent and continuing course of conduct evidencing an unwarrantable, unreasonable or unlawful use of the property to the annoyance, inconvenience, discomfort or damage of others, the primary purpose of which is intended to harass the owner or other tenants or occupants of the same or adjacent building."[697] In

---

693 Nyack Plaza v. Parker, 856 N.Y.S.2d 25 (App. Term, 9th & 10th Jud. Dists. 2007). *Cf.* Greenport Preserv., L.P. v. Heyward, 160 N.Y.S.3d 734 (App. Term, 9th & 10th Jud. Dists. 2021) (non-payment proceeding is improper type of proceeding when Landlord terminated tenancy prior to commencement of summary proceeding).

694 *See* RSC [9 N.Y.C.R.R.] § 2524.2[c](2).

695 *See generally* Metellus v. Torres-Springer, 171 A.D.3d 618, 97 N.Y.S.3d 466 (1st Dep't 2019) (although not required, Tenant afforded multiple opportunities to cure the nuisance conduct, but failed to do so).

696 Hollis Partners, LLC v. Artis, 152 N.Y.S.3d 546 (App. Term, 2d, 11th & 13th Jud. Dists. 2021) (dismissing proceeding alleging eight (8) separate nuisance incidents where predicate notice failed to allege breaches of substantial tenancy obligations or illegal occupancy); *69 E.M. LLC*, 29 N.Y.S.3d at 849; Site 15 Affordable Assocs. LLC v. Merkinson, 2021 N.Y. Misc. LEXIS 4965 (N.Y. Civ. Ct. N.Y. Cnty. April 5, 2021).

697 *See* RSC [9 N.Y.C.R.R.] § 2524.3(b); *see* Tzifil Realty Corp. v. Rodriguez, 155 N.Y.S.3d 525 (App. Term, 2d, 11th & 13th Jud. Dists. 2021); Giga Greenpoint Realty, LLC v. Mounier, 110 N.Y.S.3d 867 (App. Term, 2d, 11th & 13th Jud. Dists. 2018).

other words, to prevail, the Petitioner must demonstrate either substantial damage to the premises resulted from the Tenant's gross negligence (or any higher standard such as "knowledge" and/or "intent") or the Tenant's conduct "interfered with the use or enjoyment" of the premises over a period of time.[698]

Threatening the safety and comfort of others may substantiate a nuisance claim.[699] For example, making repeated threats and participating in "physically violent conduct" towards the property manager was held to constitute an actionable nuisance.[700] Although there is no bright-line rule, it has been held that a "handful of [obnoxious noise] complaints over the course of more than one year" did <u>not</u> constitute an ongoing pattern that threatened the comfort and safety of the other occupants.[701]

A nuisance holdover proceeding based upon the Tenant's smoking within the premises was similarly dismissed when the Housing Part concluded that "[s]moking in the privacy of [her] own apartment was

---

698 *See* Sharp v. Norwood, 89 N.Y.2d 1068, 659 N.Y.S.2d 834 (1997); *Giga Greenpoint Realty, LLC*, 110 N.Y.S.3d at 867 (a single noise incident does <u>not</u> constitute a nuisance); Tanya Towers, Inc. v. Hurtado, 114 N.Y.S.3d 819 (N.Y. Civ. Ct. N.Y. Cnty. 2019) (dismissing proceeding where Landlord failed to demonstrate Tenant created alleged fire hazards and "harbor[ed] two finches and one pigeon").

699 Frank v. Park Summit Realty Corp., 175 A.D.2d 33, 573 N.Y.S.2d 655 (1st Dep't 1991); 529 W. 29th LLC v. Reyes, 100 N.Y.S.3d 475 (App. Term, 1st Dep't 2019) (holding that the Tenant, who suffered from schizophrenia and mood disorders, engaged in nuisance conduct by starting two (2) building fires in three (3) months). *Cf.* 121 Irving MGM, LLC v. Perez, 115 N.Y.S.3d 805 (App. Term, 2d, 11th & 13th Jud. Dists. 2019) (Tenant's preparation and sale of more than a dozen lunches outside the commercial premises six (6) days per week was <u>not</u> a nuisance, in part, due to the absence of any complaints).

700 Peters v. Owens, 18 N.Y.S.3d 581 (App. Term, 1st Dep't 2015) (ongoing "belligerent and aggressive" behavior towards Tenants and building staff constitutes a nuisance); Mautner-Glick Corp. v. Tunne, 966 N.Y.S.2d 347 (App. Term, 2d, 11th & 13th Jud. Dists. 2012) (Tenant's abusive conduct towards the superintendent's spouse and building staff substantiated nuisance claim).

701 150 W. 21st LLC v. John Doe, 31 N.Y.S.3d 922 (App. Term, 1st Dep't 2016); Timston Corp. v. Kienzle, 2019 N.Y.L.J. LEXIS 2645 (N.Y. Civ. Ct. N.Y. Cnty. July 31, 2019) ("mutual disdain" and "relatively few undesirable instances" during the forty-two (42) year tenancy did not amount to a nuisance). *Cf.* 443 E. 78 Realty LLC v. Tupas, 14 N.Y.S.3d 610 (App. Term, 1st Dep't 2015) (the collection of refuse and debris "from the floor to ceiling" constitutes a nuisance).

not so unreasonable in the circumstances presented."[702] Overly broad conclusory allegations that the Tenant acted in "some undefined 'anti-social, disruptive, destructive, and/or illegal behavior'" are similarly inadequate.[703] On the other hand, a conclusory denial, without more, fails to demonstrate a meritorious defense.[704]

The spouse or the adult child of the primary Tenant does <u>not</u> automatically assume the lease of a rent-regulated apartment following the eviction. Instead, family members' rights are governed by 9 N.Y.C.R.R. § 2204.6(d), which provides that a family member assumes succession rights where he or she co-occupied the premises as a primary residence for at least the two (2) years (one (1) year if the Tenant is a senior citizen or disabled) immediately <u>prior</u> to the Tenant's death or removal.[705] The determination of whether continuous occupancy is satisfied typically presents issues of fact.

---

702 Priceman Family, LLC v. Kerrigan, 135 N.Y.S.3d 762 (App. Term, 2d, 11th & 13th Jud. Dists. 2020).

703 *69 E.M. LLC*, 29 N.Y.S.3d at 849.

704 *See* ADM Mgmt. Corp. v. Mathews, 116 N.Y.S.3d 484 (App. Term, 1st Dep't 2019).

705 *See generally* 5539-181 & 182 Prospect Park W. Brooklyn, LLC v. Caseres, 159 N.Y.S.3d 612 (App. Term, 2d, 11th & 13th Jud. Dists. 2022) (granting possession to Landlord where the testimony of the Tenant's son "lacked credibility, and there was insufficient documentary evidence to connect occupant to the apartment for actual living purposes for the relevant two-year period"); K & L Chan Realty Inc. v. Lee, 126 N.Y.S.3d 604 (App. Term, 1st Dep't 2020) (son failed to "adduce any documentary evidence showing that he resided in the apartment during the relevant period . . ., and the court rejected the testimonial evidence of respondent and his mother because [the testimony] was inconsistent, faulty and flawed"); M. M. & I. Realty Co., L.L.C. v. Gargano, 998 N.Y.S.2d 556 (App. Term, 2d, 11th & 13th Jud. Dists. 2014) (reversing Housing Part Order granting possession of rent-regulated apartment to Landlord because the ex-wife of the nuisance Tenant was entitled to succession rights and an opportunity to cure the default). *See* RSC [9 N.Y.C.R.R.] § 2204.6(d)(1),(3).

17. REFUSAL TO RE-NEW RENT-STABILIZED PREMISES (LANDLORD'S PRIMARY RESIDENCE) (90–150 DAYS)

A Tenant in a rent-stabilized apartment must be offered a renewal lease provided the Tenant continues to pay rent.[706] There is an exception where an owner seeks to recover possession "due to [an] immediate and compelling necessity" to occupy the dwelling either as his or her own primary residence or the primary residence of an immediate family member.[707] In such a situation, the owner is not required to offer the Tenant a renewal lease.[708] The HSTPA limits the number of units that may be recovered for this purpose to a single dwelling.[709]

In New York City, the Landlord must provide the Tenant written notice to vacate the premises, commonly referred to as a "Golub notice," between ninety (90) and one hundred fifty (150) days prior to the expiration of the lease where the owner intends to use the apartment as a primary residence .[710] The statute does not require a specific form of service, but the case law, relying upon RSC § 2523.5, has held that the Golub notice may be served either personally or by regular mail.[711]

If the Tenant or the spouse of the Tenant (or other family member

---

706 RSC [9 N.Y.C.R.R.] § 2524.1. The Appellate Term for the First Department held that the Landlord's offer to re-new the rent-stabilized apartment, when timely accepted, established an enforceable lease agreement notwithstanding the Landlord's prior notice of non-renewal two (2) years earlier. *See* Isaly-Liceaga v. Pickarski, 115 N.Y.S.3d 796 (App. Term, 1st Dep't 2019).

707 RSC § 2524.4. The term "immediate family" includes a spouse, son, daughter, stepson, stepdaughter, father, mother, stepfather, stepmother, brother, sister, grandfather, grandmother, grandson, granddaughter, father-in-law, mother-in-law, son-in-law, and daughter-in-law. *See id.* at § 2520.6(n).

708 *Id.* at § 2524.4(a).

709 HSTPA (L. 2019, c. 36, Part I, § 2); NYC Admin. Code § 26-511[c][9][b]. *See* Fried v. Lopez, 106 N.Y.S.3d 591 (N.Y. Civ. Ct. Kings Cnty. 2019) (dismissing holdover proceeding where the termination notice stated an intent to recover "all apartments in the building").

710 RSC § 2524.2[c](3); *see* Muccioli v. Gobrial, 2020 N.Y. Misc. LEXIS 12026 (Queens Cnty. Sup. Ct. Sept. 25, 2020).

711 1691 Fulton Ave. Assoc., LP v. Watson, 61 N.Y.S.3d 191 (N.Y. Civ. Ct. Bronx Cnty. 2017); Kuper v. Bravo, 2019 N.Y.L.J. LEXIS 959 (N.Y. Civ. Ct. Queens Cnty. March 29, 2019).

occupying the property) is a senior citizen,[712] disabled,[713] has occupied the building for at least fifteen (15) years, or suffers from a medically diagnosable impairment attributed to anatomical, physiological, or psychological conditions (other than alcohol, gambling, or controlled substances), then this provision is not applicable and the owner must offer to re-new the lease.[714]

There are several factors to consider in evaluating a good-faith attempt to recover the dwelling as a "primary residence." In *Sendowski v. Pilzer*, the Appellate Term for the First Department affirmed a final judgment of possession where the owner elected not to re-new the lease so that his daughter could use the premises as her primary residence.[715] The factors cited as evidence of good faith included the proximity of the premises to both the employment and the residences of the Landlord's adult children.[716]

However, the opposite result occurred in *Feria v. Johnson*, where the Landlord failed to demonstrate that his son was actually planning to reside at the premises.[717] Of note, the HSTPA allows for injunctive and declaratory relief, damages, and reasonable attorney's fees when "fraudulent" statements are made in connection with the Landlord's application to re-claim a rent-stabilized apartment as a primary residence.[718]

18. REFUSAL TO RE-NEW RENT-STABILIZED PREMISES (NOT TENANT'S PRIMARY RESIDENCE) (30 DAYS AND 90–150 DAYS)

A Landlord may decline to re-new the lease for a rent-stabilized apartment where the Tenant does not utilize the premises as a primary

712 A person 62 years of age or older. *See* RSC [9 N.Y.C.R.R.] § 2520.6(p).

713 The term "disabled person" is defined as "a person who has an impairment which results from anatomical, physiological or psychological conditions, other than addiction to alcohol, gambling, or any controlled substance . . ., and which are expected to be permanent and which prevent such person from engaging in any substantial gainful employment." *See id.* at § 2520.6(q).

714 HSTPA (L. 2019, c. 36, Part I, § 2); *see also* RSC § 2524.4(a).

715 16 N.Y.S.3d 794 (App. Term, 1st Dep't 2015).

716 *Id.*

717 52 N.Y.S.3d 246 (App. Term, 2d, 11th & 13th Jud. Dists. 2017).

718 HSTPA (L. 2019, c. 36, Part I, § 1).

residence.[719] Although "primary residence" is not statutorily defined within the RSC, case law has construed a person's primary residence as a dwelling in which the occupant has "an ongoing, substantial, physical nexus with the...premises for actual living purposes."[720]

The Landlord must serve two (2) predicate notices prior to the commencement of a holdover proceeding if the Tenant fails to vacate. In addition to the Golub notice pursuant to RSC § 2524.2[c](2) indicating the intent not to re-new the tenancy (which must be served between ninety (90) and one hundred fifty (150) days prior to the expiration of the lease), the Landlord must also serve a thirty (30) day notice stating that a holdover proceeding will be commenced due to the Tenant's failure to utilize the premises as a primary residence.[721]

Service of the notices may be effectuated either by personal delivery or regular mail.[722] Since the RSC allows the two (2) notices to be "combined," the requirements of the thirty (30) day notice may be interpreted as giving the Tenant *at least* thirty (30) days notice because the Golub notice may not be served fewer than ninety (90) days prior to the expiration of the lease.[723] In *700 Brooklyn Realty, LLC v. Bklyn Realty, LLC*, the Appellate Term for the Second, Eleventh and Thirteenth Judicial Districts noted that the failure to serve the notices in a timely manner "[f]orecloses the landlord's opportunity to commence a non-primary residence proceeding until a renewal lease is executed and the same window opens again prior to the expiration of the renewal lease."[724]

---

719 RSC § 2524.4[c].

720 284 Parkway Assocs. v. Despinosse, 154 N.Y.S.3d 579 (App. Term, 2d, 11th & 13th Jud. Dists. 2021); 9 Richardson St., LLC v. DeLeon, 132 N.Y.S.3d 513 (App. Term, 2d, 11th & 13th Jud. Dists. 2020).

721 *700 Brooklyn Realty, LLC*, 154 N.Y.S.3d at 732.

722 *See Muccioli*, 2020 N.Y. Misc. LEXIS at 12026; *1691 Fulton Ave. Assoc., LP*, 61 N.Y.S.3d at 191.

723 RSC § 2524.4[c].

724 *700 Brooklyn Realty, LLC*, 154 N.Y.S.3d at 732; Bedford Oak, LLC v. Hernandez, 114 N.Y.S.3d 187 (N.Y. Civ. Ct. Bronx Cnty. 2019).

19. MILITARY FAMILIES (30 DAYS)

A lease entered into by, or on behalf of, an individual who entered military service following the execution of the rental agreement may be terminated by the Tenant, at any time, by providing written notice.[725] This provision, which includes both residential and commercial premises,[726] applies equally to leases executed on behalf of the spouse of an individual who entered the military after signing the lease.[727]

The notice of termination may be mailed to the Landlord or the Landlord's agent via regular United States mail due to there being no requirement of formal service or certified mailings.[728] The termination date is typically thirty (30) days after the next rent payment is due following the delivery or mailing of the termination notice. If the rental agreement does not include a monthly rent payment, then the termination date is the final day of the month that follows the month the termination notice was mailed or delivered.[729]

725 NEW YORK STATES SOLDIERS' AND SAILORS' CIVIL RELIEF ACT [MILITARY LAW] § 310.

726 *Id.* The section includes "dwelling [residential], professional, business, agricultural, or similar" leaseholds. *Id.* at § 310(1).

727 *Id.*

728 *Id.* at § 310(2).

729 *Id.*

CHAPTER 7

PROPER AND NECESSARY PARTIES

The Landlord must name each "proper" and "necessary" party in a summary proceeding, which includes all known Tenants.[730] The Court lacks jurisdiction over an occupant who was neither named in the Petition nor served with the Notice of Petition and Petition, unless that individual voluntarily consents to the jurisdiction of the Court and joins the proceeding.[731]

A distinction is made between known Tenants and other occupants, commonly referred to as Undertenants, because a Tenant may sublet the premises or permit other occupants to take possession unbeknownst to the Landlord. Only named individuals in a written rental agreement or those who orally agreed to a tenancy less than one (1) year in duration are considered Tenants. All others in possession, including family members living at the premises who do not appear on the lease, are Undertenants. An Undertenant may be named as a party in the proceeding, but it is not required.

A. TENANTS

The Landlord's naming of each and every Tenant in a summary proceeding is a jurisdictional requirement.[732] Although Tenants are jointly and severally liable for a money judgment (i.e., the Landlord may enforce the judgment against any or all of the Tenants until the judgment

730 Bay Ridge Chicken Grill, Inc. v. Cirrus Data Int'l, LLC, 26 N.Y.S.3d 723 (App. Term, 2d, 11th & 13th Jud. Dists. 2015).

731 *See* Efaplomatidis v. Aires Mexicanos Rest. Corp., 95 N.Y.S.3d 124 (App. Term, 2d, 11th & 13th Jud. Dists. 2018) (consenting to the jurisdiction of the Court and being "substituted into the caption").

732 255 Huguenot St. Corp. v. Rwechungura, 110 N.Y.S.3d 862 (App. Term, 9th & 10th Jud. Dists. 2018) (summary proceeding dismissed where Landlord failed to name the movant's husband, a co-Tenant on the lease).

is satisfied),[733] the Landlord may not pick and choose against which Tenants to commence a summary proceeding. This is the case even where the Landlord leases the premises to multiple Tenants and a portion of the rent has been paid by some of the Tenants. Due to the fact Tenants are both "proper" and "necessary" parties in a summary proceeding, each Tenant must be afforded an opportunity to be heard.[734]

It is to the Landlord's benefit to name all of the Tenants because only those persons named in the proceeding may appear on the warrant of eviction. The spouse of a Tenant need not be named unless he or she has an "independent possessory right" to the premises.[735] The same is true for both the parents[736] and adult children[737] of the Tenant residing at the premises. Minor children should not be named in the summary proceeding because they are not parties to the rental agreement and will be removed during the eviction with their parent or guardian.[738]

---

733 *See* Priegue v. Paulus, 988 N.Y.S.2d 525 (App. Term, 9th & 10th Jud. Dists. 2014); Armour v. McDermott, 906 N.Y.S.2d 770 (App. Term, 9th & 10th Jud. Dists. 2009) (Tenants named on the lease are presumed to be joint obligors due to their status as tenants in common). A joint obligor that pays more than its proportionate share is entitled to contribution from another joint obligor. *See* NY Artistic, LLC v. Archetype, LLC, 2014 N.Y. Misc. LEXIS 3070 (N.Y. Cnty. Sup. Ct. July 7, 2014).

734 *See generally* 45th & Broadway Assocs. v. Skyline Enters., 544 N.Y.S.2d 975 (N.Y. Civ. Ct. N.Y. Cnty. 1989); Sethi v. Kaur, 839 N.Y.S.2d 437 (Nassau Cnty. Dist. Ct. 2007).

735 Randazzo v. Galietti, 55 N.Y.S.3d 694 (App. Term, 2d, 11th & 13th Jud. Dists. 2017); Kuprewicz v. Muktadir, 2002 N.Y. Misc. LEXIS 1672 (App. Term, 2d & 11th Jud. Dists. September 19, 2002).

736 JLNT Realty, LLC v. Liautaud, 26 N.Y.S.3d 213 (App. Term, 2d, 11th & 13th Jud. Dists. 2015).

737 *See* Loira v. Anagnastopolous, 204 A.D.2d 608, 612 N.Y.S.2d 189 (2d Dep't 1994); Friedman v. Yosef, 31 N.Y.S.3d 921 (App. Term, 2d, 11th & 13th Jud. Dists. 2016) (rent-stabilized property); *JLNT Realty, LLC*, 26 N.Y.S.3d at 213; New York City Hous. Auth. v. Kilafofski, N.Y.L.J., June 6, 1996, at 36 (App. Term, 2d & 11th Jud. Dists. 1996); Crossroads Assocs., LLC v. Amenya, 16 N.Y.S.3d 791 (Peekskill City Ct. 2015).

738 Daley v. Billinghurst, 799 N.Y.S.2d 159 (App. Term, 2d, 11th & 13th Jud. Dists. 2004); *see* Lilakos v. City of New York, 808 Fed. Apprx. 4 (2d Cir. 2020) (noting that "[t]he weight of lower state court authority counsels that a minor child has an independent possessory right to reside in the family home"). *Cf.* Dunn v. 583 Riverside Dr. LP, 117 N.Y.S.3d 524 (N.Y. Civ. Ct. N.Y. Cnty. 2019) (naming a minor child as a party in an eviction proceeding may not result in adverse consequences to the Landlord because it is possible for an emancipated minor to possess an interest in defending the proceeding separate from the interests of his or her parents).

A summary proceeding may not be maintained against a Tenant who, with the knowledge of the Landlord, assigns (as opposed to sublets) the lease and all obligations thereunder to a third party. When the assignment occurs prior to the commencement of the summary proceeding, the Landlord may only proceed against the assignee.[739] The Landlord may, however, seek monetary damages against the assignor in a plenary action.

1. ROOMMATE RULE (IMMEDIATE FAMILY PLUS ONE)

The Roommate Rule, which was codified in the Omnibus Housing Act of 1983 and set forth at RPL § 235-f, is "[d]esigned to prevent evictions of residential tenants who have nontraditional living arrangements with co-occupants of the apartment for reasons of economy, safety, and companionship."[740] The rule applies exclusively to residential premises, including those subject to the Multiple Dwelling Law.[741]

The Roommate Rule includes a Tenant and his or her roommate. The rule is not extended to temporary visitors or guests,[742] and further does not justify an attempt to circumvent a lease provision that prohibits subletting.[743]

Pursuant to the Roommate Rule, a residential leasehold entered into by one (1) Tenant who resides at the premises, or whose spouse resides at the premises, as his or her "primary residence" permits the additional

739 C & D Car Wash, Inc. v. Mroczkowski, 94 A.D.3d 935, 942 N.Y.S.2d 183 (2d Dep't 2012); *see generally* Dun-Donnelly Pub'g Corp. v. Kenvic Assocs., 225 A.D.2d 373, at 374, 639 N.Y.S.2d 42 (1st Dep't 1996); I & T Petroleum Inc. v. Lascalia, 880 N.Y.S.2d 873 (Nassau Cnty. Sup. Ct. 2009).

740 *See* OH 161st St. LLC v. Brooks, 94 N.Y.S.3d 803 (N.Y. Civ. Ct. Bronx Cnty. 2019) (*citing* Omnibus Housing Act of 1983, L. 1983, ch. 403, § 1).

741 *See* Barrett Japaning, Inc. v. Bialobroda, 68 A.D.3d 474, 892 N.Y.S.2d 35 (1st Dep't 2009); Bronx 1071 Franklin Ave., L.P. v. Nana, 110 N.Y.S.3d 795 (N.Y. Civ. Ct. Bronx Cnty. 2018) (refusing to enforce lease provision prohibiting a roommate).

742 *OH 161st St. LLC*, 94 N.Y.S.3d at 803 (holding that the Roommate Rule was not applicable because the individual in question regularly signed the "guest book" when visiting, and the Tenant indicated that his guest did not live in the apartment). A guest is defined as a person "temporarily received and entertained at one's home but who is not a regular occupant." *Id.*

743 Armstrong Realty, Inc. v. Roche, 2021 N.Y. Misc. LEXIS 867 (Kings Cnty. Sup. Ct. March 3, 2021).

occupancy of the Tenant's immediate family members, plus one (1) additional occupant (roommate) and that occupant's dependent children.[744] A "roommate" is defined as a person "other than a tenant or a member of a tenant's immediate family, occupying a premises with the consent of the tenant or tenants."[745]

A residential lease agreement entered into by two (2) or more Tenants permits the "[i]mmediate family of tenants, occupants and dependent children of occupants [to take possession as well]; provided that the total number of tenants and occupants, excluding occupants' dependent children, does not exceed the number of tenants specified in the current lease or rental agreement."[746] At least one (1) of the Tenants and/or their spouse must occupy the premises as a primary residence.[747]

The Appellate Division, First Department has held that a Landlord may terminate the lease where the Tenant profits from unlawfully subletting a rent-stabilized apartment.[748] In *Goldstein*, the Court rejected the Tenant's claim that the ninety-three (93) "transient, short-term, paying guests" that resided in the premises over a year and a half were her "roommates."[749] Although a lease provision waiving the Roommate Rule is unenforceable, the Landlord reserves the right to "restrict occupancy" to comply with federal, state, and local ordinances.[750]

---

744 RPL § 235-f(3). *See* Roxborough Apts. Corp. v. Becker, 296 A.D.2d 358, 745 N.Y.S.2d 173 (1st Dep't 2002) (noting that the Tenant had three (3) roommates which is a violation of RPL § 235-f).

745 RPL § 235-f(1)(b).

746 *Id.* at § 235-f(4).

747 *Id.*

748 Goldstein v. Lipetz, 150 A.D.3d 562, 53 N.Y.S.3d 296 (1st Dep't 2017).

749 *Id.*; *see also* Aurora Assocs. LLC v. Hennen, 157 A.D.3d 608, 70 N.Y.S.3d 186 (1st Dep't 2018) (holding that "[w]hen regulated tenants rent space on a short-term basis to transient individuals at rates higher than allowed by applicable regulations, that conduct is 'in the nature of subletting rather than taking in roommates, and constitute[s] profiteering and commercialization of the premises,' which is an 'incurable violation'").

750 RPL § 235-f(8).

2. SENIOR CITIZENS

Real Property Law § 227-a permits the Tenant's early termination of a residential lease where the Tenant or the Tenant's spouse reaches (or will reach) the age of sixty-two (62) during the lease term.[751] A lease provision waiving this right is "void as contrary to public policy."[752]

The lease termination date must be at least thirty (30) days after the due date of the next rent payment.[753] The Tenant may invoke this right in either of two (2) ways. The Tenant may provide documentation from a physician certifying that due to medical reasons, the Tenant requires assistance performing daily activities and is unable to reside independently in the premises and, as a result, will be moving into the residence of a family member.[754] The termination notice must further include a notarized statement from the family member that: (1) verifies the familial relationship and (2) confirms that the Tenant and/or the Tenant's spouse will be moving into the family member's residence "for a period of not less than six months."[755]

Alternatively, the Tenant may terminate the lease by providing proof that he or she will be moving into an adult care facility pursuant to section 2(21) of the Social Services Law,[756] a residential health care facility pursuant to Public Health Law § 2801, or other qualifying subsidized housing

---

751 *Id.* at § 227-a(1).

752 *Id.* at § 227-a(4).

753 *Id.* at § 227-a(2); *see* Plotkin v. Fairfield at Setauket, LLC, 819 N.Y.S.2d 212 (App. Term, 9th & 10th Jud. Dists. 2006) (two-week notice inadequate pursuant to RPL § 227-a(2)).

754 RPL § 227-a(1); *see* Windsor Realty LLC v. Carroll, 801 N.Y.S.2d 244 (N.Y. Civ. Ct. Kings Cnty. 2005) (dismissing small claims action due to noncompliance with the notice and documentation requirements pursuant to RPL §§ 227-a and 227-a(2)).

755 RPL § 227-a(2).

756 Effective July 1, 2023, an "adult care facility" is defined as "a family type home for adults, a shelter for adults, a residence for adults, an enriched housing program or an adult home, which provides temporary or long-term residential care and services to adults who, though not requiring continual medical or nursing care as provided by facilities licensed pursuant to article twenty-eight of the public health law or articles nineteen, twenty-three and thirty-one of the mental hygiene law, are by reason of physical or other limitations associated with age, physical or mental disabilities or other factors, unable or substantially unable to live independently." *See* SOCIAL SERVS. LAW § 2(21).

unit.[757] The termination notice must be accompanied by an executed copy of the lease or contract between the Tenant and facility demonstrating the Tenant's admission or pending admission in the residential facility.[758]

B. SUBTENANTS

A Subtenant is a "proper" but not a "necessary" party in a summary proceeding.[759] This means that the Landlord may (not required) include the Subtenant as a party in the Petition provided all of the Tenants are also named in the Petition.

The Landlord may not under any circumstance commence a summary proceeding against a Subtenant without also naming the Tenants because the Landlord is not in privity with a Subtenant.[760] It is for this reason that when a primary tenancy is terminated, as a matter of law, the subtenancy is also terminated.[761] Only Subtenants named in the summary proceeding may be evicted pursuant to a warrant of eviction issued against the Tenant.[762]

Where the summary proceeding is dismissed against the Tenants, the

757 RPL § 227-a(1).

758 *Id.* at § 227-a(2). *See Windsor Realty LLC*, 801 N.Y.S.2d at 244 (failure to provide documentation demonstrating admission or pending admission results in denial of claim).

759 *See* 117-119 Leasing Corp. v. Reliable Wool Stock, LLC, 139 A.D.3d 420, 30 N.Y.S.3d 622 (1st Dep't 2016); 1234 Broadway LLC v. Ying, 31 N.Y.S.3d 922 (App. Term, 1st Dep't 2016); Kew Gardens Portfolio Holdings, LLC v. Bucheli, 151 N.Y.S.3d 861 (N.Y. Civ. Ct. Queens Cnty. 2021); Citywide Preserv. LLC v. Fall, 48 N.Y.S.3d 265 (N.Y. Civ. Ct. N.Y. Cnty. 2016).

760 Triborough Bridge & Tunnel Auth. v. Wimpfheimer, 633 N.Y.S.2d 695, 696-97 (App. Term, 1st Dep't 1995); *see* 7001 E. 71st St., LLC v. Millenium Health Servs., 138 A.D.3d 573, 28 N.Y.S.3d 604 (1st Dep't 2016); 170 W. 85th St. Tenants Assoc. v. Cruz, 173 A.D.2d 338, 569 N.Y.S.2d 705 (1st Dep't 1991).

761 *117-119 Leasing Corp.*, 139 A.D.3d at 420, 30 N.Y.S.3d at 622; *170 W. 85th St. Tenants Assoc.*, 173 A.D.2d at 338, 569 N.Y.S.2d at 705.

762 98-48 Queens Blvd. LLC v. Parkside Mem. Chapels, Inc., 137 N.Y.S.3d 679 (N.Y. Civ. Ct. Queens Cnty. 2021) (noting that "[d]ue process requires only that, for the warrant to be effective against a subtenant, licensee or occupant, [they] be made a party to the proceeding, either by naming [them] in and serving [them] with the petition and notice of petition or by joining [them] as a party during the pendency of the proceeding") (*quoting 170 W. 85th St. Tenants Ass'n*, 173 A.D.2d at 338, 569 N.Y.S.2d at 705); Farchester Gardens, Inc. v. Elwell, 525 N.Y.S.2d 111 (Yonkers City Ct. 1987).

proceeding must also be dismissed against the Subtenant.[763] However, if the proceeding is dismissed only against the Subtenant, then the proceeding may continue against the Tenants.[764]

A judgment of possession and a warrant of eviction, without a money judgment, is typically the relief sought against Subtenants. Although not common, the Tenant may commence a summary proceeding in the Housing Part to evict a Subtenant.[765] This is the case because the Tenant's possessory interest in the premises is greater (or "superior") than that of the Subtenant.

Tenants and Subtenants may assert claims against one another regarding damages, but typically these claims are heard in a plenary action outside the context of a summary proceeding. Interestingly, where a commercial Subtenant agrees to be bound by "all of the provisions and restrictions in the master lease," including a liquidated damages provision, the Subtenant may be liable for damages to the entire property, even where the holdover only impacted a portion of the premises.[766]

A peculiar situation arises when the Landlord prevails against the Tenants but the Subtenant, who was <u>not</u> named in the summary proceeding, refuses to thereafter vacate the premises. Notwithstanding the possible establishment of a tenancy by sufferance, the Subtenant may continue to occupy the premises even after the Tenants have been evicted. If in fact a tenancy by sufferance was created, the Petitioner may bring another summary proceeding to regain possession after giving the Subtenant thirty (30) days written notice.[767] Otherwise, the

---

763 *See* Tefft v. Apex Pawnbroking & Jewelry Co., Inc., 75 A.D.2d 891, 428 N.Y.S.2d 52 (2d Dep't 1980).

764 *1234 Broadway LLC*, 31 N.Y.S.3d at 922 (summary proceeding continued against Tenant following dismissal against "John Doe"); 2110 Arthur Assets LLC v. Vista Mgmt. Corp., 66 N.Y.S.3d 655 (N.Y. Civ. Ct. N.Y. Cnty. 2017).

765 *See, e.g.*, Sow v. Thanvi, 31 N.Y.S.3d 924 (App. Term, 2d, 11th & 13th Jud. Dists. 2016) (commercial non-payment proceeding dismissed absent agreement between Tenant and Subtenant for the payment of rent); Subway Rests., Inc. v. Mannetti, 2003 N.Y. Misc. LEXIS 1115 (App. Term, 9th & 10th Jud. Dists. July 11, 2003); Jewish Bd. of Family & Children Servs. v. S.B., 2021 N.Y.L.J. LEXIS 1216 (N.Y. Civ. Ct. Bronx Cnty. Dec. 29, 2021) (proceeding dismissed due to defective predicate notice).

766 PHH Mtg. Corp. v. Ferro, Kuba, Mangano, Skylar, Gacovino & Lake, P.C., 113 A.D.3d 831, 979 N.Y.S.2d 536 (2d Dep't 2014).

767 *See* Chapter 6, subdiv. C(9), *supra*.

Landlord may be required to commence an ejectment proceeding in a court of competent jurisdiction.

Unique to rent-stabilized premises within New York City, a Tenant may sublet the apartment provided (1) the premises are simultaneously maintained as the Tenant's primary residence and (2) the rent charged to the Subtenant does not exceed the regulated rent, plus a ten percent (10%) surcharge where the premises are provided fully furnished.[768] The premises may not be subleased for more than two (2) of the four (4) years preceding the expiration of the sublease.[769]

C. "JOHN DOE" AND "JANE DOE"—UNNAMED RESPONDENTS

The Landlord may identify unknown individuals in possession of the premises, in both the predicate notice and the Notice of Petition and Petition, as "John Doe" and "Jane Doe." Service of the appropriate documents, and the requisite number of copies of each, must be provided to each "Doe" in the same manner as a named individual.[770] Parenthetically, a non-attorney friend of a "John Doe" or "Jane Doe" lacks standing to appear in the Housing Part on the occupant's behalf.[771]

The Landlord must move to amend the caption to substitute the proper name of an occupant identified as a "Doe" when the individual's name is learned.[772] The failure to do so may result in the dismissal of the proceeding against the "Doe." A dismissal is even more likely when the Landlord learned of the "Doe's" name prior to the commencement of the summary proceeding.[773] However, a summary proceeding may

768 RSC [9 N.Y.C.R.R.] § 2525.6(a),(b). A violation may result in an award of treble damages. *Id.*

769 RSC [9 N.Y.C.R.R.] § 2525.6[c]; *see generally* Stahl Assocs. LLC v. Alexandersson, 125 N.Y.S.3d 532 (N.Y. Civ. Ct. N.Y. Cnty. 2020).

770 *See generally* Oehlrich v. Rosas, 116 N.Y.S.3d 870 (Middletown City Ct. 2019).

771 *See* Medhat O'Kelly, As Administrator of the Estate of Magdy O'Kelly v. John Doe, 36 N.Y.S.3d 408 (App. Term, 2d, 11th & 13th Jud. Dists. 2016).

772 66 Fort Washington Assocs, LLC v. Acevedo, 131 N.Y.S.3d 778 (App. Term, 1st Dep't 2020).

773 CPLR § 1024. *See 1234 Broadway LLC*, 31 N.Y.S.3d at 922; Cymo Trading Corp. v. Manhattan Inn Hostel, LLC, 943 N.Y.S.2d 791 (App. Term, 1st Dep't 2012); Netherland Props. LLC v. Karalesis, 115 N.Y.S.3d 835 (N.Y. Civ. Ct. Bronx Cnty. 2019); 2264 G LLC v. Issac Deli & Grocery Corp., 97 N.Y.S.3d 57 (N.Y. Civ. Ct. Bronx Cnty. 2018).

continue against the Tenant where the case is dismissed against the "Doe" because the "Doe" is a "proper" but not a "necessary" party.[774]

D. GUARANTORS

A summary proceeding may not be maintained against the Guarantor of a rental agreement unless the Guarantor has an independent possessory interest in the premises.[775] The Landlord may instead commence a plenary action to enforce the guaranty in a court of competent jurisdiction.[776] This may occur either prior to the termination of the lease[777] or, if the lease contained a survival clause that continued the Tenant's and Guarantor's obligations, following lease termination.[778]

774 *See 1234 Broadway LLC*, 31 N.Y.S.3d at 922; FS 45 Tiemann Place LLC v. Gomez, 967 N.Y.S.2d 866 (App. Term, 1st Dep't 2013) (summary proceeding may continue against the Tenant where an individual who is not a necessary party was omitted from the action); *Triborough Bridge & Tunnel Auth.*, 633 N.Y.S.2d at 696-97.

775 PB 2180 Pitkin Ave., LLC v. Tress, 107 N.Y.S.3d 616 (App. Term, 2d, 11th & 13th Jud. Dists. 2019); State Realty, LLC v. Ger, 55 N.Y.S.3d 694 (App. Term, 2d, 11th & 13th Jud. Dists. 2017); MTC Commons, LLC v. Millbrook Training Ctr. & Spa, Ltd., 31 N.Y.S.3d 922 (App. Term, 9th & 10th Jud. Dists. 2016); Phoenix Indus., Inc. v. Ultimate Sports, LLC, 859 N.Y.S.2d 906 (App. Term, 9th & 10th Jud. Dists. 2008); Westbury Senior Living, Inc. v. Clements, 56 N.Y.S.3d 455 (Nassau Cnty. Dist. Ct. 2017); 26-44 Lincoln Ave., LLC v. Iranian Jewish Ctr. of Roslyn, Inc., 901 N.Y.S.2d 911 (Nassau Cnty. Dist. Ct. 2009).

776 *See* Green 333 Corp. v. RNL Life Science, Inc., 186 A.D.3d 1334, 128 N.Y.S.3d 896 (2d Dept 2020); Hawthorne Gardens, LLC v. Salman Home, Inc., 94 A.D.3d 425, 941 N.Y.S.2d 489 (1st Dep't 2012) (Guarantor liable for accelerated rent through end of lease term even though the guaranty was "[o]nly for the first two years of the lease").

777 2402 E. 69th St., LLC v. Corbel Installations, Inc., 183 A.D.3d 859, 124 N.Y.S.3d 632 (2d Dep't 2020) (lease provided that "[n]o amendments of the lease would relieve the guarantors or guarantors' obligations").

778 *See* H.L. Realty, LLC v. Edwards, 131 A.D.3d 573, 15 N.Y.S.3d 413 (2d Dep't 2015) (summary judgment in favor of Landlord against Guarantor where lease contained a survival clause and the parties' stipulation terminating the rental agreement did not terminate the obligations of either the Tenant or the Guarantor); *see also* Seabring, LLC v. Elegance Rest. Furniture Corp., 188 A.D.3d 744, 135 N.Y.S.3d 161 (2d Dep't 2020) (guarantor remained liable for "holdover rent" following expiration of lease where agreement provided the guaranty continued as long as Tenant "remained in possession" of the premises); Brusco v. Soclof, 899 N.Y.S.2d 57 (App. Term, 1st Dep't 2009). As a practical matter, the obligations of a Guarantor may be alleviated where "the original obligation is altered without his or her consent." *H.L. Realty, LLC*, 131 A.D.3d at 573, 15 N.Y.S.3d at 413 (holding that since the stipulation of settlement in the summary proceeding did not explicitly diminish Guarantor's obligation to pay liquidated damages, the Guarantor continued to remain liable under the terminated lease).

Otherwise, the right to enforce not-yet accrued lease provisions against the Guarantor (and Tenant) may be forfeited upon the termination or expiration of the rental agreement.[779]

Depending on the guaranty provision, the "[g]uarantor's liability may exceed the scope of the [Tenant's] liability."[780] In addition, liability may attach where the Tenant took possession of the premises prior to the execution of the guaranty.[781]

There have been occasions where a Guarantor has appeared in the Housing Part, either voluntarily or after improperly being named as a Respondent in a summary proceeding. Even where the Guarantor expresses an intent to avail herself to the jurisdiction of the Housing Part, perhaps to avoid being named as a defendant in a subsequent plenary action, the summary proceeding must be dismissed against the Guarantor because the Court may not expand its jurisdictional authority, even with the consent of the parties.[782]

E. FAMILY MEMBERS

As a general matter, a family member may not evict another family member in a summary proceeding where the occupancy arises out of the "familial relationship," such as when an adult child has lived in the family home since birth.[783] The absence of an identifiable Landlord and Tenant relationship between the family members necessitates dismissal of the eviction proceeding due to a lack of subject matter jurisdiction.

779 *See generally* 300 E. 96th St. LLC v. Saka, 28 N.Y.S.3d 651 (App. Term, 1st Dep't 2015) (summary judgment denied due to issues of fact regarding the guaranty and its application to the renewal lease).

780 Chip Fifth Ave. LLC v. Quality King Distribs., Inc., 158 A.D.3d 418, 70 N.Y.S.3d 196 (1st Dep't 2018); International Plaza Assocs., L.P. v. Lacher, 104 A.D.3d 578, 961 N.Y.S.2d 427 (1st Dep't 2013).

781 MF 385 First Ave. LLC v. Mason Rest. Corp., 200 A.D.3d 423, 154 N.Y.S.3d 777 (1st Dep't 2021).

782 *See PB 2180 Pitkin Ave., LLC*, 107 N.Y.S.3d at 616; *26-44 Lincoln Ave., LLC*, 901 N.Y.S.2d at 911.

783 *See* O'Neill v. O'Neill, 36 N.Y.S.3d 48 (N.Y. Civ. Ct. Queens Cnty. 2016) (dismissing summary proceeding to evict adult son who had resided in family home for over thirty (30) years).

Instead, the family member seeking possession may commence an ejectment proceeding in an appropriate court of competent jurisdiction. In an ejectment proceeding commenced by either the owner or the occupant, money damages may be awarded (unlike a summary proceeding).[784]

On the other hand, the Housing Part has jurisdiction over a summary proceeding brought against a family member whose occupancy was not the result of the "familial relationship."[785] For example, where either (1) a parent and adult child entered into a rental agreement for a specific period of time or (2) a recent college graduate returned home with the mutual understanding that he or she would only remain in the parents' home "temporarily" (e.g., until enough money is saved to find another residence), a summary proceeding on proper notice may be appropriate.

Although summary proceedings are generally an emotional experience, the emotion is heightened when family members are involved. These matters often involve Family Court and/or Criminal Court issues, including Orders of Protection, which may impact the right to possess the property. The Housing Part will not modify or supersede another Court's Order.

Case law has extended the breadth of "familial relationships" beyond that of a stereotypical traditional family. Below is a brief synopsis of family member eviction cases. The cases are neither exhaustive nor cumulative, but rather a sampling of efforts to evict family members in summary proceedings. The reader should be mindful that situations concerning the family dynamic are fact specific and changes in circumstance (or agreement) may result in a different outcome.

---

784 For a discussion on ejectment proceedings, *see* Chapter 1, subdiv. E(2)(a), *supra*.

785 *See generally* Readick v. Green, 152 N.Y.S.3d 877 (App. Term, 1st Dep't 2021) (noting that the "RPAPL contains no language exempting individuals with some family relationship to petitioner from eviction, whether under RPAPL § 711 or RPAPL § 713"); Pugliese v. Pugliese, 37 N.Y.S.3d 208 (App. Term, 2d, 11th & 13th Jud. Dists. 2016) (summary proceeding to evict Petitioner's mother would have been permitted had there been credible proof of a Landlord and Tenant relationship).

1. FAMILIAL EXCEPTION DEFENSE

a. SPOUSE

A spouse may not be evicted in a summary proceeding.[786] In *Rosenstiel v. Rosenstiel,* the Appellate Division, First Department extended this protection to separated spouses.[787] The Court reasoned that the occupation of the marital home by a spouse exists "[b]ecause of special rights incidental to the marriage contract and relationship" that cannot be abridged as long as the marital relationship remains intact.[788]

Following the termination or nullification of a marriage, a summary proceeding to regain possession may be appropriate depending upon the terms of the divorce settlement.[789] For example, a holdover proceeding against a former wife was dismissed where the wife and her ex-husband shared the family home as a married couple for approximately sixteen (16) years, during which time, the former wife financially contributed to the household.[790]

---

786 Lopez v. Reyes, 2012 N.Y.L.J. LEXIS 5602 (N.Y. Civ. Ct. Bronx Cnty. 2012).

787 20 A.D.2d 71, at 76-77, 245 N.Y.S.2d 395 (1st Dep't 1963). *But see* Halaby v. Halaby, 44 A.D.2d 495, 355 N.Y.S.2d 671 (4th Dep't 1974) (summary proceeding may be maintained against a spouse where the couple entered into a license agreement in connection with the divorce proceeding); Aloni v. Oliver, 138 N.Y.S.3d 788 (App. Term, 1st Dep't 2021) (granting summary judgment in favor of Petitioner where Respondent falsely claimed to be Petitioner's spouse).

788 *Rosenstiel*, 20 A.D.2d at 71, 245 N.Y.S.2d at 395.

789 *See, e.g.*, Abdul-Karim v. Mitchell, 113 N.Y.S.3d 478 (Greenburgh Just. Ct. 2019) (denying post-judgment motion to vacate warrant because the familial exception does not apply to a spouse following the divorce; rather the Court looks to the resulting divorce decree regarding ownership and possession of the marital residence).

790 *See* Nauth v. Nauth, 981 N.Y.S.2d 266 (N.Y. Civ. Ct. Bronx Cnty. 2013); *see also* Saoidoh v. Saoidoh, 26 N.Y.S.3d 727 (N.Y. Civ. Ct. Bronx Cnty. 2015) (dismissing summary proceeding against former spouse and daughter where the family home, which was acquired during the marriage, was not addressed in the Judgment of Divorce).

b. SIBLINGS (FACT SPECIFIC)

In *Morris v. Morris*, the Housing Part dismissed the licensee holdover proceeding against the Petitioner's brother, a seventy-six (76) year-old disabled veteran, after concluding it would be unjust to evict the brother from the family home where he had resided for more than sixty (60) years.[791] Similarly, in *Kakwani v. Kakwani*, the licensee holdover proceeding to evict the Petitioner's sister-in-law was dismissed.[792] The Court reasoned that since the Respondent entered the premises due to her marriage to Petitioner's brother where they had lived as a family for four (4) years, the familial relationship precluded an eviction by summary proceeding.[793]

c. CHILDREN AND GRANDCHILDREN (FACT SPECIFIC)

Efforts to evict children and grandchildren, for the most part, have been unsuccessful. As a matter of law, a parent may <u>not</u> evict his or her minor child without a Court Order.[794] This protection is afforded to all children whether born in or out of wedlock.[795] With regard to adult children, in *Sirota v. Sirota*, the Appellate Term held that the familial exception prohibited a parent from evicting the children who had

791 95 N.Y.S.3d 724 (N.Y. Civ. Ct. Bronx Cnty. 2018).

792 967 N.Y.S.2d 827 (Nassau Cnty. Dist. Ct. 2013); *see also* Bradly v. Lumer, 2019 N.Y. Misc. LEXIS 1717 (Suffolk Cnty. Dist. Ct. March 22, 2019) (dismissing summary proceeding where Respondent resided with his wife and children in father-in-law's home for ten (10) years); Rinis v. Toliou, 61 N.Y.S.3d 193 (N.Y. Civ. Ct. Kings Cnty. 2017) (dismissing summary proceeding to evict stepchild who entered possession due to the familial relationship); Opperisano v. Opperisano, 2017 N.Y.L.J. LEXIS 1074 (N.Y. Civ. Ct. Kings Cnty. April 26, 2017) (dismissing summary proceeding against the spouse of Petitioner's son, who was incarcerated, from the home where she resided with her son, in-laws, and brother-in-law).

793 *Kakwani*, 967 N.Y.S.2d at 827. The Housing Part was <u>not</u> persuaded by the Respondent's husband (i.e., Petitioner's brother) having "moved out of the master bedroom and into another room in the house" prior to the commencement of the summary proceeding. *Id.*

794 Sears v. Okin, 847 N.Y.S.2d 899 (App. Term, 9th & 10th Jud. Dists. 2007) (dispute involving domestic partners); *see* Isler v. Isler, 2008 N.Y. Misc. LEXIS 7511, at *3 (N.Y. Cnty. Sup. Ct. Dec. 11, 2008).

795 *See* FAMILY CT. ACT §§ 413, 513. *See* Jimenez v. Weinberger, 417 U.S. 628, 94 S.Ct. 2496 (1974).

lived in the family home for nearly thirty (30) years.[796] In *Williams v. Williams*, the summary proceeding to evict adult grandchildren was dismissed because the grandchildren had resided in the residence with their grandparents as a family for more than a decade since age eleven (11).[797]

2. FAMILIAL EXCEPTION DEFENSE NOT APPLICABLE

Irregardless of the specific familial-type relationship (other than spouse), under certain circumstances a summary proceeding may be available. For example, in *Piotrowski v. Little*, the summary proceeding to evict the Petitioner's co-resident same-sex partner was permitted.[798] In denying the Respondent's motion to dismiss the licensee holdover proceeding, the Housing Part concluded that the "summary eviction remedy of RPAPL § 713(7) applies to all common law licenses except those provided greater protections through specific legislative action."[799]

a. FAMILIAL RELATIONSHIP NOT A FACTOR IN POSSESSION

As discussed above, an eviction proceeding may proceed where the "familial relationship" was not a consideration for the occupant's possession. For example, in *Yu v. Zhan*, the Nassau County District Court denied the Respondent stepmother's motion to dismiss the holdover proceeding because her possession was initiated out of concerns regarding the school district, and not the family dynamic.[800] In that case, the parties' rental agreement did not include a rent provision, but rather

---

796 626 N.Y.S.2d 672, 673 (N.Y. Civ. Ct. Kings Cnty. 1995), *modified*, 644 N.Y.S.2d 950 (App. Term, 2d & 11th Jud. Dists. 1996).

797 822 N.Y.S.2d 415 (N.Y. Civ. Ct. N.Y. Cnty. 2006).

798 911 N.Y.S.2d 583 (Middletown City Ct. 2010).

799 *Id.*

800 112 N.Y.S.3d 441 (Nassau Cnty. Dist. Ct. 2018).

the stepmother paid the equivalent of rent directly to the school.[801]

Several years earlier, the Nassau County District Court held that a daughter-in-law could be evicted in a holdover proceeding where she failed to demonstrate that "[t]he parties lived together 'in a family unit' with 'some indicia of permanence or continuity,'" which is the "primary basis for finding that a family member was exempt from licensee status."[802] In *Heckman v. Heckman*, the Appellate Term for the Ninth and Tenth Judicial Districts similarly rejected the familial exception defense asserted by the daughter-in-law of the deceased former owner where "it [was] clear that [the] occupant fit into one of the RPAPL 711 or 713 categories."[803]

The familial exception defense was also rejected in *Nurse v. Dacres*, where "there [was] no familial relationship at all" between the Petitioner adult son of the deceased former owner and Respondents, the spouse and adult child (from a prior relationship) of the deceased caretaker and daughter-in-law of the former owner who had taken care of Respondent's parents (her in-laws) rent-free in the subject premises.[804] Specifically with regard to the Respondent former spouse of the caretaker, who took possession of the premises approximately seven (7) years following his mother's passing, the Housing Part concluded that "[t]he fact that his now deceased wife took care of his mother for money and free rent followed by her caring for petitioner for free rent in no way creates a family relationship between non-blood relatives."[805]

---

801 *Id.*; *see also* Chambers v. Sherland, 129 N.Y.S.3d 241 (N.Y. Civ. Ct. Bronx Cnty. 2019) (determination whether the $2,000 monthly payments were "rent" necessitated a hearing). In *Stanislaus v. Stanislaus*, the Housing Part dismissed the holdover proceeding brought by the co-executrix of the estate to remove her brother from their mother's home because the Petition improperly alleged that the Respondent was a month-to-month tenant, when, in fact, he was a licensee. 110 N.Y.S.3d 895 (Nassau Cnty. Dist. Ct. 2018). But for the pleading error and improper predicate notice, the Court would have denied the motion to dismiss the proceeding because the familial exception was not applicable. *Id.*

802 Lally v. Fasano, 875 N.Y.S.2d 750, 753 (Nassau Cnty. Dist. Ct. 2009).

803 50 N.Y.S.3d 793 (App. Term, 9th & 10th Jud. Dists. 2017) (holding that the familial exception did not apply to daughter-in-law).

804 130 N.Y.S.3d 653 (N.Y. Civ. Ct. Kings Cnty. 2020).

805 *Id.*

b. LACK OF "SUPPORT OBLIGATION"

The limitations of the familial exception defense were also discussed in the *Heckman* decision, where the Appellate Term opined that for the familial exception to apply, in addition to a close family dynamic, a "support obligation" between the parties is required.[806] In *Chambers v. Sherland*, the Housing Part clarified that the mere fact that the parties are "family" members does not give rise to the familial exception defense.[807] Rather, there must be a clear showing of a legal support obligation.[808] The Appellate Term for the Second, Eleventh and Thirteenth Judicial Districts had previously held that notwithstanding the family connection, it was possible that an adult daughter could evict her mother in a summary proceeding, and would have permitted same, had there been sufficient evidence of an oral agreement establishing a tenancy-at-will between them.[809]

c. LICENSEES

In *Great Jones St. Realty Corp. v. Chimsanthia*, the Appellate Term for the First Department succinctly concluded that the familial exception defense does not apply where the Respondent is a licensee.[810] The Court reasoned that since the "RPAPL contains no language exempting individuals with some familial relationship to a petitioner from eviction as licensees," a holdover proceeding was proper where the license expired upon the death of Respondent's spouse notwithstanding Respondent's claim that her in-laws were principals of Petitioner.[811]

Finally, in a highly unusual situation, the Suffolk County Surrogate's

806 *Heckman*, 50 N.Y.S.3d at 793; *see also* Dictor v. Martin, 88 N.Y.S.3d 857 (Nassau Cnty. Dist. Ct. 2018) (summary proceeding permitted against long-term partner where there was no issue of support). *But see Morris*, 95 N.Y.S.3d at 724 (declining to follow *Heckman*).

807 *Chambers*, 129 N.Y.S.3d at 241.

808 *Id.*

809 *Pugliese*, 37 N.Y.S.3d at 208.

810 157 N.Y.S.3d 851 (App. Term, 1st Dep't 2022); *Aloni*, 138 N.Y.S.3d at 788.

811 *Great Jones St. Realty Corp.*, 157 N.Y.S.3d at 851.

Court granted summary judgment in favor of the Petitioner, the administrator of her brother's estate, against an occupant and her adult children. In *Estate of Rudin*, the decedent and the occupant had been in a relationship, but a few days prior to the decedent taking his life, he obtained a Stay Away Order of Protection against the occupant which forced her from the premises.[812] Following the decedent's death, the occupant and her adult children unlawfully re-entered the premises. Deeming the matter akin to an ejectment proceeding, the Surrogate's Court granted possession to the Petitioner Estate, and, in the process, rejected the familial exception defense, noting that: (1) title to the premises was passed, by operation of law, upon decedent's death, to his sister as his distributee and (2) the unlawful re-entry of the occupants.[813]

F. EXPRESS TRUST

Where the premises are placed in an express trust, the trust generally vests in the trustee.[814] Accordingly, the proper party to sue (or be sued) is the trustee named in the trust agreement, and the failure to name the trustee as a party on behalf of the trust will result in a dismissal of the proceeding.[815]

---

812 2018 N.Y.L.J. LEXIS 2849 (Suffolk Cnty. Surrogate's Ct. Aug. 24, 2018).

813 *Id.*

814 ESTATE, POWERS AND TRUST LAW ("EPTL") § 7-2.1(a).

815 CPLR § 1004; *see* Hilda Townsend Revocable Trust v. Johnson, 126 N.Y.S.3d 623 (N.Y. Civ. Ct. Queens Cnty. 2020); Salanitro Family Trust v. Gorina, 29 N.Y.S.3d 849 (App. Term, 2d, 11th & 13th Jud. Dists. 2015); Ronald Henry Land Trust v. Sasmor, 990 N.Y.S.2d 767 (App. Term, 2d, 11th & 13th Jud. Dists. 2014); *see* Deutsche Bank AG v. Vik, 2017 N.Y. Misc. LEXIS 2258 (N.Y. Cnty. Sup. Ct. June 9, 2017).

CHAPTER 8

PLEADINGS AND DISCOVERY

The overwhelming majority of summary proceedings are commenced by the Petitioner filing a Notice of Petition and Petition.[816] Alternatively, the Petitioner may seek permission of the Court to initiate the proceeding by Order to Show Cause in lieu of a Notice of Petition.[817] The Clerk of the Court assigns each proceeding an index number at the time of filing. The filing fee in the New York City Housing Parts, the City Courts Outside New York City, and the District Courts is $45.00.[818]

RPAPL § 732 provides that where the "appropriate appellate division shall so provide in the rules of a particular court," the Notice of Petition and Petition in a non-payment proceeding will be returnable within ten (10) days of service.[819] The Appellate Division, First Department adopted RPAPL § 732 in Part 208 of the Uniform Rules for the New York City Civil Courts, and, therefore, that section is applicable to non-payment proceedings commenced in New York City.[820] In these cases, if the Tenant fails to appear (where service is proper), then a judgment must

816 In 2005, to comport with Supreme and County Court protocols, civil actions in the City and District Courts were deemed to have been commenced at the time of "filing" (as opposed to "service"). As a general matter, in the Justice Courts the proceeding continues to be commenced upon "service" of the Notice of Petition and Petition. *See* Chapter 9, *infra*.

817 RPAPL § 733(2). The statute provides that the Court "may" permit the Petitioner to proceed in this manner. *Id.*

818 *See* N.Y. City Civ. Ct. Act § 1911(b); Uniform City Ct. Act § 1911(a)(1); Uniform Dist. Ct. Act § 1911(a)(2). In the Justice Courts, the filing fee is $20. Uniform Just. Ct. Act § 1911(a)(1)(a).

819 RPAPL § 732 (HSTPA, L. 2019, c. 36, Part M, § 14). Prior to July 14, 2019, the return date for non-payment proceedings was five (5) days following service.

820 22 N.Y.C.R.R. § 208.42; Marshall v. Simmons, 134 N.Y.S.3d 617 (N.Y. Civ. Ct. Kings Cnty. 2020).

be rendered in favor of the Landlord and, absent circumstances warranting a longer stay pursuant to RPAPL § 753, the Court may stay issuance of the warrant of eviction up to ten (10) days from the date of service.[821] If the Tenant appears and the Landlord prevails in the proceeding, then the Court may stay issuance of the warrant of eviction up to five (5) days from the date of the determination, absent good cause for a longer stay.[822]

A. NOTICE OF PETITION

The purpose of the Notice of Petition is to provide the Tenant or occupant, referred to as the Respondent in a summary proceeding, ample notice of the proceeding and the relief sought. The Notice of Petition must provide: (1) the time and location of the hearing; (2) notice that the failure to assert and establish a defense may preclude the Respondent from asserting the defense or claim in another proceeding; and (3) a description of the premises for the purpose of venue.[823] The Notice of Petition in a non-payment proceeding in New York City must further state that a judgment will be entered if the Respondent fails to appear, and the Court may stay execution of the warrant of eviction up to ten (10) days from the date of service; or if the Respondent appears, the stay may be up to five (5) days from the date of determination, unless good cause is shown for a further stay.[824]

Only a judge, an attorney, or the Clerk of the Court (for *pro se* Petitioners) may issue the Notice of Petition.[825] RPAPL § 731(1) expressly prohibits the party prosecuting the proceeding (i.e., the Petitioner) from issuing the Notice of Petition,[826] and, in New York City, an attorney is prohibited from doing same.[827]

821 RPAPL § 732(3); *see* Elmsford Apt. Assocs., LLC v. Cuomo, 469 F. Supp.3d 148 (S.D.N.Y. 2020); Mosaver Realty v. Luxury Kitchen C., 167 N.Y.S.3d 708 (N.Y. Civ. Ct. Queens Cnty. 2022).

822 RPAPL § 732(2).

823 *Id.* at § 731(2); *see generally* Steinmetz v. Santiago, 13 N.Y.S.3d 853 (N.Y. Civ. Ct. Kings Cnty. 2015).

824 RPAPL § 732(4).

825 *Id.* at § 731(1).

826 *See* Laufer v. Mierzejewski, 128 N.Y.S.3d 437 (Pound Ridge Just. Ct. 2020) (holding that an attorney representing himself as a *pro se* Petitioner in a summary proceeding may not issue the Notice of Petition).

827 N.Y. City Civ. Ct. Act § 401[c]; 239 S. 1st St. LLC v. Ribot, 841 N.Y.S.2d 828 (N.Y. Civ. Ct. Kings Cnty. 2007).

B. THE PETITION

The Petition expands upon the Notice of Petition by asserting specific allegations and the "transactions intended to be proved."[828] The Petition must include the following information: (1) the Petitioner's interest in the premises;[829] (2) Respondent's interest in the premises and relationship to the Petitioner;[830] (3) a description of the premises, including whether the premises is subject to regulation;[831] (4) sufficient facts upon which the proceeding is based;[832] and (5) a statement of the relief sought.[833]

The available relief in a summary proceeding is limited to: (1) a final judgment of possession, which means lawful possession of the premises; (2) a warrant of eviction; and (3) a money judgment for unpaid

---

828 June-July Trust v. Fletcher, 141 N.Y.S.3d 832 (App. Term, 9th & 10th Jud. Dists. 2021).

829 RPAPL § 741(1). *See* 148 S. Emerson Partners, LLC v. 148 S. Emerson Assoc., LLC, 157 A.D.3d 889, 69 N.Y.S.3d 868 (2d Dep't 2018); Willie Lilley, Care of My Ideal Prop. v. Molina, 115 N.Y.S.3d 801 (App. Term, 2d, 11th & 13th Jud. Dists. 2019); Pri Villa Ave., L.P. v. Cocchia, 155 N.Y.S.3d 35 (N.Y. Civ. Ct. Bronx Cnty. 2021).

830 RPAPL § 741(2). *See* Jaikarran & Sons, Inc. v. Beecham, 110 N.Y.S.3d 783 (App. Term, 1st Dep't 2018); Brookwood Coram I, LLC v. Oliva, 15 N.Y.S.3d 710 (App. Term, 9th & 10th Jud. Dists. 2015); 287 Realty Corp. v. Livathinos, 967 N.Y.S.2d 870 (App. Term, 2d, 11th & 13th Jud. Dists. 2013); Cintron v. Pandis, 950 N.Y.S.2d 490 (App. Term, 9th & 10th Jud. Dists. 2012); Jeffco Mgmt. Corp. v. Local Dev. Corp. of Crown Heights, 881 N.Y.S.2d 364 (App. Term, 2d, 11th & 13th Jud. Dists. 2009); 1692 Rockaway LLC v. Prashad, 142 N.Y.S.3d 925 (N.Y. Civ. Ct. Kings Cnty. 2021); Aero Mgmt. Co. v. Moghadasian, 129 N.Y.S.3d 250 (N.Y. Civ. Ct. Queens Cnty. 2020).

831 RPAPL § 741(3). *See* Harway Terrace, Inc. v. Petropiento, 155 N.Y.S.3d 29 (App. Term, 2d, 11th & 13th Jud. Dists. 2021); Marie France Realty Co. v. 325 E. 14th St. Corp., 126 N.Y.S.3d 840 (App. Term, 1st Dep't 2020); 156 Nassau Ave. HDFC v. Tchernitsky, 112 N.Y.S.3d 859 (App. Term, 2d, 11th & 13th Jud. Dists. 2019); 5670 58th St. Holding Corp. v. ASAP Towing Servs., Inc., 68 N.Y.S.3d 378 (App. Term, 2d, 11th & 13th Jud. Dists. 2017).

832 RPAPL § 741(4); Oakwood Terr. Hous. Corp. v. Monk, 36 N.Y.S.3d 48 (App. Term, 9th & 10th Jud. Dists. 2016); Ropshitz v. Schwartz, 927 N.Y.S.2d 819 (App. Term, 9th & 10th Jud. Dists. 2011); McFadden v. Sassower, 907 N.Y.S.2d 101 (App. Term, 9th & 10th Jud. Dists. 2010); Jamaica Ave., LLC v. H. Carpets Inc., 153 N.Y.S.3d 834 (N.Y. Civ. Ct. Queens Cnty. 2021); Jasper, L.P. v. Davis, 114 N.Y.S.3d 576 (N.Y. Civ. Ct. Bronx Cnty. 2019); Davidson v. Myers, 2019 N.Y.L.J. LEXIS 626 (Nassau Cnty. Dist. Ct. March 6, 2019).

833 RPAPL § 741(5); *see generally* Harbor Tech LLC v. Correa, 134 N.Y.S.3d 652 (N.Y. Civ. Ct. Kings Cnty. 2020).

rent and use and occupancy.[834] The money judgment may further include any additional allowable items "other than base rent," such as statutory costs and disbursements, and, in commercial cases, reasonable added rent items.[835]

Statutory interest may also be awarded to a prevailing Petitioner in a non-payment proceeding.[836] In a holdover proceeding, where a monetary award is sought, the Petition may assert both: (1) the amount of unpaid rent owed prior to the expiration or termination of the lease (rent arrears) and (2) the fair market value for the continued use and occupation of the premises without a rental agreement through the date of the judgment (use and occupancy).

The Petition must adequately allege each of the aforementioned elements to satisfy the statutory pleading requirements. Otherwise, the proceeding may be dismissed. For example, summary proceedings have been dismissed where: (1) the Petition erroneously alleged that the Respondent was a Tenant instead of a licensee;[837] (2) the Petition described the occupant as a "Tenant" without proof of an actual Landlord and Tenant relationship;[838] (3) the Petition failed to allege that a termination notice was served;[839] (4) the Petition failed to allege that an appropriate predicate notice was served;[840] (5) the Petition omitted any reference to an appropriate governmental regulatory authority, such as

834 RPAPL § 741(5); *see generally* Mayes v. UVI Holdings, Inc., 280 A.D.2d 153, 723 N.Y.S.2d 2001 (1st Dep't 2001); Poughkeepsie Hous. Auth. v. Lee, N.Y.L.J., Dec. 18, 1998, at 36 (App. Term, 9th & 10th Jud. Dists. 1998).

835 *See, e.g.*, Milonis v. 3273-3285 Westchester Ave. Realty Corp., 138 N.Y.S.3d 787 (App. Term, 1st Dep't 2021). For a discussion about the money judgment in a summary proceeding, *see* Chapter 5, *supra*.

836 *See* APF 286 Mad LLC v. RIS Real Props., 990 N.Y.S.2d 436 (N.Y. Civ. Ct. N.Y. Cnty. 2014).

837 *See, e.g.*, Stanislaus v. Stanislaus, 110 N.Y.S.3d 895 (Nassau Cnty. Dist. Ct. 2018).

838 *1692 Rockaway LLC*, 142 N.Y.S.3d at 925.

839 *See* 1646 Union, LLC v. Simpson, 113 N.Y.S.3d 459 (App. Term, 2d, 11th & 13th Jud. Dists. 2019); Parkview Apts. Corp. v. Pryce, 95 N.Y.S.3d 125 (App. Term, 9th & 10th Jud. Dists. 2018).

840 Chen v. Salvador, 145 N.Y.S.3d 780 (N.Y. Civ. Ct. Queens Cnty. 2021); Rochdale Vill. Inc. v. Sterling, 114 N.Y.S.3d 579 (N.Y. Civ. Ct. Queens Cnty. 2019).

Section 8, rent stabilization, or other government program;[841] and (6) the Petition did not provide either the reason or the date for the early termination of the Section 8 Tenant's subsidy.[842]

On the other hand, an inadvertent scrivener's error may be capable of amendment in lieu of dismissal,[843] and the failure to include "the name of the village [or hamlet] in the address for the property...does not constitute a fatal defect, particularly [when] the address was fully set forth elsewhere in the petition."[844] In *Trafalgar Co. v. Malone*, the Housing Part denied the Tenant's motion to dismiss the proceeding where the improper description of the premises "matche[d] that in the expired lease."[845]

Although the pleading requirements are specific, the Appellate Term for the Ninth and Tenth Judicial Districts has held that the mistaken use of the term "rent" (which implies the parties have a valid Landlord and Tenant relationship), as opposed to "use and occupancy," did <u>not</u> necessarily warrant dismissal of a licensee holdover proceeding.[846] The Court reasoned that when viewed in its entirety, the Petition could <u>not</u> be "[d]eemed a judicial admission of the existence of a landlord-tenant relationship, as the petition sets forth at length the basis for petitioner's claim that occupant is a licensee [and not a Tenant]."[847]

---

841 *Cintron*, 950 N.Y.S.2d at 490 (in a proceeding involving a mobile home governed by RPL § 233, the Court noted that the "regulatory status" is significant in determining the Tenant's rights); 101-08 LLC v. Rodriguez, 157 N.Y.S.3d 695 (N.Y. Civ. Ct. Queens Cnty. 2021) (Petition failed to allege that the premises was subject to rent stabilization); Bennett v. Brooks, 153 N.Y.S.3d 833 (Mt. Vernon City Ct. 2021) (failed to allege the Respondent's Section 8 status); AR Vernon, LLC v. Carter, 131 N.Y.S.3d 537 (Mt. Vernon City Ct. 2020) (failed to allege in Petition that the premises was subject to rent regulation); Routolo v. Garzillo, 2017 N.Y.L.J. LEXIS 659 (N.Y. Civ. Ct. Kings Cnty. 2017) (proceeding dismissed where the Petition erroneously alleged the premises was "decontrolled" by an order of the Division of Housing and Community Renewal).

842 *See* 2025 Regent, LLC v. Bennet, 930 N.Y.S.2d 177 (App. Term, 2d, 11th & 13th Jud. Dists. 2011); 1507 Johns LLC v. Hernandez, 2017 N.Y.L.J. LEXIS 3761 (N.Y. Civ. Ct. Kings Cnty. Dec. 22, 2017).

843 *See, e.g.*, M & O Enters. Inc. Shopper Vill. Div. Profit Sharing Plan v. Coletta, 110 N.Y.S.3d 798 (Nassau Cnty. Dist. Ct. 2018).

844 Birchwood Ct. Owners, Inc. v. Toner, 37 N.Y.S.3d 206 (App. Term, 9th & 10th Jud. Dists. 2016).

845 *See* 2021 N.Y. Misc. LEXIS 6654 (N.Y. Civ. Ct. N.Y. Cnty. March 2, 2021).

846 East Ramapo Cent. Sch. Dist. v. Mosdos Chofetz Chaim, Inc., 36 N.Y.S.3d 344 (App. Term, 9th & 10th Jud. Dists. 2016).

847 *Id.*

1. PREDICATE NOTICE

In a non-payment proceeding, the Petition must allege that both a proper rent demand and a late-rent reminder were provided to the Tenant.[848] The same is true regarding the various types of predicate notices associated with holdover proceedings.[849] In both proceedings, the Landlord must further state the manner of service or, at minimum, attach the affidavit of service to the Petition.[850] The failure to do so is not a jurisdictional defect, and if the affidavit is inadvertently omitted from the Petition, the Landlord may cure the defect by attaching the affidavit of service to its opposition to the Tenant's motion to dismiss the proceeding.[851]

Prior to the 2019 changes implemented by the HSTPA, the conclusory assertion that "[r]ent has been demanded personally from the tenant since the same became due" was sufficient for pleading purposes.[852] Whether the demand was actually made and, if so, whether it was done properly, was a matter for the Court to determine at the hearing (rather than on a motion to dismiss).[853] At present, the same practice continues regarding the sufficiency of written predicate notices in all summary proceedings; namely, the Petition must allege that a proper and timely predicate notice was previously served, and the hearing is the forum for determining whether the notice was served as alleged.

---

848 *Oakwood Terr. Hous. Corp.*, 36 N.Y.S.3d at 48 (dismissing non-payment proceeding where Petitioner failed to prove or plead a rent demand was made); Pepe v. Miller & Miller Consulting Actuaries, Inc., 221 A.D.2d 545, at 546, 634 N.Y.S.2d 490, 491 (2d Dep't 1995). *See generally* Abdelgader v. Arola, 146 N.Y.S.3d 768 (N.Y. Civ. Ct. Queens Cnty. 2021).

849 For a discussion regarding predicate notices, *see* Chapter 6, *supra*.

850 *See* Kentpark Realty Corp. v. Lasertone Corp., 779 N.Y.S.2d 324, 326 (App. Term, 2d & 11th Jud. Dists. 2004); Sears, Jr. v. Okin, 800 N.Y.S.2d 357 (App. Term, 9th & 10th Jud. Dists. 2004).

851 Reckson Operating P'ship, L.P. v. LJC Corp., 856 N.Y.S.2d 26 (App. Term, 9th & 10th Jud. Dists. 2007).

852 Davidson v. Myers, 112 N.Y.S.3d 878 (Nassau Cnty. Dist. Ct. 2019). The Landlord must establish the timeliness and appropriateness of the rent demand at the hearing.

853 Dolan § 32:15, at 501 (4th ed. 2010).

2. VERIFICATION

The Petition must be verified by a person authorized pursuant to RPAPL § 721 (most commonly, the Petitioner) or by the Petitioner's attorney.[854] The failure to properly verify the Petition is not a jurisdictional defect.[855] However, pursuant to CPLR § 3022, the Petition may be deemed a nullity where the Tenant immediately raises an objection to the verification, which has been defined as "within 24 hours of the receipt of the defective pleading."[856] Unlike civil practice in other courts, an attorney may verify the Petition where the Petitioner and attorney are situated in the same county.[857]

An attorney's verification may delay the proceeding in the event of a default. For instance, where the Respondent defaults in a non-payment proceeding, the Court will typically award a default judgment, without an inquest, provided the pleadings are facially sufficient, the Notice of Petition includes the requisite information, and proper service is alleged.[858] However, where the Petition is verified by counsel, it has been held that a default judgment should not be awarded unless the application is accompanied by a sworn affidavit or the testimony of an individual with personal knowledge of the claims.[859] If such a person is not present in Court at the time of the default, the Court may deny the default application without prejudice to renew at a future inquest or upon the submission of a sworn affidavit from the Landlord or property manager.[860]

---

854 RPAPL § 741; 1346 Park Pl. HDFC v. Wright, 34 N.Y.S.3d 561 (App. Term, 2d, 11th & 13th Jud. Dists. 2016); *Mosaver Realty*, 167 N.Y.S.3d at 708.

855 *See generally M & O Enters. Inc. Shopper Vill. Div. Profit Sharing Plan*, 110 N.Y.S.3d at 798.

856 Knoll Manor Assocs. of NY v. Goldstein, 155 N.Y.S.3d 528 (App. Term, 9th & 10th Jud. Dists. 2021); *1346 Park Pl. HDFC*, 34 N.Y.S.3d at 561.

857 RPAPL § 741; Fang Realty Corp. v. Prime Six Inc., 151 N.Y.S.3d 862 (N.Y. Civ. Ct. Kings Cnty. 2021).

858 RPAPL § 732(3); Brusco v. Braun, 84 N.Y.2d 674, 621 N.Y.S.2d 291 (1994).

859 77 Commercial Holding, LLC v. Central Plastic, Inc., 4 N.Y.S.3d 464 (App. Term, 2d, 11th & 13th Jud. Dists. 2014); Sella Props. v. DeLeon, 890 N.Y.S.2d 254, 255-56 (App. Term, 2d, 11th & 13th Jud. Dists. 2009); *Kentpark Realty Corp.*, 779 N.Y.S.2d at 326.

860 1081 Flatbush Ave., LLC v. Jadoo, 946 N.Y.S.2d 67 (App. Term, 2d, 11th & 13th Jud. Dists. 2011); *see* 285 Schenectady LLC v. Williams, 38 N.Y.S.3d 833 (N.Y. Civ. Ct. Kings Cnty. 2016) (granting default judgment based upon submission of sworn affidavit from an individual with firsthand knowledge of the claims); 104 Realty LLC v. Brown, 981 N.Y.S.2d 637 n.14 (N.Y. Civ. Ct. Kings Cnty. 2013).

3. AMENDING THE PETITION

At or prior to the hearing, where both the Petitioner and Respondent are present, the Petitioner may amend the Petition to include the rent and any additional permissible items that have accrued since the commencement of the summary proceeding. As a practical matter, the Petitioner does not have to make another rent demand for newly accrued rent.[861] The Petition may further be amended to conform to the proof adduced at the hearing.[862]

Leave to amend the Petition should be "freely" granted without advanced notice to the Respondent provided there is no prejudice or undue surprise.[863] An amendment may be made orally but, regardless of form, a request to amend the Petition must be timely.[864] For example, a request to include the new month's rent on the 1st day of the month should be denied because typically the rent is not considered late until the 2nd day of the month or other date specified within the rental agreement.

Amendments with respect to parties' names and the proper spelling of names are routinely granted. For example, the Petitioner was

861 *See* 36 Main Realty Corp. v. Wang Law Office, PLLC, 19 N.Y.S.3d 654 (App. Term, 2d, 11th & 13th Jud. Dists. 2015); 576 E. 187th St. Bronx, LLC v. Hizam Deli Grocery Corp., 106 N.Y.S.3d 550 (N.Y. Civ. Ct. Bronx Cnty. 2018) (an amendment to the Petition (as opposed to the rent demand) required to include rent newly accrued prior to the hearing); Building Mgmt. Co., Inc. v. Benmen, 959 N.Y.S.2d 87 (N.Y. Civ. Ct. N.Y. Cnty. 2012); JDM Washington St., LLC v. 90 Washington Rest. Assocs., 950 N.Y.S.2d 647 (N.Y. Civ. Ct. N.Y. Cnty. 2012). *But see* 59 Maiden Lane Assoc., LLC v. Maiden Farm, Inc., 106 N.Y.S.3d 554 (N.Y. Civ. Ct. N.Y. Cnty. 2019) (noting contrary to common practice, the Court was "constrained" by a 1979 Appellate Term ruling—*1587 Broadway Rest. Corp. v. Magic Pyramid, Inc.*, 1979 N.Y. Misc. LEXIS 2993 (App. Term, 1st Dep't 1979)—to hold that a new rent demand was required for newly accrued rent).

862 Regatta Prop. LLC v. 21 S. End Hudson, Inc., 113 N.Y.S.3d 486 (N.Y. Civ. Ct. N.Y. Cnty. 2019) (application to conform pleadings to amend caption to reflect Respondent's proper name); *JDM Washington St., LLC*, 950 N.Y.S.2d at 647 (granting motion to conform pleadings to the proof, but case dismissed due to a discrepancy in the dollar amount recoverable).

863 DuPont Realty, LLC v. Garcia, 152 N.Y.S.3d 544 (App. Term, 2d, 11th & 13th Jud. Dists. 2021) (amendment to assert multiple dwelling status); *36 Main Realty Corp.*, 19 N.Y.S.3d at 654.

864 *See, e.g.*, Regensburg v. Rzonca, 836 N.Y.S.2d 489 (Suffolk Cnty. Dist. Ct. 2007); Jefferson House Assocs., LLC v. Boyle, 800 N.Y.S.2d 348 (Ossining Just. Ct. 2005).

permitted to substitute the proper name of the person to whom the property was transferred after a certified copy of the transfer deed was provided.[865] An amendment to substitute the proper name for a "John Doe" is similarly permissible.[866]

An amendment may also be granted to correct a mistake in the address or description of the property, either pre- or post-judgment, provided there is no prejudice to the Respondent.[867] For example, in *Najjar v. Cooper*, the Court granted the Landlord's cross-motion to amend the Petition to reflect that the apartment was situated on the first floor.[868] In *Gnosis, LLC v. Soforte*, the Petitioner's post-judgment motion to amend the judgment and warrant to include the proper village and street suffix was similarly granted.[869]

However, a request to add or substitute the name of an individual who was neither served nor listed in the caption is not permitted without that individual's informed consent to jurisdiction (personal jurisdiction), even where the individual voluntarily appeared in Court.[870] In addition, an amendment to include newly accrued rent or use and occupancy is typically not permitted when the Tenant is not present.[871]

---

865 Blue Mountain Homes, LLC v. Betancourt, 16 N.Y.S.3d 791 (App. Term, 9th & 10th Jud. Dists. 2015).

866 66 Ft. Wash. Assocs., LLC v. Acevedo, 131 N.Y.S.3d 778 (App. Term, 1st Dep't 2020); 1168 Rockaway Ave. Corp. v. Singh, 54 N.Y.S.3d 611 (N.Y. Civ. Ct. Kings Cnty. 2017).

867 Najjar v. Cooper, 950 N.Y.S.2d 724 (App. Term, 2d, 11th & 13th Jud. Dists. 2012); Gnosis, LLC v. Soforte, LLC, 958 N.Y.S.2d 307 (Nassau Cnty. Dist. Ct. 2010).

868 *Najjar*, 950 N.Y.S.2d at 724.

869 *Gnosis, LLC*, 958 N.Y.S.2d at 307 (noting that ample notice had been provided, including additional notices listing the appropriate address).

870 An unserved, non-party's voluntary appearance in Court in and of itself does not constitute consent to the jurisdiction of the Court. *Cf.* 16 Lincoln Sq. Assocs. v. Amrep Corp., 493 N.Y.S.2d 692 (N.Y. Civ. Ct. N.Y. Cnty. 1985) (holding that personal jurisdiction was not obtained where the named-Respondent's only appearance was to seek an adjournment for the purpose of making a motion to dismiss the Petition).

871 *See generally* Mustafa v. Plein, 950 N.Y.S.2d 492 (App. Term, 2d, 11th & 13th Jud. Dists. 2012) (in a holdover proceeding, default judgment limited to the amount in the Petition); Port Chester Hous. Auth. v. Turner, 734 N.Y.S.2d 805 (App. Term, 9th & 10th Jud. Dists. 2001) (same result in a non-payment proceeding).

C. ANSWER

The Respondent may file responsive pleadings, including an Answer, in a summary proceeding. The purpose of answering the Petition is threefold: (1) to frame the issues before the Court; (2) preserve the right of appeal; and (3) preserve the right to assert related claims in another action. The Respondent in a summary proceeding may submit an Answer at or before the hearing, either orally or in writing, by denying all or a portion of the allegations and asserting affirmative defenses.[872] The late filing of the Answer (after the initial Court date) generally does not result in prejudice to the Petitioner.[873] However, there is no requirement to submit an Answer, and the failure to do so may not be the basis for a default.

Where the Answer is asserted orally, "the substance thereof shall be recorded by the clerk" and "maintained in the case record."[874] A written Answer, unlike the Petition, need not be verified.[875] Notwithstanding the Housing Part's limited authority to grant equitable relief, the Respondent may assert any affirmative defense, whether based in law or equity, in a summary proceeding.[876]

A personal jurisdiction defense, such as defective service, may be waived if not asserted in the Answer or at the initial Court appearance.[877] The Appellate Term for the First Department has held that where the defense of personal jurisdiction is not timely raised in the original Answer, the Tenant is precluded from asserting the defense in

872 *See* RPAPL § 743 (HSTPA, L. 2019, c. 36, Part M, § 16); 655 Country Rd., Inc. v. Caltagirone, 101 N.Y.S.3d 701 (App. Term, 9th & 10th Jud. Dists. 2018).

873 Barker v. Cruz, 167 N.Y.S.3d 382 (N.Y. Civ. Ct. Bronx Cnty. 2022).

874 RPAPL § 743.

875 *See* Stein v. Jeff's Express, Inc., 955 N.Y.S.2d 713 (App. Term, 2d, 11th & 13th Jud. Dists. 2012); Neck Rd. One Realty v. Magna Physical Therapy PC, 2019 N.Y.L.J. LEXIS 1655 (N.Y. Civ. Ct. Kings Cnty. May 15, 2019).

876 *See* RPAPL § 743; Yacoob v. Persaud, 950 N.Y.S.2d 611 (App. Term, 2d, 11th & 13th Jud. Dists. 2012); Seward Pk. Hous. Corp. v. Flowers on Essex, LLC, 15 N.Y.S.3d 714 (N.Y. Civ. Ct. N.Y. Cnty. 2014).

877 Iodice v. Academics R Us, Inc., 26 N.Y.S.3d 724 (App. Term, 1st Dep't 2015); Chen v. Ray, 26 N.Y.S.3d 212 (App. Term, 1st Dep't 2015).

an Amended Answer.[878] The doctrine of *res judicata* further prohibits the assertion of a claim in a subsequent plenary action that could have been raised in the summary proceeding.[879]

The defense that the predicate notice is defective need not be asserted (but should be) because establishing by a preponderance of the evidence that a proper predicate notice was served is an element of the Petitioner's *prima facie* case.[880] As a result, a defective predicate notice may result in the dismissal of the summary proceeding, even where the Tenant fails to assert the defense.

Effective July 14, 2019, the Legislature codified that the Respondent is not required to file an Answer in a summary proceeding.[881] Prior to that date, a Petitioner could require an Answer when: (1) demanded in the Notice of Petition and (2) the Petition was served between eight (8) and twelve (12) days before the return date.[882] This is no longer the case. However, the reader should be mindful that if the Tenant serves an Answer, but fails to appear on the return date, a default judgment may be entered.[883]

1. MOTION TO DISMISS

In lieu of filing an Answer, the Respondent may move to dismiss the proceeding. A motion to dismiss is typically based upon defects in service and/or the Petition. Although the Court may determine from a cursory review whether proper service is alleged and the Petition states

878 *Iodice*, 26 N.Y.S.3d at 724.

879 *See* IG Second Generation Partners, L.P. v. La Motta, 133 A.D.3d 415, 21 N.Y.S.3d 2 (1st Dep't 2015); Tewksbury Mgmt. Group, LLC v. Rogers Invests. NV LP, 110 A.D.3d 546, 973 N.Y.S.2d 591 (1st Dep't 2013).

880 W54-7 LLC v. Schick, 829 N.Y.S.2d 399 (App. Term, 1st Dep't 2006).

881 RPAPL § 743 (HSTPA, L. 2019, c. 36, Part M, § 16).

882 Pursuant to CPLR §§ 3012(d), 2004 and 2005, an extension to file a late pleading in a proceeding may be obtained where a reasonable excuse is shown or in the interests of justice, including law office failure. Although no longer applicable due to the 2019 changes, it was well-established that a *pro se* Tenant's request for an adjournment on the initial Court date for the purpose of seeking counsel extended the time to answer. *See* In-Towne Shopping Ctrs. Co. v. DeMottie, 851 N.Y.S.2d 70 (App. Term, 9th & 10th Jud. Dists. 2007).

883 191 St. Assocs. LLC v. Cruz, 29 N.Y.S.3d 848 (App. Term, 1st Dep't 2016).

a *prima facie* case, disputes concerning material issues of fact require a hearing.[884] For example, the Landlord's submission of the rental agreement, without an accompanying affidavit, was sufficient to withstand a motion to dismiss where the rental agreement contradicted the Tenant's claims.[885]

The Court may not consider a defense asserted for the first time either in support of a motion to re-new a prior Order of the Court[886] or in reply papers following receipt of opposition to a motion to dismiss.[887] The denial of Respondent's motion to dismiss the proceeding (or for summary judgment) is typically not an adjudication on the merits and, therefore, the same arguments may be re-asserted at the hearing.[888] The rule prohibiting a party from making successive summary judgment motions is applicable to summary proceedings, and will be upheld where an Amended Answer is served, provided there are no new issues regarding the possessory claim.[889]

The return date of the motion is typically the initial date the parties are due to appear in Court, or a date shortly thereafter. If the parties cannot agree on a return date, the Court will select a reasonable return date. The Court may further direct a briefing schedule to avoid delay and/or confusion.

884 *See* 145 E. 16th St. LLC v. Nanda, 110 N.Y.S.3d 780 (App. Term, 1st Dep't 2018); 706 Realty Corp. v. Mohammed, 941 N.Y.S.2d 541 (App. Term, 1st Dep't 2011).

885 1935 Andrews Ave. Equities v. Diaz, 31 N.Y.S.3d 922 (App. Term, 1st Dep't 2016).

886 Tenth St. Holdings, LLC v. McKowen, 31 N.Y.S.3d 924 (App. Term, 1st Dep't 2016).

887 *See* Patchogue Assocs. v. Sears, Roebuck and Co., 951 N.Y.S.2d 314 (App. Term, 9th & 10th Jud. Dists. 2012) (summary proceeding); Ramos v. New York City Hous. Auth., 162 A.D.3d 884, 80 N.Y.S.3d 85 (2d Dep't 2018) (personal injury action); Master v. Boiakhtchion, 122 A.D.3d 589, at 590, 996 N.Y.S.2d 116, 117 (2d Dep't 2014) (same).

888 *See* Karagiannis v. Nasar, 943 N.Y.S.2d 816 (App. Term, 2d, 11th & 13th Jud. Dists. 2012).

889 Bruckner Realty LLC v. Cruz, 13 N.Y.S.3d 849 (App. Term, 1st Dep't 2015), *aff'd*, 139 A.D.3d 413, 29 N.Y.S.3d 162 (1st Dep't 2016), *aff'd*, 28 N.Y.3d 1138, 46 N.Y.S.3d 835 (2016). *Cf.* 885 Park Ave. Brooklyn, LLC v. Goddard, 53 N.Y.S.3d 794 (App. Term, 2d, 11th & 13th Jud. Dists. 2017) (successive summary judgment motions permitted where Landlord submitted evidence that the building was exempt from rent stabilization and that "[g]ranting the motion would 'further the ends of justice while eliminating an unnecessary burden on the resources of the courts'"). *See generally* Myrtle Ave. Shop, Inc. v. Sherhan, 116 N.Y.S.3d 483 (App. Term, 2d, 11th & 13th Jud. Dists. 2019).

The Landlord may similarly move for summary judgment on its claims. In *East Midtown Plaza Hous. Co. v. Gamble*, the Appellate Term for the First Department granted the Landlord's motion where the evidence "conclusively established that the apartment premises were used for prostitution on an ongoing basis, the tenant knew of and acquiesced in [the] illegal activity, and, indeed, [the Tenant] received a portion of the proceeds."[890] In *Chew v. McKenzie*, the Landlord's cross-motion for summary judgment was granted because it was undisputed that the Tenant violated the rental agreement by subleasing the rent-stabilized apartment for approximately two (2) years.[891]

2. COUNTERCLAIMS

RPAPL § 743 authorizes the assertion of oral or written counterclaims on the return date of the summary proceeding.[892] Unlike the Petitioner's claims, the Respondent may be awarded damages on a counterclaim.[893] However, equitable counterclaims[894] and counterclaims for money damages "arising out of torts unrelated to possession of the premises or [the] collection of rent" are prohibited.[895]

Counterclaims are <u>not</u> limited to the time period for which unpaid rent is sought, and the Court's maximum dollar jurisdictional limit in civil actions, which in many of the local Courts equals $15,000 ($50,000 in New York City), excluding costs and interest, does <u>not</u> apply to

890 78 N.Y.S.3d 621 (App. Term, 1st Dep't 2018).

891 941 N.Y.S.2d 536 (App. Term, 1st Dep't 2011) (permanent stay on warrant of eviction where Tenant cured the defect). *Cf.* 12 E. 86th St. LLC v. Brenner, 114 N.Y.S.3d 793 (App. Term, 1st Dep't 2019) (denying summary judgment due to "[m]ixed questions of law and fact, including whether the nature and frequency of the stabilized tenant's rental of space in her apartment on a short term basis to transient individuals constituted commercialization of the premises and profiteering"); 13775 Realty, LLC v. Foglino, 36 N.Y.S.3d 48 (App. Term, 1st Dep't 2016) (hearsay evidence insufficient to establish Landlord's *prima facie* entitlement to summary judgment).

892 *See* RPAPL § 743 (the Tenant's oral Answer may include counterclaims); *655 Country Rd., Inc.*, 101 N.Y.S.3d at 701.

893 RPAPL § 743.

894 Dolan § 43:38, at 137-38 (4th ed. 2010).

895 Wheeler v. Linden Plaza Preserv. LP, 172 A.D.3d 608, 102 N.Y.S.3d 17 (1st Dep't 2019); *see* Ndiaye v. 2123 FDB MPPH LP, 115 N.Y.S.3d 584 (App. Term, 1st Dep't 2019).

Respondent's counterclaims (similar to the Petitioner's claims),[896] with the exception of the Justice Courts where counterclaims are limited to $3,000.[897] The portion of a counterclaim asserted in the Justice Court in excess of $3,000 is deemed waived.[898] In *2094-2096 Boston Post Rd., LLC*, the Appellate Term directed the Housing Part to permit the Tenant to withdraw any portion of the excessive counterclaim prior to ruling on the underlying motion.[899]

The assertion of an unrelated counterclaim may constitute a waiver of a personal jurisdiction defense,[900] and once waived, whether intentional or otherwise, the defense may not be revived by the Tenant's withdrawal of the counterclaim.[901] The Appellate Term, First Department noted that challenging the service of the predicate notice does not constitute a waiver of personal jurisdiction defenses because the predicate notice does not "implicate" personal jurisdiction.[902]

If a counterclaim is dismissed prior to an adjudication on the merits, the Tenant may re-assert the claim in a plenary action. For example, a request to amend the Answer to assert a counterclaim on the eve of the hearing, without explanation, was denied as untimely without prejudice to filing in a plenary action.[903] However, where the Tenant timely asserts counterclaims in the summary proceeding "but fail[s] to appear at trial," the doctrine of *res judicata* prohibits the re-assertion of the

896 N.Y. City Civ. Ct. Act § 204; Uniform City Ct. Act § 204; Uniform Dist. Ct. Act § 204; Uniform Just. Ct. Act § 204.

897 N.Y. City Civ. Ct. Act § 208; Uniform City Ct. Act § 208; Uniform Dist. Ct. Act § 208; *see also* Uniform Just. Ct. Act § 208.

898 2094-2096 Boston Post Rd., LLC v. Mackies Am. Grill, Inc., 41 N.Y.S.3d 452 (App. Term, 9th & 10th Jud. Dists. 2016); Siodlak v. Light, 31 N.Y.S.3d 924 (App. Term, 9th & 10th Jud. Dists. 2016).

899 *2094-2096 Boston Post Rd., LLC*, 41 N.Y.S.3d at 452.

900 Halberstam v. Kramer, 969 N.Y.S.2d 803 (App. Term, 2d, 11th & 13th Jud. Dists. 2013) (assertion of counterclaims for mental and emotional distress constitute a waiver of the right to challenge the "adequacy of the service").

901 *Id.*; ROL Realty Co., LLC v. Gordon, 920 N.Y.S.2d 244 (App. Term, 1st Dep't 2010) (withdrawing unrelated counterclaim does not "revive" personal jurisdictional objection).

902 Nguyen v. Perparim, 116 N.Y.S.3d 467 (App. Term, 1st Dep't 2019).

903 *See* LGS Realty Partners LLC v. Kyle, 26 N.Y.S.3d 725 (App. Term, 1st Dep't 2015).

claims in a subsequent proceeding.[904]

A lease provision barring counterclaims is generally enforceable.[905] There is an exception where the counterclaims are "inextricably intertwined" with the Petitioner's claims for unpaid rent and/or use and occupancy, in which case, the counterclaims may be permitted.[906]

D. DISCOVERY

The pre-hearing exchange of documents and/or examinations before trial (depositions) may assist the parties. However, absent consent from counsel for the parties, there is no formal discovery requirement in a summary proceeding unless the Court orders same pursuant to CPLR § 408.[907]

A party seeking discovery must demonstrate that: (1) the Petitioner established a cause of action or that the Respondent has an affirmative defense; (2) a need for information is directly related to the cause of action or claim; (3) the requested discovery is narrowly tailored; (4) prejudice will result if discovery is denied; and (5) the Court may implement measures to minimize any prejudice to the non-moving

---

904 32nd Jabez Corp. v. Meekang, Inc., 194 A.D.3d 414, 143 N.Y.S.3d 203 (1st Dep't 2021).

905 Joseph v. Lyu, 97 N.Y.S.3d 55 (App. Term, 2d, 11th & 13th Jud. Dists. 2018) (dismissing Tenant's counterclaims where lease contained a "no counterclaim" provision); Man Chit Cheng v. Chang, 880 N.Y.S.2d 225 (App. Term, 2d & 11th Jud. Dists. 2008).

906 1035 Third Ave. LLC v. Pure Green NYC 62nd St. Corp., 199 A.D.3d 505, 154 N.Y.S.3d 441 (1st Dep't 2021); All 4 Sports & Fitness, Inc. v. Hamilton, Kane, Martin Enters., Inc., 22 A.D.3d 512, at 513-14, 802 N.Y.S.2d 470, 471 (2d Dep't 2005) (common area maintenance charges inextricably intertwined with Landlord's claim for rent); *2094-2096 Boston Post Rd., LLC,* 41 N.Y.S.3d at 452. *Cf.* Lucas v. Florent, Inc., 860 N.Y.S.2d 813 (N.Y. Civ. Ct. N.Y. Cnty. 2008) (counterclaim for lost business is not inextricably intertwined with claim for unpaid rent).

907 Discovery permitted where information sought regarding the use of the premises is "[p]eculiarly within the tenant's knowledge." *See* Quality and Ruskin Assocs. v. London, 800 N.Y.S.2d 259, 261 (App. Term, 2d & 11th Jud. Dists. 2005) (internal citations omitted). In addition, Tenants were granted "limited discovery relating to the apartment improvements that were the basis" for a rent overcharge claim. *See* 2701 Grand Assoc. LLC v. Morel, 31 N.Y.S.3d 924 (App. Term, 1st Dep't 2016).

party.[908] While discovery typically pertains to documents, records, and an inspection of the premises, an independent medical examination was directed where the Tenant placed his medical condition at issue.[909] As a general matter, absent "extraordinary" circumstances, a bill of particulars may <u>not</u> be amended after discovery has been completed and the case is certified ready for trial.[910]

In *7 E. 86th Realty, LLC v. Leof*, discovery relating to the Tenant's cell phone records was permitted to determine whether the Tenant "primarily reside[d] in the Subject Premises."[911] In *Park Central 1 LLC v. Williams*, the Landlord was permitted to depose the Tenant because the Tenant "possesse[d] particular knowledge which could shed light on the occupancy issues raised in connection with her son's succession claim…."[912]

On the other hand, in *Ryer 26, LLC v. Acosta*, the Landlord's motion to depose the Tenant was denied, and the Tenant's cross-motion to dismiss the proceeding was granted, where the Landlord failed to

908 603 New Jersey Ave., LLC v. Hall, 165 N.Y.S.3d 228 (App. Term, 2d, 11th & 13th Jud. Dists. 2022) (Tenant's assertion of a "colorable claim of fraud in the initial setting of the rent" warrants discovery); Lonray, Inc. v. Newhouse, 229 A.D.2d 440, 644 N.Y.S.2d 900 (2d Dep't 1996); Zada Assocs. v. Meluccio, 28 N.Y.S.3d 651 (App. Term, 1st Dep't 2015) (discovery regarding unauthorized alterations); 72A Realty Assocs. v. Lucas, 26 N.Y.S.3d 216 (App. Term, 1st Dep't 2015) (discovery regarding counterclaim asserting rent overcharge); New York Univ. v. Farkas, 468 N.Y.S.2d 808 (N.Y. Civ. Ct. N.Y. Cnty. 1983). *But see* Inwood Gardens, Inc. v. Udoh, 26 N.Y.S.3d 213 (App. Term, 1st Dep't 2015) (discovery denied where request was "overbroad and burdensome, or sought irrelevant information").

909 Windsor Plaza v. Pinies, N.Y.L.J., June 5, 2014, at 1, col. 3 (N.Y. Civ. Ct. N.Y. Cnty. 2014) (Tenant claimed he temporarily left the premises due to "health concerns" and illegal subletting of the apartment); *see* WHGA Renaissance Apts., L.P. v. Jackson, 37 N.Y.S.3d 809 (App. Term, 1st Dep't 2016) (discovery permitted where the Tenant, who was diagnosed with paranoid schizophrenia, placed her mental condition and ability to form the requisite knowledge at issue).

910 Blumenthal v. 1979 Marcus Ave. Assoc., LLC, 203 A.D.3d 1122, 163 N.Y.S.3d 420 (2d Dep't 2022); King v. Marwest, LLC, 192 A.D.3d 874, 143 N.Y.S.3d 673 (2d Dep't 2021).

911 38 N.Y.S.3d 833 (N.Y. Civ. Ct. N.Y. Cnty. 2016) (the relevant discoverable period was stipulated).

912 128 N.Y.S.3d 772 (App. Term, 1st Dep't 2020); 1560 Wallco LLC v. Guzman, 135 N.Y.S.3d 795 (N.Y. Civ. Ct. Bronx Cnty. 2020).

timely serve a notice of non-renewal.[913] In *901 Bklyn Realty, LLC v. Bklyn Realty, LLC*, discovery was improper (and unnecessary) because the succession rights defense is not a cognizable defense to a proceeding based upon illegal subletting.[914]

The parties may agree to voluntarily participate in discovery and exchange documents without Court intervention prior to a hearing. Irregardless, counsel should be guided accordingly when seeking information from an unrepresented litigant without judicial oversight. In *Missionary Sisters, Inc. v. Fauerbach*, the Appellate Term admonished counsel for requesting and obtaining documents from an eighty-six (86) year-old unrepresented Tenant without a Court Order.[915]

A party may serve a Notice to Admit pursuant to CPLR § 3123, without leave of Court, provided the notice is served no fewer than three (3) days prior to the return date. A Notice to Admit, which is intended to eliminate undisputed issues, may not seek information regarding the "ultimate conclusions" or questions "going to the heart of the matter."[916] The response to a Notice to Admit must be served no later than one (1) day prior to the return date.[917]

Effective January 1, 2019, any document produced in response to a demand for documents authored or created by the party is presumed to be authentic when introduced at trial by the adverse party.[918] The presumption of authenticity may be rebutted by a preponderance of the evidence.[919] The parties should be mindful of the duty to preserve and

913 2018 N.Y.L.J. LEXIS 2705 (N.Y. Civ. Ct. Bronx Cnty. Aug. 9, 2018) (affirmation of counsel insufficient to grant discovery); Department of Hous. Preserv. & Dev. of the City of New York v. Rosenfeld, 168 N.Y.S.3d 647 (N.Y. Civ. Ct. Kings Cnty. 2022) (discovery request denied based upon the Tenant's failure "to show ample need").

914 119 N.Y.S.3d 811 (App. Term, 2d, 11th & 13th Jud. Dists. 2019).

915 41 N.Y.S.3d 450 (App. Term, 1st Dep't 2016) (as a remedy, the Court suppressed documents pending the filing of a formal discovery motion).

916 Hyatt Ave. Assocs., LLC v. Rahman, 17 N.Y.S.3d 579 (App. Term, 2d, 11th & 13th Jud. Dists. 2015) (in non-primary residence holdover proceeding, improper to seek admission regarding the number of days the Tenant resided at the rent-stabilized apartment).

917 CPLR §§ 408, 3123.

918 *Id.* at § 4540-a.

919 *Id.*

retain documents reasonably anticipated for litigation because the intentional or negligent "disposal of crucial items of evidence...before the adversary has an opportunity to inspect them" may result in a spolitation sanction, including, but not limited to, dismissal or directed verdict (or other warranted sanction).[920]

E. JURY TRIAL

Although highly unusual in a summary proceeding, either party may demand that the case be tried before a jury. If the Petitioner requests a jury trial, the demand may be made at any time prior to the hearing provided the applicable jury fee is paid.[921] Otherwise, a jury trial is waived.[922] The Respondent's demand for a jury trial must be made at the time of the Answer.[923]

In the New York City Housing Parts, the City Courts Outside New York City, and the District Courts, the cost for a jury trial is $70.00.[924]

920 *See generally* Astacio v. Birdie 141 Broadway Assocs., 2020 N.Y. Misc. LEXIS 1671 (N.Y. Cnty. Sup. Ct. April 27, 2020) (*citing* Kirkland v. New York City Hous. Auth., 236 A.D.2d 170, 666 N.Y.S.2d 609 (1st Dep't 1997)). The party seeking sanctions for the destruction of relevant documentation must demonstrate that "the party having control over the evidence possessed an obligation to preserve it at the time of its destruction, that the evidence was destroyed with a 'culpable state of mind,' and 'that the destroyed evidence was relevant to the party's claim or defense such that the trier of fact could find that the evidence would support that claim or defense.'" Pegasus Aviation I, Inc. v. Varig Logistica S.A., 26 N.Y.3d 543, 26 N.Y.S.3d 218 (2015); *see* Aponte v. Bronx Preserv. Hous. Dev. Fund Corp., 202 A.D.3d 401, 162 N.Y.S.3d 38 (1st Dep't 2022).

921 *See* N.Y. City Civ. Ct. Act § 1303; Uniform City Ct. Act § 1303; Uniform Dist. Ct. Act § 1303; *see also* Uniform Just. Ct. Act § 1303.

922 *See* N.Y. City Civ. Ct. Act § 1303; Uniform City Ct. Act § 1303; Uniform Dist. Ct. Act § 1303. *See also* Uniform Just. Ct. Act § 1303; Mangano v. Ikinko, 958 N.Y.S.2d 308 (Ossining Just. Ct. 2010).

923 *See* N.Y. City Civ. Ct. Act § 1303; Uniform City Ct. Act § 1303; Uniform Dist. Ct. Act § 1303; *see also* Uniform Just. Ct. Act § 1303. *See* Dexter 345 Inc. v. Belem, 964 N.Y.S.2d 58 (App. Term, 1st Dep't 2012) (jury trial request denied); Tanenbaum Assocs., L.L.P. v. Yudenfreund, 831 N.Y.S.2d 363 (App. Term, 2d & 11th Jud. Dists. 2006); Washington v. Palanzo, 746 N.Y.S.2d 875 (App. Term, 9th & 10th Jud. Dists. 2002).

924 N.Y. City Civ. Ct. Act § 1911(h); Uniform City Ct. Act § 1911(a)(8); Uniform Dist. Ct. Act § 1911(a)(6).

In the Justice Courts, the fee for a trial by jury is $10.00.[925] Since a jury trial must be scheduled in advance, at times, it may be used by the Respondent as a negotiating tactic. While there may be various motivations for the actions taken by either party, the right to a jury trial is both statutory and permissible provided a timely demand is made and the appropriate jury trial fee is paid. The parties should note that a lease provision barring a trial by jury, similar to a lease provision barring counterclaims, will typically be enforced.[926]

925 Uniform Just. Ct. Act § 1911(g).

926 Gago v. 3 Hassell Pl., LLC, 121 N.Y.S.3d 517 (App. Term, 9th & 10th Jud. Dists. 2020); Inwood Gardens, Inc. v. Udoh, 26 N.Y.S.3d 213 (App. Term, 1st Dep't 2015); *Man Chit Cheng*, 880 N.Y.S.2d at 225; P & J Hous. Partners, LLC v. Alvarado, 941 N.Y.S.2d 539 (App. Term, 1st Dep't 2011); 117-119 Leasing Corp. v. Reliable Wool Stock, LLC, 2018 N.Y. Misc. LEXIS 5628 (N.Y. Cnty. Sup. Ct. Nov. 26, 2018); 2401 Davidson Assocs. v. Rice, 2018 N.Y.L.J. LEXIS 3839 (N.Y. Civ. Ct. Bronx Cnty. Nov. 21, 2018).

CHAPTER 9

SERVICE REQUIREMENTS— "10 AND 17 RULE"

In 2012, there were between 15,000 and 20,000 process servers within the United States.[927] By 2019, the number of process servers had decreased to fewer than 9,000, and the average age was forty-six (46).[928]

In a majority of the Housing Parts, a summary proceeding is commenced when the Notice of Petition and Petition are "filed" with the Court (not when the papers are "served").[929] However, in the Justice Courts, the commencement continues to be based upon the "service" of the pleadings.[930]

A. PERSONAL JURISDICTION

The Notice of Petition and Petition must be formally served upon each Respondent, and effectuating proper service is strictly enforced. Service is not an element of the Petitioner's case, but rather the mechanism for acquiring personal jurisdiction over the Respondent.[931]

927 *See* Elka Torpey, "*You're a What? Process Server*," Occupational Outlook Quarterly, Bureau of Labor Statistics, at 46 (Spring 2012). The article based estimates upon "industry sources" because the United States Bureau of Labor Statistics does not collect specific data on process servers. *Id.*

928 "*Process Server Demographics and Statistics in the US*," Zippia (Dec. 14, 2021), at https://www.zippia.com/process-server-jobs/demographics/. The 2019 study revealed that 61% of process servers were male, and the average annual salary was $57,621. *Id.*

929 *See* 92 Bergenbrooklyn, LLC v. Cisarano, 21 N.Y.S.3d 810 (App. Term, 2d, 11th & 13th Jud. Dists. 2015).

930 Livian v. Soblesohn, 2021 N.Y. Misc. LEXIS 6209 (N.Y. Civ. Ct. Queens Cnty. Dec. 3, 2021). For a discussion about the impact of the Landlord's acceptance of moneys following the "commencement" date of the summary proceeding, *see* Chapter 11, subdiv. [C](1)(B), *infra*.

931 *See* Gristmill Realty, LLC v. Roa, 133 N.Y.S.3d 383 (App. Term, 9th & 10th Jud. Dists. 2020).

A Respondent may waive personal jurisdiction defenses.[932] For example, where the Respondent appears on the return date, but does not timely challenge service, the defense of a lack of personal jurisdiction is deemed waived (i.e., the Respondent has consented to the proceeding).[933] The rationale being that since the purpose of service is to provide the Respondent with adequate notice of the claims and the date and location of the hearing, that goal is achieved when the Respondent appears in Court.

On the other hand, the Court must consider whether personal jurisdiction was established when: (1) the Respondent fails to appear on the return date or (2) the Respondent appears and makes a timely objection about the service.[934] In both scenarios, the Court initially verifies the sufficiency of the service through a review of the process server's affidavit of service.

If the Respondent fails to appear and proper service is alleged within the affidavit of service, then the Court may entertain the Petitioner's application for a default judgment. If the service is not in compliance with the applicable laws, then the proceeding will be dismissed. Alternatively, when the Respondent appears, on either the return date or perhaps by the second Court date, a good faith, non-conclusory basis for disputing the appropriateness of the alleged service must be presented to preserve the defense. It has been held that a "sworn, non-conclusory and factually specific denial of service" requires the testimony of the process server at a traverse hearing.[935]

932 *See, e.g.*, 744 E. 215 LLC v. Simmonds, 119 N.Y.S.3d 828 (N.Y. Civ. Ct. Bronx Cnty. 2019) (asserting unrelated counterclaim constitutes waiver of personal jurisdiction defense). *Cf. Gristmill Realty, LLC*, 133 N.Y.S.3d at 383 (Tenant's failure to appear does not constitute waiver of personal jurisdiction defense); Nguyen v. Perparim, 116 N.Y.S.3d 467 (App. Term, 1st Dep't 2019) (disputing service of predicate notice does not waive personal jurisdiction defense).

933 *See* West Haverstraw Preserv., LP v. Diaz, 94 N.Y.S.3d 541 (App. Term, 9th & 10th Jud. Dists. 2018); Citi Land Servs., LLC v. McDowell, 926 N.Y.S.2d 343 (App. Term, 2d, 11th & 13th Jud. Dists. 2011).

934 *See, e.g.*, Fang Realty Corp. v. Prime Six Inc., 151 N.Y.S.3d 862 (N.Y. Civ. Ct. Kings Cnty. 2021).

935 Fountain Terr. Owners, Inc. v. Balic, 101 N.Y.S.3d 699 (App. Term, 2d, 11th & 13th Jud. Dists. 2018); *see* S & H Clinton Assoc., LLC v. Cherry, 148 N.Y.S.3d 823 (App. Term, 9th & 10th Jud. Dists. 2021); Lawler v. Canfield, 114 N.Y.S.3d 621 (Watertown City Ct. 2019).

At a traverse hearing, the Petitioner bears the burden of demonstrating the lawfulness of the service (by a preponderance of the evidence).[936] As stated above, where it is concluded following the hearing that the service was inadequate, the Court is devoid of personal jurisdiction, and the proceeding will be dismissed "without prejudice."[937] As a result, another summary proceeding may be commenced following service of a new predicate notice and the payment of the requisite filing fee. Otherwise, the case may proceed to a hearing on the merits.

B. MANNER OF SERVICE

In New York, there are three (3) permissible ways to formally effectuate service (including service of predicate notices and the Notice of Petition and Petition): (1) personal delivery upon the Respondent; (2) substituted service; and (3) conspicuous place service, commonly referred to as "nail and mail" (but more accurately described as "affix and mail").[938] Since a party to the proceeding may not serve the Notice of Petition and Petition, the Petitioner will typically retain a licensed process server.[939] However, any individual over the age of eighteen (18), and not a party to the proceeding, may effectuate service.[940]

936 *See generally* Federal Natl. Mortgage Assn. v. Greenfield, 203 A.D.3d 1139, 163 N.Y.S.3d 423 (2d Dep't 2022); Serlin Bldg. Ltd. Partnership v. Little, 120 N.Y.S.3d 727 (N.Y. Civ. Ct. Kings Cnty. 2020).

937 *See, e.g.*, Resnick Seaport, LLC v. 199 Roast LLC, 146 N.Y.S.3d 768 (N.Y. Civ. Ct. N.Y. Cnty. 2021). For scheduling and practical purposes, in many Courts the traverse hearing is conducted immediately before the hearing on the merits (trial). If service is found adequate, then the case proceeds immediately to trial. If service is insufficient, then a trial is unnecessary because the proceeding will be dismissed due to a lack of personal jurisdiction.

938 RPAPL § 735.

939 CPLR § 2103(a).

940 *Id.* Within a city of more than one (1) million residents, a non-party, non-attorney who: (1) receives income for process serving or (2) has "effectuated service of process in five or more actions or proceedings in the twelve month period immediately preceding the service in question" is considered a process server. N.Y. General Business Law [Article 8-A] § 89-bb. In New York City, a process server must maintain a date-stamped version of service records and documents in electronic format (including G.P.S. coordinates) and further a copy of same within a separate "bound paginated volume" that memorializes service details in chronological order. *See* NYC Admin Code § 20-406.3; 6 Rules of the City of New York ("RCNY") §§ 2-233, 2-233a; *see* Mathew v. Valentin, 2019 N.Y.L.J. LEXIS 4638 (N.Y. Civ. Ct. Queens Cnty. Jan. 15, 2020).

In 2019, the HSTPA extended the service periods for the Notice of Petition and Petition. As a result, excluding non-payment proceedings in New York City, service must be completed no fewer than ten (10) days but not more than seventeen (17) days prior to the original return date (first Court appearance).[941] This rule replaced what was formally known as the "5 and 12 Rule."[942]

In determining whether service was timely completed, the Court does not include the "day of reckoning" (i.e., the date service is completed), but the day the proceeding is to be heard is counted.[943] If the final day is a "Saturday, Sunday, or public holiday," then the time to complete service is extended to the next business day.[944] Service of "legal process" may not be made on Sunday or other religious observance day.[945] It has been held that placing mailings in the mailbox on a Sunday does not violate the prohibition against service on "the first day of the week."[946]

941 RPAPL § 733(1) (HSTPA, L. 2019, c. 36, Part M, § 15); Pimor Assocs. v. Delvalle, 2021 N.Y.L.J. LEXIS 277 (N.Y. Civ. Ct. Queens Cnty. April 7, 2021).

942 Prior to June 14, 2019, service had to be completed between no fewer than five (5) but no more than twelve (12) days prior to the return date.

943 General Construction Law § 20. *See* JPMorgan Chase Bank v. Lowell, 309 A.D.2d 541, 765 N.Y.S.2d 315 (1st Dep't 2003); 25-31 Ontario St. v. Anthony, 115 N.Y.S.3d 645 (Cohoes City Ct. 2019).

944 General Construction Law § 20.

945 General Business Law § 11. Since the Notice of Petition and Petition are "legal process," they may not be served on Sunday under any circumstance. However, the Appellate Division, Second Department permitted service of a termination notice on Sunday absent a showing of prejudice where the lease did not specify that the notice was "legal process" or require service to be completed in accordance with statutory requirements. *See* Glenball, Ltd. v. TLY Coney, LLC, 57 A.D.3d 843, 874 N.Y.S.2d 128 (2d Dep't 2008). The decision stands for the proposition that documents that are not "legal process" may be served on Sunday. *Id.*; *cf.* Di Perna v. Black, 62 N.Y.S.2d 69 (App. Term, 1st Dep't 1946) (service of a termination notice on Sunday regarding a rent-stabilized apartment is defective); FPTK, LLC v. Paradise Pillows, Inc., 862 N.Y.S.2d 808 (N.Y. Civ. Ct. Kings Cnty. 2005) (same). *See generally* JPMorgan Chase Bank, N.A., v. Lilker, 153 A.D.3d 1243, 61 N.Y.S.3d 578 (2d Dep't 2017) (in foreclosure proceeding, holding that service on the Sabbath upon a person known to observe the Sabbath "constitutes malice" and is a misdemeanor pursuant to General Business Law § 13, which is imputed upon the process server).

946 *See* Kyriacou v. Kangelaris, 645 N.Y.S.2d 405 (Nassau Cnty. Dist. Ct. 1996) ("[p]rocess server's prompt deposit of the mail was clearly designed to allow the mailing to reach the respondents at the earliest possible moment and his diligence does not violate the purpose of the Legislature's proscription against Sunday service").

Barring holidays, the service period may be determined based upon the day of the week the proceeding will be heard. For example, if the return date is Monday, then service must typically be completed between the 2nd and 3rd preceding Fridays. A Tuesday return date requires service to be completed between the 2nd and 3rd preceding Saturdays, which is extended to the next business day if service is performed by means other than personal delivery.[947] This is because service by suitable age and discretion or conspicuous place service is completed after the affidavit of service is filed with the Court.[948] Both Wednesday and Thursday return dates appear to require service to be completed between the 2nd and 3rd preceding Mondays.[949] Finally, a Friday return date requires service to be completed between the 2nd and 3rd preceding Tuesdays.

1. PERSONAL DELIVERY

Personal delivery is the preferred method of service. This is achieved by handing the Notice of Petition and Petition to the Respondent. The papers need not be personally delivered at the premises.[950] Service in this manner is considered "complete" when the papers are handed, or personally delivered, to the Respondent, which must be done not less than ten (10) but no

---

947 General Construction Law § 25-a; Madison Plaza Commercial Owners, LLC v. EB Leasing, LLC, 958 N.Y.S.2d 61 (App. Term, 1st Dep't 2010). *See also* Ross v. State Div. of Hous. & Cmty. Renewal, 125 A.D.3d 434, 998 N.Y.S.2d 888 (1st Dep't 2015) (no extension of time to complete service when a holiday occurs within the time period to serve other than the final day).

948 RPAPL § 735(2)(b).

949 Applying the "10 and 17" Rule to a Wednesday return date, service would have to be completed between the 2nd and 3rd preceding Sundays, thus service is extended pursuant to General Construction Law § 25-a to the next business day (i.e., Monday).

950 *See* AMB Fund III New York III & IV, LLC v. WWTL Logistics, Inc., 942 N.Y.S.2d 307 (App. Term, 2d, 11th & 13th Jud. Dists. 2012) (service on the corporation's general manager at the place of business, rather than the subject premises, satisfied personal service requirements pursuant to CPLR § 311(a)(1)); City of New York v. DeNoble, 801 N.Y.S.2d 777 (App. Term, 1st Dep't 2005) (noting that RPAPL § 735 "does not require that such in-hand delivery of the Notice of Petition and Petition be effectuated at the subject property"); 126 Spruce St., LLC v. Club Centr., LLC, 830 N.Y.S.2d 506 (Nassau Cnty. Dist. Ct. 2007).

more than seventeen (17) days prior to the return date.[951] Although service is considered "complete" when the papers are handed to the Respondent, the term "complete" is not entirely accurate because the process server must further file proof of service with the Clerk of the Court in the form of a sworn affidavit of service within three (3) days of the service.[952]

Notwithstanding RPAPL § 735(2)(a), which requires the affidavit of service to be filed within three (3) days of the personal delivery, it has been held that the failure to comply with this provision constitutes a mere ministerial error, and will likely warrant the denial of a motion to dismiss.[953] The Petitioner may move to cure the defect by moving back the filing date of the affidavit of service *nunc pro tunc*.[954] However, courts in the First Judicial Department have taken the opposite approach; i.e., requiring the filing of the affidavit of service to be completed within the three (3) day period.[955]

2. SUBSTITUTED SERVICE

Substituted service is an alternative method of service. Unlike the personal delivery method, substituted service is considered "complete" when the affidavit of service is filed with the Clerk of the Court.[956] Strict compliance with the statute is generally required.[957]

---

951 RPAPL §§ 733, 735(2)(a).

952 *Id.* at § 735(2)(a).

953 Siedlecki v. Doscher, 931 N.Y.S.2d 203 (App. Term, 2d, 11th & 13th Jud. Dists. 2011); Martin, Jr. v. Sandoval, 9 N.Y.S.3d 594 (Peekskill City Ct. 2015) (service proper where the affidavit of service was filed five (5) days following delivery); Mangano v. Ikinko, 958 N.Y.S.2d 308 (Ossining Just. Ct. 2010) (late affidavit of service "deemed to have been timely filed" where the Notice of Petition and Petition were properly served).

954 *Martin, Jr.*, 9 N.Y.S.3d at 594.

955 *See, e.g.*, 2198 Cruger Assocs. v. Xhurreta, 2019 N.Y.L.J. LEXIS 4387 (N.Y. Civ. Ct. Bronx Cnty. Dec. 9, 2019) (*citing* Riverside Syndicate, Inc. v. Saltzman, 49 A.D.3d 402 (1st Dep't 2008)).

956 RPAPL § 735(2)(b).

957 *See Riverside Syndicate, Inc.*, 49 A.D.3d at 402, 852 N.Y.S.2d at 840; Berkeley Assocs. Co. v. Di Nolfi, 122 A.D.2d 703, at 705-06, 505 N.Y.S.2d 630, 632 (1st Dep't 1986); Ron Rose Group, Inc. v. Gavish & G-R Bea Corp., 2002 N.Y. Misc. LEXIS 553 (App. Term, 9th & 10th Jud. Dists. March 13, 2002); *but see* ZOT, Inc. v. Watson, 867 N.Y.S.2d 379 (N.Y. Civ. Ct. Kings Cnty. 2008) (holding the late filing of the affidavit of service does not render the court devoid of jurisdiction).

Substituted service is a byproduct of an unsuccessful effort to personally deliver the papers. For example, if the Respondent is not at home when service is attempted, the process server may leave the papers with the individual who answers the door provided that person is of an appropriate age and has the appropriate judgment.[958] Although a precise description of a "person of suitable age and discretion" is not clearly defined, leaving the Notice of Petition and Petition with a spouse, adult child, or other mature adult at the residence, or with the office manager or other acceptable employee at a place of business, will generally suffice.[959]

The same number of copies of both the Notice of Petition and Petition must be left with a person of suitable age and discretion as there are Respondents being served in this manner. In other words, if two (2) Tenants are named in the summary proceeding and are being served by substituted service, then the process server must leave two (2) copies of the Notice of Petition and Petition. In addition, the process server must mail two (2) copies of the papers to each Respondent at the subject premises the following business day; one (1) copy via registered or certified mail, and one (1) by regular mail.[960] For commercial properties, a copy of the papers must also be mailed to the Tenant's known corporate address within the State (when at a location other than the subject premises) by certified or registered mail, and regular mail, the following business day.[961]

---

958 *See* Rosenberg v. Chervil, 134 N.Y.S.3d 614 (App. Term, 9th & 10th Jud. Dists. 2020).

959 *Siedlecki*, 931 N.Y.S.2d at 203; George Doulaveris & Son, Inc. v. P.J. 37 Food Corp., 961 N.Y.S.2d 722 (App. Term, 2d, 11th & 13th Jud. Dists. 2013); Milonis v. 3273-3285 Westchester Ave. Realty Cop., 119 N.Y.S.3d 395 (N.Y. Civ. Ct. Bronx Cnty. 2019). *Cf.* O'Connell v. Singletary, 926 N.Y.S.2d 345 (App. Term, 9th & 10th Jud. Dists. 2011) (substituted service on person of suitable age and discretion at the premises after Respondent surrendered possession was not proper service).

960 RPAPL § 735(1).

961 *Id.* at § 735(1)(b); *see* Saba Realty Partners, LLC v. International Gold Star, Inc., 130 N.Y.S.3d 878 (App. Term, 2d, 11th & 13th Jud. Dists. 2020) (dismissing commercial non-payment proceeding where Landlord failed to mail the Notice of Petition and Petition to the Tenant's premises and its principal place of business within the State by registered or certified mail, and regular first class mail, following service upon a person of suitable age and discretion); *George Doulaveris & Son, Inc.*, 961 N.Y.S.2d at 722 (service defective where follow-up mailings bore the name of an entity other than the corporate Tenant); F & Realty Corp. v. 1014 Flatbush Ave., Inc., 969 N.Y.S.2d 802 (App. Term, 2d, 11th & 13th Jud. Dists. 2013) (dismissing proceeding because the papers were not mailed to Respondent's known corporate address following substituted service).

Service is complete when the process server files with the Court a sworn affidavit of service within three (3) days of the mailing.[962] Again, all of this must be completed no more than seventeen (17) days but no fewer than ten (10) days prior to the initial Court date.

3. CONSPICUOUS PLACE SERVICE ("NAIL AND MAIL")

The third and final method of service is conspicuous place service, which is commonly referred to as "nail and mail" or "affix and mail." If on the initial attempt at service no one answers the door, the process server must make at least one (1) additional attempt at service during a different time of day. On the second visit if there is still no answer, and the Petitioner is willing to forego a money judgment if the Tenant fails to appear in Court, the process server may either fasten the papers to the door or slide them beneath the entrance of the residence (one (1) copy per Respondent).[963] The process server may not "wedge" the papers between the door knob and door frame without the use of tape or other fastening device.[964]

Conspicuous place service is "the least desirable method of service, when compared with in-hand or substitute service."[965] As such, a process server must utilize "reasonable" efforts to serve a Respondent at a time and place when the occupant is expected to be present.[966] There

---

962 RPAPL §§ 733, 735.

963 *See* 156 Nassau Ave. HDFC v. Tchernitsky, 112 N.Y.S.3d 859 (App. Term, 2d, 11th & 13th Jud. Dists. 2019); Plotch v. Dellis, 75 N.Y.S.3d 779 (App. Term, 2d, 11th & 13th Jud. Dists. 2018); *Fang Realty Corp.*, 151 N.Y.S.3d at 862; Latchman v. Hardnet, 143 N.Y.S.3d 863 (N.Y. Civ. Ct. Queens Cnty. 2021); *Mathew*, 2019 N.Y.L.J. LEXIS at 4638; *see generally* Cornhill LLC v. Sposato, 54 N.Y.S.3d 548 (Rochester City Ct. 2017).

964 *See* Carlhart Realty Corp. v. Parks, 119 N.Y.S.3d 827 (N.Y. Civ. Ct. Queens Cnty. 2019); Bruckner by the Bridge, LLC v. Gonzales, 18 N.Y.S.3d 577 (N.Y. Civ. Ct. Bronx Cnty. 2015).

965 Bel Air Leasing LP v. Johnston, 157 N.Y.S.3d 346 (N.Y. Civ. Ct. Kings Cnty. 2021) (*citing* Eight Assocs. v. Hynes, 102 A.D.2d 746, 476 N.Y.S.2d 881 (1st Dep't 1984)).

966 RPAPL § 735. *See 156 Nassau Ave. HDFC*, 112 N.Y.S.3d at 859; Joseph v. Lyu, 97 N.Y.S.3d 55 (App. Term, 2d, 11th & 13th Jud. Dists. 2018); Doji Bak, LLC v. Alta Plastics, 41 N.Y.S.3d 449 (App. Term, 9th & 10th Jud. Dists. 2016); 809-811 Kings Hwy., LLC v. Pulse Laser Skin Care, 901 N.Y.S.2d 906 (App. Term, 2d, 11th & 13th Jud. Dists. 2009).

must further be a "reasonable expectation of success" that the person sought to be served will be present at the premises at the time service is attempted.[967] In other words, if the process server has knowledge that the Tenant will not be present when service is attempted, attempting service at such time is improper.[968] In addition, attempting service exclusively during normal working hours is inadequate, and may result in defective service.[969]

The use of "nail and mail" service at a commercial property is similarly defective when the Landlord and/or Landlord's representatives were aware that the Tenant was not present and/or had previously vacated the premises when service was attempted.[970] The Appellate Term for the Ninth and Tenth Judicial Districts concluded that attempts at service where there is not "at least a reasonable expectation of success in finding a person on the premises to whom delivery may be made"

967 214 Knickerbocker, LLC v. Molly's Milk Truck Sweet & Savory, 144 N.Y.S.3d 796 (App. Term, 2d, 11th & 13th Jud. Dists. 2021) (service attempts deemed unreasonable and defective where the Tenant did not have access to the premises due to Landlord's changing of the locks); Kew Gardens Terrace Owners Corp. v. McGrath, 129 N.Y.S.3d 627 (N.Y. Civ. Ct. Queens Cnty. 2020).

968 *See, e.g.*, Brooklyn Heights Realty Co. v. Gliwa, 92 A.D.2d 602, 459 N.Y.S.2d 793, 794 (2d Dep't 1983) (attempts at service exclusively when a person is reasonably expected to be at work); *214 Knickerbocker, LLC*, 144 N.Y.S.3d at 796 (Tenant lacked access to the premises); George Washington Bridge Bus Station Develop. Venture LLC v. Inho Beauty Inc., 120 N.Y.S.3d 581 (N.Y. Civ. Ct. N.Y. Cnty. 2019) (service defective where Petitioner, knowing that the "Tenant's business [was] not yet open to the public," failed to serve the papers at the commercial Tenant's known alternative location); Gomiela v. Ottimo, Index No. 94061212 (Southampton Just. Ct. Nov. 8, 1994) (unreported decision) (dismissing summary proceeding against occupant of a summer rental "[u]sed primarily on weekends" where all attempts at service were made on weekdays).

969 *Brooklyn Heights Realty Co.*, 92 A.D.2d at 602, 459 N.Y.S.2d at 793.

970 255 Huguenot St. Corp. v. Rwechungura, 110 N.Y.S.3d 862 (App. Term, 9th & 10th Jud. Dists. 2018) (Petitioner was aware that the Tenant was "outside of the country" when service was effectuated); *Doji Bak, LLC*, 41 N.Y.S.3d at 449; *George Washington Bridge Bus Station Develop. Venture LLC*, 120 N.Y.S.3d at 581; 91 Fifth Ave. Corp. v. Brookhill Prop. Holdings LLC, 28 N.Y.S.3d 263 (N.Y. Civ. Ct. N.Y. Cnty. 2016) (holding that an attempt at service "pre-destined to failure" is the "equivalent of no attempt at all"). *Cf. Kew Gardens Terrace Owners Corp.*, 129 N.Y.S.3d at 627 (service at property appropriate where occupants "maintained dominion and control over the premises and there were persons of suitable age and discretion living there with a connection to the Prime Respondents").

fails to satisfy the reasonable application standards of RPAPL § 735.[971]

Although only two (2) reasonable attempts at personal service are required before utilizing conspicuous place service, where service is completed in this manner, a money judgment may not be awarded in the event the Respondent fails to appear in Court. Rather, a money judgment may only be obtained on default following conspicuous place service where the heightened "due diligence" standards for service are satisfied, which includes, but is not limited to, at least one (1) additional attempt at service (i.e., a minimum of three (3) attempts over two (2) days) before resorting to "nail and mail."[972]

Due diligence refers to the "quality" of the attempts to effectuate personal service, and not the quantity or frequency of the efforts.[973] The Appellate Division, Second Department has held that to satisfy due diligence, the process server must further make "genuine inquiries about the defendant's whereabouts and place of employment" prior to resorting to nail and mail service.[974] The Appellate Terms for both the Second, Eleventh and Thirteenth Judicial Districts and the Ninth and Tenth Judicial Districts have similarly held that at least one (1) of the attempts at service must be at the Respondent's place of employment or business, or new residence, if known.[975]

Leaving the Notice of Petition and Petition on an outer fence surrounding the premises is sufficient where the fence "blocks" the process

971 *Doji Bak, LLC*, 41 N.Y.S.3d at 449; *255 Huguenot St. Corp.*, 110 N.Y.S.3d at 862 (pursuant to CPLR § 308(5), service by electronic mail may be permitted where Landlord has difficulty serving Tenant outside of the country); *Joseph*, 97 N.Y.S.3d at 55.

972 *Plotch*, 75 N.Y.S.3d at 779; Avgush v. Berrahu, 847 N.Y.S.2d 343 (App. Term, 2d, 11th & 13th Jud. Dists. 2007); *see* Borg v. Feeley, 2017 N.Y. Misc. LEXIS 2431 (App. Term, 1st Dep't June 23, 2017); Stephen LLC v. Zazula, 2018 N.Y. Misc. LEXIS 1428 (N.Y. Cnty. Sup. Ct. April 19, 2018); Suero v. Rivera, 162 N.Y.S.3d 684 (N.Y. Civ. Ct. Queens Cnty. 2022).

973 *Bel Air Leasing LP*, 157 N.Y.S.3d at 346.

974 Faruk v. Dawn, 162 A.D.3d 744, 79 N.Y.S.3d 249 (2d Dep't 2018); Jamaica Seven LLC v. Douglas, 155 N.Y.S.3d 528 (N.Y. Civ. Ct. Queens Cnty. 2021); *Bel Air Leasing LP*, 157 N.Y.S.3d at 346.

975 1653 Realty, LLC v. Hernandez, 117 N.Y.S.3d 790 (App. Term, 2d, 11th & 13th Jud. Dists. 2019) (plenary action for unpaid rent); Merrbill Holdings, LLC v. Toscano, 100 N.Y.S.3d 610 (App. Term, 9th & 10th Jud. Dists. 2018); *see also Cornhill LLC*, 54 N.Y.S.3d at 548.

server's access to the front door.[976] Moreover, where a building's exterior door impedes the process server's ability to reach the Tenant's particular unit, the "outer bounds of [the] tenant's actual dwelling place [is] deemed to extend to the exterior door of the building" or alternative location where the process server's "progress is arrested."[977]

Similar to substituted service, two (2) copies of the Notice of Petition and Petition must be mailed the following business day to each Respondent at the premises; one (1) via registered or certified mail, and one (1) by regular mail.[978] The process server must further file a sworn affidavit of service within three (3) days of the mailings.[979] Once again, all of this must be completed between ten (10) and seventeen (17) days prior to the initial return date in Court.

C. DEFAULT JUDGMENTS

The Respondent's failure to appear on the return date may result in a default judgment in favor of the Landlord. This means that the Landlord will be awarded a judgment of possession and a warrant of eviction provided service was proper.[980]

---

976 *See* Res Land, Inc. v. SHS Baisley, LLC, 939 N.Y.S.2d 743 (App. Term, 2d, 11th & 13th Jud. Dists. 2011).

977 Rattner v. Fessler, 202 A.D.3d 1011, 163 N.Y.S.3d 575 (2d Dep't 2022) (mortgage foreclosure proceeding); Greenwood Realty Co. v. Katz, 187 A.D.3d 1153, 131 N.Y.S.3d 225 (2d Dep't 2020); 322 W. 47th St. HDFC v. Loo, 31 N.Y.S.3d 924 (App. Term, 1st Dep't 2016).

978 RPAPL § 735(1). Where the Tenant's foreign address (in France) was known, Landlord was required to mail a copy of the Notice of Petition and Petition to that alternative address the day after leaving the papers at the premises. Horatio Arms, Inc. v. Celbert, 972 N.Y.S.2d 813 (App. Term, 1st Dep't 2013). *Cf.* 305 MK Secure Holdings, LLC v. Chen, 108 N.Y.S.3d 261 (App. Term, 1st Dep't 2018) (no additional mailings required where Tenant did not provide an alternative address).

979 RPAPL § 735(2)(b). *See* Valane v. Cruz, 2018 N.Y.L.J. LEXIS 2629 (N.Y. Civ. Ct. Bronx Cnty. Aug. 2, 2018) (service defective where completed one (1) day late; at the time service was to be completed not more than twelve (12) days prior to the return date); Abakporo v. Gardner, 875 N.Y.S.2d 818 (N.Y. Civ. Ct. Kings Cnty. 2008); Zajaczkowska v. Zeranska, 2007 N.Y. Misc. LEXIS 7819 (N.Y. Civ. Ct. Kings Cnty. Oct. 4, 2007).

980 159 W. 23rd LLC v. Spa Ciel de NY Corp., 120 N.Y.S.3d 700 (App. Term, 1st Dep't 2020) (two (2) attempts at service on the corporate Tenant during normal business hours satisfied the "reasonable" application standard); *809-811 Kings Hwy., LLC*, 901 N.Y.S.2d at 906 ("nail and mail" service after two (2) unsuccessful attempts during normal business hours on two (2) different days sufficient for a possessory judgment).

The Petitioner may further be entitled to a money judgment for unpaid rent and/or use and occupancy when service was effectuated by: (1) personal delivery; (2) substituted service; or (3) conspicuous place service (provided the heightened "due diligence" requirements for alternate service pursuant to CPLR § 308(4) were satisfied, including proof that at least three (3) reasonable attempts at personal delivery were made over two (2) days at different times of the day, and not on Sunday or public holiday, prior to nail and mail service).[981] As of June 14, 2019, a Landlord may not be awarded attorney's fees in any forum where the Tenant defaults in a summary proceeding involving residential property.[982]

Unless previously amended, a money judgement on default for rent arrears and use and occupancy is limited to the amount sought in the Petition.[983] To obtain a money judgment where service is adequate, the Petitioner must further file with the Court a non-military affidavit attesting that the process server made a reasonable inquiry regarding the Tenant's military status.[984] Since there is no fixed time to file the non-military affidavit, the failure to file the affidavit by the return date is not a jurisdictional defect. Instead, the Court may adjourn the case to allow for the filing of the affidavit, at which time, should the Tenant again fail

---

981 CPLR § 308; *see* PHH Mortgage Corp. v. Johnson, 190 A.D.3d 990, 136 N.Y.S.3d 899 (2d Dep't 2021) (four (4) attempts at service at different times and days, including a Saturday, satisfied due diligence); Wilmington Trust Co. v. Gewirtz, 193 A.D.3d 1110, 147 N.Y.S.3d 606 (2d Dep't 2021) (same); Florestal v. Coleman-Florestal, 124 A.D.3d 578, 2 N.Y.S.3d 153 (2d Dep't 2015) (several attempts at service, including two (2) Saturdays, a weekday evening, and a weekday morning, satisfied the due diligence requirements); Wells Fargo Bank, N.A. v. Cherot, 102 A.D.3d 768, 957 N.Y.S.2d 886, 887 (2d Dep't 2013) (three (3) attempts to effect personal service at the appellant's residence at various times on different days, including a Saturday, satisfied due diligence); *Avgush*, 847 N.Y.S.2d at 343 (five (5) attempts over two (2) days sufficient service for a money judgment). *But see* RH Apts., LP v. Eliot, 946 N.Y.S.2d 69 (Rochester City Ct. 2012) (use and occupancy denied absent testimony or a sworn affidavit from a person with firsthand knowledge that the occupants continued to occupy the premises following commencement of the summary proceeding).

982 *See* RPL § 234 (HSTPA, L. 2019, c. 36, Part M, § 8).

983 Mustafa v. Plein, 950 N.Y.S.2d 492 (App. Term, 2d, 11th & 13th Jud. Dists. 2012); Port Chester Hous. Auth. v. Turner, 734 N.Y.S.2d 805 (App. Term, 9th & 10th Jud. Dists. 2001).

984 *See* Riverton Sq. LLC v. McLeod, 57 N.Y.S.3d 677 (App. Term, 1st Dep't 2017); Pascal v. Law Offices of Gilbert C. Parris, 2020 N.Y. Misc. LEXIS 17539 (N.Y. Cnty. Sup. Ct. May 26, 2020); *Jamaica Seven LLC*, 155 N.Y.S.3d at 528.

to appear, a default judgment may be entered.[985]

The content of the affidavit of service is *prima facie* proof that service was performed in the manner described, and on the date and time alleged.[986] The Respondent may rebut the service, but to do so, more than conclusory denials are required.[987] However, under no circumstance may a judgment and warrant be issued where the Petition is defective on its face.[988]

Dissimilar from the other Judicial Departments, in the Fourth Judicial Department, personal delivery service may be required for the Landlord to be awarded a money judgment on default. In 1929, in the *Matter of McDonald*, the Appellate Division, Fourth Department established this rule for default judgments.[989] Notwithstanding this precedent, there seems to be a recent shift at the trial court level within that Judicial Department towards granting money judgments on default

985 Unitrin Advantage Ins. Co. v. 21st Century Pharmacy, 158 A.D.3d 450, 67 N.Y.S.3d 826 (1st Dep't 2018); Avgush v. De La Cruz, 924 N.Y.S.2d 307 (App. Term, 9th & 10th Jud. Dists. 2011).

986 Iodice v. Academics R Us, Inc., 26 N.Y.S.3d 724 (App. Term, 1st Dep't 2015); 104 Realty, LLC v. Johnson, 954 N.Y.S.2d 760 (App. Term, 2d, 11th & 13th Jud. Dists. 2012); Iris Holdings 961 42nd LLC v. Hernandez, 2018 N.Y.L.J. LEXIS 1737 (N.Y. Civ. Ct. Kings Cnty. May 23, 2018).

987 One W. Bank, FSB v. Rotondaro, 188 A.D.3d 710, 131 N.Y.S.3d 601 (2d Dep't 2020); 63rd St. Realty, LLC v. Yanush, 100 N.Y.S.3d 611 (App. Term, 2d, 11th & 13th Jud. Dists. 2018).

988 Gristmill Realty, LLC v. Roa, 133 N.Y.S.3d 383 (App. Term, 9th & 10th Jud. Dists. 2020); Lakeview Affordable Hous., LLC v. Turner, 121 N.Y.S.3d 510 (App. Term, 9th & 10th Jud. Dists. 2020); 101-08 LLC v. Rodriguez, 157 N.Y.S.3d 695 (N.Y. Civ. Ct. Queens Cnty. 2021).

989 225 A.D. 403, 233 N.Y.S. 368 (4th Dep't 1929).

where service is effectuated by means other than personal delivery.[990] The reader should be mindful of subsequent decisions from the Fourth Judicial Department on this topic. Interestingly, where there is a "split" in the Judicial Departments, it is axiomatic that the Courts follow the precedent set by the Appellate Division within their own Department. If a particular issue has not been decided within the Department, then the doctrine of *stare decisis* would require the Court to adhere to the precedent set by another Department, until either the Court of Appeals or the local Appellate Division rules on the issue.[991]

Another interesting situation results when the Respondent appears in Court following service by "nail and mail" delivery after two (2) unsuccessful attempts at personal delivery. If the Respondent consents to the issuance of a judgment of possession and a warrant of eviction, but disputes the monetary relief, then the Respondent may be in a more favorable position by defaulting so as to avoid a money judgment in the summary proceeding (Landlord may commence a plenary action). On the other hand, if the Tenant appears, then a prevailing Petitioner may be awarded a money judgment.

This is not to suggest that it is in the best interests of the Respondent to default because the Respondent would then waive the opportunity to

990 In 2009, approximately 80 years following the *McDonald* decision, the Niagara County Court rejected the legal principle that personal delivery was necessary to award a money judgment on default in a summary proceeding. *See* Expressway Vill., Inc. v. Denman, 893 N.Y.S.2d 736, 738 (Niagara Cnty. Ct. 2009). In 2016, the Rochester City Court re-adopted the *McDonald* ruling when it denied a Landlord's application for a money judgment where service was not achieved by personal delivery. *See* Cornhill LLC v. Sposato, 26 N.Y.S.3d 831 (Rochester City Ct. 2016). However, on appeal, the Monroe County Court reversed and remitted the proceeding back to the Rochester City Court for a new determination on the Landlord's application for a money judgment. *See* Cornhill LLC v. Sposato, 51 N.Y.S.3d 828 (Monroe Cnty. Ct. 2017). On remand, the Rochester City Court again denied the Landlord's application for a money judgment, but for different reasons; namely, the process server's failure to attempt to ascertain the Respondent's place of employment prior to resorting to conspicuous place service. *See Cornhill LLC*, 54 N.Y.S.3d at 548. The Rochester City Court further acknowledged that three (3) attempts at service may be sufficient for a money judgment on default provided due diligence is satisfied. *Id.*; *see also* MJC Supply, LLC v. Powis, 2019 U.S. Dist. LEXIS 28743 (E.D.N.Y. Feb. 20, 2019) (*citing* the *Cornhill, LLC* decision for the same proposition).

991 The Park Central 1 LLC v. Williams, 128 N.Y.S.3d 772 (App. Term, 1st Dep't 2020); Halpern v. Tunne, 966 N.Y.S.2d 346 (App. Term, 2d, 11th & 13th Jud. Dists. 2012).

assert defenses in the proceeding (and possibly a related action) and the right to appeal because an appeal may not be taken from a default judgment.[992] Moreover, the Tenant may continue to remain liable for damages in a subsequent plenary action. As with most legal circumstances, the party should seek the advice of counsel.

992 CPLR § 5511; 1764 Majors Path Corp. v. Petrinolis, 36 N.Y.S.3d 408 (App. Term, 9th & 10th Jud. Dists. 2016). For further discussion on appeals, *see* Chapter 14, subdiv. D, *infra*.

CHAPTER 10

MANUFACTURED HOMES AND MOBILE PARKS

Eviction proceedings, and the relevant laws contained within both Article 7 of the RPAPL and the RPL, apply to the removal of occupants from manufactured homes and mobile homes.[993] Real Property Law § 233 *et seq*. specifically pertains to the owners and occupants of a manufactured home park, which is defined as a "contiguous parcel of privately owned land [] used for the accommodation of three (3) or more manufactured homes occupied for year-round living."[994]

In this context, the Petitioner typically owns the manufactured home park ("manufactured home park owner" or "Landlord"), and the Respondent "rents space in [the] manufactured home park…for the purpose of parking [the] manufactured home [he or she owns] or… rents a manufactured home in a manufactured home park from a manufactured home park owner or operator" ("occupant" or "Tenant").[995] In other words, the occupant of the manufactured home may (but does not have to) own the manufactured home which is the subject of the summary proceeding within the Petitioner's manufactured home park.[996] Another scenario involves "rent to own contracts," whereby it is agreed that the occupant will become the owner of the manufactured home <u>after</u> certain conditions are satisfied or following the passage of a specified period of time.[997]

---

993 *See generally* Lyke v. Anderson, 147 A.D.2d 18, at 23, 541 N.Y.S.2d 817 (2d Dep't 1989).

994 RPL § 233(a)(3).

995 Hillcrest Homes, LLC v. Albion Mobile Homes, Inc., 117 A.D.3d 1434, at 1435-36, 984 N.Y.S.2d 755 (4th Dep't 2014).

996 RPL § 233(a)(1).

997 *Id.* at § 233(a)(6).

A. MANUFACTURED HOMES COMPARED TO MOBILE HOMES

Real Property Law § 233(a) defines a manufactured home as a "structure, transportable in one (1) or more sections, which in the traveling mode, is eight (8) body feet or more in width or forty (40) body feet or more in length, or, when erected on site, is 320 or more square feet, and which is built on a permanent chassis and designed to be used as a dwelling with or without a permanent foundation when connected to the required utilities."[998] A manufactured home "includes the plumbing, heating, air-conditioning, and electrical systems contained therein."[999]

On the other hand, a mobile home is "[a] moveable or portable unit, manufactured prior to January 1, 1966, designed and constructed to be towed on its own chassis, comprised of frame and wheels, connected to utilities, and designed and constructed without a permanent foundation."[1000] A mobile home may contain parts that fold or collapse while towed or parts that are "[s]eparately towable components that may be joined into one (1) integral unit that may be separated again for repeated towing."[1001] A mobile home may only be used for residential purposes.[1002] When referring to eviction proceedings, although distinct, the terms "manufactured home" and "mobile home" are used interchangeably here because "mobile homes" are included within the statutory definition of "manufactured homes."[1003]

998 *Id.* at § 233(a)(4).

999 *Id.*

1000 *Id.* at § 233(a)(5).

1001 *Id.*

1002 *Id.*; *see generally* Lazy Acres Park, LLC v. Ferretti, 118 A.D.3d 1406, 988 N.Y.S.2d 364 (4th Dep't 2014).

1003 RPL § 233(a)(4).

B. LEASE TERMS AND CONDITIONS

Absent exigent circumstances, the Landlord may not enter the manufactured home without the occupant's consent.[1004] In an eviction proceeding, the Tenant may assert the affirmative defenses of the implied warranty of habitability and retaliatory eviction, where applicable, in addition to making a claim for reciprocal attorney's fees if the Petitioner is unsuccessful, similar to RPL § 234.[1005] When a manufactured home park contains six (6) or more lots, the Landlord must maintain the security deposit in an interest-bearing account.[1006]

1. INITIAL AND RENEWAL LEASES

The initial lease, and all renewal lease offers, between a manufactured home park owner and the Respondent must be in writing, and include a statement of the Tenant's rights approved by the Commissioner of Housing and Community Renewal.[1007] In addition, a renewal lease of at least twelve (12) months must be offered to a manufactured home owner in good standing.[1008] When a proposed renewal lease is declined, whether explicitly or where the Tenant does not accept (and return signed) the lease within thirty (30) days of the offer, upon expiration, the tenancy continues on a month-to-month basis.[1009] Conversely, if the

---

1004 *Id.* at § 233(j).

1005 *Id.* at §§ 233(m),(n),(o); *see* Higgins v. Peranzo, 179 A.D.2d 871, 579 N.Y.S.2d 453 (3d Dep't 1992) (retaliatory eviction); Clarkson Mobile Home Park, Inc. v. Ecklund, 532 N.Y.S.2d 615 (Monroe Cnty. Ct. 1987) (warranty of habitability).

1006 RPL § 233(g)(4)[c].

1007 *Id.* at § 233(e)(1).

1008 *See* State of New York v. Magley, 105 A.D.2d 208, 484 N.Y.S.2d 251 (3d Dep't 1984); Amityville Mobile Home Civic Assn. Corp. v. Frontier Park Corp., 2014 N.Y. Misc. LEXIS 1636 (Suffolk Cnty. Sup. Ct. March 25, 2014); A.K.A.B. & E. Mobile Home Rentals, Inc. v. Marshall, 452 N.Y.S.2d 144 (Poughkeepsie Just. Ct. 1982). A renewal lease must be offered to a manufactured home owner, then in good standing, but currently without a lease, on or before October 1st, or, in all other situations, provided the manufactured home owner is in good standing, ninety (90) days prior to the expiration of the existing lease. *See* RPL § 233(e)(2). With regard to the non-payment of rent, "good standing" means not being more than one (1) month behind on the rent. *Id.* at § 233(e)(2)(ii).

1009 RPL § 233(e)(2); *see generally* Pedote v. STP Assoc., LLC, 959 N.Y.S.2d 91 (Nassau Cnty. Sup. Ct. 2012).

Landlord fails to provide a timely lease renewal, then the tenancy continues beyond the lease expiration date.[1010]

2. RENT INCREASES

Rent increases for manufactured homes are governed by RPL § 233-b, which generally limits the increase (including the rent, costs, fees, assessments, and utilities) to three percent (3%).[1011] However, a rent increase may be as high as six percent (6%), subject to challenge, where the manufactured home park owner demonstrates increased operating expenses, property taxes, or capital improvement costs.[1012]

3. FEES

The fees, charges, and assessments associated with the manufactured home park must be disclosed prior to entering the rental agreement.[1013] During the tenancy, an increase in fees and assessments may be imposed after the manufactured home park owner provides the Tenant ninety (90) days written notice.[1014] The Tenant's utilities and facility charges may not be increased unless a rental agreement has been offered.[1015]

Late fees must be included within the rental agreement to be enforced, but a late fee may not exceed three percent (3%) (previously five percent (5%)).[1016] A late fee may not be collected where the rent is tendered within ten (10) days of the due date.[1017]

1010 RPL § 233(e)(4).

1011 *Id.* at § 233(e)(5); *Clarkson Mobile Home Park, Inc.*, 532 N.Y.S.2d at 615 (rent increase invalid where lease was not offered to mobile home Tenants).

1012 RPL § 233-b(2),(6). A rent increase exceeding six percent (6%) requires Court approval. *Id.* at § 233-b(6).

1013 *Id.* at § 233(g)(2).

1014 *Id.* at § 233(g)(3).

1015 *Id.*

1016 *Id.* at § 233[r]. The late fee may not be compounded and is not considered "additional rent." *Id.*

1017 *Id.*

4. RENT RECEIPTS

The manufactured home park owner must provide the Tenant a written rent receipt when the rent (or any other fee or charge associated with the manufactured home park) is paid by means other than personal check.[1018] The receipt must be signed by the recipient and include the date, amount, premises, and period for which the payment was tendered.[1019]

C. GROUNDS FOR EVICTION

The HSTPA sets forth the following permissible grounds to evict an occupant of a manufactured home: (1) the failure to pay rent; (2) the premises are used as a bawdy-house or any illegal business; (3) the Tenant is in violation of a federal, state, or local law in a manner that is detrimental to the safety and well-being of other occupants at the park; (4) the Tenant violated a lease term and failed to cure the violation after receiving proper notice; or (5) a change in land use (for purposes other than a manufactured home park) after providing at least two (2) years notice.[1020]

The rent demand period for manufactured homes is longer than for other rental properties. Where a manufactured home park owner seeks to evict a Tenant due to the non-payment of rent, the owner must provide a thirty (30) day written notice (as opposed to fourteen (14) days), and the notice must be formally served in the manner set forth in RPAPL §735.[1021]

In the event the manufactured home park is available for sale, the proposed purchaser must submit a letter certifying whether the purchaser will seek a change in land use within sixty (60) months of the closing. This letter must be submitted prior to the owner's acceptance

1018 *Id.* at § 233(q).

1019 *Id.*

1020 *Id.* at § 233(b)(2)-(6).

1021 *Id.* at § 233(b)(2).

of the offer or counteroffer.[1022] Where the purchaser fails to provide a certification of intent prior to the sale, an eviction proceeding may not be commenced due to a change in land use for five (5) years following the closing.[1023] The owner's acceptance of an offer must further include written notice that the manufactured home owners have a right to match the purchase offer.[1024]

As indicated previously, an eviction proceeding based upon a Landlord's proposed change in land use generally requires two (2) years notice.[1025] Formal service of the notice must be completed in accordance with RPAPL § 735, and the notice must be simultaneously served upon all impacted occupants.[1026] The Court may direct that the Tenant receives a stipend not to exceed $15,000 due to the change in land use.[1027] To determine the precise amount of the stipend, the Court must consider the following: (1) the cost to relocate the manufactured home; (2) the number of manufactured homes within the park receiving a stipend; (3) the purchase price for the park; (4) the value of the real property; (5) the value of the development rights of the property;

1022 *Id.* at § 233-a(2).

1023 *Id.* at § 233(b)(6)(ii).

1024 *Id.*; *see* Willow Woods Manufactured Homeowners' Assn. Inc. v. R & R Mobile Home Park, Inc., 81 A.D.3d 930 (2d Dep't 2011). The manufactured home owners have the right to form a homeowners' association consisting of at least fifty-one percent (51%) of the manufactured home owners regarding the purchase (if one does not already exist). RPL § 233-a(3). A manufactured home park owner may not deny a manufactured home owner from selling the manufactured home when twenty (20) days notice of the intent to sell is provided. *Id.* at § 233[i]. However, the manufactured home park owner may reasonably reserve the right to deny the sale for the remainder of the tenancy, but "[p]ermission may not be unreasonably withheld." *Id.*; *see* Higgins v. Orsland, 183 A.D.2d 175, 589 N.Y.S.2d 640 (3d Dep't 1992); Frontier Park v. Assessor, Town of Babylon, 707 N.Y.S.2d 808 (Nassau Cnty. Sup. Ct. 2000). The manufactured home park owner may not receive either a commission or a fee from the sale of the manufactured home, unless the owner acted as an agent, and the relationship was memorialized within the contract. RPL § 233[i].

1025 RPL § 233(b)(6) (previously six (6) months); *see* STP Assoc., LLC v. Hess, 994 N.Y.S.2d 230 (App. Term, 9th & 10th Jud. Dists. 2014); *Amityville Mobile Home Civ. Assn. Corp.*, 2014 N.Y. Misc. LEXIS at 1636; *Pedote*, 959 N.Y.S.2d at 91 (six (6) months).

1026 RPL § 233(b).

1027 *See id.* at § 233(b)(6)(iii).

and (6) any other relevant factor.[1028] A warrant of eviction may not be executed to remove the Tenant until the stipend has been paid.[1029]

D. RULES PERTAINING TO EXECUTION OF THE WARRANT OF EVICTION

An eviction from a manufactured home may only occur between sunrise and sunset.[1030] The HSTPA modified RPAPL § 749 to provide that following the expiration of all applicable stays, the Sheriff or Marshal must provide a manufactured home owner a ninety (90) day notice prior to executing the warrant of eviction.[1031] However, if the conditions at the premises "[p]ose an imminent threat to the health, safety, or welfare of the other manufactured home tenants," then the Court may reduce the notice period to not less than thirty (30) days.[1032] Finally, where the occupant is renting the manufactured home from the manufactured home park owner (i.e., the Tenant does not own the manufactured home), then the notice period is only seventy-two (72) hours.[1033]

On occasion, the parties will reach a settlement that includes the transfer of ownership in the manufactured home to the Landlord. Although the parties may reach any resolution, the Housing Part does not have the authority to direct or otherwise enforce such a transfer of property rights (only issues of possession).

1028 *Id.* at § 233(b)(6)(iii)(b).

1029 *Id.* at § 233(b)(6)(iii)(a). In the event the summary proceeding does not result in the eviction of the manufactured home owner, the stipend must be returned to the manufactured home park owner. *Id.* at § 233(b)(6)(iii)[C].

1030 *Id.* at § 233(d).

1031 *Id.* at § 233(d)(1).

1032 *Id.* at § 233(d)(2).

1033 *Id.* at § 233(d)(4).

CHAPTER 11

AFFIRMATIVE DEFENSES

In a summary proceeding, the Tenant or occupant may assert any legal or equitable defense.[1034] For example, if the Respondent asserts that he or she is the owner of the premises as a defense, then the defense must be considered although the Court does not have jurisdiction to affirmatively rule on the issue of title or who is the lawful owner of the premises.[1035] The affirmative defenses identified in this chapter are some of the more common defenses asserted in summary proceedings. They do not comprise an exhaustive list.

Effective June 14, 2019, where the Tenant vacates a residential property in violation of a rental agreement, the Landlord must attempt to mitigate the damages by taking "reasonable and customary actions" to re-rent the premises to a new Tenant at the fair market rate or the previously agreed rent, whichever is less.[1036] An agreement with a new Tenant to lease the premises will generally abdicate the former Tenant's financial obligations under the lease, except for the difference in the rents.

The party claiming to have been damaged (i.e., the Landlord) has the burden of proof with respect to mitigation.[1037] The duty to mitigate

1034 *See* Yau v. Yau, 154 N.Y.S.3d 578 (App. Term, 2d, 11th & 13th Jud. Dists. 2021) (the affirmative defense of constructive eviction may be asserted in a summary proceeding); Fizzinoglia v. Capozzoli, 94 N.Y.S.3d 538 (App. Term, 9th & 10th Jud. Dists. 2018).

1035 Jacob Marion, LLC v. El Bey, 36 N.Y.S.3d 47 (App. Term, 2d, 11th & 13th Jud. Dists 2016).

1036 RPL § 227-e (HSTPA, L. 2019, c. 36, Part M, § 4); *see generally* 14 E. 14th St. Unit 509 LLC v. Toporek, 2021 N.Y. Misc. LEXIS 7035 (N.Y. Cnty. Sup. Ct. July 15, 2021); Felice v. Warf, 106 N.Y.S.3d 837 (Middletown City Ct. 2019).

1037 RPL § 227-e.

may not be waived in a rental agreement, and a lease provision to the contrary is void as a matter of public policy.[1038]

For commercial properties, absent a lease provision requiring mitigation, the Landlord has no duty to mitigate its damages.[1039] The Court of Appeals reasoned that there is no requirement to re-let or attempt to re-rent commercial premises because the rental agreement, in part, is "[r]ecognized as a present transfer of an estate in real property."[1040]

A Respondent may waive certain statutory and/or contractual defenses if not asserted in a timely manner.[1041] For example, the defenses of a lack of personal jurisdiction due to improper service;[1042] lack of standing;[1043] and the failure to verify the Petition,[1044] are waived when not timely asserted. In addition, the Landlord may be deemed to have waived the right to terminate the tenancy, notwithstanding a non-waiver provision within the lease, where the Landlord accepts rent with

1038 *Id.* For actions commenced prior to June 14, 2019, the Landlord had no duty to mitigate damages. *See* Rios v. Carillo, 53 A.D.3d 111, 861 N.Y.S.2d 129 (2d Dep't 2008); *Felice*, 106 N.Y.S.3d at 837.

1039 *See* University Sq. San Antonio, Tx. LLC v. Mega Furniture Dezavala, LLC, 198 A.D.3d 1284, 155 N.Y.S.3d 252 (4th Dep't 2021); Center for Specialty Care, Inc. v. CSC Acquisition I, LLC, 187 A.D.3d 46, 130 N.Y.S.3d 7 (1st Dep't 2020); VBGO Penn Plaza, LLC v. Salon Media Group, Inc., 2019 N.Y. Misc. LEXIS 841 (N.Y. Cnty. Sup. Ct. March 1, 2019); *see* L'Aquila Realty, LLC v. Jalyng Food Corp., 148 A.D.3d 1004, 50 N.Y.S.3d 128 (2d Dep't 2017) (Tenant remained liable post-lease termination where Landlord was not required to mitigate damages).

1040 Holy Props. Ltd., L.P. v. Kenneth Cole Prods., Inc., 87 N.Y.2d 130, at 133, 637 N.Y.S.2d 964, 966 (1995).

1041 Hickey v. Trahan, 31 N.Y.S.3d 921 (App. Term, 9th & 10th Jud. Dists. 2016); Otufale v. Whetstone, 906 N.Y.S.2d 781 (App. Term, 1st Dep't 2010).

1042 Iodice v. Academics R Us, Inc., 26 N.Y.S.3d 724 (App. Term, 1st Dep't 2015) (defense waived when not asserted in the Answer, and Tenant may not assert the defense for the first time in an Amended Answer); *Otufale*, 906 N.Y.S.2d at 781; Citi Land Servs., LLC v. McDowell, 926 N.Y.S.2d 343 (App. Term, 2d, 11th & 13th Jud. Dists. 2011) (lack of personal jurisdiction defense waived when not asserted in the Answer); Forest Hills S. Owners, Inc. v. Ishida, 943 N.Y.S.2d 791 (App. Term, 2d, 11th & 13th Jud. Dists. 2011) (improper service of rent demand). *See also* CPLR § 3211(e) (listing circumstances where the defense of lack of personal jurisdiction is waived).

1043 Chen v. Ray, 26 N.Y.S.3d 212 (App. Term, 1st Dep't 2015).

1044 *See* Morse v. Brozzo, 94 A.D.3d 1184, 942 N.Y.S.2d 246 (3d Dep't 2012).

knowledge of a breach by the Tenant.[1045] This is because the "[k]nowing acceptance of rent without any effort to terminate the lease justifies the inference that the landlord has elected to hold the tenant to the lease," and therefore waives the violation.[1046] Whether a waiver has occurred is a question of fact.[1047]

There are limitations on the ability to waive certain claims or defenses. For example, the lack of subject matter jurisdiction may not be waived under any circumstance,[1048] and deficiencies in the predicate notice generally may only be waived where the parties agree to resolve the proceeding via a stipulation of settlement.[1049]

A. RESIDENTIAL PREMISES

1. ILLEGAL APARTMENTS

As a practical matter, outside New York City, there is no prohibition against a Landlord collecting rent for an "illegal" apartment. In other words, a Tenant is not relieved of the obligation to pay rent merely

1045 56 Bogart St., LLC v. Vandyke, 110 N.Y.S.3d 201 (App. Term, 2d, 11th & 13th Jud. Dists. 2018); State Farm Fire & Cas. Co. v. Firmstone, 9 A.D.3d 812, 780 N.Y.S.2d 820 (3d Dep't 2004) (holding that generally "accepting rent with knowledge of conduct violative of the lease constitutes a waiver by the landlord of the default even if the lease contains a nonwaiver provision"); *but see* 159 W. 23rd LLC v. Spa Ciel De NY Corp., 120 N.Y.S.3d 697 (App. Term, 1st Dep't 2020) (no-waiver clause enforced); 1890 Adam Clayton Powell LLC v. Penant, 37 N.Y.S.3d 166 (App. Term, 1st Dep't 2016) (enforcing lease provision that provides the acceptance of rent does not constitute a waiver).

1046 Jefpaul Garage Corp. v. Presbyterian Hosp., 61 N.Y.2d 442, at 448, 474 N.Y.S.2d 458, 461 (1984); Lee v. Wright, 108 A.D.2d 678, at 680, 485 N.Y.S.2d 543, 544 (1st Dep't 1985).

1047 Fundamental Portfolio Advisors, Inc. v. Tocqueville Asset Mgmt., L.P., 7 N.Y.3d 96, at 104-05, 817 N.Y.S.2d 606 (2006); 145 E. 16th St. LLC v. Nanda, 110 N.Y.S.3d 780 (App. Term, 1st Dep't 2018). *Cf.* 1371 Franklin Ave. LLC v. Pugh, 120 N.Y.S.3d 751 (N.Y. Civ. Ct. Bronx Cnty. 2020) (Tenant's continued payment of rent via Zelle did not constitute a "voluntary abandonment" of Landlord's termination notice and intent to regain possession of the premises).

1048 Some of the statutory provisions of the New York City Rent Stabilization Code, such as the requirement that the Landlord serves a notice terminating the tenancy, may not be waived even with consent. *See, e.g.*, Kings Hwy. Realty Corp. v. Riley, 950 N.Y.S.2d 723 (App. Term, 2d, 11th & 13th Jud. Dists. 2012).

1049 *See* Predicate Notices Chapter 6, *supra*.

because the Landlord failed to obtain a rental permit or the premises lacked a proper certificate of occupancy.

Although illegal apartments may pose safety and health risks, these matters are properly adjudicated by the local governing municipality in a civil and/or criminal action for civil penalties, fines, compliance, and, in egregious cases, a jail sentence.[1050] Landlord and Tenant disputes and code enforcement matters are often interrelated as evidenced by the number of Landlords who also appear as defendants in town and municipal matters regarding alleged code violations; including renting without a permit, building without a permit, and the lack of a certificate of occupancy. Of note, a local village ordinance conditioning either the issuance or the renewal of a rental permit upon the owner's "forced consent" to a warrantless inspection of the premises is unconstitutional.[1051]

1050 *See, e.g.*, People v. Mazzone, 152 N.Y.S.3d 213 (App. Term, 9th & 10th Jud. Dists. 2021).

1051 *See* ATM One, LLC v. Incorporated Vill. of Hempstead, 91 A.D.3d 585, 936 N.Y.S.2d 263 (2d Dep't 2012) (*citing* Sokolov v. Village of Freeport, 52 N.Y.2d 341, 438 N.Y.S.2d 257 (1981)). *Cf.* Mamakos v. Town of Huntington, 2018 U.S. App. LEXIS 6730 (2d Cir. March 19, 2018) (upholding town code provision requiring certification of compliance from designated town official or licensed third-party engineer to obtain rental permit in lieu of a non-consensual search of the premises); Hafez v. City of Schenectady, 2018 U.S. Dist. LEXIS 49918 (N.D.N.Y. March 27, 2018) (ordinance requiring rental permit held constitutional where a search warrant could be sought if there is "reasonable cause" of a violation of the City Code at the premises); Pashcow v. Town of Babylon, 53 N.Y.2d 687, 439 N.Y.S.2d 103 (1981) (local ordinance upheld where inspection was <u>not</u> required to obtain rental permit); Infinite Green, Inc. v. Town of Babylon, 201 A.D.3d 892, 162 N.Y.S.3d 424 (2d Dep't 2022) (rental permit ordinance constitutional where Landlord given the option of providing a certification from a state-licensed engineer or having a Town inspection); Wisoff v. City of Schenectady, 116 A.D.3d 1187, 984 N.Y.S.2d 207 (3d Dep't 2014) (city ordinance upheld where "consent" or a "valid search warrant" was required to conduct an administrative inspection); McLean v. City of Kingston, 57 A.D.3d 1269, 869 N.Y.S.2d 685 (3d Dep't 2008) (ordinance requiring inspection of rental properties every two (2) years upheld because the remedy for non-compliance was to seek a search warrant).

a. SUBJECT PREMISES LACKS A RENTAL PERMIT

For properties outside New York City, where an illegal apartment (no rental permit) is either a single-family or a two-family residence, the Court will typically award a prevailing Landlord rent arrears where both a proper rent demand and a five (5) day late-rent reminder pursuant to RPL § 235-e were served on the Tenant.[1052] The same holds true for multiple dwellings which, according to Multiple Dwelling Law § 4(7), are three (3) or more families living independently within towns or municipalities with fewer than 325,000 residents.[1053]

However, the Landlord of an illegal apartment is <u>not</u> always entitled to a money judgment. For example, unpaid rent may <u>not</u> be awarded where a provision within the local governing body's administrative code makes it unlawful to collect rent for an illegal apartment.[1054] Where such a statutory provision is applicable, the rent previously paid by the Tenant is unrecoverable notwithstanding the illegal status of the premises.[1055] If the illegal apartment is a multiple dwelling within

1052 Atif v. Disapio, 114 N.Y.S.3d 555 (App. Term, 9th & 10th Jud. Dists. 2019); Messerschmidt v. Romney, 112 N.Y.S.3d 410 (App. Term, 9th & 10th Jud. Dists 2018); Hayes v. Ramsey, 110 N.Y.S.3d 206 (App. Term, 9th & 10th Jud. Dists. 2018); Thomas v. Brown, 29 N.Y.S.3d 850 (App. Term, 1st Dep't 2015); Madden v. Juillet, 13 N.Y.S.3d 850 (App. Term, 9th & 10th Jud. Dists. 2015); Pickering v. Chappe, 908 N.Y.S.2d 523, 524-25 (App. Term, 2d, 11th & 13th Jud. Dists. 2010). The five (5) day late rent reminder is codified at RPL § 235-e.

1053 Multiple Dwelling Law §§ 3(1),(8); 302(1)(b); 325(2).

1054 *See, e.g.*, Village of Southampton, N.Y. Town Code, §§ 270-3, 270-13 (2008). Section 270-13 of the Southampton Town Code provides, in pertinent part, "The following shall be conditions precedent to the collection of rent for the use and occupancy of a rental property: A. The existence of a valid rental permit for the rental property. [and] B. The tendering of a written receipt in exchange for any rent payment offered in cash." *See also* Wowaka & Sons, Inc. v. Pardell, 242 A.D.2d 1, at 6-7, 672 N.Y.S.2d 358, 361 (2d Dep't 1998) (illegal contract that violates statutory provisions that are merely *malum prohibitum* is enforceable). The Appellate Division, Second Department held that the Southampton Town Code permits a Tenant to assert a private cause of action for damages against a Landlord who rents a residence in violation of the local law. *See* Ader v. Guzman, 135 A.D.3d 671, 23 N.Y.S.3d 292 (2d Dep't 2016). The same Court held that "absent concealment," the Landlord's real estate agent has no duty "to investigate whether the premises had a valid rental permit." Ader v. Guzman, 135 A.D.3d 668, 22 N.Y.S.3d 576 (2d Dep't 2016); *see* RPL § 443(4)(b) (broker disclosure requirements for rental properties).

1055 *Atif*, 114 N.Y.S.3d at 555; ZB Prospect Realty LLC v. France, 2020 N.Y. Misc LEXIS 16133 (N.Y. Civ. Ct. N.Y. Cnty. Sept. 14, 2020).

a "city, town, or village" having more than 325,000 residents,[1056] the Landlord is similarly prohibited from recovering rent and/or use and occupancy.[1057] The prohibition against recovering rent for illegal rental properties applies to "the entire building, not just in the illegally altered apartments."[1058]

Another exception that may bar the award of rent is predicated upon ordinary contract principles, such as where the Landlord misrepresents that the apartment is "legal" when the apartment is in fact "illegal."[1059] Under these circumstances, a possessory judgment may be awarded, but the Court may decline to award a money judgment for the unpaid rent.[1060]

b. SUBJECT PREMISES LACKS A CERTIFICATE OF OCCUPANCY

Prior to executing a rental agreement for residential property containing three (3) or fewer rental units, the Landlord must provide the Tenant a conspicuous notice (boldface font) stating that a certificate of occupancy has been obtained for the premises.[1061] A lease provision waiving such notice is void.[1062] The statute does <u>not</u> set forth specific penalties for non-compliance.

Outside New York City, the failure to obtain a certificate of occupancy does <u>not</u> bar the recovery of either rent or possession in a

---

1056 Multiple Dwelling Law §§ 3(1),(8).

1057 *See Thomas*, 29 N.Y.S.3d at 850; Malden v. Wykoff S.P., LLC, 192 A.D.3d 1002, 146 N.Y.S.3d 143 (2d Dep't 2021) (property located in New York City); Sheila Props., Inc. v. A Real Good Plumber, Inc., 59 A.D.3d 424, at 425-26, 874 N.Y.S.2d 145, 147-48 (2d Dep't 2009) (same); Trafalgar Co. v. Malone, 155 N.Y.S.3d 272 (App. Term, 1st Dep't 2021) (directing return of use and occupancy for property lacking a rental permit within New York City).

1058 208 Himrod St., LLC v. Irizarry, 988 N.Y.S.2d 526 (App. Term, 2d, 11th & 13th Jud. Dists. 2014); Multiple Dwelling Law § 302(1)(b).

1059 *See* Casilia v. Webster, LLC, 140 A.D.3d 530, 32 N.Y.S.3d 494 (1st Dep't 2016).

1060 *See* Leva v. Kramer, 899 N.Y.S.2d 60 (Nassau Cnty. Dist. Ct. 2009).

1061 *See* RPL § 235-bb.

1062 *Id.*

summary proceeding.[1063] In fact, excluding the aforementioned exceptions, the Tenant remains liable for the rent for at least as long as the Tenant remains in possession.[1064] This rule similarly applies where a single-family dwelling is utilized as an unlawful two-family rental apartment.[1065]

The reader should be mindful of the Appellate Division, Second Department decision in *Martin v. Easy Living Homes, Inc.*, where the owner was denied use and occupancy for a rental property that lacked a certificate of occupancy. The *Martin* decision is distinguishable from the typical illegal apartment case outside New York City because the plaintiff-purchaser was seeking specific performance of the sale of the premises, and the parties did not have a Landlord and Tenant relationship. Moreover, the entire structure lacked a certificate of occupancy due to the builder's failure to complete construction and its knowing allowance of the unlawful occupancy.[1066]

The lack of a certificate of occupancy is not grounds for the Tenant to recover the security deposit.[1067] However, if the Tenant vacates the premises after discovering the unlawful status of the property, then the security deposit may be recovered in a plenary action.[1068]

1063 *Casilia*, 140 A.D.3d at 530, 32 N.Y.S.3d at 494; Barrett Japaning, Inc. v. Bialobroda, 54 N.Y.S.3d 609 (App. Term, 1st Dep't 2017); *Madden*, 13 N.Y.S.3d at 850; Corbin v. Briley, 747 N.Y.S.2d 134 (App. Term, 9th & 10th Jud. Dists. 2002). *But see Trafalgar Co.*, 155 N.Y.S.3d at 272 (property within New York City).

1064 *See generally* Phillips & Huyler Assocs. v. Flynn, 225 A.D.2d 475, 640 N.Y.S.2d 26 (1st Dep't 1996) (suggesting a different outcome had evidence of the Landlord's misrepresentation been presented); Municipal Metallic Bed Mfg. Corp. v. Dobbs, 253 N.Y. 313 (1930). *Cf.* Seoul Garden Bowery Inc. v. Ng, 2020 N.Y. Misc. LEXIS 2637 (N.Y. Cnty. Sup. Ct. June 8, 2020) (dismissing fraudulent misrepresentation claim against Landlord where the Tenant was aware that the premises lacked a valid certificate of occupancy).

1065 *See, e.g., Thomas*, 29 N.Y.S.3d at 850; *Pickering*, 908 N.Y.S.2d at 523; *Corbin*, 747 N.Y.S.2d at 134; Corsini v. Gottschalk, N.Y.L.J., Dec. 20, 1999, at 32 (App. Term, 9th & 10th Jud. Dists. 1999).

1066 Martin v. Easy Living Homes, Inc., 15 A.D.3d 360, at 361, 790 N.Y.S.2d 467, 468-69 (2d Dep't 2005).

1067 *See Pickering*, 908 N.Y.S.2d at 523; Schweighofer v. Straub, 885 N.Y.S.2d 713 (App. Term, 9th & 10th Jud. Dists. 2009).

1068 *Ader*, 135 A.D.3d at 671, 23 N.Y.S.3d at 292; Sethi v. Naman, 890 N.Y.S.2d 371 (App. Term, 9th & 10th Jud. Dists. 2009). For a discussion on security deposits, *see* Chapter 16, *infra*.

2. IMPLIED WARRANTY OF HABITABILITY

The warranty of habitability is frequently asserted as an affirmative defense in residential non-payment proceedings.[1069] The defense is not available in commercial cases.[1070] The warranty of habitability is not intended to be a complete defense, but rather, the Tenant seeks an abatement of all or a portion of the unpaid rent due to the defective conditions of the premises. It has been held that a complete rent abatement is inappropriate where the Tenant remains in possession.[1071]

The conditions giving rise to the defense of the warranty of habitability must be continuous, rather than episodic.[1072] An occupant who is not a party to the rental agreement may not assert the defense.[1073] The defense is similarly unavailable in a holdover proceeding to avoid an eviction, but may be asserted to refute that portion of the claim for unpaid rent.[1074]

The implied warranty of habitability imposes three (3) requirements regarding the condition of the premises. The premises must be: (1) fit for human habitation; (2) fit for the uses reasonably intended; and (3) may not subject the occupants to conditions that are dangerous,

---

1069 RPL § 235-b. The warranty of habitability is not a viable defense in either holdover proceedings or proceedings involving commercial property. *See* Goethals Mobile Park, Inc. v. Staten Island Meadowbrook Park Civ. Assn., Inc., 208 A.D.2d 896, at 897-98, 618 N.Y.S.2d 409, 411 (2d Dep't 1994) (holdover proceeding); 76th St. Owners' Corp. v. Elshiekh, 910 N.Y.S.2d 765 (N.Y. Civ. Ct. Bronx Cnty. 2010) (holdover proceeding); Azour, LLC v. Tax Sister, Inc., 909 N.Y.S.2d 282, 284 (App. Term, 2d, 11th & 13th Jud. Dists. 2010) (commercial property).

1070 146 Mulberry St., LLC v. Angelo of Mulberry St., Inc., 120 N.Y.S.3d 589 (N.Y. Civ. Ct. N.Y. Cnty. 2020).

1071 Mateo v. Anokwuru, 64 N.Y.S.3d 453 (App. Term, 1st Dep't 2017).

1072 *See generally* Hersh v. One Fifth Ave. Apt. Corp., 2016 N.Y. Misc. LEXIS 1706 (N.Y. Cnty. Sup. Ct. May 5, 2016); Metz v. Duenas, 707 N.Y.S.2d 598, 599-600 (Nassau Cnty. Dist. Ct. 2000).

1073 *See* Cambridge Hgts. HDFC v. McCormick, 112 N.Y.S.3d 412 (App. Term, 2d, 11th & 13th Jud. Dists. 2018).

1074 Kirkview Assocs. LP v. Amrock, 160 A.D.3d 1108, 75 N.Y.S.3d 288 (3d Dep't 2018) (holding the "County Court correctly observed that [the defenses of constructive eviction and the implied warranty of habitability] cannot forestall an eviction in a holdover proceeding, but overlooked that they [pose] viable 'defenses to the recovery of rent' in such proceeding").

hazardous, or detrimental to life or safety.[1075] If any of the above conditions are not satisfied, the Tenant is entitled to an abatement of rent provided the Landlord was notified of the defective conditions and the defects were not corrected within a reasonable period of time.[1076] A Subtenant may assert the warranty of habitability defense in response to the Tenant's claim for rent arrears.[1077]

A rent abatement will not be awarded where the Landlord was unaware of the defective conditions.[1078] The Appellate Term for the Second, Eleventh and Thirteenth Judicial Districts has held that to prevail on a warranty of habitability claim, the Tenant "[m]ust offer proof as to the dates, severity and duration of the conditions complained of . . ., and show that notice of the conditions was given to the landlord."[1079] The Tenant has the burden of demonstrating the extent of the defective conditions and adequate proof to compute "the appropriate [amount of] damages."[1080] In determining the amount of the rent abatement, the

1075 RPL § 235-b. *See generally* Goldhirsch v. St. George Tower and Grill Owners Corp., 142 A.D.3d 1044, 37 N.Y.S.3d 616 (2d Dep't 2016).

1076 *See* Gawad v. Aviad, 960 N.Y.S.2d 50 (App. Term, 2d, 11th & 13th Jud. Dists. 2012); Salgado v. Cambridge Manor Apts. II, Inc., 127 N.Y.S.3d 252 (Middletown City Ct. 2020); Mack v. Park Ave. and Seventy-Seventh St. Corp., 2019 N.Y. Misc. LEXIS 431 (N.Y. Cnty. Sup. Ct. Jan. 30, 2019) (issue of fact whether co-op responded in timely manner to complaints of water damage from a neighboring apartment).

1077 Israel Realty LLC v. Shkolnikov, 108 N.Y.S.3d 648 (App. Term, 1st Dep't 2018).

1078 72A Realty Assocs., L.P. v. Mercado, 1 N.Y.S.3d 876 (App. Term, 1st Dep't 2014); BRG 321, LLC v. Brown, 2015 N.Y. Misc. LEXIS 2665 (N.Y. Civ. Ct. N.Y. Cnty. March 4, 2015).

1079 Bloorian v. Pittman, 146 N.Y.S.3d 369 (App. Term, 2d, 11th & 13th Jud. Dists. 2021); EB Mgmt. Props., LLC v. Maruf, 142 N.Y.S.3d 273 (App. Term, 2d, 11th & 13th Jud Dists. 2021); Green Garden Corp. v. Mansoor, 116 N.Y.S.3d 484 (App. Term, 2d, 11th & 13th Jud. Dists. 2019); Shalom Aleichem LLC v. Soto, 123 N.Y.S.3d 461 (N.Y. Civ. Ct. Bronx Cnty. 2020).

1080 Parkville Realty Ass'n v. Woodward, 140 N.Y.S.3d 349 (App. Term, 2d, 11th & 13th Jud. Dists. 2021) (dismissing warranty of habitability counterclaim where Tenant failed to establish that the damages were attributable to the defective conditions); Ulukaya v. Pan Am Equities, 126 N.Y.S.3d 300 (App. Term, 1st Dep't 2020) (denying warranty of habitability claims following the credible testimony of the building manager regarding the condition of the premises); 200-220 W. 26 LLC v. Carney, 119 N.Y.S.3d 805 (App. Term, 1st Dep't 2019) (denying warranty of habitability claims for toxic chemicals and conspiracy claims against neighbors due to the Tenant's "uncorroborated and...entirely incredible" testimony).

Court must also consider the "[e]ffectiveness of [the] steps taken by the landlord to abate those conditions."[1081]

A rent abatement is inappropriate for the period where the Tenant was either uncooperative with the Landlord's efforts to address the conditions or interfered with the repairs.[1082] Abatements have similarly been denied where the Tenant only asserted "vague" non-specific statements regarding the defective conditions,[1083] and vacated the premises prior to a storm, only to return after the power was restored.[1084]

The warranty of habitability defense may only be asserted for defects related to the essential functions of the premises.[1085] For example, the defense has been successfully asserted: for ceiling leaks;[1086] failing to provide heat and hot water;[1087] rotted-wood subflooring;[1088] overpowering

---

1081 2590 35th St., LLC v. Veleva, 160 N.Y.S.3d 736 (App. Term, 2d, 11th & 13th Jud. Dists. 2022).

1082 *See* LGS Realty Partners LLC v. Kyle, 26 N.Y.S.3d 725 (App. Term, 1st Dep't 2015); Joan A. Bebry, LLC v. Kruglova, 938 N.Y.S.2d 227 (App. Term, 2d, 11th & 13th Jud. Dists. 2011); 150-15 79th Ave. Owners Corp. v. James, 927 N.Y.S.2d 818 (App. Term, 2d, 11th & 13th Jud. Dists. 2011); *Mack*, 2019 N.Y. Misc. LEXIS at 431 (summary judgment denied in plenary action due to questions concerning the impediments to the cooperative board's efforts to make the requisite repairs). *Cf.* De Socio v. 136 E. 56th St. Owners, Inc., 111 N.Y.S.3d 515 (N.Y. Civ. Ct. N.Y. Cnty. 2018) (awarding a fifty percent (50%) rent abatement for damages to the walls, water leaks, and mold where both parties were at fault).

1083 *See* 227J LLC v. Barker, 58 N.Y.S.3d 876 (App. Term, 1st Dep't 2017); Crotona Park Redevelopment, LLC v. Williams, 121 N.Y.S.3d 847 (N.Y. Civ. Ct. Bronx Cnty. 2020).

1084 Adler v. Ogden CAP Props., 126 A.D.3d 544, 2 N.Y.S.3d 902 (1st Dep't 2015).

1085 *See generally* Solow v. Wellner, 86 N.Y.2d 582, at 588-89, 635 N.Y.S.2d 132, 134-35 (1995); Chittle v. Choi, 2020 N.Y. Misc. LEXIS 1183 (N.Y. Sup. Ct. Kings Cnty. Feb. 24, 2020); 65E92, LLC v. Kroell, 7 N.Y.S.3d 245 (N.Y. Civ. Ct. N.Y. Cnty. 2015).

1086 Grinberg v. Eissenberg, 68 N.Y.S.3d 619 (App. Term, 2d, 11th & 13th Jud. Dists. 2018).

1087 Salvan v. 127 Mgmt. Corp., 101 A.D.2d 721, 475 N.Y.S.2d 30 (1st Dep't 1984); 13 E. 9th St. LLC v. Seelig, 114 N.Y.S.3d 817 (N.Y. Civ. Ct. N.Y. Cnty. 2019); Leris Realty Corp. v. Robbins, 408 N.Y.S.2d 166, 167-68 (N.Y. Civ. Ct. N.Y. Cnty. 1978) (good faith attempt to provide heat and hot water by replacing the boiler did not excuse the breach).

1088 Graham Ct. Owners Corp. v. Thomas, 94 N.Y.S.3d 788 (N.Y. Civ. Ct. N.Y. Cnty. 2019) (awarding a ten percent (10%) rent abatement for the forty-four (44) months the sub-flooring was rotted and mold was present in the kitchen).

odors in the water;[1089] gaseous odors emanating from the stove;[1090] defective refrigerators;[1091] noisy refrigerators and defective electric outlets;[1092] failing to provide gas;[1093] mold;[1094] bedbugs;[1095] second-hand smoke;[1096] defective sewer pipes;[1097] broken front doors;[1098] partially operational intercoms;[1099] absence of light and ventilation due to nearby construction;[1100] broken windows;[1101] lead-based paint;[1102] flooding due to a rainstorm (opening in roof);[1103] flooding due to the conduct

---

1089 Newkirk v. Scala, 90 A.D.3d 1257, 935 N.Y.S.2d 176 (3d Dep't 2011).

1090 Jacob v. Sealey, 28 N.Y.S.3d 648 (App. Term, 1st Dep't 2015).

1091 *See* 133 W. 145 LLC. v. Davis, 115 N.Y.S.3d 807 (App. Term, 1st Dep't 2019) (reducing the eighty-five percent (85%) rent abatement awarded by the Housing Part, in part, because the notice was "vague and unparticularized").

1092 Wallace 18 LLC v. Tucker, 120 N.Y.S.3d 716 (N.Y. Civ. Ct. Bronx Cnty. 2020).

1093 Inwood Ventura II LLC v. Jackson, 114 N.Y.S.3d 823 (N.Y. Civ. Ct. N.Y. Cnty. 2019); Peekskill Hous. Auth. v. Zambrano, 2019 N.Y. Misc. LEXIS 2706 (Peeksill City Ct. May 28, 2019).

1094 Cornell v. 360 W. 51st St. Realty, LLC, 95 A.D.3d 50, 939 N.Y.S.2d 434 (1st Dep't 2012), *rev'd on other grounds*, 22 N.Y.3d 762, 986 N.Y.S.2d 389 (2014); Rogers Plaza LLC v. Sam, 2022 N.Y.L.J. LEXIS 279 (N.Y. Civ. Ct. Kings Cnty. March 30, 2022).

1095 JWD & Sons, Ltd. v. Alexander, 941 N.Y.S.2d 538 (Westchester Cnty. Sup. Ct. 2011); Jefferson House Assocs., LLC v. Boyle, 800 N.Y.S.2d 348 (Ossining Just. Ct. 2005); *Cf.* Gawad v. Aviad, 960 N.Y.S.2d 50 (App. Term, 2d, 11th & 13th Jud. Dists. 2012) (warranty of habitability claim dismissed where Tenant failed to notify Landlord of the bedbug problem).

1096 Reinhard v. Connaught Tower Corp., 2011 N.Y. Misc. LEXIS 5683 (N.Y. Cnty. Sup. Ct. Nov. 30, 2011); Upper E. Lease Assocs., LLC v. Cannon, 924 N.Y.S.2d 312 (Nassau Cnty. Dist. Ct. 2011), *aff'd*, 961 N.Y.S.2d 362 (App. Term, 9th & 10th Jud. Dists. 2012). *Cf.* 555-565 Assoc., LLC v. Kearsley, 18 N.Y.S.3d 578 (N.Y. Civ. Ct. N.Y. Cnty. 2015) (denying second-hand smoke warranty of habitability claim due to the unreliability of the witness' testimony).

1097 Gottesman v. The Graham Apts., Inc., 16 N.Y.S.3d 792 (N.Y. Civ. Ct. Kings Cnty. 2015).

1098 Westside v. Ross, 2019 N.Y.L.J. LEXIS 1100 (N.Y. Civ. Ct. N.Y. Cnty. April 9, 2019).

1099 Maxwell Dev., L.P. v. France, 111 N.Y.S.3d 517 (N.Y. Civ. Ct. N.Y. Cnty. 2018) (awarding a one percent (1%) rent abatement for the defective intercom).

1100 Sutton Fifty-Six Co. v. Garrison, 93 A.D.2d 720, 461 N.Y.S.2d 14 (1st Dep't 1983).

1101 *Atif*, 114 N.Y.S.3d at 555 (App. Term, 9th & 10th Jud. Dists. 2019) (five (5) of the residence's seven (7) windows could not be opened).

1102 Chase v. Pistolese, 739 N.Y.S.2d 250, 252-53 (Watertown City Ct. 2002).

1103 Richardson v. Akelius Real Estate Mgt. LLC, 150 N.Y.S.3d 893 (N.Y. Civ. Ct. N.Y. Cnty. 2021).

of another Tenant;[1104] pet odors from a prior Tenant;[1105] odors from a nearby dumpster;[1106] inoperable air conditioners during the summer;[1107] excessive late night noise;[1108] excessive noise due to construction during weekends and early morning hours;[1109] cockroaches;[1110] and insect infestations.[1111]

The defense is not intended for an occasional rodent that appears in the premises or the inability to use or enjoy the dwelling's amenities and services, such as a door attendant, swimming pool, or gym. The Landlord may further be liable where the defective conditions were caused by a third-party; i.e., someone other than the Tenant or his guests.[1112] A successor Landlord may be liable for warranty of habitability claims arising prior to the Landlord's ownership where the purchase was "subject to existing tenancies."[1113] The appropriate calculation of the rent abatement is "[t]he difference between the fair market value of the premises in fully habitable condition, as measured by the rent reserved under the lease, and the value of the premises during the period of the breach."[1114]

1104 Heights 170 LLC v. York, 920 N.Y.S.2d 241 (App. Term, 1st Dep't 2010).

1105 Tonetti, Jr. v. Penati, 48 A.D.2d 25, 367 N.Y.S.2d 804 (2d Dep't 1975) (dogs); Kekllas v. Saddy, 389 N.Y.S.2d 756 (Nassau Cnty. Dist. Ct. 1976) (cats).

1106 Mayourian v. Tanaka, 727 N.Y.S.2d 865 (App. Term, 9th & 10th Jud. Dists. 2001).

1107 Whitehouse Estates, Inc. v. Thomson, 386 N.Y.S.2d 733 (N.Y. Civ. Ct. N.Y. Cnty. 1976).

1108 Nostrand Gardens Co-Op v. Howard, 221 A.D.2d 637, 634 N.Y.S.2d 505 (2d Dep't 1995). *Cf. Green Garden Corp.*, 116 N.Y.S.3d at 484 (denying warranty of habitability claim where Tenant failed to establish the noises were "excessive" or that Landlord failed to respond to Tenant's complaints).

1109 Diaz v. Avalonbay Communities, Inc, 119 N.Y.S.3d 829 (N.Y. Civ. Ct. N.Y. Cnty. 2019).

1110 *Rogers Plaza LLC*, 2022 N.Y.L.J. LEXIS at 279.

1111 *Wallace 18 LLC*, 120 N.Y.S.3d at 716 (five percent (5%) rent abatement for vermin infestation); *Maxwell Dev., L.P.*, 111 N.Y.S.3d at 517; Town of Islip Comm. Dev. Agency v. Mulligan, 496 N.Y.S.2d 195, 196-97 (Suffolk Cnty. Dist. Ct. 1985).

1112 *Heights 170 LLC*, 920 N.Y.S.2d at 241 (flooding caused by neighboring Tenant).

1113 Dunbar Owner LLC v. Jones, 52 N.Y.S.3d 246 (App. Term, 1st Dep't 2017).

1114 Edstrom v. St. Nick's Alliance Corp., 194 A.D.3d 518, 149 N.Y.S.3d 26 (1st Dep't 2021); Mateo v. Anokwuru, 64 N.Y.S.3d 453 (App. Term, 1st Dep't 2017); *Maxwell Dev., L.P.*, 111 N.Y.S.3d at 517 (denying rent abatement where Tenant disposed of "chicken bones" in the toilet).

The failure to assert an implied warranty of habitability defense in a summary proceeding may preclude the Tenant from raising the claim on appeal.[1115] The Tenant need not vacate the premises to establish the defense,[1116] and a setoff for the breach of the warranty of habitability is not limited to the months for which rent is demanded.[1117]

A lease provision that shifts the burden for making repairs under the warranty of habitability is unenforceable,[1118] and the warranty may not be waived in a rental agreement.[1119] The party asserting the defense will typically introduce photographs and other documentary proof to corroborate the testimony describing the defective conditions.[1120]

The warranty of habitability may be asserted as both an affirmative defense and a counterclaim for damages in a summary proceeding.[1121] Otherwise, after vacating the premises, the Tenant may commence a plenary action for money damages due to the Landlord's breach of the warranty of habitability unless the claim was previously adjudicated or waived pursuant to a stipulation of settlement.[1122] A counterclaim alleging a breach of the warranty of habitability may include the return of previously paid rent.[1123]

1115 *See Hickey*, 31 N.Y.S.3d at 921.

1116 *Maxwell Dev., L.P.*, 111 N.Y.S.3d at 517. However, a complete rent abatement is not available unless the Tenant vacates the premises. *Mateo*, 64 N.Y.S.3d at 453; *Diaz*, 119 N.Y.S.3d at 829.

1117 Warner v. Lyon, 115 N.Y.S.3d 806 (App. Term, 2d, 11th & 13th Jud. Dists. 2019).

1118 *See* Grinberg v. Eissenberg, 68 N.Y.S.3d 619 (App. Term, 2d, 11th & 13th Jud. Dists. 2018).

1119 Hameroff v. Swaminathan, 115 N.Y.S.3d 809 (App. Term, 2d, 11th & 13th Jud. Dists. 2019).

1120 *See generally* RGB Mgmt. Corp. v. D2D Bridgemarket Assoc., LLP, 2020 N.Y. Misc. LEXIS 6085 (N.Y. Cnty. Sup. Ct. Sept. 15, 2020) (on motion to dismiss proceeding, "[t]here is no bright-line rule for the types of documents that will qualify as documentary evidence, and emails and letter correspondence have been held to qualify as such").

1121 *See, e.g.*, 2590 35th St. v. Veleva, 160 N.Y.S.3d 736 (App. Term, 2d, 11th & 13th Jud. Dists. 2022); Stefanis v. Cavicchio, 2022 N.Y.L.J. LEXIS 254 (Yonkers City Ct. March 23, 2022).

1122 *See Newkirk*, 90 A.D.3d at 1257, 935 N.Y.S.2d at 176.

1123 101 Cooper St., LLC v. Beckwith, 58 N.Y.S.3d 874 (App. Term, 1st Dep't 2017); Sheffield v. Pucci, 114 N.Y.S.3d 817 (N.Y. Cnty. Sup. Ct. 2019).

A summary proceeding involving residential property is automatically stayed (not dismissed) where the utilities are "shut off" due to the Landlord's failure to pay (if the Landlord was required to pay for the utilities).[1124] The proceeding remains stayed until the outstanding invoices are paid and the utilities are restored to "working order."[1125]

3. LACHES (STALE RENT)

The doctrine of laches precludes "[e]nforcement of a right where there has been an unreasonable and inexcusable delay that results in prejudice to an opposing party."[1126] The defense may be asserted in a summary proceeding to deny a money judgment where rent arrears are considered to be stale; i.e., the Landlord did not seek unpaid rent in a timely manner and the Tenant reasonably believed the Landlord would not be seeking the arrears.[1127]

Noting that there is no pre-determined formula or calculation for determining stale rent, the New York City Housing Part held that "[a] s an equitable doctrine, the length of the actionable delay differs for every individual case."[1128] The law is intended to dissuade a Landlord from deliberately delaying suit to accrue higher rents that the Tenant could not possibly pay.

Laches is an equitable defense based upon the principle of fairness.[1129] The defense includes a burden shifting analysis. To establish

1124 *See* RPAPL § 756 (HSTPA, L. 2019, c. 36, Part M, § 22).

1125 *Id.*

1126 Saratoga Cnty. Chamber of Commerce v. Pataki, 100 N.Y.2d 801, 766 N.Y.S.2d 654 (2003) (noting the differences between the doctrine of laches, which is "a delay independent of statute," and the statute of limitations, which is a "fixed statutory period[] within which actions must be brought").

1127 *See generally* Kings & Queens Holdings, Inc. v. Ahmad, 53 N.Y.S.3d 503 (N.Y. Civ. Ct. Richmond Cnty. 2017).

1128 Park N. Realty v. Cheik, 2018 N.Y.L.J. LEXIS 2116 (N.Y. Civ. Ct. N.Y. Cnty. June 20, 2018); T & G Realty Co. v. Hawthorn, 116 N.Y.S.3d 872 (N.Y. Civ. Ct. N.Y. Cnty. 2019). *But see* STP Assocs., LLC v. Holacek, 885 N.Y.S.2d 713 (Nassau Cnty. Dist. Ct. 2009) (holding where there are more than three (3) months of unpaid rent, the rent is presumed to be stale, which shifts "[t]o [the] Landlord the burden of establishing diligence in bringing the proceeding").

1129 Similar to other equitable defenses, the defense of laches is not available in either small claims actions or plenary actions within a court of limited jurisdiction. Robinson v. Robles, 906 N.Y.S.2d 844, 846-47 (Rochester City Ct. 2010).

the defense, the Tenant must demonstrate that: (1) the Landlord has a valid claim, such as the non-payment of rent; (2) the Landlord delayed in asserting its rights although there was opportunity to do so; (3) the Tenant's lack of knowledge or notice that the Landlord would assert a claim for the rent; and (4) injury or prejudice to the Tenant if the relief is granted, which may include the inability to pay the arrears because the Tenant reasonably believed that the Landlord would not attempt to collect the rent.[1130]

Where the Tenant satisfies its initial burden, the Petitioner must provide a "reasonable excuse for the delay" and offer counter arguments to the supporting claims.[1131] The Court will then make a determination whether the delay was reasonable under the circumstances.

The laches defense is available only in residential cases.[1132] Where successfully asserted, the Landlord may be awarded a judgment of possession, a warrant of eviction, and a money judgment for only the portion of the rent arrears sought in a timely manner. In other words, the stale portion of the rent is "severed" from the summary proceeding, and the Landlord is barred from "[r]ecovering a possessory judgment for arrears found to be stale."[1133] The Landlord may attempt to seek the stale rent in a subsequent plenary action.[1134]

1130 *See generally* Jean v. Joseph, 117 A.D.3d 989, 986 N.Y.S.2d 547 (2d Dep't 2014); Dwyer v. Mazzola, 171 A.D.2d 726, 567 N.Y.S.2d 281 (2d Dep't 1991) ("[m]ere delay alone, without actual prejudice [or injury] does not constitute laches") (citations omitted); Matter of County of Orange (Al Turi Landfill, Inc.), 75 A.D.3d 224, at 237-39, 903 N.Y.S.2d 60, 69-70 (2d Dep't 2010); S & H Clinton Assocs., LLC v. Cherry, 148 N.Y.S.3d 823 (App. Term, 9th & 10th Jud. Dists. 2021) (Tenant failed to demonstrate "unreasonable delay" or "prejudice arising from such delay"); Ollie Assocs. LLC v. Santos, 116 N.Y.S.3d 865 (N.Y. Civ. Ct. Bronx Cnty. 2019) (denying summary judgment due to issues of fact regarding the defense); 2275 Washington, LLC v. Gomez, 71 N.Y.S.3d 925 (N.Y. Civ. Ct. Bronx Cnty. 2017); Layla Assocs., LLC v. Costa, 984 N.Y.S.2d 632 (N.Y. Civ. Ct. Bronx Cnty. 2013).

1131 *See* 817 W. End Co LLC v. DeLong, 2021 N.Y.L.J. LEXIS 381 (N.Y. Civ. Ct. N.Y. Cnty. May 5, 2021); *2275 Washington, LLC*, 71 N.Y.S.3d at 925.

1132 UBO Realty Corp. v. Fulton, 1993 N.Y. Misc. LEXIS 665 (App. Term, 1st Dep't 1993) (laches defense not available in a commercial case); 59 Maiden Lane Assocs., LLC v. Maiden Farm, Inc., 106 N.Y.S.3d 554 (N.Y. Civ. Ct. N.Y. Cnty. 2019); Brenner v. General Plumbing Corp., 13 N.Y.S.3d 849 (N.Y. Civ. Ct. Kings Cnty. 2015); Vinroz, LLC v. Gutierrez, 886 N.Y.S.2d 72 (Nassau Cnty. Dist. Ct. 2009).

1133 Webster Ave. Holdings v. Pough, 2018 N.Y.L.J. LEXIS 3034 (N.Y. Civ. Ct. Bronx Cnty. Sept. 12, 2018).

1134 *Id.*; Abart Holdings LLC v. Hall, 791 N.Y.S.2d 867 (App. Term, 1st Dep't 2004).

4. LIFE TENANT

A Life Tenant is entitled to possession of the premises for the duration of his or her life. The "[s]ubstance of a life estate consists in the life tenant's right to exclude all others from the possession of the subject property for the duration of his or her own life."[1135]

A life estate may be created by trust, deed, or will, and is terminated in the following ways: (1) upon the death of the life tenant; (2) the surrender or forfeiture of the premises by the life tenant; or (3) a provision within the instrument that created the life estate.[1136] In *Kurek v. Luszcyk*, the Petitioner alleged that the parties executed a "clarification" document following the creation of the life estate requiring the Life Tenant to pay monthly rent. The Appellate Term affirmed the dismissal of the non-payment proceeding because the original conveyance was "clear and unambiguous," and, as a result, gave no credence to any of the purported rent obligations referred to within the "clarification" document.[1137]

In *Fallarino v. Fallarino*, the holdover proceeding against Petitioner's nephew was dismissed because the Petitioner's mother, a non-party to the proceeding, had been granted a life estate to the premises.[1138] As a result, the Appellate Term for the Ninth and Tenth Judicial Districts considered the Petitioner a remainderman "without any right to possession of the premises for the duration of [his mother's] life and, thus, [lacked] standing to bring [the] summary proceeding."[1139]

1135 Torre v. Giorgio, 51 A.D.3d 1010, 858 N.Y.S.2d 765 (2d Dep't 2008); Franklin v. Marques, 100 N.Y.S.3d 609 (Kings Cnty. Sup. Ct. 2018).

1136 Kurek v. Luszcyk, 28 N.Y.S.3d 550 (App. Term, 2d, 11th & 13th Jud. Dists. 2015) (*citing* 56 N.Y. Jur 2d, Estates, Powers, and Restraints on Alienation, §§ 36, 40).

1137 *Id.*

1138 56 N.Y.S.3d 414 (App. Term, 9th & 10th Jud. Dists. 2017).

1139 *Id.* The Court further held that Petitioner's bearing his mother's Power of Attorney did not "[p]ermit him to commence this proceeding in his own name." *Id.*

5. MAINTENANCE AND COMMON CHARGES (OWNER OF CONDOMINIUM/COOPERATIVE FAILS TO PAY)

The New York Condominium Act provides that where a non-occupying Landlord-owner fails to pay the condominium's monthly association fees; such as maintenance, common charges, assessments, and late fees, within sixty (60) days of the allowable grace period set forth within the condominium rules, the condominium's managing board may demand that the Tenant pay all future rent to the condominium association until the fees are paid in-full.[1140] The payments "relieve" the Tenant of rent obligations to the Landlord and constitute an absolute defense in a non-payment proceeding.[1141] If the Tenant fails to comply with the condominium's demand, then the condominium association may seek to evict the Tenant.[1142]

Disputes regarding payment may be commenced via a special proceeding in the Housing Part or a declaratory judgment action in the Supreme Court. The non-occupying owner is entitled to a meeting with the condominium's managing board within thirty (30) days of the owner's written notice disputing the claim.[1143] No more than three (3) business days following the final payment, the condominium association <u>must</u> provide written notice to both the non-occupying owner and the Tenant.[1144]

The laws governing rent-stabilized properties are <u>not</u> applicable to condominium and cooperative apartments.[1145] With regard to cooperative and shareholder agreements, it has been held that the cooperative board and its shareholders are "landlord and tenant to the extent that [the cooperative board] may maintain a summary proceeding against

---

1140 RPL §§ 339-kk(b),[c].

1141 *Id.* at § 339-kk(e); Desiano v. Fitzgerald, 37 N.Y.S.3d 671 (Peekskill City Ct. 2016).

1142 *See* The Board of Mgrs. of 222 Riverside Dr. Condominium v. Holland, 2014 N.Y. Misc. LEXIS 1814 (N.Y. Cnty. Sup. Ct. April 17, 2014).

1143 RPL § 339-kk[c].

1144 *Id.*

1145 *See The Board. of Mgrs. of 222 Riverside Dr. Condominium*, 2014 N.Y. Misc. LEXIS at 1814 (*citing* Fast Props., N.V. v. Freidus, 103 A.D.2d 729, 478 N.Y.S.2d 301 (1st Dep't 1984)).

[a shareholder]."[1146] In *Vernon Manor Coop. Apts., Section II, Inc. v. Brisport*, the Mt. Vernon City Court held that the monthly maintenance or carrying charge constitutes rent, and that a dispute regarding such payment is subject to Landlord and Tenant principles and laws.[1147] In the resulting non-payment proceeding, the cooperative board was granted summary judgment, and the warrant of eviction was stayed ten (10) days to allow the shareholder to pay the arrears.[1148]

6. NEW YORK SOLDIERS' AND SAILORS' CIVIL RELIEF ACT

A Landlord may not evict "a person in military service or the spouse, children, or other dependents of a person in military service" from a residential property except with leave of Court.[1149] The law is intended to ease some of the burdens that have been placed on the men and women of all branches of our military, including reservists and members of organized State militias, who have put their lives on hold to defend our nation.[1150]

The statute provides that the proceeding may be stayed for a maximum of six (6) months, or the Court may issue any "other order as may be just" where the Respondent's military service "materially affected" the ability to pay rent.[1151] The protections afforded under the law are not intended as a defense for the non-payment of rent due to reasons other than military service.

Although Military Law § 309(2) applies to the non-payment of rent, it has been held that the general stay provision of Military Law § 304 is applicable to holdover proceedings.[1152] A person who "knowingly takes

1146 Earl W. Jimerson Hous. Co., Inc. v. Butler, 425 N.Y.S.2d 924 (App. Term, 2d Dep't 1979).

1147 112 N.Y.S.3d 877 (Mt. Vernon City Ct. 2019).

1148 *Id.*

1149 NEW YORK STATES SOLDIERS' AND SAILORS' CIVIL RELIEF ACT [MILITARY LAW] § 309(1).

1150 *Id.* at § 300.

1151 *Id.* at § 309(2).

1152 New York City Hous. Auth. v. Kostyan, 2007 N.Y. Misc. LEXIS 8785 (N.Y. Civ. Ct. Queens Cnty. Dec. 18, 2007) (granting ninety (90) day stay where Tenant's failure to appear was due to active military duty).

part" or "attempts" to take part in the eviction of a member of the military without leave of Court may be guilty of a misdemeanor, which is punishable by a maximum fine of $1,000 and/or one (1) year in jail.[1153]

7. PETS (MULTIPLE DWELLINGS) (NEW YORK CITY)

In New York City multiple dwellings, which are three (3) or more families living independently within a building, a lease provision barring household pets may not be enforced where the Tenant harbored a pet "openly and notoriously" for at least three (3) months with no adverse action taken by the Landlord.[1154] The Tenant has the initial burden of proving the Landlord's waiver.[1155] For the pet waiver to be successfully invoked, the Landlord must have "knowledge" (actual or constructive) of the Tenant's harboring of the pet.[1156] However, where the pet "[c]auses damage to the subject premises, creates a nuisance or interferes substantially with the health, safety or welfare of other tenants or occupants of the same or adjacent building," the pet waiver is not applicable.[1157]

1153 MILITARY LAW § 309(3).

1154 NYC ADMIN. CODE § 27-2009.1(b); *see* Bray Realty, LLC v. Pilaj, 42 N.Y.S.3d 711 (App. Term, 2d, 11th & 13th Jud. Dists. 2016) (dismissal of prior summary proceeding does not extend time for Landlord to commence new proceeding for violation of lease "no pet" rule); RPDG, LLC v. Kuravsky, 41 N.Y.S.3d 452 (App. Term, 2d, 11th & 13th Jud. Dists. 2016) (waiver occurs where Landlord learned Tenant had a dog more than three (3) months prior to commencement of summary proceeding); Garvey v. Rodriguez, 2019 N.Y.L.J. LEXIS 3639 (N.Y. Civ. Ct. Kings Cnty. Sept. 9, 2019) (waiver where Landlord acknowledged Tenant's pitbull in a stipulation from a prior summary proceeding). *See also* 79 W. 12th St. Corp. v. Kornblum, 201 A.D.3d 543, 157 N.Y.S.3d 378 (1st Dep't 2022) (granting Tenant's motion to dismiss cooperative building's action to remove dogs due to amended pet-friendly House Rules, and the "[l]ack of evidence that the old rule was being enforced.").

1155 Morris I LLC v. Baez, 113 N.Y.S.3d 833 (N.Y. Civ. Ct. Bronx Cnty. 2019).

1156 NYC ADMIN. CODE § 27-2009.1(b); 149th St., LLC v. Rodriguez, 31 N.Y.S.3d 922 (App. Term, 2d, 11th & 13th Jud. Dists. 2016) (knowledge of pet imputed to Landlord where Landlord's agents and/or employees were aware of the dog); 184 W. 10th St. Corp. v. Marvits, 59 A.D.3d 287, 874 N.Y.S.2d 403 (1st Dep't 2009) (Tenant's cats).

1157 NYC ADMIN. CODE § 27-2009.1(d).

8. RENT RECEIPTS

For residential properties, the Landlord must provide the Tenant with a receipt where the rent is paid by means other than personal check.[1158] If the rent is paid by personal check, then the Tenant must request a receipt and, once requested, the request is deemed continuous for the duration of the tenancy.[1159] The Landlord must maintain a "record" of all cash payments of rent for three (3) years.[1160]

Where the rent is paid directly to the Landlord or the Landlord's agent, the receipt must be given "immediately" to the Tenant.[1161] If the rent is paid indirectly, then the Landlord has fifteen (15) days from delivery to provide a receipt. The receipt must state the date, amount paid, location of the premises, period for which rent was paid, and include the signature and title of the person receiving the rent.[1162]

The 2019 Amendments do not specify a penalty for non-compliance with RPL § 235-e. In *Robinson v. Robles*, the Rochester City Court opted not to penalize the Landlord for failing to provide rent receipts due to the Tenant's default.[1163] Similarly, in *Reed v. Ragsdale*, absent a "clear" violation of the law, the Landlord was entitled to a money judgment for the unpaid rent.[1164] In *Lawler v. Caufield*, the Housing Part opted to refrain from considering a sanction for the Landlord's failure to provide rent receipts where the Tenant admitted owing the rent claimed due.[1165]

On the other hand, in both *Brinkman v. Cahill* and *Palmieri v. Hernandez*, the Courts held that any "doubt [regarding compliance]

1158 RPL § 235-e; 181 Washington Heights Assocs. LLC v. The Children's Place, Inc., 150 N.Y.S.3d 232 (N.Y. Civ. Ct. N.Y. Cnty. 2021) (the requirement to provide rent receipts pursuant to RPL § 235-e does not extend to commercial premises).

1159 RPL § 235-e(b).

1160 *Id.*

1161 *Id.* at § 235-e[c].

1162 *Id.* at § 235-e(a).

1163 906 N.Y.S.2d 844 (Rochester City Ct. 2010).

1164 695 N.Y.S.2d 240 (Newark Just. Ct. 1999).

1165 114 N.Y.S.3d 621 (Watertown City Ct. 2019).

should be resolved in favor of the tenant."[1166] This view was adopted in *Mayflower Props., LLC v. Pacheco*, where the Housing Part held that all issues of disputed fact concerning rent payments would be ruled in favor of the Tenant due to the Landlord's failure to provide receipts.[1167] In doing so, no rent was awarded for any month a receipt was required but not provided. Another trial court proposed a rebuttable presumption that the rent was deemed paid when the Landlord failed to provide rent receipts.[1168]

9. RETALIATORY EVICTION

The Landlord may not serve a notice to quit, substantially alter the terms of a rental agreement, or commence a proceeding in retaliation for any of the following protected acts: (1) a complaint by or on behalf of the Tenant made in good faith to a governmental agency regarding the Landlord's alleged violation of a health or safety law, regulation, code, or ordinance; (2) action taken to enforce the Tenant's rights pursuant to the rental agreement; or (3) the Tenant's participation in a Tenant's or resident's association.[1169] In addition, the Landlord may not refuse to re-new an existing lease or offer a renewal lease with "an unreasonable rent increase" in retaliation for the above conduct.[1170]

The defense of retaliatory eviction may be asserted in a holdover proceeding involving residential premises excluding owner-occupied

---

1166 Brinkman v. Cahill, 543 N.Y.S.2d 636, 637 (Arcadia Just. Ct. 1989); Palmieri v. Hernandez, 485 N.Y.S.2d 915, 916 (Mt. Vernon City Ct. 1984).

1167 117 N.Y.S.3d 459 (N.Y. Civ. Ct. N.Y. Cnty. 2019).

1168 Gummerson v. Strecker, 806 N.Y.S.2d 445 (Auburn City Ct. 2005).

1169 RPL §§ 223-b(1),(2) (HSTPA, L. 2019, c. 36, Part M, § 2). *See, e.g.*, Gilliam v. Duncan, 2020 N.Y.L.J. LEXIS 916 (N.Y. Civ. Ct. Kings Cnty. May 5, 2020) (dismissing summary proceeding commenced in retaliation for Tenant's refusal to pay unlawful "$200.00 side deal payment"). *Cf.* Miller v. Delarosa, 94 N.Y.S.3d 539 (N.Y. Civ. Ct. Bronx Cnty. 2018) (denying motion to dismiss holdover proceeding due to issues of fact regarding Tenant's harassment claim); Loscalzo v. Rodriguez, 13 N.Y.S.3d 850 (App. Term, 9th & 10th Jud. Dists. 2015) (retaliatory eviction not applicable where Tenant's claims "did not involve an alleged violation by landlord of a health or safety law or regulation, or the enforcement of a right under the rental agreement").

1170 *See* RPL §§ 223-b(1),(2).

dwellings with fewer than four (4) units.[1171] The rationale for excluding smaller owner-occupied dwellings (i.e., fewer than four (4) units) is that the public interest may not be served by "keeping together in one house [the] landlord and the tenant who is suing" on the grounds of retaliatory eviction.[1172]

The defense is similarly unavailable in a non-payment proceeding.[1173] In other words, the defense of retaliatory eviction does not constitute a justification for withholding rent.[1174] The exception to this rule is where the Landlord's non-payment claim is frivolous or otherwise a pretext for commencing an unlawful proceeding. In addition, the defense may not be asserted where the summary proceeding is based upon a breach by the Tenant or the Tenant's guests, or where the tenancy was terminated pursuant to the terms of the lease as a result of a bona fide transfer of ownership.[1175]

The HSTPA expanded protections against retaliatory evictions by recognizing the assertion of the implied warranty of habitability defense as protected Tenant activity.[1176] The new law further extended to one (1) year (formerly six (6) months) the period in which a substantial alteration to the tenancy, or an attempt to substantially alter the tenancy, results in a rebuttable presumption that the Landlord acted in

1171 *Id.* at § 223-b(6). *See* Sills v. Dellavalle, 9 A.D.3d 561, at 561-62, 780 N.Y.S.2d 193, 194-95 (3d Dep't 2004) (retaliatory eviction claim not available in proceeding involving owner-occupied dwellings with fewer than four (4) units). A retaliatory eviction claim may not be asserted in a summary proceeding involving commercial property. *See* Tirse v. Andrews, 128 A.D.3d 1112, 8 N.Y.S.3d 711 (3d Dep't 2015); Mitchell Gardens No. 3 Coop. Corp. v. Moskowitz, 2018 N.Y.L.J. LEXIS 2768 (N.Y. Civ. Ct. Queens Cnty. Aug. 15, 2018); New York Teachers Hous. Corp. v. Perez, 101 N.Y.S.3d 700 (N.Y. Civ. Ct. Bronx Cnty. 2018).

1172 Weil v. Kaplan, 670 N.Y.S.2d 666, 668 (App. Term, 9th & 10th Jud. Dists. 1997).

1173 Chelsea Ridge NY, LLC v. Clarke, 983 N.Y.S.2d 201 (App. Term, 9th & 10th Jud. Dists. 2013); 390 W. End Assocs. v. Raiff, 636 N.Y.S.2d 965, 967 (App. Term, 1st Dep't 1995).

1174 RPL § 223-b(4).

1175 *Id.* at § 223-b(6).

1176 *Id.* at §§ 223-b(1),(2) (HSTPA, L. 2019, c. 36, Part M, § 2).

retaliation of protected Tenant activity.[1177] The defense has further been extended to an eviction from a parking space ancillary to a residential lease.[1178]

Retaliatory conduct in violation of RPL § 223-b may result in civil damages, including reasonable attorney's fees, costs, injunctive relief, and other equitable remedies.[1179] The Tenant must affirmatively assert the defense or it is deemed waived. Otherwise, the Tenant may elect to assert the claim as a counterclaim in the summary proceeding. However, the reader should be mindful that the Housing Part may not grant injunctive or declaratory relief.[1180]

A lease provision charging a fee for making a bona fide complaint against the Landlord is unenforceable.[1181] The statute of limitations for a retaliatory eviction claim is one (1) year following the unlawful eviction.[1182] Where the Tenant enters into a Stipulation of Settlement consenting to a judgment of possession in favor of the Landlord, the claim is waived because the Tenant "[c]onceded the validity of the proceeding on which the final judgment was based."[1183]

1177 *Id.* at § 223-b(5); Tapia v. Roman, 2022 N.Y.L.J. LEXIS 469 (N.Y. Civ. Ct. Kings Cnty. April 26, 2022) (granting Tenant's unopposed motion for summary judgment where Landlord commenced holdover proceeding within one (1) year of Tenant's "numerous housing code violation complaints").

1178 *See* Raderman v. Talia Mgmt. Co., 651 N.Y.S.2d 850 (N.Y. Cnty. Sup. Ct. 1996); *Mitchell Gardens No. 3 Coop. Corp.*, 2018 N.Y.L.J. LEXIS at 2768 (holding whether occupancy of the premises is ancillary to the "residential lease or a separate commercial lease" is an issue for the trier of fact); *New York Teachers Hous. Corp.*, 101 N.Y.S.3d at 700 (denying claim due to lack of evidence).

1179 RPL § 223-b(3).

1180 *See generally* 601 W. 160 Realty Corp. v. Henry, 731 N.Y.S.2d 581 (App. Term, 2d & 11th Jud. Dists. 2001).

1181 RPL § 223-b(5-a). A Landlord or Landlord's agent who attempts to collect a fee for asserting a bona fide complaint is subject to civil liability equal to as much as three (3) times the amount of the fee. *Id.*

1182 CPLR § 215(7). *See* Munoz v. 221 W. 16th Realty LLC, 24 A.D.3d 112, 804 N.Y.S.2d 248 (1st Dep't 2005).

1183 *Cf.* Witters v. Yatrakis, 867 N.Y.S.2d 21 (App. Term, 2d & 11th Jud. Dists. 2008). Although the Tenant reserved the right to pursue a retaliatory eviction claim in the stipulation, the proceeding was dismissed due to the failure to state a claim upon which relief may be granted. *Id.*

10. SUCCESSION RIGHTS (RENT-STABILIZED) (NEW YORK CITY)

In New York City, where the Tenant permanently vacates a rent-stabilized apartment, a "family member"[1184] who simultaneously resided within the premises as his or her primary residence for at least the immediate past two (2) years may be named the Tenant on the renewal lease.[1185] The term "family member" has been expanded beyond traditional family relationships to include any person who resided within the premises with the Tenant as a primary residence and demonstrates an "emotional and financial commitment, and interdependence between [them]."[1186]

The factors commonly considered for non-traditional family members include: (1) longevity of the relationship; (2) sharing or relying upon one another to pay expenses and common necessities; (3) intermingling of finances and accounts; (4) engaging in family activities and functions; (5) formalizing legal documents and responsibilities; (6) holding themselves out to be family members; (7) caring for one another; and (8) any other behavior evincing the "intention of creating a long-term, emotionally-committed relationship."[1187] An intimate relationship is neither required nor considered.[1188]

1184 The Rent Stabilization Code's definition of a "family member" includes, but is not limited to, the Tenant's spouse, son, daughter, stepson, stepdaughter, father, mother, stepfather, stepmother, brother, sister, grandfather, grandmother, grandson, granddaughter, father-in-law, mother-in-law, son-in-law, or daughter-in-law. *See* RSC [9 N.Y.C.R.R.] § 2520.6(o)(1); *see also* 9 N.Y.C.C.R. § 2204.6(d)(3).

1185 RSC [9 N.Y.C.R.R.] § 2523.5(b)(1). *See* Jourdain v. State Div. of Hous. & Cmty. Renewal, 159 A.D.3d 41, 70 N.Y.S.3d 239 (2d Dep't 2018) (disabled senior citizen who lived in the apartment with Tenant (her daughter), and remained after Tenant permanently vacated, entitled to succession rights); Underhill-Washington Equities, LLC v. State Div. of Hous. & Cmty. Renewal, 157 A.D.3d 705, 69 N.Y.S.3d 81 (2d Dep't 2018) (brother of Tenant who resided in the apartment for more than thirty (30) years); *see also* JIMS Realty LLC v. Barrett, 90 N.Y.S.3d 879 (N.Y. Civ. Ct. Kings Cnty. 2019) (daughter resided in apartment for more than forty (40) years, the last thirteen (13) of which the Landlord accepted rent from her in her own name).

1186 RSC [9 N.Y.C.R.R.] § 2520.6(o)(2).

1187 *Id.*; *see* 530 Second Ave. Co., LLC v. Zenker, 160 A.D.3d 160, 74 N.Y.S.3d 41 (1st Dep't 2018); Confe Realty Corp. v. Jimenez-Nunez, 2019 N.Y.L.J. LEXIS 2862 (N.Y. Civ. Ct. N.Y. Cnty. Aug. 14, 2019) (succession rights applied in non-payment proceeding).

1188 RSC [9 N.Y.C.R.R.] § 2520.6(o)(2); *see, e.g.*, Naroznik v. Prockett, 15 N.Y.S.3d 713 (App. Term, 2d, 11th & 13th Jud. Dists. 2015).

The burden of demonstrating succession rights rests with the party making the claim.[1189] There is a split between the First and Second Judicial Departments regarding when the "permanent vacating" of the premises occurs.[1190] The Appellate Division, First Department holds that a family member seeking succession rights may not include the period where the primary Tenant continues to pay rent after vacating the premises.[1191] On the other hand, the Appellate Division, Second Department has ruled that the period where the primary Tenant vacates the premises, but continues to maintain some connection to the property, may be included in computing the two-year look-back period.[1192] In determining prejudice resulting from a succession claim (which the Landlord may assert as a basis to deny succession rights), a successor's concealment of "his or her occupancy to the detriment of the Landlord" may be considered.[1193]

Where the Tenant is either a senior citizen (age 62 or older)[1194] or a "disabled person,"[1195] succession rights may apply provided the family member resided with the Tenant for at least one (1) year immediately prior to the vacating.[1196] The time period for computing compliance with the residency requirement is not interrupted when the family member "temporarily" relocates due to the following: (1) active military duty; (2) enrollment as a full-time student; (3) a Court Order

1189 Fieldbridge Assocs., LLC v. Sanders, 139 N.Y.S.3d 474 (App. Term, 2d, 11th & 13th Jud. Dists. 2021).

1190 Park Cent. I LLC v. Williams, 128 N.Y.S.3d 772 (App. Term, 1st Dep't 2020).

1191 *See, e.g.*, 186 Norfolk LLC v. Euvin, 192 A.D.3d 414, 139 N.Y.S.3d 801 (1st Dep't 2021).

1192 *Jourdain*, 159 A.D.3d at 41, 70 N.Y.S.3d at 239.

1193 *See* Pers Realty LLC v. Granville, 154 N.Y.S.3d 411 (N.Y. Civ. Ct. Kings Cnty. 2021).

1194 RSC [9 N.Y.C.R.R.] at § 2520.6(p).

1195 The term "disabled person" is defined as "a person who has an impairment which results from anatomical, physiological, or psychological conditions, other than addiction to alcohol, gambling, or any controlled substance, which are demonstrable by medically acceptable clinical and laboratory diagnostic techniques, and which are expected to be permanent and which prevent such person from engaging in any substantial gainful employment." *See id.* [9 N.Y.C.R.R.] at § 2520.6(q).

1196 *Id.* [9 N.Y.C.R.R.] at § 2523.5(b)(1); 1150 Brighton Co. v. Persits, 148 N.Y.S.3d 330 (App. Term, 2d, 11th & 13th Jud. Dists. 2021).

unrelated to the lease; (4) employment requirements; (5) hospitalization; or (6) other reasonable grounds.[1197]

In *Limani Realty, LLC v. Zayfert*, succession rights were denied where the Tenant's adult son temporarily relocated to attend school as a "part-time" student during the two-year look-back period.[1198] Succession rights were similarly denied where the Tenant's adult son resided at the subject premises for fewer than sixteen (16) months prior to his mother's permanent vacatur,[1199] and where the Tenant's name was forged on renewal leases.[1200]

On the other hand, the Appellate Division, First Department granted succession rights where the family member and Tenant resided together for eight (8) years prior to the Tenant's passing, during which time they shared household expenses, traveled and celebrated birthdays and holidays together, and the Tenant's hospital records listed the occupant as her "partner."[1201] A similar outcome was reached where the occupant was previously romantically involved with the primary Tenant, and then upon their breaking-up, vacated the premises only to return to the apartment fifteen (15) years later "exhibit[ing] many of the

1197 RSC [9 N.Y.C.R.R.] § 2523.5(b)(2).

1198 970 N.Y.S.2d 345 (App. Term, 2d, 11th & 13th Jud. Dists. 2012) (evidence failed to demonstrate the premises were used as adult son's primary residence "from the time he reached the age of majority until the end of the look-back period").

1199 550 Equities LLC v. Washington, 126 N.Y.S.3d 301 (App. Term, 1st Dep't 2020). The son's request for senior citizen succession rights denied because he was sixty-one (61) years-old when his mother vacated the premises; and not sixty-two (62) years-old as required by RSC 2520.6(p). *Id.*

1200 West 48th Holdings LLC v. Herrera, 122 N.Y.S.3d 480 (App. Term, 1st Dep't 2020) (primary Tenant vacated premises more than ten (10) years before claim for succession rights).

1201 WSC Riverside Dr. Owners LLC v. Williams, 125 A.D.3d 458, 3 N.Y.S.3d 342 (1st Dep't 2015); *see* 408 St. John's Place, LLC v. Estate of Bartholomew, 129 N.Y.S.3d 619 (App. Term, 2d, 11th & 13th Jud. Dists. 2020) (daughter and granddaughter granted succession rights notwithstanding the primary Tenant's application statement that she lived "alone"); 585 W. 204th LLC v. Peralta, 43 N.Y.S.3d 766 (App. Term, 1st Dep't 2016) (Tenant's adult son established succession rights where he resided in the rent-regulated apartment from birth, including the two (2) years immediately preceding his mother's death); Infinity Corp. v. Danko, 9 N.Y.S.3d 593 (App. Term, 1st Dep't 2015) (succession rights granted where the occupant and Tenant "enjoyed a family-type relationship" for nearly twenty (20) years).

behaviors associated with a traditional marriage."[1202] Likewise, succession rights were granted where the Tenant and family member lived together for approximately twenty-five (25) years, and the family member was the Tenant's sole care giver.[1203] The Court noted that the Tenant and occupant had become life partners two (2) years prior to the Tenant's passing.[1204]

The absence of documentary evidence does not "[u]ndermine a succession rights claim when the totality of the testimonial evidence... establishes the requisite emotional and financial commitment."[1205] In *Hitchcock Plaza Inc. v. Fortune*, the Tenant's niece was awarded succession rights based "in large measure on the court's assessment of the credibility of the witnesses" where she and her uncle shared household expenses, were traveling companions, and attended religious ceremonies together.[1206] Succession rights were also granted to the Tenant's adult son absent the production of "customary items of documentary proof of primary residence,...[where he] was unemployed for a long period of time and lacked substantial assets."[1207]

Finally, succession rights were awarded to a nephew who lived with his aunt for twenty-five (25) years and "cooked and shopped for her, took her to doctors' appointments, regularly ate dinner with her, did her laundry, and paid rent and utilities for the apartment."[1208] The Appellate

---

1202 *530 Second Ave. Co., LLC*, 160 A.D.3d at 160, 74 N.Y.S.3d at 41.

1203 *Naroznik*, 15 N.Y.S.3d at 713.

1204 *Id.* Nieces and nephews are not identified as traditional family members. *See* RSC [9 N.Y.C.R.R.] § 2520.6(o).

1205 1035 Washington Realty, LLC v. Weston, 128 N.Y.S.3d 144 (App. Term, 2d, 11th & 13th Jud. Dists. 2020); Jeremy Props. LC v. Franklin, 151 N.Y.S.3d 617 (N.Y. Civ. Ct. N.Y. Cnty. 2021).

1206 15 N.Y.S.3d 711 (App. Term, 1st Dep't 2015) (holding that the "modest intermingling of finances" was not sufficient to negate the overall family-like relationship); *see* PACST 1244-46, 1356, LLC v. Swinton, 31 N.Y.S.3d 923 (App. Term, 2d, 11th & 13th Jud. Dists. 2016) (great-niece qualified for succession rights after establishing "the requisite emotional and financial commitment and interdependence between her and tenant").

1207 *Fieldbridge Assocs., LLC*, 139 N.Y.S.3d at 474.

1208 354 Atl. Ave., LLC v. Noronha, 116 N.Y.S.3d 849 (App. Term, 2d, 11th & 13th Jud. Dists. 2019).

Term for the Second, Eleventh and Thirteenth Judicial Districts was not influenced by the lack of an "intermingling of finances," noting that "many adults who live with their parents do not choose to intermingle their finances."[1209]

11. TENANT PASSES AWAY DURING THE TENANCY

Unless agreed otherwise, the death of the Tenant prior to the expiration of the rental agreement neither terminates the rental agreement nor alleviates the obligation to pay rent. Instead, the rental agreement passes to the estate of the decedent, and the executor, administrator, or other legal representative of the estate may maintain the premises until the expiration of the lease or such other time as it may be properly terminated or cancelled.[1210] Accordingly, the estate is substituted for the decedent as a party to the rental agreement, and the benefits and obligations thereunder may be enforced.[1211]

If the Tenant passes away prior to the commencement of a summary proceeding, the proceeding is a nullity; a defect that is incapable of being cured whether by stipulation or other manner.[1212] As a general matter, a successor Tenant is not liable for the predecessor's arrears (unless obligated pursuant to an agreement) because the successor was not a party when the arrears accrued. Since "a successor in interest is not a tenant until he becomes a party to a lease…and because [the] tenant did not become a party until after the arrears sought had accrued, a nonpayment proceeding does not lie" for the predecessor's arrears.[1213] Moreover, a lease provision that binds "successors and assigns" to its terms is unenforceable where the estate became a party to the lease

1209 *Id.*; *1035 Washington Realty, LLC*, 128 N.Y.S.3d at 144.

1210 Westway Plaza Assocs. v. Doe, 179 A.D.2d 408, 578 N.Y.S.2d 166 (1st Dep't 1992).

1211 *See* De Christoforo v. Shore Ridge Assocs., 116 A.D.2d 123, at 126, 500 N.Y.S.2d 528, 530 (2d Dep't 1986).

1212 356-358 SJP, LLC v. Stewart, 130 N.Y.S.3d 595 (App. Term, 2d, 11th & 13th Jud. Dists. 2020).

1213 71 W. 68th St., LLC v. Roach, 72 N.Y.S.3d 518 (App. Term, 1st Dep't 2017); East Harlem Pilot Block Bldg. IV HDFC Inc. v. Diaz, 9 N.Y.S.3d 592 (App. Term, 1st Dep't 2015).

after the rent arrears accrued.[1214]

However, where rent arrears are owed at the time of the Tenant's passing and the premises "is occupied by a person[s] with a claim to possession," a summary proceeding may be commenced for rent arrears against the occupants, and for possession only against the estate. This means that the occupants lawfully in possession of the premises may also be named in the non-payment proceeding, but the possessory judgment and warrant of eviction may not be used to remove such individuals.[1215] Effective June 14, 2019, there is no longer a mandatory stay or temporary prohibition against the commencement of a summary proceeding following the Tenant's passing where an executor has not been named (the Landlord previously had to wait three (3) months).

If the lease expired prior to the Tenant's death, then the decedent's estate is not a necessary party and need not be named in the summary proceeding.[1216] This is because the "[p]ossessory claim of the estate lapsed upon termination of decedent's lease."[1217] In addition, if the premises are leased to a husband and wife, they take possession as tenants by the entirety.[1218] Thus, upon the passing of one (1) of the spouses, the decedent's possessory right is automatically transferred to the surviving spouse.[1219]

Recent case law has addressed the opposite scenario where the co-owner joint tenant (Landlord) of the premises passed away during the term of the lease, which she had entered into with her caretaker (Tenant) unbeknownst to the co-owner. In what appears to be a case of first impression, in *Harmon v. Misholy*, the Suffolk County District Court held that the execution of the lease did not sever the joint

1214 *71 W. 68th St., LLC*, 72 N.Y.S.3d at 518.

1215 RPAPL § 711(2).

1216 *See* Marine Terr. Assocs. v. Kesoglides, 884 N.Y.S.2d 552 (App. Term, 2d, 11th & 13th Jud. Dists. 2009); Ryerson Towers, Inc. v. Estate of Laura Brown, 612 N.Y.S.2d 99 (App. Term, 2d & 11th Jud. Dists. 1994).

1217 Ellis v. Disch, 851 N.Y.S.2d 57 (App. Term, 1st Dep't 2007); *see also Marine Terr. Assocs.*, 884 N.Y.S.2d at 553; 1820 First Ave. Inc. v. Mendoza, 2015 N.Y. Misc. LEXIS 3416 (N.Y. Civ. Ct. N.Y. Cnty. Sept. 22, 2015).

1218 229 W. 109 St. Realty Corp. v. Ichida, 127 N.Y.S.3d 691 (App. Term, 1st Dep't 2020).

1219 *Id.*; Vernum v. Freyer, 139 N.Y.S.3d 522 (Warren Cnty. Sup. Ct. 2021).

tenancy and, as a result, upon the co-owner's passing, all rights to the premises automatically reverted to the surviving joint tenant, which effectively terminated the caretaker's right to possession.[1220]

12. TENANT SAFE HARBOR ACT ("TSHA")

The TSHA bars eviction due to the non-payment of rent where the residential Tenant or lawful occupant suffered a "financial hardship" during the COVID-19 Period.[1221] In other words, a residential Tenant who suffered a financial hardship during the COVID-19 Period (i.e., March 7, 2020—January 15, 2022) may not be evicted for the failure to pay rent during that period.[1222]

The burden of establishing a financial hardship rests with the Tenant.[1223] When the affirmative defense is successfully established, the Court may award a prevailing Landlord a money judgment for the full amount of rent owed, but may not issue a judgment of possession or a warrant of eviction.[1224]

In determining financial hardship, the Court considers the Tenant's or lawful occupant's: (1) income prior to the COVID-19 Period; (2) income during the COVID-19 Period; (3) liquid assets; (4) eligibility and receipt of government financial assistance, including cash assistance, supplemental nutrition assistance, disability assistance, home energy assistance, unemployment insurance, and emergency rental assistance; and (5) any additional relevant factors.[1225] Demonstrable proof of one (1) of the above factors is sufficient to invoke the affirmative defense.[1226]

1220 166 N.Y.S.3d 504 (Suffolk Cnty. Dist. Ct. 2022). The lease was signed by the holder of a Power of Attorney on behalf of the joint tenant (co-owner), who passed away approximately one (1) month into the five-year tenancy. *Id.*

1221 Tenant Safe Harbor Act (A.10290B/S.8192) (Ch. 127 of the Laws of 2020); *see* Cabrera v. Humphrey, 192 A.D.3d 227, 140 N.Y.S.3d 609 (3d Dep't 2021) (the TSHA "[i]s limited to summary eviction proceedings based on nonpayment and does not apply to holdover proceedings").

1222 TSHA § 2(1); *see generally* 111-50 Realty Corp. v. Melgar, 139 N.Y.S.3d 778 (N.Y. Civ. Ct. Queens Cnty. 2020).

1223 *110-50 Realty*, 139 N.Y.S.3d at 778.

1224 TSHA §§ 1, 3.

1225 *Id.* at § 2(2).

1226 *See 110-50 Realty*, 139 N.Y.S.3d at 778.

13. VICTIM OF DOMESTIC VIOLENCE

In 2015, the State Legislature enacted RPAPL § 744, which prohibits a Landlord from evicting a residential Tenant based upon the Tenant's status as a victim of domestic violence.[1227] RPL § 227-d defines a victim of domestic violence as any person who "is or has been, or is a parent accompanied by a minor child or children who is or has been, in a situation in which such person or child is a victim of an act that would constitute a violent felony offense [Penal Law § 72.02] or a family offense [Family Court Act § 812(1)], and such act is alleged to have been committed by a member of the same family or household [Family Court Act § 812(1)]."[1228]

RPAPL § 744 is a defense in a residential summary proceeding where it is demonstrated that but for the Tenant's status as a victim of domestic violence, the Landlord would not have sought an eviction. The defense is rebutted where the Landlord demonstrates a "lawful ground" for the eviction.[1229] The defense further does not apply to owner-occupied residential dwellings with two (2) or fewer residential units.[1230]

The Respondent asserting the defense bears the burden of demonstrating that: (1) he or she is a Tenant at the subject premises; (2) a victim of domestic violence; and (3) the proceeding to recover possession would not have been commenced but for the Respondent's status as a victim of domestic violence.[1231] In *85 EP LLC v. Cano*, the defense was denied where the Respondent was "employed as a superintendent by petitioner, and occupied the apartment [in which Petitioner sought removal] as an incident" of the employment.[1232] Since the occupancy of real property "incident to employment is recognized as a circumstance in which no landlord-tenant relationship exists," the Respondent was unable to demonstrate that she was a Tenant, and, as a result, a defense

---

1227 RPAPL § 744(1).

1228 *Id.*

1229 *Id.* at §§ 744(1),(2).

1230 *Id.* at § 744(4).

1231 *Id.* at §§ 744(1),(2).

1232 124 N.Y.S.3d 635 (N.Y. Civ. Ct. Kings Cnty. 2020).

pursuant to RPAPL § 744 was not proper.[1233]

B. COMMERCIAL PREMISES

1. BREACH OF COVENANT TO REPAIR

Absent a lease provision specifying the circumstances upon which the Tenant may withhold rent, a commercial Tenant that remains in possession must continue to pay rent where the Landlord breaches the rental agreement by failing to make required repairs.[1234] In other words, the Landlord's failure to make the repairs is not a defense in a non-payment proceeding.

It is well-established that the covenant to pay rent is independent of the covenant to make repairs as long as the Tenant remains in

---

1233 *Id.* (*citing* RPAPL § 713(11)); *see also* Mangan Realty, LC v. Anthony, 104 N.Y.S.3d 873 (N.Y. Civ. Ct. Bronx Cnty. 2019) (Tenant failed to demonstrate status as a victim of domestic violence; specifically that physical contact that would constitute a violent felony was attributable to an individual that would qualify as a "family offense"). *Cf.* KDG Albany, LP v. Dixon, 89 N.Y.S.3d 835 (Albany City Ct. 2018) (dismissing holdover proceeding where RPAPL § 744 defense successfully asserted).

1234 *See* Fifth Line, LLC v. Fitch, 167 A.D.3d 847, 91 N.Y.S.3d 135 (2d Dep't 2018) (holding that "[g]enerally, a [commercial] tenant's duty to continue to pay rent is not suspended if the tenant remains in possession of the leased premises, even if the landlord breaches its obligations under the lease, unless there is an express provision in the lease declaring the circumstances under which the tenant may withhold rent"); Soundview Cinemas, Inc. v. AC I Soundview, LLC, 149 A.D.3d 1121, 53 N.Y.S.3d 157 (2d Dep't 2017) (HVAC system inoperable and leaking roof). A lease provision that provides the rent must be paid even where the commercial Landlord has failed to make repairs to the premises will generally be enforced. *See, e.g.*, Harlington Realty Co., LLC v. Lawrence Plumbing Supply Inc., 201 A.D.3d 435, 156 N.Y.S.3d 748 (1st Dep't 2022); Blue Water Realty, LLC v. Salon Mgmt. of Great Neck, Corp., 189 A.D.3d 496, 139 N.Y.S.3d 9 (1st Dep't 2020) (same). Parenthetically, the Court of Appeals recently reaffirmed that a commercial Tenant obligated to pay the real property taxes for the premises pursuant to the rental agreement has the right to challenge the assessment in accordance with Article 7 of the Real Property Tax Law (not limited to the property owner). *See* DCH Auto v. Town of Mamaronek, 2022 N.Y. LEXIS 1172 (June 16, 2022).

possession.[1235] Any damages sustained by the Tenant may be asserted as a counterclaim, if not barred by the rental agreement, or in a plenary action in a court of competent jurisdiction.

2. FAILURE TO EXERCISE OPTION TO RE-NEW LEASE

A commercial Tenant's failure to timely exercise a lease renewal provision may be forgiven, in equity, where the omission: (1) was due to "inadvertence," "negligence," or "honest mistake;" (2) will result in forfeiture by the Tenant; and (3) the absence of prejudice to the Landlord.[1236] A "forfeiture" occurs where the Tenant, in good faith and with the intention of renewing the lease, makes improvements to the premises, and, as a result, non-renewal will cause "substantial loss."[1237]

In *135 E. 57th St. LLC v. Daffy's Inc.*, the Appellate Division, First Department excused an untimely lease renewal where the delay was due to an inadvertent calendaring error, the Tenant acted in good faith, and there was no discernible prejudice.[1238] A similar outcome resulted in *Laundry Mgmt.-N. 3rd St., Inc. v. BFN Realty Assocs., LLC*, where the Appellate Division, Second Department concluded that the Landlord was not prejudiced when the Landlord entered into a contract for the sale of the premises after receiving the Tenant's written notice of its

---

1235 Universal Comms. Network, Inc. v. 229 W. 28th Owner, LLC, 85 A.D.3d 668, 926 N.Y.S.2d 479 (1st Dep't 2011); Westchester Cnty. Indus. Dev. Agency v. Morris Indus. Bldrs., 278 A.D.2d 232, 717 N.Y.S.2d 279 (2d Dep't 2000); 91 E. Main St. Realty Corp. v. Angelic Creations by Lucia, 884 N.Y.S.2d 565, 566 (App. Term, 9th & 10th Jud. Dists. 2009); Kato Int'l LLC v. Gerard Fox Law, P.C., 2020 N.Y. Misc. LEXIS 2447 (N.Y. Cnty. Sup. Ct. May 26, 2020). A lease provision reserving the Landlord's right to enter the premises to make repairs does not necessarily establish a duty to make the repairs. *See* Han v. Kemp, Pin & Ski, LLC, 142 A.D.3d 688, 36 N.Y.S.3d 883 (2d Dep't 2016) (out-of-possession Landlord generally has no responsibility to maintain commercial premises in a "reasonably safe condition"); Cabral v. Zerega Realty LLC, 2021 N.Y. Misc. LEXIS 5472 (Bronx Cnty. Sup. Ct. Nov. 4, 2021).

1236 *See* Laundry Mgmt.-N. 3rd St., Inc. v. BFN Realty Assocs., LLC, 179 A.D.3d 776, 116 N.Y.S.3d 352 (2d Dep't 2020); Waterfalls Italian Cuisine, Inc. v. Tamarin, 149 A.D.3d 1141, 53 N.Y.S.3d 347 (2d Dep't 2017); J.N.A. Realty Corp. v. Cross Bay Chelsea, Inc., 42 N.Y.2d 392, 397 N.Y.S.2d 958 (1977).

1237 *Laundry Mgmt.-N. 3rd St., Inc.*, 179 A.D.3d at 776, 116 N.Y.S.3d at 352; *J.N.A. Realty Corp.*, 42 N.Y.2d at 392, 397 N.Y.S.2d at 958.

1238 91 A.D.3d 1, 934 N.Y.S.2d 112 (1st Dep't 2011).

intent to re-new the lease.[1239] The Appellate Division further concluded that the loss of "long-standing good will associated with the premises" is a factor to consider in determining whether a forfeiture will result.[1240]

Approximately twelve (12) years prior to the *Laundry Mgmt.-N. 3rd St., Inc.* decision, the same Appellate Division had held that the Tenant's failure to deliver the renewal notice to Landlord's attorney by the negotiated means and format (i.e., certified mail) was not excusable.[1241] In *2039 Jericho Turnpike Corp.*, the Court reasoned that since there was no credible evidence suggesting that a renewal notice had been provided, it could not reasonably be concluded that the Landlord waived those lease requirements.[1242]

The same result was reached with respect to an out-of-possession Tenant.[1243] In *Baygold Assocs.*, the Tenant failed to establish that a forfeiture would result because there was no indication that the improvements made to the premises "decades" earlier were completed with the intent of renewing the lease.[1244] Although the occupants had sustained monetary damages, the Court of Appeals concluded that "[t]he forfeiture rule was crafted to protect tenants in possession who make improvements of a 'substantial character' with an eye toward renewing a lease, not to protect the revenue stream of an out-of-possession tenant…."[1245]

1239 *Laundry Mgmt.-N. 3rd St., Inc.*, 179 A.D.3d at 776, 116 N.Y.S.3d at 352.

1240 *Id.*

1241 2039 Jericho Turnpike Corp. v. Caglayan, 64 A.D.3d 609, 882 N.Y.S.2d 311 (2d Dep't 2009).

1242 *Id.*

1243 Baygold Assocs., Inc. v. Congregation Yetev Lev of Monsey, Inc., 19 N.Y.3d 223, 947 N.Y.S.2d 794 (2012).

1244 *Id.*

1245 *Id.*

C. ADDITIONAL AFFIRMATIVE DEFENSES

1. ACCEPTANCE OF PAYMENT FOLLOWING TERMINATION/EXPIRATION OF LEASE

Whether the Landlord may accept moneys following the expiration or termination of the rental agreement depends on the parties' intent and the timing of the payments relative to the commencement of the summary proceeding. As discussed below, the acceptance of payment is limited when the Landlord wishes to pursue an eviction proceeding.

a. ACCEPTANCE OF SUBSEQUENT MONTH'S RENT PRIOR TO COMMENCEMENT OF SUMMARY PROCEEDING

The Landlord may continue to accept rent payments until the termination date set forth in the termination notice.[1246] However, the acceptance of rent for a period subsequent to the termination of the lease, but prior to the commencement of a summary proceeding, re-establishes the tenancy on a month-to-month basis. Accordingly, the termination notice would be voided, and the summary proceeding may be dismissed.[1247] Nonetheless, a holdover proceeding may continue where the Landlord initially accepts (and inadvertently deposits) the payment, but returns the funds within a reasonable period of time.[1248]

1246 ATM Four, LLC v. Miller, 961 N.Y.S.2d 356 (Nassau Cnty. Dist. Ct. 2012). *See* Top Value Homes, Inc. v. Continental Petroleum Corp., 784 N.Y.S.2d 924 (Nassau Cnty. Dist. Ct. 2004). *See also* DOLAN § 30:16, at 429-30 (4th ed. 2010).

1247 *See* RPL § 232-c; *see also* Gennarelli v. Cherkovsky, 65 N.Y.S.3d 491 (Nassau Cnty. Dist. Ct. 2017); Vita v. Dol-Fan, III, Inc., 852 N.Y.S.2d 589, 590-91 (App. Term, 9th & 10th Jud. Dists. 2007); *Top Value Homes, Inc.*, 784 N.Y.S.2d at 924.

1248 Macleay Woods Hous. Co., Inc. v. Franks, 851 N.Y.S.2d 58 (New Rochelle City Ct. 2007) (payment returned approximately fourteen (14) days after receipt did not warrant dismissal). *Cf.* East Bay Assocs. v. Johnson, 2000 N.Y. Misc. LEXIS 696 (App. Term, 9th & 10th Jud. Dists. 2000) (checks held for seven (7) weeks and three (3) weeks, respectively, warranted dismissal).

b. ACCEPTANCE OF SUBSEQUENT PAYMENT AFTER COMMENCEMENT OF SUMMARY PROCEEDING

It is generally accepted that the acceptance of payment following commencement of a holdover proceeding is permitted without voiding the termination notice or creating a new tenancy. This outcome is supported by RPAPL § 711(1), which provides that the "[a]cceptance of rent after commencement of the special proceeding upon this ground [holdover following expiration of lease] shall not terminate such proceeding nor effect any award of possession."[1249] In other words, the money accepted to occupy the premises following commencement of a summary proceeding, absent an intent to enter into a new Landlord and Tenant relationship, is either prior rent arrears or, if for a new period, considered to be use and occupancy (as opposed to rent), which the Landlord may accept at any time.[1250]

This raises the question when is a summary proceeding "commenced?" The issue presented itself following the 2005 amendments to the New York City Civil Court Act, which converted the New York City Housing Parts from "service" to "filing" Courts and, as a result, the Courts were asked to resolve whether a termination notice is vitiated when the Landlord accepts payment after the filing of the summary proceeding, but prior to the service of the Notice of Petition and Petition.[1251]

In *92 Bergenbrooklyn, LLC v. Cisarano*, the Appellate Term for the Second, Eleventh and Thirteenth Judicial Districts held that the "commencement date" is dependent upon the context in which the issue arises, and, more specifically, in the instant matter, at the time of "service" (and, as a result, the predicate notice was vitiated and the

---

1249 RPAPL § 711(1) (emphasis added).

1250 *Id.*

1251 In 1994, RPAPL § 731 was amended by deleting the phrase "service of" in reference to the commencement of a summary proceeding. *See* 92 Bergenbrooklyn, LLC v. Cisarano, 21 N.Y.S.3d 810 (App. Term, 2d, 11th & 13th Jud. Dists. 2015).

summary proceeding was dismissed).[1252] In its decision, the Court noted that the statutory change to a filing Court did not change the rules regarding when a Landlord may accept rent without vitiating the termination notice.[1253] The Court reasoned that for these purposes, the proceeding commences upon "service" (not filing) because only then is there certainty that the Tenant is on notice of the summary proceeding.[1254]

2. AUTOMATIC LEASE RENEWAL

Pursuant to General Obligations Law § 5-905, a residential or commercial lease provision that states the rental agreement automatically re-news upon expiration is not enforceable unless the Landlord provides the Tenant a written reminder of the lease renewal provision between fifteen (15) and thirty (30) days from the date of renewal. The notice must be given to the Tenant by either personal service, registered mail, or certified mail.[1255] The failure to provide the written notice "renders the automatic renewal clause...unenforceable as against public

1252 *Id.* (holding that "[b]y accepting the [next month's] rent before the service of the papers on tenant, landlord vitiated its notice of termination"); Livian v. Soblesohn, 2021 N.Y. Misc LEXIS 6209 (N.Y. Civ. Ct. Queens Cnty. Dec. 3, 2021) (same); Langdoc v. Warden, 141 N.Y.S.3d 678 (Albany City Ct. 2021) (same).

1253 *92 Bergenbrooklyn, LLC*, 21 N.Y.S.3d at 810.

1254 *Id.*; *see* 1834 Caton v. Edwards, 2019 N.Y.L.J. LEXIS 1727 (N.Y. Civ. Ct. Kings Cnty. May 22, 2019); *see also* Arverne Ltd. Profit Hous. Corp. v. Taft's Dental, P.C., 99 N.Y.S.3d 851 (N.Y. Civ. Ct. Queens Cnty. 2019). The Appellate Term for the Ninth and Tenth Judicial Districts adopted the same rule regarding the acceptance of rent after filing the proceeding, but prior to service of the Notice of Petition and Petition. *See* Scarborough Manor Owners Corp. v. Robson, 59 N.Y.S.3d 877 (App. Term, 9th & 10th Jud. Dists. 2017). However, in *Scarborough Manor Owners Corp.*, the motion to dismiss the summary proceeding was denied because the Tenant's payments were deposited into a bank lockbox unbeknownst to the Landlord, and, as a result, "there was no knowing acceptance of rent and [the] tenant could have had no legitimate expectation that her payment of rent would give rise to a month-to-month tenancy." *Id.*; Sebco Hous. Dev. Fund Co., Inc. v. Acosta, 121 N.Y.S.3d 774 (App. Term, 1st Dep't 2020) (same).

1255 GOL § 5-905.

policy of this State."[1256]

When notice is not provided, the Tenant has the option of remaining in possession or vacating the premises because the "[L]andlord places himself in the position, when he does not give notice...of abiding by the Tenant's choice of what [the Tenant] wishes to do."[1257] If the Tenant elects to stay, then a month-to-month tenancy is created upon the Landlord's acceptance of the rent payment.[1258]

3. BANKRUPTCY

If the Tenant files for bankruptcy during the pendency of a summary proceeding, the proceeding is automatically stayed.[1259] This is the case even where the Landlord was unaware of the bankruptcy filing.[1260] However, if the bankruptcy filing occurred prior to the commencement of the summary proceeding, then the proceeding will typically be dismissed.[1261] Due to the Court's retention of jurisdiction, there have been occasions where summary proceedings commenced after the bankruptcy filing have been stayed (as opposed to dismissed). For example, this was the outcome where the commencement of the proceeding was in good faith and the Petitioner ceased to prosecute upon learning of

---

1256 *Id.*; Hain v. Zwitzer, 875 N.Y.S.2d 820 (Rochester City Ct. 2008); Malone Assocs. v. Grand Union Co., 249 A.D.2d 830, at 831, 671 N.Y.S.2d 861, 862 (3d Dep't 1998); J.H. Holding Co. v. Wooten, 291 N.Y. 427, 430 (1943) (RPL § 230 "was enacted solely for the protection of the tenant"). *Cf.* Stop & Shop Supermkt. Co., LLC v. Goldsmith, 2013 U.S. Dist. LEXIS 90820 (S.D.N.Y. June 24, 2013). RPL § 230 was substantially transferred into General Obligations Law § 5-905, which became law, effective September 27, 1964.

1257 Mobil Oil Corp. v. Lione, 322 N.Y.S.2d 82, 86 (Suffolk Cnty. Dist. Ct. 1971); *see generally Stop & Shop Supermarket Co. LLC*, 2013 U.S. Dist. LEXIS at 90820.

1258 *Mobil Oil Corp.*, 322 N.Y.S.2d at 84-85.

1259 11 U.S.C. § 362(a).

1260 Carr v. McGriff, 8 A.D.3d 420, 781 N.Y.S.2d 34 (2d Dep't 2004); Chen v. Dickerson, 847 N.Y.S.2d 334, 336 (App. Term, 9th & 10th Jud. Dists. 2007) (automatic bankruptcy stay prohibits "commencement and continuation" of an action against the debtor arising prior to the bankruptcy proceeding); Kocher v. Smith, 980 N.Y.S.2d 252 (Poughkeepsie City Ct. 2014).

1261 *Chen*, 847 N.Y.S.2d at 334 (*citing* Carr, 8 A.D.3d at 420, 781 N.Y.S.2d at 34).

the bankruptcy filing.[1262]

Pursuant to 11 U.S.C. § 362(b)(22), an exception to the automatic stay exists (i.e., the stay does not apply and an eviction may occur) where the bankruptcy filing occurred after the judgment of possession and warrant of eviction were issued.[1263] Interestingly, there is an exception to the exception (i.e., the stay applies and the eviction may not occur) where the Tenant had the right to cure the default and deposited with the Bankruptcy Court the past due rent for the thirty (30) day period following the bankruptcy petition.[1264]

If the Tenant files for bankruptcy during the summary proceeding and a Subtenant is named as a co-Respondent, then the proceeding will be stayed against the Tenant and either stayed or, if proper, dismissed against the Subtenant because the Landlord may not proceed directly against a Subtenant.[1265] The Landlord may seek an Order from the Bankruptcy Court lifting the stay if the property is separate from the estate.[1266]

A discharge in bankruptcy eliminates the Tenant's personal liability for rent arrears and other monetary debts under the rental agreement. Upon authorization of the Bankruptcy Court, the Landlord is permitted to seek an eviction in a summary proceeding, but the Landlord may not collect unpaid rent or other monetary relief.[1267] As a result, following the bankruptcy discharge or other Order lifting the stay, the

---

1262 *Id.*; *see also* In re City of Schnectady, 201 A.D.3d 1, 158 N.Y.S.3d 279 (3d Dep't 2021) (in tax collection proceeding, holding that since "[t]he court was not deprived of jurisdiction [by the bankruptcy], it should not have dismissed the proceeding....").

1263 North Tower Phase III Assoc. v. Petrov, 930 N.Y.S.2d 175 (N.Y. Civ. Ct. N.Y. Cnty. 2011); Santodonato v. Voelker, 881 N.Y.S.2d 366 (Nassau Cnty. Dist. Ct. 2009).

1264 11 U.S.C. § 362(l)(1); *North Tower Phase III Assoc.*, 930 N.Y.S.2d at 175.

1265 *See generally* Tefft v. Apex Pawnbroking & Jewelry Co., Inc., 75 A.D.2d 891, 428 N.Y.S.2d 52, 53 (2d Dep't 1980) ("[a] subtenant incurs no liability directly to a paramount lessor for performance of covenants contained in the original lease").

1266 *Cf.* Rindenow v. Alenick, 100 N.Y.S.3d 611 (App. Term, 9th & 10th Jud. Dists. 2018) (summary proceeding proper where Bankruptcy Court lifted the stay prior to the foreclosure sale).

1267 *See* Cey Realty Assocs., LLC v. Pettway, 29 N.Y.S.3d 846 (App. Term, 1st Dep't 2015) (permanently staying execution of warrant of eviction where Tenant paid, and Landlord accepted, rent arrears following the bankruptcy); 428 E. 66th St. LLC v. Meirowitz, 824 N.Y.S.2d 762 (App. Term, 1st Dep't 2006).

Landlord may "[p]ursue any remedy to which it is entitled under state law for breach of the tenant's obligation to pay rent, except a remedy against the debtor personally to collect the money due."[1268]

4. LANDLORD DID NOT OWN PREMISES WHEN PROCEEDING COMMENCED

Although demonstrating lawful "title" or ownership of the premises is typically an element of the Landlord's case, ownership is not required to maintain a summary proceeding because RPAPL § 721 explicitly permits, *inter alia*, a "landlord or lessor" to bring a summary proceeding without requiring ownership.[1269] It is a fundamental principle of Landlord and Tenant Law that the Housing Part may not determine issues of "title,"[1270] but rather the Court may adjudicate the issue solely for the purpose of determining which party is entitled to "possession."[1271]

Thus, the Tenant may assert that the Landlord is not the owner or lacks a superior interest in the premises as an affirmative defense, but the Tenant may not affirmatively claim that it is the "owner" in a

1268 Dulac v. Dabrowski, 4 A.D.3d 308, 774 N.Y.S.2d 487 (1st Dep't 2004) (the underlying debt "is not extinguished" when the debtor's debts are personally discharged) (emphasis added); *428 E. 66th St., LLC*, 824 N.Y.S.2d at 762.

1269 RPAPL § 721 (listing eleven (11) categories of individuals and entities that may commence a summary proceeding). *See* Chickery v. Prestige Catering, 143 N.Y.S.3d 771 (App. Term, 2d, 11th & 13th Jud. Dists. 2021); Tacfield Assocs., LLC v. Davis, 990 N.Y.S.2d 440 (App. Term, 2d, 11th & 13th Jud. Dists. 2014); Mirra v. Pattee, 862 N.Y.S.2d 815 (App. Term, 2d & 11th Jud. Dists. 2008); 1113 Walton Co. v. Cruz, 162 N.Y.S.3d 924 (N.Y. Civ. Ct. Bronx Cnty. 2022) (holding that Jane Doe may be a party in a non-payment proceeding, but rent arrears may not be awarded against her due to the absence of a Landlord and Tenant relationship).

1270 *See* 459 Webster Ave., LLC v. Green, 117 N.Y.S.3d 791 (App. Term, 9th & 10th Jud. Dists. 2019); Chopra v. Prusik, 801 N.Y.S.2d 692, 693 (App. Term, 2d & 11th Jud. Dists. 2005); 905 Mother Gaston Corp. v. More, 165 N.Y.S.3d 831 (N.Y. Civ. Ct. Kings Cnty. 2022).

1271 Nissequogue Boat Club v. State of New York, 14 A.D.3d 542, at 544, 789 N.Y.S.2d 71, 73 (2d Dep't 2005); Yacoob v. Persuad, 950 N.Y.S.2d 611 (App. Term, 2d, 11th & 13th Jud. Dists. 2012); Thane v. Thane, 149 N.Y.S.3d 883 n.2 (N.Y. Civ. Ct. Queens Cnty. 2021).

summary proceeding.[1272] The defense is further limited by the principle of estoppel to deny the Landlord's title, which precludes the defense where the Tenant entered into the rental agreement acknowledging, accepting, and benefitting from the Landlord's title and the Landlord's permission to grant possession.[1273]

In *Ty Blds. II, Inc. v. 55 Day Spa, Inc.*, the Appellate Division, Second Department affirmed the denial of the Tenant's cross-motion to dismiss the amended complaint where the corporate Landlord was not formally in existence when the parties entered into the rental agreement.[1274] Noting that the amended complaint included identical claims regarding the agreement, the Court held that where the Tenant previously acknowledged the business entity in its business dealing, the Tenant "[s]hould not be allowed to quibble or raise immaterial issues on matters which do not concern [it] in the slightest degree or affect [its] substantial rights."[1275]

Asserting the defense that the Tenant is the "owner" of the subject premises by adverse possession is not without risk. If the Housing Part rules in favor of the Landlord, then the Tenant may be collaterally estopped from raising the issue of title in any other action or forum.[1276] However, if the Tenant prevails in the summary proceeding, then the issue of title may be raised again in a subsequent declaratory judgment

1272 Fountains-Clove Rd. Apts., Inc. v. Gunther, 47 N.Y.S.3d 212 (App. Term, 2d, 11th & 13th Jud. Dists. 2017); *459 Webster Ave.*, LLC, 117 N.Y.S.3d at 791; Jacob Marion, LLC v. El Bey, 36 N.Y.S.3d 47 (App. Term, 2d, 11th & 13th Jud. Dists. 2016) (default judgment vacated where Respondent plausibly asserted she was the lawful owner of the premises); Muzio v. Rogers, 867 N.Y.S.2d 376 (App. Term, 9th & 10th Jud. Dists. 2008).

1273 The parties are required to abide by the terms of their negotiated relationship for as long as it continues. *See* DOLAN § 5:8, at 253-54 (4th ed. 2010); *Tacfield Assocs., LLC*, 990 N.Y.S.2d at 440. The defense of a lack of ownership may be waived in a post-foreclosure holdover summary proceeding where the Tenant had ample opportunity, but failed to assert, the defense in the foreclosure action. *See* M & T Mtg. Corp. v. Larkins, 910 N.Y.S.2d 763 (App. Term, 2d, 11th & 13th Jud. Dists. 2010).

1274 167 A.D.3d 679, 90 N.Y.S.3d 47 (2d Dep't 2018).

1275 *Id.* (*quoting* Boslow Family Ltd. P'ship v. Glickenhause & Co., 7 N.Y.3d 664, at 668, 827 N.Y.S.3d 94 (2006)).

1276 *See Nissequogue Boat Club*, 14 A.D.3d at 543-44, 789 N.Y.S.2d at 73.

action in Supreme Court,[1277] provided the action is filed within sixty (60) days of entry of the Housing Part's decision.[1278]

5. LANDLORD DIVESTED OF OWNERSHIP DURING SUMMARY PROCEEDING

Unless directed otherwise, CPLR § 1018 authorizes the continuation of a summary proceeding where the Landlord sells or otherwise transfers ownership of the premises during the pendency of the proceeding.[1279] Although not required, ideally, the parties would bring the transfer to the attention of the Court such that a substitution may occur without disruption.[1280] Regardless, in *Tabak v. Steele*, the Appellate Term for the First Department held that the Landlord could continue to pursue monetary relief during the pendency of the appeal without substituting the transferee because the "delay did not affect the continued progress of the proceeding."[1281] The dispute in that matter was limited to the monetary relief, and the judgment was binding on the

1277 To demonstrate title by adverse possession not founded or based upon a written instrument, the Tenant must establish: (1) "acts sufficiently open" to put a reasonable owner on notice or (2) the subject premises was "protected by a substantial enclosure." *See* RPAPL §§ 521, 522 (as amended in 2008); Marone v. Kally, 109 A.D.3d 880, 971 N.Y.S.2d 324 (2d Dep't 2013). In addition, the Tenant must establish by clear and convincing evidence that the possession was hostile and under a claim of right, actual, open and notorious, exclusive and continuous for at least ten (10) years. *See* Estate of Becker v. Murtagh, 19 N.Y.3d 75, 945 N.Y.S.2d 196 (2012); Montanaro v. Rudchyk, 189 A.D.3d 1214, 136 N.Y.S.3d 330 (2d Dep't 2020); Children's Magical Garden, Inc. v. Norfolk St. Dev., LLC, 164 A.D.3d 73, 82 N.Y.S.3d 354 (1st Dep't 2018); Scalamander Cove, LLC v. Bachmann, 119 A.D.3d 547, 987 N.Y.S.2d 902 (2d Dep't 2014).

1278 RPAPL § 747(2) provides that "[t]he judgment shall not bar an action, proceeding or counterclaim, commenced or interposed within sixty days of entry of the judgment, for affirmative equitable relief which was not sought by counterclaim in the proceeding because of the limited jurisdiction of the court" (emphasis added). *See* Haque v. Rob, 83 A.D.3d 895, 920 N.Y.S.2d 707 (2d Dep't 2011) (*citing* Henry Modell & Co. v. Minister, Elders & Deacons of the Ref. Prot. Dutch Church of City of N.Y., 68 N.Y.2d 456, at 462-63, 510 N.Y.S.2d 63, 66-67 (1986)); L.G. v. C.G.G., 63 N.Y.S.3d 305 (Kings Cnty. Sup. Ct. 2017).

1279 CPLR § 1018 (section states that "[u]pon any transfer of interest, the action may be continued by or against the original parties unless the court directs the person to whom the interest is transferred to be substituted or joined in the action"); *see generally* Tabak v. Steele, 901 N.Y.S.2d 903 (App. Term, 1st Dep't 2009); Buywise Holding, LLC v. Harris, 31 A.D.3d 681, 821 N.Y.S.2d 213 (2d Dep't 2006).

1280 *See, e.g.*, U.S. Bank Trust, N.A. v. Zaidi, 2017 N.Y. Misc. LEXIS 4187 (Suffolk Cnty. Sup. Ct. Oct. 12, 2017).

1281 *Tabak*, 901 N.Y.S.2d at 903.

transferee.[1282]

Alternatively, the Housing Part may transfer the summary proceeding to the Civil Part of the Court, assign a new index number, and convert the matter into a plenary action for money damages.[1283] The Petition would be deemed the Complaint, and the Tenant would have no fewer than twenty (20) days to formally interpose an Answer. The monetary relief awarded would be capped on the date the Landlord was divested of ownership. Finally, the transfer would be without prejudice to the transferee commencing its own proceeding for possession provided the claim was neither previously waived nor abandoned.

The caveat to proceeding in this manner is that the local Court's authority in a plenary action is limited to the maximum jurisdictional dollar amount of the Court, and the Court lacks subject matter jurisdiction over the dispute where a claim exceeds such amount. Moreover, the Court is without authority to *sua sponte* (i.e., on the Court's own motion) reduce or modify a claim that exceeds the statutory threshold.[1284] If the claim is voluntarily reduced to fall within the jurisdictional authority of the Court, then the Landlord may not seek the balance of the amount owed in another forum because "claim-splitting" is not

---

1282 *Id.*; Bova v. Vinciguerra, 139 A.D.2d 797, 526 N.Y.S.2d 671 (3d Dep't 1988). The reader should be mindful that except where a TSHA defense is successfully asserted, a money judgment must be issued simultaneously with a judgment of possession, and, as a result, the Petitioner must prove entitlement to both by a preponderance of the evidence. *See* Chapter 5 subdiv. B(2)(a), *supra*.

1283 East Bronx Props., Inc. v. James, 103 N.Y.S.2d 535 (N.Y. Mun. Ct. 1951).

1284 Although there is no dollar restriction on the amount of rent the Housing Part may award in a summary proceeding, the Court's monetary jurisdictional limitation is applicable to plenary actions. *See* Eastrich No. 80 Corp. v. Patrolmen's Benev. Assoc., 688 N.Y.S.2d 409 (App. Term, 1st Dep't 1999); Campbell v. Fairfield Pres. Assocs., 798 N.Y.S.2d 707 (App. Term, 2d & 11th Jud. Dists. 2004). The monetary thresholds in civil actions (other than small claims actions) is $50,000 in the New York City Civil Courts; $15,000 in the District Courts and City Courts Outside New York City; and $3,000 in the Justice Courts.

permitted.[1285] On the other hand, if the Landlord refuses to reduce the claim, the proceeding will be dismissed because the dollar amount was not reduced "by motion or stipulation."[1286]

In deciding whether to reduce the claim, the Landlord need not concern itself whether the statute of limitations has since expired. This is because when an action is dismissed due to a lack of subject matter jurisdiction, the Landlord has an additional six (6) months to commence a plenary action in a court of competent jurisdiction even where the statute of limitations has expired provided the claim otherwise would have been timely at the time the original complaint was commenced.[1287]

6. MERGER (PARTIES EXECUTE PURCHASE AGREEMENT DURING THE TENANCY)

A Landlord and Tenant relationship is terminated when the parties enter into a contract of sale for the premises. The anticipated sale of the property merges the relationship from a tenancy into that of vendor

1285 *See generally* David A. Kaminsky & Assocs., P.C. v. Brenner, 135 N.Y.S.3d 751 (App. Term, 1st Dep't 2020); Bay Crest Assoc. v. Paar, 4 N.Y.S.3d 812 (App. Term, 9th & 10th Jud. Dists. 2015) (holding that plaintiff's claims for annual assessments and attorney's fees "were part of a single cause of action" and, as a result, subject to the $15,000 monetary jurisdictional limit of plenary actions in the District Court); Rocco v. Badalamente, 867 N.Y.S.2d 20 (App. Term, 9th & 10th Jud. Dists. 2008) (the claim-splitting doctrine "[r]equires a plaintiff to join all installments due under a single contract [such as rent] at the time suit is commenced") (internal citations omitted); 1443 York Ave. Realty Co. v. Ronning, 824 N.Y.S.2d 764 (App. Term, 1st Dep't 2006).

1286 Boland v. Miller, 867 N.Y.S.2d 15 (App. Term, 9th & 10th Jud. Dists. 2008). *But see Eastrich No. 80 Corp.*, 688 N.Y.S.2d at 409 (pursuant to Article VI, § 19(f) of the New York State Constitution, a case in which the New York City Courts lack subject matter jurisdiction may be transferred to the Supreme Court). Article VI, § 19(I) of the State Constitution prohibits the District Courts, City Courts Outside New York City, and Justice Courts from exercising the same transfer authority to a higher Court. *Id.*

1287 CPLR § 205(a). *See* Parker v. Mack, 61 N.Y.2d 114, at 118, 472 N.Y.S.2d 882, 884 (1984); *Campbell*, 798 N.Y.S.2d at 707.

and vendee in possession.[1288]

The entering of the purchase agreement is the act that converts the Tenant's status to that of a vendee regardless of whether the sale is executed.[1289] As a result, where a contract is executed but the sale is not consummated, the Landlord is prohibited from evicting the former-Tenant (vendee) in a summary proceeding following the expiration of the rental agreement.[1290] A summary proceeding is similarly improper where the parties enter into a joint venture to sell the premises.[1291] However, the mere "agreement to agree" to a contract of sale in the future does not warrant dismissal of the summary proceeding.[1292]

Moreover, exceptions to the general principle exist that would permit a summary proceeding, such as where a contract was not executed, the parties entered into a contract for sale but elected to rescind the agreement and re-establish the tenancy, or where an intent to continue

1288 *See generally* Blackburn Food Corp. v. Ardi, Inc., 189 A.D.3d 1329, 139 N.Y.S.3d 303 (2d Dep't 2020) (holding that "execution of a contract of sale [for real property] between landlord and tenant serves to merge the landlord-tenant relationship into the vendor-vendee relationship and thus effectively terminates the former, unless the parties clearly intend the contrary result"); Barbarita v. Shilling, 111 A.D.2d 200, at 201-02, 489 N.Y.S.2d 86, 87 (2d Dep't 1985); Koppelman v. Barrett, Jr., 17 N.Y.S.3d 584 (App. Term, 9th & 10th Jud. Dists. 2015). *See also* Macquaire Elecs. USA v. Globalfoundries U.S. Inc., 2016 Del. Super. LEXIS 648 (New Castle (Del.) Sup. Ct. Dec. 22, 2016) (under New York law, the Tenant's exercise of a purchase option within the lease terminates the obligation to pay rent).

1289 *See* Potts v. Thomas, 66 N.Y.S.3d 410 (Nassau Cnty. Dist. Ct. 2017) (where an "agreement to agree" to purchase was made without entering into a contract, a summary proceeding remains a viable method for regaining possession). *See generally* Reis v. J.B. Kaufman Realty Co., LLC, 181 A.D.3d 740, 117 N.Y.S.3d 607 (2d Dep't 2020) ("agreement to agree" to lease extension unenforceable where material term omitted); Vizel v. Vitale, 184 A.D.3d 602, 125 N.Y.S.3d 166 (2d Dep't 2020) (holding that "[t]he parties' failure to set forth either the amount of rent to be paid during the renewal period, or an agreed formula, methodology, or objective extrinsic event by which that rent could be determined, rendered the option to renew an unenforceable agreement to agree").

1290 Kaygreen Realty Co., LLC v. IG Second Generation Partners, L.P., 2010 N.Y. Misc. LEXIS 1887 (Queens Cnty. Sup. Ct. April 9, 2010), *aff'd as modified*, 78 A.D.3d 1010, at 1015-16, 912 N.Y.S.2d 246 (2d Dep't 2010).

1291 *See* Tello v. Dylag, 15 N.Y.S.3d 715 (App. Term, 9th & 10th Jud. Dists. 2015).

1292 *See Potts*, 66 N.Y.S.3d 4 at 10.

the tenancy may be inferred from the parties' conduct.[1293] Another exception falls within the ambit of RPAPL § 713(9), which authorizes a summary proceeding where the proposed purchaser remains in possession after defaulting on contract terms that were "necessarily to be performed within ninety days."[1294]

7. MUTUAL MISTAKE/FRUSTRATION OF PURPOSE (RESCISSION OF LEASE)

The defense of mutual mistake is an equitable defense that allows for the rescission of a rental agreement where both parties made a material mutual mistake or were under a substantial mistaken impression regarding the premises at the time the rental agreement was executed.[1295] The defense is narrowly construed, but it is sustainable where the mistake "was so substantial that there was no 'true meeting of the parties' minds.'"[1296]

For the defense to succeed, the mistake must render the loss of all benefits from the agreement. In *Gap, Inc. v. 170 Broadway Retail Owner, LLC*, the Appellate Division, Second Department held that the doctrine of frustration of purpose "does not apply as a matter of law where...the tenant was not 'completely deprived of the benefit of its bargain.'"[1297] In other words, "a change in circumstances [must have made] one party's performance virtually worthless to the other, frustrating his purpose in

1293 *See generally* Matter of Rosenstein, 129 A.D.3d 847, 11 N.Y.S.3d 631 (2d Dep't 2015); Hadlick, Jr. v. DiGiantommaso, 154 A.D.2d 338, 545 N.Y.S.2d 816 (2d Dep't 1989); *Kaygreen Realty Co., LLC*, 2010 N.Y. Misc. LEXIS at 1887; Sethi v. Kaur, 847 N.Y.S.2d 899 (Nassau Cnty. Dist. Ct. 2007).

1294 Jacobs v. Andolina, 123 A.D.2d 835, at 836-37, 507 N.Y.S.2d 450, 452-53 (2d Dep't 1986); *see Koppelman*, 17 N.Y.S.3d at 584; Gorbrook Assocs., Inc. v. Silverstein, 966 N.Y.S.2d 346 (App. Term, 9th & 10th Jud. Dists. 2012) (whether the contract of sale could be finalized within ninety (90) days is an issue of fact); LaManna v. DiDonato, 842 N.Y.S.2d 674 (App. Term, 9th & 10th Jud. Dists. 2007).

1295 *See* Dandey Realty Corp. v. Nick's Hideaway, Inc., 886 N.Y.S.2d 549, 550 (App. Term, 9th & 10th Jud. Dists. 2009) (commercial lease rescinded due to mistaken belief the premises could be used as a restaurant).

1296 Lakshmi Grocery & Gas, Inc. v. GRJH, Inc., 138 A.D.3d 1290, 30 N.Y.S.3d 743 (3d Dep't 2016) (commercial lease rescinded where Landlord's representative "provided the wrong sales figures").

1297 195 A.D.3d 575, 151 N.Y.S.3d 37 (2d Dep't 2021).

making the contract."[1298]

The defense was successfully asserted where the parties intended for the premises to be used as a restaurant but, unbeknownst to them, the parcel was not capable of being re-zoned for this purpose.[1299] Similarly, a zoning law change after entering into the rental agreement may result in rescission where the "[r]easonable expectations of the parties...[are] frustrated due to circumstances beyond the control of the parties."[1300] In *K.A.M.M. Group, LLC v. Lafayette Realty, Inc.*, rescission was further granted, and the Tenant was permitted to recover its down payment, where the lease contained a mistake regarding the commencement date and the premises had been re-rented to another Tenant.[1301]

Of note, the Appellate Division, First Department has held that the unanticipated loss of income due to the COVID-19 Pandemic (and the related Executive and Administrative Orders) does not constitute sufficient grounds for the frustration of purpose defense.[1302] Moreover, a party's failure "to take advantage of 'easily accessible' means of ascertaining" information regarding the status and permitted use of a property may similarly preclude rescission.[1303] In *Ermenegildo Zegna Corp. v. L & M 825 LLC*, the Appellate Division, First Department denied

---

1298 Lin-Dan Garage Corp. v. Beneficial 21 Parking LLC, 2022 N.Y. Misc. LEXIS 2196 (N.Y. Cnty. Sup. Ct. April 26, 2022) (*citing* PPF Safeguard, LLC v. BCR Safeguard Holding, LLC, 85 A.D.3d 506, 508, 924 N.Y.S.2d 391 (1st Dep't 2011)). "[T]o invoke the doctrine of frustration of purpose, the frustrated purpose must be so completely the basis of the contract that, as both parties understood, without it, the transaction would have made little sense." *Id.* (*quoting* Center for Specialty Care, Inc. v. CSC Acquisition I, LLC, 185 A.D.3d 34, 42, 127 N.Y.S.3d 6 (1st Dep't 2020)).

1299 *Dandey Realty Corp.*, 886 N.Y.S.2d at 549.

1300 Burnside 711, LLC v. Nassau Regional Off-Track Betting Corp., 67 A.D.3d 718, at 720, 888 N.Y.S.2d 212, 213-14 (2d Dep't 2009) (premises re-zoned prior to taking possession or payment of rent).

1301 153 A.D.3d 799, 60 N.Y.S.3d 378 (2d Dep't 2017).

1302 City Natl. Bank v. Baby Blue Distribs., Inc., 199 A.D.3d 559, 158 N.Y.S.3d 65 (1st Dep't 2021); 933 Broadway, LLC v. Godiva Chocolatier, Inc., 2022 N.Y. Misc. LEXIS 1912 (N.Y. Cnty. Sup. Ct. April 7, 2022).

1303 *Lakshmi Grocery & Gas, Inc.*, 138 A.D.3d at 1290, 30 N.Y.S.3d at 743; *cf.* 1357 Tarrytown Rd. Auto, LLC v. Granite Props., LLC, 142 A.D.3d 976, 37 N.Y.S.3d 341 (2d Dep't 2016) (rescission denied where the commercial lease was subject to "restrictions of local law, zoning or ordinance" and Landlord "made no representation concerning the suitability of the premises for the [Tenant's] intended business").

summary judgment because whether the commercial Tenant exhibited "conscious ignorance" of known factors that impacted the use of the premises posed a question of fact.[1304] Finally, in *1st Ave. Enters. LLC v. Love Picin Inc.*, the defense was denied because the slow pace of construction was contemplated in the lease, and the Tenant was capable of operating its commercial bar during the construction.[1305]

8. NON-DELIVERED WRITTEN LEASE

A written rental agreement is not valid until an executed copy is delivered and accepted by both parties.[1306] Where the executed agreement is not provided to one (1) of the parties and the Tenant does not take possession of the premises, the agreement is unenforceable.[1307]

If the Tenant takes possession without receiving a copy of the executed lease, then the lease provisions are not enforceable against either party. It has been held that the act of signing the rental agreement "in the presence of both parties" is adequate delivery, particularly where the Tenant has paid a month's rent.[1308] The filing of the signed rental agreement with the Town Assessor's Office was held to constitute

1304 166 A.D.3d 562, 86 N.Y.S.3d 873 (1st Dep't 2018); Jerome M. Eisenberg, Inc. v. Hall, 147 A.D.3d 602, 48 N.Y.S.3d 71 (1st Dep't 2017).

1305 2021 N.Y. Misc. LEXIS 5537 (N.Y. Cnty. Sup. Ct. Nov. 5, 2021); *see* Gap Inc. v. Ponte Gadea N.Y. LLC, 524 F. Supp. 3d 224 (S.D.N.Y. 2021) (same).

1306 Sommerfeldt v. Pickett, 151 A.D.3d 1752, 56 N.Y.S.3d 752 (4th Dep't 2017); 219 Broadway Corp. v. Alexander's, Inc., 46 N.Y.2d 506, at 511-12, 414 N.Y.S.2d 889, 891-92 (1979). The Tenant's failure to sign the lease notwithstanding her payment of a deposit is "[a]t most, an offer to lease, [and] a deposit paid in anticipation of the lease agreement generally remains the property of the person who made the deposit." Rodriguez v. Curtis Chance Realty, 126 N.Y.S.3d 842 (App. Term, 2d, 11th & 13th Jud. Dists. 2020) (*citing* Albert v. Margaretten, 2002 N.Y. Misc. LEXIS 724 (App. Term, 9th & 10th Jud. Dists. 2002)).

1307 *See generally* Dlugosz v. O'Brien, 36 A.D.3d 1035, at 1036-37, 828 N.Y.S.2d 628, 629-30 (3d Dep't 2007) (execution and delivery of lease required); 709 Rte. 52, Inc. v. DelCastillo, 910 N.Y.S.2d 408 (App. Term, 9th & 10th Jud. Dists. 2010) (signed but undelivered lease unenforceable where the Tenant did not receive the keys or take possession); Setauket Props. Corp. v. Open Doors Mgmt., Inc., 2010 N.Y. Misc. LEXIS 3765 (Suffolk Cnty. Sup. Ct. Aug. 5, 2010).

1308 Storico Dev., LLC v. Batlle, 9 A.D.3d 908, at 909, 780 N.Y.S.2d 696, 697 (4th Dep't 2004); Levinson v. Bailey, 2012 N.Y. Misc. LEXIS 3110 (N.Y. Cnty. Sup. Ct. June 15, 2012).

sufficient delivery because the filing exhibited acknowledgment and acceptance of the binding rental agreement.[1309]

9. PETITION ASSERTS ALTERNATIVE GROUNDS FOR EVICTION

As a general matter, a Landlord may assert both non-payment and holdover claims in the Petition.[1310] The reason for allowing alternative theories is that in many situations the occupants, as opposed to the Petitioner, are "[i]n the best position to know the circumstances under which they entered into the occupancy...."[1311]

The proceeding may be dismissed if the alternative pleadings and/or accompanying predicate notices are not appropriate and "reasonable under the attendant circumstances and sufficiently detailed so as to permit Respondent to prepare a defense."[1312] Compliance with the standards for providing multiple predicate notices may be particularly challenging due to the various lengths of the notice periods. The adequacy of the pleadings and notices are determined on a case-by-case basis.[1313] An objection based upon the caption of the Petition is waived

---

1309 *Sommerfeldt*, 151 A.D.3d at 1752, 56 N.Y.S.3d at 752.

1310 *See* Kern v. Guller, 40 A.D.3d 1231, at 1232, 835 N.Y.S.2d 764, 765 (3d Dep't 2007) (holding that pleading non-payment and holdover claims in the alternative was permissible pursuant to CPLR § 3014 where the parties' month-to-month tenancy was terminated); 3657 Realty Co. LLC v. Jones, 52 A.D.3d 272, 859 N.Y.S.2d 434 (1st Dep't 2008); Kew Gardens Portfolio Holdings, LLC v. Bucheli, 130 N.Y.S.3d 878 (App. Term, 2d, 11th & 13th Jud. Dists. 2020) (pleading in the alternative the Respondent was a licensee or squatter); Jacobson v. Raff, 927 N.Y.S.2d 816 (App. Term, 9th & 10th Jud. Dists. 2011); Azour, LLC v. Tax Sister, Inc., 909 N.Y.S.2d 282 (App. Term, 2d, 11th & 13th Jud. Dists. 2010) (permitting joint trial of non-payment proceeding and subsequent holdover proceeding following termination of the tenancy); 1506 Wallco LLC v. Guzman, 135 N.Y.S.3d 795 (N.Y. Civ. Ct. Bronx Cnty. 2020).

1311 *Kew Gardens Portfolio Holdings, LLC*, 130 N.Y.S.3d at 878.

1312 *See generally* 1616 President St. Realty LLC v. Barber, 2021 N.Y.L.J. LEXIS 252 (N.Y. Civ. Ct. Kings Cnty. March 31, 2021); See Why Gerard, LLC v. Gramro Entertainment Corp., 907 N.Y.S.2d 103 (Albany City Ct. 2010), *aff'd*, 94 A.D.3d 1205, 941 N.Y.S.2d 350 (3d Dep't 2012).

1313 *See, e.g., 1506 Wallco LLC*, 135 N.Y.S.3d at 795; *See Why Gerard, LLC*, 907 N.Y.S.2d at 103. For further discussion about predicate notices where alternative theories are alleged, *see* Chapter 6, subdiv. A(4), *supra*.

if the claim is <u>not</u> raised prior to the hearing.[1314]

Interestingly, in 2006, the Appellate Term for the Ninth and Tenth Judicial Districts held in *Seaton v. Chavez* that inconsistent claims were <u>not</u> permitted.[1315] Although both the holdover and non-payment claims were eventually dismissed, the Court concluded that where a Landlord commences a summary proceeding alleging both holdover and non-payment claims, "only the nonpayment claim is maintainable."[1316] The Appellate Term thereafter clarified that the mere filing of a non-payment proceeding does <u>not</u> automatically nullify an existing holdover proceeding.[1317] Although dual proceedings are not simultaneously permitted, the Court allowed the holdover proceeding to continue because the non-payment proceeding was "immediately" discontinued (two (2) days later).[1318]

At present, provided the requisite notices are adequate and the Respondent is capable of defending the proceeding, a summary proceeding based upon alternative claims is permitted. In *145 E. 16th St. LLC v. Spencer*, the Appellate Term held that the commencement of multiple non-payment proceedings pending the appeal of the dismissal of a holdover proceeding did <u>not</u> vitiate the predicate notice or demonstrate an intent to create a new Landlord and Tenant relationship.[1319] The controversy arose when the holdover proceeding was reinstated on appeal. The Court rejected the Tenant's assertion that the non-payment proceedings, which were subsequently discontinued or dismissed without prejudice, required dismissal of the reinstated holdover proceeding

1314 Jacoby v. Cabrera, 110 N.Y.S.3d 202 (App. Term, 9th & 10th Jud. Dists. 2018) (defects pertaining to the captioning of the proceeding are not jurisdictional, and, therefore, may be waived).

1315 816 N.Y.S.2d 701 (App. Term, 9th & 10th Jud. Dists. 2006).

1316 *Id.* The same Court subsequently held that a non-payment proceeding was barred by a previously commenced ejectment proceeding because the "ejectment action is deemed a [re-entry] by [the] landlord into possession," and an election to terminate the lease. *See* Jefferson Vall. Mall Ltd. P'ship v. Franchise Acquisition Group, Inc., 874 N.Y.S.2d 667, 668 (App. Term, 9th & 10th Jud. Dists. 2008).

1317 72nd St. Assocs., LLC v. Persson, 13 N.Y.S.3d 853 (App. Term, 1st Dep't 2015).

1318 *Id.*

1319 13 N.Y.S.3d 851 (App. Term, 1st Dep't 2015).

due to the conflicting theories for relief.[1320]

10. PREMISES NOT DELIVERED BROOM-CLEANED

A lease delivery provision stating that the obligation to pay rent accrues when the Landlord provides the premises vacant and broom-cleaned within ninety (90) days of execution is enforceable. The Appellate Division, Second Department held in *1710 Realty, LLC v. Portabella 308 Utica, LLC* that the Landlord's failure to timely provide the premises "[f]ree of garbage, refuse, trash and other debris" afforded the Tenant the right to terminate the rental agreement.[1321] In that case, it was undisputed that the amount of "refuse" left by the prior occupant was "far more than just a few trash bags."[1322]

11. PREMISES RENDERED UNTENANTABLE DUE TO FIRE OR THE ELEMENTS

Where the property is destroyed or otherwise rendered unfit for occupancy due to no fault of the Tenant or the Tenant's guests, the Tenant may, without notice, surrender possession and terminate the rental agreement.[1323] The exception to this rule exists where the lease provides for an alternative remedy, in which case, the negotiated lease provision prevails.[1324] Real Property Law § 227 applies to both residential and commercial premises, but it has been held that "a commercial tenant may waive the statute by the terms of its lease agreement."[1325]

When RPL § 227 is invoked, the Tenant's obligation to pay further rent is terminated and any advanced payments must be "adjusted to the

1320 *Id.* (noting that the non-payment proceedings were commenced <u>after</u> the holdover proceeding was dismissed).

1321 189 A.D.3d 944, 138 N.Y.S.3d 523 (2d Dep't 2020).

1322 *Id.*

1323 RPL § 227.

1324 *See, e.g.*, 4261 Realty Holding LLC v. DB Real Estate Assets II LLC, 980 N.Y.S.2d 275 (Nassau Cnty. Dist. Ct. 2013) (negotiated Destruction, Fire, and Other Casualty lease provision precluded RPL § 227 claim).

1325 N.N. Int'l (USA) Corp. v. Gladden Props., LLC, 41 N.Y.S.3d 720 (N.Y. Cnty. Sup. Ct. 2016).

date of [the] surrender."[1326] This provision is commonly utilized where the property is damaged by fire, but there is no preclusion for other uncontrollable natural disasters such as hurricanes and storms. For example, RPL § 227 was available to many of the Tenants victimized by Super Storm Sandy, which in October of 2012, resulted in the displacement of thousands of New Yorkers.

If the damage caused by a natural disaster does not render the premises uninhabitable or the Tenant does not vacate the premises due to the unhabitable condition, then a residential Tenant may still be entitled to an abatement of rent based upon the warranty of habitability.[1327] In a commercial case, the New York County Supreme Court held that the COVID-19 Pandemic, and the resulting restrictions on the use of the premises, did not warrant termination where the lease did not "contemplate loss of use due to a pandemic or resulting government lockdown."[1328]

12. RECORDING OF THE LEASE

Rental agreements of three (3) or more years may be recorded pursuant to Real Property Law § 291. However, the failure to record such a lease only voids the lease as against a bona fide subsequent purchaser for value who recorded first.[1329] It does not void the lease against

1326 RPL § 227; *cf.* Goldhirsch v. St. George Tower and Grill Owners Corp., 142 A.D.3d 1044, 37 N.Y.S.3d 616 (2d Dep't 2016) (enforcing proportional rent abatement lease provision where fire renders the premises "partly or wholly untenantable").

1327 Park W. Mgmt. Corp. v. Mitchell, 47 N.Y.2d 316, 418 N.Y.S.2d 310 (1979); Rogers Plaza LLC v. Sam, 2022 N.Y.L.J. LEXIS 279 (N.Y. Civ. Ct. Kings Cnty. March 30, 2022); NYCHA Coney Island Houses v. Ramos, 971 N.Y.S.2d 422 (N.Y. Civ. Ct. Kings Cnty. 2013). *But see* Adler v. Ogden CAP Props., 126 A.D.3d 544, 2 N.Y.S.3d 902 (1st Dep't 2015) (warranty of habitability defense not available where Tenants "left their apartments before they lost electricity and they did not return until after the electricity had been restored").

1328 New WTC Retail Owner LLC v. Fal Coffee WTC LLC, 2022 N.Y.L.J. LEXIS 59 (N.Y. Cnty. Sup. Ct. Feb. 3, 2022).

1329 *See* RPL §§ 290-91; Citibank, N.A. v. Plagakis, 21 A.D.3d 393, 800 N.Y.S.2d 192 (2d Dep't 2005); Hi-Rise Laundry Equip. Corp. v. Matrix Props., Inc., 96 A.D.2d 930, 466 N.Y.S.2d 375 (2d Dep't 1983); *see generally* Cooper v. Pullar, 145 A.D.3d 1247, 42 N.Y.S.3d 677 (3d Dep't 2016); RR Reo II, LLC v. Omeje, 939 N.Y.S.2d 743 (App. Term, 2d, 11th & 13th Jud. Dists. 2011); Levy v. Pedersen, 983 N.Y.S.2d 204 (Nassau Cnty. Dist. Ct. 2013).

a Tenant. Accordingly, where a Landlord is a bona fide purchaser for value, the Tenant may not use the non-recording of the rental agreement with the prior owner as a defense for early termination or the non-payment of rent because the lease is unenforceable against the Landlord.[1330]

13. RENTER'S INSURANCE (FAILURE TO PROCURE)

For a lease forfeiture provision to be upheld, the Court must make an independent determination that: (1) the Landlord reserved the right to declare the forfeiture; (2) a clear and unambiguous "material breach" of a substantial lease obligation occurred; (3) the Landlord's prompt exercising of its rights; and (4) a determination that enforcement of the lease provision would not be unconscionable.[1331] The Court applies the doctrine of substantial performance to determine whether a breach was "material."[1332]

The Tenant's failure to provide a copy of a renter's insurance policy is not a material breach.[1333] However, the failure to maintain a continuous insurance policy, when required to do so, may be sufficient to terminate the tenancy.[1334] This is the case even where insurance is subsequently obtained because the replacement policy "[d]oes not protect [the Landlord] against the unknown universe of any claims arising during

1330 Jackson v. Robergeau, 781 N.Y.S.2d 625 (App. Term, 2d & 11th Jud. Dists. 2003); 1644 Broadway LLC v. Jimenez, 993 N.Y.S.2d 645 (N.Y. Civ. Ct. Kings Cnty. 2014).

1331 Helsam Realty Co., Inc. v. H.J.A. Holding Corp., 781 N.Y.S.2d 554, 557 (App. Term, 2d & 11th Jud. Dists. 2004) (*citing* DOLAN § 23:39, at 202-05); *cf.* Freund & Freund & Co., Inc., v. Biscuits & Baths Tribeca, LLC, 889 N.Y.S.2d 505 (N.Y. Civ. Ct. N.Y. Cnty. 2009).

1332 DOLAN § 23:39, at 203-04.

1333 Rubinstein Bros. v. Ole of 34th St., Inc., 421 N.Y.S.2d 534, 537 (N.Y. Civ. Ct. N.Y. Cnty. 1979).

1334 *See* 455 Dumont Assocs., LLC v. Rule Realty Corp., 180 A.D.3d 735, 119 N.Y.S.3d 508 (2d Dep't 2020); 117-119 Leasing Corp. v. Reliable Wool Stock, LLC, 139 A.D.3d 420, 30 N.Y.S.3d 622 (1st Dep't 2016) (the "tenant's failure to obtain insurance was not curable"); JT Queens Carwash, Inc. v. 88-16 N. Blvd., LLC, 101 A.D.3d 1089, 956 N.Y.S.2d 536 (2d Dep't 2012). *Cf.* Bliss World LLC v. 10 W. 57th St. Realty LLC, 190 A.D.3d 475, 135 N.Y.S.3d 821 (1st Dep't 2021) (Tenant fulfilled insurance obligations where lease permitted umbrella policy without specifying aggregate limits).

the period of no insurance coverage."[1335]

In *60G 542 Broadway Owner, LLC v. Prince Fashions, Inc.*, the Appellate Term for the First Department granted summary judgment in favor of the retail condominium unit owner due to the Tenant's breach of the insurance coverage provision.[1336] The Court further reasoned that the breach was incapable of being cured due to the resulting gap in insurance, which was unable to be offset in a subsequent policy.[1337] The Court opined that even had the Subtenant maintained the appropriate insurance and named the Landlord as an additional insured, that still may have been insufficient to cure the default because the Landlord is not "[r]equired to accept [a] subtenant's performance in lieu of a tenant's."[1338] Two (2) years following its decision, the Court reached the same conclusion in *159 W. 23rd LLC v. Spa Ciel De NY Corp.* due to the Tenant's failure to maintain an umbrella insurance policy.[1339]

In *455 Dumont Assocs., LLC v. Rule Realty Corp.*, the Appellate Division, Second Department terminated the tenancy due to the Tenant's failure to procure the requisite insurance notwithstanding an alternative lease provision authorizing the Landlord to acquire the insurance in Tenant's stead.[1340] The Court reasoned that since the Landlord was not required to purchase the insurance, the lease did "not preclude the landlord from exercising any other remedy in law or

---

1335 Kim v. Idylwood, N.Y., LLC, 66 A.D.3d 528, 886 N.Y.S.2d 337 (1st Dep't 2009); *see 455 Dumont Assoc., LLC*, 180 A.D.3d at 735, 119 N.Y.S.3d at 508; Juan v. 213 W. 28 LLC, 149 A.D.3d 539, 53 N.Y.S.3d 28 (1st Dep't 2017); Friendly Hands Apts. LLC v. Friendly Hands, Inc., 128 N.Y.S.3d 772 (App. Term, 1st Dep't 2020). *Cf.* Metropolitan Transp. Auth. v. Kura River Mgmt., Ltd., 292 A.D.2d 230, 739 N.Y.S.2d 668 (1st Dep't 2002) (lease forfeiture clause unenforceable due to inadequate notice).

1336 111 N.Y.S.3d 166 (App. Term, 1st Dep't 2018).

1337 *Id.*

1338 *Id.* (*quoting* 166 Enters. Corp. v. I G Second Generation Partners, L.P., 81 A.D.3d 154, 917 N.Y.S.2d 143 (1st Dep't 2011)).

1339 120 N.Y.S.3d 697 (App. Term, 1st Dep't 2020); *see also* Armstrong Realty, Inc. v. Roche, 2021 N.Y. Misc. LEXIS 867 (Kings Cnty. Sup. Ct. March 3, 2021) (noting that where the lease "[u]nequivocally require[s Tenant] to obtain and maintain specified insurance[,] the failure to obtain insurance as required by lease provision is generally considered a material breach of a lease").

1340 180 A.D.3d at 735, 119 N.Y.S.3d at 508.

equity[, and] therefore established that [the Landlord] had the grounds to terminate the lease upon a breach of the insurance procurement provision."[1341]

The reader should be mindful of an earlier conflicting decision from the New York City Housing Part where termination was denied because the lease alternatively permitted the Landlord to purchase the insurance. In *Rubenstein v. Ole of 34th St., Inc.*, the Housing Part denied the application to terminate the tenancy because the rental agreement authorized the Landlord, at the Tenant's expense, to purchase the required insurance.[1342] The Court reasoned that since there was "another easily spelled out remedy in the lease," including compensation for the additional expense in a plenary action, the drastic remedy of lease termination was inappropriate.[1343]

14. SUCCESSOR LANDLORDS

A successor Landlord acquires the premises subject to the terms and conditions of the existing tenancy, including any waiver of rights, where the successor Landlord has actual or constructive knowledge of the leasehold.[1344] The Tenant's possession of the premises at the time of the transfer constitutes, at minimum, constructive notice.[1345] The successor Landlord is bound by any oral waivers given prior to the transfer of ownership.[1346]

The introduction of an Assignment of the Rents may be required to obtain a money judgment for unpaid rent prior to the transfer. With the

---

1341 *Id.*

1342 421 N.Y.S.2d 534 (N.Y. Civ. Ct. N.Y. Cnty. 1979). *See* DOLAN § 23:39, at 203.

1343 *Rubinstein Bros.*, 421 N.Y.S.2d at 537.

1344 *See generally* Stoneybrook Realty, L.L.C. v. Cremktco, Inc., 675 N.Y.S.2d 749, 751 (App. Term, 9th & 10th Jud. Dists. 1998); 833 Mgmt., LLC v. Great Empire 65 Realty, LLC, 997 N.Y.S.2d 98 (Kings Cnty. Sup. Ct. 2014).

1345 Cooper v. Pullar, 145 A.D.3d 1247, 42 N.Y.S.3d 677 (3d Dep't 2016); Peak Dev., LLC v. Construction Exchange, 100 A.D.3d 1394, 953 N.Y.S.3d 755 (4th Dep't 2012); Stracham v. Bresnick, 76 A.D.3d 1009, at 1010-11, 908 N.Y.S.2d 95, 97 (2d Dep't 2010).

1346 *See* 5 Sunset Park Holdings, LLC v. Brito, 950 N.Y.S.2d 491 (App. Term, 2d, 11th & 13th Jud. Dists. 2012) (former Landlord orally waived requirement that written consent must be obtained prior to alterations).

possible exception where there is a waiver of rights, the Tenant generally need not be concerned that the new Landlord will unilaterally implement different terms than those agreed to by the former Landlord. For example, in *Magal Props. LLC v. Gritsyk*, the Appellate Term held that the successor Landlord was bound by the predecessor Landlord's agreement sixteen (16) years earlier authorizing specific alterations.[1347]

Pursuant to General Obligations Law § 7-108(2)(b), a successor Landlord is deemed to have knowledge of the security deposit tendered to the former Landlord where the premises is a residential dwelling, and the security deposit was: (1) deposited within six (6) months of the transfer of title; (2) identified in the rental agreement in effect at the time of the transfer of title; or (3) otherwise "supported by documentary evidence provided by the tenant." The successor Landlord is further generally responsible for the return of the security deposit.[1348]

15. TENANT MADE MORTGAGE PAYMENTS ON BEHALF OF THE LANDLORD

A summary proceeding may not be utilized to re-gain possession where the occupant's payments were monthly mortgage installments, as opposed to rent.[1349] Although the Landlord may charge rent in an amount equal to the mortgage obligations (and apply the rent towards the mortgage),[1350] the defense typically arises where the Tenant directly pays the lender on behalf of the Landlord. The defense is also frequently asserted in connection with the anticipated sale of the premises.

The Landlord's failure to pay the mortgage is not a viable defense for the Tenant in a non-payment proceeding.[1351] In addition, a Tenant is not entitled to a credit for mortgage payments made on behalf of the Landlord. In *Amherst Med. Park, Inc. v. Amherst Orthopaedics, P.C.*, the Appellate Division, Fourth Department held that notwithstanding the

1347 28 N.Y.S.3d 649 (App. Term, 1st Dep't 2015) (dismissing holdover proceeding).

1348 *See* Battle v. Smith, 950 N.Y.S.2d 721 (App. Term, 9th & 10th Jud. Dists. 2012).

1349 *See Tello*, 15 N.Y.S.3d at 715; Cazares v. Aguilar, 950 N.Y.S.2d 721 (Nassau Cnty. Dist. Ct. 2012); DOLAN § 38:15, at 584-86 (4th ed. 2010).

1350 *See* General Elec. Capital Corp. v. Loretto-Utica Res. Health Care Facility, 77 A.D.3d 1468, 909 N.Y.S.2d 274 (4th Dep't 2010).

1351 *Id.*

parties' agreement, a commercial Tenant could <u>not</u> offset the mortgage payments purportedly made by the Tenant's guarantor.[1352]

The occupant's failure to obtain a mortgage commitment for the purchase of the premises, even if agreed, may <u>not</u> be the basis for a summary proceeding.[1353] Rather, the owner must commence a plenary action or a declaratory action in a court of competent jurisdiction.

16. TENANT NO LONGER IN POSSESSION OF SUBJECT PREMISES

a. TENANT VACATED PRIOR TO COMMENCEMENT OF SUMMARY PROCEEDING

When the Tenant vacates the premises (and the Landlord accepts surrender of possession) <u>prior</u> to the commencement of a summary proceeding, the Petition must be dismissed because a summary proceeding may <u>not</u> be maintained where "possession" is not in dispute.[1354] The Landlord may commence a plenary or small claims action outside of the Housing Part for any monetary claims stemming from the leasehold.

Whether the Tenant is in possession is a factual issue.[1355] A critical factor in determining if a surrender occurred is whether the Tenant has any dominion or control over the premises. It has been held that the Tenant's physical vacating of the premises combined with an

---

1352 Amherst Med. Park, Inc. v. Amherst Orthopedics, P.C., 31 A.D.3d 1131, at 1133, 818 N.Y.S.2d 884, 885 (4th Dep't 2006).

1353 Cat Hollow Estates, Inc. v. Savoia, 46 A.D.3d 1293, at 1294, 849 N.Y.S.2d 111, 112, (3d Dep't 2007).

1354 *See* Highbridge Dev. BR, LLC v. Nisky Kilt, Inc., 172 A.D.3d 1590, 100 N.Y.S.3d 398 (3d Dep't 2019); Clark v. Singletary, 31 N.Y.S.3d 920 (App. Term, 9th & 10th Jud. Dists. 2016); O'Connell v. Singletary, 926 N.Y.S.2d 345 (App. Term, 9th & 10th Jud. Dists. 2011); Phoenix Indus., Inc. v. Ultimate Sports, LLC, 859 N.Y.S.2d 906 (App. Term, 9th & 10th Jud. Dists. 2008).

1355 *See* Riverside Research Inst. v. KMGA, Inc., 68 N.Y.2d 689, at 692, 506 N.Y.S.2d 302, 304 (1986); PK Rest., LLC v. Lifshutz, 138 A.D.3d 434, 30 N.Y.S.3d 13 (1st Dep't 2016); 535-545 Fee, LLC v. Evrotas Enters., 2018 N.Y. Misc. LEXIS 4467 (N.Y. Cnty. Sup. Ct. Jan. 23, 2018); Charles v. 95 Waring Place, LLC, 2021 N.Y.L.J. LEXIS 1218 (Yonkers City Ct. Dec. 29, 2021); South Ferry Bldg. Co. v. 44 Wall St. Fund, Inc., 535 N.Y.S.2d 685 (N.Y. Civ. Ct. N.Y. Cnty. 1988).

unsuccessful attempt to return the keys constitutes a valid surrender.[1356]

Absent a waiver, a summary proceeding is permitted where the Tenant vacates the premises but leaves behind his or her possessions. This is because the Tenant is deemed to still be in possession. As a practical matter, absent a surrender, the Landlord may only be left to guess whether the Tenant surrendered possession (abandoned the premises), which would allow the Landlord to re-claim possession;[1357] or instead had the Tenant merely temporarily left the premises, with no intent of surrendering possession, such as the taking of a vacation, which would prohibit the Landlord from re-claiming possession absent a Court Order and eviction by the Sheriff. Typically, a Landlord will error on the side of caution in such a scenario, and seek a lawful eviction in the Housing Part.[1358]

A surrender by operation of law, also referred to as an implicit surrender, occurs where the parties act in a manner (without an express agreement) inconsistent with a Landlord and Tenant relationship which "[i]ndicates their intent to deem the lease terminated."[1359] The returning of the keys in and of itself does not constitute a surrender by operation of law.[1360]

1356 Johnson v. Marcano, 101 N.Y.S.3d 699 (App. Term, 2d, 11th & 13th Jud. Dists. 2018).

1357 If an abandonment is established, due to the absence of privity of estate, the Landlord may instead pursue its remedies based on contract principles in a plenary action but "[m]ay not seek [same in] the speedier summary proceeding in the landlord-tenant court." *South Ferry Bldg. Co.*, 535 N.Y.S.2d at 685; 560 Colonial LLC v. Advance Abstract Corp., 936 N.Y.S.2d 58 (Nassau Cnty. Dist. Ct. 2011).

1358 The use of self-help in an unlawful eviction by a residential Landlord is a class A misdemeanor. RPAPL § 768. For a discussion regarding unlawful evictions, *see* Chapter 11, subdiv. C[18][c], *infra*.

1359 Fragomeni v. AIM Servs., Inc., 135 A.D.3d 1272, 23 N.Y.S.3d 496 (3d Dep't 2016); *see* Thor 680 Madison Ave. LLC v. Qatar Luxury Group S.P.C., 2020 U.S. Dist. LEXIS 92744 (S.D.N.Y. May 17, 2020); Ford Coyle Props., Inc. v. 3029 Ave. V Realty, LLC, 63 A.D.3d 782, 881 N.Y.S.2d 146, 147 (2d Dep't 2009); Clearview Farms LLC v. Wowkowych, 94 N.Y.S.3d 537 (Monroe Cnty. Sup. Ct. 2017), *aff'd*, 162 A.D.3d 1157, 74 N.Y.S.3d 903 (3d Dep't 2018); Point 128, LLC v. Sound De Point LLC, 155 N.Y.S.3d 731 (N.Y. Civ. Ct. Queens Cnty. 2021).

1360 *Ford Coyle Props., Inc., LLC*, 63 A.D.3d at 782, 881 N.Y.S.2d at 147; 34 W. 75th St. LLC v. Hynes, 2019 N.Y.L.J. LEXIS 3093 (N.Y. Civ. Ct. N.Y. Cnty. Sept. 4, 2019).

b. TENANT VACATED AFTER COMMENCEMENT OF SUMMARY PROCEEDING

The Landlord may continue to pursue its claims in a summary proceeding where the Tenant vacated the premises after the proceeding was commenced.[1361] However, the Landlord and Tenant relationship is considered terminated as of the date the Tenant vacated, and, as a result, the money judgment may not include unpaid rent or use and occupancy for a period following the surrender.[1362] An exception to this rule is where the rental agreement contains a survival clause that continues the Tenant's obligations following the termination of the lease, in which case, the Landlord may pursue the monetary claims in a plenary action.[1363]

17. TENANTS IN COMMON

A tenant in common shares equal ownership rights in the premises with one (1) or more persons and/or entities. A common example is siblings who were bequeathed equal ownership in a family residence or

1361 156 E. 37th St. LLC v. Eichner, 113 N.Y.S.3d 484 (N.Y. Civ. Ct. N.Y. Cnty. 2019); *see* 1129 N. Blvd., LLC v. Astra Group, Inc., 992 N.Y.S.2d 159 (App. Term, 9th & 10th Jud. Dists. 2014); Bahamonde v. Grabel, 939 N.Y.S.2d 226 (App. Term, 9th & 10th Jud. Dists. 2011); Harbor Tech LLC v. Correa, 134 N.Y.S.3d 652 (N.Y. Civ. Ct. Kings Cnty. 2020). As discussed in Chapter 5, subdiv. B(2)(a), when the Tenant vacates the premises during the pendency of a summary proceeding, the Landlord must be awarded a judgment of possession if a money judgment is awarded. *See* Sowalsky v. E. F. MacDonald Stamp Co., 294 N.Y.S.2d 1016 (3d Dep't 1968); *Eastrich No. 80 Corp.*, 688 N.Y.S.2d at 409; Erick James LLC v. Bruna, 141 N.Y.S.3d 294 (N.Y. Civ. Ct. Bronx Cnty. 2021) (holding that "[j]urisdiction is not divested merely because of the removal of the respondent subsequent to the commencement of the proceeding").

1362 *See* Patchogue Assocs. v. Sears, Roebuck and Co., 951 N.Y.S.2d 314 (App. Term, 9th & 10th Jud. Dists. 2012); Cornwell v. Sanford, 222 N.Y. 248 (1918). *See generally* MH Residential 1, LLC v. Barrett, 78 A.D.3d 99, at 103, 908 N.Y.S.2d 6, 9 (1st Dep't 2010) (noting that "[w]here a summary proceeding to recover possession of real property has been instituted, the landlord-tenant relationship may only be terminated by actual surrender of the premises or by issuance of a warrant of eviction").

1363 *Patchogue Assocs.*, 951 N.Y.S.2d at 314 (holding "[s]ince there was no survival clause, landlord could have sought to recover the unpaid rent in a plenary action, rather than commencing a summary proceeding, the purpose of which is to recover possession of real property").

obtained title due to their parents' passing intestate.[1364] A lessee, such as a family member who enters possession with the permission of just one (1) tenant in common, may share possession with a non-consenting tenant in common. This is commonly referred to as joint possession.

It is well-established that tenants in common have an equal right to possession of the premises, which precludes their removal in a summary proceeding.[1365] This is the case even where the tenants in common entered into an agreement for the payment of rent or use and occupancy.[1366] Due to the equal right to possession, an out-of-possession tenant in common does not "[r]elinquish any of their rights as when another co-tenant assumes exclusive possession of the property."[1367] The proper recourse to recover possession against a tenant in common is an action in partition pursuant to RPAPL § 901.[1368]

A tenant in common may not bind a non-consenting tenant in

1364 *See, e.g.*, LCD Holding Corp. v. Powell-Allen, 203 A.D.3d 811, 164 N.Y.S.3d 635 (2d Dep't 2022) (where decedent passed away intestate, ownership of the premises automatically transferred to six (6) distributees who became equal owners as tenants in common).

1365 *See* Rabin v. Rabin, 13 N.Y.S.3d 852 (App. Term, 9th & 10th Jud. Dists. 2015) (noting the parties may seek relief in the Surrogate's Court where the executor of the Estate was a tenant in common); Lee v. Tabasko, 957 N.Y.S.2d 636 (Nassau Cnty. Dist. Ct. 2010); *see generally* Pivarsky v. Island Hills Golf Club, Inc., 2013 N.Y. Misc. LEXIS 4924 (Suffolk Cnty. Sup. Ct. Oct. 15, 2013).

1366 Dolan § 38:21, at 589-90. *But see* Capsouto v. Capsouto, 202 A.D.3d 587, 164 N.Y.S.3d 99 (1st Dep't 2022) (noting that "[w]hile there is a presumption that tenants in common share equally in their common tenancy, such a presumption may be rebutted if the facts show that they hold the tenancy in unequal shares"). Factors may include "the amounts invested in the property by the...tenants in determining the shares to which they are entitled." *Id.* (*citing* McGuire v. McGuire, 93 A.D.3d 701, at 703, 939 N.Y.S.2d 572 (2d Dep't 2012)).

1367 169 MLS Realty Corp. v. One 69 Skill Corp., 197 A.D.3d 1079, 153 N.Y.S.3d 505 (2d Dep't 2021). The Appellate Division, Second Department noted that pursuant to RPAPL § 541, "[n]onpossessory cotenants are protected...by a common-law rule that presumes a cotenant's possession is possession by and for the benefit of all other cotenants." *Id.* (citation omitted). However, this protection "cease[s] after the expiration of ten years of continuous exclusive occupancy by such tenant, personally or by his [or her] servant or by his [or her] tenant, or immediately upon an ouster by one tenant of the other and such occupying tenant may then commence to hold adversely to his [or her] cotenant." *Id.*

1368 *See, e.g.*, Korn v. Korn, 190 A.D.3d 1043, 139 N.Y.S.3d 701 (3d Dep't 2021); Parker v. Parker, 145 N.Y.S.3d 757 (App. Term, 2d, 11th & 13th Jud. Dists. 2021). For a description of partition actions, *see* Chapter 1 subdiv. E(2)(b), *supra*.

common to a rental agreement with a third party. However, a tenant in common may commence a summary proceeding without the consent of the other.[1369] The ultimate relief in a summary proceeding is the termination of the lessee's "exclusive" occupancy. As a result, rather than removal, a non-consenting tenant in common may achieve joint possession with the lessee. Accordingly, a summary proceeding will be dismissed where the petitioning tenant in common is already in possession and/or shares the premises with the lessee.[1370]

18. UNLAWFUL EVICTIONS

a. CONSTRUCTIVE EVICTION

A constructive eviction occurs where the Landlord commits a wrongful act or an omission that substantially denies the Tenant's "beneficial use and enjoyment" of all or a portion of the premises.[1371] For example, where the Landlord fails to repair a perpetually leaking roof, a constructive eviction would result if the Tenant is unable to perform its operations in the premises due to the non-repair.[1372]

To assert the defense, the Tenant must vacate the portions of the premises claimed to have been denied within a reasonable period of time.[1373] A delay in vacating the premises due to "efforts to resolve the

1369 Bernadotte v. Woolford, 33 N.Y.S.3d 877 (Nassau Cnty. Dist. Ct. 2016).

1370 *Id.*

1371 *See generally* Barash v. Pennsylvania Term. Real Estate Corp., 26 N.Y.2d 77, 308 N.Y.S.2d 649 (1970) (dismissing action where plaintiff-Tenant failed to make a *prima facie* case for constructive or actual eviction).

1372 Great American Realty of E. Industry Ct., LLC v. Guzu, Inc., 187 A.D.3d 719, 130 N.Y.S.3d 348 (2d Dep't 2020) (summary judgment improper due to issues of fact whether damage from Hurricane Sandy denied Tenant's "[b]eneficial use and enjoyment of the premises, and whether the [Landlord] failed to take appropriate steps to correct the condition").

1373 *See* International Dev. Inst. v. Westchester Plaza, LLC, 194 A.D.3d 411, 149 N.Y.S.3d 411 (1st Dep't 2021); Turnwood Assocs., LLC v. Sutton Hay Day, Inc., 192 A.D.3d 1173, 141 N.Y.S.3d 339 (2d Dep't 2021); Iken v. Bohemian Brethen Presbyterian Church, 162 A.D.3d 594, 80 N.Y.S.3d 246 (1st Dep't 2018); 7001 E. 71st St., LLC v. Millenium Health Servs., 138 A.D.3d 573, 28 N.Y.S.3d 604 (1st Dep't 2016); 36 Main Realty Corp. v. Wang Law Office, PLLC, 19 N.Y.S.3d 654 (App. Term, 2d, 11th & 13th Jud. Dists. 2015); *see also* Zurel U.S.A., Inc. v. Magnum Realty Corp., 279 A.D.2d 520, at 521, 719 N.Y.S.2d 276 (2d Dep't 2001) (approximately three (3) to four (4) months is reasonable time for a commercial tenant to vacate the premises).

dispute without litigation...is a reasonable excuse."[1374] The Tenant need not abandon the entire premises, only the impacted areas.[1375]

If the Tenant continues to use the portions of the premises at issue, even if the usage is greatly diminished, then the defense of constructive eviction is not available.[1376] A commercial Tenant that remains in possession, notwithstanding the Landlord's failure to provide essential services, must continue to pay the rent.[1377]

A Subtenant may not assert a constructive eviction claim against the Landlord because a Landlord and Tenant relationship is a necessary element.[1378] Similarly, when a commercial Tenant enters into an agreement with a Subtenant in violation of the commercial lease, the Tenant's constructive eviction claim against the Landlord may be dismissed because a Tenant "[c]annot recover for interference by [a] landlord with an unlawful subtenancy."[1379] In *ERSRT 250 W. 5th St., L.L.C.*, the Tenant's constructive eviction claim was devoid of merit because the Subtenant was the only entity to be damaged by the Landlord's alleged misconduct.[1380]

1374 384 Columbus Ave. Assoc., LLC v. 101 W. 78th, LLC, 2016 N.Y. Misc. LEXIS 3202 (N.Y. Cnty. Sup. Ct. Sept. 6, 2016).

1375 *See* Minjak Co. v. Randolph, 140 A.D.2d 245, 528 N.Y.S.2d 554 (1st Dep't 1988); *N.N. Int'l (USA) Corp.*, 41 N.Y.S.3d at 720; Westbury Flats, LLC v. Dr. Steven H. Backer D.D.S., P.C., 130 N.Y.S.3d 631 (N.Y. Civ. Ct. Kings Cnty. 2020).

1376 *See* Arpino v. Cicciaro, 967 N.Y.S.2d 865 (App. Term, 9th & 10th Jud. Dists. 2012) (holding that where the commercial workshop area "ha[d] been used for its intended purposes, albeit for a drastically reduced amount of time each day during the colder months of the year, there has been no abandonment"); Kossoff v. 910 Fifth Ave. Corp., 2021 N.Y. Misc. LEXIS 6656 (N.Y. Cnty. Sup. Ct. Dec. 20, 2021); Garry v. Ryan & Henderson, P.C., 36 N.Y.S.3d 364 (Nassau Cnty. Dist. Ct. 2016).

1377 Thor 725 8th Ave. LLC v. Goonetilleke, 2015 U.S. Dist. LEXIS 25696 (S.D.N.Y. March 3, 2015) (Landlord's posting of "Retail Space Available" signs and allowing prospective Tenants to view the premises did not constitute a constructive eviction). Absent a lease provision to the contrary, the covenant to make repairs in a commercial premises is independent of the Tenant's obligation to pay rent. *See* Chapter 11, subdiv. B(1), *supra*.

1378 *7001 E. 71st St., LLC*, 138 A.D.3d at 573, 28 N.Y.S.3d at 604; MTS NY Lessee, L.P. v. Eden H., Inc., 2019 N.Y. Misc. LEXIS 5579 (N.Y. Cnty. Sup. Ct. Oct. 16, 2019).

1379 ESRT 250 W. 5th St., L.L.C. v. 13D/West 57th LLC, 148 A.D.3d 621, 50 N.Y.S.3d 363 (1st Dep't 2018).

1380 *Id.*

The statute of limitations for a constructive eviction claim is one (1) year.[1381] A Tenant that has been constructively evicted from a portion of the premises is entitled to an abatement of rent (not an entire suspension of rent which is reserved for a constructive eviction from the entire premises).[1382] Expert testimony is not required to establish the claim in a residential case, but is necessary in commercial cases to accurately determine the reasonable diminution of the rental value.[1383]

A constructive eviction claim does not arise where the rental agreement: (1) authorizes the Landlord to enter the premises to make repairs and alterations and (2) expressly precludes a rent abatement on that basis.[1384] Similarly, a lease provision that immunizes the Landlord from liability for "the installation of scaffolding or a sidewalk bridge" bars the defense of constructive eviction.[1385] It has further been held that "[a] lterations to leased premises, made with the consent of the tenant, do not amount to an eviction, no matter how extensive or the degree of interference with the tenant's occupancy."[1386]

1381 Reinhard v. Connaught Tower Corp., 150 A.D.3d 431, 51 N.Y.S.3d 412 (1st Dep't 2017); Kent v. 534 E. 11th St., 80 A.D.3d 106, 912 N.Y.S.2d 2 (1st Dep't 2010).

1382 *See Minjack Co.*, 140 A.D.2d at 245, 528 N.Y.S.2d at 554; Board of Mgrs. of Manhasset Med. Arts Condominium v. Integrated Med. Professionals, PLLC, 121 N.Y.S.3d 532 (Suffolk Cnty. Sup. Ct. 2020); *Westbury Flats, LLC*, 130 N.Y.S.3d at 631; 174 Mott Group, LLC v. Lucky 168 Rest. Corp., 856 N.Y.S.2d 500 (N.Y. Civ. Ct. N.Y. Cnty. 2008).

1383 *See* Shackman v. 400 E. 85th St. Realty Corp., 161 A.D.3d 438, 77 N.Y.S.3d 13 (1st Dep't 2018); Arbern Realty Co. v. Clay Craft Planters Co., Inc., 727 N.Y.S.2d 236, 237 (App. Term, 9th & 10th Jud. Dists. 2001); New York City Economic Dev. Corp. v. Harborside Mini Storage, Inc., 819 N.Y.S.2d 211 (N.Y. Civ. Ct. Kings Cnty. 2006).

1384 Noor Staffing Group v. 622 Third Ave., 195 A.D.3d 489, 145 N.Y.S.3d 336 (1st Dep't 2021); Board of Managers of Saratoga Condo. v. Shuminer, 148 A.D.3d 609, 51 N.Y.S.3d 34 (1st Dep't 2017); Fieldstone Capital Inc. v. Ryan & Conlon, LLP, 104 N.Y.S.3d 823 (App. Term, 1st Dep't 2019); APF 286 Mad LLC v. RIS Real Props., Inc., 13 N.Y.S.3d 849 (App. Term, 1st Dep't 2015).

1385 Empire Room, LLC v. Empire State Bldg. Co., LLC, 159 A.D.3d 648, 74 N.Y.S.3d 18 (1st Dep't 2018); *Shuminer*, 148 A.D.3d at 609, 51 N.Y.S.3d at 34 (scaffolding).

1386 *Noor Staffing Group*, 195 A.D.3d at 489, 145 N.Y.S.3d at 336; *APF 286 Mad LLC*, 13 N.Y.S.3d at 849; 737 Park Ave. Acquisition LLC v. Robert B. Jetter, M.D., PLLC, 7 N.Y.S.3d 245 (App. Term, 1st Dep't 2014).

b. ACTUAL EVICTION

An actual eviction occurs where the Tenant is wrongfully ousted from physical possession of all or a portion of the premises, such as where the Landlord changes the locks or bars the Tenant from entering. Expert testimony is not required to establish the defense.[1387] The remedy for an unlawful eviction is the complete suspension of rent even where the wrongful act only denied the Tenant's use and enjoyment of a portion of the premises.[1388]

A "trivial" intrusion or interference with the Tenant's use and enjoyment of a commercial property is not an eviction and, thus, an abatement of rent is not available.[1389] In *Eastside Exh. Corp. v. 210 E. 86th St. Corp.*, the Court of Appeals held that the Landlord's taking of twelve (12) square feet of non-essential lobby space within the 15,000 to 19,000 square foot movie theater was a "*de minimis* taking," which failed to justify an abatement of rent, and precluded the Tenant's claims for injunctive and other monetary relief.[1390] Whether the taking is *de minimis* is determined on a case-by-case basis. The Appellate Term for the Second, Eleventh and Thirteenth Judicial Districts extended the "*de minimis* taking" rule to residential leaseholds.[1391]

In *ZMoore, Ltd. v. Kingman Mgt. LLC*, the Appellate Division, First Department, dismissed the commercial Tenants' breach of lease action because the Landlord's taking constituted a minimal intrusion of

---

1387 *See* Appliance Giant, Inc. v. Columbia 90 Assocs., LLC, 8 A.D.3d 932, 779 N.Y.S.2d 611 (3d Dep't 2004); 487 Elmwood, Inc. v. Hassett, 107 A.D.2d 285, at 289, 486 N.Y.S.2d 113, 117 (4th Dep't 1985) (expert testimony required to establish damages resulting from actual eviction).

1388 *See* Frame v. Horizons Wine & Cheese, Ltd., 95 A.D.2d 514, at 518, 467 N.Y.S.2d 630, 633 (2d Dep't 1983) (where there is a partial actual eviction, the Landlord may not recover use and occupancy for the remaining portion of the premises occupied by the Tenant) (*citing Barash*, 26 N.Y.2d at 77, 308 N.Y.S.2d at 649); Israel Realty LLC v. Shkolnikov, 36 N.Y.S.3d 47 (N.Y. Civ. Ct. N.Y. Cnty. 2016).

1389 *See* Eastside Exh. Corp. v. 210 E. 86th St. Corp., 18 N.Y.3d 617, 942 N.Y.S.2d 19 (2012).

1390 *Id.*

1391 *See* Paskov v. Kreshitchki, 954 N.Y.S.2d 760 (App. Term, 2d, 11th & 13th Jud. Dists. 2012); *cf.* Goldstone v. Gracie Terr. Apt. Corp., 110 A.D.3d 101, 970 N.Y.S.2d 783 (1st Dep't 2013) (denying Tenant's motion for a preliminary injunction because the minimal taking failed to result in irreparable harm).

hallway space within "a common area not demised to [the Tenant]."[1392] The Appellate Division concluded that the four (4) feet taken in the basement of the commercial Tenant's restaurant was a "mere[] trivial interference" with the Tenant's use and enjoyment.[1393]

When the Tenant elects to withhold rent following a partial actual eviction, the Tenant may not assert a claim for damages.[1394] However, if the Tenant opts to pursue a claim for damages due to the actual eviction, then the Tenant waives the right to assert the unlawful eviction as a defense in a non-payment proceeding.[1395]

c. SELF-HELP BY LANDLORD (CRIMINAL AND CIVIL LIABILITY)

In New York, only the Sheriff or Marshal may perform or authorize an eviction pursuant to a lawful Order of the Court. For residential properties, the Landlord may not resort to self-help relief, such as changing the locks and/or removing the Tenant's possessions.[1396]

RPAPL § 768 makes the "intentional" unlawful eviction of an occupant who lawfully entered possession pursuant to a rental agreement or otherwise lawfully remained in the premises for not less than thirty (30) consecutive days, a class A misdemeanor punishable by up to one (1) year in jail and civil penalties between $1,000—$10,000 for each violation.[1397] Conduct that constitutes an unlawful eviction includes: (1) the use or threatened use of force "to induce" an occupant to vacate; (2) acting with the intent "to interfere with or disturb the comfort, repose,

1392 154 A.D.3d 603, 63 N.Y.S.3d 346 (1st Dep't 2017).

1393 *Id.*

1394 E-Z Eating 41 Corp. v. H.E. Newport, LLC, 171 A.D.3d 415, 97 N.Y.S.3d 101 (1st Dep't 2019); Schwartz v. Hotel Owners Corp., 132 A.D.3d 541, 20 N.Y.S.3d 341 (1st Dep't 2015); *Frame*, 95 A.D.2d at 514, 467 N.Y.S.2d at 633; Motichka v. MP 1291 Trust, 2020 N.Y. Misc. LEXIS 2085 (N.Y. Cnty. Sup. Ct. May 15, 2020).

1395 *Frame*, 95 A.D.2d at 514, 467 N.Y.S.2d at 633; *see* Bostany v. Trump Org. LLC, 88 A.D.3d 553, 931 N.Y.S.2d 280 (1st Dep't 2011).

1396 Clinkscale v. Sampson, 48 A.D.3d 730, 853 N.Y.S.2d 572 (2d Dep't 2008); Taffet v. Vega, 165 N.Y.S.3d 229 (App. Term, 9th & 10th Jud. Dists. 2022); Coleman v. Murray, 934 N.Y.S.2d 33 (Suffolk Cnty. Dist. Ct. 2011).

1397 RPAPL § 768 (HSTPA, L. 2019, c. 36, Part M, § 24); Watson v. NYCHA-Brevoort Houses, 138 N.Y.S.3d 830 (N.Y. Civ. Ct. Kings Cnty. 2020).

peace, or quiet" of the use and occupancy; and (3) any effort or threat of effort to deny the occupancy of the premises.[1398] The statute further requires that the property owner "[t]akes all reasonable and necessary action" to restore an unlawfully evicted occupant to a suitable occupancy within the dwelling.[1399]

A wrongfully ousted Tenant may commence a proceeding in the Housing Part by Order to Show Cause to be restored to the premises pursuant to RPAPL § 713(10) and, if necessary, direct the Sheriff or Marshal to return the Tenant to possession by removing and changing the locks.[1400] Standing to commence the proceeding is <u>not</u> contingent upon the number of consecutive days the wrongfully displaced occupant was in possession of the premises.[1401] Although the Housing Part may direct the restoration of the Tenant, who would be the Petitioner in the action, the Court may <u>not</u> award money damages.[1402] The Tenant would, however, be entitled to treble damages in a subsequent plenary action.[1403] Predicate notice is <u>not</u> required prior to commencing a proceeding to be restored to possession, but the current occupant must be named as a Respondent.[1404]

1398 RPAPL §§ 768(1)(a)(i),(ii),(iii).

1399 *Id.* at § 768(1)(b).

1400 *Id.* at § 713(10). *See* Jones v. New York City Hous. Auth., 151 N.Y.S.3d 618 (N.Y. Civ. Ct. Kings Cnty. 2021) (noting that RPAPL § 768 may subject a Landlord who utilizes self-help to criminal and civil liabilities). The authority for seeking restoration is codified at RPAPL § 713(10).

1401 Goncalves v. Soho Vill. Realty, Inc., 9 N.Y.S.3d 522 (App. Term, 1st Dep't 2015); Byas v. New York City Hous. Auth., 2020 N.Y. Misc. LEXIS 4443 (Bronx Cnty. Sup. Ct. June 26, 2020).

1402 Eze v. Spring Creek Gardens, 85 A.D.3d 1102, 925 N.Y.S.2d 888 (2d Dep't 2011); Rostant v. Swersky, 79 A.D.3d 456, at 457, 912 N.Y.S.2d 200, 201-02 (1st Dep't 2010); Cudar v. O'Shea, 951 N.Y.S.2d 312 (App. Term, 2d, 11th & 13th Jud. Dists. 2012); Viglietta v. Lavoie, 932 N.Y.S.2d 307 (App. Term, 9th & 10th Jud. Dists. 2011); Cascade Funding RM 1 2020 Alternative Holdings, LLC v. Singletary, 131 N.Y.S.3d 854 (Suffolk Cnty. Dist. Ct. 2020).

1403 RPAPL § 853. *See* Hood v. Koziej, 140 A.D.3d 563, 37 N.Y.S.3d 68 (1st Dep't 2016); *Clinkscale,* 48 A.D.3d at 731, 853 N.Y.S.2d at 573; Cohen v. Restuccia, 2021 N.Y. Misc. LEXIS 1739 (N.Y. Cnty. Sup. Ct. April 8, 2021).

1404 Bay Ridge Chicken Grill, Inc. v. Cirrus Data Int'l, LLC, 26 N.Y.S.3d 723 (App. Term, 2d, 11th & 13th Jud. Dists. 2015) (proceeding dismissed where Petitioner-Tenant failed to name current occupant as a party).

The statute of limitations for an unlawful eviction claim is one (1) year which "[b]egins to run when 'it is reasonably certain that the tenant has been unequivocally removed with at least the implicit denial of any return.'"[1405] A special proceeding to be restored to possession is improper where the individual claiming to have been unlawfully removed was not in "actual possession" or "constructive possession" at the time of the unlawful entry.[1406] Moreover, where the occupant abandoned the premises, there can be no liability for wrongful eviction or trespass.[1407]

When the Landlord is awarded a possessory judgment and a warrant of eviction from the Court, but nonetheless elects to utilize self-help, the Tenant's recourse is to commence a new proceeding in the Housing Part or other court of competent jurisdiction to be restored to possession. The Tenant may not seek such relief by way of Order to Show Cause in the Landlord's summary proceeding.[1408] For example, in *Triangle Props. #14 LLC v. Beauty Salon Depot/Beauty U.S.A., LLC*, the motion to be restored to possession following the Landlord's use of self-help was denied because the Tenants "[w]ere not removed pursuant to a judgment or order of the court,... [and as a result] the court was without authority, in [a] non-payment proceeding commenced by landlord, to direct [the] landlord to restore [the tenants] to possession."[1409]

In a commercial case, the Landlord may avail itself of a lease

1405 *PK Rest., LLC*, 138 A.D.3d at 434, 30 N.Y.S.3d at 13; *see* Kolomensky v. Wiener, 135 A.D.2d 505, 522 N.Y.S.2d 156 (2d Dep't 1987); Guzzo v. 250 E. Houston St. Assocs., L.P., 2020 N.Y. Misc. LEXIS 9757 (N.Y. Cnty. Sup. Ct. Oct. 7, 2020).

1406 Weiss v. Bretton Woods Condo. II, 203 A.D.3d 1100, 166 N.Y.S.3d 204 (2d Dep't 2022); *Viglietta*, 932 N.Y.S.2d at 307.

1407 *See* Ovcharenko v. 65th Booth Assocs., 131 A.D.3d 1144, 16 N.Y.S.3d 763 (2d Dep't 2015) (summary judgment denied where there was a question of fact whether the Tenant had abandoned the premises); Salem v. U.S. Bank Nat'l Assoc., 82 A.D.3d 865, 918 N.Y.S.2d 532 (2d Dep't 2011); Vatel v. Wills, 161 N.Y.S.3d 748 (N.Y. Civ. Ct. N.Y. Cnty. 2022) (proceeding to be restored to possession dismissed notwithstanding indicia of an illegal lockout where Tenant "voluntarily relinquished that known right when he indicated to the police and [the Landlord] that he was leaving, packed some of his belongings . . ., then returned days later, after a cool down period to voluntarily pack his own belongings").

1408 Triangle Props. # 14, LLC v. Beauty Salon Depot/Beauty U.S.A., 920 N.Y.S.2d 245 (App. Term, 9th & 10th Jud. Dists. 2010).

1409 *Id.*; Ferby v. Jonero, LLC, 998 N.Y.S.2d 306 (N.Y. Civ. Ct. Kings Cnty. 2014).

provision authorizing re-entry based upon a breach by the Tenant provided the re-entry is done in a reasonable manner and without force.[1410] In *Martinez v. Ulloa*, the Appellate Term dismissed the Tenant's special proceeding to be restored to possession absent sufficient evidence the Landlord violated the lease or that the re-entry was completed in an unreasonable and/or forceful manner. However, in that case, the Tenants were independently returned to possession with the assistance of the Police.[1411] As a result, the Court denied the Landlord's cross-motion for re-issuance of the judgment of possession because the Landlord originally used self-help without the assistance of the Court and "cannot now complain of being denied the opportunity to short circuit the procedural requirements of a summary proceeding…."[1412] Finally, a Tenant will <u>not</u> be restored to possession, even where unlawfully evicted, when awarding possession would be "futile" (e.g., the Landlord is otherwise entitled to possession).[1413]

1410 *See* Drapaniotis v. 36-08 33rd St. Corp., 48 A.D.3d 736, 853 N.Y.S.2d 356 (2d Dep't 2008); Bozewicz v. Nash Metalware Co., 284 A.D.2d 288, 725 N.Y.S.2d 671 (2d Dep't 2001); Jovana Spaghetti House v. Heritage Co. of Massena, 189 A.D.2d 1041, 592 N.Y.S.2d 879 (3d Dep't 1993); Gangi Foods, Inc. v. BSY Enters., Inc., 2008 N.Y. Misc. LEXIS 9028 (Suffolk Cnty. Sup. Ct. July 11, 2008); *Ferby*, 998 N.Y.S.2d at 306.

1411 Martinez v. Ulloa, 22 N.Y.S.3d 787 (App. Term, 2d, 11th & 13th Jud. Dists. 2015).

1412 *Id.*

1413 Fitzgerald Edibles, Inc. v. Osborne Tenants Corp., 179 A.D.3d 451, 113 N.Y.S.3d 540 (1st Dep't 2020); Shack Collective Inc. v. Dekalb Mkt. Hall, LLC, 130 N.Y.S.3d 925 (N.Y. Civ. Ct. Kings Cnty. 2020).

CHAPTER 12

TENANTS—FEDERAL AND STATE CLAIMS

Generally, counterclaims for damages may be asserted by Tenants in summary proceedings.[1414] However, some claims, such as torts unrelated to possession,[1415] equitable claims,[1416] and claims for declaratory and injunctive relief,[1417] are beyond the jurisdiction of the Housing Part, and must be commenced in another forum. As a result, there has been a litany of housing-related litigation initiated by Tenants in both the Federal and State (Supreme) Courts.

A. DISCRIMINATION CLAIMS

It is well-established that an individual does not have a constitutional right to housing.[1418] The protections afforded occupants of real property are statutorily-based and the result of case law. Several of the laws designed to protect against housing discrimination are discussed below.

1414 For a discussion regarding counterclaims, *see* Chapter 8, subdiv. C(2), *supra*.

1415 Wheeler v. Linden Plaza Preserv. LP, 172 A.D.3d 608, 102 N.Y.S.3d 17 (1st Dep't 2019); *see* Ndiaye v. 2123 FDB MPPH LP, 115 N.Y.S.3d 584 (App. Term, 1st Dep't 2019).

1416 DOLAN § 43:38, at 137-38 (4th ed. 2010).

1417 Dickson v. MacDougal St. Synagogue Beth-Midrash, 2013 N.Y. Misc. LEXIS 3472 (N.Y. Cnty. Sup. Ct. Aug. 8, 2013).

1418 *See* Nachmenson v. New York City Dep't of HRA Social Servs., 2017 U.S. Dist. LEXIS 92580 (E.D.N.Y. June 15, 2017).

1. FAIR HOUSING ACT

The Federal Fair Housing Act of 1968 ("FHA" or "Fair Housing Act") makes it unlawful to discriminate, in either the sale or rental of residential property, on the basis of race, color, religion, gender, disability,[1419] familial status, or national origin.[1420] In 2019, more than 10,000 FHA discrimination claims were filed within the United States,[1421] and nearly $16.7 million was expended to settle existing claims.[1422]

a. PRIMA FACIE CASE AND AVAILABLE REMEDIES

Section 3604 of the FHA prohibits a Landlord or owner from discriminating against a prospective residential occupant due to his or her inclusion within a protected class: (1) during negotiations; (2) the making of a purchase or lease offer; and (3) determining the "availability" of the premises.[1423] Fair Housing Act § 3617 similarly makes it unlawful to coerce, intimidate, threaten, or interfere with an occupant's quiet use and enjoyment of the premises for any of the same reasons.

The provisions of the FHA apply equally to pre-acquisition (viewing and negotiation) and post-acquisition (after the Tenant takes possession) housing discrimination. For a post-acquisition FHA claim,

1419 In 1988, Congress amended the Fair Housing Act to include discrimination on the basis of a disability as prohibited conduct. *See* Fair Housing Amendments Act of 1988, sec. 6, §§ 3604(f)(1),(2) (1988).

1420 Pub. L. No. 90-284, 82 Stat. 83 (1968) (codified as amended at 42 U.S.C. § 3601 *et seq.*).

1421 *See* Office of Fair Housing and Equal Opportunity, "*State of Fair Housing Annual Report to Congress: FY 2018—FY 2019*," U.S. Department of Housing and Urban Development ("HUD"), at 10, https://hud.gov/sites/dfiles/FHEO/documents/FEHO%20Report%20Final%20-%20Web%20Version.pdf. A breakdown of the discrimination claims reveals that 4,767 were based upon a disability; 2,002 for racial discrimination; 979 for retaliation; 853 for gender; 743 due to national origin; 756 for familial status; 313 for color; and 202 for religion. *Id.*

1422 *Id.*, at 9.

1423 The Fair Housing Act makes unlawful the "refus[al] to sell or rent after the making of a bona fide offer, or to refuse to negotiate for the sale or rental of, or otherwise make unavailable or deny, a dwelling to any person because of race, color, religion, sex, familial status, or national origin," or "discriminat[ing] against any person in the terms, conditions, or privileges of sale or rental of a dwelling, or in the provision of services or facilities in connection therewith" for any of the same reasons. 42 U.S.C. § 3604(a),(b).

it must be proven that: (1) that the Tenant was subjected to "harassment that was sufficiently pervasive and severe so as to create a hostile housing environment;" (2) the harassment was due to the Tenant's membership in a protected class; and (3) a legitimate basis for "imputing" or holding the Landlord responsible for the harassing conduct.[1424] A hostile environment is determined based upon "the totality of the circumstances,"[1425] and the Court will look to the following factors: "the nature of the conduct, the context in which the incident(s) occurred, the severity, scope, frequency, duration, and location of the conduct, and the relationships of the persons involved."[1426] This analysis is to be evaluated from "[t]he perspective of a reasonable person in the aggrieved person's position."[1427]

The available remedies in a private civil action for FHA violations include: (1) actual and punitive damages; (2) temporary and permanent injunctive relief; (3) affirmative relief (e.g., directing the Landlord to "pass policies or rules, build housing, or take other affirmative steps toward non-discriminatory housing");[1428] (4) attorney's fees; and (5) any other relief that is just.[1429] A State's Attorney General similarly has standing to file suit on behalf of individuals discriminated against due to FHA violations, and may seek monetary damages and injunctive relief on their behalf.[1430] The statute of limitations for an FHA claim is two (2) years <u>after</u> the occurrence of the housing discriminatory practice or "breach of a conciliation agreement" entered into under the FHA, whichever occurred later.[1431]

1424 A.L.M. v. Board of Managers of the Vireum Schoolhouse Condo., 2021 U.S. App. LEXIS 32829 (2d Cir. Nov. 4, 2021) (*citing* Pierre v. Lantern Group Found., Inc., 2016 U.S. Dist. LEXIS 80079 (S.D.N.Y. June 20, 2016)).

1425 *Id.*; 24 C.F.R. § 100.600(a)(2)(i).

1426 *Board of Managers of the Vireum Schoolhouse Condo.*, 2021 U.S. App. LEXIS at 32829; 24 C.F.R § 100.600(a)(2)(i)(A).

1427 24 C.F.R. § 100.600(a)(2)(i)(C).

1428 Mhany Mgmt. v. Incorporated Vill. of Garden City & Garden City Bd. of Trustees, 985 F. Supp.2d 390, 430 (E.D.N.Y. 2013).

1429 42 U.S.C. § 3613[c].

1430 *Id.* at § 3614.

1431 *Id.* at § 3613(a)(1); *see* Barry v. Cadman Towers, Inc., 136 A.D.3d 951, 25 N.Y.S.3d 342 (2d Dep't 2016).

b. BURDEN-SHIFTING ANALYSIS

A housing discrimination claim may be proven by a demonstration of either: (1) "disparate treatment" (intentional discrimination) or (2) "disparate impact."[1432] Under either measure, the burden-shifting framework set forth by the United States Supreme Court in *McDonnell Douglas Corp. v. Green* is utilized to analyze the sufficiency of the claim.[1433] This means that when the Tenant establishes a *prima facie* case of housing discrimination, the burden then shifts to the Landlord to assert a legitimate, non-discriminatory rationale for its action.[1434] In other words, the Landlord must demonstrate that its decision or policy was necessary to "achieve one or more substantial, legitimate, non-discriminatory interests."[1435] If the Landlord offers such a non-discriminatory rationale or interest, the burden then shifts back to the Tenant who may prevail where it is shown that either: (1) an alternative policy would have served the Landlord's non-discriminatory interests while having less of a "discriminatory effect" on the protected group[1436] or (2) the Landlord's purported rationale was a "pretext" for unlawful discrimination.[1437]

1432 *See* Long Island Hous. Servs. v. NPS Holiday Sq. LLC, 2021 U.S. Dist. LEXIS 171345 (E.D.N.Y. Sept. 9, 2021); Indig v. Pomona, 2019 U.S. Dist. LEXIS 200934 (S.D.N.Y. Nov. 19, 2019); Reed v. Friedman Mgmt. Corp., 2019 U.S. Dist. LEXIS 52961 (S.D.N.Y. March 28, 2019).

1433 411 U.S. 792, 93 S.Ct. 1817 (1973).

1434 Mitchell v. Shane, 350 F.3d 39 (2d Cir. 2003); Wood v. Mutual Redevelopment Houses, Inc., 2021 U.S Dist. LEXIS 174534 (S.D.N.Y. Sept. 14, 2021).

1435 24 C.F.R. § 100.500[c](2); MHANY Mgmt. v. County of Nassau, 819 F.3d 581 (2d Cir. 2016).

1436 24 C.F.R. § 100.500[c](3); *MHANY Mgmt.*, 819 F.3d at 581.

1437 *Mitchell*, 350 F.3d at 39; *see* Melton v. Shabazz, 2021 U.S. Dist. LEXIS 27453 (S.D.N.Y. Feb. 12, 2021).

c. DISPARATE TREATMENT (INTENTIONAL DISCRIMINATION)

For intentional discrimination claims, the plaintiff need only make a "modest showing that a member of a statutorily protected class was not offered the same terms, conditions, or privileges of rental of a dwelling or not provided the same services or facilities in connection therewith…giving rise to a reasonable inference of prohibited discrimination."[1438] The plaintiff must further "present evidence that animus against the protected group was a significant factor" in the discriminatory conduct.[1439]

A "disparate treatment" claim may be demonstrated through either: (1) direct evidence of discriminatory intent or (2) indirect evidence that infers discriminatory intent by the owner or Landlord.[1440] Due to the "less stringent" pleading requirements for *pro se* litigants,[1441] absent direct evidence of discrimination, the complaint asserted by an unrepresented Tenant will withstand a motion to dismiss where the requisite elements are alleged and the facts "give plausible support to a minimal inference of discriminatory motivation."[1442]

The United States Second Circuit Court of Appeals recently addressed whether intentional Tenant-on-Tenant discriminatory conduct impugns liability on a Landlord who fails to act after learning of such conduct. In *Francis v. Kings Park Manor, Inc.*, the Second Circuit held

---

1438 Khalil v. Farsh Corp., 260 F. Supp.2d 582 (W.D.N.Y. 2003) (emphasis added); *see Board of Managers of the Vireum Schoolhouse Condo.*, 2021 U.S. App. LEXIS at 32829.

1439 Regional Econ. Cmty. Action Program v. City of Middletown, 294 F.3d 35 (2d Cir. 2002); Birch Family Servs. v. Wlody, 2021 U.S. Dist. LEXIS 106513 (E.D.N.Y. June 7, 2021).

1440 *Reed*, 2019 U.S. Dist. LEXIS at 52961; *Khalil*, 260 F. Supp.2d at 582. *But see* Jones v. Volunteers of Am. Greater N.Y., 2022 U.S. Dist. LEXIS 45103 (S.D.N.Y. March 14, 2022) (FHA claim dismissed for failure to state a claim).

1441 *See, e.g.*, Tasfay v. Ramos, 2022 U.S. Dist. LEXIS 27391 (S.D.N.Y. Feb. 14, 2022).

1442 Littlejohn v. City of New York, 795 F.3d 297 (2d Cir. 2015) (emphasis added); *see* Palmer v. Mae, 2018 U.S. App. LEXIS 31479 (2d Cir. Nov. 7, 2018); *but see* Jones-Bey v. La Casse, 2021 U.S. Dist. LEXIS 55651 (S.D.N.Y. March 22, 2021) (FHA amended complaint dismissed where the allegations "relie[d] exclusively on legal conclusions" and failed to suggest or infer a discriminatory motive).

that there is no such liability and dismissed the FHA claims against a Landlord that failed to intervene on behalf of a Tenant who was racially-harassed by a fellow Tenant at the premises.[1443]

In dismissing the action, the Second Circuit reasoned that a Landlord is not presumed to have the requisite degree of control over Tenants residing within their complex to substantiate a FHA claim for intentional discrimination.[1444] The Court further refused to apply a "deliberate indifference" theory of liability because "[t]he typical powers of a landlord over a tenant—such as the power to evict—do not establish the substantial control necessary to state" a claim against the Landlord for Tenant-on-Tenant conduct.[1445]

d. DISPARATE IMPACT

To establish housing discrimination based upon a "disparate impact," the Tenant must demonstrate that, regardless of intent, the Landlord's "outwardly" neutral, non-discriminatory practice had a significant adverse or disproportionate negative impact upon individuals of a protected group.[1446] A "causal connection" between the Landlord's facially-neutral policy and its discriminatory impact must be established.[1447] In other words, the plaintiff has to sufficiently "allege facts... or produce statistical evidence demonstrating [the] causal connection" between the defendant's stated policy and the resulting discriminatory

1443 992 F.3d 67 (2d Cir. 2021).

1444 *Id.*

1445 *Id.*; Edstrom v. St. Nicks Alliance Corp., 194 A.D.3d 518, 149 N.Y.S.3d 26 (1st Dep't 2021) (dismissing FHA claim against Landlord stemming from Tenant-on-Tenant racial and sexual orientation harassment).

1446 *MHANY Mgmt.*, 819 F.3d at 581; *see generally* Xu v. Suffolk Cnty., 2021 U.S. Dist. LEXIS 58867 (E.D.N.Y. March 26, 2021) (disparate impact demonstrated by showing that "defendant's practices have a proportionally greater negative impact on minority populations").

1447 Tsombanidis v. W. Haven Fire Dep't, 352 F.3d 565 (2d Cir. 2003); *see* Texas Dep't of Hous. & Cmty. Affairs v. Inclusive Cmtys. Project, Inc., 576 U.S. 519, at 541-42, 135 S.Ct. 2507, 2523-24 (2015) (plaintiff must provide statistical data of racial disparity to prevail on an FHA disparate impact claim).

effect.[1448]

In 2020, the HUD standards for analyzing disparate impact claims were set for a major overhaul. In September 2020, HUD published the "2020 Rule" (effective October 2020), which was intended to replace the agency's 2013 Rule for analyzing disparate impact claims. The proposed 2020 Rule imposed more stringent requirements on the Tenant to sustain a disparate impact claim, including: the elimination of the definition of discriminatory effect, stricter pleading requirements, a deviation from the burden-shifting framework, the creation of new affirmative defenses for Landlords, and limitations on available relief.[1449] However, on October 25, 2020, the United States District Court for the District of Massachusetts enjoined the implementation of the 2020 Rule,[1450] and, thereafter, on June 25, 2021, HUD moved to reinstate the "previously promulgated [2013 Rule] titled, "Implementation of the Fair Housing Act's Discriminatory Effects Standard," which remains the current standard.[1451]

2. AMERICANS WITH DISABILITIES ACT

The Americans With Disabilities Act ("ADA") provides that "[n]o qualified individual with a disability shall, by reason of such disability, be excluded from participation in or be denied the benefits of the services, programs, or activities of a public entity, or be subjected to

---

1448 *Inclusive Communities Project, Inc.*, 576 U.S. at 519, 135 S.Ct. 2507. *See* Jackson v. Tryon Park Apts., Inc., 2019 U.S. Dist. LEXIS 12473 (W.D.N.Y. Jan. 25, 2019) (denying motion to dismiss racially disparate impact claim based upon apartment complex policy refusing to rent to felons); Paige v. New York City Hous. Auth., 2018 U.S. Dist. LEXIS 137238 (S.D.N.Y. Aug. 14, 2018) (motion to dismiss denied where plaintiff claimed the failure to comply with lead-paint inspection laws disproportionately impacted children).

1449 *See* "HUD's Implementation of the Fair Housing Act's Disparate Impact Standard," 85 Fed. Reg. 60288, Sept. 24, 2020, at www.federalregister.gov/documents/2020/09/24/2020-19887/huds-implementation-of-the-fair-housing-acts-disparate-impact-standard.

1450 *See* Massachusetts Fair Hous. Ctr. v. Housing and Urban Development, 496 F. Supp.3d 600 (D. Mass. 2020).

1451 *See* "Reinstatement of Discriminatory Effects Standard," 86 Fed. Reg. 33590, June 25, 2021, at www.federalregister.gov/documents/2021/06/25/2021-13240/reinstatement-of-huds-discriminatory-effects-standard.

discrimination by any such entity."[1452] The term "public entity" is defined in the ADA as "a state or local government" or "any department, agency, special purpose district, or other instrumentality of a State or States or local government."[1453] Title III of the ADA prohibits disability discrimination in "places of public accommodation."

To assert a *prima facie* ADA housing claim, it must be alleged that: (1) the Tenant is a qualified individual with a disability; (2) the Landlord is subject to the ADA; and (3) the Tenant was denied an opportunity to participate in or benefit from the Landlord's services, programs, or activities, or was otherwise discriminated against due to a disability.[1454] To substantiate the claim, the Tenant must demonstrate, *inter alia*, that the housing is a "public accommodation" and the Landlord's representatives are officials of a public entity.[1455] Where the defendant is a private Landlord, the ADA is not applicable even when the housing is subsidized by public funds.[1456]

An individual may not be liable under the ADA,[1457] and Title III of the ADA does not provide a private cause of action for damages.[1458] A State's Attorney General has enforcement authority to investigate ADA violations and standing to commence civil actions when appropriate.[1459] An ADA claim may be proven by introducing evidence of: (1)

1452 Pub. L. No. 39-116, 104 Stat. 328 (2008) (codified at 42 U.S.C. § 12101 *et seq.*). *See* 42 U.S.C. § 12132.

1453 *Id.* at § 12131(1)(a)-(b).

1454 Sykes v. New York City Hous. Auth., 2022 U.S. Dist. LEXIS 130682 (S.D.N.Y. July 22, 2022); Burris v. Hous. and Servs., Inc., 2019 U.S. Dist. LEXIS 43972 (S.D.N.Y. March 18, 2019).

1455 *See* Flynn v. Cohison, 2016 U.S. Dist. LEXIS 66011 (E.D.N.Y. May 19, 2016); Reid v. Zackenbaum, 2005 U.S. Dist. LEXIS 17177 (E.D.N.Y. Aug. 17, 2005) (dismissing ADA claim where complaint failed to allege the Tenant "[r]esided in public housing, and whether [the Landlord's] actions were in his official capacity on behalf of the New York City Housing Authority…a public entity under the ADA").

1456 *Flynn*, 2016 U.S. Dist. LEXIS at 6601 n.1.

1457 *Burris*, 2019 U.S. Dist. LEXIS at 43972.

1458 *See* 42 U.S.C. § 12188(a)(1) (same remedies available under Title III of ADA and Title II of Civil Rights Act of 1964); Powell v. National Bd. of Medical Examiners, 364 F.3d 79, 86 (2d Cir. 2004) (injunctive relief may be awarded for violations of Title III of the ADA).

1459 42 U.S.C. § 12188(b).

intentional discrimination (disparate treatment); (2) disparate impact; or (3) the Landlord's failure to make a reasonable accommodation.[1460]

The available relief for a violation of the ADA includes: (1) injunctive and declaratory relief; (2) affirmative relief directing the residence to be brought into ADA compliance and the retention of Court jurisdiction until compliance is achieved; (3) monetary damages (not punitive damages) when requested by the Attorney General; (4) civil penalties up to $50,000 for the first violation ($100,000 for a subsequent violation); (5) attorney's fees; and (6) any other relief deemed appropriate.[1461] The statute of limitations for an ADA housing discrimination claim is three (3) years.[1462]

The Landlord is required to consider an appropriate accommodation when an accommodation is necessary for a disabled Tenant to remain in the premises.[1463] As a result, the Landlord must either "reasonably accommodate the Tenant's handicap or show that no reasonable accommodation will eliminate or acceptably minimize the risk posed by the handicapped tenant."[1464] An accommodation is <u>not</u> required for a Tenant "[w]hose tenancy would constitute a direct threat to the health or safety of other individuals or whose tenancy would result in substantial physical damage to the property of others."[1465]

When an Article 81 Guardian is appointed for an "incapacitated" Tenant, the Tenant is automatically deemed to be a "handicapped" person pursuant to 42 U.S.C. § 3604(f)(2)(A) of the FHA, and, therefore, if applicable, the ADA would govern.[1466] For example, in *Prospect Union*

1460 *See generally* Fair Hous. in Huntington Comm. Inc. v. Town of Huntington, N.Y., 316 F.3d 357, 366 (2d Cir. 2003); Pierce v. Fordham Univ., Inc., 2016 U.S. Dist. 71322 (S.D.N.Y. June 1, 2016); *see also* Krist v. Kolombos Rest. Inc., 688 F.3d 89, 95 (2d Cir. 2012) (where plaintiff demonstrates there was a failure to provide a reasonable accommodation, a discriminatory intent need not be demonstrated because the ADA was <u>not</u> "intended to allow recovery only for intentional discrimination").

1461 42 U.S.C. § 12188; Leonid Treyger v. Liberty 99 Cents Paradise Inc., 2022 U.S. Dist. LEXIS 72134 (E.D.N.Y. April 18, 2022).

1462 Louis v. New York City Hous. Auth., 152 F. Supp.3d 143 (S.D.N.Y. 2016).

1463 42 U.S.C. § 3604(f)(3)(B).

1464 529 W. 29th LLC v. Reyes, 100 N.Y.S.3d 475 (App. Term, 1st Dep't 2019).

1465 42 U.S.C. § 3604(f)(9).

1466 Prospect Union Assoc. v. DeJesus, 167 A.D.3d 540, 91 N.Y.S.3d 36 (1st Dep't 2018).

Assoc., the Appellate Division, First Department directed that before determining whether execution of the warrant of eviction would be permanently stayed, a hearing was required to determine if the Article 81 Guardian could be a factor in allowing the Tenants, who had cognitive deficiencies and mobility limitations, to safely remain in the premises and in compliance with their lease obligations without risk or undue harm to other occupants.[1467]

3. REHABILITATION ACT

Section 504 of the Rehabilitation Act provides that "[n]o otherwise qualified individual with a disability . . ., shall, solely by reason of her or his disability, be excluded from the participation in, be denied the benefits of, or be subjected to discrimination under any program or activity receiving Federal financial assistance or under any program or activity conducted by any Executive agency or by the United Postal Service."[1468]

To sustain a claim under the Rehabilitation Act, the plaintiff must demonstrate that: (1) the plaintiff is a qualified individual with a disability; (2) the defendant is subject to the ADA; (3) the plaintiff was denied a benefit from or the opportunity to participate in the defendant's services or otherwise discriminated against due to a disability (e.g., a reasonable accommodation was not implemented); and (4) the

---

1467 *Id.* (noting that "[t]he issue is whether, with the involvement of the article 81 guardian and its management of their affairs, tenants can fulfill their lease obligations and avoid eviction"); *see* New York Found. for Senior Citizens v. Hamilton, 170 A.D.3d 543, 96 N.Y.S.3d 52 (1st Dep't 2019) (affirming vacating of stipulation of settlement because the Tenant, who was diagnosed with autism and suffered from intellectual development disabilities, lacked capacity to enter into the agreement and the Landlord was <u>not</u> entitled to rely upon the Article 81 Guardian's "acquiescence to the Stipulation"); 2013 Amsterdam Ave. Hous. Assn., L.P. v. King, 98 N.Y.S.3d 775 (App. Term, 1st Dep't 2019); 140 W. End Ave. Owners Corp. v. Dinah L., 114 N.Y.S.3d 844 (N.Y. Civ. Ct. N.Y. Cnty. 2019) (granting 90 day stay for elderly ward of Article 81 Guardian to find alternative housing). *Cf.* 642-654 Whippersnapper LLC v. Mahoney, 99 N.Y.S.3d 576 (App. Term, 1st Dep't 2019) (denying application to vacate stipulation of settlement absent evidence the Guardian inadvisedly entered into the agreement or failed to consider the Tenant's best interests, but stayed execution of the warrant of eviction and remanded the matter for a hearing on the issuance of a permanent stay).

1468 Rehabilitation Act of 1973, Pub. L. No. 93-112, 87 Stat. 355 (codified as amended at 29 U.S.C. § 794(a)).

defendant receives financial assistance from the Federal government.[1469] The plaintiff must further establish that the defendant's discriminatory conduct was "solely by reason of [plaintiff's] handicap."[1470]

Similar to the ADA, there is "[n]o individual liability under the Rehabilitation Act."[1471] A critical distinction between the statutes is that the defendant under the Rehabilitation Act must be a recipient of Federal funding, which includes Section 8 housing. As discussed in *Schine v. New York State Office for Dev. Disabilities*, although the statutes are typically analyzed "simultaneously," they are not identical.[1472] A Rehabilitation Act claim is generally more difficult to prove because the plaintiff must further establish that the discriminatory conduct was "solely" due to the disability.[1473]

In *United States v. 111 E. 88th Partners*, the United States District Court for the Southern District of New York denied the defendant-Landlord's motion for summary judgment where the Landlord took no action (i.e., constructive denial) on the Tenant's request to permit an emotional support dog in his rent-controlled apartment.[1474] The Tenant, who had an assortment of medical and mental health issues, submitted medical documentation and the letters of multiple physicians in support of his accommodation request.[1475] In response, the Landlord essentially ignored the Tenant's request by not making a final determination, but instead, delaying the process and repeatedly requesting additional medical documentation and intimating that a subsequent medical examination will be required in addition to a drawn out discovery

1469 *Burris*, 2019 U.S. Dist. LEXIS at 43972.

1470 Reid v. Zackenbaum, 2005 U.S. Dist. LEXIS 17177 (E.D.N.Y. Aug. 17, 2005).

1471 Zlotnick v. Crystal Run Vill., Inc., 2021 U.S. Dist. LEXIS 207432 (S.D.N.Y. Oct. 27, 2021).

1472 2017 U.S. Dist. LEXIS 2362 (E.D.N.Y. Jan. 5, 2017), *adopted by*, 2017 U.S. Dist. LEXIS 51962 (E.D.N.Y. March 31, 2017).

1473 *Id.* Where the Tenant's lone assertion is that the accommodation request, and the denial of the request, was due to a disability, the ADA and Rehabilitation Act claims may be analyzed concurrently. *Id.*

1474 2020 U.S. Dist. LEXIS 74920 (S.D.N.Y. April 27, 2020).

1475 *Id.* at *2-3. The Court noted that for at least twenty (20) years, the Tenant had three (3) dogs "[i]n his apartment without obtaining Defendant's permission." *Id.*

process.[1476]

In denying the Landlord's motion for summary judgment, the District Court reasoned that: (1) the requests for unnecessary information were a dilatory tactic and (2) issues of fact existed regarding whether the Landlord had acted in good faith. The Landlord's lack of good faith was further questioned by its simultaneous attempt to evict the Tenant in a summary proceeding.[1477]

4. STATE DISCRIMINATION CLAIMS (HUMAN RIGHTS LAW)

a. EXECUTIVE LAW § 296(5)

Independent of the Federal statutes, New York enacted Executive Law § 296(5) within Article 15 of the State Human Rights Law ("HRL") which prohibits discrimination in housing matters based on any of the following factors; race, creed, color, national origin, sexual orientation, gender identity or expression, military status, sex, age, disability, marital status, lawful source of income, or familial status. New York State discriminatory housing claims "parallel those applicable under the [Fair Housing Act]," and therefore are analyzed in a similar fashion [and often] with similar outcomes.[1478]

In *Edstrom v. St. Nicks Alliance Corp.*, after dismissing the Tenant's

1476 *Id.* at *41-43. The Tenant also filed a complaint with HUD which resulted in a stay of the eviction proceeding. The HUD charge of discrimination found reasonable cause that the Landlord sought "to intimidate [Tenant] and interfere with his right to a reasonable accommodation" by "[r]equest[ing] additional information and a potential medical examination [which] was excessive, intrusive, burdensome, and unnecessary." *Id.*, at *20. The Tenant previously supplied "`sufficient reliable documentation' to support his accommodation request." *Id.*

1477 *Id.* at *41-43 (*citing* Logan v. Matveevskii, 175 F. Supp.3d 209, 229 (S.D.N.Y. 2016) (holding "[i]n assessing whether a defendant has constructively denied a plaintiff's request for an accommodation through unreasonable delay, courts often consider whether the delay was caused by the defendant's unreasonableness, unwillingness to grant the requested accommodation, or bad faith, as opposed to mere bureaucratic incompetence or other comparatively benign reasons")); Bizelia v. Clinton Towers Hous. Co., 2022 U.S. Dist. LEXIS 98138 (S.D.N.Y. May 31, 2022) (constructive denial of accommodation request by refusing to provide a final response).

1478 *Jackson*, 2019 U.S. Dist. LEXIS at 12473; Williams v. New York City Hous. Auth., 879 F. Supp.2d 328 (E.D.N.Y. 2012) (dismissing State disparate impact claims because they are "analogs" of the FHA claims).

FHA claim (the Landlord allegedly failed to respond to complaints of race-based and sexual orientation harassment by another Tenant), the Appellate Division, First Department noted the common "framework" for assessing FHA and HRL claims, and similarly dismissed the HRL claim for the same reasons.[1479] The same outcome resulted in *Haber v. ASN 50th St. LLC*, where the Court held that because the Tenant's "[d]iscriminatory treatment claims under the FHA fail[ed] under the *McDonnell Douglas* test, and because…[the HRL uses] the same standards as the FHA, [the] discriminatory treatment claims under these latter provisions must fail as well."[1480]

Effective October 11, 2019, the HRL was amended to include protections against discrimination on the basis of "gender identity or expression" and "lawful source of income."[1481] The "lawful source of income" restriction prohibits, in part, a Landlord from refusing to rent to a prospective Tenant based upon socioeconomic status, including being the recipient of governmental financial assistance, provided the income is earned from a lawful practice.[1482]

b. EXECUTIVE LAW § 296(18)

The Appellate Division, Third Department has held, similar to a claim under the Rehabilitation Act, that notwithstanding a lease provision prohibiting pets, a Landlord's refusal to allow a Tenant an emotional support dog as a reasonable accommodation may constitute a violation of Executive Law § 296.[1483] In *Hollandale Apts. & Health Club,*

1479 194 A.D.3d 518, 149 N.Y.S.3d 26 (1st Dep't 2021).

1480 847 F. Supp.2d 578 (S.D.N.Y. 2013).

1481 Executive Law § 296(5), as amended by L. 2019, ch. 8, § 5.

1482 *Id.*

1483 Section 296(18)(2) provides, "It shall be an unlawful discriminatory practice for the owner, lessee, sub-lessee, assignee, or managing agent of, or other person having the right of ownership of or possession of or the right to rent or lease housing accommodations:…(2) To refuse to make reasonable accommodations in rules, policies, practices, or services, when such accommodations *may be necessary* to afford said person with a disability equal opportunity to use and enjoy a dwelling, including the use of an animal as a reasonable accommodation to alleviate symptoms or effects of a disability, and including reasonable modification to common use portions of the dwelling." (emphasis added).

LLC v. Bonesteel, the Court concluded that the Tenant "offered sufficient evidence that having [an emotional support] dog would affirmatively enhance his quality of life by ameliorating the effects of his disability, and thus demonstrated necessity within the meaning of...the [Human Rights Law]."[1484]

The Court further noted the broader State definition of "disability" (as compared to the Federal definition), and that the "HRL does not require a showing of a limitation in a major life activity, but instead defines disability,...as 'a physical, mental or medical impairment...[that] is demonstrable by medically accepted clinical or laboratory diagnostic techniques.'"[1485] Reliance upon the therapist's testimony and the benefits to the Tenant was sufficient to satisfy the Human Rights Law guidelines.[1486]

c. REAL ESTATE AGENTS AND BROKERS

In August 2020, as a response to an extensive investigation into discriminatory housing market practices, the State amended RPL § 441-c to permit the Department of State to revoke or suspend the licenses of real estate brokers and salespersons for violations of the HRL.[1487] This was the first time New York authorized the forfeiture of a real estate agent's licensing due to discriminatory conduct.

In addition to the revocation or suspension of the agent's real

1484 173 A.D.3d 55, 100 N.Y.S.3d 711 (3d Dep't 2019); *see* 1 Toms Point Lane Corp. v. New York State Div. of Human Rights, 176 A.D.3d 930, 112 N.Y.S.3d 250 (2d Dep't 2019) (same); New York State Div. of Human Rights v. Cooper Square Realty, Inc., 2020 N.Y. Misc. LEXIS 4719 (N.Y. Cnty. Sup. Ct. Aug. 19, 2020) (Landlord required to put mats or other floor covering in lobby).

1485 *Hollandale Apts. & Health Club, LLC*, 173 A.D.3d at 55, 100 N.Y.S.3d at 711(*citing* Executive Law § 292(21)(a)).

1486 *Id.*

1487 RPL § 491-c(1)(a).

estate license, fines up to $2,000 may be assessed for each violation.[1488] Additional legislative enactments include, but are not limited to: (1) the establishment of an Anti-Discrimination Housing Fund, which may be utilized for fair housing testing; (2) increased training and education for real estate professionals on housing and discrimination laws; and (3) requiring associate real estate brokers to supervise and serve as "office managers" for other real estate professionals within their office.[1489]

d. REVIEW OF THE HUMAN RIGHTS COMMISSION'S DECISIONS

In New York City, Administrative Code § 8-123 authorizes judicial review of an Order of the New York City Commission on Human Rights regarding claims of discrimination. As a general matter, the decision of the Human Rights Commission will be upheld where it is "supported by substantial evidence on the record considered as a whole."[1490]

In *Marine Holdings, LLC v. New York City Commis. on Human Rights*, the Court of Appeals upheld the Human Rights Commission's decision in favor of the Tenant where the substantial evidence failed to demonstrate that the proposed accommodation (i.e., installing a wheelchair accessible entrance by converting a window into a doorway with a ramp) would result in an undue hardship to the commercial Landlord's business.[1491] The statute of limitations for State Human Rights discrimination claims is thirty (30) days following service of the Commission's Order.[1492]

1488 *Id.* In 2021, subsequent legislation and amendments were enacted that increased the maximum fines per violation from $1,000 to $2,000 (RPL § 441-c(a)(1)); implemented industry standardized operating procedures and practices (RPL § 442-h); and imposed fair housing and discrimination training requirements for real estate agents and salespersons (RPL § 441(3)). An agent who has his or her license revoked is ineligible for re-licensing for one (1) year. RPL § 441-c(4).

1489 "Governor Hochul Signs Legislative Package to Combat Housing Discrimination," Dec. 21, 2021, at https://www.governor.ny.gov/news/governor-hochul-signs-legislative-package-combat-housing-discrimination.

1490 NYC Admin. Code § 8-123(e).

1491 31 N.Y.3d 1045, 76 N.Y.S.3d 510 (2018).

1492 NYC Admin. Code § 8-123(h).

B. TENANT'S SAFETY

It is well-established that a Landlord "is not required to insure the safety of tenants or visitors" at the premises.[1493] Under common law, a Landlord is merely required to "[t]ake minimal precautions to protect tenants from foreseeable harm, including foreseeable criminal conduct by a third person."[1494] In this regard, summary judgment dismissing the complaint may be granted where the Landlord had neither actual nor constructive knowledge of a defective condition.[1495]

The Landlord is responsible for implementing the safety measures enacted by Federal, State, and Local governing authorities. For example, in multiple dwellings, the building's owner must install in each apartment or separate living unit an approved smoke detector within ten (10) feet from the entrance of each bedroom and other sleeping areas.[1496] In these buildings, in addition to all single- and two-family homes in New York City, the Landlord must further install an approved carbon monoxide alarm.[1497]

It has been held that the parent company of a commercial Tenant is not liable for the tortious conduct of its subsidiary (the commercial Tenant) except where the parent company exercises sufficient control over the

---

1493 Markov v. Grecian Gardens Co., 188 A.D.3d 1032, 132 N.Y.S.3d 664 (2d Dep't 2020) (emphasis added); Ferguson v. Antaeus Realty Corp., 94 A.D.3d 806, at 806-07, 941 N.Y.S.2d 870 (2d Dep't 2012) (citation omitted).

1494 *Ferguson*, 94 A.D.3d at 806, 941 N.Y.S.2d at 870.

1495 *See* Matson v. Dermer Mgt., Inc., 200 A.D.3d 772, 155 N.Y.S.3d 98 (2d Dep't 2021) (no liability where Landlord did not know or have reason to know of defective bedroom ceiling).

1496 Multiple Dwelling Law § 68; Multiple Residence Law § 15; NYC Admin. Code § 27-2045. *See* Rohan v. Kew Realty LLC, 200 A.D.3d 1082, 155 N.Y.S.3d 824 (2d Dep't 2021); *see also* Figueroa v. Parkash, 179 A.D.3d 583, 114 N.Y.S.3d 647 (1st Dep't 2020) (holding that where the Landlord fulfills its duty of providing a functional smoke detector, "the obligation to maintain the smoke detector was assumed by [the Tenant]," and liability for the failure to continue to ensure the smoke detector was in "good working condition" going forward may only be assessed against the Landlord where the Landlord's conduct "placed [the Tenant] in a more vulnerable position than he would have been in had [the Landlord] done nothing").

1497 Executive Law § 378; NYC Admin. Code § 27-2046.1. *See generally* Schiff v. ABI One, LLC, 2016 N.Y. Misc. LEXIS 3368 (N.Y. Cnty. Sup. Ct. Sept. 21, 2016), *aff'd*, 155 A.D.3d 543, 65 N.Y.S.3d 714 (1st Dep't 2017). The reader should also consult a municipality's Local Laws for requirements pertaining to smoke and carbon monoxide detectors.

subsidiary.[1498] In *Neill v. Cinema de Lux*, the Appellate Division, Second Department dismissed the personal injury action against the parent company of the Tenant movie theater because the parent company "did not own, occupy, control, or make special use of the premises where the accident occurred,...the movie theater was being operated by its wholly owned subsidiary, and [the parent company did not owe a] duty of care to the plaintiff."[1499]

1. RES IPSA LOQUITUR (NEGLIGENCE PER SE)

When an injury is sustained at the premises, the doctrine of res ipsa loquitur, which allows for a finding of negligence based upon the mere fact that a certain event occurred, does not apply where the Landlord lacked "control" over the defective or dangerous condition.[1500] An agreement to the contrary within the lease (i.e., provision imposing liability irregardless of Landlord's "control" over the condition) may result in a different outcome.

The doctrine of res ipsa loquitur, which is a rule of evidence, permits an inference of negligence where: (1) the incident is of the kind that ordinarily does not occur absent negligence; (2) the "instrumentality" which resulted in the injury was within the exclusive control of the Landlord; and (3) the injury was not the result of a voluntary action by the plaintiff.[1501] In other words, "'unless the landlord has retained control over the premises and has a duty imposed by statute or assumed by contract or a course of conduct' to perform maintenance and repairs," liability does not attach.[1502]

2. CRIMINAL LIABILITY

A Landlord may be held criminally responsible for his or her actions or omission to act when required to do so. For example, in *People v. Kukic*, the Landlord was convicted of manslaughter after two (2) people

1498 Neill v. Cinema de Lux, 198 A.D.3d 974, 155 N.Y.S.3d 580 (2d Dep't 2021).

1499 *Id.*

1500 *See* Correa v. Matsias, 153 A.D.3d 1312, 61 N.Y.S.3d 131 (2d Dep't 2017).

1501 *Id.*; *see* Wenzel v. All City Remodeling, 195 A.D.3d 496, 145 N.Y.S.3d 342 (1st Dep't 2021); Maroonick v. RAE Realty, LLC, 2021 N.Y. Misc. LEXIS 998 (N.Y. Cnty. Sup. Ct. March 11, 2021).

1502 Taliana v. Hines REIT Three Huntington Quadrangle, LLC, 197 A.D.3d 1349, 154 N.Y.S.3d 136 (2d Dep't 2021); Grant v. 132 W. 125 Co., LLC, 180 A.D.3d 1005, at 1007, 120 N.Y.S.3d 345, 347 (2d Dep't 2020).

were killed following an explosion at the premises.[1503] The conviction was sustained, in part, because the Landlord participated in an unlawful scheme to "deliberately circumvent[] safety regulations [and] to create and operate [an] unauthorized system that diverted natural gas from the building."[1504]

3. PERSONAL INJURY CLAIMS

There have been numerous negligence and personal injury actions resulting from injuries sustained by Tenants, guests, employees, and patrons at the premises due to: assault;[1505] shootings;[1506] homicide contributed to

1503 196 A.D.3d 169, at 175, 149 N.Y.S.3d 75, 80 (1st Dep't 2021).

1504 *Id.*

1505 Astupina v. W. Farms Sq. Hous. Dev. Fund Corp., 195 A.D.3d 461, 150 N.Y.S.3d 73 (1st Dep't 2021) (notwithstanding an inoperable front and side door, granting summary judgment in favor of Landlord where "no triable issue of fact exists because there is no evidence from which a jury could conclude, without pure speculation, that the assailant was an intruder, as opposed to a tenant or invitee"); George v. 855 Ocean Ave., LLC, 165 A.D.3d 1060, 86 N.Y.S.3d 564 (2d Dep't 2018) (dismissing personal injury action because the Landlord had no notice of "[p]rior occurrences of the same or similar criminal activity at or near the subject premises"); Ramos v. New York City Hous. Auth., 147 A.D.3d 992, 48 N.Y.S.3d 198 (2d Dep't 2017) (premises security claims require a showing that the intruder "gained access to the premises through a negligently maintained entrance"); *Ferguson*, 94 A.D.3d at 806, 941 N.Y.S.2d at 870 (personal injury claims dismissed where the assailant did not gain entry "[t]hrough a negligently maintained entrance").

1506 Ballo v. AIMCO 2252-2258 ACP, LLP, 155 A.D.3d 582, 63 N.Y.S.3d 865 (1st Dep't 2017) (out-of-possession Landlord was not liable because it had no duty of care to the patron of the commercial Tenant (a bar) who was shot while on the sidewalk outside the premises).

by negligent security (inoperable door);[1507] robberies;[1508] fires;[1509] defective appliances;[1510] toxic mold;[1511] slip and falls;[1512] unlit staircases;[1513] ob-

1507 *See* Scurry v. New York City Hous. Auth., 193 A.D.3d 1, 140 N.Y.S.3d 255 (2d Dep't 2021) (denying Landlord's motion for summary judgment because while the gravity of the crime could not be anticipated, an operable locking system may have deterred the targeted attack against a former girlfriend and her children). *But see* Estate of Murphy v. New York City Hous. Auth., 193 A.D.3d 503, 148 N.Y.S.3d 19 (1st Dep't 2021) (noting a split with the Second Judicial Department, granting Landlord's motion for summary judgment where the perpetrators "would have gained access to the building by following another person in or forcing such a person to let them in[, which] negates the unlocked door as a proximate cause of the harm that befell [the decedent], and makes her assailants' murderous intent the only proximate cause").

1508 Golub v. Louis, 153 A.D.3d 903, 60 N.Y.S.3d 415 (2d Dep't 2017) (dismissing Tenant's personal injury action because the intruders gained access to the premises by breaking a window, and, therefore, the act was <u>not</u> foreseeable).

1509 Fitzsimons v. Brennan, 169 A.D.3d 873, 95 N.Y.S.3d 112 (2d Dep't 2019) (granting summary judgment in favor of defendant college dismissing wrongful death suit because the college "did not owe a duty to ensure that the [private] off-campus housing listed on its website...complied with all relevant fire safety standards"); *cf.* Daly v. E. 36th LLC, 153 A.D.3d 1145, 61 N.Y.S.3d 206 (1st Dep't 2017) (denying plaintiff Tenant's motion for summary judgment due to questions regarding whether the Landlord had notice of the deficient electrical and wiring systems).

1510 Kaplan v. Tai Props., L.L.C., 147 A.D.3d 420, 45 N.Y.S.3d 792 (1st Dep't 2017) (dismissing personal injury action for burn injuries (head) resulting from a defective gas stove because the Landlord did <u>not</u> have either a statutory or a contractual duty to repair appliances the Tenant installed).

1511 Desernio v. Ardelean, 188 A.D.3d 994, 132 N.Y.S.3d 670 (2d Dep't 2020) (denying Landlord's motion for summary judgment where Landlord failed to demonstrate "through expert evidence based on a scientifically-reliable methodology, that there was no causal link between the plaintiff's alleged injuries and his exposure to mold").

1512 Montalvo v. Texas Roadhouse Holdings, LLC, 200 A.D.3d 986, 159 N.Y.S.3d 116 (2d Dep't 2021) (dismissing claim against Landlord where the Landlord neither controlled the common area nor was responsible for illuminating the area the customer "fell as she attempted to step down from a walkway abutting the restaurant to the asphalt parking lot"); Cuello v. 708 Tremont Realty, LLC, 199 A.D.3d 604, 158 N.Y.S.3d 91 (1st Dep't 2021) (granting out-of-possession Landlord's motion for summary judgment where the Landlord had no duty to the Tenant-supermarket's customer who fell on "a wet, greasy substance on a delivery ramp" at the supermarket).

1513 Uppstrom v. Peter Dillon's Pub, 172 A.D.3d 497, 100 N.Y.S.3d 239 (1st Dep't 2019) (dismissing claim against out-of-possession Landlord where there was insufficient evidence that the alleged violations regarding the staircase were the proximate cause of plaintiff's injuries). The Appellate Division further opined that even if the staircase was improperly illuminated, liability still would not attach to the out-of-possession Landlord because "[i]nadequate lighting is not a structural or design defect." *See id.* Parenthetically, in New York City, § 27-375(f) of the Administrative Code of New York City provides that where the stairs are less than forty-four (44) inches wide, only one (1) handrail is required.

jects left on a staircase by a contractor;[1514] ceiling collapse;[1515] faulty front entrance doors;[1516] forklift operator injuries;[1517] portable water heaters;[1518]

1514 Santiago v. Post Rd. Assoc., LLC, 157 N.Y.S.3d 771, 157 N.Y.S.3d 771 (2d Dep't 2022) (holding that the Landlord established "it did not owe the Tenant's employee a duty of care because it was an out-of-possession landlord with no duty to keep the staircase free from transitory conditions").

1515 *Wenzel*, 195 A.D.3d at 496, 145 N.Y.S.3d at 342 (denying Landlord's motion for summary judgment where Landlord was notified of foot-long cracks in the ceiling prior to the collapse); *Maroonick*, 2021 N.Y. Misc. LEXIS at 998 (denying Tenant's motion for summary judgment because the ceiling was not in the Tenant's exclusive possession).

1516 King v. Marwest, LLC, 192 A.D.3d 874, 143 N.Y.S.3d 673 (2d Dep't 2021) (dismissing action against out-of-possession Landlord where Tenant employer maintained responsibility for maintenance of the front door under the lease agreement).

1517 Vargas v. Weishaus, 199 A.D.3d 620, 159 N.Y.S.3d 33 (1st Dep't 2021) (denying Landlord's motion for summary judgment where the evidence failed to demonstrate whether the accident occurred inside the premises, at the entrance, or on the sidewalk). *Cf.* Arias v. Sanitation Salvage Corp., 199 A.D.3d 554, 159 N.Y.S.3d 14 (1st Dep't 2021) (dismissing personal injury action against out-of-possession Landlord where the Tenant's employee delivery driver slipped and fell on a piece of salmon skin in an area the Tenant's employer was responsible for maintaining). In New York City, the owner of real property that abuts a public sidewalk has a duty to maintain the sidewalk in a reasonably safe condition. *See* NYC ADMIN. CODE § 7-210; Xiang Fu He v. Troon Mgt., Inc., 34 N.Y.3d 167, 114 N.Y.S.3d 14 (2019) (trial necessary to determine whether out-of-possession Landlord was negligent due to its failure to remove snow and ice from the sidewalk). A "sidewalk" is defined as the "portion of a street between the curb lines, or the lateral lines of a roadway, and the adjacent property lines, but not including the curb, intended for the use of pedestrians." NYC ADMIN. CODE § 19-101(d).

1518 Crosby v. Southport, LLC, 169 A.D.3d 637, 94 N.Y.S.3d 109 (2d Dep't 2019) (dismissing personal injury action against out-of-possession owner of commercial property where it did not: (1) have a duty to the Tenant's employee; (2) create the dangerous situation; or (3) retain control over the premises).

dog bites;[1519] falls from a loft area;[1520] faulty handrails;[1521] broken windows;[1522] and tree logs stacked along the property line.[1523] As in any action, the Landlord in a personal injury action may seek indemnification from its insurance carrier (as an additional assured) pursuant to the terms of its

---

1519 To recover under strict liability against the Landlord for injuries resulting from the Tenant's dog, the plaintiff must show that the Landlord: (1) had notice the Tenant had a dog; (2) knew or reasonably should have known the dog had "vicious propensities"; and (3) maintained sufficient control over the leased premises to permit the Landlord to either "remove or confine" the dog. *See* Elardi v. Morales, 192 A.D.3d 1074, 141 N.Y.S.3d 716 (2d Dep't 2021) (dismissing action against Landlord where the Landlord "was not aware, nor should he have been aware, that the dogs had any vicious propensities"). "Vicious propensities include the propensity to do any act that might endanger the safety of the persons and property of others in a given situation." Collier v. Zambito, 1 N.Y.3d 444, 775 N.Y.S.2d 205 (2004); *see also* Logie v. Lester, 170 A.D.3d 822, 93 N.Y.S.3d 894 (2d Dep't 2019) (dismissing personal injury action of Tenant's guest against the Landlord where the Tenant's dog bit the guest inside the residence); Toher v. Duchnycz, 172 A.D.3d 1894, 97 N.Y.S.3d 901 (4th Dep't 2019) (dismissing dog bite claim because Landlord did not have actual or constructive knowledge that the Tenants' dog had vicious propensities). *Cf.* Hunt v. Public Administrator of Kings County, 179 A.D.3d 652, 113 N.Y.S.3d 574 (2d Dep't 2020) (denying Landlord's motion for summary judgment where the evidence failed to establish that either "the dog did not have vicious propensities, or that the owner of the premises did not know or have reason to know of the dog's vicious propensities"); Loeffler v. Glasgow, 169 A.D.3d 1024, 94 N.Y.S.3d 607 (2d Dep't 2019) (denying Landlord's motion to vacate default judgment where a visitor was bitten by a dog owned by Landlord's spouse, but remitted the matter to Supreme Court for a new hearing on damages); Kraycer v. Fowler St., LLC, 147 A.D.3d 1038, 48 N.Y.S.3d 206 (2d Dep't 2017) (denying summary judgment because the plaintiff raised issues of fact whether non-parties with knowledge of the dogs' vicious propensities were "agents" of the Landlord).

1520 Hutchison v. Estate of Kursh, 198 A.D.3d 509, 152 N.Y.S.3d 796 (1st Dep't 2021) (denying summary judgment where there were issues of fact whether the condition of the loft was unsafe and the proximate cause of the fall).

1521 Amster v. Kromer, 157 A.D.3d 922, 67 N.Y.S.3d 494 (2d Dep't 2018) (dismissing Tenant's personal injury action due to a defective handrail and improperly constructed landing because the Landlord neither created the hazardous condition nor had knowledge (actual or constructive) of the faulty maintenance).

1522 Cotto v. New York City Hous. Auth., 155 A.D.3d 937, 64 N.Y.S.3d 120 (2d Dep't 2017) (dismissing Tenant's personal injury action against out-of-possession Landlord for injuries caused by a defective window when the Landlord did not create or cause the condition and further lacked actual or constructive knowledge of same).

1523 S.-B v. Radincic, 173 A.D.3d 407, 103 N.Y.S.3d 375 (1st Dep't 2019) (dismissing Tenant's personal injury action where the Landlord neither had actual nor constructive notice that the Tenant's child and his friend would "play" on the tree logs).

liability policy.[1524]

A contributory negligence claim may be maintained against an injured individual, but only where the injured person had a duty to the Landlord. For example, in *Hopkins v. Booth*, the Federal Magistrate Judge dismissed the out-of-possession Landlord's counterclaim for contributory negligence in a wrongful death action in which the Tenant's death and the injuries sustained by another occupant were the result of exposure to Legionella bacteria in the vacation rental hot tub.[1525] Since the Tenant was responsible for the maintenance of the hot tub, the Landlord was prohibited from asserting contributory negligence as an affirmative claim (but was permitted to assert the claim as an affirmative defense) because the Tenant owed no duty to the Landlord.[1526]

4. NO DUTY TO CLEAN-UP DURING A STORM

Absent a lease provision to the contrary, the Landlord has no duty to clean-up or otherwise make the premises secure while a storm is in progress.[1527] The Landlord's obligation to take "reasonable" steps to remedy the dangerous conditions does <u>not</u> resume "[u]ntil a reasonable time after the storm has ended."[1528] However, the Landlord may be responsible for resulting damages where its "clean-up efforts make the area more dangerous."[1529]

1524 *See* 71 Lafayette Ave. LLC v. New York Marine & Gen. Ins. Co., 199 A.D.3d 603, 154 N.Y.S.3d 759 (1st Dep't 2021) (Landlord entitled to indemnification from insurance company after Tenant fell through cellar door).

1525 2019 U.S. Dist. LEXIS 27894 (W.D.N.Y. Feb. 20, 2019).

1526 *Id.*

1527 Weinberger v. 52 Duane Assocs., LLC, 2011 N.Y. Misc. LEXIS 4957 (N.Y. Cnty. Sup. Ct. Oct. 13, 2011), *aff'd*, 102 A.D.3d 618, 959 N.Y.S.2d 154 (1st Dep't 2013).

1528 Lewis v. 311 Realty, LLC, 201 A.D.3d 591, 158 N.Y.S.3d 559 (1st Dep't 2022) *Weinberger*, 102 A.D.3d at 618, 959 N.Y.S.2d at 154.

1529 *Weinberger*, 2011 N.Y. Misc. LEXIS at 4957; *see generally* Encarnacion v. New York City Hous. Auth., 161 A.D.3d 485, 73 N.Y.S.3d 429 (1st Dep't 2018).

C. LEAD-BASED PAINT

1. OUTSIDE NEW YORK CITY

A Landlord may be liable for injuries resulting from a dangerous or defective condition in the property, such as lead paint, where a duty of care is established.[1530] A Landlord is liable for damages resulting from lead-based paint when the Landlord had actual or constructive notice of the lead-based paint and ample opportunity to remedy the condition, but failed to do so.[1531]

Constructive notice may be demonstrated by showing: (1) the Landlord retained the right of entry and assumed a duty to make repairs; and further knew or was aware of all of the following, that (2) the premises was constructed before lead-based paint was banned;[1532] (3) paint was peeling in the apartment; (4) lead-based paint is hazardous to children; and (5) that young children resided in the premises.[1533] In both *Rodrigues* and *Cassidy,* the Appellate Division, Fourth Department held that issues of fact precluded dismissal prior to trial.[1534]

In *Cassidy*, the Court examined both the rental agreement and the parties' conduct in assessing an out-of-possession owner's duty in tort, and determined that there were triable issues of fact regarding

1530 John v. Cassidy, 151 A.D.3d 1598, 57 N.Y.S.3d 567 (4th Dep't 2017).

1531 *See* McDowell v. Maldovan, 181 A.D.3d 1178, 121 N.Y.S.3d 456 (4th Dep't 2020).

1532 In New York City, lead-based paint was banned in residential dwellings in 1960. *See* Dakota Jade T. v. New York City Housing Auth., 148 A.D.3d 537, 49 N.Y.S.3d 446 (1st Dep't 2017); 656 W. 162nd St. Tenants Assn. v. Edelstein, 155 N.Y.S.3d 736 (N.Y. Civ. Ct. N.Y. Cnty. 2021). The federal government banned "[l]ead-based paint…for residential use in the United States in 1978 by the U.S. Product Safety Commission (16 C.F.R. 1303)." *See* Alston v. Pelkowski, 2016 N.Y. Misc. LEXIS 3573 (Suffolk Cnty. Sup. Ct. July 18, 2016).

1533 *McDowell,* 181 A.D.3d at 1178, 121 N.Y.S.3d at 456; Chapman v. Silber, 97 N.Y.2d 9, 734 N.Y.S.2d 541 (2001); Rodrigues v. Lesser, 150 A.D.3d 1686, 54 N.Y.S.3d 810 (4th Dep't 2017); Hines v. Double D & S Realty Mgmt. Group, 106 A.D.3d 1171, 964 N.Y.S.3d 298 (3d Dep't 2013) (*quoting* Robinson v. Bartlett, 95 A.D.3d 1531, 944 N.Y.S.2d 777 (3d Dep't 2012)).

1534 *Rodrigues*, 150 A.D.3d at 1686, 54 N.Y.S.3d at 810; *Cassidy*, 151 A.D.3d at 1598, 57 N.Y.S.3d at 567.

the Landlord's constructive notice of the lead-paint.[1535] In *Rodrigues*, triable issues of fact were presented in the form of "`evidence from which it may be inferred that [the owner] knew that paint was peeling on the premises'..., and 'evidence from which a jury could infer that [he] knew or should have known of the dangers of lead paint to children.'"[1536] Similarly, in *Hauerstock v. Barclay & Realty, LLC*, the Appellate Division, First Department denied a motion to dismiss the proceeding where the owners failed to establish that they lacked actual or constructive notice of the presence of lead-based paint in the antique columns they had purchased and placed within the building's lobby.[1537]

More recently, in *McDowell v. Maldovan*, the Appellate Division, Fourth Department reached a different conclusion when the lead-paint exposure action was dismissed against the co-owner who shared the premises with his father as tenants-in-common.[1538] The Court held that the movant defendant, unlike his father, demonstrated "he had no knowledge of inspections for or the existence of lead paint at the property during plaintiffs' tenancy and that he was unaware that the property was constructed at a time before lead paint was banned, that paint was peeling at the property,...and that young children lived on the property," and, therefore, regardless of the actual or constructive knowledge of the co-owner (his father), dismissal was required against the movant.[1539]

2. NEW YORK CITY (LOCAL LAW NO. 1)

In New York City, the Lead Poisoning Prevention Act, also known as Local Law No. 1, requires a Landlord to identify (and notify occupants) and remediate lead-based paint hazards, and, further, establishes liability against the Landlord of an apartment building containing lead-based paint constructed prior to 1960 (regardless of

1535 *Cassidy*, 151 A.D.3d at 1598, 57 N.Y.S.3d at 567.

1536 *Rodrigues*, 150 A.D.3d at 1686, 54 N.Y.S.3d at 810.

1537 168 A.D.3d 519, 92 N.Y.S.3d 220 (1st Dep't 2019).

1538 181 A.D.3d at 1178, 121 N.Y.S.3d at 456.

1539 *Id.* (the Court further reasoned that notice of the lead-paint by the other tenant-in-common "cannot be imputed to the [moving] defendant").

Landlord's knowledge) or between 1960 and 1977 (with Landlord's actual knowledge).[1540] Between 2013 and 2016, more than 10,000 violations were issued to New York City Landlords for "dangerous lead paint conditions."[1541]

The Landlord must remediate the lead-based paint or hazardous material upon reasonable discovery within the premises.[1542] Liability may be established under Local Law No. 1 where: (1) the building at issue contains, at minimum, three (3) apartments (multiple dwelling); (2) injury resulted from the ingestion of lead-based paint in the premises; (3) the injured was six (6) years-old or younger at the time of the exposure; and (4) the Landlord and/or owner knew or reasonably knew the injured's age.[1543]

However, the statute "does not impose absolute liability, [but] rather,...a standard of reasonableness."[1544] In other words, the Landlord may avoid liability where "the lead paint hazard existed '*despite* [the Landlord's] diligent and reasonable efforts to prevent it.'"[1545]

D. SOCIAL SERVICES LAW ("SPIEGEL LAW")—PUBLIC ASSISTANCE

In New York, eligible individuals of limited financial means may be eligible to receive federal public assistance in the form of supplemental security income.[1546] When the federal program took effect in 1974, New York discontinued its public assistance program, titled "Aid to Aged,

---

1540 NYC ADMIN. CODE §§ 27-2056.3, 27-2056.4, 27-2056.5.

1541 "*New York City's Efforts to Prevent and Respond to Childhood Lead Exposure*," Trust for America's Health (study), at https://www.tfah.org/story/nyclead.

1542 S.T. v. 1727-29 LLC, 189 A.D.3d 10, 127 N.Y.S.3d 16 (1st Dep't 2020).

1543 *1727-29 LLC*, 189 A.D.3d at 10, 127 N.Y.S.3d at 16 (granting plaintiff's partial summary judgment motion on liability); I.Z. v. W. End Residencies Hous. Dev. Fund Co., 2021 N.Y.L.J. LEXIS 1274 (N.Y. Cnty. Sup. Ct. Jan. 11, 2022) (denying Landlord's motion for summary judgment due to issues of fact regarding Landlord's actual or constructive notice of the lead-based paint within the premises).

1544 *1727-29 LLC*, 189 A.D.3d at 10, 127 N.Y.S.3d at 16.

1545 *Id.* (emphasis in original) (*citing* Juarez v. Wavecrest Mgmt. Team, 88 N.Y.2d 628, 649 N.Y.S.2d 115 (1996)).

1546 *See* N.Y. SOC. SERVS. LAW ("SSL") § 211 (2003). The rules and regulations pertaining to federal supplemental security income may be found at 42 U.S.C. § 1381, Pub. Law No. 92-603, 86 Stat. 1465 (1972).

Blind and Disabled," and adopted a new Title 6 of Article 5 of the Social Services Law ("SSL"), titled "Additional State Payments for Eligible Aged, Blind and Disabled Persons."[1547]

As a result, the State "established a state-wide program of additional state payments" for qualifying individuals.[1548] To be eligible for the additional state payments, an individual must be over the age of sixty-five (65), blind or disabled, satisfy the residency and citizenry requirements, and have countable income and/or resources at or below the mandatory minimum monthly standards.[1549]

1. VIOLATIONS AND UNSAFE BUILDING CONDITIONS

New York State public assistance payments, which include an allowance for shelter costs, may be made directly to the Landlord.[1550] Social Services Law § 143-b was enacted in 1962 to counteract the unscrupulous practice of some Landlords who received rent payments on behalf of public assistance recipients, but failed to provide the required services and/or offer a safe environment in which to live.

Social Services Law § 143-b(5) provides a defense in a non-payment proceeding where the building has "existing violations…which relate to conditions [that] are dangerous, hazardous or detrimental to life or health."[1551] Where the local health or building department notifies the Department of Social Services (or other governmental agency) of the unsafe conditions, the agency may issue a notice withholding shelter payments. The notice to withhold payments is a complete defense, subject to a determination by the Court, because neither a possessory judgment nor a money judgment may be issued for any period in which the dangerous or hazardous conditions existed.[1552]

1547 SSL §§ 207-212; *see generally* Khrapunskiy v. Doar, 12 N.Y.3d 478, 881 N.Y.S.2d 377 (2009). Additional provisions governing the amount of monthly grants and allowances are codified at SSL § 131-a, which is commonly referred to as the "safety net assistance" provision. *Khrapunskiy*, 12 N.Y.3d at 478, 881 N.Y.S.2d at 377.

1548 SSL § 207.

1549 *Id.* at § 209.

1550 *Id.* at § 143-b(1).

1551 *Id.* at § 143-b(5)(a).

1552 *Id.* at § 143-b(5)(b).

In *20 W. Props LLC v. Banks*, the Appellate Division, First Department rejected a due process constitutional challenge to Social Services Law § 143-b when the Landlord sought to recover the partial rent payments that had been withheld by the New York City Human Resources Administration ("HRA") due to multiple hazardous housing violations.[1553] The Court upheld the law, and concluded that the HRA "has a compelling interest in 'temporarily withholding payments of rent until [the] hazardous and dangerous violations are cleared.'"[1554]

A Tenant may assert the unsafe conditions as a defense in a non-payment proceeding after the governmental agency withholds payment.[1555] In *541-543 W. 150th St. LLC v. Allen*, the Appellate Term for the First Department held that the warrant of eviction was properly vacated, in part, because the rent arrears were paid in full "[e]xcept for funds withheld by the Department of Social Services pursuant to the Spiegel Law."[1556] Parenthetically, the defense is not applicable in holdover proceedings.[1557]

2. ADULT HOME OPERATORS

A certified adult home operator may terminate an Adult Care Admission Agreement with a supplemental security income recipient in limited situations, such as the failure to pay "authorized charges, expenses, and other assessments."[1558] RPAPL § 713-a and Social Services

1553 188 A.D.3d 552, 132 N.Y.S.3d 633 (1st Dep't 2020).

1554 *Id.*

1555 Notre Dame Leasing, LLC v. Rosario, 308 A.D.2d 164, 761 N.Y.S.2d 292 (2d Dep't 2003), *aff'd*, 2 N.Y.3d 459, 779 N.Y.S.2d 801 (2004); Fifty-Seven Assocs., L.P. v. Feinman, 924 N.Y.S.2d 309 (App. Term, 1st Dep't 2011) (Spiegel defense refuted where Tenant did not provide Landlord access to correct housing code violations).

1556 109 N.Y.S.3d 814 (App. Term, 1st Dep't 2018).

1557 Valentine v. Maybank, 501 N.Y.S.2d 553, 554 (Suffolk Cnty. Dist. Ct. 1986).

1558 SSL § 461-g. The grounds for terminating the Admission Agreement are: (1) the need for continuing medical or nursing care which the residence is unable to provide; (2) engaging in behavior that "poses imminent risk of death or imminent risk of serious physical harm" to oneself or others; (3) failing to pay required charges, expenses, and assessments, including, use and occupancy; (4) "repeated behavior" that directly "impairs" the well-being of the resident or others, or "substantially interferes" with the facility's operations; (5) the facility's operating certificate was revoked or voluntarily surrendered by the facility; or (6) the appointment of a receiver on behalf of the facility who is arranging the orderly relocation of residents. *Id.* at § 461-g(1).

Law § 461-h(15) provide that authorized adult home operators and their residents are not governed by conventional Landlord and Tenant relationships. As a result, an adult home seeking to terminate a resident's Admission Agreement neither commences a non-payment nor a holdover proceeding.[1559] Instead, the adult home operator, where authorized, may commence a special proceeding in the Housing Part after giving thirty (30) days written notice to the occupant.[1560]

For example, in *P & A Reckless v. Howard*, the Appellate Term for the Ninth and Tenth Judicial Districts granted the termination of the resident's Admission Agreement.[1561] The Court concluded that in light of the "overwhelming proof of the [resident's] repeated cigarette smoking violations," the resident directly impacted his own well-being and the well-being of others in the adult home, and "substantially interfered" with the facility's operation.[1562]

The New York State Admission Agreement generally requires an adult home operator to accept supplemental security income benefits in full satisfaction of the services provided. Although the resident may receive additional financial assistance in the form of a personal needs allowance ("PNA"), the adult home operator may not accept these monies under any circumstance.[1563]

If the adult home operator prevails against a supplemental security

1559 RPAPL § 713-a; SSL § 461-h(15). *See* Westbury Senior Living, Inc. v. Clements, 2017 N.Y.L.J. LEXIS 1933 (Nassau Cnty. Dist. Ct. 2017).

1560 RPAPL § 713-a; SSL § 461-g(2); *see* Oceanview Manor Home for Adults v. Vargas, 32 N.Y.S.3d 863 (N.Y. Civ. Ct. Kings Cnty. 2016). The Appellate Division, First Department dismissed as moot a preemptive declaratory judgment action against an adult home operator because "due process is insured to a resident of this type of home before their admission agreement may be involuntarily terminated." Campbell v. Blum, 91 A.D.2d 937, 457 N.Y.S.2d 816 (1st Dep't 1983).

1561 16 N.Y.S.3d 895 (App. Term, 9th & 10th Jud. Dists. 2015). *Cf. Vargas*, 32 N.Y.S.3d at 863 (dismissing Petition where the adult home "failed to make a *prima facie* showing of repeated behavior [i.e., smoking] rising to the level warranting the termination of the admission agreement").

1562 *P & A Reckless*, 16 N.Y.S.3d at 895.

1563 SSL § 131-o(2); Dworkin v. Dombrowski, 308 A.D.2d 88, at 96, 761 N.Y.S.2d 245, 251 (2d Dep't 2003) (SSL § 131-o(2) prohibits an adult facility "from contracting with [SSI recipients]...as to give rise to an obligation on their part to expend part or all of their personal allowance to pay for services or supplies").

income recipient, the adult home operator must assist the resident in finding a new residence. Instead of an eviction, the resident may continue to reside in the adult home until another suitable residence is located.[1564]

The Admission Agreement may provide that upon thirty (30) days written notice, the resident is required to pay additional charges "due to the [adult home's] increased costs of maintenance and operation." In *Lockwood v. DeLeon*, an adult home operator sought to terminate a supplemental security income recipient's Admission Agreement due to her failure to pay increased maintenance and operation costs. Although there was unchallenged testimony from a qualified State employee, the proceeding was dismissed because the adult home failed to substantiate a basis for the rate increase. The adult home's accountant acknowledged that since "maintenance and operation" costs are <u>not</u> normally defined accounting terms, the adult home had lumped "maintenance and operation" costs with its other expenses, including those for non-chargeable "supplies and services."[1565]

1564 *P & A Reckless*, 16 N.Y.S.3d at 895 (the "requirement [that the home assists in finding a new home] may provide a basis to stay execution of the warrant").

1565 *See* Lockwood v. DeLeon, Index No. BALT 654-09 (Suffolk Cnty. Dist. Ct. Nov. 17, 2009) (unreported decision).

CHAPTER 13

STIPULATIONS OF SETTLEMENT

A Stipulation of Settlement is a binding agreement (often resolving the litigation) that will generally be enforced where there is substantial non-compliance.[1566] When the Tenant consents to the entry of a judgment of possession and a warrant of eviction, often in consideration for additional time to remain in possession of the premises and/or a reduction in rent arrears, a post-judgment motion to vacate the judgment to assert affirmative defenses will typically be denied.[1567] In other words, affirmative defenses, including defects in the predicate notice, are waived as a result of the Stipulation of Settlement.[1568] An agreement need not be So Ordered by the Court to be enforced.

A hearing is required where there are issues of fact regarding compliance and/or enforcement of a stipulated resolution.[1569] For example,

1566 *See* Shalimar Leasing, LP v. Medina, 155 N.Y.S.3d 520 (App. Term, 2d, 11th & 13th Jud. Dists. 2021) (noting that "[i]t was not until after the stipulation was signed and a tenant organizer in her building reviewed the stipulation of settlement that [the Tenant] expressed dissatisfaction with its terms"); 2345 Crotona Gold, LLC v. Dross, 31 N.Y.S.3d 924 (App. Term, 1st Dep't 2016) (motion to vacate Stipulation of Settlement denied absent evidence of fraud or mistake, and Tenant's failure to timely dispute the rent increase); Option One Mortgage Corp. v. Daddi, 60 A.D.3d 920, 874 N.Y.S.2d 822 (2d Dep't 2009) (Stipulation of Settlement constitutes a waiver of affirmative defenses).

1567 *See* HSBC Bank USA, N.A. v. Posy, 55 N.Y.S.3d 692 (App. Term, 9th & 10th Jud. Dists. 2017); Michalak v. Fechtel, 911 N.Y.S.2d 693 (App. Term, 9th & 10th Jud. Dists. 2010).

1568 *See* 448 LLC v. Butcher's Choice Meat Mkt., 113 N.Y.S.3d 792 (App. Term, 1st Dep't 2019); Hernco, LLC v. Hernandez, 9 N.Y.S.3d 593 (App. Term, 2d, 11th & 13th Jud. Dists. 2015); Semen v. Dor, 943 N.Y.S.2d 794 (App. Term, 2d, 11th & 13th Jud. Dists. 2011).

1569 *See generally 448 LLC*, 113 N.Y.S.3d at 825; Agras Realty, LLC v. Susi, 128 N.Y.S.3d 143 (App. Term, 2d, 11th & 13th Jud. Dists. 2020); Durst Pyramid, LLC v. Griffin, 135 N.Y.S.3d 751 (App. Term, 1st Dep't 2020).

hearings were necessary to determine whether to accelerate a warrant of eviction when the Tenant's "objectionable conduct" raised questions of fact regarding compliance,[1570] and, again, in another proceeding, when the Tenant engaged in "harassing" conduct towards other Tenants.[1571]

A. SETTLEMENT AGREEMENTS ARE PREFERRED

Due to the high volume of cases in the Housing Parts, amongst other reasons, the Court generally encourages negotiated resolutions because the "[p]arties to a civil dispute are free to chart their own litigation course...and [it] is essential to the management of court calendars and the integrity of the litigation process."[1572] For example, in *Banana Kelly Union HDFC v. Chambers*, the stipulation to discontinue the non-payment proceeding was upheld where the agreement was entered into voluntarily and no explanation was provided for the inordinate delay in seeking to restore the proceeding to the Court's calendar.[1573] Similarly, in *Rivera v. Kaba*, the amount of rent awarded to the Landlord was reduced due to a stipulation from a prior, related summary proceeding in which the Landlord did not reserve the right to "seek any amount greater than the [use and occupancy] per month agreed upon...."[1574]

Moreover, the Appellate Term has reasoned that "[l]iteral enforcement of the terms of [a] stipulation of settlement is not unjust..., where the agreement was negotiated by sophisticated parties, all of whom were represented by counsel, and the default was neither inadvertent

1570 *See, e.g.*, Caring Communities Assocs. HDFC v. Boffa, 31 N.Y.S.3d 920 (App. Term, 2d, 11th & 13th Jud. Dists. 2016).

1571 *Durst Pyramid, LLC*, 135 N.Y.S.3d at 751.

1572 191 St. Assocs. LLC v. Cruz, 29 N.Y.S.3d 848 (App. Term, 1st Dep't 2016) (citations omitted); Thomas v. Brown, 29 N.Y.S.3d 850 (App. Term, 1st Dep't 2015); 90th St. Corp. v. 203 W. 90th St. Retail, LLC, 2019 N.Y. Misc. LEXIS 6036 (N.Y. Cnty. Sup. Ct. Nov. 4, 2019); 1700 Harrison LLC v. Whetstone, 151 N.Y.S.3d 620 (N.Y. Civ. Ct. Bronx Cnty. 2021).

1573 41 N.Y.S.3d 448 (App. Term, 1st Dep't 2016) (Landlord waited eleven (11) months before moving to revoke the stipulation).

1574 115 N.Y.S.3d 811 (App. Term, 1st Dep't 2019).

nor trivial."[1575] As such, a party does not have an automatic right to appeal from a final judgment consented to by stipulation,[1576] and a stipulation reserving the Landlord's right to seek attorney's fees in a subsequent plenary action is enforceable.[1577]

A term or condition omitted from the stipulation will not be enforced (or read into the agreement). This includes the absence of a remedy for non-compliance. Accordingly, where the parties agree that rent arrears are owed and the Tenant may continue to remain in possession provided the arrears are paid pursuant to a "payment schedule," the parties should include a provision stating the remedy (typically, a judgment of possession, a money judgment for the remaining rent arrears, and a warrant of eviction) in the event the Tenant fails to comply. Otherwise, the Court is without authority to grant such relief in the summary proceeding, even where there is ample showing of non-compliance.[1578] Instead, to regain possession of the premises, the Landlord would have to commence a declaratory judgment action in the Supreme Court (to enforce the stipulation) or a new summary proceeding in the event there is an unrelated subsequent breach of the rental agreement.[1579]

1575 580 Park Ave., Inc. v. Mirto, 116 N.Y.S.3d 843 (App. Term, 1st Dep't 2019); CS 393 LLC v. Toledano, 116 N.Y.S.3d 869 (N.Y. Civ. Ct. N.Y. Cnty. 2019).

1576 Kitty Holding Corp. v. Corriette, 138 N.Y.S.3d 790 (App. Term, 9th & 10th Jud. Dists. 2021).

1577 *See* Paramount Leasehold, L.P. v. 43rd St. Deli, 173 A.D.3d 421, 102 N.Y.S.3d 182 (1st Dep't 2019) (party does "not waive its rights to attorneys' fees by postponing its application therefor until after the merits determination"); Landlord Grand Concourse Estates LLC v. Ture, 114 N.Y.S.3d 804 (App. Term, 1st Dep't 2019); Win Feng LLC v. Lawrence, 110 N.Y.S.3d 774 (App. Term, 1st Dep't 2018). *Cf.* Rego Park Ventures, LLC v. Shany, 158 N.Y.S.3d 747 (App. Term, 2d, 11th & 13th Jud. Dists. 2022) (enforcing stipulation provision waiving the right to assert allegations in a subsequent proceeding).

1578 *See* 133 Plus 24 Sanford Ave. Realty Corp. v. Ni, 7 N.Y.S.3d 819 (App. Term, 2d, 11th & 13th Jud. Dists. 2015); Gloria Homes Apts. LP v. Wilson, 17 N.Y.S.3d 382 (App. Term, 1st Dep't 2015) ("Since the parties' intent is not clear from the face of the stipulation, the hearing court should have made findings on the issue").

1579 *See* Wallkill Affordable Senior Hous., L.P. v. Powell, 127 N.Y.S.3d 693 (App. Term, 9th & 10th Jud. Dists. 2020) (vacating judgment of possession where the stipulation provided that in the event of a breach, the proceeding "[s]hall be restored to the Court's calendar"); *133 Plus 24 Sanford Ave. Realty Corp.*, 7 N.Y.S.3d at 819; Lucky 9911 LLC v. Giron, 130 N.Y.S.3d 606 (N.Y. Civ. Ct. Queens Cnty. 2020); East 53 BSD LLC v. Hosang, 129 N.Y.S.3d 267 (N.Y. Civ. Ct. Kings Cnty. 2020).

Enforcement of a Stipulation of Settlement is determined on a case-by-case basis. Courts have upheld stipulated terms in all of the following situations: where a commercial Tenant failed to replace the awning in front of the premises;[1580] a Landlord was denied "access" to make repairs;[1581] a Tenant's repeated non-compliance with payment terms;[1582] the Tenant's substantial compliance with negotiated payment terms;[1583] the issuance of a warrant of eviction with the consent of a *pro se* Tenant, the execution of which was stayed approximately four (4) months;[1584] the waiver of the security deposit;[1585] a two-attorney Stipulation of Settlement;[1586] a liquidated damages provision valuing use and occupancy at two (2) times the value of the final rent;[1587] the movant's failure to establish a "legal" basis for vacating the stipulation;[1588] installation of a new roof by a commercial Tenant (without removing the pre-existing

---

1580 *See* Serencha Realty Corp. v. A.M. Two In One, Inc., 31 N.Y.S.3d 924 (App. Term, 1st Dep't 2016); 59-61 E. 3rd St., LLC v. Said, 29 N.Y.S.3d 847 (App. Term, 1st Dep't 2015) (two-attorney stipulation enforced against commercial Tenant where Landlord was <u>not</u> provided "free and unfettered" access to make renovations).

1581 Wira Assocs. v. Easy, 26 N.Y.S.3d 216 (App. Term, 2d, 11th & 13th Jud. Dists. 2015).

1582 Mehr Props., LLC v. Fonrose, 29 N.Y.S.3d 847 (App. Term, 2d, 11th & 13th Jud. Dists. 2015) (Tenant's fourth Order to Show Case denied following repeated defaults of the stipulation); Third Lenox Terr. Assocs. v. Johnson, 950 N.Y.S.2d 611 (App. Term, 1st Dep't 2012) (stay denied notwithstanding Landlord's initial failure to enforce Stipulation of Settlement).

1583 *See* 164-03 v. Alsamet, 148 N.Y.S.3d 330 (App. Term, 2d, 11th & 13th Jud. Dists. 2021) (restoring Tenant to possession due to compliance with stipulated payment schedule).

1584 Molinelli v. Goulbourne-Fontan, 138 N.Y.S.3d 790 (App. Term, 2d, 11th & 13th Jud. Dists. 2021).

1585 90th St. Corp. v. 203 W. 90th St. Retail, LLC, 187 A.D.3d 497, 130 N.Y.S.3d 310 (1st Dep't 2020) (absent an unjust or inequitable result, stipulation enforced where the parties "were sophisticated business persons represented by counsel").

1586 *Durst Pyramid, LLC*, 135 N.Y.S.3d at 751.

1587 723 Edibles, Inc. v. 721 Borrower, LLC, 150 N.Y.S.3d 896 (N.Y. Sup. Ct. N.Y. Cnty. 2021) (noting the "[s]tipulation's liquidated-damages provision awards use and occupancy at twice the monthly rent should the tenant not vacate as agreed, rather than seven times [the] rent [which] in the context of a commercial tenancy, is not an unenforceable penalty").

1588 Alvarez v. Strujan, 110 N.Y.S.3d 865 (App. Term, 1st Dep't 2018).

roof);[1589] an undue duress claim asserted more than one (1) year after the stipulation was signed;[1590] and when a *pro se* Tenant "understood the terms of the stipulation and received ample consideration for [the] agreement to vacate."[1591]

B. UNENFORCEABLE SETTLEMENT AGREEMENTS

There have also been numerous instances where Stipulations of Settlement have not been enforced. A Stipulation of Settlement will not be enforced, even where there is substantial compliance, when: (1) enforcement "would be unjust or inequitable" or otherwise "permit the other party to gain an unconscionable advantage";[1592] (2) the stipulation "was entered into inadvisably or...it would be inequitable to hold the parties" to its terms;[1593] or (3) where there is "evidence of fraud, [mistake], overreaching, unconscion[able conduct] or illegality."[1594] In other words, the Court retains the authority to vacate a judgment

1589 Islip Theaters, LLC v. Landmark Plaza Props. Corp., 183 A.D.3d 872, 124 N.Y.S.3d 367 (2d Dep't 2020) (noting that "[c]ontrary to the landlord's contention, the stipulation did not require that the preexisting roof be removed as a precondition to the installation of the new roof").

1590 Maxwell Dev., L.P. v. France, 111 N.Y.S.3d 517 (N.Y. Civ. Ct. N.Y. Cnty. 2018).

1591 Skeete v. Bah, 29 N.Y.S.3d 849 (App. Term, 1st Dep't 2015); 35 Jackson House Apts. Corp. v. Yaworski, 29 N.Y.S.3d 850 (App. Term, 2d, 11th & 13th Jud. Dists. 2015) (two-attorney stipulation strictly enforced against Tenant who failed to provide the licenses of repair workers), *aff'd*, 163 A.D.3d 805, 83 N.Y.S.3d 62 (2d Dep't 2018).

1592 368 Chauncey Ave. Trust v. Whitaker, 911 N.Y.S.2d 696 (App. Term, 2d, 11th & 13th Jud. Dists. 2010); Ross Realty v. KBS Tires, LLC, 108 N.Y.S.3d 264 (App. Term, 9th & 10th Jud. Dists. 2018); PK Mgmt., LLC v. Baumann, 110 N.Y.S.3d 780 (App. Term, 9th & 10th Jud. Dists. 2018).

1593 600 Hylan Assocs. v. Polshak, 851 N.Y.S.2d 74 (App. Term, 2d & 11th Jud. Dists. 2007) (granting counsel's motion to vacate Stipulation of Settlement and final judgment against the then-unrepresented Tenant where a viable laches defense was asserted); *see also* 2701 Grand Assoc. LLC v. Morel, 31 N.Y.S.3d 924 (App. Term, 1st Dep't 2016) (vacating Stipulation of Settlement and final judgment for rent-regulated premises where the Tenant, now represented by counsel, asserted rent overcharge claim following an 88% rent increase).

1594 *See* Chelsea 19 Assocs. v. James, 67 A.D.3d 601, at 602, 889 N.Y.S.2d 564, 566 (1st Dep't 2009) (Tenant's "loss of possession is not a forfeiture but 'merely the contracted-for consequence' of his non-compliance with the stipulation"); Hallock v. State of New York, 64 N.Y.2d 224, at 230, 485 N.Y.S.2d 510, 512-13 (1984).

and warrant, and, in the process, deny enforcement of a Stipulation of Settlement, for "good cause" or other sufficient grounds to invalidate the agreement.[1595]

Where the parties bifurcate the summary proceeding by settling the issue of possession without resolving the monetary claims, the Court no longer retains jurisdiction to issue a money judgment even where the stipulation reserves such right.[1596] Instead, the Landlord would have to commence a separate plenary proceeding for monetary relief.

In *125 Ct. St., LLC v. Nicholson*, the Appellate Term for the Second, Eleventh and Thirteenth Judicial Districts vacated two (2) stipulations and dismissed the holdover proceeding where the Landlord charged "preferential" rent in excess of the legally permissible "[r]egulated rent listed in the last preceding registration statement."[1597] Similarly, stipulations have not been enforced where: the attorney lacked actual and/or apparent authority to enter into the agreement;[1598] the guardian *ad litem* lacked capacity to enter into the Stipulation on behalf of the ward;[1599] the Tenant retained counsel after entering into the Stipulation;[1600] the Landlord refused to submit the requisite W-9 Form for payment of the rent arrears;[1601] the *pro se* Tenant was evicted the day before enter-

1595 Saavedra v. Mor, 150 N.Y.S.3d 211 (App. Term, 2d, 11th & 13th Jud. Dists. 2021).

1596 Steinmetz v. Oyala, 142 N.Y.S.3d 273 (App. Term 2d, 11th & 13th Jud. Dists. 2021).

1597 115 N.Y.S.3d 817 (App. Term, 2d, 11th & 13th Jud, Dists. 2019).

1598 *See* Bank of New York v. Betancourt, 950 N.Y.S.2d 721 (App. Term, 9th & 10th Jud. Dists. 2012). *But see* Roxborough Apts. Corp. v. Hussein, 110 N.Y.S.3d 775 (App. Term, 2d, 11th & 13th Jud. Dists. 2018) (two-attorney stipulation enforced where Tenant's attorney, at minimum, had apparent authority to enter into the agreement to resolve the non-payment proceeding); 150-15 Flushing LLC v. Batista, 101 N.Y.S.3d 700 (App. Term, 2d, 11th & 13th Jud. Dists. 2018) (enforcing two-attorney stipulation absent proof that Landlord's counsel lacked apparent authority to enter into the agreement).

1599 New York Found. For Senior Citizens v. Hamilton, 170 A.D.3d 543, 96 N.Y.S.3d 52 (1st Dep't 2019).

1600 1901 Hennessy LLC v. Vicente, 122 N.Y.S.3d 487 (App. Term, 1st Dep't 2020) (holding that the Court "favorably exercise[s] our discretion to relieve [the Tenant] of her uncounseled decision to consent to a possessory judgment, and allow her to defend the holdover petition on the merits").

1601 Dino Realty Corp. v. Khan, 3 N.Y.S.3d 259 (App. Term, 2d, 11th & 13th Jud. Dists. 2014); Eubanks v. Kinsler, 2020 N.Y.L.J. LEXIS 1083 (N.Y. Civ. Ct. Kings Cnty. July 1, 2020).

ing into a stipulation waiving "several meritorious defenses;"[1602] the Department of Social Services approved payment of the arrears;[1603] the stipulation with a *pro se* Tenant included a money judgment "substantially in excess" of the amount demanded within the Petition;[1604] the Landlord failed to file an annual rent registration barring the rent increase;[1605] the *pro se* Tenant agreed to a "time is of the essence" provision within the stipulation;[1606] the money judgment negotiated by the Landlord's attorney and *pro se* Tenant included impermissible items;[1607] and to avoid an unnecessary eviction.[1608]

In addition, the Appellate Term for the First Department held in a plenary action that the Tenant was <u>not</u> liable for post-surrender rent, nearly one (1) year after vacating the premises, notwithstanding the parties' agreement in a <u>prior</u> non-payment proceeding that the settlement was "without prejudice to claims for past and future rents."[1609] The Court deemed the vacating to be a surrender by operation of law, and, as a result, the agreement preserving claims for future rent was <u>not</u> a resolution of the issue (or admission), but rather a "clear acknowledgment by the parties that any monetary claims arising from the proposed surrender have yet to be decided."[1610] As a result, and further noting that the Landlord had subsequently received rents from a new

---

1602 Chauncey Equities, LLC v. Murphy, 112 N.Y.S.3d 861 (App. Term, 2d, 11th & 13th Jud. Dists. 2019).

1603 Gerard Ct. Assocs., LLC v. Hamer, 31 N.Y.S.3d 921 (App. Term, 1st Dep't 2016).

1604 Rochdale Vil. v. Baker, 2021 N.Y. Misc. LEXIS 4474 (N.Y. Civ. Ct. Queens Cnty. May 4, 2021).

1605 Samson Mgmt. v. Cordero, 112 N.Y.S.3d 422 (App. Term, 9th & 10th Jud. Dists. 2018).

1606 Trump Park Ave. LLC v. Summers, 2016 N.Y.L.J. LEXIS 4991 (N.Y. Civ. Ct. N.Y. Cnty. March 17, 2016).

1607 Nu Horizons Manor v. Adderly, 951 N.Y.S.2d 87 (Suffolk Cnty. Dist. Ct. 2012).

1608 332 EDC Realty Corp. v. Barlow, 990 N.Y.S.2d 440 (N.Y. Civ. Ct. Kings Cnty. 2014) (holding that the Petitioner should accept the late payment so as to avoid an unnecessary eviction where the Tenant changed his mind and opted to remain in possession).

1609 *See* Rockaway One Co. LLC v. Alston, 116 N.Y.S.3d 844 (App. Term, 1st Dep't 2019).

1610 *Id.* (opining that "it would 'def[y] logic' for defendant to vacate her stabilized apartment of many years, while also agreeing to pay rent for one year after her vacatur").

Tenant, the Court limited the money judgment to the amount owed for the months the Tenant occupied the premises.[1611]

A stipulation that waives the protections afforded under the Rent Stabilization Code, even when the waiver may be beneficial to the Tenant, is similarly unenforceable.[1612] In *1010 Realty, LLC v. Dixon*, the stipulation authorizing an eviction if the Tenant (who had obtained possession by asserting succession rights) "unreasonably rejected" a lease for a two-bedroom apartment was not enforced.[1613] Noting that the Tenant had a legal right to a renewal lease under the Rent Stabilization Code, the Court concluded that an eviction was improper because "an agreement by the tenant to waive the benefit of any provision of the [Rent Stabilization Law] or [the RSC] is void," and further unenforceable as a matter of public policy.[1614]

C. THE COURT'S DISCRETIONARY AUTHORITY

The Court is not "[b]ound by language in the stipulation stating that any default shall be deemed material"[1615] or that a resulting default should be "deemed *de minimis*."[1616] In addition, the Court may not unilaterally modify the terms of the parties' agreement to make a stipulation enforceable.[1617]

Amendments to the Petition should be memorialized in the stipulation or, at minimum, placed on the record. For example, if the Petition

---

1611 *Id.*

1612 RSC [9 N.Y.C.R.R.] § 2520.13; *see* 8 Beach St. Realty Inc. v. Blagg, 20 N.Y.S.3d 291 (App. Term, 1st Dep't 2015).

1613 147 N.Y.S.3d 866 (App. Term, 2d, 11th & 13th Jud. Dists. 2021); 164-03, LLC v. Poblete, 122 N.Y.S.3d 487 (App. Term 2d, 11th & 13th Jud. Dists. 2020) (restoring Tenant to possession because a waiver of benefits is unenforceable under the RSC).

1614 *1010 Realty, LLC*, 147 N.Y.S.3d at 866.

1615 Boston Rd. Brooklyn, L.P. v. Steptoe, 92 N.Y.S.3d 702 (App. Term, 2d, 11th & 13th Jud. Dists. 2017); 135 Amersfort Assoc., LLC v. Jones, 20 N.Y.S.3d 292 (App. Term, 2d, 11th & 13th Jud. Dists. 2015).

1616 GHR Co., LLC v. Sannon, 95 N.Y.S.3d 125 (App. Term, 2d, 11th & 13th Jud. Dists. 2018).

1617 *135 Amersfort Assoc., LLC*, 20 N.Y.S.3d at 292 (holding that the Court may not unilaterally change the date of rent payments).

alleges rent arrears for the months of April and May, but the settlement is not reached until June, and it is further agreed that June's rent is to be included within the Stipulation of Settlement, then the Petitioner must amend the Petition to include the rent for June. Otherwise, the June portion of the money judgment may not be enforced in the event there is a dispute regarding compliance.[1618]

It is prudent to require dispositive Stipulations of Settlement to be in writing. It goes without saying that the parties should carefully draft the stipulation to ensure that the agreement accurately reflects that which was agreed.[1619] Any ambiguity within a Stipulation of Settlement may be construed against the drafter.[1620] It is equally well-established that the Court will typically rely upon an otherwise unambiguous Stipulation of Settlement absent clear evidence that the document does not accurately reflect the parties' agreement.[1621] To the extent the Court's pre-printed Stipulation of Settlement Form contradicts any handwritten notations, the handwritten notes usually take precedent.[1622]

D. RPAPL § 746—SETTLEMENTS INVOLVING UNREPRESENTED LITIGANTS

The Legislature passed RPAPL § 746 to reduce ambiguity in settlement agreements by requiring the Court to "fully describe the terms of the stipulation" (other than for an adjournment or a stay of the proceeding) to *pro se* litigants. Accordingly, where a *pro se* litigant reaches a settlement, the individual may not simply send written correspondence

1618 Nathanson v. Mitchell, 836 N.Y.S.2d 487 (Nassau Cnty. Dist. Ct. 2007); *see* 201 W. 136 St. Realty MNGMNT LLC v. Roman, 957 N.Y.S.2d 267 (N.Y. Civ. Ct. N.Y. Cnty. 2012).

1619 *See generally* 23rd Chelsea Assocs. LLC v. Stone, 115 N.Y.S.3d 811 (App. Term, 1st Dep't 2019) (remanding case to Housing Part to determine, in part, whether the *pro se* Tenant's purported signature on the stipulation was "genuine").

1620 125-127 Allen St. Assocs. v. Lin, 122 N.Y.S.3d 488 (App. Term, 1st Dep't 2020).

1621 Banos v. Rhea, 25 N.Y.3d 266, 11 N.Y.S.3d 515 (2015); 615 Pelham Realty, Inc. v. Herring, 984 N.Y.S.2d 634 (App. Term, 1st Dep't 2014).

1622 *See* Hudson Towers Hous. Co., Inc. v. VIP Yacht Cruises, Inc., 63 A.D.3d 413, 881 N.Y.S.2d 46 (1st Dep't 2009).

or submit the Stipulation of Settlement to the Clerk of the Court. Instead, the parties must appear, and the Court will affirmatively explain the terms of the agreement.

1. PRO SE LITIGANTS MUST BE PRESENT

If a *pro se* litigant reaches a settlement but fails to appear before the Court, then the case may be adjourned to another date. A default judgment will typically not be granted against the non-appearing Respondent due to the proposed stipulation. A subsequent non-appearance may result in a default, and the relief granted would typically mirror the terms of the parties' agreement to the extent the Court has the authority to grant such relief. The parties should be mindful that a money judgment is limited to the amount sought in the Petition, unless previously amended, notwithstanding an agreement to include another month's rent in the proposed stipulation.

2. COURT COLLOQUY

Effective March 22, 2022, RPAPL § 746 was amended, and the statute now lists the topics of inquiry that must be included within the Court's on the record colloquy prior to accepting a Stipulation of Settlement involving an unrepresented litigant.[1623] Previously, the inquiry was left to the discretion of the Court.

The colloquy with the *pro se* litigant must include all of the following inquiries: (1) confirmation of the parties' identities and whether all necessary parties have been named in the proceeding; (2) the authority of the signatory, if the named party is not present (presumably this pertains to a litigant that is represented by counsel but is not present); (3) the *pro se* litigant's right to a hearing, and that the right will be waived if the parties settle the claims; (4) whether the adversary's counsel (or client) misrepresented any of the facts, engaged in coercive conduct, or placed undue pressure upon the unrepresented litigant; (5) an inquiry into the *pro se* litigant's acquiescence and/or objections to the allegations in the Petition; (6) confirmation that the *pro se* litigant was fully

1623 *See* RPAPL § 746.

apprised of the available "claims or defenses," and the consequences (waiver) if the stipulation is accepted; (7) a full and accurate description of the stipulated terms; (8) in a non-payment proceeding, whether the *pro se* litigant intends to apply for public assistance or other financial assistance to satisfy the rent arrears; and (9) an inquiry into the *pro se* litigant's understanding of the implications of a judgment, and the legal requirement that a satisfaction of judgment must be provided when the arrears are paid in full.[1624]

In the interests of justice, the Court may omit from the inquiry any "topic" that is rendered irrelevant due to prior Court appearances, the history of the case, or for other satisfactory reasons.[1625] A reason for the omission must be stated on the record. The statute further permits the judge's Court Attorney to conduct the conference.[1626] However, a Court Attorney is not a "[s]ubstitute for an allocution by the Court and, where [a conference with a Court Attorney] is used, the results shall be reported to the court, which shall note on the record that such conference occurred."[1627]

The provisions of RPAPL § 746 are not applicable where both parties are represented by counsel. When both sides have counsel, it is customary to confirm on the record that the attorneys explained the terms and obligations of the stipulation to their clients.

E. A SPOUSE MAY NOT BIND ANOTHER SPOUSE TO A SETTLEMENT

Where the Tenants are spouses, but only one (1) of the spouses appears in Court, the appearing spouse may not sign a stipulation on behalf of (or otherwise bind) the non-appearing spouse.[1628] When proper service is alleged, the Court will typically enter a default judgment

1624 *Id.* at § 746(2).

1625 *Id.* at § 746(4).

1626 *Id.* at § 746(3).

1627 *Id.*

1628 *See* GOL § 3-305; Pinpoint Techs. 3, LLC v. Mogilevsky, 15 N.Y.S.3d 714 (App. Term, 2d, 11th & 13th Jud. Dists. 2015) (breach of contract). Parenthetically, a parent may not appear on behalf of her adult daughter who is also a party in the proceeding. *See 2701 Grand Assoc. LLC*, 31 N.Y.S.3d at 924.

against the non-appearing spouse similar to the terms agreed to by the appearing spouse.[1629] In several of the Housing Parts, the money judgments may be for different amounts because only the amount sought in the Petition, unless previously amended, may be awarded against a non-appearing Tenant. However, the reader should be mindful that Tenants to a rental agreement are united in interest, and, as a result, the liability of one (1) may be conferred equally upon all. Accordingly, where only some of the Tenants appear in Court, the resulting judgments, including the monetary relief, may be identical.[1630]

To avoid potential windfalls, the Court may require confirmation on the record that if the appearing spouse complies with the Stipulation of Settlement, then the Petitioner will not seek to enforce the judgment and warrant against the non-appearing spouse. These same principles apply when the Respondents are not married.[1631]

F. LANDLORDS' ACCEPTANCE OF FUTURE MONEY

Although a money judgment in a summary proceeding is limited to arrears that have already accrued, the parties may include within the Stipulation of Settlement a provision regarding the payment of future months' rent or use and occupancy. This typically arises when additional moneys will become due prior to full compliance with the stipulation. As discussed below, although perhaps referred to within the stipulation, future moneys may not be included within the money

1629 *See 2701 Grand Assoc. LLC*, 31 N.Y.S.3d at 924 (vacating judgment against both Tenants, including the non-appearing co-Tenant, where rent overcharge claim asserted); *but see* Linden Lefferts, LLC v. Cox, 924 N.Y.S.2d 724 (App. Term, 2d, 11th & 13th Jud. Dists. 2011) (Subtenant's motion to vacate default granted where his spouse, also a Subtenant, entered into an agreement with the Landlord and other occupants).

1630 *See* Rossi v. Scott, 52 N.Y.S.3d 248 (App. Term, 9th & 10th Jud. Dists. 2017); Oakwood Terrace Hous. Corp. v. Monk, 36 N.Y.S.3d 48 (App. Term, 9th & 10th Jud. Dists. 2016); Priegue v. Paulus, 988 N.Y.S.2d 525 (App. Term, 9th & 10th Jud. Dists. 2014).

1631 *See* Fieldbridge Assoc., LLC v. Robinson, 155 N.Y.S.3d 524 (App. Term, 2d, 11th & 13th Jud. Dists. 2021) (money judgment against non-appearing Respondent vacated where non-party family member (not the Respondent) signed the stipulation).

judgment issued by the Housing Part in a summary proceeding under any circumstance.

1. STIPULATION CONSENTING TO A JUDGMENT AND WARRANT WITH STAY

Presume in a non-payment proceeding the parties reach a settlement that includes a final judgment of possession, a money judgment, and a warrant of eviction, and the enforcement of the warrant of eviction is stayed for a definite period (e.g., three (3) months) to give the Tenant an opportunity to pay the arrears without an eviction. For this hypothetical, further presume the parties agree that the Landlord is entitled to compensation for each additional month the Tenant remains in possession during the three (3) month stay. Finally, one (1) week after entering the agreement, the judgment and warrant of eviction are issued at the Landlord's request with the appropriate stays on execution.

In both residential and commercial non-payment proceedings (whether resolved by settlement, motion, or following a hearing on the merits), the Court must vacate the judgment and warrant of eviction if the Tenant pays (or deposits with the Court) the full amount of arrears or satisfies the money judgment prior to the execution of the warrant of eviction, unless the rent had been withheld in "bad faith."[1632] For residential properties, to avoid this occurrence, the Landlord will typically seek to include provisions within the stipulation that state: (1) any moneys received for a period following the issuance of the judgment is deemed "use and occupancy" (as opposed to rent) and (2) that "future payments are not intended to revive the tenancy."[1633] Otherwise, if the acceptance of a subsequent payment is construed as an intent to enter into a new tenancy, then both the judgment of possession and warrant

1632 RPAPL § 749(3) (HSTPA, L. 2019, ch. 36, § 19, Part M).

1633 As discussed in Chapter 5, *supra*, the term "rent" represents payment to occupy property pursuant to a Landlord and Tenant agreement (which would vitiate the judgment and warrant) and "use and occupancy" represents the reasonable value to occupy real property absent such an agreement (acceptance by the Landlord does not vitiate the judgment or warrant). In other words, the acceptance of subsequent "rent" payments nullify the judgment of possession and warrant of eviction due to the establishment of a new tenancy.

of eviction may be nullified.[1634] The money judgment in favor of the Landlord would, however, remain unaffected.

For commercial properties, the Landlord's acceptance of rent for a future month following issuance of the judgment is permitted provided the parties did not intend to continue the tenancy. In other words, a commercial Landlord may accept the payment of rent following issuance of the judgment and warrant without vitiating the warrant provided there is no intent to revive the tenancy.[1635]

A prevailing Landlord in a non-payment proceeding may refrain from submitting a proposed judgment and warrant for a "reasonable period" of time and continue to accept the payment of rent without jeopardizing the award. However, once issued, an inordinate delay prior to the execution of the warrant may result in a "stale warrant." In some locations, the Sheriff will not enforce a warrant three (3) months following issuance. Upon a satisfactory explanation, however, the Court may issue a duplicate warrant. The parties should familiarize themselves with the local rules and protocols regarding the issuance and enforcement of judgments and warrants.

2. STIPULATION ACKNOWLEDGING RENT ARREARS ARE OWED (WITHOUT A JUDGMENT)

Another common scenario occurs when the parties reach an agreement on the amount of the rent arrears, but the Tenant is given time to pay the arrears prior to the issuance of a judgment and warrant. The consideration for the additional time is typically the immediate issuance of a final judgment of possession, a money judgment, and a warrant of eviction, without stay, if the Tenant fails to make a scheduled payment. To obtain the judgment, the Landlord will typically submit an

---

1634 Compare with RPAPL § 711(1), which states that in a holdover proceeding based upon the occupants' rental agreement expiring, the Landlord's "[a]cceptance of rent after commencement of the special proceeding upon this ground shall not terminate such proceeding nor effect any award of possession to the landlord or to the new lessee, as the case may be."

1635 *See* First Citizens Nat'l Bank v. Koronowski, 46 A.D.3d 1474, at 1475, 848 N.Y.S.2d 494, 495 (4th Dep't 2007).

ex parte (without notice) affidavit of non-compliance.[1636]

A finding of non-compliance may only be based upon the Tenant's failure to pay the rent arrears. Non-compliance may not be based on the failure to pay a future month's rent.[1637] Accordingly, a Landlord may seek to include a provision within the stipulation that states: "all payments going forward will first be applied towards the current month's rent, and any additional monies thereafter shall be applied to the arrears." This means that the Tenant must be current on both the rent and the rent arrears to be in compliance with the stipulation.[1638]

For example, in *368 Chauncey Ave. Trust v. Whitaker*, the judgment and warrant of eviction were upheld where the stipulation provided that "any monies received would first be applied to the current rent."[1639] The Appellate Term denied a stay on the execution of the warrant because the Tenant failed to substantially comply with the payment of rent arrears.[1640] Absent such a provision, the monies would first be applied towards the arrears which would require the Landlord to commence a new summary proceeding if the Tenant failed to pay a subsequent month's rent.[1641]

The parties' agreement may alter this outcome where the payments are allocated in an alternative manner. In *78-14 Roosevelt, LLC v. Hamilton-Madison House, Inc.*, the Appellate Term for the Second, Eleventh and Thirteenth Judicial Districts denied the Landlord's non-compliance claim because the stipulation provided that following a specific payment, the remainder of the rent arrears were deemed to have been fully satisfied.[1642] As

---

1636 An affidavit of non-compliance is a sworn statement of a person with firsthand knowledge of the breach, and, as such, an attorney affirmation is generally insufficient. *See PK Mgmt., LLC*, 110 N.Y.S.3d at 780 (failed to submit affidavit of non-compliance).

1637 Fairgate Assocs., Inc. v. Adams, 2002 N.Y. Misc. LEXIS 914 (App. Term, 1st Dep't July 29, 2002); *201 W. 136 St. Realty MNGMNT LLC*, 957 N.Y.S.2d at 267.

1638 *See* 1215 Realty Assocs., LLC v. Thomas, 934 N.Y.S.2d 35 (App. Term, 2d, 11th & 13th Jud. Dists. 2011) (motion to stay execution of warrant of eviction denied where Tenant failed to pay rent while arrears were outstanding); *368 Chauncey Ave. Trust*, 911 N.Y.S.2d at 696.

1639 911 N.Y.S.2d 696 (App. Term, 2d, 11th & 13th Jud. Dists. 2010).

1640 *Id.*

1641 *600 Hylan Assocs.*, 851 N.Y.S.2d at 74; AMML Realty Corp. v. Townsend, 117 N.Y.S.3d 808 (Mt. Vernon City Ct. 2019); *Nathanson*, 836 N.Y.S.2d at 487.

1642 100 N.Y.S.3d 611 (App. Term, 2d, 11th & 13th Jud. Dists. 2018).

a result, the Tenant's failure to pay a subsequent month's rent did not constitute a breach of the stipulation (but rather Landlord could assert the claim in a new non-payment proceeding).[1643]

When the stipulation extends into a new month or months, the Respondent may be inclined to pay the arrears in full before the next month's rent accrues. This is because once the arrears are satisfied, the non-payment proceeding is immediately deemed resolved, and any additional or future breaches would necessitate a new proceeding. In other words, if the arrears are paid in full, for example, in June (regardless of whether they are paid early or on schedule), then the failure to pay July's rent would not constitute a default of the Stipulation of Settlement, and the Landlord would have to commence a new non-payment proceeding.

Consider the following hypothetical situation: the parties enter into a Stipulation of Settlement on April 15th where it is agreed: (1) the monthly rent is $1,500; (2) $500 in rent arrears are owed; and (3) the arrears will be paid in two (2) equal installments of $250 on May 15th and June 15th. Further presume it is agreed that the monies paid going forward will first be applied to the current month's rent and then towards the arrears, and that the rent for May and June is due on May 1st and June 1st, respectively.

If the arrears ($500) are paid before June 1st, then the Tenant will have complied with the stipulation, and the failure to pay the June rent may not be a basis for granting a judgment or warrant of eviction. Instead, the Landlord would have to commence a new proceeding on proper notice.

However, if in the same scenario the Tenant paid the May rent ($1,500) on May 1st, plus $250 in arrears on May 15th and an additional $1,500 on June 1st, and no additional payments were tendered thereafter, then the Tenant would not be in compliance, and a judgment and warrant may be issued. This is because after applying the June 1st payment ($1,500) towards June's rent, the Tenant would be delinquent on the second payment of rent arrears ($250) as of June 16th.

1643 *Id.* Since the Tenant had already been evicted, the Landlord's remedy was to commence a plenary action for damages for the subsequent non-payment of rent. *Id.*

CHAPTER 14

COURTROOM PROCEDURES AND PROTOCOLS

Although appearing without counsel is strongly discouraged, individuals are permitted to represent themselves in a summary proceeding. However, a non-attorney may not represent another individual.[1644] In addition, a person holding a Power of Attorney (if not also a duly admitted attorney authorized to practice law) is prohibited from commencing a summary proceeding or representing another individual because that would constitute the unauthorized practice of law.[1645] A Power of Attorney may grant the holder the limited authority to sign

1644 *See* Porter v. New York City Hous. Auth., 169 A.D.3d 455, 95 N.Y.S.3d 2 (1st Dep't 2019); Carroll St. Props. v. Velez, 101 N.Y.S.3d 699 (App. Term, 2d, 11th & 13th Jud. Dists. 2018).

1645 Whitehead v. Town House Equities, Ltd., 8 A.D.3d 369, 777 N.Y.S.2d 917 (2d Dep't 2004); Fallarino v. Fallarino, 56 N.Y.S.3d 414 (App. Term, 9th & 10th Jud. Dists. 2017); Pinpoint Techs. 3, LLC v. Mogilevsky, 15 N.Y.S.3d 714 (App. Term, 2d, 11th & 13th Jud. Dists. 2015) (breach of contract claim); 91 E. Main St. Realty Corp. v. Angelic Creations by Lucia, 884 N.Y.S.2d 565, 567 (App. Term, 9th & 10th Jud. Dists. 2009); *see also* Ontario Heights Homeowners Assoc. v. Town of Oswego Planning Bd., 77 A.D.3d 1465, at 1466, 908 N.Y.S.2d 514, 515 (4th Dep't 2010) (party who is not an attorney may not represent co-Petitioners). Of note, the unauthorized practice of law in New York is a misdemeanor. JUD. LAW §§ 478, 485. A civil remedy for the unauthorized practice of law is also available under Judiciary Law § 476-a. In *Harvey v. Proto Prop. Servs.*, the Appellate Term noted an exception applicable to small claims matters in which a party may request that a non-attorney "related by consanguinity or affinity" represent his or her interests, and the Court shall grant the request where it "[f]inds that due to the age, mental or physical capacity or other disability of such party that it is in the interests of justice to permit such representation" 116 N.Y.S.3d 478 (App. Term, 2d, 11th & 13th Jud. Dists. 2019) (*citing* NEW YORK CIV. CT. ACT § 1815). *See also* UNIFORM CITY CT. ACT § 1815; UNIFORM DIST. CT. ACT § 1815; UNIFORM JUST. CT. ACT § 1815.

and/or verify documents on behalf of the party.[1646]

The Appellate Term for the Second, Eleventh and Thirteenth Judicial Districts has held that partnerships and limited partnerships must appear by counsel.[1647] Corporations and limited liability companies must also appear by counsel, except in the Justice Courts where the corporation may appear by an "officer, director or employee of the corporation provided that the appearance by a non-lawyer…shall be deemed to constitute the requisite authority to bind the corporation in a settlement or trial."[1648] An agent of a corporate Landlord, unless a duly admitted attorney, may not commence a summary proceeding on behalf of the entity or in the agent's name on behalf of the entity.[1649] The improper *pro se* filing of a pleading on behalf of a corporate entity is capable of amendment by counsel.[1650]

1646 Aviles v. Santana, 61 N.Y.S.3d 190 (N.Y. Civ. Ct. Bronx Cnty. 2017).

1647 *Carroll St. Props.*, 101 N.Y.S.3d at 699; Ernest & Maryanna Jeremias Family P'ship, L.P. v. Sadykov, 11 N.Y.S.3d 792 (App. Term, 2d, 11th & 13th Jud. Dists. 2015) (holding that as a matter of "policy and uniformity," since partnerships and limited partnerships were "largely subsumed within the definition of voluntary associations when Civil Practice Act § 236 was enacted," these entities require counsel); Oehlrich v. Rosas, 116 N.Y.S.3d 870 (Middletown City Ct. 2019). *Cf.* Net Leased Real Estate Props., Operating P'ship v. Air Chef, Inc., 2014 N.Y. Misc. LEXIS 2793 (N.Y. Cnty. Sup. Ct. June 20, 2014) ("[a] partnership that is not a registered limited liability partnership may appear *pro se* in a civil action").

1648 CPLR § 321(a). *See* Hamilton Livery Leasing, LLC v. State of New York, 151 A.D.3d 1358, 58 N.Y.S.3d 624 (3d Dep't 2017); Michael Reilly Design, Inc. v. Houraney, 40 A.D.3d 592, at 593-94, 835 N.Y.S.2d 640, 641 (2d Dep't 2007). See also Uniform Just. Ct. Act § 501.

1649 *See* Lehtonen v. Dellaquila, 128 N.Y.S.3d 410 (App. Term, 9th & 10th Jud. Dists. 2020); *Carroll St. Props.*, 101 N.Y.S.3d at 699; Inland Diversified Real Estate Serv., LLC v. Keiko New York, Inc., 36 N.Y.S.3d 407 (App. Term, 9th & 10th Jud. Dists. 2016); *Oehlrich*, 116 N.Y.S.3d at 870.

1650 *Hamilton Livery Leasing, LLC*, 151 A.D.3d at 1358, 58 N.Y.S.3d at 624 (holding that a corporation's *pro se* filing of the complaint may be cured by counsel's subsequent notice of appearance and signature affixed to the pleading); Plank, LLC v. Dutch Vill., LLC, 113 N.Y.S.3d 485 n.2 (Albany Cnty. Sup. Ct. 2019) (same).

A. CALL OF THE CALENDAR

There is no formula for handling a Housing Part calendar. However, at all times, judges must "require order and decorum" in the courtroom and "[b]e patient, dignified and courteous to litigants, jurors, witnesses, lawyers and others with whom the judge deals in an official capacity."[1651] This Chapter is intended to provide an overview of courtroom procedure and an insight as to what an individual may expect in Court. The descriptions should not in any way be construed as a comment or opinion on any courtroom procedure.

During the first call of the Calendar, which begins at approximately 9:30 a.m., Stipulations of Settlements are typically heard first, followed by attorney applications for adjournments.[1652] The remainder of the Calendar is then called. The parties are routinely directed to conference their case prior to the second call of the Calendar, which does not begin before 10:30 a.m. In some locations, the Judge may direct the parties to participate in mediation or other form of alternative dispute resolution available in the courthouse.

Adjournment requests are entertained during first call from both counsel and *pro se* litigants. Either party in a summary proceeding is entitled to one (1) adjournment "[a]t the time issue is joined" (i.e., for practical purposes, the return date of the Petition).[1653] Real Property Actions and Proceedings Law § 745(1) provides that the adjournment must be for not less than fourteen (14) days, unless the parties consent to a shorter adjournment. The granting or denial of subsequent ad-

---

1651 22 N.Y.C.R.R. [Rules of Judicial Conduct] § 100.3(B)(2),(3); *see* Matter of Miller, 35 N.Y.3d 484, 133 N.Y.S.3d 218 (2020) (directing removal of judge whose [m] isconduct in the aggregate [including inappropriate behavior and conduct towards Court staff and misreporting of financials], along with his prior disciplinary history, [] 'exhibited a pattern of injudicious behavior...which cannot be viewed as acceptable conduct by one holding judicial office'"); Matter of O'Connor, 32 N.Y.3d 121, 87 N.Y.S.3d 140 (2018) (imposing "severe sanction" of removal from judicial office where "jurist [] exhibited a pattern of injudicious behavior...[that constitutes] an abuse of the power of his office in a manner that...has irredeemably damaged public confidence in the integrity of [the judge's] court") (*quoting* Matter of Jung, 11 N.Y.3d 365, 870 N.Y.S.2d 819 (2008)).

1652 For a discussion on Stipulations of Settlement, *see* Chapter 13, *supra*.

1653 RPAPL § 745(1) (HSTPA, L. 2019, c. 36, Part M, § 17).

journment requests is left to the discretion of the Court.[1654] In deciding a request for a discretionary adjournment, the Court may consider whether the request is "made for the purpose" of delaying the proceedings or the failure to exercise due diligence.[1655]

In New York City, there are additional requirements regarding adjournments. For example, where the Respondent is granted two (2) adjournments or sixty (60) days passes from the first Court appearance, whichever is sooner (not including the days the matter was adjourned at the Petitioner's request), the Court may, upon request, direct that the Respondent deposit with the Court the rent or use and occupancy that will thereafter accrue.[1656] A request for an adjournment on the return date for the purpose of retaining counsel is not considered one (1) of the two (2) allotted adjournments.[1657]

The failure to pay use and occupancy directed by the Court does not constitute a basis for dismissing the Tenant's defenses or counterclaims.[1658] Moreover, the Court has discretion, for "good cause" shown,

---

1654 *Id.* (the statute uses the phrase "[a] party's second or subsequent request for [an] adjournment").

1655 *See* Tuscan Realty Corp. v. O'Neill, 731 N.Y.S.2d 830 (App. Term, 2d & 11th Jud. Dists. 2001); *see also* Slaughter v. Pekich, 128 N.Y.S.3d 780 (App. Term, 9th & 10th Jud. Dists. 2020) (in small claims action, improvident exercise of discretion to deny Tenant's request at trial for an adjournment to retrieve photographs and receipts after the Court ruled it would not review these items on the Tenant's cell phone); New York City Hous. Auth. v. Deraffele, 134 N.Y.S.3d 614 (App. Term, 1st Dep't 2020) (proper to grant brief adjournment to allow party an opportunity to secure a witness familiar with the parties' agreement).

1656 RPAPL § 745(2)(a); *see* Myrtle Venture Five, LLC v. Eye Care Optical of NY, Inc., 11 N.Y.S.3d 796 (App. Term, 2d, 11th & 13th Jud. Dists. 2015) (Court prematurely directed the deposit of use and occupancy where the minimum number of days, not including consent adjournments, had not elapsed following service). Any portion of the rent or use and occupancy paid with a government housing subsidy may not be included within the deposit. *See* RPAPL § 745(2)[c]. A deposit is not required where the Respondent demonstrates that the Petitioner is not a proper party or asserts any of the following defenses: (1) actual eviction; (2) actual partial eviction; (3) constructive eviction; (4) a defense pursuant to SSL § 143-b (section titled, "Avoidance of Abuses in Connection With Rent Checks"); (5) existence of hazardous violations; (6) rent overcharge; (7) illegal apartment; or (8) lack of jurisdiction. *See* RPAPL § 745(2)(a).

1657 RPAPL § 745(2).

1658 *Id.* at § 745(2)(f).

to extend the Respondent's time to tender the deposit.[1659] However, an "excessive" number of adjournment requests by the Landlord may result in the dismissal of the summary proceeding and an award of costs in favor of the Tenant.[1660]

If the Tenant does not appear at first call, the Court may inform the Landlord of any defects in service which unless waived will result in a dismissal. Notwithstanding the defective and/or inadequate proof of service, the Landlord may be inclined to wait until second call in the event the Tenant appears and waives the service deficiencies. Otherwise, the summary proceeding will be dismissed, without prejudice, which means the Landlord may commence a new proceeding (after serving another predicate notice) and the parties may return to Court within a few weeks.

If the Respondent appears without asserting a timely objection to the service defects (typically at the first or second Court appearance), the defense of a lack of personal jurisdiction is waived and the proceeding may continue.[1661] The defense is deemed waived if not timely asserted even when the delay was due to the parties engaging in unsuccessful settlement discussions.[1662] Not surprisingly, some Tenants may be inclined to proceed notwithstanding the defective service due to the more favorable negotiating position and/or to avoid potentially having to return to Court in a subsequent proceeding.

Where the rent is paid in full after a non-payment proceeding was commenced, the Petitioner may seek to withdraw the action. The withdrawal is typically without prejudice to commencing another summary proceeding, if necessary, but only after a new predicate notice is

---

1659 *Id.* at § 745(2)(d)(ii); 1588-1600 AMS LLC v. Gil, 167 N.Y.S.3d 296 (App. Term, 1st Dep't 2022).

1660 RPAPL § 745(2)(e).

1661 *See* Washington v. Palanzo, 746 N.Y.S.2d 875 (App. Term, 9th & 10th Jud. Dists. 2002).

1662 *Id.*; S & S Enters. Realty, Inc. v. Stevenson, 98 N.Y.S.3d 502 (Mt. Vernon City Ct. 2018) (holding that where the Respondent's actions "evinced" an intent to participate in the summary proceeding and "submit to the court's jurisdiction," a motion to dismiss due to a lack of personal jurisdiction will be denied).

served.[1663] If a request is made to discontinue the action "with prejudice" (i.e., precluding another proceeding for the same period or breach), the Tenant must demonstrate prejudice to a substantial right or other special circumstances.[1664]

The second call of the Calendar initially mirrors the first call. Stipulations of Settlement are considered first followed by attorney applications for adjournments. Thereafter, attorney applications for default judgments are entertained where the pleadings are facially sufficient and proper service is alleged.[1665] Applications for default judgments typically may not be considered until at least one (1) hour after the proceeding is initially called, or at least 10:30 a.m.[1666]

The remainder of the Calendar is then called a second time. Oral argument on Orders to Show Cause, which are usually submitted by Respondents seeking to vacate a default judgment or requesting additional time to remain in the premises, and motions to dismiss are then heard, followed by hearings.

1663 *See generally* Elnazer v. Quoquoi, 17 N.Y.S.3d 267 (App. Term, 2d, 11th & 13th Jud. Dists. 2015) (withdrawing the Petition is the procedural equivalent to discontinuing the action without prejudice).

1664 655 Country Rd. Inc. v. Caltagirone, 101 N.Y.S.3d 701 (App. Term, 9th & 10th Jud. Dists. 2018) (due to a "total lack of merit to landlord's claim," the Court granted motion to dismiss the summary proceeding with prejudice); *see generally* Deutsche Bank Nat'l Trust Co. v. Holcomb, 178 A.D.3d 773, 111 N.Y.S.3d 891 (2d Dep't 2019); New York Mortgage Trust, Inc. v. Dasdemir, 116 A.D.3d 679, 985 N.Y.S.2d 86 (2d Dep't 2014); Expedite Video Conf. Servs., Inc. v. Botello, 67 A.D.3d 961, 890 N.Y.S.2d 82 (2d Dep't 2009).

1665 Martine Assocs. LLC v. Minck, 785 N.Y.S.2d 648, 649 (App. Term, 9th & 10th Jud. Dists. 2004); *see* 140 East Hartsdale Ave., LLC v. Brooks, 119 N.Y.S.3d 379 (App. Term, 9th & 10th Jud. Dists. 2019); Bel Air Leasing LP v. Johnston, 157 N.Y.S.3d 346 (N.Y. Civ. Ct. Kings Cnty. 2021). To be awarded a default judgment, the Landlord must provide sufficient proof that the Tenant is not in the military. *See* Riverton Sq. LLC v. McLeod, 57 N.Y.S.3d 677 (App. Term, 1st Dep't 2017); Pascal v. Law Offices of Gilbert C. Parris, 2020 N.Y. Misc. LEXIS 17539 (N.Y. Cnty. Sup. Ct. May 26, 2020).

1666 *See* Uniform Civil Rules for the District Court § 212.42(a); Uniform Civil Rules for the City Courts Outside the City of New York § 210.42(a); Riverwalk on the Hudson, Inc. v. Culliton, 87 N.Y.S.3d 852 n.1 (Albany City Ct. 2018).

B. HEARINGS

1. ROLE OF THE COURT

The overwhelming majority of summary proceedings are resolved prior to a hearing. However, in those instances where an amicable resolution is not attainable, the Petitioner must prove its case at a hearing by a fair preponderance of the evidence.[1667] Represented and *pro se* litigants are held to the same standards.[1668] In rendering its decision, whether orally on the record or in a written decision, the Court must state the "ultimate or essential facts relied upon."[1669]

During the hearing, the Court accepts (or rejects) evidence and assesses the credibility of witnesses.[1670] The Court has no obligation to explain the burden of proof or the admissibility of evidence to a *pro se*

1667 *See* Mautner-Glick Corp. v. Glazer, 31 N.Y.S.3d 922 (App. Term, 1st Dep't 2016), *aff'd*, 148 A.D.3d 515, 48 N.Y.S.3d 587 (1st Dep't 2017); Tello v. Dylag, 15 N.Y.S.3d 715 (App. Term, 9th & 10th Jud. Dists. 2015); Chelsea Ridge NY, LLC v. Clarke, 983 N.Y.S.2d 201 (App. Term, 9th & 10th Jud. Dists. 2013); 6 W. 20th St. Tenants Corp. v. Dezertzov, 146 N.Y.S.3d 464 (N.Y. Civ. Ct. N.Y. Cnty. 2021).

1668 Samuels v. Mpantas, 154 N.Y.S.3d 582 (App. Term, 9th & 10th Jud. Dists. 2021); Limani Realty, LLC v. Zayfert, 970 N.Y.S.2d 345 (App. Term, 2d, 11th & 13th Jud. Dists. 2012) ("a *pro se* litigant 'acquires no greater right than any other litigant'"); Boltz v. Ascolesi, 847 N.Y.S.2d 895 (App. Term, 2d & 11th Jud. Dists. 2007) (*pro se* litigants are "[n]ot entitled to any greater rights than any other party, and cannot get concessions at the expense of another party's rights") (citations omitted).

1669 CPLR § 4213(b); *see* Kolchin v. Bay Ridge Nissan, Inc., 148 N.Y.S.3d 819 (App. Term, 2d, 11th & 13th Jud. Dists. 2021) (small claims action); Rodriguez v. Curtis Chance Realty, 126 N.Y.S.3d 842 (App. Term, 2d, 11th & 13th Jud. Dists. 2020) (new trial required where Appellate Court was unable to determine trial court's reasoning for its decision); Dexter 345, Inc. v. Hanlon, 110 N.Y.S.3d 484 (App. Term, 1st Dep't 2018) (Housing Part "failed to comply with the mandate of CPLR § 4213(b) when it rendered a decision that left 'unanswered and unresolved' the landlord's claim that tenant did not maintain the subject premises as her primary residence"); 129th St. Cluster Assocs. v. Levy, 26 N.Y.S.3d 214 (App. Term, 1st Dep't 2015) (appeal held in abeyance and the proceeding remanded to the Housing Part for a decision in compliance with CPLR § 4213(b)); RBD Realty Consultants, Inc. v. Espinal, 949 N.Y.S.2d 565 (App. Term, 1st Dep't 2012) (proceeding returned to the Housing Part for a new hearing due to the Court's "cryptic decision" and failure to provide any insight, explanation, or rationale for its decision); Karole v. 340 W. End Ave., LLC, 165 N.Y.S.3d 688 (N.Y. Civ. Ct. N.Y. Cnty. 2022) (small claims matter for the return of the Tenant's security deposit).

1670 *See* West 115 11-13 Assoc. LLC v. Pierre, 115 N.Y.S.3d 797 (App. Term, 1st Dep't 2019); Giga Greenpoint Realty, LLC v. Mounier, 110 N.Y.S.3d 867 (App. Term, 2d, 11th & 13th Jud. Dists 2018); Grove Equities LLC v. Butensky, 110 N.Y.S.3d 783 (App. Term, 1st Dep't 2018).

litigant.[1671] However, in its discretion, the Court may provide a *pro se* litigant "some latitude" with respect to protocol and procedure.[1672] In addition, the Court may take an active role at the hearing, particularly, but not exclusively, where one (1) or more of the parties are unrepresented by eliciting and clarifying the testimony of the witnesses when it is "[p]roper or necessary…to facilitate or expedite the orderly progress of the trial."[1673]

The Housing Part may dismiss a summary proceeding at the close of the Petitioner's case where the evidence fails to substantiate the claims.[1674] However, the Court may not dismiss a case where factual and/or legal disputes have been raised without holding an evidentiary hearing (trial).[1675] If the Court's decision is not supported by the evidence or is contrary to the pertinent law, an Appellate Court may reverse the decision and either rule in favor of the opposing party or remit the matter to the Housing Part for a new hearing before the same

1671 *Limani Realty, LLC*, 970 N.Y.S.2d at 345.

1672 *Id.*

1673 Accardi v. City of New York, 121 A.D.2d 489, at 491, 503 N.Y.S.2d 818, 820 (2d Dep't 1986) (*quoting* People v. Ellis, 62 A.D.2d 469, at 470, 404 N.Y.S.2d 862, 863 (1st Dep't 1978)); Carlson, Sr. v. Porter, 53 A.D.3d 1129, at 1132, 861 N.Y.S.2d 907, 910 (4th Dep't 2008); Tonkin v. Lofthouse, 34 A.D.3d 1309, 823 N.Y.S.2d 716 (4th Dep't 2006); Kalikow Family P'ship, LP v. Seidemann, 18 N.Y.S.3d 579 (App. Term, 2d, 11th & 13th Jud. Dists. 2015); Agudas Chasidei Chabad of the United States v. Congregation Lubavitch, Inc., 127 N.Y.S.3d 252 (N.Y. Civ. Ct. Kings Cnty. 2020).

1674 *See, e.g.*, Hecsomar Realty Corp. v. Camerena, 113 N.Y.S.3d 463 (App. Term, 1st Dep't 2019) (where at the close of Petitioner's case the evidence demonstrated that the occupant did not enter possession with permission of the lawful Tenant, who had passed away five (5) months earlier, the licensee holdover proceeding was dismissed). *Cf.* Bilkis v. Trantham, 120 N.Y.S.3d 579 (N.Y. Civ. Ct. Queens Cnty. 2019) (permitting Petitioner to amend the Petition to avoid dismissal due to a defective pleading).

1675 Guzman v. Perez, 119 N.Y.S.3d 686 (App. Term, 9th & 10th Jud. Dists. 2019) (holding that it was "[e]rror for the court to enter a final judgment based on tenant's failure to make the court-ordered deposit"); Carlos v. Primus, 97 N.Y.S.3d 55 (App. Term, 9th & 10th Jud. Dists. 2018) (reversing final judgment and remitting matter to the Housing Part because it was error to grant judgment in favor of the Landlord based upon the Tenant's failure to make a court-ordered deposit). The *Carlos* case was adjudicated outside New York City. However, prior to July 14, 2019, it was possible in New York City for a judgment to be issued in favor of the Landlord without a hearing (trial) if the Tenant failed to make the Court-ordered deposits. *See* RPAPL § 745(2). The law has since been amended so this is no longer the case.

or a different judge.[1676] For example, a final judgment of possession was vacated where the Housing Part erroneously accepted evidence exclusively from the Tenant, thereby shifting the burden of proof.[1677] The Appellate Term concluded that it was reversible error to award a possessory judgment where the Landlord was not required to prove its case.[1678]

The Appellate Court may also reinstate an erroneously dismissed petition.[1679] For example, the Appellate Term for the First Department reversed the Housing Part's *sua sponte* dismissal of the summary proceeding following six (6) days of hearings where the Landlord failed to serve a proper termination notice.[1680] In *80th Inc. v. Witter*, the Appellate Term concluded that the Housing Part was required to provide the Landlord an opportunity to address the deficiency before dismissing the proceeding because the defense was not raised by the Respondent.[1681]

Provided counsel is present, the Landlord's failure to appear at the hearing does not necessitate a dismissal of the proceeding. Petitioner's counsel may attempt to prove a *prima facie* case exclusively through the testimony of the Respondent and other witnesses as well as the documentary exhibits. However, as a practical matter, the Landlord would be bound by the Tenant's testimony that "all of the rent was paid" if the Court were to find the testimony credible. These same principles apply when the Tenant fails to appear, but his or her counsel is present. Instead of a default, Respondent's counsel may cross-examine the

1676 *See* 818 Woodward, LLC v. Gerges, 55 N.Y.S.3d 691 (App. Term, 2d, 11th & 13th Jud. Dists. 2017); New York City Hous. Auth. v. Martinez, 26 N.Y.S.3d 725 (App. Term, 1st Dep't 2015).

1677 1764 Majors Path Corp. v. Petrinolis, 36 N.Y.S.3d 408 (App. Term, 9th & 10th Jud. Dists. 2016).

1678 *Id.*

1679 *See, e.g.*, 222 Stanhope II, LLC v. Bagamery, 155 N.Y.S.3d 29 (App. Term, 2d, 11th & 13th Jud. Dists. 2021).

1680 *See* 80th Inc. v. Witter, 22 N.Y.S.3d 137 (App. Term, 1st Dep't 2015) (holding that "Courts are 'not in the business of blindsiding litigants, who expect us to decide their [cases] on rationales advanced by the parties, not arguments their adversaries never made'") (citation omitted).

1681 *Id.*

Petitioner and call additional witnesses on the Tenant's behalf.

With regard to "last minute" adjournment requests, the decision to grant or deny an adjournment (beyond a request for an adjournment made on the initial Court date) is left to the discretion of the Court. For example, the denial of adjournment requests was proper where the Tenant: (1) sought to retain new counsel during the hearing;[1682] (2) subpoena an additional witness mid-trial;[1683] and (3) when the Tenant caused the previous delays that resulted in a prior mistrial.[1684] Denial of Landlords' requests for adjournments was similarly appropriate where the relevancy of the testimony of the potential witness was unclear and counsel for the Landlord's predecessor's "[a]dmitted that he had not attempted to contact the prior tenant or confirm that tenant's attorney would be producing him at trial."[1685]

The discretion to deny a "last minute" adjournment request is <u>not</u> without limits. For example, an adjournment should have been granted where Tenant's counsel was unavailable due to being "engaged" in another Court.[1686] In *1346 Park Pl. HDFC v. Wright*, after denying the request for an adjournment in part due to counsel's failure to submit an affirmation of engagement, the Housing Part gave the Tenant an ultimatum of discharging counsel and proceeding *pro se* or the Court would prohibit her participation. The Tenant refused to discharge counsel, and at essentially what became a default judgment application, the Landlord was awarded possession.[1687] The Appellate Term reversed, vacated the judgment, and directed a new hearing.[1688]

1682 *See* West 88th St., LLC v. Henriquez, 5 N.Y.S.3d 331 (App. Term, 1st Dep't 2014).

1683 Issac v. Bishop, 135 N.Y.S.3d 568 (App. Term, 9th & 10th Jud. Dists. 2020).

1684 Chen v. Ray, 26 N.Y.S.3d 212 (App. Term, 1st Dep't 2015).

1685 Beverly Holding NY, LLC v. Blackwood, 115 N.Y.S.3d 810 (App. Term, 2d, 11th & 13th Jud. Dists. 2019).

1686 1346 Park Pl. HDFC v. Wright, 34 N.Y.S.3d 561 (App. Term, 2d, 11th & 13th Jud. Dists. 2016).

1687 *Id.*

1688 *Id.* (holding it is "[a]n improvident exercise of discretion to deny an adjournment where the evidence to be presented is material, where the adjournment is not sought in order to delay the proceedings and where the party seeking the adjournment has acted with due diligence to protect its interest").

2. EVIDENTIARY ISSUES

The rules of evidence apply to summary proceedings.[1689] An evidentiary principle often misunderstood is that "admissibility" is not the same as "reliability." In other words, the mere introduction of testimony or an exhibit into evidence does not require the trier of fact to accept that evidence as being truthful or to give that evidence any weight whatsoever. The reader should be mindful that the trier of fact (i.e., the Judge in a non-jury trial) may only consider the evidence introduced at the hearing in rendering a final determination. The amount of weight given any particular item of evidence is left to the sole discretion of the arbiter. Prior to a verdict, the Court has the discretion to permit a party to re-open its case after resting for the purpose of correcting any perceived deficiencies.[1690]

a. HEARSAY

It is well-established that an out-of-court statement of a non-party offered for the truth of the matter asserted is not admissible. However, a hearsay statement offered as evidence of the witness' state of mind, rather than for the truth of the statement itself, may be admissible as an exception to the hearsay rule.[1691] This situation arises in a variety of contexts. For example, the hypothetical out-of-court statement of an unavailable non-party witness may be admissible in a non-payment proceeding where the Tenant claims that he was told the apartment

---

1689 Cobble Hillbillies, LLC v. Interior Design, 782 N.Y.S.2d 600 (N.Y. Civ. Ct. Kings Cnty. 2004) (rules of evidence apply at hearings, including an inquest in a summary proceeding).

1690 *See generally* Hyatt Ave. Assocs., LLC v. Rahman, 17 N.Y.S.3d 579 (App. Term, 2d, 11th & 13th Jud. Dists. 2015) (application to re-open Tenant's case denied where the purpose of the request was to re-introduce documents the Court previously refused to admit).

1691 *See* Benitez v. Whitehall Apts. Co., LLC, 862 N.Y.S.2d 813 (N.Y. Cnty. Sup. Ct. 2008) (out-of-court statement of Landlord's superintendent regarding the building's security cameras was properly considered on a motion for summary judgment because the testimony was introduced to demonstrate the victim's state of mind when entering the elevator), *aff'd*, 56 A.D.3d 273, 866 N.Y.S.2d 668 (1st Dep't 2008); Dexter 345 Inc. v. Cruz, 119 N.Y.S.3d 17 n.1 (N.Y. Civ. Ct. N.Y. Cnty. 2019); 116 Madison St., LLC v. Seid, 901 N.Y.S.2d 900 (N.Y. Civ. Ct. N.Y. Cnty. 2009).

was "illegal" or that the property was in foreclosure. If the out-of-court statement was offered to demonstrate the Tenant's reasoning for not paying the rent, as opposed to the status of the premises or that the rent was not paid, then the statement may be admissible. It is worth repeating that admitting the testimony does not mean the testimony will be deemed credible by the trier of fact.

b. SUBPOENAS

Parties may subpoena witnesses and business records. When the subpoena demands the production of documents maintained by a governmental agency, such as a police report or proof of payment by the Department of Social Services, the subpoena must be "So Ordered" by the Court and may be submitted on one (1) day notice to the agency.[1692] The governmental records are generally admissible as evidence without the preparer being called to testify provided a certification or authentication is submitted from the head of the agency.[1693] Otherwise, as in any other action, an attorney may issue subpoenas without leave of Court, and a *pro se* litigant must always obtain Court approval to compel the production of documents and/or testimony at a hearing.

c. BUSINESS RECORDS

Another common evidentiary issue involves the introduction of the rental agreement and other records. Typically, the Landlord will introduce the lease as a contract between the parties after laying a proper foundation and authenticating the signatures.[1694]

1692 CPLR § 2307. *See* Townsend v. B-U Realty Corp., 128 N.Y.S.3d 156 (N.Y. Cnty. Sup. Ct. 2020) (subpoena for records of the Division of Housing and Community Renewal); 59 Maiden Lane Assoc., LLC v. Maiden Farm, Inc., 106 N.Y.S.3d 554 (N.Y. Civ. Ct. N.Y. Cnty. 2019) (Court Ordered subpoena for documents from the New York City Department of Finance).

1693 CPLR § 2307; CPLR Rule 4518. *See generally* New York Cnty. Dist. Attorney's Office v. Rodriguez, 536 N.Y.S.2d 933, 937-38 (N.Y. Civ. Ct. N.Y. Cnty. 1988); *see* Barcher v. Radovich, 183 A.D.2d 689, at 690-91, 583 N.Y.S.2d 276, 278 (2d Dep't 1992).

1694 *See* Alfaro v. Lavacca, 186 A.D.3d 1591, 129 N.Y.S.3d 846 (2d Dep't 2020) (affidavit failed to lay proper foundation to admit lease agreement pursuant to CPLR Rule 4518(a)); Tuscan Realty Corp. v. O'Neill, 731 N.Y.S.2d 830 (App. Term, 2d & 11th Jud. Dists. 2001); Cordova v. 1212 Bedford Realty LLC, 126 N.Y.S.3d 620 (N.Y. Civ. Ct. Kings Cnty. 2020); Asal Realty LLC v. Kaune, 125 N.Y.S.3d 840 (N.Y. Civ. Ct. Bronx Cnty. 2020).

The rental agreement may otherwise be introduced as a business record exception to the hearsay rule pursuant to CPLR Rule 4518(a) through the testimony of a property manager or other agent sufficiently familiar with the company's business records "[t]o aver that the record is what it purports to be[,] that it came out of the entity's files," and that the document was prepared in the regular course of the Landlord's business.[1695] More specifically, it has been held that to satisfy the "[f]oundational requirements of the business records exception to the hearsay rule, the record must (1) be made in the regular course of business (i.e., it must 'reflect a routine, regularly conducted business activity' that is 'needed and relied on in the performance of functions of the business'), (2) it must be the regular course of the business to make such a record ('a double requirement of regularity' that 'the record be made pursuant to established procedures for routine, habitual, systematic making of such a record'), and (3) the record must be 'made at or about the time of the event being recorded.'"[1696]

A copy of an official government document may be utilized for authentication purposes provided an officer or a deputy of an officer with legal custody testifies as to the "correctness" of the copy, the document bears an official raised seal, and a certificate of the Clerk of the Court is included.[1697] In *Plotch v. Dellis*, an alternative method for introducing a photocopy of the referee's deed following foreclosure was discussed

1695 CPLR Rule 4518; APF 286 MAD, LLC v. Chittur & Assocs., P.C., 28 N.Y.S.3d 647 (App. Term, 1st Dep't 2016); DeLeon v. Port Auth. of New York and New Jersey, 306 A.D.2d 146, 761 N.Y.S.2d 54 (1st Dep't 2003); *see also* Resnick Seaport, LLC v. 199 Roast LLC, 146 N.Y.S.3d 768 (N.Y. Civ. Ct. N.Y. Cnty. 2021) (declining to admit electronic records of third party pursuant to CPLR Rule 4518(a) where the process server was unable to lay a proper foundation for the business records); 1449 Fulton LLC v. Yaya, 115 N.Y.S.3d 831 (N.Y. Civ. Ct. Kings Cnty. 2019) (rent ledger was <u>not</u> admitted where Landlord failed to produce a witness with firsthand knowledge of its contents and/or where the ledger was maintained).

1696 Beach v. Touradji Capital Mgt., LP, 117 N.Y.S.3d 803 (N.Y. Cnty. Sup. Ct. 2019) (*quoting* People v. Kennedy, 68 N.Y.2d 569, 510 N.Y.S.2d 853 (1986)). In *Beach*, the Court noted that the business records exception to the hearsay rule "grew out of considerations of necessity and trustworthiness—the necessity for alternatives to permit large and small businesses to prove debts by their records of account, and the unusual degree of trustworthiness and reliability of such records owing to the fact that they were kept regularly, systematically and contemporaneously." *Id.*; *see* CPLR Rule 4518(a).

1697 CPLR at Rule 4540(a),(b).

where the official copies served upon the Respondent did not bear a raised seal. In that case, the Appellate Term held that the copies were admissible pursuant to CPLR § 2105, which provides an alternative method for certifying an unsealed copy where counsel submits a sworn certificate stating that she compared the original to the copy, and the copy is a true and complete copy.[1698]

d. BEST EVIDENCE RULE

Under an exception to the Best Evidence Rule, where the original rental agreement is either lost or destroyed, a duplicate may be introduced as a secondary source provided: (1) an adequate explanation for the non-production is provided; (2) the non-production was not the result of bad faith on the part of the party seeking to admit the document; and (3) the accuracy of the secondary source is demonstrated.[1699] In *Casanas v. Carlei Group, LLC*, the Appellate Division, First Department admitted into evidence a photocopy of the purported 100-year lease between the parents and their offspring that listed the annual rent as $100.[1700] The Appellate Court, relying upon the trial court's determination on the credibility of the witnesses, including a handwriting expert, concluded that the lease was properly admitted because "the images of the parents' signatures on the photocopy of the lease were consistent with their known signatures and [the absence of any] evidence that the images of their signatures or the document itself was manipulated."[1701]

A secondary source is generally not admissible where the proponent of the document fails to adequately explain the unavailability of the

1698 Plotch v. Dellis, 75 N.Y.S.3d 779 (App. Term, 2d, 11th & 13th Jud. Dists. 2018). The referee's deed attached to the Petition and filed with the Court included the certifying official's signature with a raised seal. *Id.*; *see generally* Deutsche Bank Nat'l Trust Co. v. Karibandi, 188 A.D.3d 650, 134 N.Y.S.3d 464 (2d Dep't 2020).

1699 *See generally* Aviation Distribs. Inc., Formed 1945 v. Aviation Distribs. Inc., Formed 2014, 203 A.D.3d 418, 164 N.Y.S.3d 579 (1st Dep't 2022); Schozer v. William Penn Life Ins. Co. of New York, 84 N.Y.2d 639, 620 N.Y.S.2d 797 (1994).

1700 200 A.D.3d 442, 158 N.Y.S.3d 95 (1st Dep't 2021).

1701 *Id.*

original document.[1702] However, in *B.N. Realty Assocs. v. Lichtenstein*, the Appellate Division, First Department held that the introduction of the rental agreement as a secondary source was proper, notwithstanding the absence of an explanation for the failure to produce the original, where the Tenant admitted owing the rent arrears and the counterclaim arose from the same agreement.[1703]

A reliable photocopy or computer printout of a lost or destroyed rental agreement or other business record may be introduced pursuant to CPLR Rule 4539.[1704] This exception is applicable to "[c]opies of documents made by an accurate reproduction process, such as photocopying, provided the documents are those of a business and the copying was done in the regular course of business. When utilized, the proponent is exempt from the requirement of producing the original or explaining its absence."[1705]

e. PHOTOGRAPHS AND VIDEOS

Photographs and video may be utilized to confirm or refute the condition of the premises.[1706] Photographs are sometimes further introduced to demonstrate unauthorized alterations and renovations.[1707]

1702 *See* 76-82 St. Marks, LLC v. Gluck, 147 A.D.3d 1011, 48 N.Y.S.3d 210 (2d Dep't 2017) (copy of commercial lease guaranty not admitted where movant failed to adequately demonstrate that the "proffered evidence" was "a reliable and accurate portrayal of the original").

1703 96 A.D.3d 434, at 434-35, 949 N.Y.S.2d 1, 2 (1st Dep't 2012).

1704 *See, e.g., APF 286 MAD, LLC*, 28 N.Y.S.3d at 647.

1705 174 LLC v. Roberts, 809 N.Y.S.2d 482 (N.Y. Civ. Ct. Bronx Cnty. 2005). *See also* CPLR Rule 4539. *Cf.* Ramchandani v. Piran Fashions, Inc., 999 N.Y.S.2d 798 (App. Term, 2d, 11th & 13th Jud. Dists. 2014) (copies of rent checks inadmissible where the copies were not authenticated by competent testimony or supporting affidavit).

1706 *See generally* 1710 Realty, LLC v. Portabella 308 Utica, LLC, 189 A.D.3d 944, 138 N.Y.S.3d 523 (2d Dep't 2020); West 88th St., LLC v. Henriquez, 5 N.Y.S.3d 331 (App. Term, 1st Dep't 2014); 98-48 Queens Blvd. LLC v. Parkside Mem. Chapels, Inc., 137 N.Y.S.3d 679 (N.Y. Civ. Ct. Queens Cnty. 2021); Hibbert v. Powell, 2021 N.Y.L.J. LEXIS 594 n.4 (N.Y. Civ. Ct. Bronx Cnty. June 23, 2021) (video of attempted burglary at premises admitted into evidence); 156 E. 37th St. LLC v. Eichner, 113 N.Y.S.3d 484 (N.Y. Civ. Ct. N.Y. Cnty. 2019). In *Spears v. Cumberland Farms, Inc.*, the Orange County Supreme Court gave a negative inference charge at trial due to the destruction of video surveillance containing "[t]he most probative physical evidence as to the conditions of the premises when the plaintiff fell; the nature of the condition, and notice that the defendant may have had to the condition"). 2020 N.Y. Misc. LEXIS 18640 (Orange Cnty. Sup. Ct. April 22, 2020).

1707 Zada Assocs. v. Melucci, 28 N.Y.S.3d 651 (App. Term, 1st Dep't 2015).

Photographs and videos are admissible provided they "fairly and accurately" depict the condition of the subject matter on the date in question.[1708] If the movant asserts that the photograph and/or video accurately portrays the condition of the premises at the relevant time, then the Court may admit the photograph or video regardless of when and by whom it was taken or filmed.[1709]

f. AUDIO RECORDINGS

In New York, it is lawful to record a conversation, without notice, where at least one (1) party to the conversation consents to the recording.[1710] However, to introduce the audio recording at a hearing, a proper foundation must be provided through clear and convincing evidence regarding the relevancy, authenticity, completeness, and accuracy of the recording.[1711] If the conversation was recorded <u>without</u> at least one (1) party's consent, or otherwise obtained in an unlawful manner in violation of section 250.05 of the Penal Law (eavesdropping), then the audio recording is inadmissible.[1712]

1708 Read v. Ellenville Nat'l Bank, 20 A.D.3d 408, 799 N.Y.S.2d 78 (2d Dep't 2005); Lott-Coakley v. Ann-Gur Realty Corp., 886 N.Y.S.2d 67 (Bronx Cnty. Sup. Ct. 2009). *Cf.* Torres v. Hickman, 162 A.D.3d 821, 79 N.Y.S.3d 62 (2d Dep't 2018) (in personal injury action, video excerpt inadmissible where movant failed to properly authenticate the video).

1709 *But see* Leven v. Tallis Dept. Store, 178 A.D.2d 466, 577 N.Y.S.2d 132 (2d Dep't 1991) (unauthenticated photographs taken two (2) years following the accident improperly admitted into evidence).

1710 *See* PENAL LAW § 250; People v. Lasher, 58 N.Y.2d 962, 460 N.Y.S.2d 522 (1983).

1711 *See generally* People v. Ely, 68 N.Y.2d 520, 510 N.Y.S.2d 532 (1986); People v. Covlin, 205 A.D.3d 578, 168 N.Y.S.3d 70 (1st Dep't 2022); People v. Hurlbert, Jr., 81 A.D.3d 1430, 916 N.Y.S.2d 713 (4th Dep't 2011); Samra v. Messeca, 17 N.Y.S.3d 385 (App. Term, 1st Dep't 2015) (recorded conversation between Tenant and Landlord's agent admissible).

1712 CPLR § 4506(1); People v. Azeez, 193 A.D.3d 752, 146 N.Y.S.3d 284 (2d Dep't 2021) (recordings of "controlled" telephone calls at the police station between the complainant and defendant admitted where the complainant participated "with the knowledge that they were being recorded"); People v. Badalamenti, 27 N.Y.3d 423, 34 N.Y.S.3d 360 (2016) (holding that the vicarious consent doctrine permitted introduction of an otherwise improperly taken audio recording between the criminal defendant and a five-year old when the child's father in good faith believed his son was in peril).

C. PAROL EVIDENCE

Although parol evidence is a rule of "substantive law," and not a rule of evidence, it is important to note that issues of lease interpretation and contemporaneous agreements are frequently raised in summary proceedings. It is well-established that where a written rental agreement is clear, complete, and unambiguous, the Court will not consider any additional or extraneous oral or written statements that may contradict the lease terms.[1713] In other words, "[a]bsent fraud or mutual mistake, where the parties have reduced their agreement to an integrated writing, the parol evidence rule operates to exclude evidence of all prior or contemporaneous negotiations between the parties offered to contradict or modify the terms of their writing."[1714] Moreover, a clear and unambiguous merger clause depicting the writing as the parties' full and complete agreement will generally bar parol evidence intended to establish a contradictory intent.[1715]

Ambiguity in the drafting of an agreement is to be construed against the drafter.[1716] However, where a lease provision is ambiguous or vague, the Court may consider parol evidence to assist in the interpretation of

1713 Madison Ave. Leasehold, LLC v. Madison Bentley Assoc., LLC, 8 N.Y.3d 59, 828 N.Y.S.2d 254 (2006) (parol evidence may not be used to create ambiguity within an otherwise clear and unambiguous rental agreement); CDC Develop. Props., Inc. v. American Independent Paper Mills Supply Co., Inc., 184 A.D.3d 623, 125 N.Y.S.3d 722 (2d Dep't 2020) (lease agreement clear and unambiguous); Hoeg Corp. v. Peebles Corp., 153 A.D.3d 607, 60 N.Y.S.3d 259 (2d Dep't 2017) (parol evidence not available where "the written retainer agreement is a complete written instrument"); GMDC Two Corp. v. Pensato, 2018 N.Y. Misc. LEXIS 806 (Kings Cnty. Sup. Ct. Feb. 15, 2018) ("[e]xtrinsic evidence and parol evidence may not be considered in determining the meaning of a written contract when ambiguity does not exist").

1714 Lopez v. Platinum Volkswagen, 26 N.Y.S.3d 214 (App. Term, 9th & 10th Jud. Dists. 2015) (citations omitted).

1715 *See, e.g.*, 1450 Broadway, LLC v. Tripoint Capital Advisors, LLC, 2022 N.Y. Misc. LEXIS 438 (N.Y. Cnty. Sup. Ct. Jan. 28, 2022).

1716 *See* Goldhirsch v. St. George Tower and Grill Owners Corp., 142 A.D.3d 1044, 37 N.Y.S.3d 616 (2d Dep't 2016); Fac Preserv. HDFC v. Moreno, 150 N.Y.S.3d 496 (App. Term, 2d, 11th & 13th Jud. Dists. 2021); Kossoff v. 910 Fifth Ave. Corp., 2019 N.Y. Misc. LEXIS 2988 (N.Y. Sup. Ct. June 6, 2019); 819 Realty Group v. Beast Fitness Evolved LLC, 2019 N.Y.L.J. LEXIS 2406 (N.Y. Civ. Ct. Kings Cnty. July 10, 2019).

the parties' written agreement.[1717] For example, parol evidence was permitted in determining whether a commercial lease included approximately 165 square feet in the building plans.[1718] Parol evidence was also permitted to clarify the "dollar amount of the monthly payments and the meaning of the [lease] term 'six month grace period.'"[1719]

D. APPEALS

A party may appeal an Order of the Court by filing a Notice of Appeal and paying the appropriate fee within thirty (30) days of service of the Notice of Entry.[1720] The party must further serve a copy of the transcript of the minutes on the opposing party and execute a Stipulation of Settlement of the Transcript.[1721] If the parties cannot agree on settling the minutes, then the party seeking the appeal must make a motion to the Court to Settle the Transcript of Minutes.

1717 International Business Machines Corp. v. Global Foundries U.S. Inc., 204 A.D.3d 441, 167 N.Y.S.3d 13 (1st Dep't 2022) (general and vague contract clauses "do not preclude the use of parol evidence to establish the fraudulent inducement claim"); Liberty Equity Restoration Corp. v. Pil Soung Park, 160 A.D.3d 628, 75 N.Y.S.3d 47 (2d Dep't 2018) (parol evidence "admissible to supplement and interpret the terms of the parties' agreements" regarding the paying of a mortgage); First Am. Commercial Bancorp, Inc. v. Saatchi & Saatchi Rowland, Inc., 55 A.D.3d 1264, 865 N.Y.S.2d 424 (4th Dep't 2008) (parol evidence required to clarify sublease boundaries and description); Great S. Bay Family Med. Practice, LLP v. Raynor, 35 A.D.3d 808, 826 N.Y.S.2d 729 (2d Dep't 2006) (parol evidence permitted for "the interpretation of the handwritten changes" to the lease); Fisher v. Burke, 151 N.Y.S.3d 620 (N.Y. Civ. Ct. Kings Cnty. 2021) (context of text messages may be considered where the texts were ambiguous "about a mutual intent to create a landlord/tenant relationship").

1718 Clean Act Inc. v. 4126 Realty Corp., 164 A.D.3d 1179, 81 N.Y.S.3d 900 (1st Dep't 2018).

1719 *See* Kasiotis v. Jones, Jr., 5 N.Y.S.3d 328 n.2 (Sullivan Cnty. Ct. 2014) (citation omitted); *see also* 1626 Second Ave. LLC v. Salsberg, 105 A.D.3d 432, 962 N.Y.S.2d 135 (1st Dep't 2013) (parol evidence permitted to "clarify" lease guaranty).

1720 CPLR § 5513.

1721 *See* Goldman v. Malagic, 112 N.Y.S.3d 862 (App. Term, 1st Dep't 2019) (dismissing appeal due to the Tenant's failure to submit a copy of the trial (hearing) transcript and exhibits).

1. WHERE TO FILE APPEAL

The appropriate Court to take the appeal depends on the location and origination of the trial court. For example, an appeal of an Order of the District Courts, which are exclusively situated within the Second Judicial Department, and the New York City Civil Courts, are made to the appropriate Appellate Term.[1722]

Although the Appellate Division in each of the four (4) Judicial Departments has the authority to establish an Appellate Term for the purpose of hearing appeals, only the First and Second Departments have exercised this authority. Appeals from the City Courts outside New York City and the Justice Courts are made to the appropriate County Court, except where the Court is located within the First or Second Judicial Departments.[1723]

2. LEGAL STANDARDS

The Appellate Court will give "substantial deference" to the Housing Part, which had the opportunity "[t]o observe and evaluate the testimony and demeanor of the witnesses [that] affords it a better perspective from which to assess their credibility."[1724] Typically, the Appellate Court will not overturn the Housing Part's decision "[u]nless such determination could not have been reached under any fair interpretation

1722 UNIFORM DIST. CT. ACT § 1701; N.Y. CITY CIV. CT. ACT § 1701. The Appellate Division, Second Department created the Appellate Term for the purpose of such appeals pursuant to 22 N.Y.C.R.R. § 730.1. The Appellate Division, First Department established an Appellate Term pursuant to 22 N.Y.C.R.R. § 640.1. Parenthetically, if the Appellate Terms in the First and Second Judicial Departments did not exist, then appeals from the New York City Civil Courts would be made in the Appellate Division, First Department (N.Y. CITY CIV. CT. ACT § 1701) and appeals from the District Court would be made in the County Court (UNIFORM DIST. CT. ACT § 1701).

1723 UNIFORM CITY CT. ACT § 1701; UNIFORM JUST. CT. ACT § 1701.

1724 34-15 Parsons Blvd., LLC v. Zhao, 165 N.Y.S.3d 226 (App. Term, 2d, 11th & 13th Jud. Dists. 2022); 700 Bklyn Realty, LLC v. Forsythe, 161 N.Y.S.3d 691 (App. Term, 2d, 11th & 13th Jud. Dists. 2022); Miller v. Jefferson, 112 N.Y.S.3d 413 (App. Term, 2d, 11th & 13th Jud. Dists. 2018); Primova v. McShur, 101 N.Y.S.3d 701 (App. Term, 2d, 11th & 13th Jud. Dists. 2018).

of the evidence."[1725]

An appeal may not be taken from a default judgment entered against a non-appearing Tenant.[1726] Instead, the defaulting Respondent may move in the Housing Part to vacate the default and, if the motion to vacate the default judgment is denied, then an appeal from that Order may be taken.[1727] The failure to "[o]ppose the [] appeal filed in the Appellate Term or otherwise participate in the proceedings before that court" bars that party from appealing the Appellate Court's determination.[1728]

With the exception of subject matter jurisdiction, the failure to assert a defense in the summary proceeding renders the defense unavailable on appeal.[1729] Where there are multiple Tenants, whom by definition are united in interest, the Court may vacate or modify the judgments against all, including those Tenants that did not pursue an appeal.[1730] For example, in *Priege v. Paulus*, the money judgment was reduced against the non-appealing Tenant because the Appellant and non-appealing Tenant shared a common interest in the leasehold.[1731]

1725 Mautner-Glick Corp. v. Glazer, 31 N.Y.S.3d 922 (App. Term, 1st Dep't 2016); Hillside Park 168 v. Khan, 148 N.Y.S.3d 326 (App. Term, 2d, 11th & 13th Jud. Dists. 2021); Parkchester Preserv. Co. L.P. v. Adams, 28 N.Y.S.3d 649 (App. Term, 1st Dep't 2016). *Cf.* DiLorenzo v. Windermere Owners, LLC, 174 A.D.3d 102, 104 N.Y.S.3d 65 (1st Dep't 2019) (noting that limiting Appellate Review to a fair interpretation of the evidence is appropriate where the ruling at issue was based upon credibility determinations, and not inferences to be drawn from the facts).

1726 CPLR § 5511; Manhattan Mini Stor., LLC v. Ebrain Consult., LLC, 113 N.Y.S.3d 813 (App. Term, 1st Dep't 2019); 1764 Majors Path Corp. v. Petrinolis, 36 N.Y.S.3d 408 (App. Term, 9th & 10th Jud. Dists. 2016).

1727 *See, e.g.*, Ratnam Assocs. v. Discount King USA, Inc., 126 N.Y.S.3d 608 (App. Term, 9th & 10th Jud. Dists. 2020).

1728 141 Ave. A Assoc. v. Klein, 158 A.D.3d 541, 68 N.Y.S.3d 723 (1st Dep't 2018) (Tenant was not an "aggrieved party" pursuant to CPLR § 5511 due to the failure to participate in the Landlord's appeal at the Appellate Term).

1729 Hickey v. Trahan, 31 N.Y.S.3d 921 (App. Term, 9th & 10th Jud. Dists. 2016).

1730 Rossi v. Scott, 52 N.Y.S.3d 248 (App. Term, 9th & 10th Jud. Dists. 2017); Priegue v. Paulus, 988 N.Y.S.2d 525 (App. Term, 9th & 10th Jud. Dists. 2014).

1731 *Priegue*, 988 N.Y.S.2d at 525; *see also Oakwood Terr. Hous. Corp.*, 36 N.Y.S.3d at 48 (proceeding dismissed against both the appealing Tenant and her non-appealing spouse where Petitioner failed to prove or plead a rent demand was made).

3. STAY PENDING APPEAL

A Respondent seeking to stay enforcement of the money judgment pending an appeal may deposit the amount awarded with the Housing Part. However, depositing the funds does not stay the eviction.[1732] A request to stay execution of the warrant of eviction, thereby prohibiting the eviction until after the appeal is decided, must be made to the Appellate Term or other appropriate Appellate Court. The Appellate Court may direct the payment of use and occupancy as a condition for granting a stay.

The appeal may be rendered moot if the Tenant is evicted during its pendency because the determination by the Appellate Court "will not affect the rights of the parties."[1733] The same may hold true where the Tenant voluntarily vacates the premises during the appeal.[1734]

1732 CPLR § 5519.

1733 Michalak v. Fechtel, 911 N.Y.S.2d 693 (App. Term, 9th & 10th Jud. Dists. 2010). In *Coleman v. Ceraolo*, the Appellate Term concluded that the appeal was moot because the Tenant failed to comply with the Court's terms of the stay. 906 N.Y.S.2d 778 (App. Term, 1st Dep't 2010).

1734 Parkchester Preserv. Co. L.P. v. Adams, 28 N.Y.S.3d 649 (App. Term, 1st Dep't 2016).

CHAPTER 15

STAYS AND ORDERS TO SHOW CAUSE

In 2017, approximately 21,000 of the more than 230,000 residential summary proceedings commenced in New York City (or 9.1%) resulted in an eviction.[1735] The following year, there were a similar number of residential evictions. In 2018, Bronx County had the highest eviction rate among the New York City Boroughs, with one (1) eviction per every seventy-nine (79) residential units. Manhattan had the lowest rate at one (1) eviction per 345 residential units.[1736]

Although the Housing Part may not provide declaratory relief, for "good cause" the Court may stay enforcement of a warrant of eviction at any time prior to its execution, or, if the warrant was already executed, restore the Tenant to possession.[1737] The statute does not pose limitations on the duration of a stay, but the stay should only be in effect for a "reasonable" period of time under the circumstances. The Court further for "good cause" has inherent discretion to stay the re-letting or renovating of the premises for a "reasonable period of time."[1738]

1735 *See* Residential Evictions (2017 -2019), New York City Council website, https://council.nyc.gov.

1736 *Id.* There was an eviction for every 180 residential units in Brooklyn; every 209 units in Queens; and every 266 units in Staten Island (Richmond County). *Id.*

1737 RPAPL § 749(3) (HSTPA, L. 2019, c. 36, Part M, § 19). *See* Tzifil Realty Corp. v. Rodriguez, 126 N.Y.S.3d 842 (App. Term, 2d, 11th & 13th Jud. Dists. 2020) (in proceeding to be restored to possession, the Tenant's contempt application was denied due to improper service). *Cf.* 214 Knickerbocker v. Molly's Truck Sweet & Savory, 144 N.Y.S.3d 796 (App. Term, 2d, 11th & 13th Jud. Dists. 2021) (where removal was due to an unlawful lockout, Tenant seeking to be restored to possession must make the application in a separate special proceeding, and not a motion to vacate the default judgment); Otero v. Hope Founders HDFC, 2021 N.Y.L.J. LEXIS 474 (N.Y. Civ. Ct. N.Y. Cnty. March 29, 2021) (same).

1738 RPAPL § 749(1); Kerr v. Nicholson, 160 N.Y.S.3d 579 (N.Y. Civ. Ct. Kings Cnty. 2022).

A. ORDERS TO SHOW CAUSE (VACATING JUDGMENTS)

1. FOURTEEN (14) DAY WRITTEN NOTICE (SHERIFF'S NOTICE)

Following the expiration of all applicable stays, the Sheriff or Marshal must provide the Respondent with a fourteen (14) day written notice prior to the eviction.[1739] The warrant of eviction must describe the premises from which removal is sought and provide the earliest date the eviction may occur.[1740] The Sheriff's Notice must be formally served in the same manner as the Notice of Petition and Petition and the warrant may only be executed on a business day (Monday—Friday) between sunrise and sunset.[1741]

Prior to the 2019 Amendments, the Appellate Term held that the "failure to properly serve the [Sheriff's] notice [did] not affect the validity of the final judgment."[1742] For example, in *Capital 2000, LLC v. Tatum*, the Court denied the Respondent's post-eviction motion to be restored to possession, notwithstanding the improper service of the Sheriff's Notice, because the Respondent had entered into a Stipulation of Settlement agreeing to vacate the premises.[1743] Although not dispositive, the Court further noted that the Tenant delayed seeking relief until after the eviction was completed.[1744] A similar outcome resulted following the 2019 Amendments in *Molinelli v. Goulbourne-Fontan* when the same Court reasoned that the failure to serve the Sheriff's Notice did not "affect the validity of a final judgment, and it afford[ed] no basis for granting tenant's motion to be restored, as she was required to vacate by

1739 RPAPL § 749(2)(a); *see generally* Dixon v. County of Albany, 192 A.D.3d 1428, 145 N.Y.S.3d 639 (3d Dep't 2021). Prior to June 14, 2019, the Sheriff was merely required to provide 72 hours notice.

1740 RPAPL § 749(1); *see generally* Point 128, LLC v. Sound De Point LLC, 155 N.Y.S.3d 731 (N.Y. Civ. Ct. Queens Cnty. 2021). The Sheriff need not wait until the "earliest date" the "execution" of the warrant may occur listed in the warrant before serving the Fourteen (14) Day Notice. As a practical matter, absent falling on a weekend or holiday, the "earliest date" the execution of the warrant may occur is the fifteenth (15th) date following the expiration of the stay or the issuance of the warrant without a stay. *See* General Construction Law § 20.

1741 RPAPL § 749(2)(a).

1742 *See* Capital 2000, LLC v. Tatum, 41 N.Y.S.3d 718 (App. Term, 2d, 11th & 13th Jud. Dists. 2016) (emphasis added).

1743 *Id.*

1744 *Id.*

[a date certain pursuant to stipulation] and failed to do so."[1745]

In addition, the Appellate Division, Third Department has held that filing an affidavit of service following service of the Sheriff's Notice is "superfluous" and, therefore, "not required."[1746] In *Dixon v. County of Albany*, the Respondent sought a stay because the affidavit of service for the Sheriff's Notice, which was served by "nail and mail" delivery, was not filed with the Court within three (3) days of service. The Appellate Division reasoned that dissimilar from the affidavit of service for the Notice of Petition and Petition, the Sheriff's Notice occurs after a final determination.[1747] Accordingly, the Court concluded that "[f]iling the affidavit of service at the conclusion of service of a warrant of eviction is not required, and the 14-day notice begins the day following the date of service, posting or mailing, whichever is later."[1748]

At any time, but typically after service of the Sheriff's fourteen (14) day notice, a Respondent may submit an *ex parte* Order to Show Cause to vacate a default judgment and/or request additional time to remain in possession of the premises. In a default situation, the failure to assert a personal jurisdiction defense in the motion papers accompanying the Order to Show Cause may constitute a waiver of the defense.[1749] The Court's decision to sign the Order to Show Cause and issue a stay upon execution of the judgment and warrant is governed by, *inter alia*, CPLR § 2201, which generally authorizes a stay of the proceedings "upon such terms as may be just." The decision to issue a stay is left to the discretion of the Housing Court,[1750] and the service requirements set forth by the Court are generally strictly enforced.[1751]

1745 138 N.Y.S.3d 790 (App. Term, 2d, 11th & 13th Jud. Dists. 2021).

1746 *Dixon*, 192 A.D.3d at 1428, 145 N.Y.S.3d at 639.

1747 *Id.*

1748 *Id.*

1749 Lakeview Affordable Hous., LLC v. Turner, 121 N.Y.S.3d 510 (App. Term, 9th & 10th Jud. Dists. 2020).

1750 Papandrea-Zavaglia v. Arroyave, 168 N.Y.S.3d 789 (N.Y. Civ. Ct. Kings Cnty. 2022).

1751 *Tzifil Realty Corp.*, 126 N.Y.S.3d at 842 (in contempt action, holding that "where the court orders service by a particular date, all components of service must be accomplished by that date," but a mere "technical infirmity" in service may be overlooked and the court maintains jurisdiction); Torres v. Sedgwick Ave. Dignity Developers LLC, 163 N.Y.S.3d 885 (N.Y. Civ. Ct. Bronx Cnty. 2022) (denying contempt motion due to improper service).

If a stay is issued, the warrant of eviction remains in effect but may not be executed until the motion is decided and the stay is lifted. In other words, the eviction is delayed for as long as the stay remains in place.[1752] Where the Court declines to sign the Order to Show Cause and/or issue a stay, the declination is not "the law of the case," and the Court must still render a decision on the underlying motion.[1753] If an Order to Show Cause brought by a *pro se* Respondent is not signed by the Housing Part (i.e., the Court declines to impose a stay prior to the motion's return date), in some locations, including the District Courts, the motion papers will be sent to the Appellate Term for review.

The Court may require the payment of use and occupancy as a condition for the additional time the Tenant remains in possession of the premises.[1754] However, the failure to pay the use and occupancy (or post an undertaking) does not constitute a basis for either denying or refusing to consider the underlying motion.[1755]

Personal appearances are generally required for oral argument on the return date of an Order to Show Cause.[1756] Where the Tenant is only seeking to vacate a money judgment, personal appearances may be waived.

There are exceptions to the requirement of a fourteen (14) day Sheriff's Notice for manufactured home parks. The notice period in these cases is generally expanded to at least ninety (90) days prior to the eviction, but the Court may reduce this period to thirty (30) days where the park's Owner seeks to evict a Tenant who owns the mobile

---

1752 *See, e.g.*, BNS Bldgs., LLC v. Morgan, 847 N.Y.S.2d 900 (App. Term, 2d & 11th Jud. Dists. 2007) (affirming conditional stay upon proof of payment Landlord previously refused to accept); Deutsche Bank Nat'l Trust Co. v. Oliver, 879 N.Y.S.2d 674, 676-77 (Nassau Cnty. Dist. Ct. 2009) (staying execution of warrant where Respondent demonstrated ample explanation for the request, including caring for her 92-year old mother who suffered from dementia).

1753 1901 Hennessy LLC v. Vicente, 122 N.Y.S.3d 487 (App. Term, 1st Dep't 2020).

1754 The 6465 Realty Co. v. Tsugiyama, 15 N.Y.S.3d 715 (App. Term, 1st Dep't 2015).

1755 Ratnam Assocs. v. Discount King USA, Inc., 126 N.Y.S.3d 608 (App. Term, 9th & 10th Jud. Dists. 2020).

1756 *See, e.g.*, 2115 Washington Realty v. Braxton, 2021 N.Y.L.J. LEXIS 766 (N.Y. Civ. Ct. Bronx Cnty. Aug. 4, 2021); 224-232 Atlantic Ave. Investors, LLC v. Gonzalez, 55 N.Y.S.3d 695 (N.Y. Civ. Ct. Kings Cnty. 2017).

home and fails to pay rent or the underlying circumstances that formed the basis for the eviction pose an immediate threat to the health, safety, or welfare of the other Tenants.[1757] Where the Tenant does not own the mobile home, the Sheriff need only provide seventy-two (72) hours notice.[1758]

If the Landlord prevails in a summary proceeding, the Clerk of the Court may issue the Respondent an "emergency letter." The emergency letter notifies the Department of Social Services, or other applicable governmental agency, that the occupant is in need of assistance finding a new residence and the earliest date an eviction may occur.

2. GROUNDS TO VACATE A DEFAULT JUDGMENT AND TRAVERSE HEARINGS

A Respondent may vacate a default judgment by providing: (1) a reasonable excuse for the non-appearance or (2) establishing a lack of jurisdiction.[1759] To be timely, the motion must be made within one (1) year of either the entry of judgment or service of a copy of the judgment.[1760] In addition to a stay on the execution of the warrant of

1757 RPL §§ 233(d)(2),(3).

1758 *Id.* at § 233(d)(4).

1759 CPLR § 5015(a)(1),(4). *See* Lotz v. Westbourne Apts., Inc., 159 A.D.3d 810, 73 N.Y.S.3d 572 (2d Dep't 2018); Mid-Hudson Props., Inc. v. Klein, 167 A.D.3d 862, 90 N.Y.S.3d 264 (2d Dep't 2018) (miscommunication regarding court appearance was reasonable excuse); Murphy v. Coalition of Landlords, 147 N.Y.S.3d 869 (App. Term, 9th & 10th Jud. Dists. 2021); 1449 Fulton v. Britton, 144 N.Y.S.3d 797 (App. Term, 2d, 11th & 13th Jud. Dists. 2021); ADM Mgmt. Corp. v. Mathews, 116 N.Y.S.3d 484 (App. Term, 1st Dep't 2019); 903 Realty, LLC v. Michael, 943 N.Y.S.2d 793 (App. Term, 2d, 11th & 13th Jud. Dists. 2011) (motion to vacate default judgment denied due to inadequate explanation for the non-appearance). *Cf.* 1825 Madison Retail, LLC v. Exclusive Dental Studios, PLLC, 114 N.Y.S.3d 553 (App. Term, 1st Dep't 2019) (noting that although the "excuse for its unreadiness" was "not particularly compelling," the Court granted motion to vacate a default due to a meritorious defense, the expeditious manner in which the relief was sought, and the absence of prejudice).

1760 CPLR § 5015(a)(1). *See* Deutsche Bank Nat'l Trust Co. v. Segal, 200 A.D.3d 852, 155 N.Y.S.3d 338 (2d Dep't 2021); Wells Fargo Bank, N.A. v. Ridenow, 186 A.D.3d 782, 127 N.Y.S.3d 343 (2d Dep't 2020); Loeffler v. Glasgow, 169 A.D.3d 1024, 94 N.Y.S.3d 607 (2d Dep't 2019). In *Loeffler*, the Appellate Division, Second Department noted that the Court maintains "'[i]nherent power to set aside excessive awards made upon default,' despite the fact that there is no reasonable excuse for the default." *Loeffler*, 169 A.D.3d at 1024, 94 N.Y.S.3d at 607.

eviction, the Respondent will typically seek the dismissal of the proceeding or, in the alternative, a hearing on the merits and/or a traverse hearing regarding service.

There is a strong public policy in favor of resolving lawsuits on the merits, as opposed to default.[1761] Excusable default may be demonstrated by a credible assertion of illness or automobile breakdown on the hearing date.[1762] Plausible explanations may further include, but are not limited to: missing a Court appearance due to a governmental agency's inspection of the premises;[1763] a spouse's failure to provide the movant with the Court papers;[1764] caring for an out-of-state elderly parent;[1765] misrepresentation by the Landlord's agent that a Court appearance was <u>not</u> required;[1766] Tenant's incarceration;[1767] waiting in the "wrong" room of the Courthouse at the time of the default;[1768] and law office failure.[1769]

Conclusory, unsubstantiated denials of service and unsworn allegations refuting service are <u>not</u> reasonable explanations for vacating a default judgment.[1770] In addition, undisclosed, incredulous "medical

---

1761 Epstein Becker & Green, P.C. v. Samson Mgmt. LLC, 188 A.D.3d 454, 131 N.Y.S.3d 892 (1st Dep't 2020); *Mid-Hudson Props., Inc.*, 167 A.D.3d at 862, 90 N.Y.S.3d at 264.

1762 *See, e.g.*, Jenkins v. Cisse, 114 N.Y.S.3d 800 (App. Term, 2d, 11th & 13th Jud. Dists. 2019) (food poisoning may constitute a reasonable excuse for failing to appear).

1763 Jacob Marion, LLC v. El Bey, 36 N.Y.S.3d 47 (App. Term, 2d, 11th & 13th Jud. Dists. 2016).

1764 Stepping Stones Assocs. v. Garcia, 971 N.Y.S.2d 75 (App. Term, 9th & 10th Jud. Dists. 2013) (judgment vacated after the arrears were paid notwithstanding the lack of a meritorious defense).

1765 Genuine Realty Corp. v. Mitchell, 111 N.Y.S.3d 164 (App. Term, 1st Dep't 2018).

1766 Westwood House LLC v. Javier, 105 N.Y.S.3d 840 (N.Y. Civ. Ct. N.Y. Cnty. 2019).

1767 2001 Story LLC v. Saul, 126 N.Y.S.3d 300 (App. Term, 1st Dep't 2020); 46 Downing St. LLC v. Thompson, 998 N.Y.S.2d 306 (App. Term, 1st Dep't 2014).

1768 Gates Towers, LLC v. Pfohl, 2016 N.Y. Misc. LEXIS 2746 (App. Term, 2d, 11th & 13th Jud. Dists. 2016).

1769 A & F Scaccia Realty Co. v. New York City Dep't of Environmental Protection, 200 A.D.3d 875, 161 N.Y.S.3d 108 (2d Dep't 2021); Government Employees Ins. Co. v. Avenue C Med., P.C., 166 A.D.3d 857, 87 N.Y.S.2d 252 (2d Dep't 2018) (miscommunication between former and present counsel); Oakdale Manor Owners, Inc. v. Raimondi, 29 N.Y.S.3d 848 (App. Term, 9th & 10th Jud. Dists. 2015).

1770 TBF Fin., LLC v. Eagle Tours, LLC, 172 A.D.3d 1269, 101 N.Y.S.3d 365 (2d Dep't 2019); Harbor Tech LLC v. Correa, 134 N.Y.S.3d 652 (N.Y Civ. Ct. Kings Cnty. 2020).

reasons;"[1771] conclusory denials that "no money is owed;"[1772] waiting eighteen (18) months to vacate the default;[1773] "conclusory assertions" that the Tenant did not receive the Petition;[1774] and intentional defaults, such as the Tenant's "refusal to participate...[due to] unparticular allegations of 'bad faith on the court,'"[1775] are similarly inadequate explanations.

Case law has imposed the additional requirement that the Respondent asserts the possibility of a "meritorious defense."[1776] In a non-payment proceeding, potential meritorious defenses include, but are not limited to: the rent was paid; the parties reached a subsequent agreement; and the warranty of habitability entitles the Tenant to an offset against some or all of the rent. In addition, a judgment and warrant may be vacated for "good cause" where the Respondent provides proof that the rent arrears were available, but not tendered, prior to the execution of the warrant due to a physical injury.[1777]

Similar outcomes may result in holdover proceedings. For example, the Appellate Term for the Ninth and Tenth Judicial Districts has held that pleading defects in the Petition[1778] and the failure to establish personal jurisdiction constitute grounds for vacating a default

---

1771 Dexter 345 Inc. v. Belem, 964 N.Y.S.2d 58 (App. Term, 1st Dep't 2012).

1772 *Jenkins*, 114 N.Y.S.3d at 800.

1773 116 John St. Owner, LLC v. Kim, 108 N.Y.S.3d 646 (App. Term, 1st Dep't 2018).

1774 Milonis v. 3273-3285 Westchester Ave. Realty Corp., 138 N.Y.S.3d 787 (App. Term, 1st Dep't 2021).

1775 *See* Sobro Local Dev. Corp. v. Bey, 7 N.Y.S.3d 245 (App. Term, 1st Dep't 2014).

1776 Citibank, N.A. v. Dervas, 204 A.D.3d 745, 164 N.Y.S.3d 475 (2d Dep't 2022); Aero Mgmt. v. Moghadasian, 160 N.Y.S.3d 741 (App. Term, 2d, 11th & 13th Jud. Dists. 2022); *Jacob Marion, LLC*, 36 N.Y.S.3d at 47; Cambridge Hgts. HDFC v. McCormick, 112 N.Y.S.3d 412 (App. Term, 2d, 11th & 13th Jud. Dists. 2018) (non-party to lease may not assert the defense of warranty of habitability).

1777 *See, e.g.*, Portillo v. Simpson, 95 N.Y.S.3d 126 (App. Term, 2d, 11th & 13th Jud. Dists 2018).

1778 *Lakeview Affordable Hous., LLC*, 121 N.Y.S.3d at 510; Parkview Apts. Corp. v. Pryce, 95 N.Y.S.3d 125 (App. Term, 9th & 10th Jud. Dists. 2018).

judgment.[1779] Where a lack of jurisdiction (personal or subject matter jurisdiction) is demonstrated, the Respondent need not substantiate a reasonable excuse for the default or the possibility of a meritorious defense.[1780] In all other situations, the failure to assert a potential meritorious defense will likely result in the motion being denied.[1781]

The process server's affidavit of service creates a presumption of proper service which requires the defaulting party to present more than "bare and unsubstantiated denials" to rebut.[1782] Where the movant raises a sufficient basis for challenging service; i.e., asserts more than conclusory denials, the Court may not rely solely upon the affidavit of service.[1783] A credible statement from the Respondent that: (1) he or she "was not home" when personal service is alleged or (2) the affidavit includes an erroneous name, address, and/or description of the person

1779 Bank of New York v. Dutan, 200 A.D.3d 636, 158 N.Y.S.3d 208 (2d Dep't 2021); 1653 Realty, LLC v. Hernandez, 117 N.Y.S.3d 790 (App. Term, 2d, 11th & 13th Jud. Dists. 2019); F & Realty Corp. v. 1014 Flatbush Ave., Inc., 969 N.Y.S.2d 802 (App. Term, 2d, 11th & 13th Jud. Dists. 2013) (vacating default judgment and dismissing Petition where Landlord failed to mail a copy of the Notice of Petition and Petition to Tenant's known corporate address following service on a person of suitable age and discretion); RR Reo, II, LLC v. Omeje, 939 N.Y.S.2d 743 (App. Term, 2d, 11th & 13th Jud. Dists. 2011) (vacating default judgment and dismissing Petition due to defective service).

1780 Fountain Terrace Owners, Inc. v. Balic, 101 N.Y.S.3d 699 (App. Term, 2d, 11th & 13th Jud. Dists. 2018) (issue of personal jurisdiction).

1781 *See, e.g.*, Founders v. Williams, 38 N.Y.S.3d 831 (App. Term, 1st Dep't 2016).

1782 HSBC Bank, N.A. v. Walker, 201 A.D.3d 795, 162 N.Y.S.3d 82 (2d Dep't 2022) (mortgage foreclosure action); 622 VCA, LLC v. Black, 166 N.Y.S.3d 436 (App. Term, 9th & 10th Jud. Dists. 2022).

1783 Tri State Flood, Inc. v. Wet Out Now Cleaning & Restoration, LLC, 157 N.Y.S.3d 327 (App. Term, 9th & 10th Jud. Dists. 2021) (movant "[m]ust swear to detailed and specific facts to rebut the statements in the process server's affidavit"); *Founders*, 38 N.Y.S.3d at 831. In a foreclosure proceeding, the Appellate Division, Second Department accepted the process server's second affidavit of service where the original was inadequate. *See* Deutsche Bank Nat'l Trust Co. v. Quinones, 114 A.D.3d 719, 981 N.Y.S.2d 107 (2d Dep't 2014). *Cf.* Thornton Americas Holdings (U.S.), LLC v. Waldron, 166 N.Y.S.3d 822 (App. Term, 2d, 11th & 13th Jud. Dists. 2022) (unsubstantiated denials of service fail to establish "entitlement to a traverse hearing"); Webster 204 Realty, LLC v. Los Muchachos Rest. Corp., 163 N.Y.S.3d 797 (N.Y. Civ. Ct. Bronx Cnty. 2022) (same).

allegedly served, is generally sufficient to grant a traverse hearing.[1784] Similarly, the sworn statement that the Tenant "was home all day, but nobody knocked on her door or otherwise attempted to serve her personally on that date," required a hearing on service.[1785] However, the conclusory statement "I was never served," without more, will not result in a traverse hearing.[1786]

At a traverse hearing, the burden is on the proponent of service to establish by a preponderance of the evidence that process was properly served.[1787] Exclusive reliance on the affidavit of service is impermissible.[1788] If the traverse is sustained, then the default judgment must be vacated, and the proceeding will be dismissed due to the lack of personal jurisdiction.

A process server in New York City must bring "all records...relating to the matter at issue" to the traverse hearing, including the log book

1784 *See, e.g.*, 91-7 Seventh Ave. LLC v. Zucca Trattoria, Inc., 162 N.Y.S.3d 920 (N.Y. Civ. Ct. N.Y. Cnty. 2022). *See also* 342 E. 67 Realty LLC v. Jacobs, 106 A.D.3d 610, 966 N.Y.S.2d 46 (1st Dep't 2013); 502 Ave. P Corp. v. AM & R Auto Repair Shop, 29 N.Y.S.3d 847 (App. Term, 2d, 11th & 13th Jud. Dists. 2015); 2437 Valentine Assoc. v. Valverde, 139 N.Y.S.3d 522 (N.Y. Civ. Ct. Bronx Cnty. 2021).

1785 West 97th St. Realty Corp. v. Aptaker, 2016 N.Y. Misc. LEXIS 230 (N.Y. Civ. Ct. N.Y. Cnty. 2016). *See generally* 156 Nassau Ave. HDFC v. Tchernitsky, 112 N.Y.S.3d 859 (App. Term, 2d, 11th & 13th Jud. Dists. 2019).

1786 *See* Medhat O'Kelly, As Administrator of the Estate of Magdy O'Kelly v. John Doe, 36 N.Y.S.3d 408 (App. Term, 2d, 11th & 13th Jud. Dists. 2016); LC & Assocs. v. Deans, 2002 N.Y. Misc. LEXIS 1693 (App. Term, 9th & 10th Jud. Dists. Sept. 19, 2002) (movant's conclusory statement "I was not served" is insufficient to vacate judgment).

1787 *Fountain Terrace Owners, Inc.*, 101 N.Y.S.3d at 699. *See* Fuentes v. Espinal, 153 A.D.3d 500, 60 N.Y.S.3d 81 (2d Dep't 2017); Frankel v. Schilling, 149 A.D.2d 657, at 659, 540 N.Y.S.2d 469, 470-71 (2d Dep't 1989); Forest Hills S. Owners, Inc. v. Ishida, 943 N.Y.S.2d 791 (App. Term, 2d, 11th & 13th Jud. Dists. 2011); Resnick Seaport LLC v. 199 Roast LLC, 2021 N.Y.L.J. LEXIS 564 (N.Y. Civ. Ct. N.Y. Cnty. June 16, 2021); *Harbor Tech LLC*, 134 N.Y.S.3d at 652.

1788 *502 Ave. P Corp.*, 29 N.Y.S.3d at 847; *see* 77 Commercial Holding, LLC v. Central Plastic, Inc., 4 N.Y.S.3d 464 (App. Term, 2d, 11th & 13th Jud. Dists. 2014); Friedman v. Eisner, 886 N.Y.S.2d 70 (App. Term, 2d, 11th & 13th Jud. Dists. 2009); Bham v. Wilson, 809 N.Y.S.2d 776, 777 (App. Term, 9th & 10th Jud. Dists. 2005).

and license where applicable.[1789] Section 208.1 of the Uniform Rules for the New York City Civil Courts provides that this requirement may be waived where good cause is shown and in the interests of justice.[1790] In New York City, a process server must further maintain and provide proof of Global Positioning System ("GPS") location and time.[1791]

3. UNDERTAKING AS A CONDITION FOR A STAY

If the Respondent is directed to post an undertaking as a condition for a stay, even where the Respondent fails to post the undertaking, the Court must decide the motion on the merits because a denial on the grounds that the undertaking was not posted constitutes reversible error.[1792] This rule is strictly enforced.

4. DECIDING THE ORDER TO SHOW CAUSE

On the return date, the parties are routinely directed to conference their case prior to oral argument. If a resolution is unobtainable and the motion is granted, then any of the following outcomes may result: (1) the judgment and warrant of eviction are vacated and the case is dismissed; (2) a hearing may be held on the merits; (3) a traverse hearing scheduled where service is sufficiently disputed; or (4) the money

---

1789 *See* UNIFORM RULES FOR NEW YORK CITY CIVIL COURT [22 N.Y.C.R.R.] § 208.29; AMB Fund III New York III & IV, LLC v. WWTL Logistics, Inc., 942 N.Y.S.2d 307 (App. Term, 2d, 11th & 13th Jud. Dists. 2012); Kenmore Assoc., L.P. v. Burke, 124 N.Y.S.3d 507 (N.Y. Civ. Ct. N.Y. Cnty. 2020); Serlin Bldg. Ltd. P'ship v. Littlem 2020 N.Y.L.J. LEXIS 356 (N.Y. Civ. Ct. Kings Cnty. Feb. 19, 2020). This rule applies to process servers in any city with a minimum of one (1) million residents. *See* GENERAL BUSINESS LAW § 89-cc.

1790 *See* UNIFORM RULES FOR NEW YORK CITY CIVIL COURT [22 N.Y.C.R.R.] § 208.1; *AMB Fund III New York III & IV, LLC*, 942 N.Y.S.2d at 307; *2437 Valentine Assocs., LLC*, 139 N.Y.S.3d at 522. *But see* First Commercial Bank of Memphis, N.A. v. Ndiaye, 733 N.Y.S.2d 562 (Queens Cnty. Sup. Ct. 2001) (action dismissed due to the process server's failure to comply with statutory requirements).

1791 RULES OF THE CITY OF NEW YORK [6 R.C.N.Y] § 2-233b; *Resnick Seaport, LLC*, 146 N.Y.S.3d at 768.

1792 *See Ratnam Assocs.*, 126 N.Y.S.3d at 608; Guzman v. Perez, 119 N.Y.S.3d 686 (App. Term, 9th & 10th Jud. Dists. 2019); CO-BB Devonshire Venture, LLC v. Smith, 110 N.Y.S.3d 481 (App. Term, 9th & 10th Jud. Dists. 2018); Parkview Equities, LLC v. Coughlin, 986 N.Y.S.2d 866 (App. Term, 9th & 10th Jud. Dists. 2014); Zabolotny v. Andersen, 859 N.Y.S.2d 907 (App. Term, 9th & 10th Jud. Dists. 2008).

judgment is modified and the judgment of possession and warrant of eviction are permitted to stand.

If the motion is denied, the Court will typically lift the stay and authorize enforcement of the judgment and warrant of eviction. The Court may, in its discretion, further extend the stay notwithstanding the denial of the motion.[1793] Absent a specific ruling to the contrary, the Sheriff will typically have to provide another fourteen (14) day notice prior to executing the warrant of eviction.[1794]

B. VACATING THE WARRANT (RPAPL § 749)

Real Property Actions and Proceedings Law § 749 permits the Court, for good cause shown, at any time prior to the execution of the warrant of eviction to: (1) stay execution or vacate the warrant; or (2) following execution, restore the Tenant to possession.[1795] The statute more specifically provides with regard to non-payment proceedings that where the full amount owed is paid (or deposited with the Court) prior to the execution of the warrant, the warrant must be vacated unless the Landlord demonstrates that the rent was withheld in bad faith.[1796]

Under prior law, the issuance of the warrant of eviction was the intervening event that terminated the Landlord and Tenant relationship in a non-payment proceeding.[1797] More specifically, prior to June 14,

1793 *See* 191 St. Assocs. LLC v. Cruz, 29 N.Y.S.3d 848 (App. Term, 1st Dep't 2016) (extending the stay 60 days following denial of Tenant's motion); Waterside Plaza, LLC v. Bhawnaney, 943 N.Y.S.2d 795 (App. Term, 1st Dep't 2012). *See generally* 1539 Park Pl., LLC v. Clarke, 152 N.Y.S.3d 767 (App. Term, 2d, 11th & 13th Jud. Dists. 2021); Building Mgmt. Co. Inc. v. Orelli, 108 N.Y.S.3d 648 (App. Term, 1st Dep't 2018).

1794 *See generally* 502 W. 152nd St., LLC v. Soumahoro, 98 N.Y.S.3d 500 (App. Term, 1st Dep't 2018).

1795 *See generally* 431 Audubon LLC v. Jiminian, 113 N.Y.S.3d 458 (App. Term, 1st Dep't 2019); Birchwood Ct. Owners, Inc. v. Toner, 37 N.Y.S.3d 206 (App. Term, 9th & 10th Jud. Dists. 2016).

1796 RPAPL § 749(3); 36 Apt. Assocs., JV v. Mayo, 130 N.Y.S.3d 649 (Mt. Vernon City Ct. 2020).

1797 *See* Crisafulli v. Southbridge Towers, Inc., 161 A.D.3d 690, 74 N.Y.S.3d 492 (1st Dep't 2018).

2019, in non-payment proceedings outside New York City, the Tenant typically had until the issuance of the warrant (i.e., signature affixed by the Court) to pay the arrears to avoid an eviction.[1798] This is no longer the case because RPAPL § 749(3) expanded the "payment" period until the execution of the warrant of eviction (absent "bad faith").

In *450 Clinton, LLC v. Bowe*, the Appellate Term for the Second, Eleventh and Thirteenth Judicial Districts affirmed the Housing Part's decision to vacate the warrant of eviction where the Tenant, who had resided in the rent-stabilized premises for thirty-seven (37) years, paid the arrears in full.[1799] Similarly, in *Poughkeepsie Hous. Auth. v. Johnson*, the warrant of eviction was vacated where the disabled Respondent demonstrated an ability to pay both the arrears and the rent going forward.[1800]

When appropriate, the Court may also vacate the warrant and restore the Tenant to possession following the eviction.[1801] In *2203 Belmont Realty Corp. v. Gant*, the Appellate Term, First Department granted the Tenant's motion to be restored to possession where the Tenant acted in good faith, resumed his employment after being laid off, and satisfied the arrears, costs, and Landlord's attorney's fees.[1802] In *Hillside Ave., LLC v. Mateo*, the Appellate Term conditionally granted the Tenant's motion to be restored to possession because the Tenant's failure to comply with the payment schedule was due to a scrivener's

---

1798 *See* RPAPL § 751.

1799 115 N.Y.S.3d 803 (App. Term, 2d, 11th & 13th Jud Dists. 2019) (the Court, however, did not vacate the final judgment rendered following a hearing on the merits); *see* 1588-1600 AMS LLC v. Gil, 167 N.Y.S.3d 296 (App. Term, 1st Dep't 2022).

1800 101 N.Y.S.3d 701 (App. Term, 9th & 10th Jud. Dists. 2018) (the Court did not vacate the final judgment).

1801 *See, e.g.*, In re Lafayette Boynton Hous. Corp. v. Pickett, 135 A.D.3d 518, 23 N.Y.S.3d 204 (1st Dep't 2016) (disabled Tenant paid $14,030.59 and made good faith attempts to secure financial assistance for the remaining amounts due) (*citing* Brusco v. Braun, 84 N.Y.2d 674, 621 N.Y.S.2d 291 (1994)); *Birchwood Ct. Owners, Inc.*, 37 N.Y.S.3d at 206 (directing Landlord to restore Tenant to possession provided the arrears and use and occupancy were paid within twenty (20) days).

1802 36 N.Y.S.3d 410 (App. Term, 1st Dep't 2016).

error on the money order.[1803] A similar result occurred in *Thamer Props. Corp. v. Nava* where the Tenant tendered the rent arrears two (2) weeks prior to the eviction.[1804] The Appellate Term reasoned that the Landlord's re-renting of the room to a third party was inconsequential to the Court's ultimate decision.[1805]

A Tenant seeking to be restored to the premises must name the new Tenant in possession, if any, as a party to the proceeding.[1806] In *Guoco Hempstead Prop., LLC v. Eltaiar*, the Appellate Term for the Second, Eleventh and Thirteenth Judicial Districts held that "[i]f there is a new tenant in possession, the new tenant must be joined prior to the hearing."[1807]

Motions to be restored to possession may be denied for a variety of reasons, including the Tenant's failure to act in good faith. In *Parkview Apts. Corp. v. Pryce*, the Appellate Term for the Ninth and Tenth Judicial Districts denied the motion due to "[o]verwhelming proof that the tenants" had engaged in objectionable conduct at the premises (i.e., causing noxious odors).[1808] In *GHR Co., LLC v. Sannon*, the Appellate Term for the Second, Eleventh and Thirteenth Judicial Districts similarly refused to vacate the warrant, but continued to stay its execution where the parties' settlement included a "probationary period."[1809] Moreover, in *431 Audubon LLC v. Jiminian*, the Appellate Term for the First Department extended the stay (without vacating the judgment) for ten (10) months due to the children residing within the apartment and the Tenant's ability to pay the rent arrears.[1810]

When executing the warrant, the Sheriff must check the premises

---

1803 113 N.Y.S.3d 463 (App. Term, 1st Dep't 2019) (the motion was conditionally granted on the Tenant paying arrears and eviction costs within ten (10) days).

1804 95 N.Y.S.3d 126 (App. Term, 1st Dep't 2018).

1805 *Id.*

1806 DLB of NY, LLC v. Billan, 139 N.Y.S.3d 744 (App. Term, 2d, 11th & 13th Jud. Dists. 2021).

1807 121 N.Y.S.3d 776 (App. Term, 2d, 11th & 13th Jud. Dists. 2020).

1808 95 N.Y.S.3d 125 (App. Term, 9th & 10th Jud. Dists. 2018).

1809 95 N.Y.S.3d 125 (App. Term, 2d, 11th & 13th Jud. Dists. 2018).

1810 113 N.Y.S.3d 458 (App. Term, 1st Dep't 2019).

for "companion animals" and, when animals are found in the premises, "reasonable efforts" must be undertaken to either reunite the occupant with the animals or have the companion animals transported to an appropriate animal shelter.[1811] A "companion animal" is defined as a dog or cat, or "other domesticated animal normally maintained in or near the household."[1812]

C. STAYING ISSUANCE OF THE WARRANT (RPAPL § 753)

Real Property Actions and Proceedings Law § 753 governs stays on both (1) the "issuance" of a warrant of eviction and (2) the execution to collect costs regarding residential premises. Where proper, a stay may be granted for up to one (1) year.[1813] Section 753 had applied exclusively to New York City until 2019, at which time, the geographical restrictions were removed.[1814]

A request for a stay on the issuance of the warrant arises following an "award" of possession in favor of the Petitioner. For the Court to stay the "issuance" of the warrant and/or the collection of costs, the occupant must demonstrate that: (1) the premises are used for residential purposes (other than hotels or rooming houses); (2) the application is made in good faith; and (3) "due and reasonable efforts" were unsuccessfully taken to find similarly suitable alternative housing in the neighborhood or that the denial of the request for a stay will result in "extreme hardship" to the applicant or the applicant's family.[1815]

The factors to consider in determining whether an "extreme hardship" would result include: (1) a serious ill-health or exacerbation of

1811 RPAPL § 749(2)(b).

1812 *Id.* (adopting the definition of "companion animal" set forth in AGRICULTURE AND MARKETS LAW § 350).

1813 *Id.* at § 753(1) (HSTPA, L. 2019, c. 36, Part M, § 21). The time period had formerly been up to six (6) months.

1814 *Id.*; *see* Moflhi v. Wagner, 160 N.Y.S.3d 575 (Albany City Ct. Feb. 8, 2022).

1815 RPAPL § 753; 140 W. End Ave. Owners Corp. v. Dinah L., 114 N.Y.S.3d 844 (N.Y. Civ. Ct. N.Y. Cnty. 2019). Outside a city of more than one (1) million residents, the term "neighborhood" is defined as the same town or village or, where the applicant has school-aged children, then the same "school district."

an ongoing condition; (2) a child's enrollment in school; (3) "extenuating life circumstance[s]" impacting the ability to relocate or the quality of life; and (4) substantial hardship to the Landlord.[1816] If granted, the Court may direct the occupant to deposit moneys in the form of use and occupancy with the Clerk of the Court, either in a lump sum or in installment payments, as consideration for the Tenant's occupancy of the premises during the stay period.[1817] The amount of the deposit is based upon the rent for the most recent month the occupant was in lawful possession, plus any additional amount necessary to achieve the fair market value of the premises. This amount may further include unpaid rent accrued prior to the stay.[1818]

The reader should be mindful that in a residential holdover proceeding based upon the Tenant's breach of the rental agreement, the Court must stay issuance of the warrant of eviction for thirty (30) days to afford the Tenant an opportunity to cure the breach.[1819] However, where the proceeding was predicated upon the unlawful holding over by an "objectionable" Tenant, the stay provisions pursuant to RPAPL § 753 are not applicable if the Landlord provides "competent evidence" that the occupant is, in fact, objectionable.[1820] A lease provision waiving the occupant's rights under RPAPL § 753 is void as against public policy.[1821]

1816 RPAPL § 753.

1817 *Id.* at § 753(2); *140 W. End Owners Corp.*, 114 N.Y.S.3d at 844.

1818 RPAPL § 753(2).

1819 *Id.* at § 753(4); *see, e.g.*, Grove Equities LLC v. Butensky, 110 N.Y.S.3d 783 (App. Term, 1st Dep't 2018) (holding that RPAPL § 753(4) "must be 'liberally construed to spread its beneficial effects as widely as possible") (citation omitted); Spencer Scott Group, LLC v. Nahas, 2022 N.Y. Misc. LEXIS 823 (Richmond Cnty. Sup. Ct. Jan. 24, 2022).

1820 RPAPL § 753(3).

1821 *Id.* at § 753(5); *see* 159 MP Corp. v. Redbridge Bedford, LLC, 33 N.Y.3d 353, 104 N.Y.S.3d 1 (2019).

CHAPTER 16

SECURITY DEPOSIT

A recent study revealed that approximately thirty-six percent (36%) of Tenants' security deposits are not returned.[1822] A common justification for withholding a security deposit is the Tenant's "moving out early" and the parties' agreement to use the deposit to satisfy rent arrears.[1823]

In New York, the security deposit (for both residential and commercial premises) remains the property of the Tenant for the duration of the tenancy.[1824] The Landlord holds the deposit in trust as a "protected creditor should the tenant breach the lease."[1825] Where there is damage to the premises beyond ordinary wear and tear, in order to utilize the security deposit, the Landlord must "establish the reasonable value of any of the repairs."[1826] If the Landlord fails to demonstrate both sufficient grounds for the withholding and the reasonable amount of

1822 *See* Jeff Rhode, "*20 Surprising Rental Property Owners Statistics (2022 Edition)*," Dec. 14, 2021, at https://learn.roofstock.com/blog/rental-property-owner-statistics. In 2013, approximately twenty-five percent (25%) of Tenants did not have their security deposits returned. *See* Graham Wood, "*Security Deposit Refund: 1 in 4 Renters Don't Get Their Money Back, Survey Finds*," AOL Finance, Jan. 29, 2013, at https://www.aol.com/2013-01-29-security-deposit-refund.html.

1823 Wood, "*Security Deposit Refund: 1 in 4 Renters Don't Get Their Money Back, Survey Finds*," at AOL Finance.

1824 GOL § 7-103(1); Vanchev v. Mulligan, 41 N.Y.S.3d 722 (App. Term, 2d, 11th & 13th Jud. Dists. 2016).

1825 Glass v. Janbach Props., Inc., 73 A.D.2d 106, 425 N.Y.S.2d 343 (2d Dep't 1980); Automatic Data Proc. v. York Hunter, Inc., 2004 N.Y.L.J. LEXIS 415 (N.Y. Civ. Ct. N.Y. Cnty. Feb. 5, 2004).

1826 Cuevas v. Rowinski, 135 N.Y.S.3d 223 (App. Term, 2d, 11th & 13th Jud. Dists. 2020). *See* GOL § 7-108(1-a)(f); Quijano v. Rowinski, 116 N.Y.S.3d 483 (App. Term, 2d, 11th & 13th Jud. Dists. 2019); Hermida v. Blochwitz, 61 N.Y.S.3d 191 (App. Term, 9th & 10th Jud. Dists. 2017).

expenses incurred as a result, then the funds must be returned after the Tenant vacates the premises.[1827]

A. GENERAL RULES

The security deposit (and any advance payment) for both rent-stabilized and unregulated residential properties may not exceed one (1) month's rent,[1828] and a lease provision "waiving or modifying" a Tenant's right to the security deposit pursuant to GOL § 7-108 is "absolutely void."[1829] The reader should be mindful that the HSTPA applies to residential premises, and the 2019 law changes did not alter the rules regarding security deposits for commercial properties.

The Housing Part may not include an unpaid security deposit within the money judgment even with the consent of the parties.[1830] Claims regarding the return of the security deposit are generally adjudicated in a plenary or small claims action after the Tenant vacates the premises.

1827 GOL § 7-103(1); Li v. Gao, 145 N.Y.S.3d 758 (App. Term, 9th & 10th Jud. Dists. 2021) (awarding judgment for return of security deposit where Landlord failed to demonstrate that the Tenant caused damage beyond ordinary wear and tear); *Cuevas*, 135 N.Y.S.3d at 223 (directing a new trial where Landlord was not afforded opportunity to introduce evidence regarding damage to the premises); Nunez v. 58-43 Penrod St., LLC, 132 N.Y.S.3d 510 (App. Term, 2d, 11th & 13th Jud. Dists. 2020) (awarding return of security deposit where there was no reasonable basis for withholding the funds and the Landlord "improperly withheld [the Tenant's] refrigerator"); *Quijano*, 116 N.Y.S.3d at 483 (Tenant entitled to return of security deposit where the alleged damage was "ordinary wear and tear"); Wicklund v. Mukhtyar, 61 N.Y.S.3d 193 (App. Term, 9th & 10th Jud. Dists. 2017) (Landlord failed to establish that the Tenant caused damage beyond ordinary wear and tear); Sachtschale v. Greece, 118 N.Y.S.3d 376 (N.Y. Civ. Ct. N.Y. Cnty. 2019) (Tenant awarded judgment for the security deposit where the damage was "normal wear and tear," and further holding it was inappropriate to withhold the deposit on the grounds that the Tenant "used the [premises] during the last year of her tenancy for short term rentals").

1828 GOL § 7-108(1-a)(a) (unregulated residential premises); RSC [9 N.Y.C.R.R.] § 2525.4 (rent-stabilized premises). There is an exception to the limit on the amount of the security deposit for owner-occupied cooperative apartments where the Tenant is the unit's owner who purchased "exclusive occupancy of such dwelling unit individually and with the permitted occupants pursuant to a proprietary lease or occupancy agreement…." GOL § 7-108(4) [note, there are two subdivisions 4 of this section].

1829 GOL § 7-108(3); Felder v. Fleet Mills, LLC, 148 N.Y.S.3d 824 (App. Term, 9th & 10th Jud. Dists. 2021).

1830 Hines v. Ambrose, 907 N.Y.S.2d 437 (App. Term, 9th & 10th Jud. Dists. 2010).

A violation of the maintenance and notification requirements pertaining to the security deposit may result in damages against the Landlord and, if the violation was willful, punitive damages may be imposed in an amount equal to two (2) times the deposit.[1831]

1. THE DEPOSIT MAY NOT BE UNILATERALLY APPLIED TOWARDS RENT DURING THE TENANCY

During the tenancy, a Tenant may not use the security deposit to pay the rent without the Landlord's consent. This frequently occurs where the Tenant attempts to utilize the security deposit as the final month's rent. In *Winter v. Del Regno*, the Appellate Term for the Ninth and Tenth Judicial Districts rejected this practice and held that absent consent, a Tenant may not unilaterally apply the security deposit while "still renting the apartment."[1832]

2. INTEREST-BEARING ACCOUNTS

A Landlord generally need not maintain the security deposit in an interest-bearing account.[1833] Exceptions to this rule include rent-stabilized apartments[1834] and residential buildings containing "six or more family dwelling units."[1835] In *Pritzker v. Park S. Lofts LLC*, the New York County Supreme Court held that the exception for buildings containing "six or more family dwelling units" only applies to the owners of

1831 GOL § 7-108(1-a)(g).

1832 155 N.Y.S.3d 528 (App. Term, 9th & 10th Jud. Dists. 2021).

1833 *See, e.g.*, Audthan LLC v. Nick & Duke, LLC, 110 N.Y.S.3d 503 (N.Y. Cnty. Sup. Ct. 2018).

1834 *See* RSC § 2525.4. If a security deposit greater than one (1) month's rent was paid prior to the enactment of the RSC, then the deposit "may continue in effect during the term of such lease and any renewals thereof with the same tenant." *Id.*

1835 GOL § 7-103(2-a). Buildings with mixed-uses for residential and commercial purposes are not exempt from this exception (i.e., if there are six (6) or more family dwelling units, then the security deposit must accrue interest). *See* Gihon, LLC v. 501 Second St., LLC, 103 A.D.3d 840, 962 N.Y.S.2d 238 (2d Dep't 2013).

the building.[1836] According to that decision, a Landlord who owns five (5) or fewer dwelling units within an unregulated building may not be required to place the deposit in an interest-bearing account.[1837]

3. THE FINANCIAL INSTITUTION HOLDING THE DEPOSIT (NOTICE)

Regardless of the type of account, the Tenant must be provided written notice of the amount and the financial institution (name and address) where the security deposit is maintained.[1838] The reader should be mindful that the GOL does not require the immediate return of the security deposit if the Landlord fails to provide such notice.[1839] However, the omission permits a "rebuttable inference" that the Landlord commingled the security deposit with personal funds, which, in turn, may result in the Landlord's forfeiture of any right to the deposit.[1840]

4. DEPOSIT RETURNED WHEN THE TENANT DOES NOT TAKE POSSESSION

After executing a rental agreement, the Landlord may retain the security deposit where the Tenant neither takes possession of the premises nor provides timely notice of the intent not to enter possession.[1841] The security deposit reverts back to the Tenant if the property was not

---

1836 920 N.Y.S.2d 243 (N.Y. Cnty. Sup. Ct. 2010) (reasoning "[t]he exclusion of properties with five or fewer family dwellings from application of GOL § 7-103(2-a) is consistent with the notion that it does not impose the burden of requiring the landlord to keep the security deposit in a separate interest-bearing account upon the fee owner of only a single unit, just as it clearly does not apply to the fee owner of a single-family home"); *see* Government of the Rep. of S. Africa v. Sonsino, 2011 U.S. Dist. LEXIS 105773 (S.D.N.Y. Sept. 16, 2011) (finding the *Pritzker* decision to be "persuasive").

1837 *Pritzker*, 920 N.Y.S.2d at 243. The reader should note that the decision states, in dicta, that its conclusion was inconsistent with an Attorney General Opinion (No. 17) issued forty (40) years earlier. *Id.*

1838 GOL § 7-103(2). The financial institution must have a place of business within the State. *Id.* If the security deposit is placed within an interest-bearing account, the Landlord is entitled to receive an administration expense in an amount equivalent to one percent (1%) of the deposit each year. *Id.*

1839 Sikora v. Shurtluff, 121 N.Y.S.3d 508 (App. Term, 9th & 10th Jud. Dists. 2020).

1840 *See* GOL § 7-103(2); Rubman v. Osuchowski, 163 A.D.3d 1471, 82 N.Y.S.3d 675 (4th Dep't 2018); Milkie v. Guzzone, 143 A.D.3d 863, 39 N.Y.S.3d 243 (2d Dep't 2016); Baffour v. Calenda, 126 N.Y.S.3d 299 (App. Term, 1st Dep't 2020).

1841 *See* Ally v. Latchman, 886 N.Y.S.2d 69 (App. Term, 2d, 11th & 13th Jud. Dists. 2009).

in move-in or habitable condition when the lease commenced.[1842] In addition, the security deposit (and any rent previously paid) reverts to the Tenant where the "lease was [not] executed"[1843] or the Tenant learns that the premises were rented to another party.[1844]

5. UNLAWFUL CONVERSION (COMMINGLING)

Due to the change in status "from [that of] debtor-creditor, to trustee-cestui que trust," the Landlord must refrain from commingling the Tenant's security deposit with its own funds.[1845] This is the case even where the Tenant is in breach of the rental agreement (e.g., fails to pay rent).[1846] As indicated previously, the Landlord's failure to provide notice of the financial institution where the security was deposited permits an inference that the Landlord commingled the security deposit with personal funds.[1847] Whether based upon this inference or other evidence, the Landlord forfeits any right to avail itself of a commingled security deposit and, upon demand, the Tenant is entitled to

1842 Siudym v. Sicherer, 901 N.Y.S.2d 910 (App. Term, 9th & 10th Jud. Dists. 2009); Ilacqua v. Sameyah, 880 N.Y.S.2d 873 (App. Term, 9th & 10th Jud. Dists. 2009).

1843 Harris v. Diorio, 63 N.Y.S.3d 305 (App. Term, 9th & 10th Jud. Dists. 2017).

1844 *See* Butten v. Maggio Realty LLC, 7 N.Y.S.3d 240 (App. Term, 1st Dep't 2014).

1845 In re Perfection Tech. Servs. Press, Inc., 22 A.D.2d 352, 256 N.Y.S.2d 116 (2d Dep't 1965); Finnerty v. Freeman, 673 N.Y.S.2d 843, 844 (App. Term, 9th & 10th Jud. Dists. 1998); Hansen v. Lorenzo, 901 N.Y.S.2d 906 (Suffolk Cnty. Dist. Ct. 2009); *see generally* 1710 Realty, LLC v. Portabella 308 Utica, LLC, 189 A.D.3d 944, 138 N.Y.S.3d 523 (2d Dep't 2020) (claim for commingling moot where Tenant was entitled to return of security deposit after terminating tenancy due to Landlord's failure to provide the premises "vacant, broom-clean, and free of the prior tenant's property").

1846 GOL § 7-103; *see* LeRoy v. Sayers, 217 A.D.2d 63, at 67-68, 635 N.Y.S.2d 217, 220-21 (1st Dep't 1995) (holding "[t]he tenant's noncompliance with the lease terms [is not] a defense to a landlord's breach of his duty [to keep the security deposit segregated]"); DeVries v. Jim Duffy LLC, 138 N.Y.S.3d 787 (App. Term, 1st Dep't 2021) (Tenant's "repudiation of the lease agreement" does not relieve Landlord of the obligation to segregate the Tenant's security deposit); Kelligrew v. Lynch, 784 N.Y.S.2d 921 (App. Term, 9th & 10th Jud. Dists. 2004) (holding that "[a] tenant's failure to comply with the terms of a lease is not a defense to a landlord's breach of the duty not to commingle the deposit with personal funds").

1847 *Rubman*, 163 A.D.3d at 1471, 82 N.Y.S.3d at 675.

its immediate return.[1848]

The statute of limitations on a claim for unlawful conversion (e.g., commingling a security deposit) is three (3) years from "when the conversion or taking occurred."[1849] The Landlord may cure the commingling (and revive its right to hold the deposit) by depositing the security deposit within a segregated account prior to the expiration of the rental agreement and/or demand by the Tenant.[1850] In addition, "the right to a refund [of the commingled security deposit] is immediate and shall not be delayed or postponed until the resolution of a landlord's claim for some or all of the security deposit."[1851]

A lease provision allowing for the commingling of the security deposit is null and void.[1852] In addition, the Landlord may not use a commingled security deposit as an offset against moneys the Tenant owes pursuant to

---

1848 *Id.*; *Milkie*, 143 A.D.3d at 863, 39 N.Y.S.3d at 243; Solomon v. Ness, 118 A.D.3d 773, 987 N.Y.S.2d 220 (2d Dep't 2014); Paterno v. Carroll, 75 A.D.3d 625, at 628, 905 N.Y.S.2d 653, 655-56 (2d Dep't 2010); *Perfection Tech. Servs. Press, Inc.*, 22 A.D.2d at 356, 256 N.Y.S.2d at 170; Dan Klores Assocs. v. Abramoff, 288 A.D.2d 121, at 121-22, 733 N.Y.S.2d 388 (1st Dep't 2001) (a Landlord who commingles the security deposit may not use the deposit to "offset…justifiable repair costs after the tenant vacates"); *DeVries*, 138 N.Y.S.3d at 787; Shipman v. Swift, 100 N.Y.S.3d 482 (Norwich City Ct. 2018).

1849 *See* Harlem Capital Ctr., LLC v. Rosen & Gordon, LLC, 145 A.D.3d 579, 44 N.Y.S.3d 36 (1st Dep't 2016).

1850 *See generally Harlem Capital Ctr., LLC*, 145 A.D.3d at 579, 44 N.Y.S.3d at 36; Spagnoletti v. Chalfin, 131 A.D.3d 901, 16 N.Y.S.3d 727 (1st Dep't 2015) (holding that "[e]ven if [the deposit was] not properly segregated in the first instance, defendants had the ability to cure that defect during the term of the lease"); Bartis v. Harbor Tech, LLC, 2020 N.Y. Misc. LEXIS 11304 (Kings Cnty. Sup. Ct. Nov. 17, 2020); McMaster v. Pearse, 804 N.Y.S.2d 640, 643 n.2 (N.Y. Civ. Ct. N.Y. Cnty. 2005) (*citing* MILTON R. FRIEDMAN, FRIEDMAN ON LEASES § 20.4 [Nature of Security Deposit–Statutes], at 1293 (4th ed. 1997) ("[The] Landlord's right to the security [deposit] is revived if the commingling ceases before tenant brings an action to recover the deposit. But segregation after expiration of the term and [vacating] by tenant is held too late for such revival")). *See also DeVries*, 138 N.Y.S.3d at 787 (holding that Landlord's "conclusory averments regarding his 'standard practice' in handling security deposits failed to raise a triable issue of fact" on the question of whether the commingling was cured).

1851 *McMaster*, 804 N.Y.S.2d at 640 (emphasis added); 3 Green St., LLC v. Caceres, 115 N.Y.S.3d 381 n.4 (Hastings-On-Hudson Just. Ct. 2019) (noting "[i]f Petitioner commingled the security deposit with its own funds, that represents a conversion of Respondent's property and she was entitled to an immediate refund of the deposit at that time").

1852 GOL § 7-103(3); *see Solomon*, 118 A.D.3d at 773, 987 N.Y.S.2d at 220.

the rental agreement.[1853] An offset "[a]llows entities that owe each other money to apply their mutual debts against each other, thereby avoiding the absurdity of making A pay B when B owes A."[1854] An offset is impermissible for a commingled security deposit because a trustee (i.e., the Landlord) may not offset an obligation of a trust beneficiary (i.e., the Tenant).[1855] "To allow the landlord to set off the rent against the deposit would be to treat the deposit as a debt and the landlord as a debtor, the situation [GOL § 7-103] was enacted to change."[1856]

However, a Tenant may elect to offset the commingled security deposit against any rents due and owing the Landlord.[1857] If the rent is current, then the Tenant may be awarded the security deposit as damages in a summary proceeding where asserted as a counterclaim or, otherwise, the Tenant may commence a plenary or small claims action for the return of the deposit.

Where there are multiple Landlords to a rental agreement, liability for commingling the security deposit may attach to any or all of them, even a Landlord who lacked knowledge or reason to know of the commingling.[1858] This is because a Landlord is responsible for violations of the fiduciary relationship with the Tenant, even those unknowingly

---

1853 *Perfection Tech. Servs. Press, Inc.*, 22 A.D.2d at 352, 256 N.Y.S.2d at 166, *aff'd*, 18 N.Y.2d 644, 273 N.Y.S.2d 71 (1966); 23 E. 39th St. Mgmt. Corp. v. 23 E. 39th St. Developer, LLC, 134 A.D.3d 629, 23 N.Y.S.3d 33 (1st Dep't 2015); *Baffour*, 126 N.Y.S.3d at 299.

1854 *See generally* University Sq. San Antonio, TX. LLC v. Mega Furniture Dezavala, 198 A.D.3d 1284, 155 N.Y.S.3d 252 (4th Dep't 2021); Westinghouse Credit Corp. v. D'Urso, 278 F.3d 138, 149 (2d Cir. 2002) (citations omitted).

1855 *Perfection Tech. Servs. Press, Inc.*, 22 A.D.2d at 356, 256 N.Y.S.2d at 170; *Westinghouse Credit Corp.*, 278 F.3d at 149. *See generally* Fore Improvement Corp. v. Selig, 278 F.2d 143 (2d Cir. 1960).

1856 *23 E. 39th St. Mgmt. Corp.*, 134 A.D.3d at 629, 23 N.Y.S.3d at 33.

1857 *Id.* (holding that "[t]he same logic [i.e, the Landlord may not offset the debts of the Tenant trust beneficiary] does not pertain where a tenant seeks to apply the security deposit to reduced amounts found owing to the landlord").

1858 *See McMaster*, 804 N.Y.S.2d at 647 ("[t]he obligation [of a landlord relating to security deposits]...do[es] not permit a cofiduciary to claim exemption from responsibility based upon passivity, ignorance of the law, or even the contrary advice of counsel"); Matter of the Estate of Rothko, 43 N.Y.2d 305, at 320, 401 N.Y.S.2d 449, 455 (1977) (an "executor [fiduciary] who knows that his coexecutor is committing breaches of trust and not only fails to exert efforts directed towards prevention but accedes to them is legally accountable even though he was acting on the advice of counsel"); *Hansen*, 901 N.Y.S.2d at 906 (noting that "[a]lthough the Defendant herein did not actually convert the security deposit, he is nonetheless responsible for his partner's violation of the fiduciary relationship").

committed by a another fiduciary.[1859] In addition to the return of the security deposit, the Tenant is entitled to statutory interest from the earliest date of the conversion.[1860]

6. TENANT'S CLAIM FOR RETURN OF THE DEPOSIT

Other than where a deposit has been commingled, a claim for the return of the security deposit is "premature" when asserted prior to the Tenant vacating the premises or the expiration of the tenancy.[1861] As discussed previously, after the Tenant vacates the premises, recovery of the security deposit may be sought in an appropriate Court as an affirmative claim or counterclaim.[1862]

In an action to recover the security deposit, the Landlord may be "entitled to claim unpaid rent as an offset…even in the absence of a counterclaim."[1863] However, where the rent is current, a prevailing Tenant may recover the security deposit when the Landlord fails to demonstrate damages beyond ordinary wear and tear or noncompliance with a statutory or contractual obligation.[1864] A Tenant is further entitled to a money

1859 *McMaster*, 804 N.Y.S.2d at 647.

1860 Scotti v. Barrett, 166 A.D.3d 698, 88 N.Y.S.3d 44 (2d Dep't 2018) (for conversion claim, the "[u]sual measure of damages…is the value of the property at the time and place of conversion, plus interest"); *23 E. 39th St. Mgmt. Corp.*, 134 A.D.3d at 629, 23 N.Y.S.3d at 33; Vidipax, LLC v. Brown Bear Realty Corp., 880 N.Y.S.2d 228 (N.Y. Cnty. Sup. Ct. 2009); *but see Audthan LLC*, 110 N.Y.S.3d at 503 (holding that a Tenant may only recover interest on the security deposit "as of right where the lease provides for interest, or the deposit is for the rental property which 'contains six or more family dwelling units'").

1861 Wingett v. Bartoloni, 803 N.Y.S.2d 21 (App. Term, 9th & 10th Jud. Dists. 2005); 188 Ave. A Take Out Food Corp. v. Lucky Jab Realty Corp., 2020 N.Y. Misc. LEXIS 10889 (N.Y. Cnty. Sup. Ct. Dec. 21, 2020) (noting "an action for the return of security is premature where the term has not yet expired"); Hayes v. Ramsey, 110 N.Y.S.3d 206 (App. Term, 9th & 10th Jud. Dists. 2018) (improper to award return of security deposit where Tenant listed the subject premises as her current residence, thereby "fail[ing] to establish that [the] tenancy had ended").

1862 *See generally* Posh NY, Inc. v. Lobern Dev. Co., LLC, 924 N.Y.S.2d 311 (App. Term, 9th & 10th Jud. Dists. 2011). The statute of limitations for the unlawful withholding of a security deposit is six (6) years. *See* Sharaf v. Younger, 46 N.Y.S.3d 477 (App. Term, 2d, 11th & 13th Jud. Dists. 2016).

1863 Stines v. Bowins, 157 N.Y.S.3d 326 (App. Term, 9th & 10th Jud. Dists. 2021); Johnson v. Marcano, 101 N.Y.S.3d 699 (App. Term, 2d, 11th & 13th Jud. Dists. 2018).

1864 *See, e.g.*, Albert v. Bryant, 162 N.Y.S.3d 905 (Mt. Vernon City Ct. 2022); Camacho v. Paduch, 2018 N.Y.L.J. LEXIS 2374 (Middletown City Ct. July 11, 2018).

judgment for the security deposit where the Tenant vacated the premises and terminated the tenancy after learning the unlawful status of the property, such as the Landlord's failure to obtain a valid rental permit.[1865]

The reader should be mindful that if successful on a claim for the return of a portion or the entire security deposit, the Housing Part has no authority to direct the Landlord or Landlord's counsel to pay the Tenant because declaratory and injunctive relief are beyond the jurisdictional authority of the Court.[1866] Instead, the Court may award an offset or issue a money judgment in favor of the Tenant for the amount improperly withheld.[1867]

B. GROUNDS TO WITHHOLD THE DEPOSIT

General Obligations Law § 7-108(1-a)(b) sets forth the grounds for withholding a security deposit for an unregulated residential dwelling. These grounds include: (1) "reasonable and itemized costs due to [the] non-payment of rent;" (2) repairs for property damage beyond ordinary wear and tear caused by the Tenant and/or the Tenant's guests; (3) utility charges payable directly to the Landlord pursuant to the rental agreement; and (4) costs associated with moving and storing the Tenant's belongings.[1868]

The Landlord must provide proof of the costs associated with the repairs for damage beyond ordinary wear and tear, and that the damage did not precede the Tenant's initial occupancy.[1869] Similar standards are

---

1865 Ader v. Guzman, 135 A.D.3d 671, 23 N.Y.S.3d 292 (2d Dep't 2016); Sethi v. Naman, 890 N.Y.S.2d 371 (App. Term, 9th & 10th Jud. Dists. 2009). *See* Illegal Apartments, Chapter 11, subdiv. A(1), *supra*.

1866 *See* 555 & 561 Gates, LLC v. Hamadov, 130 N.Y.S.3d 183 (App. Term, 2d, 11th & 13th Jud. Dists. 2020); LA Gem, LLC v. Fuentes, 110 N.Y.S.3d 198 (App. Term, 9th & 10th Jud. Dists. 2018).

1867 Deutsch v. G. Shore III Dev. Corp., 875 N.Y.S.2d 819 (App. Term, 9th & 10th Jud. Dists. 2008); World Realty Corp. v. Consumer Sales, Inc., 862 N.Y.S.2d 812 (App. Term, 9th & 10th Jud. Dists. 2005).

1868 GOL § 7-108 (1-a)(b); *see, e.g.*, Peltz v. Kalayjian, 116 N.Y.S.3d 481 (App. Term, 9th & 10th Jud. Dists. 2019); *Albert*, 162 N.Y.S.3d at 905.

1869 GOL § 7-108(1-a)(b) (stating, in part, "The landlord may not retain any amount of the deposit for costs relating to ordinary wear and tear of occupancy or damage caused by a prior tenant"). *See also Felder*, 148 N.Y.S.3d at 824 (failed to prove the cost to repaint the apartment); Chery v. Richards, 117 N.Y.S.3d 796 (App. Term, 9th & 10th Jud. Dists. 2019) (same).

generally utilized for commercial premises, but the commercial entities need not consider GOL § 7-108, which only applies to residential properties.[1870]

1. THE WITHHOLDING MUST RELATE TO THE SUBJECT PREMISES

The Landlord's withholding of a security deposit <u>must</u> be for a reason related to the leased premises. In *Gable v. Cahill*, the Appellate Term for the Second, Eleventh and Thirteenth Judicial Districts held that the Landlord's deductions for the "removal" of items from the backyard were improper because the "lease did <u>not</u> include the backyard as a portion of the premises being rented."[1871]

As discussed previously, where the Tenant defaults on the payment of rent, the Landlord is generally entitled to apply the security deposit (provided the security deposit was <u>not</u> commingled) as a setoff against rent arrears or in satisfaction of a judgment.[1872] However, the applicable

1870 *See, e.g.*, Harlington Realty Co., LLC v. Gotham W. Realty LLC, 2022 N.Y. Misc. LEXIS 264 (N.Y. Cnty. Sup. Ct. Jan. 19, 2022); 55 Broadway Realty LLC v. Houston Upholstery Co., Inc., 2021 N.Y. Misc. LEXIS 6318 (N.Y. Cnty. Sup. Ct. Dec. 8, 2021); Jozefovic v. White Plains Healthcare Props. I, 2021 N.Y. Misc. LEXIS 1720 (N.Y. Cnty. Sup. Ct. April 8, 2021).

1871 130 N.Y.S.3d 884 (App. Term, 2d, 11th & 13th Jud. Dists. 2020).

1872 *See* 501 Fifth Ave. Co., LLC v. Aslam, 136 A.D.3d 535, 25 N.Y.S.3d 180 (1st Dep't 2016) (security deposit applied to damages accrued during the tenancy); Ring v. Anabil USA, Inc., 29 A.D.3d 408, 815 N.Y.S.2d 68 (1st Dep't 2006) (security deposit applied to unpaid rent where commercial tenancy terminated early); Markowitz v. Landau, 171 A.D.2d 564, 567 N.Y.S.2d 268 (1st Dep't 1991) (holding the deposit "provides a fund from which the landlord can draw for unpaid rent or damages and which puts the landlord into the status of a secured creditor"); *Stines*, 157 N.Y.S.3d at 326 (security deposit may be offset against unpaid rent); James Bohl, CPA, P.C. v. Poffenbarger, 100 N.Y.S.3d 609 (App. Term, 9th & 10th Jud. Dists. 2018) (applied as offset against utilities); 511 W. 25th St. Owner LP v. WestKids25, LLC, 2019 N.Y. Misc. LEXIS 3928 (N.Y. Cnty. Sup. Ct. July 15, 2019) (lease permitted Landlord to apply the security deposit to post-vacatur damages); 88 Third Realty, LLC v. Bekiyants, 2018 N.Y. Misc. LEXIS 6509 (N.Y. Cnty. Sup. Ct. Dec. 21, 2018) (holding that "[w]hen a landlord holds a security deposit at the time a court issues a judgment for unpaid rent, the security deposit is subtracted from the judgment if the landlord has 'applied' the security deposit to the arrears"); Lyras v. Yoo, 2020 N.Y. Misc. LEXIS 10265 (Rye City Ct. Dec. 2, 2020) (security deposit offset against unpaid rent); Carr v. Torrey, 98 N.Y.S.3d 500 (Parma Justice Ct. 2018) (deposit applied towards rent arrears); *see also 188 Ave. A Take Out Food Corp.*, 2020 N.Y. Misc. LEXIS at 10889 (noting that "[w]hile usually nothing will prevent a landlord from applying the security deposit to the arrears, 'interest on the arrears should not [be] calculated prior to the application of a credit for the security deposit'").

statutes and rental agreement should be reviewed for limiting restrictions prior to applying the security deposit for any purpose.[1873]

In a highly unusual matter, the Appellate Term for the Ninth and Tenth Judicial Districts addressed a situation where the Landlord refused to utilize the security deposit in satisfaction of the money judgment, notwithstanding the Tenant's consent, where there were no additional viable claims against the Tenant.[1874] In *D & B Enters., No. 2. v. Cablam, Inc.*, the Court held that the Landlord had no choice but to acquiesce (i.e., use the security deposit to satisfy the money judgment) because the lack of any viable future claims rendered the return of the security deposit a "liquidated" claim, and liquidated claims may be utilized to satisfy a money judgment without the consent of the creditor Landlord.[1875] On the other hand, where there are outstanding claims, or potentially viable future claims, against the Tenant, the return of the security deposit is considered an "unliquidated" claim which requires the consent of the judgment creditor (i.e., the Landlord) to be used in satisfaction of the judgment.[1876]

1873 *See* 14 E. 4th St. Unit 509 LLC v. Toporek, 203 A.D.3d 17, 159 N.Y.S.3d 419 (1st Dep't 2022) (noting that the lease provided "the security deposit cannot be applied to arrears") (emphasis added); Jeffrey Mgmt. Corp. v. One Commercial Realty Servs. LLC, 2022 N.Y. Misc. LEXIS 428 (N.Y. Cnty. Sup. Ct. Jan. 26, 2022) (holding that "the terms of the guarantee must control, and may prohibit an offset where the landlord may recover from the guarantor without first applying the security deposit") (*citing 501 Fifth Ave. Co., LLC*, 136 A.D.3d at 535, 25 N.Y.S.3d at 180 (Landlord "had a right under the lease to determine when and how the security deposit would be applied towards the tenant's outstanding lease obligations . . .")).

1874 *See* D & B Enters. No. 2 v. Cablam Inc., 729 N.Y.S.2d 239 (App. Term, 9th & 10th Jud. Dists. 2001) (the lease did not include a survival clause).

1875 *Id.*; Gramatan Realty Corp. v. Morrell, 106 N.Y.S.3d 729 (Mt. Vernon City Ct. 2018) (holding that "[w]here the rental agreement is terminated and there is no claim for damage to property against Tenants, the security deposit may be used in full or partial satisfaction of a judgment because under that scenario the right to recover the security deposit is considered a liquidated claim").

1876 *D & B Enters. No. 2*, 729 N.Y.S.2d at 239 (holding "[o]rdinarily, the right to recover a security deposit might be deemed unliquidated [and, as a result, the landlord's consent is required to use the security deposit in satisfaction] because the landlord might have a claim for damage to the property or for unpaid rent which has yet to be adjudicated").

2. REQUISITE STEPS TO WITHHOLD THE DEPOSIT (RESIDENTIAL PROPERTY)

The Landlord must provide written reports and allow for a series of inspections, both pre- and post-possession, as a prerequisite to withholding the Tenant's security deposit at the conclusion of the tenancy. As described earlier, the Landlord's noncompliance with the statutory requirements may result in civil liability, plus punitive damages in an amount equal to two (2) times the deposit for willful noncompliance.[1877]

a. INITIAL INSPECTION AND REPORT (PRIOR TO POSSESSION)

The Landlord is required to offer an opportunity for a joint inspection of the premises both: (1) prior to the Tenant taking possession, and again (2) following notice of either party's intent to terminate the tenancy.[1878] Where the Tenant requests an inspection prior to taking possession, "the parties shall execute a written agreement before the tenant begins occupancy of the unit attesting to the condition of the property and specifically noting any existing defects or damages."[1879] Any defects or damages listed within the initial report ("Initial Report") may not constitute a basis for withholding the security deposit after the Tenant vacates the premises.[1880] The Initial Report is admissible as "[e]vidence of the condition of the premises at the beginning of the occupancy" in a proceeding related to the return of the security deposit.[1881]

b. SECOND INSPECTION AND REPORT (NOTICE TO TERMINATE)

When either party notices an intent to terminate the tenancy, the Landlord must "within a reasonable time" provide written notice of the Tenant's right to request another inspection prior to vacating the premises.[1882] If the Tenant requests an inspection, the inspection must

1877 GOL § 7-108(1-a)(g).

1878 *Id.* at §§ 7-108(1-a)[c],(d).

1879 *Id.* at § 7-108(1-a)[c].

1880 *Id.*

1881 *Id.*

1882 *Id.* at § 7-108(1-a)(d).

take place, provided at least forty-eight (48) hours written notice is given, between one (1) and two (2) weeks before the termination of the lease.[1883]

Following the inspection, the Landlord must prepare an "itemized [written] statement specifying repairs or cleaning that are proposed to be the basis of any deductions from the tenant's deposit" ("Second Report").[1884] The purpose of the Second Report is to afford the Tenant an opportunity to cure any defects and make necessary repairs prior to the termination of the tenancy, and, together with the Initial Report, both Reports are admissible in a proceeding for the return of the security deposit.[1885]

c. FINAL REPORT AND NOTICE OF WITHHOLDING

No more than fourteen (14) days after the Tenant vacates the premises, the Landlord must provide a separate "itemized statement" setting forth the basis and amount of each withholding from the security deposit ("Third Report").[1886] The remaining portion of the security deposit, if any, must be returned to the Tenant within the same time period.[1887] The failure to timely provide the Third Report, and any remaining portion of the security deposit held by the Landlord, results in the forfeiture of the Landlord's "right to retain any portion of the security deposit."[1888]

In *Bauer v. Gerber*, the Tenant was granted summary judgment for the return of the security deposit due to the Landlord's noncompliance with the fourteen (14) day requirement pursuant to GOL § 7-108(1-a)

1883 *Id.* If fewer than two (2) weeks notice is provided, then the inspection need not take place between one (1) and two (2) weeks prior to the termination of the tenancy. *Id.*

1884 *Id.*; *Albert*, 162 N.Y.S.3d at 905 (disallowing withholding of security deposit, except a portion for a broken door which the Tenant did not dispute, where the Landlord failed to provide written notice of the right to inspect the premises following the notice to terminate or a detailed statement of the purported defective conditions).

1885 GOL § 7-108(1-a)(d).

1886 *Id.* at § 7-108(1-a)(e).

1887 *Id.* at § 7-108(1-a)(e).

1888 *Id.*

(e).[1889] In that case, the Landlord provided the Third Report more than twenty-two (22) days after the Tenant vacated the premises, and further indicated that the remaining portion of the security deposit would be returned on an unspecified future date.[1890] Due to the noncompliance, the Court awarded the Tenant actual damages, including attorney's fees pursuant to RPL § 234.[1891]

The Appellate Division, First Department has clarified that the automatic forfeiture provision for the Landlord's noncompliance with GOL § 7-108(1-a) is exclusively set forth within subdivision (e); the failure to provide an itemized statement and return the remaining portion (if any) of the security deposit within fourteen (14) days after the tenant vacates the premises.[1892] In *14 E. 4th St. Unit 509 LLC*, the Court succinctly concluded that "by the plain terms of the statute only the obligations in subdivision (e) are subject to a penalty of forfeiture" for noncompliance.[1893] Accordingly, since the Landlord violated another subsection of the statute (i.e., subdivision (d), the failure to provide notice of an opportunity to inspect the premises within a reasonable period of time following notification of an intent to terminate the tenancy), the Court permitted the Landlord to withhold and utilize the security deposit (and awarded a money judgment for the difference) as an offset against property damage beyond ordinary wear and tear attributable to the Tenant.[1894]

1889 2021 N.Y.L.J. LEXIS 1299 (N.Y. Civ. Ct. Kings Cnty. Jan. 19, 2022).

1890 *Id.* The statute does not specify the manner and form in which the itemized statement must be provided. GOL § 7-108(1-a).

1891 *Bauer*, 2021 N.Y.L.J. LEXIS at 1299; GOL § 7-108(1-a)(g). The Court denied the Tenant's request for punitive damages after concluding the noncompliance was not willful. *Id.*; *cf.* Elena v. Milo Mgmt. LLC, 2021 N.Y.L.J. LEXIS 337 (Yonkers City Ct. April 22, 2021) (denying claim for return of the security deposit where the Landlord "provide[d] creditable testimony and evidence explaining the reason for the [three (3) day] delay" in providing an itemized statement of damages and returning the remaining portion of the deposit).

1892 *14 E. 4th St. Unit 509 LLC*, 203 A.D.3d at 17, 159 N.Y.S.3d at 419.

1893 *Id.*

1894 *Id.*

APPENDIX

SAMPLE FORMS

FORMS—TABLE OF CONTENTS[1895]

1895 The forms provided are neither all encompassing nor necessarily applicable to your particular situation. The reader should consult with an attorney and, further, refer to the local and other laws regarding a specific matter, including, but not limited to, rent control and rent stabilization laws where applicable.

I. PREDICATE NOTICES

A. FOURTEEN (14) DAY RENT DEMAND (Non-payment)

TO: SEAN JONES, SHANNON JONES

JOHN DOE #1-3 and JANE DOE # 1-3, being fictitious persons, intended to be any other occupants in the premises known as __ ________ Street, Apt. __, ___________, New York ____, ____ County (the "Subject Premises")

Re: Rental Agreement, dated ________, between the Landlord, __________ and Tenants, ____________________, regarding the Subject Premises, a residential property

PLEASE TAKE NOTICE, that you have failed to make the payment of rent as obligated under your rental agreement for the Subject Premises and, that, as a result, the following arrears are due and owing the Landlord:

January, _____, rent	$ __________
February, _____, rent	$ __________
March, _____, rent	$ __________
Total due:	$__________

PLEASE TAKE FURTHER NOTICE, that pursuant to Real Property Actions and Proceedings Law § 711(2), demand is hereby made for you to pay the above rent arrears on or before ________, ___, 20__, such date being at least fourteen (14) days from the date of service upon you of this rent demand or, alternatively, you must vacate and surrender possession of the Subject Premises to the Landlord. The failure to pay the aforementioned amount by ________, ___, 20__, will result in a summary proceeding being commenced to recover possession of the Subject Premises, a warrant to evict, and all rent and other relief available, plus interest and costs, that the Landlord is entitled pursuant to the rental agreement whether in the summary proceeding and/or a subsequent plenary action.

Dated:

____

Owner/Landlord or authorized individual
on behalf of the Owner/Landlord

B. FIVE (5) DAY LATE NOTICE (NON-PAYMENT) (RESIDENTIAL)[1896]

February __, 20__

VIA CERTIFIED MAIL RETURN RECEIPT REQUESTED

TO: SEAN JONES, SHANNON JONES

JOHN DOE #1-3 and JANE DOE # 1-3, being fictitious persons, intended to be any other occupants in the premises known as __ ________ Street, Apt. __,

___________, New York _____ County (the "Subject Premises")

Re: Five (5) Day Late Rent Notice

Rental Agreement, dated ________, between the Landlord, __________ and Tenants, ____________________, regarding the Subject Premises, a residential property

Dear Mr./Ms. ___________:

This notice is provided pursuant to Real Property Law § 235-e(d) to inform you that your payment of the _______ 20__ rent for the Subject Premises, in the amount of $__________, is now **more than five (5) days** past due. Upon receipt of this five (5) day Late Notice, payment in full is to be remitted to the undersigned at __. ____________ Street, East Islip, NY 11730.

Dated:

____

Owner/Landlord or authorized individual on behalf of the Owner/Landlord

1896 For residential properties, both a fourteen (14) day Rent Demand and a five (5) day Late Notice must be provided prior to the commencement of a non-payment proceeding.

C. LANDLORD'S NOTICE TO TERMINATE MONTH-TO-MONTH TENANCY (RESIDENTIAL) (30-, 60- OR 90-DAY NOTICE)

TO: SEAN JONES, SHANNON JONES

JOHN DOE #1-3 and JANE DOE # 1-3, being fictitious persons, intended to be any other occupants in the premises known as __ ________ Street, __________, New York ____, Apt. ____ (the "Subject Premises")

Re: Month-to-Month Rental Agreement, dated ________, between the Landlord, __________ and Tenants, __________________, regarding the Subject Premises, a residential property

PLEASE TAKE NOTICE, that the undersigned Landlord elects to terminate your tenancy of the Subject Premises, which is presently being held by you pursuant to a month-to-month agreement. This notice is being provided not less than __ [*thirty (30) OR sixty (60) OR ninety (90)*] days prior to the termination date of ________, __, 20__ [*in most jurisdictions, the date selected should coincide with the final day of the monthly term; i.e., if the tenancy began on the 1st, then select the 31st (or 30th where applicable), etc.*].

PLEASE TAKE FURTHER NOTICE that Tenants have been in possession of the premises for a duration of _________________ months /years [*if the Tenants have occupied the premises for a duration of one (1) year or less, then a 30 day notice is required OR if the Tenants have occupied the premises for more than one (1) year but fewer than two (2) years, then a 60 day notice is required OR if the Tenants have occupied the premises for more than two (2) years, then a 90 day notice must be provided*].

PLEASE TAKE FURTHER NOTICE, that you and all other persons occupying the Subject Premises must vacate and surrender the Subject Premises on or before ______, __, 20__, a date not less than ____ [*thirty (30) OR sixty (60) OR ninety (90)*] days from the date the herein Notice was served upon you.

PLEASE TAKE FURTHER NOTICE, that the failure to quit and vacate the Subject Premises by the above date will result in the Landlord commencing a summary proceeding to have you evicted from the Subject Premises for holding over past the termination of your tenancy and for possession, a money judgment for all monetary relief, including unpaid rent and use and occupancy, together with all other reasonable relief the Owner/Landlord is entitled.

Dated:

____

Owner/Landlord or authorized individual on behalf of the Owner/Landlord

D. LANDLORD'S NOTICE TO TERMINATE MONTH-TO-MONTH TENANCY (COMMERCIAL) (NEW YORK CITY) (30 DAYS)

TO: XYZ Corp.

JOHN DOE #1-3 and JANE DOE # 1-3, being fictitious persons, intended to be any other occupants in the premises known as __ ________ Street, __________, New York ____, Apt. ____ (the "Subject Premises")

Re: Month-to-Month Rental Agreement, dated ________, between the Landlord, __________ and Tenant, ___________________, regarding the Subject Premises, a residential property

PLEASE TAKE NOTICE, that the undersigned Landlord elects to terminate your tenancy of the Subject Premises, which is presently being held by you pursuant to a month-to-month agreement. This notice is being provided not less than thirty (30) days prior to the termination date of ________, __, 20__ [*the date selected should coincide with the final day of the monthly term; i.e., if the tenancy began on the 1st, then select the 31st (or 30th where applicable), etc.*].

PLEASE TAKE FURTHER NOTICE, that you and all other persons occupying the Subject Premises must vacate and surrender the Subject Premises on or before ______, __, 20__, a date not less than thirty (30) days from the date the herein Notice was served upon you.

PLEASE TAKE FURTHER NOTICE, that the failure to quit and vacate the Subject Premises by the above date will result in the Landlord commencing a summary proceeding to have you evicted from the Subject Premises for holding over past the termination of your tenancy and for possession, a money judgment for all monetary relief, including unpaid rent and use and occupancy, together with all other reasonable relief the Owner/Landlord is entitled.

Dated:

____

Owner/Landlord or authorized individual on behalf of the Owner/Landlord

E. LANDLORD'S NOTICE TO TERMINATE MONTH-TO-MONTH TENANCY (COMMERCIAL) (OUTSIDE NYC) (ONE MONTH)

TO: XYZ Corp.

JOHN DOE #1-3 and JANE DOE # 1-3, being fictitious persons, intended to be any other occupants in the premises known as __ ________ Street, __________, New York ____, Apt. ____ (the "Subject Premises")

Re: Month-to-Month Rental Agreement, dated ________, between the Landlord, __________ and Tenant, __________________, regarding the Subject Premises, a residential property

PLEASE TAKE NOTICE, that the undersigned Landlord elects to terminate your tenancy of the Subject Premises, which is presently being held by you pursuant to a month-to-month agreement. This notice is being provided not less than one (1) month prior to the termination date of ________, __, 20__ [*the date selected should coincide with the final day of the monthly term; i.e., if the tenancy began on the 1st, then select the 31st (or 30th where applicable), etc.*].

PLEASE TAKE FURTHER NOTICE, that you and all other persons occupying the Subject Premises must vacate and surrender the Subject Premises on or before ______, __, 20__, a date not less than one (1) month from the date the herein Notice was served upon you.

PLEASE TAKE FURTHER NOTICE, that the failure to quit and vacate the Subject Premises by the above date will result in the Landlord commencing a summary proceeding to have you evicted from the Subject Premises for holding over past the termination of your tenancy and for possession, a money judgment for all monetary relief, including unpaid rent and use and occupancy, together with all other reasonable relief the Owner/Landlord is entitled.

Dated:

____

Owner/Landlord or authorized individual on behalf of the Owner/Landlord

F. LANDLORD'S NOTICE NOT TO RE-NEW TENANCY (RESIDENTIAL) (30-, 60- OR 90-DAY NOTICE)

TO: SEAN JONES, SHANNON JONES

JOHN DOE #1-3 and JANE DOE # 1-3, being fictitious persons, intended to be any other occupants in the premises known as ___________ Street, ___________, New York _____, Apt. _____ (the "Subject Premises")

Re: Rental Agreement, dated _________, between the Landlord, ___________ and Tenants, ____________________, regarding the Subject Premises, a residential property

PLEASE TAKE NOTICE, that pursuant to Real Property Law § 226-c, the undersigned Landlord elects <u>not</u> to re-new your tenancy of the Subject Premises which is due to expire on _________, __, 20__.

PLEASE TAKE FURTHER NOTICE that Tenants have been in possession of the premises for a duration of __________________ months/years or the rental agreement is for a duration of __________________ months/years [*if the Tenants have occupied the premises for a duration of one (1) year or less and the lease is for a duration of one (1) year or less, then at least a 30 day notice is required OR if the Tenants have occupied the premises for more than one (1) year but fewer than two (2) years or the lease* was *for at least one (1) year but for a duration less than two (2) years, then at least a 60 day notice is required OR if the Tenants have occupied the premises for more than two (2) years or the lease was for a duration of at least two (2) years, then at least a 90 day notice must be provided*].

PLEASE TAKE FURTHER NOTICE, that you and all other persons occupying the Subject Premises must vacate and surrender the Subject Premises on or before _______, __, 20__, a date not less than _____ [*thirty (30) OR sixty (60) OR ninety (90)*] days from the date the herein Notice was served upon you.

PLEASE TAKE FURTHER NOTICE, that the failure to quit and vacate the Subject Premises by the above date will result in the Landlord commencing a summary proceeding to have you evicted from the Subject Premises for holding over past the termination of your tenancy and for possession, a money judgment for all monetary relief, including unpaid rent and use and occupancy, together with all other reasonable relief the Owner/Landlord is entitled.

Dated:

____

Owner/Landlord or authorized individual on behalf of the Owner/Landlord

G. LANDLORD'S RENT INCREASE OF AT LEAST 5% (RESIDENTIAL)

TO: SEAN JONES, SHANNON JONES

JOHN DOE #1-3 and JANE DOE # 1-3, being fictitious persons, intended to be any other occupants in the premises known as __ ________ Street, __________, New York ____, Apt. ____ (the "Subject Premises")

Re: Rent Increase—Rental Agreement, dated ________, between the Landlord, __________ and Tenants, ____________________, regarding the Subject Premises, a residential property

PLEASE TAKE NOTICE, that pursuant to Real Property Law § 226-c, effective January __, 20__, the monthly rent for the Subject Premises shall increase from $______ per month to $______ per month, an increase 5% or greater from the current rent ("Rent Increase").

PLEASE TAKE FURTHER NOTICE that Tenants have been in possession of the premises for a duration of ________________ or the rental agreement is for a duration of ________________ [*if the Tenants have occupied the premises for a duration of one (1) year or less and the lease is for a duration of one (1) year or less, then at least a 30 day notice is required OR if the Tenants have occupied the premises for more than one (1) year but fewer than two (2) years or the lease* was *for at least one (1) year but for a duration less than two (2) years, then at least a 60 day notice is required OR if the Tenants have occupied the premises for more than two (2) years or the lease was for a duration of at least two (2) years, then at least a 90 day notice must be provided*].

PLEASE TAKE FURTHER NOTICE, that the Rent Increase coincides with the expiration of the current Rental Agreement, and that renewal of the Rental Agreement is subject to the Tenant's agreement to said Rent Increase. This Notice is provided at least ____ [*thirty (30) OR sixty (60) OR ninety (90)*] days prior to the expiration date of the current Rental Agreement.

Dated:

____

Attorneys for Landlord

TENANT ACKNOWLEDGED

AND ACCEPTED

By: ____________________

Name: ____________________

Position: ____________________

Date and Time: ______________

H. TEN (10) DAY NOTICE TO REVOKE LICENSE AGREEMENT (HOLDOVER)

TO: **SEAN JONES, SHANNON JONES**
JOHN DOE #1-3 and JANE DOE # 1-3, being fictitious persons, intended to be any other occupants in the premises known as __ ________ Street, ___________, New York ____, Apt. ____ (the "Subject Premises")

Re: License Agreement, dated ________, between the Owner/Licensor, __________ and Occupants, ____________________, regarding the Subject Premises, a residential property

PLEASE TAKE NOTICE, that you and all other persons occupying the Subject Premises must quit and vacate the Subject Premises on or before ________, __, 20__, a date not less than ten (10) days from the date the herein ten (10) day Notice was served upon you, on the grounds that your license to possess the Subject Premises has been revoked. [*modify accordingly if the Occupant is a squatter or the Subject Premises had been foreclosed upon and the Occupant is not a bona fide Tenant*].

PLEASE TAKE FURTHER NOTICE, that the failure to quit and vacate the Subject Premises by the above date will result in a summary proceeding being commenced to recover possession of the Subject Premises, together with a money judgment and further all other reasonable relief the Owner/Licensor is entitled.

Dated:

____
Owner/Licensor or other authorized individual

I. NOTICE TO QUIT POSSESSION (POST-FORECLOSURE) (HOLDOVER) (10-DAYS, 90-DAYS OR LONGER)

TO: SEAN JONES, FRANK "DOE"

JOHN DOE #1-3 and JANE DOE # 1-3, being fictitious persons, intended to be any other occupants in the premises known as __ _______ Street, ____________, New York ____, Apt. ____ (the "Subject Premises")

Re: Post-foreclosure of the Subject Premises—Notice to Quit Possession and Vacate the Subject Premises, a residential property

PLEASE TAKE NOTICE, that the Subject Premises described in Schedule "A" annexed hereto has been sold to BANK ______, pursuant to a Judgment of Foreclosure and Sale, dated _____________, that was duly entered in the Clerk's Office of Suffolk County on ____________, relating to a foreclosure action entitled ____________v. _____________, Index No. __-_____. Pursuant to the aforementioned Judgment, a sale was held on _______________, and the referee duly delivered a deed to Bank ______. **A certified copy of the Referee's Deed is attached hereto and is now exhibited to you.** The Judgment of Foreclosure and Sale states, *inter alia*, that the subsequent purchaser at said sale shall be let into full possession of the entire Subject Premises.

PLEASE TAKE FURTHER NOTICE, that pursuant to the Protecting Tenants at Foreclosure Act of 2009, Pub. Law No. 111-22, §§ 701-04, 123 Stat. 1660 (2009) ("PTFA"), as reinstated by the Economic Growth, Regulation Relief and Consumer Protection Act of 2018, Pub. Law No. 115-174,12 U.S.C. §§ 5201 *et. seq*. (2018), and pursuant to §§ 221, 713 and 1303 of the New York State Real Property Actions and Proceedings Law ("RPAPL"), if you are occupying the Subject Premises as a bona fide tenant, then you have until _______, __, 20__, that being a date not less than ____ [*if occupant is not a bona fide Tenant, then 10 days notice OR if occupant is a bona fide Tenant, then the longer of 90 days or the time remaining on the lease unless the new owner seeks to occupy the premises as a primary residence in which case 90 days notice is required*] days from the date a copy of this Notice to Quit Possession was served upon you, to quit and vacate the Subject Premises.

PLEASE TAKE FURTHER NOTICE, that if you are a bona fide Tenant or your lease qualifies under New York State Law, and your lease term expires <u>after</u> the above date, you may have the right to continue to occupy the Subject Premises for the greater of the remainder of the lease term or a period of ninety (90) days, under the same terms and conditions that were in effect at the time of entry of the Judgement of Foreclosure and Sale or if no such Judgment was entered, upon the terms and conditions that were in effect at the time of the transfer of ownership of such property.

The PTFA defines a bona fide Tenant as one who: (a) entered into the rental agreement with the former owner before the Notice of Foreclosure; and (b) is not the former owner or the child, spouse or parent of the former owner; and [c] the rental agreement was the result of an arms-length transaction; and (d) the rent is not substantially less than the fair market rent for the property or your rent is reduced or subsidized due to a Federal, State or local subsidy.

According to RPAPL § 1305, for a lease to qualify for the ninety (90) day Notice period: (a) you must not be the owner of the Subject Premises and (b) the rent must not be substantially less than the fair market rent for the Subject Premises unless the Subject Premises is subject to a Federal or State statutory system of subsidy or other federal or state statutory scheme.

The name and address of a new owner, any person or entity which becomes a successor-in-interest after the issuance of the [*ten (10) or ninety (90), or longer*] day Notice provided for in this subdivision shall notify all Tenants of its name and address and shall assume such interest subject to the right of the Tenant to maintain possession as provided herein. Please contact the undersigned upon receipt of this Notice to discuss your lease and financial obligations.

If you do not contact us, then you must vacate the Subject Premises by the above date. Bank ____ hereby demands that all occupants and all persons occupying the Subject Premises under you, including all family members, lessees, licensees, etc., to quit and surrender possession of the Subject Premises to Bank ______ on or before the above vacate date. The Subject Premises is to be left in broom clean condition. You are not to remove anything attached to or used in connection with the Subject Premises or covered by the mortgage that has been foreclosed.

PLEASE TAKE FURTHER NOTICE, that unless each person occupying the Subject Premises quits and vacates the Subject Premises on or before the above date, Bank ______ will commence a summary proceeding to have you evicted from the Subject Premises and further seek all monetary relief, including, but not limited to, use and occupancy of the Subject Premises, that the Bank may be entitled.

Dated:

____

Attorneys for BANK ______

The undersigned, an attorney duly licensed to practice law within the State of New York hereby certifies pursuant to CPLR § 2105 that I have compared the accompanying deed to the original of same referred to within this Notice to Quit Possession—[*10 Day or 90 Day*] Notice and have found same to be a true and complete copy.

Dated: ____

J. NOTICE TO CURE

TO: COMPANY XYZ

JOHN DOE #1-3 and JANE DOE # 1-3, being fictitious persons, intended to be any other occupants in the premises known as __ ________ Street, ___________, New York ____, Suite ____ (the "Subject Premises")

Re: Rental Agreement, dated ________, between the Landlord, __________ and Tenant, ____________________, regarding the Subject Premises, a commercial property

PLEASE TAKE NOTICE, that pursuant to Paragraph ___ of your rental agreement for the Subject Premises duly executed on ______ __, 20__, and further applicable law, Notice is hereby given that you have materially violated said rental agreement in that you violated Paragraph __ of the rental agreement in that you [*specify the breach*].

PLEASE TAKE FURTHER NOTICE, that the following includes an accurate description of the facts establishing the breach: [*state the factual allegations resulting in the breach*]. The breach is on-going, and the Landlord continues to incur damages as a result.

PLEASE TAKE FURTHER NOTICE, that you must cure this breach on or before ______ __, 20__, as specified within the rental agreement, and the failure to cure the breach by this date will result in the rental agreement terminating and the Landlord commencing a summary proceeding to have you evicted from the Subject Premises and for all other relief available from the Court.

PLEASE TAKE FURTHER NOTICE, that pursuant to Paragraph __ of the rental agreement, you are responsible for all costs, including attorney's fees, incurred by the Landlord as a result of your breach.

Dated:

____

Attorneys for Landlord

K. TENANT'S NOTICE TO TERMINATE MONTH-TO-MONTH TENANCY (OUTSIDE NYC)

TO: LANDLORD
For the premises known as __ _______ Street, _________, New York ____, Apt. ____ (the "Subject Premises")

Re: Month-to-Month Rental Agreement, dated ________, between the Landlord, __________ and Tenant, ____________________, regarding the Subject Premises, a residential property

PLEASE TAKE NOTICE, that the undersigned Tenant elects to terminate the tenancy for the Subject Premises, which is presently a month-to-month tenancy.

PLEASE TAKE FURTHER NOTICE, that Tenant and all other persons occupying the Subject Premises shall vacate and Landlord shall accept surrender of the Subject Premises on or before ______ __, 20__,[1897] a date not less than one (1) month from the date the herein Tenant's Notice to Terminate Month-to-Month Tenancy was served upon you.

PLEASE TAKE FURTHER NOTICE, that the Tenant's obligations under the Rental Agreement shall cease to exist on the termination date. Notwithstanding the termination of the month-to-month tenancy, the Tenant reserves the right to seek all relief, monetary and/or otherwise, in the appropriate forum for any breaches of the Landlord's duties and obligations in connection with the Rental Agreement. Kindly contact the undersigned to arrange an inspection of the Subject Premises.

Dated:

____

Tenant or authorized individual on behalf of the Tenant

1897Presumably, the Tenant must select a termination date of at least one (1) month in duration from the service of the notice and which falls on the final day of the term. For example, if the month-to-month tenancy began on February 1st and the Tenant causes to be served a termination notice on February 6th, then the termination date would be March 31st, April 30th, May 31st, June 30th or July 31st etc., i.e., at least one (1) month notice and the last day of the term.

II. TENANT'S NOTICE OF SURRENDER OF THE PREMISES

TO: COMPANY XYZ

Landlord

Re: Surrender of Premises located at __ ________ Road, ______, New York (a commercial property)

Dear ____________,

As of this date, the __th day of __________, 20__, Tenant ____ hereby surrenders the above premises and all rights to possession thereof and returns same to the Landlord, _________. As per our discussion, Tenant's possessions have been removed from the premises. Enclosed please find all sets of the keys that were in the Tenant's possession for the subject premises. The premises have been returned in broom-swept condition. Kindly return my client's security deposit upon receipt.

Very truly yours,

Counsel for Tenant __________

LANDLORD COMPANY XYZ
ACKNOWLEDGED RECEIPT AND KEYS RECEIVED

By: ________________________

Name: _____________________

Position: ____________________

Date and Time: _________________

III. NOTICE OF PETITION AND PETITION

A. NON-PAYMENT PROCEEDING

SUFFOLK COUNTY SIXTH DISTRICT COURT
PATCHOGUE, NEW YORK

Petitioner,	Index No. BRLT __-_____
- against -	***NOTICE OF PETITION***
Respondent.	**(Non-Payment Proceeding)**

To the Respondent: [name(s) and address(es) of each Respondent]

PLEASE TAKE NOTICE, that a hearing at which you must appear and answer will be held at the Suffolk County Sixth District Court, 150 West Main Street, Patchogue, New York, on _______, __, 20__ at 9:30 a.m., upon the annexed Petition, which requests a final judgment to evict you from and award the Petitioner the possession of the subject premises located at __ ________ Road, _______, New York _____ County of Suffolk, and, more specifically, [*description as appropriate*—Apartment No. ___; the _____ rooms on the ____ floor, first floor, second floor, etc.], and such other and further relief as requested in the Petition and/or the Court deems proper and appropriate.

PLEASE TAKE FURTHER NOTICE, that Petitioner also seeks, as set forth in the Petition, a money judgment against you in the sum of $_________, with interest thereon from [*first day unpaid rent was due*].

PLEASE TAKE FURTHER NOTICE, that your answer to the Petition may set forth any applicable defense(s), unless waived by the applicable laws or otherwise, and further assert a counterclaim(s) against the Petitioner.

PLEASE TAKE FURTHER NOTICE, that if you fail at such time to interpose and establish any defense that you may have to the allegations set forth in the Petition, you may be precluded from asserting such defense(s) or claim(s) on which it is based in any other proceeding or action.

PLEASE TAKE FURTHER NOTICE, that your failure to appear may result in a final judgment by default for the petitioner evicting you from the premises and ordering you to pay the amount demanded in the Petition.

DATED:

____

Issuing Judge/Clerk/Attorney

SUFFOLK COUNTY SIXTH DISTRICT COURT
PATCHOGUE, NEW YORK

Petitioner,	Index No. BRLT __-_____
- against -	***PETITION***
Respondent.	**(Non-Payment Proceeding)**

Petitioner, _____________ ("Petitioner" or "Landlord"), by his/her/its attorneys ________, LLP, asserts and alleges the following:

1. Petitioner is the owner and Landlord of the parcel of residential real property located at __ ____________Road, ______, New York ___, County of Suffolk, Town of __________, which is within the territorial jurisdiction of the Court.

2. More specifically, the residential property at the aforementioned address is a single family residential property [*or other*], bearing [*description as appropriate*—Apartment No. ___; the _____ rooms on the ____ floor, first floor, second floor, etc.] (the "Subject Premises").

3. Respondent [*list every Tenant's name(s)*] ("Respondent" or "Tenant") is the Tenant of the Subject Premises, having entered into possession of the Subject Premises pursuant to an [*oral or written*] rental agreement, dated on or about _____ (the "Lease") between Petitioner and Respondent.

4. The Lease is for a period of ___ months/years, commencing _____, __, 20__.

5. Within the aforementioned Lease, Respondent promised to pay Landlord (*Landlord's predecessor*) as rent the sum of $__________ each [*month or weekly or other arrangement*] on or before the __th day of each month for the duration of the Lease (the "Rent").

6. Respondent is presently in possession of the Subject Premises, and has been in possession since _______.

7. Pursuant to the Lease, Petitioner is entitled to but Respondent has failed and/or refuses to pay the Rent due and owing Petitioner for each of the following periods:

(Month) __________, 20___ (Amount) $______________

(Month) __________, 20___ (Amount) $______________

(Month) __________, 20___ (Amount) $______________

8. Respondent has defaulted in his obligations pursuant to the Lease as set forth above and the total now due and owing Petitioner for rent arrears is $____.

9. Petitioner has provided notice to Respondent by service of the attached written notice by certified mail stating that the Petitioner has not received rent payment five (5) days after the due date set forth in the Rental Agreement [*attach Five Day Notice(s) and proof of certified mailing*].

10. Petitioner has further duly demanded that Respondent to surrender possession or pay the unpaid Rent for each month indicated above since same has become due by service of a written fourteen (14) day Rent Demand that was served on the Respondent in accordance with Real Property Actions and Proceedings Law ("RPAPL") § 735 [*attach Fourteen (14) Day Rent Demand(s) and affidavit of service*].

11. Respondent continues to remain in possession of the Subject Premises without the consent or permission of the Landlord.

12. There are no known applications for relief pursuant to the Emergency Rental Assistance Program ("ERAP") pending at this time that would prohibit or bar the commencement of the herein summary proceeding [*include for as long as ERAP is in effect*].

13. The Subject Premises is not subject to rent control because [*insert that which is applicable*—the Subject Premises is located in a community which has not adopted the Emergency Tenant Protection Act of 1974 ("ETPA"); the building in which the Subject Premises is located was constructed after December 31, 1973; or the building in which the Subject Premises is located has fewer than six (6) units].

or

13. Petitioner is in full compliance with the Emergency Tenant Protection Act of 1974 ("ETPA"), as amended, and [*insert that which is applicable*—the Rent demanded herein is not greater than the maximum rent permitted by law; the Subject Premises is subject to rent control and the Rent demanded herein does not exceed the maximum rent prescribed by the New York State Divisions of Housing and Community Renewal (DHCR) and/or Homes and Community Renewal (HCR); or the Subject Premises is presently subject to the Emergency Tenant Protection Act of 1974 (ETPA), as amended, because ________________ and the Petitioner/Owner of the Subject Premises has registered the Rent and services with the DHCR and/or HCR pursuant to ETPA and the Tenant Protection Regulations thereunder; is in compliance with ETPA; and the Rent demanded herein does not exceed the legal regulated rent permitted the Petitioner under said Law, Regulations and appropriate Rent Guidelines Board Orders].

WHEREFORE, Petitioner requests (1) a final judgment of possession in Petitioner's favor; (2) issuance of a warrant to remove Respondent(s) from possession of the Subject Premises; and (3) a money judgment for rent arrears and/or fair value and use and occupancy in the sum of $_______________, with interest from [*the first date that the unpaid rent was due*], plus costs and disbursements herein.

Dated:__________

ATTORNEY'S FIRM NAME

____

Attorneys for Petitioner _______

By: _________________________

Address

City, State Zip Code

Telephone Number

Facsimile Number

STATE OF NEW YORK)

ss:

COUNTY OF _________)

[*Petitioner or duly authorized Agent for Petitioner*], being duly sworn, states that deponent has read the foregoing Petition, and that the contents of the Petition are true to deponent's own knowledge except as to those matters that are alleged upon information and belief, and as to those matters, deponent believes them to be true.

____

Petitioner (signature)

Print Name/Title

Sworn to before me this __th day

of _____________, 20__

____

Notary Public

B. HOLDOVER PROCEEDING

SUFFOLK COUNTY SIXTH DISTRICT COURT
PATCHOGUE, NEW YORK

Petitioner,	Index No. BRLT __-_____
- against -	***NOTICE OF PETITION***
Respondent.	**(Holdover Proceeding)**

To the Respondent: [name(s) and address(es) of each Respondent]

PLEASE TAKE NOTICE, that a hearing at which you must appear and answer will be held at the Suffolk County Sixth District Court, 150 West Main Street, Patchogue, New York, on _______, __, 20__ at 9:30 a.m., upon the annexed Petition, which requests a final judgment to evict you from and award the Petitioner the possession of the subject premises located at __ ________ Road, _______, New York _____ County of Suffolk, and, more specifically, [*description as appropriate*—Apartment No. ___; the _____ rooms on the ____ floor, first floor, second floor, etc.], and such other and further relief as requested in the Petition and/or the Court deems proper and appropriate.

PLEASE TAKE FURTHER NOTICE, that Petitioner also seeks, as set forth in the Petition, a money judgment against you in the sum of $_________, with interest thereon from [*first day unpaid rent was due*], plus the reasonable value of use and occupancy.

PLEASE TAKE FURTHER NOTICE, that your answer to the Petition may set forth any applicable defense(s), unless waived by the applicable laws or otherwise, and further assert a counterclaim(s) against the Petitioner.

PLEASE TAKE FURTHER NOTICE, that if you fail at such time to interpose and establish any defense that you may have to the allegations set forth in the Petition, you may be precluded from asserting such defense(s) or claim(s) on which it is based in any other proceeding or action.

PLEASE TAKE FURTHER NOTICE, that your failure to appear may result in final judgment by default for the petitioner evicting you from the premises and ordering you to pay the amount demanded in the Petition.

DATED:

____
Issuing Judge/Clerk/Attorney

SUFFOLK COUNTY SIXTH DISTRICT COURT
PATCHOGUE, NEW YORK

Petitioner,	Index No. BRLT __-_____
- against -	***PETITION***
Respondent.	**(Holdover Proceeding)**

Petitioner, _____________ ("Petitioner" or "Landlord"), by his/her/its attorneys ________, LLP, asserts and alleges the following:

1. Petitioner is the owner and Landlord of the parcel of residential real property located at __ _____________Road, ______, New York ______, County of Suffolk, Town of ___________, which is within the territorial jurisdiction of the Court.

2. More specifically, the residential property at the aforementioned address is a single family residential property [*or other*], bearing [*description as appropriate*—Apartment No. ___; the _____ rooms on the ____ floor, first floor, second floor, etc.] (the "Subject Premises").

3. Respondent(s) [*list every Tenant's name(s)*] ("Respondent(s)" or "Tenant(s)") is the Tenant of the Subject Premises, having entered into possession of the Subject Premises pursuant to an [*oral or written*] rental agreement, made on or about _____, __, 20__ and ending on _____, __, 20__ at the rental of $________ for each month payable on the __th day of each month (the "Lease") between Petitioner and Respondent(s).

4. Respondent(s) ________ is/are the Undertenants of the aforesaid Tenants.

5. The term for which said premises were rented by the Respondent(s) expired on _____, __, 20__ as a result of [*(1) the agreed upon time period of the verbal/ written agreement has ended; (2) the agreed upon time period of the lease has ended; (3) a breach caused by Tenant following proper Notice (a copy of which is attached; or (4) other*].

6. [*if applicable*] At least thirty (30) days [or *sixty (60) days or ninety (90) days*] written notice prior to the expiration of the rental agreement was served upon the Respondent(s) in a manner provided for by law informing Respondent(s) that the Petitioner elected to [*terminate or not re-new*] the tenancy, and that unless Respondent(s) vacated the Subject Premises on the day which said term expired, Petitioner would commence a summary proceeding to remove Respondent(s) therefrom.

7. Respondent(s) continues to remain in possession of the Subject Premises without the permission of the Petitioner following the expiration or termination of said term.

8. There are no known applications for relief pursuant to the Emergency Rental Assistance Program ("ERAP") pending at this time that would prohibit or bar the commencement of the herein summary proceeding [*include for as long as ERAP is in effect*].

9. The Subject Premises is not subject to rent control because [*insert that which is applicable*—the Subject Premises is located in a community which has not adopted the Emergency Tenant Protection Act of 1974 ("ETPA"); the building in which the Subject Premises is located was constructed after December 31, 1973; or the building in which the Subject Premises is located has fewer than six (6) units].

or

9. Petitioner is in full compliance with the Emergency Tenant Protection Act of 1974 ("ETPA"), as amended, and [*insert that which is applicable*—the Rent sought herein is not greater than the maximum rent permitted by law; the Subject Premises is subject to rent control and the Rent demanded herein does not exceed the maximum rent prescribed by the New York State Divisions of Housing and Community Renewal (DHCR) and/or Homes and Community Renewal (HCR); or the Subject Premises is presently subject to the Emergency Tenant Protection Act of 1974 (ETPA), as amended, because _______________ and the Petitioner/Owner of the Subject Premises has registered the Rent and services with the DHCR and/or HCR pursuant to ETPA and the Tenant Protection Regulations thereunder; is in compliance with ETPA; and the Rent demanded herein does not exceed the legal regulated rent permitted the Petitioner under said Law, Regulations and appropriate Rent Guidelines Board Orders].

WHEREFORE, Petitioner requests (1) a final judgment of possession in Petitioner's favor; (2) issuance of a warrant to remove Respondent(s) from possession of the Subject Premises; and (3) a money judgment for rent arrears and/or fair value and use and occupancy in the sum of $_______________, with interest from [*the first date that the unpaid rent was due*], plus costs and disbursements herein.

Dated:__________

ATTORNEY'S FIRM NAME

____

Attorneys for Petitioner ________
By: ___________________________
Address
City, State Zip Code
Telephone Number
Facsimile Number

STATE OF NEW YORK)
ss:
COUNTY OF __________)

[*Petitioner or duly authorized Agent for Petitioner*], being duly sworn, states that deponent has read the foregoing Petition, and that the contents of the Petition are true to deponent's own knowledge except as to those matters that are alleged upon information and belief, and as to those matters, deponent believes them to be true.

____

Petitioner (signature)
Print Name/Title

Sworn to before me this __th day
of _______________, 20__

____

Notary Public

IV. ANSWER WITH COUNTERCLAIMS[1898]

A. NON-PAYMENT PROCEEDING

SUFFOLK COUNTY SIXTH DISTRICT COURT
PATCHOGUE, NEW YORK

________________________________	Index No. BRLT __-_____
Petitioner,	**ANSWER**
- against -	**<u>WITH COUNTERCLAIMS</u>**
Respondent.	**(Non-payment Proceeding)**
________________________________	

Respondent, _____________ ("Respondent"), by his/her/its attorneys, _________________, P.C., hereby interposes in response to Petitioner's Petition the following Answer with Counterclaims.

1. Respondent denies knowledge and information sufficient to form a belief as to the truth of the allegations set forth in paragraphs 1, 12 and 13 of the Petition.

2. With respect to the allegations set forth in paragraph 2 of the Petition, Respondent admits occupying the Subject Premises pursuant to a rental agreement with Petitioner. Respondent denies the remaining allegations set forth in that paragraph of the Petition.

3. Respondent denies the allegations set forth in paragraphs 3, 4, 5, 6, 9, 10 and 11 of the Petition.

4. With respect to paragraphs 7 and 8 of the Petition, Respondent respectfully refers all conclusions of law to the Court for determination, and, further to the extent that a response is required, the allegations are denied.

<u>AS AND FOR A FIRST AFFIRMATIVE DEFENSE</u>

5. Respondent hereby repeats and reiterates each and every allegation contained in paragraphs 1 through 4 as if fully set forth herein.

6. Petitioner failed to properly serve Respondent with the Notice of Petition and Petition pursuant to Real Property Actions and Proceedings Law § 735, and, as a result, the Court lacks jurisdiction over Respondent.

7. Alternatively, Respondent respectfully requests a traverse hearing.

1898 Pursuant to RPAPL § 743, an Answer is not required except in circumstances involving the non-payment of rent and where the rules of the appropriate Appellate Division require as such. If the Tenant submits an Answer, it may be done orally or in writing. RPAPL § 743.

AS AND FOR A SECOND AFFIRMATIVE DEFENSE

8. Respondent hereby repeats and reiterates each and every allegation contained in paragraphs 1 through 7 as if fully set forth herein.

9. Petitioner failed to make a proper rent demand prior to the commencement of this summary proceeding.

AS AND FOR A THIRD AFFIRMATIVE DEFENSE

10. Respondent hereby repeats and reiterates each and every allegation contained in paragraphs 1 through 9 as if fully set forth herein.

11. Petitioner failed to provide a proper five (5) day late rent reminder by certified mail prior to the commencement of this summary proceeding.

AS AND FOR A FOURTH AFFIRMATIVE DEFENSE

12. Respondent hereby repeats and reiterates each and every allegation contained in paragraphs 1 through 11 as if fully set forth herein.

13. Respondent tendered the rent claimed due herein to Petitioner but Petitioner refused to accept same by rejecting and/or returning the payments to Respondent.

AS AND FOR A FIFTH AFFIRMATIVE DEFENSE AND FIRST COUNTERCLAIM

14. Respondent hereby repeats and reiterates each and every allegation contained in paragraphs 1 through 13 as if fully set forth herein.

15. The conditions of the Subject Premises are dangerous, hazardous and detrimental to the safety of Respondent and all others entering same.

16. The aforementioned conditions include: [*list the dangerous conditions*].

17. The aforementioned conditions have been ongoing and continuous since __________.

18. Petitioner was provided ample notice of the defective conditions yet Petitioner failed to remedy the conditions thereby breaching the warranty of habitability.

19. Based upon the foregoing, Respondent is entitled to an abatement of the rent plus a money judgment for damages sustained due to Landlord's breach.

AS AND FOR A SECOND COUNTERCLAIM

20. Respondent hereby repeats and reiterates each and every allegation contained in paragraphs 1 through 19 as if fully set forth herein.

21. The applicable Lease includes a provision awarding a prevailing Petitioner reasonable attorney's fees.

22. Respondent is thus entitled to the same consideration pursuant to Real Property Law § 234.

23. Based on the foregoing, Respondent requests an award of reasonable attorney's fees in an amount to be determined by the Court.

WHEREFORE, Respondent respectfully requests judgment against Petitioner (1) dismissing the Petition or, alternatively, granting a traverse hearing on the issue of service; (2) in the event the Court is not inclined to dismiss the Petition, Respondent seeks an abatement of the alleged unpaid rent; (3) plus a money judgment in an amount to be determined by the Court on the first and second counterclaims; and (4) and such other and further relief as the Court deems just and proper.

Dated:__________

ATTORNEY'S FIRM NAME

____

Attorneys for Respondent _______
By: ________________________
Address
City, State Zip Code
Telephone Number
Facsimile Number
[*Not Required*]

STATE OF NEW YORK)
ss:
COUNTY OF _________)

[*Respondent*], being duly sworn, states that deponent has read the foregoing Answer with Counterclaims, and that the contents of the Answer with Counterclaims are true to deponent's own knowledge except as to those matters that are alleged upon information and belief, and as to those matters, deponent believes them to be true.

____

Respondent (signature)
Print Name/Title

Sworn to before me this __th day
of _____________, 20__

____

Notary Public

B. HOLDOVER PROCEEDING

SUFFOLK COUNTY SIXTH DISTRICT COURT
PATCHOGUE, NEW YORK

Petitioner,	Index No. BRLT __-_____
- against -	**ANSWER** **WITH COUNTERCLAIM**
Respondent.	**(Holdover Proceeding)**

Respondent, _____________ ("Respondent"), by his/her/its attorneys, ________________, P.C., hereby interposes in response to Petitioner's Petition the following Answer with Counterclaim.

1. Respondent denies knowledge and information sufficient to form a belief as to the truth of the allegations set forth in paragraphs 1, 9 and 10 of the Petition.

2. With respect to the allegations set forth in paragraph 2 of the Petition, Respondent admits to formerly occupying the Subject Premises pursuant to a rental agreement with Petitioner. Respondent denies the remaining allegations set forth in that paragraph of the Petition.

3. Respondent denies the allegations set forth in paragraphs 3, 5, 6, 7 and 11 of the Petition.

4. With respect to paragraphs 4 and 8 of the Petition, Respondent respectfully refers all conclusions of law to the Court for determination, and, further to the extent that a response is required, the allegations are denied.

AS AND FOR A FIRST AFFIRMATIVE DEFENSE

5. Respondent hereby repeats and reiterates each and every allegation contained in paragraphs 1 through 4 as if fully set forth herein.

6. Respondent surrendered possession of the Subject Premises prior to the commencement of the herein summary proceeding.

7. Based on the foregoing, the action must be dismissed.

AS AND FOR A SECOND AFFIRMATIVE DEFENSE

8. Respondent hereby repeats and reiterates each and every allegation contained in paragraphs 1 through 7 as if fully set forth herein.

9. To the extent a Landlord and Tenant relationship existed between Petitioner and Respondent, since Respondent tendered payment for use and occupancy

following the alleged expiration of the Lease, the tenancy was on a month-to-month basis, thereby requiring Petitioner to cause to be served upon Respondent a predicate notice terminating the tenancy prior to the commencement of the herein summary proceeding.

10. Since Respondent has been in possession of the Subject Premises for the three (3) year period from _______ __, 20__, through the present date, the Petitioner was required to serve a ninety (90) day [*or sixty (60) day or thirty (30) day depending on the length of tenancy and how long occupied the premises*] Notice prior to commencing the instant proceeding.

11. Petitioner failed to cause to be served upon Respondent a ninety (90) day [*or sixty (60) day or thirty (30) day depending on the length of tenancy and how long occupied the premises*] Notice of termination pursuant to Real Property Law § 226-c(2)(d) prior to commencing this proceeding. The failure to serve such notice requires dismissal of the action.

12. Alternatively, in the event Petitioner claims there was service of a proper predicate notice, Respondent respectfully requests a traverse hearing.

AS AND FOR A THIRD AFFIRMATIVE DEFENSE

13. Respondent hereby repeats and reiterates each and every allegation contained in paragraphs 1 through 12 as if fully set forth herein.

14. Petitioner commenced this summary proceeding in retaliation for Respondent filing a complaint with the local Code Enforcement agency regarding dangerous conditions within the Subject Premises that are in violation of the local Town Code.

15. Respondent made the aforementioned complaint on or about _________ __, 20__, two (2) months prior to the commencement of this summary proceeding.

16. The Subject Premises is not an owner-occupied property with fewer than four (4) units.

17. The stated reasons for the commencement of this summary proceeding are a pretext for the true reason which is contrary to law and in violation of the exercise of Respondent's lawful rights.

18. Accordingly, the Petition must be dismissed.

AS AND FOR A FIRST COUNTERCLAIM

19. Respondent hereby repeats and reiterates each and every allegation contained in paragraphs 1 through 18 as if fully set forth herein.

20. The relevant Lease includes a provision awarding a prevailing Petitioner reasonable attorney's fees.

21. Respondent is thus entitled to the same consideration pursuant to Real Property Law § 234.

22. Based on the foregoing, Respondent requests an award of reasonable attorney's fees in an amount to be determined by the Court.

WHEREFORE, Respondent respectfully requests judgment against Petitioner (1) dismissing the Petition or, alternatively, granting a traverse hearing; (2) a money judgment in an amount to be determined by the Court on the counterclaim; and (3) such other and further relief as the Court deems just and proper.

Dated:__________

ATTORNEY'S FIRM NAME

____

Attorneys for Respondent _______
By: _________________________
Address
City, State Zip Code
Telephone Number
Facsimile Number
[*Not Required*]

STATE OF NEW YORK)

ss:

COUNTY OF _________)

[*Respondent or Respondent's Attorney*], being duly sworn, states that deponent has read the foregoing Answer with Counterclaim, and that the contents of the Answer with Counterclaim are true to deponent's own knowledge except as to those matters that are alleged upon information and belief, and as to those matters, deponent believes them to be true.

____

Respondent (signature)

Print Name/Title
Sworn to before me this __th day
of ______________, 20__

____

Notary Public

V. STIPULATION OF SETTLEMENT

SUFFOLK COUNTY SIXTH DISTRICT COURT
PATCHOGUE, NEW YORK

____

Petitioner,

- against -

Respondents.

____

Index No. BRLT __-_____

STIPULATION OF SETTLEMENT

It is hereby stipulated[1899] and agreed by and between the undersigned parties that the above-captioned action is settled as follows:

1. The Petition is amended to include the current month's rent of ___________ in the amount of $_________ which became due following the commencement of this summary proceeding.

2. Respondent consents to the jurisdiction of the Court, waives any and all jurisdictional defenses, and withdraws the counterclaims.

3. Subtenant ___________, having consented to the jurisdiction of the Court, further consents that his proper name shall be substituted for the "John Doe" named in the Notice of Petition and Petition.

4. Respondent ________ and Subtenant __________ consent to the immediate entry of a judgment of possession in favor of the Petitioner and the issuance of a warrant of eviction. The execution of the warrant of eviction shall be stayed until ______ __, 20__. Tenant _________ further consents to entry of a money judgment against him in the amount of $ ________.

or

Respondent ____ and Subtenant _______ are currently in possession of the subject premises, and Tenant ________ acknowledges owing Petitioner rent arrears in the sum of $_________, and further agrees to pay such arrears on or before ______ __, 20__. Payments are to be made in the following manner: [*payment schedule—dates, amount and form of payment*]. In the event Tenant ___________ fails to pay the rental arrears as agreed above, then the Petitioner,

1899 Pursuant to Real Property Actions and Proceedings Law § 746, if either or both parties appear *pro se*, the Court must "conduct[] an allocution on the record," in accordance with the litany of topics set forth in that section, with the unrepresented litigant(s) to ascertain that the party is knowingly, voluntarily, and intelligently entering into the agreement.

upon submission of an affidavit of non-compliance, will be entitled to a judgment of possession and issuance of a warrant of eviction against Tenant _______ and Subtenant ________, plus a money judgment against Tenant _______ only, in the amount of $ ______ [*amount in the Petition as amended on the record, the Petition amount, or a lower amount*], with credit given for any partial payments made. The parties further agree that all monies received from this date forward will first be applied to the current month's rent with the remainder towards the arrears. It is expressly agreed that the failure on the part of the Tenant to pay future rent may <u>not</u> be a basis for default under the terms of this Stipulation of Settlement nor may future rent be included in a monetary judgment.

5. Tenant ______ further waives his right to the return of the security deposit in the amount of $ _______.

Date: _______________

_______________________	_______________________
Petitioner	Attorney for Petitioner
_______________________	_______________________
Respondent	Attorney for Respondent
_______________________	_______________________
Subtenant	Attorney for Subtenant

VI. JUDGMENT OF POSSESSION AND WARRANT OF EVICTION

SUFFOLK COUNTY DISTRICT COURT
JUDGMENT OF POSSESSION

____

Petitioner,

- against -   Index No. BRLT __-_____

Respondent.

____

WHEREAS a Notice of Petition and Non-Payment Petition duly verified and proof of service having been filed with this court and the issue having been decided by the Hon. _____ ________, District Court Judge on September __, 20__, a final order is made, after a hearing in favor of Petitioner.

WHEREAS Petitioner _______ has an address at __ ___________ Rd., ______, NY _____.

WHEREAS Respondents _______ have an address at __ _________ St., _____, NY _____.

NOW, upon the motion Petitioner's counsel, _________, Esq., __ ___________ Rd., ______, NY _____,

IT IS HEREBY ADJUDGED that possession of the premises, described in the Petition located at __ _________________ Street, _____, NY _____, said property is further described as: Apartment located on the second floor, be awarded to the Petitioner, along with a monetary judgment in the amount of $10,500.00 for a total judgment of $10,500.00.

AND IT IS FURTHER ORDERED that a warrant of eviction shall issue removing all named Respondents from the described premises. The execution of the warrant is stayed to and including __/__/20__.

Date of Decision: 9/__/20__

____

J.D.C.

Judgment entered at Suffolk County District Court—6th District, 150 West Main Street, Patchogue, NY 11772, in the State of New York in the total amount of $10,500.00 on September __, 20__ at 2:06 pm.

____

Clerk of the Court

SUFFOLK COUNTY DISTRICT COURT
WARRANT OF EVICTION

Petitioner,	Index No. BRLT __-_____
- against -	Original Issuance
	WARRANT OF EVICTION
Respondent.	Non-Payment

TO THE SHERIFF OF SUFFOLK COUNTY

Final decision in favor of the Petitioner has been granted based on the judgment of possession entered in the Suffolk County District Court—6th District on 9/__/20__, which awarded Petitioner the delivery of the premises:

Therefore, you are commanded to remove the Respondent(s) listed below:

(1) Sean Jones, Shannon Jones, John Doe

And all other persons from the following described premises, located in the County of Suffolk and to put said Petitioner in full possession thereof:

(1) 14 Smith Lane, _______, NY _________

Said property is further described as: Apartment located on the second floor

THE EARLIEST DATE THE EVICTION MAY OCCUR IS _________, 20__.[1900]

Witness,

Hon. _____ ________District Court Judge

Dated:

____

J.D.C.

1900 RPAPL § 749(1) provides that the warrant must state "the earliest date upon which execution may occur pursuant to the order of the court". Practically, the eviction will take place after the "earliest date" unless the Sheriff served the fourteen (14) day notice on the earliest date possible.

VII. SHERIFF'S FOURTEEN (14) DAY EVICTION NOTICE

Sheriff's Office, County of ______________

Accredited Law Enforcement Agency

Civil Enforcement Section

___ Smith Road

_________, NY ____

____

Sheriff

14-DAY EVICTION NOTICE

File No.: ______________________________

Respondent(s) ______________________________

Property Address ______________________________

____

In compliance with provisions of New York State Law, I as Sheriff of the County of ________________, do hereby give notice that you have fourteen (14) days, including any period which occurs on a Saturday, Sunday or public holiday, to vacate these premises.

At the expiration of the aforesaid fourteen (14) days if the premises are not vacated, I have no alternative but to forcibly evict you pursuant to court directed mandate.

SHERIFF OF ______ COUNTY
BY: __________________________
Deputy Sheriff/Rank/Shield/Command
DATE: ______________
TIME: ______________

VIII. ORDER TO SHOW CAUSE TO VACATE JUDGMENT

HON. ______________________,
JUDGE OF THE SUFFOLK COUNTY DISTRICT COURT
At a Motion Term of the District Court
of the State of New York, County of Suffolk

____

Petitioner,

- against -

Respondent.

____

Index No. BRLT __-_____

ORDER TO SHOW CAUSE
TO VACATE DEFAULT

Upon the affidavit of Respondent ___________________________, sworn to on ___________, and upon all prior papers and proceedings,

Let the Petitioner show cause at a Motion Term of this Court to be held at the Courthouse located at _____________, _______, New York, on the __th day of ______ __, 20__, at 9:30 am, or as soon thereafter as the parties can be heard, why an order should not be entered vacating the default and/or the judgment granted in favor of the Petitioner and dismissing the proceeding, or setting the matter down for a hearing, and why the Respondent should not be awarded such other and further relief as may be just and proper.

Sufficient reason being presented for the relief requested, it is,

ORDERED, that pending the hearing and determination of this motion, the Sheriff and Petitioner and all of his/her agents are stayed from conducting any proceedings to enforce the judgment, and further it is

ORDERED, that Respondent serve a copy of this Order, and the papers upon which it is based, on Petitioner at _______________, ______, New York __, and the Sheriff of _________ County at ______________, ________, New York _____, by personal delivery by the __th day of ___________, 20__.

All papers the Petitioner wishes to submit in opposition to the Respondent's motion must be forwarded to the Court and Respondent's counsel prior to the hearing date. Personal appearance is required and oral statements will be considered on the return date of the motion.

Order signed at ______________, New York

Date: __________

Enter,

____

J.D.C.

SUFFOLK COUNTY SIXTH DISTRICT COURT
PATCHOGUE, NEW YORK

Petitioner,	Index No. BRLT __-_____
- against -	**AFFIDAVIT IN SUPPORT OF MOTION TO VACATE DEFAULT**
Respondent.	

____________________ being duly sworn, deposes and says:

1. I am the Respondent in the above-captioned summary proceeding wherein Petitioner seeks a final judgment of possession, a money judgment for alleged unpaid rent and a warrant to evict me from the subject premises.

2. Your deponent resides at the subject premises, located at _______________, __________, New York ____. Together with my family, including my spouse and three (3) children, we have lived at this address for the past four (4) years.

3. This is an action for the non-payment of rent pursuant to a lease agreement I entered into with the Petitioner-Landlord.

4. On ______ __, 20__, a default judgment, including a judgment of possession, a money judgment in the amount of $10,500 and a warrant of eviction, without stay, was entered by this Court.

5. I did not appear [*must state a reasonable explanation for not appearing—* e.g.,] because I was not served with the Notice of Petition and Petition. I only learned of this proceeding when I called the Landlord to complain that the heat was not operational the past few days and the temperature within the premises (during the winter months) would not exceed 60 degrees Fahrenheit. The Landlord told me that I had to leave the premises because the Petitioner prevailed in Court. I attempted to explain to the Landlord that I did not receive any notices about a Court date, to which the Landlord responded, "Just leave!" I have now reviewed the Court's file, and note that the affidavit of service alleges that I was personally served with the Notice of Petition and Petition on ______ __, 20__, at 3:15 pm at the property address. The process server is mistaken as I was at work on that date at that time. I do not arrive home until about 6:00 pm. In addition, the description in the affidavit of service indicates that a male approximately 45 years of age weighing about 200 pounds and standing 6' tall was served. As you will discover if I am given the opportunity to defend myself, I am 30 years of age, 5' 8" tall and weigh approximately 175 pounds. No one at the property meets the description either. I further did not receive any of the court papers by mail. At

minimum, I am requesting a traverse hearing because I was not served and am disputing the allegations set forth in the affidavit of service.

6. I also have a meritorious defense to the action. [*must state the possibility of a meritorious defense*—e.g., The rent is paid in full.] I have attached a copy of the cancelled checks and rent receipts that show I am current on the rent. In addition, the Petitioner did not provide either a fourteen (14) day rent demand or a five (5) day delinquent notice for the payment of rent prior to commencing this proceeding. For these reasons, the required predicate notices were not provided and this failure further requires dismissal of the proceeding.

7. No previous application for this relief has been made.

WHEREFORE, deponent respectfully requests an order vacating the judgment entered on the __th day of ____________, 20__, and dismissing the proceeding, or such other relief as may be just and proper.

Dated:

____
Respondent

Sworn to before me this __th day
of ______________, 20__

Notes:

In January 2021, RPAPL § 1305 was amended to require service of the predicate notice upon a bona fide Tenant of residential property following a foreclosure auction "in the same manner as required" by RPAPL § 1303(4), which is, by (1) certified mail, return receipt requested and (2) first-class mail to the Tenant's address at the property.

Notes:

Notes:

Notes:

Notes: